BOOKS KIDS WILL SIT STILL FOR

BOOKS KIDS WILL SIT STILL FOR™

The Complete Read-Aloud Guide

SECOND EDITION

Judy Freeman

R. R. BOWKER
New York

Published by R. R. Bowker,
a division of Reed Publishing (USA) Inc.
Copyright © 1990 by Judy Freeman
All rights reserved
PRINTED AND BOUND IN THE UNITED STATES OF
AMERICA
Second printing, May 1992

The following poems have been reprinted with the permission of the publishers:

"Thoughts on Getting Out of a Nice Warm Bed in an Ice-Cold House to Go to the Bathroom at Three O'Clock in the Morning" reprinted with permission of Atheneum Publishers, an imprint of Macmillan Publishing Company, from IF I WERE IN CHARGE OF THE WORLD AND OTHER WORRIES by Judith Viorst. Copyright © 1981 by Judith Viorst.

The poem "Homework! Oh, Homework!" by Jack Prelutsky from THE NEW KID ON THE BLOCK. Copyright © 1984 by Jack Prelutsky. Reprinted by permission of Greenwillow Books, William Morrow & Co. Published in Great Britain by William Heinemann Ltd.

The first verse of the poem "Alligator Pie" by Dennis Lee from ALLIGATOR PIE. Copyright © 1974 by Dennis Lee. Reprinted with permission of Macmillan of Canada, a Division of Canada Publishing Corporation.

"Down by the Bay" by Raffi from DOWN BY THE BAY. Text: Copyright © Crown 1987. Music: Troubadour Records Ltd., Willowdale, Ontario, Canada. Reprinted by permission.

"Library" from SMALL POEMS AGAIN by Valerie Worth, illustrated by Natalie Babbitt. Poems copyright © 1975, 1986 by Valerie Worth. Illustrations copyright © 1986 by Natalie Babbitt. Reprinted by permission of Farrar, Straus and Giroux, Inc.

Library of Congress Cataloging-in-Publication Data

Freeman, Judy
    Books kids will sit still for : the complete read-aloud guide / by Judy Freeman. — 2nd ed.
        p.   cm.
    Includes bibliographical references and indexes.
    ISBN 0-8352-3010-4
    1. Children's literature—Bibliography.   2. Bibliography—Best books—Children's literature.   3. School libraries—Book lists.
4. School libraries—Activity programs.   5. Oral reading.
I. Title
Z1037.F847   1990
011.62—dc20
                                        90-2373
                                        CIP

Cover illustration by Ketti Kupper

ISBN 0-8352-3010-4

90000

9 780835 230100

To my right hand man, Izzy,
who never complained about being a book-widower,
and kept a sense of humor through deadlines and disaster.

CONTENTS

ANNOTATED READ-ALOUD LISTS

BIBLIOGRAPHY AND INDEXES

LIST OF ILLUSTRATIONS

PREFACE

IT IS NOT ENOUGH FOR A LIBRARIAN SIMPLY TO STOCK BOOKS FOR children to read or for a teacher to teach reading with only a basal at his or her side. Children must be inundated with books constantly, and with a great deal of good-natured fervor, if we expect them to become more than just language decoders.

The easiest and most effective method of interesting children in reading good books is to read aloud to them. Children love hearing a book dramatized and brought to life. A more difficult book becomes accessible to everyone, not just the top readers. Children's books, read aloud daily, profoundly affect children in ways that spelling words and phonics exercises never can.

Queries from interested teachers and librarians include: How do we know which books to read, and after we read them, then what? How do we get the kids hooked? We must cover so much curriculum in the course of a year; how do we justify using children's books alongside the required texts? And what educational advantages will we find?

I wrote *Books Kids Will Sit Still For* to answer some of those questions. In 1975 while working in another New Jersey school district, I began compiling what became a brief, mimeographed, graded list of books for the teachers in my school who were interested in reading aloud. Like most librarians, I am a compulsive and unrepentant list-maker, and over the years my 10-page list of books grew and ran rampant.

At Van Holten School, the list continued to evolve into what it is now: a manual of ways to fool around with books, with explanatory chapters on read-aloud techniques, booktalking, creative dramatics, storytelling, poetry, and nonfiction. The chapter "101 Ways to Celebrate Books" lists additional creative writing and other literature-based activities. Altogether, the first nine chapters comprise a short course on specific strategies to encourage children's response to literature. Literature-shy adults will gain confidence in their talents to innovate with books.

Next, there is a series of graded, annotated lists containing over 2,000 of my personal, tried-and-true, kid-tested favorites for reading aloud. No title was included unless I read it, loved it, and tried it out on an unsuspecting class or two to see if it "flew." Many teachers at my school and librarians in my children's literature classes at the Rutgers School of Communication, Information and Library Studies also tested titles, along with my suggested literature extension activities, and reported back on their students' reactions. Those titles that passed muster are included here.

Each entry consists of the author(s), complete title, illustrator, publisher, copyright date, ISBN if the book is in print, annotation, and up to five subject headings under which the book is listed in the Subject Index. Where applicable, the number of chapters, pages, stories, and/or number of sittings required to complete a title are also included.

Each entry's annotation includes a simple plot statement. Also incorporated are practical ideas for sharing the books with children to develop their comprehension and creativity, and tie into subject areas such as language arts, library skills, science, social studies, art, music, and even physical education.

A majority of the annotations cite related titles that fit in as either companions, follow-ups, or extensions on that subject or theme. Most of these related titles appear as main entries, each with an annotation that provides still more relevant activities and titles. A related title lacking a main entry listing is shown in the annotation with publisher's name and publication date in parentheses. For additional tie-ins, check the Subject Index.

All of the fiction lists include both "fiction" and "easy fiction/picture book" titles, as the two categories overlap. Chapter books are usually found on the fiction shelves of the library, whereas stories that can be finished in one sitting are most often in "easy fiction," though there are many exceptions to these rules.

Lists are overlapping in terms of recommended grade levels (Pre–K, K–1, 1–2, 2–3, and so on). It is often folly to prescribe an age level for a book, as many books can be enjoyed by all ages, though at different levels of comprehension. My aim has been to peg each book to the two grades I have found to be most suited to it, in terms of the literal comprehension and the maturity levels of children.

Folk and fairy tales are split into two separate chapters. The first, "Folk & Fairy Tales, Myths and Legends: Single Stories," consists of single, illustrated versions of tales, most in picture-book format, which can be read aloud in one sitting. The second, "Folk & Fairy Tales, Myths and Legends: Collections," contains folktale collections in which from three to over four dozen stories are compiled into a single volume. Many of these tales are broad based in appeal, so each citation includes a more liberal grade-level interest span. When you select a collection to read aloud, choose only those stories you can't resist, and let your students discover the rest.

The authors listed in the two folklore chapters are actually retellers, since no one knows who originally composed the stories, some of which are hundreds of years old. Translators' names are also included where applicable. In the interests of easy access, all the German folktales collected by the brothers Jacob and Wilhelm Grimm are listed under "Grimm, Jacob," and the myriad editions of Aesop's fables are grouped under "Aesop," regardless of how they were listed on the books' title pages. Likewise, Mother Goose collections are listed under the name "Mother Goose" instead of the collectors or illustrators.

On the poetry list, note that "comp." for compiler is written after many of the authors' names. This indicates that the author listed did not write the poems, but collected and edited them from other sources. Because so many picture books are told in rhyme, I decided to move single, picture-book renditions of narrative poems, like Robert W. Service's *The Cremation of Sam McGee* and Clement C. Moore's *The Night Before Christmas*, in with the fiction grade-level lists instead of keeping them in the poetry chapter. You will find them all in the Subject Index, listed under "Narrative Poetry."

Nonfiction books, also listed by author, will contain references to other titles on the same or similar topics that appear elsewhere in the chapter.

Although many titles on my lists are available in paperback editions, these were not usually noted here, as they go in and out of print even faster than hardbacks. If you can't find a book in hardback, check *Books in Print* at your library or bookstore to see if it's obtainable in paperback.

The four indexes at the back of the book (Author, Title, Illustrator, and Subject) should help you in your search for the perfect read-aloud. The Subject Index is extensive, listing not only author and title, but grade level as well.

All of the books listed in the Professional Bibliography are ones I have read and can highly recommend as valuable shelf allies in the ongoing search for good children's books and new ideas on how to use them.

Although the book is geared toward teachers and librarians, it should also prove useful to parents, scout and camp counselors, and anyone else who works with children in preschool through sixth grade. There is such limited time in the school day as it is that teachers must plan carefully to get the most out of every minute. Every title I have included is one I feel is worth the time away from the textbooks. It's up to you to decide which books fit each occasion.

In October 1988, I had the good fortune to be invited to speak at the Kaleidoscope 4 Conference in Calgary, Alberta, Canada. The theme of that memorable children's literature conference was "Imagining and Creating: Connections of the Heart and Mind." At that time, I had just started with my reading and research for this edition of *Books Kids Will Sit Still For*, and after returning from the conference, I plunged into the bottomless lake of children's literature with renewed zeal. Since then, I've spent untold hours making connections between books and readers, children and teachers, books and books. One book reminds me of another, which gives me an idea for a project, until, like a huge rolling snowball, I've accumulated a pastiche of titles all interconnected by theme, style, characters, or plot. Each time I reexamine a title, I see other ties and relations.

Now it's your turn to use my connections, and in turn, to make new ones. Should you find to your dismay that some of your favorite read-alouds do not appear on these pages, or if you have developed a cache of innovative methods to make these or other books come alive, I would be pleased and honored if you would write to me, care of R. R. Bowker, to share your thoughts. I am always on the hunt for titles I might have missed, dismissed, or been unable to locate in time, and will consider including them in the next edition. I'm also always curious to know which books bloom and which ones bomb for your children and why.

When you read the books suggested here, you will find yourself amused, astonished, enthralled, tickled, enlightened, and enmeshed in stories along with your children. A love of children's literature is contagious and, if you're careful, may well result in an epidemic that will spread to everyone in your school. All schools should encounter and prosper from such an enjoyable disease.

> Judy Freeman
> Elementary School Librarian
> Van Holten School, Bridgewater, New Jersey

ACKNOWLEDGMENTS

WHAT WAS SUPPOSED TO BE A SIMPLE, UPDATED SECOND EDITION OF *Books Kids Will Sit Still For* has turned into a many-armed creature, and more than tripled in size. The following people helped it grow:

My favorite public librarians in the world, those intrepid book hounds at the Somerset County Library in New Jersey, who not only didn't hide when they saw me coming in to request another hundred books, but shared their Rollos and treated me like one of the gang: Robin DelGuidice, Nina Lowe, Jackie Davie-Ruggero, Marcia Zorn, Pat Cosenza, Marge Newcombe, and Mary Ann Mruk.

Gary Chmielewski and Steve and Suzanne Hynes of the Follett Library Book Company, who lent me books, galleys, and loads of moral support.

The Somerset County Library Children's Bookwriters Group, whose members read and critiqued hundreds of pages without flinching: Nancy Cooney, Paula DePaolo, Joan Elste, Dot Leef, Margie Palatini, Wendy Pfeffer, Penny Pollock, Shirley Roffman, Pam Swallow, and Virginia Troeger; plus Joan Carris, who started the whole ball rolling before she moved away.

At Bowker, my publisher Marion Sader, who was so tenacious in helping me out of sticky situations, and my editor and fellow New Jersey-ite Nancy Bucenec.

Alice Yucht, my "Booktalks Unlimited" partner, critic, and pal.

Lois Schochet, Jane Scherer, and Carol Shields, who made periodic checks on the "Attic Girl" to make sure she hadn't stopped working or breathing.

Joan Grace, who made sure the library was still ticking and kept me from running down.

Loreli Stochaj for her Funky Fonts and new slant on old books.

Dennis Helms for sage advice and astonishing lunches.

Tracy and Yvette Cathers for their flying fingers.

Amy Lippincott for helping with the cards.

My Macintosh for only crashing once.

My parents, Bob and Gladys; sister Sharron; brother Richard; siblings-in-law Steven Alloy, Ann Guthrie, and Sam and Margaret Feldman, who took no offense at my clicking keyboard every time they called.

The students and staff at Van Holten School in Bridgewater, New Jersey, for their book sense, friendship, and enthusiasm; plus the Bridgewater–Raritan School District administrators for granting the sabbatical that got me started.

J.F.

INTERACTING WITH
CHILDREN'S LITERATURE

Illustration from I'LL MEET YOU AT THE CUCUMBERS by Lilian Moore, illustrated by Sharon Wooding. Atheneum, 1988. Reprinted by permission.

INTRODUCTION:
RAISING READERS

SINCE THE MID-1970S I HAVE BEEN A BOOK CHEERLEADER FOR children, teachers, and parents. I am the human card catalog who can whip out the pertinent title when a befuddled six-year-old says, "You read it to us last year and it was pink." I'm the one who slaves to coax reluctant fifth-graders out of "Sweet Valley Twins" and into Lois Lowry's "Anastasia" books. I quietly cheer each time a teacher and class gush over a new book they are sharing aloud. Last spring, there I was in the picture one kindergartner drew to go along with his caption, "The Librarian and a lizard are in quicksand."

Is there such a thing as being a born librarian, all those nasty stereotypes notwithstanding? I see myself and my colleagues as "new wave" librarians, determined that our libraries will be landmarks for all students and teachers who come our way. We tout reading as a pursuit of pleasure, and not just for taking tests, filling in endless odious worksheets, and backstroking through another predigested basal reader.

What turns people into readers? The experts say the more books in your house and the more your parents read, the better chance you have. But many of our students have no books at home, parents who don't read, and TVs that are never turned off. Do we throw up our hands and consider these kids unreachable?

My mother grew up with no books in her house. Her earliest book memory is the time her father took her to the drugstore and told her to pick out anything she wanted.

"I want a book," she told him.

"A book? What do you want a book for? How about a toy?"

"I want my own book," she repeated stubbornly, so he bought her one. She hasn't stopped reading since, and she and my father made sure to pass on that gift to all three of their children.

She recalls herself as an adolescent, hunkered down in a comfortable chair, feet tucked under, the way she sits even now, immersed in one thick tome or another, and eating dry saltines.

"Go out and play," her mother would holler. "Bookworm! You'll ruin your eyes."

We all ruined our eyes in my family. I don't know if it was from all the books, but each person in my family is more nearsighted than the next. If it was the books, it's been worth it.

There were books everywhere in my parents' house as I was growing up. Behind my parents' bed, instead of a headboard, there were built-in bookshelves. Luxury was lying on their bed on a cold, rainy day, reading a thick old book with a wide floppy binding in which I would hide achingly sour, little round wrapped lemon candies called Napoleons. I'm far kinder to my book bindings now, but back then I found it necessary to conceal the candies from my cavity-fearing mother. One by one, I'd extract the candies from the bottom of the binding and stuff the wrapper down the top. My mother was right. I did rot my teeth, but I read a lot of memorable books that way, from Dickens to Dostoyevsky.

From our weekly Tuesday night family trips to the public library followed by ice cream cones, and the unforgettable day in first grade when I learned to read the word "said" and a whole world of dialogue opened up before me, books have made such a difference in my life that I want to pass on my obsession to the new generation of kids who are being wined and dined on music videos and slasher movies.

At many universities across the country, undergraduate and graduate students preparing to be our next generation of teachers are not required to take a course in children's literature. The philosophy seems to be that it's sufficient to give education majors the basic "How to Teach Reading" courses, whereas the real books children like to read—the literature—are deemed too unimportant for a separate course of study.

Once again, the tide turns. In school districts where teachers and librarians have been too fixated with standardized tests to take any curricular time for "frills" like reading aloud or using actual children's books in class, administrators now whisper that perhaps our children are learning to hate reading and perhaps using real children's books might help reverse that. The California Reading Initiative and the Whole Language Approach are welcome new buzzwords in the latest reading revolution.

Reading is far more than just a skill to be mastered. Reading for enjoyment is a free ticket to other cities, states, countries, or far-off worlds, and it allows us to inhabit the minds of even the most introspective characters. Just as many of us recall rote learning of poetry with distaste, so can learning to read be unpleasant and filled with anguish for children today. We envision our students as future book consumers, aspiring to more than the latest supermarket romances, but if they read only junk as children, their adult tastes will probably be just as undemanding. And so we, the literary-minded teachers, librarians, and parents, are in the plum position to remedy negative attitudes toward reading and give our children the times of their lives by immersing them in all the best children's books our libraries and bookstores have to offer.

In Bridgewater-Raritan, the New Jersey school district where I work, the school administration has always been tremendously supportive of those innovative souls who use children's literature as a booster or as a base to their subject matter. Even so, many teachers are all too reluctant to try anything "fun" with books, fearing, perhaps, it might be construed as "frivolous."

What a trauma it is for a librarian to hear an already-macho, overbasalized third-grade boy claim indifferently, "Oh, I don't need to take out any library books. I can get a book from home if I want one." Or the new fifth-grader who announces defiantly, "Yeah, we had a library in our old school. We had to go there once a week to get books, but I never read 'em."

Are these children lost to reading? Not if they have a librarian who, through booktalking, storytelling, and other stimulating book-based mania, can lure them back. Or if they land a teacher like Linda Forte at my school.

When Linda reads a book aloud, her students offer to pass up lunch, gym, and even going home. She's a smart cookie, though. Slapping the book shut right at a thrilling moment, she lets her listeners suffer and gives them another compelling reason to come to school the next day. Somehow, she makes time for reading aloud, collecting every floating classroom moment. By reorganizing priorities a bit, every teacher, no matter how overworked, can find time each day to read aloud a chapter, a paragraph, or at least a good poem.

One must perform frequent magic to make the books we hawk memorable, each year adding more spells to the repertoire. In the Van Holten School Library such enchantment includes: poetry parties; an all-school "Book Train," where all 500 of us line the corridors, snuggle up against the walls, and read; the fifth grade "In What Book Game," based on plot statements each child writes about fiction books he or she has read; and the handsome, annotated Summer Reading List booklets that the district librarians compile and hand out to every student for free-choice summer reading.

Many of the teachers at Van Holten thrive on frequent book thrills. One such third-grade teacher, Evelyn Balunis, loves to dress up. One fine day, after I read James Marshall's *Miss Nelson Is Missing* to her class, the library door crashed open and in flew a woman in an ugly black dress, striped socks, and long fingernails. "I am your new teacher, Miss Viola Swamp," she shrieked. "Everybody sit up straight!"

The students sat up, shocked, but only momentarily, until they realized it was just Mrs. Balunis being unpredictable again. Evelyn spent the entire day in character, springing into other classrooms to cackle at surprised teachers, "My name is Miss Viola Swamp. Listen, honey, if you're not feeling so great, if your brats are giving you a hard time and you have a little stomachache or a sore throat, you just give me a call. I'll straighten out this class in no time flat."

Mrs. Balunis is perfectly calm and sane much of the time, but there's a spark in her eye. Her students will never forget her.

When you use children's books as a natural part of the school day, the advantages multiply. Teachers have the obligation to give their students this long-reaching gift. Once our children leave elementary school, it's almost too late. But for those who grow up harboring an early-learned passion for reading, it will always be there, a vicarious vacation after the school day, after the job, after the babies are in bed. We are the ones who can pass on this legacy.

With over 3,500 children's books published each year, one must be extraordinarily selective when culling out the best. Out of every ten recommended fiction titles I read, an average of one fits in that special niche of being a good read-aloud. Of the other nine, five are usually penny dreadful—a combination of poor illustrations and trite writing—and the other four range from acceptable to exquisite, but not as read-alouds. There are plenty of wonderful books out there for children to read to themselves (and far more dreary ones), but for a teacher or librarian to read one aloud, it must have exceptional merits.

I am intrigued and amused by the often wildly contrasting opinions about any one book in the reviewing publications. *School Library Journal* (*SLJ*) loves and stars it; *Booklist* loathes and pans it, and vice versa. But I don't put great stock in anyone else's opinion until I have read it myself.

Each spring, Alice Yucht (middle school librarian, *Library Talk* magazine columnist, and my Booktalks Unlimited "partner-in-crime") and I develop and present an all-new edition of our "Winners & Losers" children's literature conference for teachers and librarians. We show and review, and praise or pan, the 150-or-so books that have been cited by the American Library Association, *Booklist*, *Hornbook*, and *SLJ* as their year's best-of-the-best picks, and describe ways to use them with kids. We are always struck by the small number of books that are selected by all four lists, and the vast majority that only make it onto one.

Just what is it that constitutes a read-aloud? In fiction, the style must rise above formula writing, with characters one would be excited to meet in person. A good writer is one who clearly describes characters, scenes, and events so we can see them happening in our mind's eye. A great writer is one who helps us become those characters and live out their lives with them as we read. There is room for both types when reading aloud. Not every book must be a masterpiece, though one looks for a certain richness that will elevate a child's understanding of other people and the world around.

I look for tight plots that make sense within the frameworks of their stories; dialogue that rings true; premises that one can accept, no matter how bizarre, because the supporting details are right; story lines that are original or at least handled in a fresh, new way; and a clear, fluid writing style. I reject many books because the plot unravels and fizzles out before the ending. Others work well for one-to-one reading but not in a group setting.

I start out each new book optimistically, wanting to be pulled in and seduced, but I am often disappointed. If I've read too many bad or mediocre books at one time, my resulting gloomy mood can carry over into a new book, causing me to pan something I should have read more closely. Later, either guilt, a child, or a colleague will tell me to have another look, and back I go, to read the book again and give it another chance. I've rediscovered several good books that way.

My reasons for selecting a title are intentionally diverse. We read aloud so children can hear great literature, develop a poetic ear for words put together in a rich, orderly, felicitous fashion, and learn to relax around books. Still, not every selection can be a classic, though many classics are listed in the Read-Aloud Lists, side by side with titles that might be considered frivolous. One must vary children's literary fare. Too many hard-slogging tomes can be as tedious as too much fluff. One needs a balance, interspersing all genres, styles, and moods.

If it's a picture book, the illustrations must not only add resonance and meaning to the story, but they must be clear enough for a class to make them out. With great reluctance, I omitted several of Steven Kellogg's and Kevin Henkes's books because the illustrations were simply too light, tiny, and detailed to decipher from farther away than two or three feet. For a small group or one-on-one reading they are marvelous, but my focus is on books a larger group can share. Even then, with some titles it is necessary for the children to sit as close to you as possible. (I call this intimate regrouping the "Sardine Approach to Literature.")

Many books were included simply because they made me laugh out loud. Tying titles into the curriculum may be an educationally wise and useful idea, but to me, one of the best legacies we can leave to our children is a license to laugh, dream, and fantasize. A sense of humor, nurtured by a teacher or librarian who sees the importance of laughter in school, is a gift that can carry us through tense times.

Certain books, including "problem" fiction and fairy tales, help children work their way through tough personal roadblocks in their own lives and develop a sense of empathy for others. An essential side effect of shared literature is the sense of community and closeness that a class feels after experiencing the emotional ups and downs of books like Betsy Byars's *Cracker Jackson* or the fairy tale *Beauty and the Beast*. "What would you do if that happened to you?" is a question that brings into play students' developing standards and sense of moral fairness, which they then intuitively apply to their own lives. Reading aloud good literature stretches us all. Children from other cultures and times in history become familiar companions when we share their sagas.

Recently, two tenth-grade boys, now tall, handsome, and worldly-wise, dropped in to my library to reminisce. As they pored over the fiction shelves seeking out former favorites, one came across Judy Blume's taboo-breaking classic of junior high angst, *Are You There God? It's Me, Margaret*. He pointed to it and said affectionately, "Ah, I remember that one—my first sexual experience!" His friend replied, "Yeah, that one was good. I used to take all those 'girl's' books out and sign them out with a girl's name so no one would know I was reading them."

Many boys feel they must hide their interest in reading books about girls, while girls tend to be more open-minded with their choices. Boys who won't read a "girl's" book on their own will get to see how the "other half" lives when the teacher reads such a book aloud. Care must be taken in selection, however, as many contemporary fiction books deal with personal matters such as a first menstrual period or the search for a one-size-fits-all training bra, and girls would be mortified to hear you give voice to those incidents in class. I decided against inclusion of many such personal books, feeling they were better read alone than as a group.

What thrills one class or teacher may seem dull or outrageous to another, depending on taste, interest, and the children's levels of sophistication. For this reason, do not expect to love every book on the lists. Likewise, do not feel obligated to restrict your fiction choices to those books on your grade-level lists. If you are a first-grade teacher, for instance, also look at the Pre–K and 2–3 fiction lists as well as the K–1 and 1–2 lists. Public librarians often face a wide age range for many of their story hours and need to plan accordingly.

Upper-grade teachers should not miss reading the more subtle or mature picture books listed for grades K–3. Older children often appreciate these stories more than the younger children for whom they were originally intended, and on a long, stressful day, nothing beats the snap of a good, funny picture book. Be sure to check under Picture Books for All Ages in the Subject Index, where many of these titles are identified.

Assigning grade levels to a book can be a tricky business, especially when limiting fiction books to only two grades. Most of the time, this works fine. For example, although you can read James Howe's *Bunnicula* to younger children, they will not be as in tune with the wordplays and worldly-wise humor as will fourth- and fifth-graders. Sixth-graders may love the book but feel it a bit young for their tastes. I originally put Roald Dahl's *The BFG* on the grades 3–4 fiction lists, but the teacher of the third-grade class that field-tested it felt her children were missing a great deal of the humor. Fourth- and fifth-graders rolled on the floor.

On a literal level, first-graders enjoyed Pat Cummings's *C.L.O.U.D.S.* about Chuku, the assistant skymaker who grows bored painting the same bland New York City skies each day, but second- and third-graders were much sharper in picking up nuances and understanding the ironic humor. As part of their weather studies unit, fourth-graders liked the story, but they did not respond with the same fervor. You will therefore find it on the grades 2–3 list.

If the book is part of a series, I often listed only one book, with reference to the others given in the annotation. There is no point in reading aloud more than one "Great Brain" or all seven "Narnia" books, unless your students are so hooked that they twist your arm to continue with the sequel. You want that first title to lead them to read all the others themselves. Still, many sequels stand on their own, and those I included. Louis Sachar's *Wayside School Is Falling Down* is just as bizarre and wonderful as the first one, *Sideways Stories from Wayside School*, and they both deserve attention.

Although many old and out-of-print books are being re-released these days, far more newer titles are going out of print sooner, causing great problems for librarians. Many of my favorites on the lists are currently unavailable, though I keep reordering them in hopes that a stray copy will turn up in the jobber's warehouse, or a publisher will note which titles are still being requested and take steps to bring them back. We should all compile lists of our favorite out-of-print titles and send them to each publisher. Keep an eye out for the biannual back-in-print columns in *SLJ* and *Booklist* to see if your efforts worked. It's worth the try.

For a more systematic approach, if you can spend the money, there are many book dealers, listed in the classifieds of *SLJ* and the *New York Times Book Review*, who specialize in finding out-of-print children's books. In addition, many books you never suspected of being treasures are now hidden away on your library shelves, awaiting discovery.

For those teachers who claim they don't have time to read aloud, much less try any of the book-related activities that enthrall and motivate students, perhaps some priorities should be reexamined. Those who are nervous about incorporating children's books into the curriculum and justifying a literature-based approach to teaching can find no fault with such behavioral objectives as developing literature appreciation, evaluation, and listening skills; identifying the climax; describing or drawing inferences about the main characters, plot, and the setting of a story; comparing and contrasting styles of writing; or introducing literary genres—all of which we do every time we read aloud.

Science is more interesting when the explanations of the earth's phenomena are introduced through the folklore that people once believed, along with the more traditionally accepted top-notch nonfiction books. Every subject is enhanced when literature is used as a connecting thread. Let each suggestion you borrow from the Read-Aloud Lists be just the first step in an exponential explosion of book enrichment activities you weave into your children's lives.

If children never hear their language read aloud, arranged in all those delicious, meaty phrases that constitute the best of our literature, then all the phonics drills on earth won't help them expand their vocabularies and imaginations, appreciate a thought well put, or whet a hunger for words, spoken and spelled.

Carol Shields, then a fourth-grade teacher, had been indifferent to children's books for years. Her classes were always fun and well-behaved in the library, but a spark was missing. In desperation, I foisted upon her one book by a lunatic author, and she was hooked. Daniel Pinkwater's *Lizard Music* was the culprit, and it became the first in a long line of books this teacher has read to her students over the past 10 years. Her students were ecstatic, and an annual class of readers has evolved.

Carol's taste in books now veers toward the bizarre whenever possible. She lives within walking distance of school, along with her husband and two cats. One afternoon, she started reading aloud to her class the tantalizing first chapter of Roald Dahl's *The Witches*. She reached the part where the narrator cautions the reader that any woman can be a witch, even the lovely schoolteacher reading aloud at that very moment.

The students snickered at this, but one earnest boy leapt from his chair, knocking it over, and pointed an accusing finger at Carol. "That's right!" he cried. "That's right! She could be a witch! She has two black cats in her yard. I've seen them!"

Well, maybe he's right. Because those students clamored after Roald Dahl's books for months afterward, and everyone knows "kids don't read anymore these days." We all need to use that combination of witchcraft, nonsense, and book skulduggery to keep our students spellbound so that, one day, they will be reading aloud to their children, too.

Illustration from RED RIDING HOOD copyright © 1987 by James Marshall. Published by Dial Books for Young Readers. All rights reserved. Used with permission.

READING ALOUD:
TRICKS OF THE TRADE

AUTHORITIES ASSUME THAT ALL TEACHERS, LIBRARIANS, AND PARENTS are experts at reading aloud. After all, how complicated can it be? And yet, I have observed librarians reading in dull, disinterested monotones, and teachers reading picture books to young children sprawled across the room at their desks, too far away to see the illustrations. Parents have said to me, "I should read aloud to my kid? He already knows how to read. He's not a baby anymore."

After much prodding, one reluctant teacher finally decided to read an adventure story aloud to the class. When I asked several children how they were enjoying the story, they said, "Oh, the book is good, but our teacher reads in *such* a boring voice!"

You are the one who can counteract that and make books matter. Every year you can push a little harder to excite children and their parents about books, and every year you will pick up a few more ideas and techniques to keep yourself fresh and motivated. The possibilities are dizzying.

GETTING STARTED

There are no hard-and-fast rules for reading aloud, but a few guidelines never hurt. My mother's commonsense admonition "Always read with expression!" was directed to me as a first-grader, but it has stood me in good stead.

Your oral reading style should fit your personality. Don't feel obligated to offer a unique voice for each character or to act out each scene dramatically as you read. The words of a good read-aloud should grab your listeners even if your delivery does not equal Olivier's. When you maintain good pitch, volume, and expression as you read, your students will demonstrate their approval by their rapt attention.

Having the children sit close enough to see the details in the pictures fosters a community feeling and allows them to respond to your reading. In my library, the "Story Rug" is where we sit, in three rows so everyone can see, and it's a magical place to be. That section, surrounded by the easy fiction and fiction shelves, is our private little enclave. When I greet a class at the door and tell them to go to the Story Rug, they rush to settle in there, happily anticipating a new story, book, or booktalk. The Story Rug is more personal for stories than the tables; it's a place where we can let down our defenses and get in the mood to read.

In a classroom, children should also sit close to the teacher as he or she reads. This is not a time for students to daydream at their desks, draw pictures, or do homework while they listen halfheartedly. Teachers who allow this behavior are demonstrating to their classes that reading aloud is not really so important, when just the opposite is true.

Once the reading begins, remember to make frequent eye contact to further involve your listeners. I hold picture books up to one side, level with my shoulder, with the bottom tilted slightly toward me to deflect any glare, and turn my head sideways so that I can read the text while the children examine each illustration.

READING ALOUD: COMMON PITFALLS

One good reason for reading a new book to yourself before trying it aloud is to get a feel for the language and to hone your use of expression. If you do select a book that you have never read before and find yourself bored to tears as you read it to your students, don't be surprised if they seem restless or uninterested.

When a longer title does not work out as planned, stop reading it and choose another one. No one says you must finish every book you start. End at a reasonable chapter and tell your listeners if they want to find out what happens, they can borrow the book from you and finish the story themselves.

For some books, judicious editing may help tighten the action. If, however, you find yourself omitting long sections, paraphrasing major passages, and simplifying vocabulary right and left, your selection is most likely too difficult for your audience. Although it's a good idea to read a cross section of books that will challenge your listeners, be careful not to choose books far over their heads. It's true that your children will most often love the books you do, but if they are only comprehending a storyline at its most literal level, the best approach is to save that book for a later year. Why push children to absorb ideas and concepts that are well above their academic and maturity levels when there are so many other more appropriate selections clamoring to be read? This does not mean that you need to "dumb down" your reading choices, but choose what will most stimulate your class without putting them on overload. Many books are worth waiting for until such time as the children have the background to make the story most meaningful.

A crackerjack teacher I know proposed to read *The Hobbit* to her class of very bright second- and third-graders. I cautioned her against it, as I felt the vocabulary and nature of the fantasy were well beyond their ability to comprehend, but she was determined to give it a try. Several weeks later, she returned the book for another selection, saying it wasn't worth all the detailed explanations she had to dole out along the way.

The first time I read aloud the spare novella *Stone Fox* by John Reynolds Gardiner, I wondered if I might have trouble with the devastating ending, where, 10 feet from the dogsled race finish line, Little Willie's beloved dog Searchlight collapses and dies of exertion. The answer came as my fourth-graders sat breathless, desperate to know if Little Willie would win the $500 that would save his grandfather's farm and life. With one gulping sob, I overflowed with tears, just as I cry for Charlotte when she dies, every time I reread *Charlotte's Web* to myself. Sniffling and hoarse-voiced, I whispered through the final pages, wiping my eyes, clutching my shredded tissue, and trying, without much success, not to look like a total fool. The children had never seen me do that before, though they were also shaken by the sudden, tragic ending. Moral: If you know you can't do it, don't read aloud sad bits from books, unless you don't mind crying with the kids.

Another type of editing problem may emerge when you neglect to read, or at least skim, a new book before using it with a class. In these modern times, off-color words or passages that you might prefer not to read aloud will crop up at the most inopportune times. Forewarned, if you choose, you can edit out these words, sentences, or even longer sections wihout making an issue of them, or you may decide not to select the book as a read-aloud. The two main characters in *How to Eat Fried Worms* by Thomas Rockwell invoke the word *bastard* in the heat of an argument. If that word bothers you, even in context, change it to *creep* or whatever you consider less offensive.

On a grander scale, in an uproarious chapter from Roald Dahl's *The BFG*, the Big Friendly Giant explains to Sophie, the little orphan girl he has kidnapped, about whizpoppers, or what happens to him after he drinks the downwardly fizzing drink, frobscottle. If you are not prepared for the inevitable flatulence jokes from your fourth- or fifth-graders, perhaps you will want to avoid this book, though you will be missing out on a story filled with the most hilariously convoluted language since Casey Stengel.

Sometimes it is the children who are embarrassed by a story. Third- or fourth-graders will almost certainly be shocked by and snicker at the scene in Hans Christian Andersen's *The Wild Swans* when the queen sends lovely Elise into the marble bath where one toad grasps her hair, the second her forehead, and the third her breasts. The accompanying illustration is discreet enough, but you may choose to paraphrase or otherwise amend the passage for the sake of not disrupting an otherwise grand story.

There are certain parts and functions of the body that children would rather not have adults acknowledge, and they are careful not to discuss these when they think we are within hearing range. I still remember Benjy Freeman's (no relation) aghast look the day he had to read aloud the word *bosom* in sixth grade. To save face, he mispronounced it on purpose, but the teacher stopped him, corrected his pronunciation, and made him repeat it. We all held our breath, thrilled and shamed for him as he said the dreaded word aloud.

Kids today are not substantially less squeamish, though I note with interest the words that make my students squirm: *love* and *kiss* being two major offenders. Three cheers for Elizabeth Levy for allowing the word *queer* back into children's vocabularies, it being taboo for the longest time, with her first-rate "Something Queer" mystery series. My students don't think twice when they ask for those titles. Sadly, however, this is an isolated case.

Overexposure to inappropriate violence and adult themes in movies and TV has resulted in many of our students clamoring for more of the same in the library. How many of us have gone to "R"-rated movies and counted all the young children who have been brought along by their parents in lieu of hiring a baby-sitter? Six-year-olds have said to me with alarming frequency these days, "Don't you have any books where the bad guys get shot and there's blood everywhere and they have lots of knives and they kill everybody and cut off their arms and stuff?" "Sorry," I say, "We don't go for such gore around here. How about a nice scary monster book instead?"

Teenagers may find modern-day slice-and-dice movies amusing, but children are not inured to the terrifying mess when they watch. Though bravado precludes them from admitting it, they are scared silly by "Jason" and "Freddy Kruger." Indeed, why shouldn't they be? This is not children's fare, and it is abusive for any parent to allow young children to see it. Children who don't yet know the distinction between reality and illusion lose their innocence far too early.

Reading aloud a diversity of books in school begins to counter some of the harmful messages children are hearing from their VCRs. For a while at least, in the security of our classrooms, we can offer a more hopeful, less warped picture of the world.

RAISING READERS

Each time you finish a new read-aloud, make it available to your students who will love hearing the echo of your voice as they read through it another time. Reading aloud is the most potent way to influence children to become readers themselves, and showing knowledge of and respect for books rubs off on children. We often don't recognize our power in influencing children's lives until a former student, now in high school, drops in to say, "I still remember that book you read us in third grade," and you realize it was over eight years ago.

New students in the library say, "Have you read all these books?" whenever I recommend favorites to them. "Just about," I tell them. "How can I tell you what's worth reading if I haven't read it myself?" They seem astonished that an adult would want to read or admit to loving books meant for children. Even so, it takes time before children trust your recommendations. When I started working as a librarian, many times I'd gush over this book or that only to see the student I'd "sold" it to quietly return it to the shelves when the coast was clear. The longer you know your students, the more they will accept and then seek out your judgments on books.

We professional educators are the ones most responsible for the success or failure of our students as readers for pleasure. We can make the allure of reading so intense that our kids are hard put to resist it. When I meet older children or adults who profess a loathing or disdain for reading or a reluctance to read for pleasure, I feel sorry that no teacher ever penetrated their protective shells. All it takes is one committed teacher to propel them into books and take away the stigma of being a "bookworm."

When I ask a child to tell me about one great book she has read and she tells me she hates to read and has never found a book she loved, I say, "It must be that you just haven't found the right kinds of books for you yet." It is a test of our mettle to match up each child to that perfect first book. There is no 100 percent success rate, but we keep on plugging.

New student Peter, a real outdoors kind of kid with a passion for camping and fishing, was a good reader, but when I asked him what he liked to read he said, "I only read nonfiction. I've never read a good fiction book in my life." I took a chance and told him a bit about Elizabeth Speare's riveting historical tale of a 12-year-old boy's survival in the Maine woods, *The Sign of the Beaver*. Reluctantly, he took it, just to be polite, I think. The following week Peter appeared in the library. "This is the *best* fiction book I've ever read," he exclaimed.

"It's the only fiction book you ever read," I reminded him. "Are you up to trying another one?" He was. I gave him Jean Craighead George's *My Side of the Mountain*, and another fiction reader was born.

Peter could have spent the rest of his life scorning fiction as irrelevant and unnecessary. Plenty of people do. The ability to enjoy and lose oneself in fiction, through which the world becomes a more interesting place, is the mark of sophistication in a young reader.

One September, Patrick, a new fifth-grader, told me that he had read and liked some Steven King novels, and that seemed pretty heavy going for a 10-year-old kid. He seemed an unusually discerning reader so I steered him to some of our hard-hitting fiction, and he was receptive. Three or four weeks later he told me that he'd never read so much in his whole life as in the last month.

"Hang on," I said. "I thought you always read like this."

"Nah," he told me. "I liked to read but I never did it much before now. And now I can't stop."

Because of my assumption that this boy was a great reader, I treated him like one, and it was a self-fulfilling prophecy. We need to treat all of our students this way, and because we're wild about books, they will be, too.

When teachers read aloud frequently, fool around with language, tell riddles and stories, try tongue twisters, and sing silly songs, their students show more creativity and are more willing to plunge into library-led poetry readings, storytelling, and creative drama. They tend to be more focused on stories, more imaginative, and less structured in their responses. As a desirable side effect, they also are more likely to mesh well as a group and show greater tolerance and affection for each other.

Children who hear no additional literature read in class or at home are often not sure when something is funny, are less willing to join in on a story's repeated refrain, or to take a chance on selecting longer, more challenging books. They prefer to read something familiar, or, in the case of many boys, take out a series of football books to examine the photographs.

Then again, sometimes we overestimate or take for granted how well our students comprehend. A third-grade teacher in my school was conducting a reading group and they had just finished a poignant scene in their reading book. One sentence described the main character, stating, "A lump rose in his throat." Afterward, the teacher asked a student, "Tell me about that scene. What was in the boy's throat?" Without hesitating, he replied, "A rose."

When you read aloud, don't expect to reach every child you teach, though often the one you are sure is paying no attention is actually listening very carefully and might surprise you later with his response. Plenty of nonreaders eschew books because they associate them with failure, and so reading becomes a hated and dreaded chore. Unless someone reads aloud to them—you, for example—when will they ever start to see otherwise?

ASK A SILLY QUESTION . . . QUESTIONING TECHNIQUES

One problem that teachers and librarians have with reading aloud is the inclination to turn every story into a reading lesson. After a story, we do not need to ask all of those probing questions to test our listeners' comprehension. Each book need not tie into an important subject. Reading aloud for the sheer pleasure it gives is a powerful motivator.

With many books, silence is the best response. As you close the book, a hush falls over the room, children sigh with pleasure, and then sit back to mull over and relive the story in their own heads. To dive in with questions afterward is intrusive and annoying.

However, when we do want to discuss a story, we need to be aware of a more broad-based range of questioning techniques. Warm-ups and follow-ups are two aspects of reading aloud that are most often given short shrift.

In Tom Birdseye's *Airmail to the Moon*, Ora Mae Cotton of Crabapple Orchard accuses her brother and sister of stealing her first-out baby tooth, right from under her pillow. She vows when she finds the culprit, "I'm gonna open up a can of gotcha and send him airmail to the moon," though, much to her embarrassment, the tooth is in her own pocket the whole time. The subject of loose teeth is a loaded one with children, and reading a book about it opens you up to becoming an unofficial tooth-examiner for the rest of the year!

Beginning the story by asking, "Has anyone here lost a tooth?" is an obvious opener, but it will get everyone's instant attention. Kids talk about their teeth the way we older folk discuss our ailments. However, if we look at the reasons we ask questions—to extend children's thinking processes and open them up to new ideas —a more interesting set of questions then might be: (1) Have you ever lost something important that you searched for all over the place and then found in either a very sensible place or a very weird place? (2) Of all the teeth you've lost so far, which one do you remember most and why?

After several dissertations on the preceding questions, children will focus in further if you say, "While I'm reading the story, try to figure out, from all your experience, just where Ora Mae's lost tooth could be." By personalizing the story in this way, children are more likely to relate to the character and discuss her plight with insight and sympathy.

After a story like Eloise Greenfield's *Grandpa's Face*, we might make stabs at questioning our kindergartner's comprehension, basal reader-style, saying, "How did Tamika feel when she saw her grandpa making that face in the mirror?" One child will invariably reply, "Sad," and if you question that, another will say, "No, happy." Then you might say, puzzled, "Happy? Do you think so?" for in the story, Tamika is terrified when she sees her actor grandpa, in preparation for a part, peer into the mirror with a look of hatred on his face, which she misinterprets as his real feelings. "No, she was mad," comes the final response.

I call this the "Happy, Sad, Mad, Glad" Syndrome, where children try to read your face to tell you what they think you want to hear. At this point, children are not responding out of identification with the characters, but because they know you expect them to say something.

When selecting books to read aloud, it is in our best interest to consider how we want to showcase each title, and develop strategies to make it most meaningful to children. In terms of planning, one useful guide is the six-level hierarchy of questioning, originally set forth in Benjamin Bloom's *The Taxonomy of Educational Objectives* (Longman, 1956):

1. KNOWLEDGE: This incorporates the literal questions on which we tend to rely too much, such as the 5 Ws, with little emphasis on the "why." If you plan to act out a story, having children retell the sequence of events is

necessary to measure their recall. Much questioning never goes beyond this basic level, unfortunately, when we ask students to rattle off facts but not much more.

2. COMPREHENSION: Here we ascertain whether or not the children understood the main idea of the story and the characters' stated reasons for acting, and have them describe or summarize parts of a story.

3. APPLICATION: Now we take the events from the story and ask children to relate them to their own experiences, to something they've seen, done, or said before. They can predict the outcome and use clues to figure out the turns of a plot.

4. ANALYSIS: Looking back over what they've read or heard, children draw conclusions about characters' motives and look for evidence to support their claims. They can compare and contrast one story with another, figuring out what parts were the same or different. Here's where many of the "why" questions fit in.

5. SYNTHESIS: Using what they have learned, children can create new ideas, by writing, drawing, debating, or thinking aloud, such as coming up with a sequel to a story, telling a story from another character's point of view, composing a song about a story, or acting out a folktale using improvised dialogue.

6. EVALUATION: Finally, students can offer their own opinions and judgments, with reasons to support their ideas. Comparing one book with another they've heard, they can discuss what makes one title superior to another.

Too often we base our questions on levels one and two, and neglect the other more challenging and creative levels that require children to identify with characters and apply what they have read to their own lives. It is better to ask no questions at all than to make students rehash the plot and dredge up tedious answers out of a sense of pedagogical duty.

Sometimes the questions I ask are to see if children have "gotten" the funny parts. Many times, wordplays or humorous bits need to be explained to children, who then laugh forever, as if they had understood it in the first place. A sense of humor must be developed through repeated exposure to funny things.

A more serious book like Barbara Cooney's *Miss Rumphius* begs to be discussed so children who have come away with a solely literal interpretation of the story can begin to think about its message: that we are all responsible for making the world a better place. When I read this story to one second-grade class, several children jumped up at the end and gave me a hug. Something about the story touched them in what I'd like to think was a lasting way, though it was only after we had talked about it a while that they started to see that the word *beautiful* does not need to mean only visible aesthetics.

You might ask *some* of the following six types of questions to provoke a discussion:

1. KNOWLEDGE: How is Miss Rumphius related to little Alice, the narrator of the story? (Miss Rumphius is her Great Aunt.) What three things did Miss Rumphius set out to do when she grew up? (She intended to go to faraway places, to live beside the sea when she grew old, and do something to make the world more beautiful.)

2. COMPREHENSION: Why did Miss Rumphius decide to plant lupine seeds along the Maine coast? (Her father told her when she was young that she should do something to make the world more beautiful. This was her way of fulfilling his request.) Describe how she made her decision to plant those seeds. (She was sick in bed with a bad back and when she recovered she found her favorite flowers, lupines, growing far from where she had originally planted them in her garden. The wind and birds had apparently carried the seeds. This gave her the idea.)

3. APPLICATION: Have you ever known anyone like the "Lupine Lady," who did something to help others without being asked or paid for it?

4. ANALYSIS: When Miss Rumphius was sick in bed with a bad back, what do you think she thought about? What does it mean, to do something that will make the world more beautiful?

5. SYNTHESIS: When little Alice, Miss Rumphius's grandniece, grows up, what do you think she might do to make the world more beautiful? What can *you* do to make the world more beautiful?

6. EVALUATION: Do you think Miss Rumphius succeeded in making the world more beautiful? Why or why not?

Most other stories do not need all that fuss made over them for the sake of gauging children's comprehension. Too many questions take the fun out of hearing a story, as too many written book reports make reading good books a terrible chore. Young children are not always equipped to evaluate an author's style or an illustrator's use of color. They'll give you a gut reaction, but don't expect them to give a detailed verbal analysis of a story. Instead, ask them to draw a picture of the scariest, funniest, most interesting part of a story, and they will eloquently answer all of your probing questions with a set of eight crayons, especially if the tips aren't broken yet. You need to evaluate each book on its own merits to decide how you want to incorporate it into your children's lives.

GETTING TO KNOW YOU—AUTHORS AND ILLUSTRATORS

Friend and librarian colleague Jane Scherer wrote the following words to the tune of "The Farmer in the Dell" to teach first-, second-, and third-graders the parts of a book. It works wonderfully, especially when you sing it several times, increasing the speed each time.

The author writes the book, the author writes the book;
Hi ho librario, the author writes the book.

The illustrator draws, the illustrator draws;
Hi ho librario, the illustrator draws.

The publisher puts it together, the publisher puts it together;
Hi ho librario, the publisher puts it together.

The copyright tells us when . . . they made the book and then,
Hi ho librario, let's sing it once again!

Get in the habit of name dropping. Whenever you talk about a book, give the author and illustrator their due by mentioning their names and even a bit of suitable gossip about them. Before long, students will begin to do the same, giving recognition to the people responsible for a book's creation. Books do not drop from the sky, contrary to children's perceptions, and once readers are aware of the work behind writing, illustrating, and publishing, they will have more respect for the books you read to them and the ones they read alone.

Tell them that Avi spent only one full day writing his soccer novel *S.O.R. Losers*, but 14 years working on the fantasy *Bright Shadow*. That Gordon Korman was 13 years old when he wrote the side-splitting *This Can't Be Happening at Macdonald Hall* for an English assignment, and it led to his career as a writer. That Jean Little, who writes so eloquently about children with handicaps, is herself blind. Or that Dr. Seuss's real name is Theodore Seuss Geisel, and sometimes he writes under the name Theo Le Sieg, which is Geisel spelled backward. These odd bits of trivia make the author memorable.

When I held up a copy of Karen Ackerman's Caldecott Medal-winning *Song and Dance Man* to show to a second-grade class, one boy piped up, "Hey, I know him. He's the guy who illustrated *Air Mail to the Moon*." He was right, of course, and Stephen Gammell should be honored to note that children recognize his scratchy colored pencil style of illustration.

Teachers might select a dozen significant authors and illustrators to highlight over the course of the school year. School librarians should do the same, with different authors for each grade. When I made a list of all the authors and illustrators I would like my students to recognize, there were well over 100 names I considered important.

An edited list follows (by no means comprehensive) of some of those authors and illustrators who have made a lasting contribution to children's literature and have accumulated a body of significant work. The grade levels are suggestions only. Obviously, Amy Schwartz will appeal as much to first- as to second-graders, and Johanna Hurwitz writes books for many ages, not just third grade. Draw up your own list based on your reading; this is just to get you started.

Authors and Illustrators Worth an Extra Fuss

(Key: Authors = A, Illustrators = I, Authors/Illustrators = A/I)

PRESCHOOL THROUGH KINDERGARTEN: Marc Brown (A/I), Eric Carle (I), Donald Crews (A/I), Don Freeman (A/I), Dick Gackenbach (A/I), Kevin Henkes (A/I), Shirley Hughes (A/I), Pat Hutchins (A/I), David McPhail (A/I), Maurice Sendak (A/I), Nicki Weiss (A/I), Rosemary Wells (A/I).

GRADE 1: Verna Aardema (A), Adrienne Adams (A/I), Harry Allard and James Marshall (A/I team), Jose Aruego and Ariane Dewey (A/I team), Lorna Balian (A/I), Eileen Christelow (A/I), Ezra Jack Keats (A/I), Leo Lionni (A/I), Patricia C. McKissack (A), James Marshall (A/I), Mercer Mayer (A/I), Daniel Pinkwater (A/I), Beatrix Potter (A/I), Amy Schwartz (A/I), Marjorie Weinman Sharmat (A), James Stevenson (A/I), Vera B. Williams (A/I), Audrey and Don Wood (A/I team), Ed Young(A/I).

GRADE 2: Carol and Donald Carrick (A/I team), Barbara Cooney (A/I), Tomie dePaola (A/I), Paul Galdone (A/I), Stephen Gammell (I), Steven Kellogg (A/I), Arnold and Anita Lobel (A/I, sometimes as a team, sometimes separately), Peggy Parish (A), Bill Peet (A/I), Allen Say (A/I), Dr. Seuss (A/I), William Steig (A/I), Chris Van Allsburg (A/I), Judith Viorst (A), Benard Waber (A/I), Paul O. Zelinsky (A/I), Margot Zemach (A/I).

GRADE 3: Hans Christian Andersen (A), Beverly Cleary (A), Barbara Dillon (A), Jacob and Wilhelm Grimm (A), Johanna Hurwitz (A), Trina Schart Hyman (I), Richard Kennedy (A), Rudyard Kipling (A), Patricia Lauber (A), Julius Lester (A), A. A. Milne (A), Jack Prelutsky (A), Shel Silverstein (A).

GRADE 4: Michael Bond (A), Ellen Conford (A), Scott Corbett (A), Roald Dahl (A), John D. Fitzgerald (A), Jean Fritz (A), James Howe (A), Jean Little (A), Barbara Park (A), Robert Newton Peck (A), Daniel Pinkwater (A/I), Joseph Rosenbloom (A), Alvin Schwartz (A), Seymour Simon (A), Alfred Slote (A), Robert Kimmell Smith (A), Donal J. Sobol (A), Jean Van Leeuwen (A), E. B. White (A), Laura Ingalls Wilder (A).

GRADES 5 AND 6 (All A): Lloyd Alexander, Avi, Natalie Babbitt, Lynne Reid Banks, Bill Brittain, Betsy Byars, Sid Fleischman, Russell Freedman, Mary Downing Hahn, Dick King-Smith, Gordon Korman, Lois Lowry, Phyllis Reynolds Naylor, Katherine Paterson, Cynthia Rylant, Marilyn Sachs, Mary Stolz, Mildred Taylor, Valerie Worth.

USING PROPS AND OTHER GIMMICKS

Serious pack rats will recognize the syndrome called Collector's Mania. Every time I run into an unusual item at a flea market, garage sale, or store, I mull over what book, story, or lesson it could accompany. I've found rubber animals, fake noses, giant sunglasses, a cardinal hat with flapping wings, turkey feathers, a "Poohsticks" tea towel from London, and a miniature replica of the Dead Sea Scrolls complete with clay storage vase from Israel. Often I collect things first and then figure out how I can use them with my students later. Shanna, a fifth-grade student, once gave me a gray furry wind-up mouse. I knew immediately this was no ordinary toy. It was the mouse that became real in Leo Lionni's *Alexander and the Wind-Up Mouse*, and I now use it to introduce that story.

Another present was a glass magic wand with purple sparkly stars inside. Not only does that wand lead children to find good books on the shelves—it pulls me along and "points" whenever it spots a magical title—but it is also the practical jokester father's magic wand when I tell and sing Pete Seeger's *Abiyoyo*.

A set of real deer antlers and a handful of peacock feathers were just the thing to introduce and follow-up David Small's *Imogene's Antlers*. We started out listening to the ocean roar in a large seashell before launching into Verna Aardema's African folktale *Bimwili and the Zimwi*, of a little girl who leaves a shell by the seaside, and is then kidnapped by an awful creature when she runs back to retrieve it. Another wonderful wind-up toy is the set of chattering teeth I demonstrate as a warm-up to Nurit Karlin's *The Tooth Witch*.

To go along with Leone Castell Anderson's *The Wonderful Shrinking Shirt*, a first-rate tellable story with plenty of audience participation, I sewed a miniature yellow flannel shirt with purple stripes. By the end of the story, when the shirt has decreased to doll-size, too small to fit anyone, I pull out my creation. "Where did you get that," the children howl disbelievingly. "Baby Wilbur lent it to me," I say. "He made me promise not to get it dirty. There's no telling what might happen if we have to wash it again!"

When booktalking, I often hold up realia to help introduce titles: an antique key for Lynne Reid Banks's *The Indian in the Cupboard*, a pocket watch for Elizabeth

George Speare's *The Sign of the Beaver*, a pair of black eyeglass frames and a composition book for Louise Fitzhugh's *Harriet the Spy*, a pig nose for Mary Stolz's *Quentin Corn*, a ripe tomato for Mordecai Richler's *Jacob Two-Two Meets the Hooded Fang*, a snow-swirled glass globe for Barbara Dillon's *What's Happened to Harry?*

There is no rule that one must use such objects with a story, but reading aloud engenders an even greater sense of adventure and suspense when you pull out a surprise now and again. Matching *every* story with a prop or handout is unnecessary overkill. Ask yourself, "Will this extra touch enhance my story or overwhelm it?"

IN SEARCH OF MAGIC BOXES

As my stock of tie-in items grew, I began to cast about for some sort of treasure chest—a Magic Box of sorts—that could be used to add to the mystery of a presentation. My search ended in a friend's classroom when I stumbled upon a large, bread-box size wooden box with a lift-up lid on hinges.

That first Magic Box is a wonder. It has held the pasta pot filled with uncooked spaghetti when I read Tomie dePaola's *Strega Nona*; bean cards, one for each child to keep, with ordinary red beans pasted on them to remember Lorinda Bryan Cauley's *Jack and the Beanstalk*; and the two sleigh bells from Chris Van Allsburg's *The Polar Express*. (One bell jingled, the other did not, thanks to a small puddle of Elmer's that glued the inside ball to the metal.) It becomes a Booktalk Treasure Box when children have to find specific fiction books listed on task cards and place them inside. After they finish, we adjourn to the Story Rug where I pull each book out of the box, tell a sentence or so about it, and hand it out to the student who wants it first.

When I taught a course at Rutgers on fiction genres, one of my students, librarian Cathy Darby, displayed her final project. She had collected, designed, and constructed eight stupendous Booktalk Boxes, one for each genre of fiction, and planned the props and books to go along with each one. To introduce each genre during the year, she planned to bring out the relevant box and, with great fanfare, open it and retrieve the props that went along with each book as she booktalked the title.

Here are some of her ideas, which you may borrow and extend. In each box, there are props, both collected and handmade, for from five to eight books.

1. ANIMAL STORIES, REALISTIC AND FANTASY
   Box: Live animal carrying case.
   Titles and Props: *Wally* (Judie Wolkoff)—string of Christmas lights, rubber dinosaur that looks like a trachodon; *Cat Walk* (Mary Stolz)—frilly baby bonnet, can of cat food.
2. ADVENTURE, MYSTERY, SUSPENSE, AND HORROR
   Box: Dark green antique toolbox found in a garage sale, draped inside with black satin, fake cobwebs, a clanking chain, a few spiders, and a bat.
   Titles and Props: *The View from the Cherry Tree* (Willo Davis Roberts)—bottle of ketchup, binoculars; *Peppermints in the Parlor* (Barbara Brooks Wallace)—peppermint candies, large pair of long-blade scissors.
3. FANTASY
   Box: Medieval-looking, colorful, huge, rectangular metal cookie tin from Germany.

Titles and Props: *Mail-Order Wings* (Beatrice Gormley)—bottle of "Aero Joy" Juice, newly designed label taped over the original juice label, bird feather; *The Wizard Children of Finn* (Mary Tannen)—flashlight, sneaker.

4. SCIENCE FICTION

Box: Large white plastic cylinder-shaped container with green lid, redesigned with Styrofoam and foil to resemble a rocket.

Titles and Props: *The Green Book* (Jill Paton Walsh)—small blank-paged book, packet of vegetable seeds; *Fat Men from Space* (Daniel Pinkwater)—McDonald's Styrofoam burger container, candy bar.

5. HUMOR

Box: "Joker" box, made out of a large hat box with a papier-mâché head of a laughing joker attached.

Titles and Props: *Skinnybones* (Barbara Park)—baseball shirt, bag of "Kittyfritters" dry cat food; *Banana Twist* (Florence Parry Heide)—bananas, plastic replica of a banana split.

6. CONTEMPORARY FICTION

Box: Brightly colored school knapsack.

Titles and Props: *Lenny Kandell, Smart Aleck* (Ellen Conford)—pocketknife, tape recorder microphone; *Veronica Ganz* (Marilyn Sachs)—plastic fish skeleton, pink underpants.

7. CONTEMPORARY FICTION, PROBLEMS

Box: Picnic Basket.

Titles and Props: *The Summer of the Swans* (Betsy Byars)—watch, orange sneaker; *Hang Tough, Paul Mather* (Alfred Slote)—baseball, bottle of aspirin.

8. HISTORICAL FICTION

Box: Carpetbag.

Titles and Props: *War Horse* (Michael Morpurgo)—piece of barbed wire, horse, French and German coins; *What Happened in Hamelin* (Gloria Skurzynski)—plastic rat, metal pennywhistle or flute.

Once you find your first magic box, they seem to turn up everywhere. At Crabtree and Evelyn's, I found one that looked like an old-fashioned tome, with marbelized paper, a leatherlike binding, and a hinged lid. An antique store yielded a heavy metal box with embossed paintings by Rembrandt. One of my favorites is a plastic Rolykit box that from the outside looks like a hexagonal treasure chest, but it opens by unrolling until it is a long, flat rectangle, like a jelly roll undone. Inside are tiny compartments for screws or fishing supplies. I use it when telling children about the unpredictability of stories and how the best books are full of surprises. Then I undo the box, a side at a time, and they gasp. I have found a large red, heavy-duty plastic box, like a cat-carrying case, but with large black dinosaurs stenciled on the sides, at a Nature Company store. (If you don't receive their catalog, call 1-800-227-1114 and put yourself on the mailing list. You won't be disappointed.) It is now my nonfiction box, through which I can introduce the 10 Dewey categories or hone in on a particular subject, like mammals or science experiments. Children are tantalized by the mystery of what's in there and sit spellbound as each book or prop is extracted.

Mini-boxes are also a treat. I filled a small red metal chest with miniature objects, one for each letter of the alphabet, such as assorted plastic animals, a tiny

Chinese umbrella, a nut, and a question mark cut out of heavy colored cardboard. After chanting Susan Hoguet's *I Unpacked My Grandmother's Trunk* with a first-grade class who easily recalled all 26 items in sequence, I opened the mini-trunk, and each child reached in and pulled out one object. Standing in a circle, they identified their pieces, and then we played the memory game, each child holding up the proper item as we came to it. At the end, we repacked the trunk in reverse alphabetical order.

FEED ME

There is no rule that says you must reward children each time you complete a successful book or lesson, but sometimes the addition of an incentive or a handout marks the occasion as one to remember.

One morning, as I read aloud a chapter of Janice May Udry's *Angie* to a fourth-grade class, the smell of fresh toast began to waft toward the Story Rug. (In the chapter, Angie, who every day for breakfast had toast, peanut butter, and cereal, invented a whole raft of breakfast delights for her school breakfast chart assignment, including pickled pretzels, eel and toadstool stew, alligator à la mode, and stuffed boa contrictor.) When my class asked who was making toast, I led them over to the tables. There, courtesy of Mrs. Balunis, were cups of cereal and squares of toast with peanut butter on top, enough for each person in the class. "It's Angie's breakfast!" they shouted, and dug in with relish.

Wordless books often get short shrift in the library. Speech teachers love to use them with students, but by and large, children turn them down, saying, "I want a book with words to a story in it, not just pictures." Wordless books do tell stories, of course, though the reader must fill in the words, which is a valuable activity in itself. Wanting to introduce my kindergartners to wordless books that they could then take home and "read" aloud to their parents, I showed them a variety of my favorites, such as Noriko Ueno's *Elephant Buttons* and Lynd Ward's *The Silver Pony*. Holding up Emily Arnold McCully's *Picnic*, about a mouse family that sets out for a day in the country but loses its youngest member for a time, I explained that wordless books are like television with the sound turned down. We can hear what all the characters are saying if we look at the pictures carefully and listen to our imagination. As I showed each page, I turned an invisible knob and magically, the children supplied the dialogue, with some side coaching from me.

Picnic was great fun to read, and the children clamored for wordless books for weeks after that, but it was the follow-up that they could not get over. We put down an old sheet as our picnic blanket, and I brought out a picnic basket filled with a mouse's picnic for them to sample. Each child received a small plate with a tiny grape, a miniature carrot stick, cheese wedgelet, apple chunk, a one-inch peanut butter and jelly sandwich, and two fingernail-size Toll House cookies, each harboring one chocolate chip. We washed it all down with mini-glasses of lemonade, sang picnic songs, and pretended we were mice.

Penelope Proddow's Greek myth, *Demeter and Persephone*, told in Homeric verse, meant more to the fifth-graders when they could see what a pomegranate looked like before we started reading. Afterward, we cut it open, and each person ate six seeds to mark the start of winter. Most had never seen a pomegranate before.

(Don't wear good clothes if you use this idea. Pomegranates squirt and stain like mad.)

CLOTHES MAKE THE WOMAN

Children notice everything about their teachers, from new shoes to good moods. You can capitalize on their fascination with your life by carrying it over to what you read and why.

Look at Ms. Frizzle in the "Magic School Bus" books. She's the teacher who specializes in taking her class on field trips through the water system, into the earth, and inside the human body. In every scene, the flamboyant Frizzle wears a striking new dress, coordinated with the subject she is covering that day. Teachers everywhere would give their eyeteeth to discover her shopping secrets. Who else finds dresses covered with octopi, nuts and bolts, dinosaurs, or even noses, eyes, and ears? And her shoes! They've been festooned with lizards, screwdrivers, and Venus's-flytraps. ("Take a look at her shoes," says one child to another during their outside picnic in *The Magic School Bus Inside the Human Body*. "Please! I'm eating!" the girl replies, refusing to acknowledge the humanlike tongues attached to the uppers of her teacher's high heels.)

One can predict what Ms. Frizzle is planning next by checking out her new outfit. You may not have access to a magic bus that shrinks or expands as needed, but you might, for instance, wear crazy jewelry that coordinates with the story you're reading—a cat pin for Mary Calhoun's *Cross-Country Cat*, with a pair of ski-pole earrings, for instance, or a bunch of dandelions pinned to your shirt for Carol Chapman's *Barney Bipple's Magic Dandelions*. When students realize you like weird jewelry and collectibles, they'll bring you strange presents, too.

I'm partial to my Chinese dragon dress, which seems made for dragon book-talks and Jay Williams's *Everyone Knows What a Dragon Looks Like*; the red-and-white striped knee socks for George Selden's *Sparrow Socks*; and the necklace from India with the giant white rabbit, a natural for Rafe Martin's *Foolish Rabbit's Big Mistake*. Shopping has become an adventure.

If you can't drum up the right outfit, but you have props, puppets, or other hidden objects you want to display, make yourself a story apron. Start with a basic butcher's apron, the kind with the pocket on the front, and with colored material, add three to five more large pockets in which you can secrete your treasures. Whenever your children find you wearing the story apron, they'll be eager to see what marvels you have planned. If you put Velcro pieces on the outside of the pockets, you can even become a human flannel board.

AND THEY'RE EVEN GOOD FOR YOU!

Studies show that the more children read, the better their vocabulary, phonics, and comprehension skills become, and the easier schoolwork is to handle. Share these facts with your students. I tell them the following:

"There are three things in this world I am crazy about: chocolate ice cream sodas with mocha chip ice cream, Belgian chocolates, and books. Ice cream sodas are delicious, but they're very fattening and all that sugar isn't great for you. Belgian chocolates are heavenly, but they're terrible for your teeth, and besides that, they cost a fortune. And then there are books.

"Books are not fattening. They are free, at least in the library. They are delicious and enchanting and fun and satisfying. Not only that, they make you smart. Read one good fiction book tonight, and tomorrow when you come to school, you will be a little smarter. (That is, unless you were so busy reading you didn't bother to do your homework. This will make your teacher yell, and is not a great idea.) Turn off the TV and read two books this week, and not only will you have a good time, but your brain power will increase. Without lifting a finger, except to turn the pages, of course, you will become a bit more brilliant and a better reader every time you finish a new book.

"Imagine that. Something that feels good, doesn't cost anything, makes you more intelligent, and helps you do better in school. All you have to do is curl up in a comfortable chair, open your book, and enjoy yourself. That's what I call a good deal!"

Children who think reading books is sissy stuff change their tunes when they meet up with a book-obsessed teacher or librarian. By sheer force of personality, we can help our students, especially the older, more jaded ones, to see that reading is not only pleasurable but a hip thing to do.

Illustration from THE SHOW-AND-TELL WAR AND OTHER STORIES ABOUT
ADAM JOSHUA by Janice Lee Smith, illustrated by Dick Gackenbach. Harper &
Row, Publishers, 1988. Reprinted by permission of HarperCollins Publishers.

A CHAPTER OR TWO
MAY SUFFICE

OFTEN IN THE LIBRARY, WHERE THERE IS RARELY THE TIME TO READ aloud an entire book, I'll settle in with, say, a fifth-grade class and read through the beginning of a captivating story like Lynne Reid Banks's *The Indian in the Cupboard*, in which a tiny plastic toy Indian is inadvertently brought to life by Omri, a nine-year-old English boy. When I finish the chapter, hands shoot up. "Can I have that book?" children plead.

What with team teaching, computer instruction, pull-out programs, and special subjects, the school day is fragmented into many pieces, making sustained teaching more difficult. Teachers often seek to eliminate unnecessary "extras," but reading aloud must not be permitted to fit into that category. It is as academically vital, if not more so, as reading groups and spelling tests.

If you must save time, cut down on the length of your sessions, but try with all your might to read *something* aloud to your students every single day.

Picture books don't take long to finish, but upper-grade teachers are often reluctant to invest the time to read aloud longer chapter books, one after another. School librarians who see their students once a week for 40 minutes do not have enough time to read aloud long books, but there is time enough to introduce authors and their books through booktalks and one-chapter read-alouds.

Reading aloud one representative chapter from a book is a middle ground between booktalking and reading the whole book aloud. Children still get a taste of the author's style and start to become friends with the characters. This first encounter, like meeting any fascinating new acquaintance, makes them eager to get to know the heroes and villains. One chapter is often enough to get students hooked. As long as you can leave them dangling in suspense or sighing with satisfaction, they'll need to know what happens next, which is when you offer up the book to the highest bidder.

Not just any chapter will do. Be selective when searching for the perfect grabber. What you want is an excerpt full of action, humor, and the unusual twist. Keep a sharp lookout for that self-sufficient chapter in addition to the one that keeps you contemplating the outcome. Pamela Pollack did just that when she compiled *The Random House Book of Humor for Children*, a first-rate collection of chapters and other funny bits from assorted children's books and poems.

The suggestions that follow have been selected solely from books on the Read-Aloud Lists in this book, though you will undoubtedly come across many other wonderful chapters in books that you would not otherwise need to read aloud in their entirety. The search for satisfying chapters is endless; to get you started, here is a hodgepodge of books that start out wonderfully and get even better.

A-CHAPTER-OR-TWO READ-ALOUDS FOR GRADES 2–4

Classic Humor and a Taste of the Olden Days

Everyone knows about A. A. Milne's *Winnie-the-Pooh* and *The House at Pooh Corner*, but millions have relied on the Disney movies for their information and have missed being seduced by the charm, wit, and commonsense silliness of the originals. On a snowy day, I still read "In Which a House Is Built at Pooh Corner for Eeyore" and sing "The More It Snows (Tiddley Pom)," just as my mother did for me, way back in my wistful memory. For a special birthday, bring in a jar of honey and a balloon to go along with "In Which Eeyore Has a Birthday and Gets Two Presents." All of the other chapters have their own allure, so try out different ones every year.

After 40 years, Beverly Cleary's early books like *Henry Huggins* and *Beezus and Ramona* are still fresh and delightful. Mrs. Amato, my venerable librarian back in elementary school, was hard put to find another author I took to as warmly, though I still recall my delight at Anna Elizabeth Bennett's *Little Witch* and Gertrude Chandler Warner's *The Boxcar Children*, two books children still find grand.

Cleary was special, and still is. My sister Sharron was Beezus to my Ramona, and some of my early memories have blended together with tales about the Quimby clan. Sharron still hasn't quite forgiven me for burning the head of her ballerina doll on a light bulb, of which I have no memory, though I can picture it as clearly as the time Ramona pushed her best rubber doll Bendix into the baking batter of Beezus's birthday cake while playing at "Hansel and Gretel."

I do remember thrusting my open palms into the two chocolate layers cooling on the cake rack, making prints like those white plaster of Paris hand molds children still make in kindergarten. My mother was making the cake for her bridge group, and she frosted over my Ramona-like deed so no one would know. Ramona's mother made applesauce when her daughter took one bite out of every apple in the cellar basket.

To isolate a few chapters, I would pick the following:

1. *Beezus and Ramona*: "Beezus and Her Little Sister." Sick to the teeth of reading aloud to Ramona the insipid story *The Littlest Steam Shovel*, Beezus takes her to the public library where she immediately selects *Big Steve the Steam Shovel*. Determined never to return her new favorite book, the unrepentant Ramona scribbles in crayon on every page.
2. *Henry Huggins*: "Henry's Green Christmas." Getting the lead in the school Christmas play is Henry's worst nightmare come true, and he tries his best to get out of it. His mutt Ribsy saves the day when he accidentally overturns a gallon of green paint all over his master.
3. *Ramona the Pest*: "Ramona's Great Day." In which Ramona takes her new kindergarten teacher Miss Binney at a more literal level than most. When Miss Binney tells her, "Sit here for the present," Ramona won't budge from her chair as she awaits her teacher's gift, sure that Miss Binney likes her best.

This is also the first time a child in a story ever asked the kind of practical question that is on every child's mind. Miss Binney reads aloud Virginia Lee Burton's classic *Mike Mulligan and His Steam Shovel* where Mike and his trusty machine Mary Ann undertake to dig the town hall cellar in only one day. Ramona's hand shoots into the air. "I like the way Ramona remembers to raise her hand when she has a question," the teacher remarks in positive reinforcement style. Ramona beams and drops her bombshell. "Miss Binney, I want to know—how did Mike Mulligan go to the bathroom when he was digging the basement of the town hall?" An excellent question.

For another oldie but goodie, take your pick of stories from Betty MacDonald's "Mrs. Piggle-Wiggle" series about the plump little lady who lives in an upside-down house and knows more about children than any of us. She has remedies for answer-backers, slow-eater-tiny-bite-takers, fighter-quarrelers, and then there's the dreaded "Radish Cure" for children who refuse to take their baths. Written over 40 years ago by the author of *The Egg and I* (if you never read the book, perhaps you recall the Claudette Colbert/Fred MacMurray movie), these hilarious behavior-mod stories are short and filled with bewildered parents and their marauding children, all of whom learn their lessons, thanks to the miraculous Mrs. P.-W.

Children are always intrigued by descriptions of other schools and teachers. They listen in enthusiastic horror to tales of others, way back when, unjustly punished by paddling or the strap. In *Farmer Boy*, one of the "Little House" books by Laura Ingalls Wilder, students' sympathies will lie with Almonzo's kind new teacher, Mr. Corse, who never beats the children. Threatened by five strapping 16-year-olds who come to school each year to thrash the new teacher and break up the place, Mr. Corse shows them a trick or two of his own when he dispenses a little discipline in the form of a 15-foot blacksnake ox-whip. Read Chapter One: "School Days" and then Chapter Four: "Surprise."

Current Humor Chapters

To tie modern-day children into the old fairy tales, read the first two or three short chapters of Catherine Storr's *Clever Polly and the Stupid Wolf*, in which a nitwit of a wolf tries every fairy tale-related trick that he knows, from growing a ladder rung to planting a bean seed, to gobble up his succulent young target.

How to Eat Fried Worms by Thomas Rockwell is enough to put even the hardiest gourmand off one's feed for a while, as Billy accepts a 50-dollar bet to eat 15 nightcrawlers in 15 days. Your students may not flinch, but if you start feeling queasy, stop after the first worm. My library assistant Joan Grace gives candy gummy worms to each hardy child who finishes this book and describes to her some of the more interesting worm recipes sampled by the main character.

Still in the food department, the first two chapters in Ann Cameron's *The Stories Julian Tells* are winners. First, Julian and his little brother Huey accidentally eat the entire lemon pudding their father has concocted, and as a punishment, they face a good whipping and beating. That is, the wily father instructs his apprehensive sons to whip the egg whites and beat the other ingredients together to replace the first batch. Chapter Two is a tailor-made first step into the care and feeding of the library's card catalog. Julian tells his gullible little brother that a garden catalog is a book filled with magical cats that will leap out of the pages and plant his garden for him. I keep a Burpee catalog in school to show what a real seed catalog looks like. (Write to W. Atlee Burpee Co., Warminster, PA 18974, or call 1-800-888-1447 and they'll put you on their mailing list.) There's also a black-stuffed catalog cat named Licorice who oversees our card catalog. I remind reticent users that Licorice knows where everything is in the catalog, and if they can't find what they're looking up, to ask his assistance.

The gentle humor and matter-of-fact charm of the first few chapters from Janwillem Van de Wetering's *Hugh Pine* will make you want to drive straight to the Maine woods in search of the hamlets of Rotworth and Sorry. Hugh Pine, the only intelligent, hat-and-coat-clad porcupine among his lesser-brained associates, has taught himself to walk upright and even to speak English with his new companion, postmaster Mr. McTosh.

Animals can be more than they seem in Barbara Dillon's Halloween comedy-thriller *What's Happened to Harry?* where a witch turns young Harry into a poodle and then takes over his human body to cause major mischief in town. Chapter One, with its lulling description of Halloween candy, will make everyone drool.

On the realistic fiction front, after trying every angle to make his loose tooth fall out, Adam Joshua is stunned when he swallows it while eating a bowl of Mate's Mighty Munchies for breakfast. *The Monster in the Third Dresser Drawer and Other Stories about Adam Joshua* is Janice Lee Smith's first book in the series about a boy whose new baby sister gives him anxiety and whose day-to-day exploits give first- and second-graders grins. I am also entirely taken with "The Library Caper" from *The Show-and-Tell War*, where Adam Joshua checks out a Superman book and then, unable to bear giving back the best book he ever read, steals it for a time until he can copy down each page.

Chapters from Donald J. Sobol's "Encyclopedia Brown" mystery series are good training for future Holmesian followers, because listeners must use logic and deductive reasoning skills to crack each of the 10 cases per book. Detailed solutions are appended for those of us who are not as swift as the clever young son of Idaville's police chief. In the same vein, start out with a chapter or two from the "Einstein Anderson" books, Seymour Simon's science sleuth series.

School Stories

Sideways Stories from Wayside School by Louis Sachar is an outrageous tale of the top-floor class in a building that was inadvertently built 30 stories high, with one classroom per floor, instead of 30 rooms side by side on one level. (The architect got confused.) Each of the 30 chapters is about a child or two from the classroom on the top floor, where the miserable Mrs. Gorf presides. In just the first two chapters, Mrs. Gorf turns her students into apples only to have the tables turned on herself, and the nifty Mrs. Jewls takes over. The first chapter of the sequel, the equally insane *Wayside School Is Falling Down!*, finds Mrs. Jewls teaching her class about gravity by pushing a computer out the window. Third- through sixth-graders will howl over this one, and you should experience vicarious pleasure as well.

Also guffawingly funny is the April Fools' Day chapter in *Peter Potts* by Clifford Hicks, a perfect climax to the usual April 1 antics your students are known to pull. Don't read it until the first week of April, or you will find yourself fielding one practical joke after another.

Children are gratified to see an authority figure stumped or outsmarted every so often, and that's what happens to Mr. Wendell, William's teacher in *Fat Men from*

Space by Daniel Pinkwater. With his new filling, William finds he can clench his teeth and receive radio stations in his mouth, which makes playing a practical joke on the all-knowing Mr. Wendell a necessity. This book is not broken into chapters, so read from the beginning to the last paragraph on page 19, ending with, "And now the number-one tune on the charts, I'll Never Forget Your Nose."

Lynn Hall has invented one pip of a character for *In Trouble Again, Zelda Hammersmith?*, the first of a series. Narrator third-grader Zelda and her loving mom live in the Perfect Paradise Trailer Park where Zelda does nothing but get into scrapes. An appropriate chapter to read right before report cards is "Zelda and the Awful F." Devastated by an "F" in math, sure her mother will no longer love her, she first "loses" the card in the sewer, and then, after being given a replacement at school, decides to fake a car accident for sympathy. If her mother is relieved to find she's unharmed, Zelda reasons, she just might forget to be mad about her bad grade. The resulting reaction is more than she envisions, and Zelda finds out, along with your pupils, that a bad grade is not the end of the world.

Milo is always having dumb accidents. So when a library book called *Be a Perfect Person in Just Three Days* falls on his head, he checks it out and gives it a try. Steven Manes's first chapter will make your not-so-perfect cherubs clamor for details.

A-CHAPTER-OR-TWO READ-ALOUDS FOR GRADES 4–6

Short Stories

From books of short stories, I've culled some favorites. Check the Subject Index under Short Stories for more suggestions. Don't feel restrained by the following recommendations; all of these collections' short stories are worth the nod.

The title story in Ruth Ainsworth's *The Phantom Carousel and Other Ghostly Tales*, about a boy and the special wooden horse he rides at a local fair, is a haunting one with a suitably mystical and touching ending. Alfred Slote's title story in *The Devil Rides with Me and Other Fantastic Stories* is about an earnest young skier who makes an inadvertent bargain with Satan himself. Speaking of the Devil, any of the selections from Natalie Babbitt's *The Devil's Storybook* will prove startling and worth a chew.

Not for the delicate constitution did Lance Salway write his seven sly, creepy tales, *A Nasty Piece of Work and Other Ghost Stories*. A rowdy class will settle down fast when you scare their socks off with the title story about Martin who doesn't believe in the powers of Oliver's carved magic stick until thousands of flies buzz his room one fright-filled night.

Terry Jones's *Fairy Tales* consists of 30 atypical fantasies, each only two to three oversize pages long, and adorned with a large, dreamy Michael Foreman watercolor. If you are a fan of "Monty Python's Flying Circus" on PBS, you'll recognize Jones, a member of the troupe, and appreciate his cockeyed sense of humor here as well. "Happy ever after" is not how many of these tales end, and children will have plenty to say about the stories of lost fortunes, indecisive heroes, and wizards who get their just deserts. Select a few at random and compare them to traditional fairy tales.

You might need to watch "Masterpiece Theatre" to perfect the Cockney accent of Michael Fish, the professional fingersmith in Roald Dahl's story "The Hitchhiker," from the collection *The Wonderful Story of Henry Sugar and Six More*. Even without the accent, your listeners will pay diligent attention to this tale of two men who run afoul of the law.

Taking the law into their own hands, Sherlock Holmes addicts will be delirious to discover William Kotzwinkle's collection of five "Inspector Mantis" mysteries in *Trouble in Bugland*. Here is one of those books that deserves the moniker "for the special reader," as the bug-tinged language is as archaic and full of English-style description as any tale of Conan Doyle's great detective. Puns and wordplays abound—in the first story, "The Missing Butterfly," the circus owner is P. T. Barnworm—and the structure, humor, and interplay between Mantis and his faithful assistant Dr. Hopper are modeled after the original. Each story is fairly long and involved, but this is just the ticket to introduce alert children to the delights of Victorian-style mystery and will lead some straight to 221-B Baker Street.

In another specialized animal collection, Lloyd Alexander's *The Town Cats and Other Tales*, you will have a dramatic field day imitating the clucking, tight-fisted shopkeeper outwitted by a cunning feline in "The Cat and the Golden Egg."

Finally, there's Cynthia Rylant's elegant, understated *Children of Christmas*. For years I searched for compelling, nonreligious Christmas stories to read to my fifth-graders. Rylant's six brilliant, present-tense, slice-of-life vignettes will make your consumers sit back and reflect on children and former children who are not so fortunate. All of the stories are matter-of-fact memorable, but especially "Silver Packages," about a young mountain boy who grows up to repay his debt to his community. Read at least two stories aloud; you may find you want to read the whole book. It's not that long, and there's plenty to ponder over in each story.

Humorous Chapters

Looking over John D. Fitzgerald's *The Great Brain*, the first of seven fictionalized books about the author and his money-grubbing, ever-chiseling marvel of an older brother as they grew up Catholic in mostly Mormon turn-of-the-century Utah, may put you off at first. The print is so small and cramped-looking. But children who are undeterred by the format will love these books, and the infectiously funny chapter "Revenge Can Be Sour" can help break down the resistance of others. John D. decides that for once he will get a childhood disease before his brothers do so he can be recovering just as they come down with the sickness—in this case, mumps. His plan backfires when brother Tom D. gets wind of what he has done, gives him three days of the unbearable "silent treatment," and cons him out of his pride-and-joy Indian beaded belt.

Two chapters especially stand out in Robert McCloskey's classic *Homer Price*: "The Case of the Sensational Scent" where pet skunk Aroma captures four robbers single-tailed, and "The Doughnuts" with which many children are familiar, thanks to the Weston Woods film. I'm especially partial to the spooneristic sheriff who says things like, "Yep! . . . that was sure one smell job of swelling," and to Homer's Uncle Ulysses who runs a lunchroom full of modern automatic labor-saving devices, including a doughnut machine that runs "just as regular as a clock can tick."

Many children have never savored the joys of skinny-dipping, and after hearing "Janice Riker Strikes Again" from Robert Newton Peck's *Soup and Me*, some might still be reluctant to give it a try. Of course, having a big bruiser like Janice steal your underwear and throw the rest of your clothes in the water is not the best way to end up. Stranded on The Log in the middle of Putt's Pond, Rob and his best friend Soup can't do a thing about it.

One author who never fails to make children laugh aloud is Barbara Park. Her first chapter of *Operation: Dump the Chump* will reduce a fourth-grade class to hiccups. Oscar loathes his little brother Robert, who has always taken great pleasure in humiliating him. The first time they met, infant Robert went to the bathroom on Oscar's lap. And how about last Christmas when Robert swiped Oscar's new Santa Christmas cards and wrote "Merry Christmas POOPOO HED" on every one? After years of suffering these indignities, Oscar is plotting his ultimate revenge. In Chapter One of *Skinnybones*, Alex Frankovitch writes an outrageous entry to the Kitty Fritters TV Contest, for which he dumps a 10-pound bag of the dry cat nibbles all over the kitchen floor so he can find the entry blank. His cat Fluffy scoffs down so many that she throws up on his shoe.

Betsy Byars is another master of humor, often interspersed with serious topics. The second chapter of *The 18th Emergency* lays bare hero Mouse's massive problem. As Mouse explains to best friend Ezzie, he was in the upstairs corridor at school when, noticing the chart of prehistoric man hanging on the wall, he whipped out his pen and wrote the name "Marv Hammerman" next to the picture of Neanderthal man. Hammerman is the biggest, toughest kid in the sixth grade. He's flunked a lot. Unfortunately, Hammerman happened to be standing right behind Mouse at the time, and now he and his buddies are on Mouse's trail.

On the other side of the fence, there's *Veronica Ganz*, a girl with a mission. As the self-proclaimed class bully, she feels obligated to pound the tar out of every newcomer, including that sassy little shrimp Peter Wedermeyer. The problem is, as author Marilyn Sachs so masterfully tells us in that satisfying first chapter, that Peter is not one bit awestruck by Veronica's brawn. "Veronica Ganz doesn't wear pants," he taunts her, and she swears vengeance, only to end up with a bushel of fish garbage dumped on her head.

The first two chapters of Florence Parry Heide's *Banana Twist* are as nutty as they come. Jonah D. Krock, son of health-food and exercise-crazed, TV-hating parents, is determined to get accepted to the exclusive Fairlee boarding school where, unbeknownst to his folks, a boy can eat all the junk food he craves and there's a color TV in every room. In the meantime, he makes the acquaintance of the world's creepiest neighbor, the apparently banana-fixated Goober Grube. You'll find yourself laughing helplessly, and you may not be able to stop reading at the end of Chapter Two.

Since Lois Lowry's *All about Sam* is one of the all-time greats, it seems almost criminal not to read the whole thing aloud. Here's Anastasia Krupnik's little brother from the moment of his birth, when he can only communicate by saying "Waaaahhhh," to the last page when he signals his own name by flashlight in Morse code. If you can only give a taste of the book, however, read Chapter Three where Sam misunderstands his mother's explanation of how water pipes work. He gleefully flushes Anastasia's goldfish Frank down the toilet to give him the rare honor of going into the pipes, under the ground, into the ocean, up into the sky, and then raining back down.

Fantasy Chapters

I have yet to meet a reader who wasn't entranced by William Sleator's *Into the Dream*, where classmates Paul and Francine discover they are having the same recurring nightmare. The first short chapter, which can be booktalked just as easily as read, is a classic setup for the partnership the two unwilling classmates must forge, as there is no one else who can help them discover why their dream is getting worse.

Lloyd Alexander's books plead to be read aloud, as anyone who has read *The First Two Lives of Lukas-Kasha* can attest. After lazy bounder Lukas pays his penny to a marketplace conjurer and is dunked in a pail of water, he finds himself inexplicably drowning in an ocean by an unfamiliar shore. Pinching himself hard, he finds that his dream is very real.

By the end of the first chapter, Quentin finds his family's farm veritably drowning in cash after a leprechaun grants his wish for *All the Money in the World*, a clever yarn of greed and trickery by Bill Brittain. This talented author evokes the fairy tale aura of misty New England in *Devil's Donkey*, about the calamitous consequences a young unbeliever faces when he cuts a branch off the forbidden witches' tree. In the first chapter or two, depending on how far you want to go, Dan'l Pitt's confrontation with Old Magda the witch, mediated by his uncle, narrator Stew Meat, is a rousing one. The hag calls into play her special powers to transform the headstrong young boy into a donkey when he utters the words "dang blast."

Katie is no witch, but she has lived her almost 10 years knowing she is different from other children. When people look at her, they are taken aback by the strange color of her eyes and the feeling that she is odd. In Chapter One of *The Girl with the Silver Eyes* by Willo Davis Roberts, we learn about Katie's most outstanding ability. Using her eyes, she can move objects without touching them, a talent she has tried unsuccessfully to hide all her life and that appears to be growing stronger.

Then there's Gregory, a boy with no special talents to mention, except an inkling of how to use his wits to stay alive. Unfortunately, Gregory ignores a "Keep Out" sign by the Bear Lair display in the toy store and finds himself in the living room of a live, full-size, intelligent, boy-hungry bear. Luckily, Sir Rosemary comes to the rescue in full armor, but by the end of the first chapter of *Into the Painted Bear Lair* by Pamela Stearns, Gregory's problems are just beginning. There seems to be no way back to the toy store, and the bear plans to eat Gregory as soon as the boy gets over his bogus case of the sniffles.

Not all bears are unfriendly. Paddington's problem is that he is prone to accidents and calamities. *A Bear Called Paddington*, the first of Michael Bond's popular series, lets us know what we're in for in the second chapter, "A Bear in Hot Water," where our hero has a bit of a problem turning off the bath faucets in time. Each "Paddington" book has several dryly amusing chapters for reading aloud, and *Paddington's Storybook* is a collection of some of the best.

Historical Fiction Chapters

Max and Me and the Time Machine, as told by writing partners Gery Greer and Bob Ruddick, is filled with a blending of "thees" and "thous" and modern-day slang. Verily, the boys' trip back to "merry olde" England of 1250 A.D. is a funny one. Read the first three chapters, or skip the first one if you're short on time.

Losing both her parents in a boating accident at sea is just the start of bad times for poor little rich girl Emily Luccock in the fog-filled, Victorian-styled melodrama *Peppermints in the Parlor* by Barbara Brooks Wallace. Shipped off to San Francisco to live with her adored aunt and uncle in their mansion, Sugar Hill Hall, Emily finds her aunt a shadow of her former self, her uncle missing, and a hideous snake-eyed witch of a woman running the house as an old folks' home. In just the first two chapters, Emily is shorn of her long golden braids by the venomous Mrs. Meeching, becomes a servant, and learns the pink-and-white-striped peppermint drops that tempt her from the parlor's crystal bowl are forbidden to "charity brats" like her. Promise a similar peppermint drop to all who finish this crackling mystery on their own.

In a more traditional adventure story, 16-year-old Rudi Matt has no memory of his courageous father who died trying to reach the summit of the Citadel 15 years earlier. Working as a dishwasher at the Swiss village's hotel in the mid 1860s, Rudi is drawn to study each face of the mountain, the last unconquered peak of the Alps, and dreams of climbing it one day, despite his mother's fears for his safety. He gets his chance when he saves the life of Englishman and world-famous mountaineer Captain Winter, who has fallen into a glacial crevasse near the mountain. Chapter Two, "A Boy and a Man," details Rudi's selfless rescue and pumps up the listener's adrenaline for the heartstopping ascents that will follow in *Banner in the Sky* by James Ramsey Ullman.

Most people think the story of the Pied Piper is only a fairy tale, but author Gloria Skurzynski traveled all the way to Hamelin, Germany, to research her riveting fiction version of *What Happened in Hamelin*. Based on the actual events of 1284 when all the children from the rat-infested town were led away, the book is narrated by Geist, the orphaned baker's apprentice, who is befriended by the piper and ultimately left behind. Character descriptions in the first chapter are unforgettable and horrifying.

Let the above titles start you on a reading binge, but be sure to diversify your read-aloud agenda. If you always read only one or two chapters, you will be depriving your children of completing the grand tour. Understandably, your listeners will be frustrated and hunger for more.

Vary the fare, alternating from booktalking to reading single chapters and entire books of all genres. Even the best books get monotonous if you stick to just one type. Try some historical, some hysterical, a pinch of sci-fi, a sip of fantasy, a few stray animal tales, a couple of contemporary, a soupçon of mystery, and an adventure or two. Stretch your students and yourself as well.

Illustration from THE CHOCOLATE TOUCH by Patrick Skene Catling, illustrated by Margot Apple. Illustrations © 1952 by Margot Apple. By permission of Morrow Jr. Books, William Morrow & Co.

BOOKTALKING

OBVIOUSLY, IN ONE YEAR NO TEACHER OR LIBRARIAN COULD READ aloud all the books on one grade level of the Read-Aloud Lists. (The texts for kindergarten through second-grade books, however, are brief enough to facilitate the completion of scores of books in the course of the school year.) If you would like to familiarize your students with great numbers of titles, and stir up unquenchable interest at the same time, start booktalking.

Booktalks are the educator's equivalent of coming attractions at the movies. After just one minute of plugging, you will have 15 eager children pleading with you to let them read the book you have just described. It takes little time to prepare and deliver several one-minute booktalks, and your students will pass the books around to each other for weeks to come.

Keep up the encouragement and they will start delivering spontaneous booktalks to each other. Take advantage of their interest and allow volunteers to booktalk their latest discoveries to the group. It beats oral book reports, which are a variation on the theme but tend to be delivered in a bored or nervous monotone. Teach your kids your own booktalking tips and tricks as if you're letting them in on a big secret, and in no time your group will be tossing around book recommendations like M&Ms. Next, set up booktalk swap sessions between classes. You just might spark a schoolwide reading revolution.

Anybody can booktalk. You do it every time you recommend a book to someone, and certainly there is no trick to that. Yet, when I've conducted booktalking workshops and courses for teachers and librarians, some people always say, "Well, sure, *you* can do booktalks. But I don't have the time (or the patience . . . talent . . . guts . . . skill . . . knowledge . . . need . . . student interest) to do it myself." Horsefeathers! Booktalking is a cinch, as long as you don't allow yourself to become overawed by it.

In my elementary school library, I had always made time to tell my students about grand new books, reading aloud passages, relating tickling incidents, showing and telling the best I had to give. Then, during book selection time, I was in the midst of the mob, shilling titles right and left, issuing fast plot teasers to make each book a hot item. But, to me, this wasn't real booktalking. Real booktalking was for experts. Real booktalking was *serious*.

When I took Mary Kay Chelton's course in booktalking at Rutgers, I learned the difference between booktalking for teens and for elementary schoolers is merely one of style and formality. For teens, you need to be more polished and professional. Second- through sixth-graders are more accepting and forgiving, so you can relax and give looser, less-stylized talks, in the conversational tone you use when telling a spouse or friends some bit of gossip.

And remember that those short blurbs you spill out to borrowers are booktalks, too, and are just as important as any formal all-class session, for they are personally tailored to each child. When teachers, while waiting for their students to sign out their library books, spend the time grading papers or chatting with peers, they are missing out on a most vital opportunity to interact with their children. This is a prime time to reinforce the notions that reading groups and real books do have more than some slight connection and that teachers also appreciate good literature. Librarians and teachers both need to "work the crowd" during browsing time, looking through and waxing enthusiastic about the books their students have chosen, recommending new titles, assessing reading levels, and cheering on reticent readers.

Too often, we fall back on timeworn approaches to monitor our children's reading because that's how it's always been done. How many times have you heard yourself saying, "Put that book back right away. I will not have you reading another football book. Now go find a nice *story*." The boy grabs the first book that comes to hand, stashes it in the back of his desk, and resolves never to read a word of it. "How do I reach him?" you wonder.

Or, "You may not use that book for your book report. It only has 97 pages, and I told you to read one with over 100 pages. Find something else." The student picks out the first book she can find with 107 pages, big print, and giant margins. "Is the length really so important?" you question yourself.

There must be a better way to get kids excited about books.

If we want our children to be book hounds, we must set that example, showing them daily that we love to read, that we like to read "their" books as well as our own, and that we care about their reading experiences. Positive encouragement always works better than negative, of course, but sometimes we feel at a loss as how best to influence our students' reading tastes. Booktalking is one way to get close to a class, show them which books matter to you, and make those books seem irresistibly tantalizing.

GETTING STARTED

Here are 10 basic and relatively painless steps for prospective booktalkers to follow.

1. Select some hilarious, exciting, terrifying, terrific, mystifying, thrilling, heart-rending, quality titles (including nonfiction and poetry as well as fiction) that you have read and that are on your students' varied interest and reading levels. Don't bother with books you haven't read. Students often sense your unfamiliarity, and besides, it's not cricket to recommend something you haven't experienced firsthand. They could do as well just by reading the front book flap. The titles recommended in this book's Read-Aloud Lists make first-rate booktalks, though these are only a small but select percentage of booktalkable titles and books children will enjoy reading on their own.

2. Skim through the first third of each book to refamiliarize yourself with plot, characters, and setting, all the while searching for short, action-filled scenes enticing enough to retell. All three editions of Joni Bodart's *Booktalk!* (listed in the Professional Bibliography) include scores of already written booktalks you can crib at leisure. This is fair game, though you will soon see the booktalks you create are every bit as good.

3. Keeping your personal platitudes to the barest minimum, compose a 30-second to 10-minute description of a dramatic incident, a plot overview, or a character study that will involve your listeners and make them eager to know more.

4. The longer your booktalk is, the more detailed it will be. I like to look for a complete episode that I can tell as a story, although a short description fits the bill perfectly for some books. Some books only need one tantalizing sentence to get your audience salivating. Throw in a handful of these 10- to 30-second flashes to keep them breathless. Even a long booktalk does not tell too much. If you find yourself explaining what happened to each character and revealing the second half of the book, cut it short. Why should anyone bother to read the book if you've already clued them in on everything that happens?

5. Try to duplicate the flavor of the original prose in your retelling. If you are describing a particularly funny, riveting, scary, or poignant moment, the audience will want to experience those emotions. Be dramatic when the scene calls for it, but don't overdo it. Listeners want to focus on the story, not your acting. Every so often, when it fits, you can include a short key passage to read aloud. Mark it with a paper clip on the side of the page next to your starting sentence to avoid fumbling for the right place. Only read aloud when the book says it better than you can. The more proficient you get, the less you'll need to fall back on reading aloud, although if not overused, it does add texture to your presentation. Elementary school children sometimes feel they're being cheated if you don't read anything aloud.

6. Learn the names of your characters so it sounds like you're recounting experiences with old friends. When you get stuck, as we all do now and again, casually open to the front book flap where, if you are lucky, such vital statistics will reside. If not, keep talking as you idly leaf through a few pages until you find what you need. The children won't know it's not part of your planned speech unless you tell them, so don't tell them. If you are feeling insecure, write any necessary "crib notes" on a slip of "Post-it" paper and stick it on the back cover.

7. Practice your booktalks until you get the hang of them. While rehearsing, be on the alert and correct any rocking or swaying, nervous and unnecessary hand movements, mumbling, lack of eye contact, and inappropriate nail biting or jewelry fumbling. As in storytelling, you might find it useful to make an audiotape of your practice talk to time how long it takes to cover each book and to get an idea of what speaking quirks you want to iron out. The tape recorder might be brutal, but it's more honest than you'll ever be. If you find you come across as unsure or jittery, don't advertise it— overcome it. You teach because you like to be in front of children. Take

advantage of the natural reverence in which children hold you and don't be afraid of making a fool of yourself every so often.

8. When you deliver your booktalk, make sure to clearly state the title and author of each book and show the cover at some point during your discourse. If you just booktalked Gordon Korman's *This Can't Be Happening at Macdonald Hall*, take the opportunity to show off other Korman titles in passing.

9. After you finish, distribute the books fairly to the children who want them. Try raffling for a change, by picking a number, letter, month, state, river, or color for potential readers to guess. Include as categories curriculum tie-ins for quick reinforcement, such as continents, countries, mammals, or planets. Books become all the more alluring when one must win them to read. Sometimes I fix the contest. That fourth-grade boy who loathes books impulsively decides that Bruce Coville's *The Monster's Ring* sounds too good to miss. He tentatively raises his hand as you sum up with, "Russell turned into a monster on Halloween. Whoever can guess the other holiday I'm thinking about right now gets to check out the book." When it's his turn to guess and he blurts out, "The Fourth of July?" you say, "Charlie, you must have read my mind," and hand over the book, even though you had planned on St. Patrick's Day as your answer. *Never* let your students know you sometimes give weighted favor to those who might best benefit from particular titles, and don't overdo it. Most of the time, let yourself be surprised by who wins.

10. Keep a record of the talks you give to each class so you don't forget and try to sell the same book twice. It's a good idea to note the reading and interest levels and the types of books you use so you can keep your selection varied. Make a master list of all the books you love, then base your booktalks on these, adding to the list every time you stumble on new treasures. And quit worrying. The more you booktalk, the easier it gets to pull one together quickly.

SUBLIMINAL BOOKTALKS

It is possible to booktalk without saying a word. By having only the most appetizing books at your beck and call, you are advertising their desirability every time you hold one up.

I've never been able to understand how anyone could prefer teaching the parts of a title page using those lame little generic title page dittos and worksheets when you can hand out honest-to-goodness real books. Why teach about indexes, glossaries, and tables of contents using your drab old textbooks when you can dig through the best of the library's nonfiction books to do the same thing, exposing children to fresh topics that they can swap among themselves? Hand-picking each title you distribute is a form of silent booktalking. My two rules of thumb are to incorporate real books in every aspect of teaching and to select only top-rate titles that you can recommend without hesitation.

In my library, the children know that each of the scores of books on display along the tops of shelves and counters has the "Freeman Guarantee," meaning I already read it and loved it, making it a possible good choice for checkout. "Oh, great!" I say each time children choose these books, "Now there's more room to put other favorites on display!" And I do.

SHORT TALKS

The fastest and easiest type of booktalk to throw together is the 30-second to 2-minute talk. If you give four or five at a shot, you'll have spent very little time introducing more books than you could read aloud in several months. Short talks can be done when there are a few minutes left before lunch or the last bell, to warm up a class, or to showcase a batch of new, unrelated titles you just came across. Many of the annotations on the Read-Aloud Lists in this book make acceptable 10-second short talks, though you might want to give a tad more detail.

I work short talks into my library lessons as a base to everything I teach. Introducing encyclopedia skills to fourth grade? Out comes Donald J. Sobol's "Encyclopedia Brown" series about America's Sherlock Holmes in sneakers, with a few sentences on how young Leroy solves his cases, and those books are snapped up. Reviewing the parts of a catalog card to third-graders, I "find" a gold coin on the floor, which happens to remind me of Patrick Skene Catling's *The Chocolate Touch*. After everyone's wondering what else John Midas might turn into chocolate, I "discover" a giant catalog card for that very book, cut into puzzlelike components of author, title, illustrator, publisher and copyright date, annotation, and call letters, which we then assemble in proper order on the flannel board.

Not only does it take next to no time to introduce each lesson with a book tie-in, it perks up interest in what you're doing next. For every curricular subject you teach, there are good books out there waiting to be introduced. (Check the Subject Index in the back of this book.)

For younger children below second grade, 30-second short talks can be effective, though the children are often dismayed that you don't want to read the whole book to them. When you're reading a new story aloud, hold up several related titles, show a picture or two, and tell about them briefly as a supplement to the main event. The more books you introduce in each class, the more they'll read.

Following are a sampling of short talks you might give to fourth-, fifth-, or sixth-graders. Be sure to incorporate the title and author into each short talk, and hold up the book so children can examine the cover.

Thirty-Second Short Talks: Three Examples

Professor Flybinder's Fantastic, Fully Guaranteed Time Machine, which best friends Steve and Max pick up at a garage sale for a mere $2.50, really works! They set the dial for 1250 A.D. and land up in "jolly olde" England. Steve has taken over the armor-clad body of valiant Sir Robert, about to enter into a jousting match with the black-hearted Hampshire Mauler. And Max? He's become Steve's trusty horse! *Max and Me and the Time Machine* by Gery Greer and Bob Ruddick is their first wild and woolly adventure, followed by *Max and Me and the Wild West*.

Night after night, Paul has been having the same terrible dream, though each night it feels more threatening, urgent, and real. Voices whisper words he can't understand. The word *Stardust* blinks to his left, and there's a person whose identity he can't make out standing beside him. Then Francine, a girl in his class he neither knows nor likes, approaches him at recess and tells him she, too, is having the same horrifying dream. *Into the Dream* by William Sleator is for those nights when you are afraid to close your eyes.

Harry's Great-Uncle George, whom he has never met, has just died and in his will left Harry his most cherished possession. Is it a private jet? A treasure chest overflowing with precious jewels? A Rolls Royce? No, it's a parrot. An extremely intelligent African Gray parrot, as it turns out, answering to the name of Madison, after the fourth president of the United States. Madison is a bit different from your average parrot. He not only talks as well as any human, he reads, picks out tunes on the piano, answers the telephone, and even plays a mean game of chess. As author Dick King-Smith tells it, he becomes *Harry's Mad*, the greatest pal a kid could have . . . until he's bird-napped by a burglar.

One-Minute Short Talks: One Example

For those of you who have always been fascinated with the life of Helen Keller, here is another astonishing biography; Edith Fisher Hunter's *Child of the Silent Night: The Story of Laura Bridgman*. Since she was two years old, Laura Bridgman was not only blind, but completely deaf and unable to talk. With no sense of smell or taste, the only sense Laura still had was the sense of touch. She was born in 1829, almost 50 years before Helen Keller, and until she was seven, there was no hope she could ever be taught to communicate, even though she was intelligent and eager to learn. When she could not make herself understood, she would fly into a violent rage. Then Dr. Samuel Gridley Howe heard about her plight. As the director of the New England Asylum for the Blind, now known the world over as the Perkins School for the Blind, Dr. Howe was eager to see if it would be possible to educate her. Laura was accepted there as a student. Laura Bridgman not only became the first blind and deaf person to be able to make herself understood, but was taught to read and write as well, and took part in teaching other children at the school. She is proof that we can achieve great things, in spite of our handicaps.

THEME BOOKTALKS

Next try a theme booktalk by pulling together several short talks that contain a common thread such as loneliness, food, pets, fear, new friends, or weird neighbors. The possibilities are limitless, including curriculum tie-ins to a subject that the class is studying, and don't forget to consider poetry, biography, and nonfiction as complements to your fiction selections. Link together all the books in your presentation, almost like telling a long segmented story, with an introduction and a windup ending. In the following 6- to 10-minute booktalk designed for fourth-graders, the reading levels range from third through fifth grades, and genres include humor, fantasy, nonfiction, science fiction, adventure, and mystery. The theme loosely connecting all five books, which otherwise have very little in common, is trees.

Trees Booktalk

(Introduction: 10 seconds)   Now that spring is finally here, I find myself waiting for the flowering trees outside the library to bloom. That's how I know summer is on its way.

(Ease into Book 1: 30 seconds—A quick tease)   Imagine what it would be like if all the trees near your house stayed green and leafy, even through the snows of January. When the Finch family moved into their new house, that's just what they found. Even on the coldest days of the year, flowers bloomed outside their house and the snow melted immediately. You see, the Finches had a volcano steaming in their basement. They never needed to worry about heating bills because the temperature in the house always hovered around 80°. For a while, the volcano seemed harmless enough. Read Roger Drury's book *The Finches' Fabulous Furnace* to discover what happened during that fateful year when the volcano started growing.

(Book 2: One minute and 30 seconds—Show photographs from the book as you talk)   On March 20, 1980, there was a strong earthquake in southern Washington State that awoke a volcano from a 123-year sleep. Perhaps you've heard of Mount St. Helens and its tremendous eruption on May 18 of that year. Perhaps you've wondered what happens when a real volcano blows its top. Before the explosion, Mount St. Helens was like a massive pressure cooker, building up superheated water beneath the rock. When it came, the 15-minute blast flattened forests of gigantic fir trees, 180 feet tall, like they were matchsticks. The resulting avalanche deposited a 24-square-mile accumulation of trees, rock, and dirt an average of 150 feet deep. Mudflows tore out steel bridges, demolished houses, and carried trucks along as if they were toys. Fifty-seven people died as a result, as well as countless wild animals and most of the plants and trees over 230 square miles. Patricia Lauber's *Volcano: The Eruption and Healing of Mount St. Helens* explains how the disaster happened, and how that devastated area has gradually come back to life.

(Book 3: One minute)   On the small, newly discovered planet that Patty, the youngest child, names Shine, the new inhabitants are lucky survivors who left Earth by spaceship four years earlier. After escaping The Disaster, an explosion far more destructive than Mount St. Helens's, each voyager was permitted to take only one book and very few other personal belongings. They left Earth knowing they could never return. There would be no healing of the planet Earth this time. Now they must adapt to the planet Shine, their new home, where the grass and flowers are sharp and brittle like glass. The trees are so hard, they can't be cut with a saw and can only be felled with the help of fire. There are no clouds and it never rains in the daytime. The only life they find is a type of jellyfish that they burn and use for fuel to light their lamps. At first it seems possible to make a new life here, but then things begin to go wrong. Seeds from Earth sprout and die. Food from the spaceship is running low. Can they survive on this strange new planet? The children have the answer in Jill Paton Walsh's future tale, *The Green Book*.

(Book 4: One minute)   Back on Earth, it was one snow-covered winter tree that almost cost Warton his life in the book *A Toad for Tuesday* by Russell E. Erickson, the first in the series about the two toad brothers, Warton and Morton. The two toads spent a cozy winter in their snug underground house, feasting on Morton's baked goodies, until Warton took it into his head to venture out in the cold and

snow with a basket of beetle brittle for their Aunt Toolia. Nothing Morton could say would discourage this foolhardy notion, even though toads never go outside in freezing weather. Warton was so determined, he made himself a pair of skis from oak tree roots and ski poles from porcupine quills, and then he set out on his mission. He had not even made it halfway when disaster struck. A hungry owl spied Warton whizzing by, snatched him up in his talons, and deposited him in a filthy hideaway at the top of a tall oak tree. Warton was a prisoner—until Tuesday, that is—for Tuesday was the nasty owl's birthday, and on that day, that owl planned to eat one nice juicy toad to celebrate.

(*Book 5: One minute and 30 seconds*)   Warton the toad wanted only to escape from that oak tree. But Rob, in the book *The View from the Cherry Tree* by Willo Davis Roberts, used the cherry tree as his escape from everyone else around him. You see, Rob's sister, Darcy, was getting married, and the whole household was in an uproar, preparing for the big day. It seemed that whatever Rob did, he was underfoot or in trouble. The cherry tree was one place he could hide, alone, without anyone nagging, pestering, or hollering at him. Up in the tree, he also had a perfect opportunity to spy, unseen, on everyone below: on his father and uncle arguing, on his sister and her fiancé, and even on awful old lady Calloway, the nasty next-door neighbor who made his life miserable with her scolding and surly threats. It was in the cherry tree that Rob happened to witness the sight of an unidentified pair of man's hands that pushed the old woman out of her first floor window. Rob watched in horror as the cord of the old woman's ever-present binoculars caught on a tree branch, causing her to strangle to death. An accident, everyone said. She must have fallen, they all agreed, even the police. Only Rob knew the truth—that old lady Calloway had been murdered—and no one seemed to believe his story . . . except for the anonymous killer who now began to stalk Rob, too.

(*Conclusion: 15 seconds*)   As you can see from these books, trees can be places of danger and mystery, as well as shelter and shade. So why don't you borrow one of these copies, settle into a nice cozy spot under an oak, or even a cherry tree, and have a good read?

Naturally, many other books would tie into a "trees" theme booktalk just as well. For grades 2 to 4, possibilities include Clyde Robert Bulla's King Arthur story, *The Sword in the Tree*, Barbara Dillon's *The Teddy Bear Tree*, James Flora's tale of a vine run amok, *The Great Green Turkey Creek Monster*, or Louis Slobodkin's *The Space Ship Under the Apple Tree*, which is where alien Marty crash-lands.

For grades 4 to 6, these would also work well: Lloyd Alexander's *The Wizard in the Tree*, Jean Craighead George's back-to-the-wilderness survival account, *My Side of the Mountain*, Sonia Levitin's *Jason and the Money Tree*, about a boy who plants a 10-dollar bill that takes root, Philippa Pearce's fantasy *Tom's Midnight Garden*, or Diane Wolkstein's collection of Haitian folktales, *The Magic Orange Tree*.

Any book that includes an episode involving a tree is fair game, like Barbara Park's *Don't Make Me Smile*, where Charlie Hickle is so distraught over his parents' impending divorce that he runs away to the park and hides in one. Or how about Carlo Collodi's classic, *The Adventures of Pinocchio*, about the puppet who asks for trouble and gets it in every possible way. He began life as a block of wood. Janwillem Van de Wetering's *Hugh Pine*, a Maine porcupine more intelligent than most, retreats to his tree when he wants to be alone. Allen turns from human boy to human plant thanks to his photosynthesis science project in *Top Secret* by John Reynolds Gardiner. Elizabeth George Speare's historical survival story, *The Sign of the Beaver*, which has a "Robinson Crusoe" subtheme as does *The Green Book*, also has a gripping tree scene where 12-year-old Matt climbs up to cadge honey from a beehive with disastrous results.

Often it works best to gather an assortment of books you'd like to use and *then* figure out what they have in common. Most books have many theme tie-ins. For instance, *The Finches' Fabulous Furnace* also deals with explosions, moving, seasons, and the Fourth of July; *Volcano* incorporates survival, geology, and conservation and natural phenomena; *The Green Book* is about survival, planets, books, and brave new worlds; *A Toad for Tuesday* touches on sports, flying, reptiles and amphibians, birds, and making friends; *The View from the Cherry Tree* covers sibling relationships, murder, mystery, cats, pets, spying, weddings, and neighbors. Your chosen themes can be as broad or as limited as you like.

LONGER BOOKTALKS

Long talks can be based on just one or two books, described in more detail than short talks. Lasting from 3 to 10 minutes, long talks examine an entire episode or series of scenes in a book, resulting in greater emotional involvement on the parts of both teller and listener. You may select a compelling passage to read aloud, and it helps to briefly showcase several back-up titles as well.

Bunnicula, by James and Deborah Howe, and the first of a pun-loaded series, makes a delightful longer talk. First read aloud the editor's introduction and then describe the circumstances under which the Monroe family found a bunny on a seat at a Dracula movie and took it home to Chester, the neurotic psychology-spouting cat, and Harold, the tale's narrator and family dog, both of whom discover that the rabbit was, in fact, a vegetarian vampire. Hold up each sequel and tell a sentence or so about each one.

One of the great fantasies of all time, Brian Jacques's *Redwall* deserves a long talk. I lead up to it by first combining several short talks to develop a brief presentation on the great mouse novels of all times, starting with Robert Lawson's *Ben and Me* (1939), through E. B. White's *Stuart Little* (1945), past Beverly Cleary's "Ralph" trilogy, Robert C. O'Brien's *Mrs. Frisby and the Rats of NIMH* and its sequel, Jane L. Conly's *Rasco and the Rats of NIMH*, Roger Drury's *The Champion of Merrimack County*, and Jean Van Leeuwen's "Great" trilogy. Fourth- and fifth-grade boys in particular have a great fascination for fictional mice, and they are thrilled to discover all the masterpieces in the field.

Redwall is the penultimate mouse book. The middle volume in the trilogy, it is the tale of Matthias, a young novice mouse at Redwall Abbey, who matures into a hero when the abbey comes under attack by Cluny the Scourge and his hideous band of marauding rats. Never has a villain been more vicious and devoid of redeeming qualities than Cluny, a Portuguese rat with a fearsome tail that he uses to put fear into the hearts and bodies of enemies and allies alike. At 351 pages, *Redwall* is not a novel for the faint at heart, as it has a cast of hundreds and as many names to learn as a Russian novel. A long talk—where you introduce headstrong Matthias and describe the abbey's founding by Martin the Warrior, whose portrait is woven into the Abbey's ancient tapestry—interspersed with readings about

Cluny in Chapters Two and Four and the second half of Chapter Eight is enough to inspire courageous readers to tackle the tome. Unfortunately, most teachers will not choose to read *Redwall* aloud due to its length, though it is more than worth the time spent in terms of language enrichment and sheer pleasure.

AUTHOR BOOKTALKS

The author talk is an agreeable way to introduce readers to a batch of books by a single author. Often you can booktalk a series, like Lloyd Alexander's "Prydain Chronicles" (*The Book of Three, The Black Cauldron, The Castle of Lyr, Taran Wanderer,* and *The High King*), Gordon Korman's "Bruno & Boots" series (*This Can't Be Happening at Macdonald Hall* up to *The Zucchini Warriors*), Lois Lowry's "Anastasia" books, C. S. Lewis's "Narnia" books, or John D. Fitzgerald's autobiographical "Great Brain" series.

Beverly Cleary's "Ramona" books are still the greatest, and the egg-cracking scene in *Ramona Quimby, Age 8* is one of the best examples of booktalking nirvana. (Bring along a hard-boiled and an uncooked egg and teach your students to tell the difference. The raw one spins slowly and erratically while the hard-boiled one spins smoothly. If they don't believe you, pick up the hard-boiled one and ask if someone wants to try cracking it on his head, à la Ramona. If no one volunteers, do it yourself.)

Use the booktalk as a starting point to delve into the author's style, characters, personal life, and interests in some depth. Random House's "Meet the Newbery Author" filmstrip series sometimes does it better than you can, with photographs, anecdotes, and the author's own voice in interviews. To find out gossip about an author, check in Ann Commire's multivolume reference series, *Something about the Author,* published by Gale.

GENRE BOOKTALKS

Talk about the types of fiction books kids like, or read, or know about, and they'll most likely come up with many of the following genres, which you very handily can record on the board: realistic, fantasy, humorous, contemporary, school stories, problem novels, handicaps, science fiction, historical, biographical or autobiographical, adventure, suspense, horror, mystery, animal, and sports.

Fiction books can be slotted into one of two major categories: realistic or fantasy. Literature is not so cut-and-dried that we can say a book is just a mystery or an animal story. Most books fit into two or more subcategories. Sylvia Cassedy's *Behind the Attic Wall*—where rebellious orphan Maggie moves in with her aunts, attends school, and communicates with the living dolls upstairs—contains elements of mystery, fantasy, humor, and contemporary problems. It's a realistic fantasy, if that's a fair description.

A valuable booktalk for second through fourth grades is one that starts with a discussion of the difference between realistic fiction and fantasy. As you booktalk each title, including some on animals, both talking and ordinary, and humans, both magic-endowed and normal, ask children to identify its category. Younger children are often surprised to find that fiction does not always include talking pigs and mice, but can be about school kids just like them.

To present a more complex genre booktalk for fourth- through sixth-graders, with the more detailed list of genres on the board, whip out a sample title of each type and booktalk it in one or two sentences. Now lug out a pile of 10 or so additional books, each one selected to fit into one major category. Give a one- to two-sentence booktalk for each one, and ask students to identify which categories it best fits into and why.

As an example: Bored with being home sick in bed, Rachel wishes for something to happen. Before she knows it, she is riding astride a unicorn in a place where grunting pigs float by in the air. What kind of book is Emily Rodda's *The Pigs Are Flying!* and how do you know it?

Caution: Be vigilant that this booktalk does not drag into a lessonlike session and is perked up with only your most bright-eyed titles. This is essentially a teaching booktalk, but don't let your students suspect this. Keep it light and very fast-paced and hand out the books as you go.

"Ten Ways to Pick a Great Book" Talk

When the children walk into the library, many undergo "Library Mind-Lock," a condition where one doesn't know how or where to start looking for the books of one's dreams, what with all those impenetrable shelves, thousands of spines facing out, giving away few secrets. Thank heavens for teachers and librarians who ease the pain by saying, "What kind of book are you in the mood for today?" instead of "You want a good book? Go look one up in the card catalog."

Library Mind-Lock worsens when time is pressing and the teacher worriedly consults her watch, signaling time to go. Many children suffer from extreme cases simply because no one has ever helped them sort out strategies for making intelligent reading choices. They pick up a likely contender, look at the last page, see that it has only 86 pages and big print, and that's the only evaluative criterion they've ever considered. A booktalk discussion session will ease their pain and help them see browsing time in a more benign light.

There are at least 10 ways to pick out a good book. Ask your students to think of some and list their suggestions on the board. Prepare in advance for this booktalk by pulling out 10 to 20 books that fit neatly into your own 10 categories, out of the 11 detailed below. Your list and your students' list are sure to coincide on most points. Allow for free-wheeling discussion of titles they've read that fit in each category and be prepared to leap over to the shelves to pluck off additional titles as they come up.

I present this type of booktalk once a year with third, fourth, or fifth grades. As we compile our list on the board, I bring out my own stack of books, correlate each one, in a very few sentences, with the appropriate item listed, and then raffle off or hand out copies like mad. Students are always impressed to hear that some of the methods they use for selecting reading matter are valid and helpful to others. In no particular order, here is my list:

1. **It has a good cover.** You can *tell* people not to judge a book by its cover, but it's much harder to get them to believe it. Face it, the jacket sells or kills the book for adults as well as kids. Booktalking a book with a rotten jacket will help to sell it, but if you just put the book out on display, chances are no one

will go near it. Some books with exceptionally winning dust jackets to which my students have been drawn include: Lynne Reid Banks, *The Fairy Rebel*; Bill Brittain, *Dr. Dredd's Wagon of Wonders*; Bruce Coville, *The Monster's Ring*; Roald Dahl, *The Witches*; Barbara Park, *Skinnybones*; Daniel Pinkwater, *Fat Men from Space*; William Sleator, *Among the Dolls*; Jane Sutton, *Me and the Weirdos*; Janwillem Van de Wetering, *Hugh Pine*; Elizabeth Winthrop, *The Castle in the Attic*.

2. **The title sounds good.** For instance, who could pass up *The Monster Garden*; *I'm Going to Be Famous*; *Harvey's Horrible Snake Disaster*; *Mail-Order Wings*; *In Trouble Again, Zelda Hammersmith*; *Germy Blew It*; *Deadly Stranger*; *Chicken Trek*; *After Fifth Grade, the World!*; or *The Bodies in the Besseldorf Hotel*.

3. **It was recommended by a friend.** If your friend has similar tastes, then you will always have plenty to read. Once teachers start talking books on a daily basis, students will do the same and try to convince their friends to read what they do. Peer raves are the most influential kind. For those children who are not already on to this trick, reading the sign-out card to see who else took the book out and how many times it was renewed is another instant way to gauge public opinion.

4. **It was made into a movie.** This can work for or against a book, from "I loved that movie and can't wait to read the book," to "I already saw that movie. Why should I read the book?" Stress that the book is almost always superior to the movie, because there's no way to include all the levels of a story in a mere two-hour film.

Movies often go that extra mile and destroy the integrity of a special book. Disney so babied *Winnie-the-Pooh* that many self-respecting third- and fourth-graders sniff, "I'm too old to read *that*." Too many movies made from children's books suffer from terminal "cutes" and are difficult for adults to watch without gagging. Leading children back to the original text to compare and evaluate is a useful antidote.

If you show a filmstrip of a book, such as one of the excellent Random House or Pied Piper adaptations of award-winning books, be sure to have one or more copies of the book *on hand* to give out. If you tell the class that the book is available on the library shelves, they'll probably forget all about it at browsing time. Seize the moment and capitalize on their interest right then. Books with movie tie-ins include:

Lloyd Alexander, *The Book of Three* and *The Black Cauldron*, the first two titles of five in the *Chronicles of Prydain* (cartoon movie)
William Armstrong, *Sounder* (movie)
Betsy Byars, *The Midnight Fox* (TV movie)
Carlo Collodi, *The Adventures of Pinocchio* (Walt Disney cartoon movie)
Roald Dahl, *Charlie and the Chocolate Factory* (movie known as *Willie Wonka and the Chocolate Factory*)
Walter Farley, *The Black Stallion* (movie)
John Reynolds Gardiner, *Stone Fox* and *Top Secret* (TV movies)
Fred Gipson, *Old Yeller* (movie)
E. L. Konigsburg, *From the Mixed-Up Files of Mrs. Basil E. Frankweiler* (movie)

C. S. Lewis, *The Lion, the Witch and the Wardrobe* (cartoon movie and English TV miniseries)

Astrid Lindgren, *Pippi Longstocking* (movie)

Robert McCloskey, *Homer Price* (movie of "The Doughnuts" chapter)

Stephen Manes, *Be a Perfect Person in Just Three Days* (TV movie)

Barbara Robinson, *The Best Christmas Pageant Ever* (TV movie)

George Selden, *The Cricket in Times Square* (cartoon movie)

Marlene Fanta Shyer, *Welcome Home, Jellybean* (TV movie)

Jane Wagner, *J.T.* (TV movie)

E. B. White, *Charlotte's Web* (cartoon movie)

5. **It was excerpted in the basal reader.** This one is even riskier than number 4, but it works with some children. Basal readers, working valiantly to improve their stodgy images, now mostly use selections from children's books instead of their own labored prose from the "Dick and Jane" years. However, children's most common library reaction to the suggestion that they take out one of these books is, "I already read that. We had it in our reading book." If reminded that they only read one chapter and that the rest of the book is even better, *sometimes* they'll believe you.

6. **You know and like the author's other books.** Children who have read and laughed themselves silly over Barbara Park's *Operation: Dump the Chump* will most likely find *The Kid in the Red Jacket* and *Skinnybones* just as appealing. Get in the habit of bandying about authors' names as well as titles whenever you read aloud or introduce new books.

7. **You've read and liked other books of that series/in that genre/with that theme/or on that subject.** These days authors are churning out "series" books, and children do love reading more than one book with the same characters. Remember Nancy Drew and the Hardy Boys? They're still around, though today's hot items include "The Babysitters Club," "Sweet Valley Twins," and the zillions of "Choose Your Own Adventure" clones. There's nothing wrong with these series; they're not great literature but fun, undemanding reads that, if you do your homework, you can turn into first steps for better choices. Children who hate to read can be turned around when they find books they can get through without pain. The trick is to use them to steer your readers to the good stuff. If it's a series they're after, look to the following quality offerings:

Robert Arthur (and others), "The Three Investigators" thriller/mystery series

Michael Bond, "Paddington Bear" series

Betsy Byars, *The Not-Just-Anybody Family* and sequels in the "Blossom" family quartet

Ann Cameron, "Julian" series (*The Stories Julian Tells*, etc.)

Beverly Cleary, "Ramona," "Henry Huggins," and "Ralph" series

Judy Delton, *Backyard Angel* and sequels in the "Angel" series

John D. Fitzgerald, "The Great Brain" series

Clifford B. Hicks, "Alvin Fernald" series

E. W. Hildick, "McGurk" mystery series

James Howe, *Bunnicula* and sequels

Dean Hughes, "Nutty" series

Johanna Hurwitz, "Russell," "Nora," and "Teddy" series

Suzy Kline, "Herbie Jones" and "Horrible Harry" series
Gordon Korman, "Bruno & Boots" series (*This Can't Be Happening at Macdonald Hall*, etc.)
Lois Lowry, "Anastasia" series
Betty MacDonald, "Mrs. Piggle-Wiggle" series
Stephen Manes, "Oscar Noodleman" series (*Chicken Trek*, etc.)
Phyllis Reynolds Naylor, *Witch's Sister* quartet
Mary Norton, "The Borrowers" series
George Selden, *The Cricket in Times Square* and sequels
Seymour Simon, "Einstein Anderson" series
Janice Lee Smith, "Adam Joshua" series
Jean Van Leeuwen, *The Great Cheese Conspiracy* and sequels
Laura Ingalls Wilder, *Little House in the Big Woods* and sequels
Jay Williams and Raymond Abrashkin, "Danny Dunn" series

One time-saving way to help children locate fiction books on favorite genres or themes is by using the book spine stickers, put out by major library supply companies, with colorful logos for sports, adventure, humor, animals, science fiction, fantasy, and mystery. To find a funny book, borrowers skim the spines for the pink laughing face stickers. This is another form of silent booktalking, as long as you put stickers only on those books you can vouch for.

8. **The book flap or back cover blurb sounds good.** Train students to whip open the cover of hardbacks and read the jacket copy or flip to the back cover of paperbacks. Book blurbs are just punchily written booktalks. When you're lucky, the publishing company publicists get the wording just right, and the book sells itself.

9. **The chapter titles sound unusual.** This is a bit far-fetched, but some books specialize in cunning chapter titles, and all you need to do to churn up curiosity is to open to the table of contents and read it aloud. Entertaining ones include: Florence Parry Heide's *Banana Twist* (Something We Don't Tell Parents; The Banana Boy; It Was Hopeless So I Didn't Try Too Hard); Clifford B. Hicks's *Peter Potts* (Chapter 2: Good Ways to Pull a Loose Tooth, Requiring Only Some Fishline, a Live Chicken, and a Barbell); James Howe's *Nighty-Nightmare* (Nobody Here but Us Chickens; Once Upon a Time in Transylvania); and Phyllis Reynolds Naylor's *The Bodies in the Besseldorf Hotel* (The Body Snatchers; One Thousand Kisses; Dead; The Missing Body).

10. **The first sentence or paragraph or page is intriguing.** Surprisingly few books start off with a bang on page one. Not many children are patient beyond the first chapter nowadays. Consider it a blessing if the first page is a grabber. These never fail:

> "There's nights up in this corner of New England when the mists seethe and writhe their way down from the mountains, and the dogs start to howling, and the hair on the backs of cats stand straight up as they scream and spit at things invisible to human eyes. On those nights, the people of our village of Coven Tree gather inside their houses and lock their doors and are afraid. For it's then that the Devil stalks among the hills and forests, looking for souls to claim." (Bill Brittain, *Devil's Donkey*)

"One summer two boys and a girl went to a foster home to live together.
    One of the boys was Harvey. He had two broken legs. He got them when he was run over by his father's new Grand Am." (Betsy Byars, *The Pinballs*)

"The Herdmans were absolutely the worst kids in the history of the world. They lied and stole and smoked cigars (even the girls) and talked dirty and hit little kids and cussed their teachers and took the name of the Lord in vain and set fire to Fred Shoemaker's old broken-down toolhouse." (Barbara Robinson, *The Best Christmas Pageant Ever*)

Additional first-page winners include: Ellen Conford, *Me and the Terrible Two*; Roger Drury, *The Champion of Merrimack County*; Lee Harding, *The Fallen Spaceman*; Ted Hughes, *The Iron Giant*; Beverly Keller, *The Genuine, Ingenious Thrift Shop Genie, Clarissa Mae Bean and Me*; Daniel Pinkwater, *The Slaves of Spiegel*; Marilyn Sachs, *Veronica Ganz*; Marjorie Weinman Sharmat, *Chasing After Annie*; Jane Sutton, *Me and the Weirdos*; Gertrude Chandler Warner, *The Boxcar Children*.

11. **It's on display in the library**. Happily, the "Freeman Guarantee" proves to be a powerful incentive in many cases.

The success of your booktalks can be gauged instantly by how eager your listeners are to gain possession of each title. If no one wants to take out a certain book or two, either your booktalk was not up to standard or the topic did not hit a nerve with anyone. Perhaps you oversold it and told too much of the plot. Could you have selected one that was way beyond your audience's level of comprehension? (A librarian friend tells the story of a coworker in her high school who, when told the incoming class of all-boy, remedial-reader tenth-graders liked war stories, attempted to booktalk *War and Peace*.)

A book can be a roaring success with one class and a dud with the next. Maybe the kids or you were in a bad mood. Without letting yourself get paranoid, figure out the problem and resolve to do better next time. Make sure there is a next time; as with any contact sport, the more you work out, the better you play. Most important, don't be discouraged. Children who act blasé for your first talk will drop their defenses once they realize the books you recommend are good ones. Pretty soon you'll have them drooling on command as soon as you hold up a new title.

BOOKTALK RECORD-KEEPING

If you like to keep records of what you do, then begin a file of booktalk cards so you will not have to start from scratch each year. Pull out the cards you need and you will have an instant refresher of what you want to say without rereading the whole book. *Witch's Sister* makes a marvelously terrifying short or long talk.

SAMPLE BOOK TALK FILE CARD

Naylor, Phyllis Reynolds.   Grade Level: 4–6
WITCH'S SISTER
Atheneum, 1979.

THEMES: Witchcraft, Siblings, Suspense

BLURB: After Lynn and her best friend Mouse investigate, they become convinced that Lynn's 14-year-old sister has been learning witchcraft from Mrs. Tuggle, a deceptively sweet old lady who lives up the hill.

CHARACTERS: Lynn Morley (12 years old, precise, imaginative)
Mouse Beasley (Lynn's best friend, timid, sloppy dresser)
Judith Morley (Lynn's older sister, aloof, suspected of witchcraft by Lynn)
Mrs. Tuggle (English, older woman, sinister, a possible witch)
Mrs. Morley (Lynn's mother, children's book author)
Stevie Morley (Lynn's six-year-old brother)

BOOKTALK: 1. Lynn suspects her sister Judith of learning witchcraft, not just sewing, from Mrs. Tuggle. List reasons Lynn gives: pp. 3, 5, 15.
2. Lynn and Mouse spy on Judith and Mrs. Tuggle, only to see them sticking pins, voodoo-style, into a doll: pp. 35–38.
3. Include mention of other trilogy titles: *Witch Water*, *The Witch Herself*, and *The Witch's Eye*.

Most of the books on my Read-Aloud Lists for grades 2 through 6, plus those on the nonfiction, poetry, and folklore lists, make wonderful booktalks with a bit of planning and a touch of the old soft shoe. Your students will let you know by their reading how much they appreciate and enjoy your efforts.

CREATIVE DRAMATICS
AND CHILDREN'S LITERATURE

ALL THE COMPREHENSION SKILLS BOOKLETS IN THE WORLD WON'T help students fathom cause and effect the way acting out a story will. Using creative drama to extend a story allows children to develop new criteria for interpreting characters and understanding their actions, as well as gain intuitive knowledge of story structure and plot. As a group activity, creative drama provides children with the freedom to try out ideas without fear of ridicule.

You've just finished reading aloud to your third-graders Burton Turkle's *Do Not Open*, a startling story of a sensible woman who calmly outwits the terrifying creature she has released from a bottle found on the beach. Instead of asking, "Why did the voices inside the bottle keep changing?" or "Was Miss Moody scared of the monster?" you ask the class to break into pairs—Miss Moody versus the still-bottled creature. After several minutes of debating time where each "monster" finally convinces each doubting but curious "Miss Moody" to release him from the bottle, they trade roles, and each "Miss Moody" tricks her creature into becoming a mouse. While the pairs are arguing, you look around, but don't impose yourself on any of the discussions.

Afterward, you get back together as a group and ask the children how it went. *Now* you hear them answer questions eagerly and talk nonstop about how each character responded to the situation, for they have experienced those changes firsthand.

NARRATIVE PANTOMIME

Narrative pantomime—where you narrate the events from a story, either word-for-word or self-edited to fit the situation, while the actors put it into motion—is the easiest technique to direct and perform. Look for a story or episode with scads of action, a simple plot, and little or no dialogue.

Although you may feel self-conscious and unsure the first time you lead your crew in a narrative pantomime, these feelings will soon flee when you note the actors' ecstatic faces and hear them exclaim, "Let's do it again." After reading a story aloud, you can usually complete a narrative pantomime tour de force in less than 10 minutes. More complex productions take longer, but if you start out simply, you will find the activities easy to complete successfully.

Many stories can be read aloud verbatim, without any changes. *Old Mother Hubbard and Her Dog*, with versions by Tomie dePaola, Paul Galdone, Lennart Hellsing, and Evaline Ness, is one of those. After reading the story and having children join you on the ". . . but when she came back . . ." refrain, tell them they will now become the dogs while you read the story and play the part of Old Mother Hubbard. Go over the rules, such as not touching anyone else, and ask them to think how they might pantomime the parts where the dog rides a goat or stands on his head. Request two volunteers to demonstrate their solutions, so all can see the difference between jumping on a child's back and pretending to do so. By working out potential problems in advance, you minimize the chances of children becoming overzealous or attempting a headstand.

When acting out a pantomime, remind children that it is like a silent movie, and they should refrain from talking so they can hear each direction as you read. If you'd like them to chant along or include sound effects, let them know. You are the director and, as such, must set the sights for each presentation. *Old Mother Hubbard* ends well for a dramatic piece, with the dame curtsying and the dog bowing, after which you can either do it again or sit down and ask everyone which parts they felt were the most satisfying, funny, or real. Give each child a chance to respond.

Set up behavior guidelines for your students; when you clap hands, bang a drum, or say "Freeze," all children are to stop instantly and listen for directions. Practice that with them so they know what to expect. Go over any other rules, such as not interfering with anyone else or not crawling under tables or chairs. Before you begin, have students space themselves so they are not within touching distance of other children.

Any child who cannot follow along without "cutting up" should sit down on a "time out" chair until he or she is ready to participate. Enforce this in a kind, nonthreatening way, without letting yourself appear annoyed or upset, by calmly leading the child over to the designated chair and saying quietly, "When you do that it spoils the mood for the rest of us. Take some time to think about what you should be doing, and when you think you're ready to join in again, come back to the group." Children will want to be part of the action, and they'll usually simmer down fast after being spectators for a spell.

Whereas most children are raring to go whenever you announce a new dramatics scene, sometimes a child will balk and be reluctant to join in. He or she may be scared, shy, cynical, or looking for extra attention. Again, keep your response low key. Suggest to the child to feel free to join in at any time. Often, children will choose to stay seated but pantomime along with the group. Children in wheelchairs are able to participate in this way, as one can be just as expressive with the hands and head as with the entire body.

Short Takes: Simple Narrative Pantomime

Narrative pantomime can mean acting out images as basic as eating an apple or a drippy ice cream cone, preening your feathers and fanning out your tail as peacocks, or playing a short piece on an invisible piano. Impromptu mini-pantomimes like these keep listeners alert and involved and can be a nice way to stretch and relax after a test or a tough morning.

With young children, rhymes and fingerplays are popular dramatics choices. Mother Goose is bursting with possibilities. (Look under Fingerplays and Nursery

Rhymes in the Subject Index for a list of titles.) As Little Jack Horners, we hold onto our Christmas pies, stick in our thumbs, pull out our plums, and chomp them right down. As Jack Be Nimble, we jump over our invisible candlesticks. *Humpty Dumpty* can be done as a group, with half comprising the giant tottering egg and the other half the soldiers who gamely try to piece the shell together. For *Little Miss Muffet*, break into pairs: Miss Muffet versus the spider. Each time the spider sits beside her and scares her away, change roles so the spider now becomes Miss Muffet, spooning up her mush.

Don't neglect poetry as another splendid source of quick takes. Pantomime emotions, actions, and reactions. Sometimes the entire poem tells a tale worth playing. "True Story" from Shel Silverstein's *Where the Sidewalk Ends* allows children to re-enact a cowboy's perilous adventures, and even to die at the end. "The Case of the Crumbled Cookies" from X. J. Kennedy's *Ghastlies, Goops & Pincushions*, where actors playing Sam Supersleuth dust the cookie crumbs for fingerprints, only to recognize that they are the culprits, is another poem with action. So are Evelyn Beyer's "Jump or Jiggle," Dorothy Aldis's "Dangerous," Karen Gundersheimer's "Happy Winter, Steamy Tub," and many more besides from Jack Prelutsky's collection *Read-Aloud Rhymes for the Very Young*. For older children, "Foul Shot" by Edwin A. Hoey from Lilian Moore's *Go with the Poem* and "The Base Stealer" by Robert Francis from Joanna Cole's *A New Treasury of Children's Poetry* are compelling, each slowing down the excitement of a split-second sports play into separate movements.

Picture books are rife with possibilities. While reading *Cross-Country Cat* by Mary Calhoun, it may occur to you that the children need a minute of firsthand skiing experience. Put the book down and say, "All right, cats, put on your left ski. Good. Now your right. Let's stand up very carefully and take our first steps. Excellent. Do you think you can glide?" If they are eager, lead them in a quick glide around the room. Sit down and resume the story.

While doing an author talk on the delicious books of Arnold Lobel, I love to read my second-graders *Mouse Tales*, which consists of the seven short bedtime stories Papa Mouse tells to his children, one for each mouse. The fifth story, "The Journey," about a mouse who drives, roller skates, tramps, runs, and walks all the way to his mother's house, is so spinningly silly, we act it out twice, giggling all the way home. The whole trip takes all of five minutes, and it puts us all in a sunny mood for the rest of the day. When next we meet, I am invariably greeted with, "Hello, Miss Freeman. You are looking fine. And what nice new feet you have!"

Single-word or short-phrase pantomimes are fun for warm-ups. A book like Sally Noll's *Jiggle Wiggle Prance*, with all its action verbs, or Sandra Boynton's *A Is for Angry*, with one descriptive adjective per alphabet letter, is quick and easy to do, as children change their expressions and motions for each word.

For preschool through second grade, exploring nonverbal communication with Marie Hall Ets's *Talking without Words* can help you establish classroom discipline signals at a glance. Children act out each situation with the appropriate motions. One typical page reads " 'Come here' I say to my dog. But I don't say it with words. I just click my tongue and pat my knee and he comes." Compile a list of other silent messages to follow up the original book-based pantomime and ask for volunteers to act them out for the rest of the group to guess. Possibilities include: "Stop!" "Oh, no!" "Go away." "That hurts." "I feel sick." "I like you." Children will surely offer their own variations. Finally, show them some of *your* classroom-based, nonverbal signals, ranging from, "Good thinking!" and "I think you're pretty terrific!" to "Knock it off now or else!"

Whatever Sidney put in his Changing Box would change into something else when he pressed a button. After changing his baby sister into a lamp and his football into a toaster, Sidney and his dog Wally crawled into the Changing Box and switched places so Sidney could be *Dog for a Day*. Introduce or follow up Dick Gackenbach's cheerful story by asking your children to crawl into their own invisible Changing Boxes. Each time you push the main button, announce what you are changing them into, and have them clamber out as animals and other animate or inanimate objects. Accept children's suggestions as you go, if you like.

Daniel Pinkwater uses a similar motif in his inspired *Tooth-Gnasher Superflash*. Accompanied by nervous car salesman Mr. Sandy, Mrs. Popsnorkle, and the five little Popsnorkles, Mr. Popsnorkle test-drives a flashy new car and finds, to his great satisfaction, that it turns into a dinosaur, an elephant, a turtle, and a giant flying chicken. Rev up your engines and start driving, being very careful not to touch anyone else's car. (Again, remind your drivers that the "time out" chair is for anyone who can't remember that important rule—"real" car drivers get tickets if they drive unsafely.) Practice stopping at red lights, using turn signals, and beeping the horn. Each time you discover a new color button on the dashboard, push it and announce what the vehicle will become. Start out with the animals in the story, throw in a few exotic ones like a snake, a kangaroo, or a porpoise, and end up with the chicken, parking at the car dealer and turning off the engine. This is great fun for everyone and you will laugh yourselves silly.

Holding on his lap a photo album that the photographer has brought along, Pig Pig gazes at each picture before he says "cheese" and *wham* . . . finds himself in that picture. Hanging by his overalls strap from the top of a church steeple, perching precariously on an airplane wing, in the middle of a rowboat, and atop a chocolate cake are places Pig Pig ends up in David McPhail's *Pig Pig and the Magic Photo Album*. Bring in a loaded or unloaded camera and announce each scene. Count to three, say "cheese," and the actors will become Pig Pig in a freeze frame, tableau-style pose while you snap their pictures.

All ages delight in the tall tales of adventure-prone Grandpa from James Stevenson's *Could Be Worse* and *We Can't Sleep*. The children each become Grandpa and react to everything that happens to him as you read. Who wouldn't like riding on a shark's fin, weightlifting a walrus, or riding a paper airplane home to bed? The rest of the "Grandpa" books will fly off the shelves afterward.

William Joyce's *George Shrinks* is but a nine-sentence story, written as a letter of instructions from absent parents to an oldest son. He is to wash, dress, eat, clean up, and look after his little brother. The hitch in the plans is that when George wakes up, he finds that his dream of being small has come true. Mouse-size, he carries out his parents' demands, brushing his teeth with a now-huge toothbrush, washing gargantuan dishes in a swimming pool-size sink, and narrowly escaping disaster with the family cat, before becoming himself again. After hearing the book once or twice, and marveling over the difficulties of performing everyday chores for a thumb-size person, children will get a first-rate gross motor skills workout by acting out the story in pantomime.

For Grades 4–6

As you read aloud or booktalk to older children, be on the lookout for descriptive scenes that your students can act out. This provides an interesting interlude in your reading and helps them visualize a graphic scene. After describing Andrea's flight plans in Beatrice Gormley's *Mail-Order Wings* to your fourth- to sixth-grade students, add a novel twist by having them pantomime applying wings to their shoulders, not being able to remove them, and flying around the room.

From Willo Davis Roberts's *The Magic Book*, Alex Graden's singular experience at the library's used-book sale is another good candidate. Each time the old book mysteriously falls to the floor, Alex places it back on the table, until the third time when he opens the flap and finds, in spidery, faded script, the words, "This book belongs to Alexander W. Graden." Why a faded, musty old book, published in London in 1802, should have Alex's name in it should be one of the questions children puzzle over as they act out the brief scene.

In Michael Bond's *A Bear Called Paddington*, there's a marvelous scene in which the bumbling bear takes his very first tub bath, with predictable results. Children love bailing out of the flood with their imaginary floppy hats.

Monster-loving fourth- and fifth-graders will appreciate Russell's plight when his magic ring causes him to become a heinous fang-filled monster one full-mooned Halloween. In Chapter Two of Bruce Coville's *The Monster's Ring*, pages 12 to 15 describe his transformation, which, with just a minor amount of cutting, you can reread while your listeners act it out. First, horns break through his forehead, then hair sprouts on his face and hands, and his fingernails become sharp claws. Children will take fiendish delight in drawing before and after self-portraits.

Editing and Improving Scenes

Editing is essential in many cases to speed up the action so children are not standing around pondering their next moves. You will find that most children will be unself-conscious once they get involved and realize that no one is scrutinizing their actions for mistakes or to criticize. Each person becomes too wrapped up in the story to take notice of anyone else. When editing a story—which you can do as you are reading it aloud for the pantomime—omit or paraphrase the talky sections, condense the time span if necessary, and cut or add description to make the action flow logically and sequentially.

Catastrophe Cat by Dennis Panek has very few words, so to act out the cat's fur-raising city adventure, you must supply your own running narration. Young children love all the havoc he raises, and you'll appreciate the calm ending, with the cat back home at last, snoozing away.

During the month of April, primary classes fall over themselves laughing when you read David Cleveland's *The April Rabbits*. Each day, as the month progresses, Robert sees more and more bunnies doing the strangest things, such as tap dancing on his windowsill, flying, playing basketball, and singing on the garage roof. Once you've shared this giddy little romp, reread it aloud while your students become the rabbits. The only editing you need is a bit of descriptive padding in places, where the action is shown in the illustration rather than in the text. "Eight rabbits left their bikes in the driveway on the eighth" might profit from the elaboration, "Eight rabbits zoomed up the driveway on their bikes on the eighth. They jumped off, kicked down the kick stand, and then ran to hide in a tree."

After you've acted out the story, if the children are enthusiastic, run through it again. It's a good idea to offer them positive suggestions for improvement—no personal comments, just some new ideas on which to focus. For example, "This time, make your rabbits even sneakier when they hide at the end. Remember, you can't hide under anything like chairs or tables. If you make yourself feel small, then you will seem invisible. Also, each time your rabbit does something unrabbitlike, such as paddling a canoe or trying on Robert's underwear, make each action seem real. Try to see the peanut butter and radish sandwiches you make, and even though you can't pick up any real books when the rabbits are at the library, remember how it feels to pick up a giant stack of books."

After your encouragement, the next time you act out the scene, the students will take their roles more seriously. Usually, little character development occurs in simple narrative pantomime; it's only a literal interpretation of the story. Yet after you finish, you will find that your children have a sharper sense of setting and sequence and can imbue main characters with personality.

Acting out picture books can be enjoyed by all ages. When I was introducing the parts of a catalog card to my third-graders, I first read aloud the picture book *Humphrey, the Dancing Pig* by Arthur Getz, about a pig who decides to dance until he is as thin as the cat. He tries the hula, rock and roll, ballet, and other dances, until he is so lithe that the farmer puts him to work catching vermin. After discussing the parts of the book including author, illustrator, publisher, copyright date, and call number, we constructed a huge oak tag author card based on the title page. Then, to unwind from our labors, we acted out the story. Children all played the part of Humphrey; I was the farmer/narrator. Editing the text, I condensed a week's worth of dancing into the time frame of a single day and ended the story with Humphrey asleep in his corn crib, fat and contented once more. When possible, end an active production like this with the characters sitting or sleeping, to give everyone a chance to wind down.

If you've ever read the humorous 1889 English novel *Three Men in a Boat*, written by Jerome K. Jerome, and even if you haven't, don't miss Wallace Tripp's illustrated riotous rabbity excerpt, *My Uncle Podger*. Because the humor depends on typically British understatement, I often wondered if the narration, concerning inept Uncle Podger's all-day attempt to hang a picture, was over children's heads. A narrative pantomime in which everybody re-enacts the gentleman rabbit's furious struggles clarifies the funny parts, rendering them even more tickling. You will need to perform some judicious editing, paraphrasing dialogue into action, so that Uncle P. can remain center stage. Most of us are acquainted with at least one similar pompous buffoon, and the acting can lead into an entertaining character analysis.

How I Hunted the Little Fellows, an autobiographical story by Russian author Boris Zhitkov, makes a fascinating drama for grades 3 to 5, with some careful editing, which you will need to consider in advance. Young Boria convinces himself that a crew of tiny men live inside the model ship that his grandfather has forbidden him to touch. In actuality, he has concocted the whole story in his imagination. After reading the story aloud, ask your listeners why Boria thought there were little fellows in the ship and how else he could have proved their existence. Next, have them imagine that Boria's supposition was true and have them take the parts of the little fellows hiding below deck as you read the scene aloud.

Beforehand, mark the pertinent passages, starting with:

I was sure that the cabin could open and that the little fellows were living inside . . . I waited to see if one looked out the window. Surely they would look out from time to time. When nobody was home, they probably went out on deck and climbed the rope ladders to the masts. But if they heard the slightest noise, then—whisk—quick as mice, they would duck back into the cabin, crouch down, and keep quiet.

Then, read the description of the little fellows chopping up the hard candy that Boria has left for them, and the one that details their sitting all day on benches, shoulder to shoulder, until they sneak up on deck and leave their tiny footprints in the ink-soaked mat. Next comes some real action as Boria shakes the steamer upside down while the little fellows hold on tight, still not making a sound.

For an understanding of the destruction he causes, have the children now become Boria as you read aloud the passage where he dismantles the boat, up to his despairing realization that the little fellows do not, and never did, exist. Afterward, sit back down and discuss why his fantasy became so real to him and how he might have owned up his dreadful deed to his grandmother. Finally, students can write or tell about the worst things they ever did, and how they made up for them.

Pairs Pantomime

Narrative pantomime need not always be a solo venture, with all children playing the same part. Children can also work in pairs or groups, depending on the story to be performed. Pairs pantomime is especially satisfying because actors can switch roles midway and experience two characters for the price of one.

In James Daugherty's *Andy and the Lion*, the updated confrontation between Andy and the thorny-pawed big cat provides a perfect theatrical interlude. Before acting out the scene, students need to be prepped to avoid the pitfalls of acting out of character. They should discuss how the boy can be startled by the hidden lion's tail, how boy and lion can chase each other around an imaginary rock without being caught (as do hunter and bear around a tree in Wilson Gage's *Cully Cully and the Bear*), how Andy can carefully dethorn the lion's paw, and how the lion can pretend to lick Andy's face. Miraculous possibilities will be suggested. Ask a volunteer pair to demonstrate feasible solutions. One child may show how the lion could crouch, with one hand or foot extended to suggest a tail; when the lion moves its "tail," the other child will jump back in alarm. If you end up with a trio or two, don't hesitate to designate two lions or two Andys for that group. One child may even want to play the dog.

When my second-graders acted out the chapter, the children were genuinely startled by how believable the scene was to them. One boy exclaimed, "I was really scared when that lion twitched his tail!"

After we finished the first run-through, I offered a few suggestions for improvement, such as, "This time, get a better grip on the thorn before you pull so both of you really feel it when it finally comes out." They switched parts and we tried again. The text needs no editing; it has action and just the right amount of dramatic tension. When we regrouped to discuss our favorite moments, they were at no loss for words.

For pairs pantomime, look for stories with dynamic duos; James Marshall's "George and Martha" or Arnold Lobel's "Frog and Toad" tales are fine examples. Mirra Ginsburg's *The Chick and the Duckling* fits the bill for the younger set.

Miriam Nerlove based her *I Made a Mistake* on a jump rope rhyme:

59

> I went to the bathroom to brush my hair,
> I made a mistake . . . and brushed a bear.

For each couplet, one child can be the active narrator, the other the resulting "mistake," including lamb, swan, frog, and mouse. Children can then compose new rhymes and act them out. In preparation, after reading the story the first time, have the children read it with you, but before each couplet, tell them in what mood they should recite it, such as angry, surprised, terrified, or amused. When you finally act out the story, you can assign these emotions as well, which gives the pantomime more depth.

Most children love to try mirror exercises. Use them with A. A. Milne's *Winnie-the-Pooh* as he does his daily stretching exercises before the mirror or with Jack Kent's *Jim Jimmy James*. If you can get a copy to show, both the Marx Brothers' movie *Duck Soup* and the "I Love Lucy" episode with Lucy and Harpo have hilarious scenes where two identically costumed characters meet unexpectedly and mirror each other's actions.

First demonstrate the activity by having the whole group mirror you. Next, ask partners to face each other; as one child begins to move, the partner must attempt to mirror each motion. Start out slowly, then have everyone speed up a bit. Now switch so the follower becomes the leader. When they've got the hang of it, announce that neither one is to be the leader this time, but they must mirror each other and keep moving regardless. The role of leader thus passes back and forth between the members of each twosome in an unspoken exchange of power. Try it yourself—it's trickier than it looks.

Then there is *The Incredible Painting of Felix Clousseau* by Jon Agee. In this odd and infatuating book, the unknown painter of the title creates masterworks that come to life. Ridiculing his painting of a duck, the judges at the Royal Palace's Grand Contest of Art are stunned when not only does the painting quack, but the duck walks off the canvas. Clousseau becomes famous until his paintings begin to cause chaos. Volcanoes erupt, waterfalls drip, and cannons explode off the surfaces. Clousseau is jailed until his painting of the sleeping dog awakens to capture a thief bent on stealing the king's crown. Released from prison, the artist trudges back to his studio and returns to his painting—literally.

Bring in a large picture frame or canvas stretcher to use as your representative canvas. Each pair must decide what one object or person their painting will represent. One pair at a time can create a canvas as the rest of the group watches; one person acts as artist and arranges his partner into the agreed subject. The audience must guess what this painting represents—soldier, tree, the Statue of Liberty, dinosaur, at which point the painting will "come alive."

For longer fiction, you must keep one eye trained for pertinent passages. One good choice is Christine Nostlinger's *Konrad*, about Mrs. Bartolotti, an eccentric weaver who unexpectedly finds herself the parent of a factory-canned seven-year-old son. After the mailman delivers a large parcel, she removes the wrappings and extricates a huge gleaming can with a ring-pull. Opening the can, she is shocked by the contents: a crumpled dwarflike creature who, after Mrs. B. douses him with the enclosed nutrient solution, is transformed into a perfectly normal child.

In performing the pairs pantomime of Konrad and his new mother, the child who plays Konrad actually has two parts: first as the can and then as the contents of that can. Caution your students to perform without hamming it up, as Mrs. B. must show an emotional reaction of surprise and shock, whereas Konrad remains as stoic as his container.

Group Pantomime

Once you've tried solo and pairs pantomime, the next logical step is group pantomime, where the class works together to act out a story with a large cast. This is the simplest sort of group story to act out because children do not need to add dialogue, and you provide the sequence in your narration.

When there are many roles in a story, consider rearranging chairs in your library to make a large semicircle so children can sit on them in order of appearance in the play. This avoids the confusion of who's up next. In a classroom, if there is not a large empty space, seat children at desks in the sequence of their parts and act out the story at the front of the room so all can see. When you work out and introduce a procedure for moving desks in an orderly way into predetermined spaces, children can clear the floor effectively in a short time with little disruption.

With Alexei Tolstoi's *The Great Big Enormous Turnip,* ask for volunteers to play the turnips, the old man, old woman, their granddaughter, the dog, cat, and mouse. Cast more than one child for each role if necessary, so that everyone has a part. Warm up by having all the children pretend they are turnips, sown from seeds, leaves peeking above the earth, and slowly growing toward the sun. Pretend to pull their leaves so they lean precariously but stay embedded in the soil. Then, narrate the whole story as the group acts it out.

The group can also work together to form a unit, as in *Lazy Tommy Pumpkinhead* by William Pène du Bois, in which a lazy boy depends on machines to awaken, wash, dress, and even feed him. Have students become these machines with each child or small group performing the functions of their choice. With you in charge of the "controls," have your "machines" speed up or slow down, and request accompanying sound effects for each function.

The robot factory in Alfred Slote's *My Robot Buddy* can be created similarly, as second- and third-graders band together to manufacture the various parts of the robots. Assembly-line pantomimes are interesting because each child's actions must be interdependent of those of the rest of the group. Adding sound effects to the motions makes the activity even more compelling.

USING SOUND

Narrative pantomime is usually silent because children must listen carefully for the various clues to their next actions. In many stories, children need to use their voices as well to mimic the sounds that enrich the telling. A slapstick story like Jill Murphy's *Peace at Last* would fall flat if the listeners didn't join in on all the snoring, ticking, dripping, and tweeting noises that keep Mr. Bear from getting his 40 winks.

After I read *Peace at Last* to a first-grade class, we recorded a cassette tape of the sound effects in sequence. We all love/hate to hear ourselves on tape because our voices come out so different from the way we hear them ourselves. Children are fascinated with identifying their own recorded voices, and the actors listened very carefully to directions so their output would be a success.

First, we discussed the sequence of the noises and practiced how a dripping faucet or ticking clock might sound. I purposely did not add my own interpretations so the children would feel free to devise their own sounds. After a short rehearsal, we taped in sequence, pushing the "pause" button after each noise. When we finished taping, we acted out the complete story in pantomime, with each child playing the part of Mr. Bear while I narrated. As each noise came up in the story, I switched on our tape so we could hear it, after which the multitude of bears exclaimed their repeated refrain of, "Oh, *no!* I can't stand *this.*"

Certain stories lend themselves to sound effects. Rolf Myller's *A Very Noisy Day* was written for that purpose, encompassing all the noises a dog might encounter in a day. When reading aloud Judith Viorst's *My Momma Says There Aren't Any Zombies, Ghosts, Vampires, Creatures, Demons, Fiends, Goblins or Things*, it's much scarier if your listeners make all of the accompanying creepy noises described so graphically in the text. Speaking of chills, Paul Galdone's *King of the Cats*, a folktale about a gravedigger who witnesses a cat funeral procession, is interspersed with harrowing meows that should be cried in unison.

Sometimes just a segment of a story or novel is appropriate for a sound effects interlude. Incorporate noises into your stories by asking the audience to participate. Children who are read to regularly know just when to join in and are eager for your sanction.

Younger students will "ba-loop" through the clam concert in *Clams Can't Sing* by James Stevenson. One second-grade teacher and class were so enamored of their cacophony, they made a 20-minute "Morning Sounds at the Beach" tape, which they sent to the author, who wrote back agreeing that clams really can sing.

Recently I made a clam puppet out of two large clam shell halves, a lot of white cloth book tape to hold the halves together, two large googly eyes, and finger loops on the top and bottom halves so the clam could "sing." Handing out two small clam shells from a beach bucket to each person makes the concert even more personal.

For grades 4 to 6, John Bellairs's *The House with a Clock in Its Walls*, a tale of wizardry and an evil sorcerer plotting the end of the world, includes a mansion filled with every type of clock, including the sinister one in the title. After reading aloud the description of the midnight chimes on pages 15 and 16, have your students recreate the mood and the clamor of all the clocks striking at once.

Several other titles with good "sound" possibilities include Robert McCloskey's scene in *Make Way for Ducklings* where the ducklings tie up Boston street traffic, Dayle-Ann Dobbs's escaped bicycle wheel escapade *Wheel Away*, and Jane Goodsell's *Toby's Toe*, which is full of bad-tempered noises as each character passes along a grumpy mood. Even science class can be enriched with the addition of a bit of bombilation when you read aloud Thomas P. Lewis's *Hill of Fire*, an easy-to-read fictional account of the eruption of Mexico's volcano Paricutin in 1943. Have your students work out how it might have sounded.

Individual sounds that blend together for a final outburst are fun to try. Both Aliki's *At Mary Bloom's* and Pamela Allen's *Bertie and the Bear* contain plenty of good noises, each of which you can assign to several children. At the end, as each group produces its animal or instrument noise, the effect is remarkable.

On a rainy day, after reading aloud or booktalking a good weather story like Mirra Ginsburg's *Mushroom in the Rain* (grades Pre–K), Bill Martin, Jr., and John Archambault's *Listen to the Rain* (grades 1–2), Judi Barrett's *Cloudy with a Chance of Meatballs* (grades 2–3), Emily Rodda's *The Pigs Are Flying* (grades 4–5), or Bill

Brittain's *Dr. Dredd's Wagon of Wonders* (grades 5–6), make rain right in your classroom. (Look up Weather in the Subject Index for more title suggestions.)

Joan Robinson, once with Creative Theater in Princeton, New Jersey, and now a librarian in Vermont, taught me this magical technique, along with most everything else I've learned about creative drama on the way. Seat your group in a circle. Start by rubbing your hands together, fingers extended. One at a time, each person to your left will imitate your motion until everyone in the circle is rubbing palms. Then, begin snapping your fingers. Everyone must keep on doing the previous motion until the person to their immediate right begins snapping. When the snapping has come full circle, begin clapping. Next, stamp your feet. Finally, one by one, reverse your actions. The full sequence is: *rub/snap/clap/stamp/clap/snap/rub*.

It may take younger children a few tries before they catch on to the fact that they must both listen to the sounds and continue each action until the person on their right changes motions. When you finish, the less imaginative ones will scoff, saying they didn't hear any rain storm. Now, do it again, but this time, tape record it. When you play the tape back, even the most jaded children will be impressed at the results, from the first mist of rain to the loud drumming noise it makes when the downpour reaches its peak.

REPETITIVE DIALOGUE

The repeated refrain "peanut butter, peanut butter, jelly, jelly" is from Nadine Bernard Westcott's elephant-filled version of the chant *Peanut Butter and Jelly*, a kitchen-bound cousin to the myriad tellings of "I'm Going on a Bear Hunt," where the audience copycats your every word and movement.

Children thrive on helping out with a story when there is a refrain to chant. Acting out a tale with much repetitive dialogue is an icebreaker for shy children, as they don't need to worry about what to say. Lines are repeated often and are easy to recall. While reading aloud or telling stories such as Tony Johnston's *Yonder*, Sonia Levitin's *Nobody Stole the Pie*, Jack Prelutsky's *The Mean Old Mean Hyena*, or Lore Segal's *All the Way Home*, you will find your listeners eager to repeat the patterns with you. George Shannon's *Lizard's Song*, about a bear who can't remember the words, has an oft-repeated chorus that *must* be sung for the best effect. And Linda Williams's *The Little Old Lady Who Was Not Afraid of Anything* comes as close to perfection as possible; a story with a chantable refrain, sound effects and body motions, a scary *Boo!* and a satisfying ending that won't scare young children more than necessary.

Cumulative sequence stories are a good choice to use with younger children who enjoy the linear structure of cause and effect. When acting out Paul Galdone's old English folktale *The Old Woman and Her Pig*, even kindergartners have no trouble remembering and reciting the entire final sequence in which the cat begins to kill the mouse who starts to gnaw the rope that attempts to hang the butcher who starts to kill the ox who commences drinking the water that tries to quench the fire that begins to burn the stick that beats the dog who bites the pig who finally jumps over the stile so the old woman can get home that night. Honest.

Folktales such as *The Gingerbread Boy* or *The Three Little Pigs* include whole sections that children know by heart. If they can tell the story with you, why not stage a simple production? Many of Paul Galdone's marvelous folktale retellings lend themselves to creative drama. The plots are simple, the illustrations clear. Try *The Monster and the Tailor*. Working in pairs, children can enact the suspenseful graveyard confrontation between the emerging monster and the frightened tailor who is frantically attempting to finish stitching a duke's trousers. "I see that, but I'll sew this," he tells the creature who then chases him back to the castle and leaves his massive handprint on the palace wall.

EXPLORING CHARACTERIZATION THROUGH SPEECH

The Interview Technique

As an alternative to a general discussion of the whys and wherefores of protagonists and antagonists, conduct an interview with yourself as the host and with your students as interviewees and audience. For instance, say you and your fifth- or sixth-graders have just completed the unsettling novel *The Monster Garden* by Vivian Alcock. Announce to the class that you have somehow managed to induce most of the characters from the book to appear on your talk show and introduce Frankie Stein, the main character, as the first guest. Ask if she's in the room and as you peer at your audience, either wait for someone to volunteer, or say, "Oh yes, there she is. Frankie, we're so glad you could make it today," and point to one of your more verbal students. You need as a first "guest" that person who will be willing to transform herself instantly into a new character without being self-conscious or tongue-tied.

Once "Frankie" is sitting in a chair next to you, facing the audience, announce that you intend to find out more about the scientist's daughter who grew her own monster with a bit of genetic goo. Start off the questioning, but tell the audience that they are also welcome to raise their hands and ask their own questions.

Once the ice is broken, many children will want to volunteer to be interviewed in character. Several students, one after another, can be interviewed as the same character, answering different questions. If a child is tongue-tied and offers one-word answers, begin with literal questions requiring responses of only a few words. Change characters frequently to allow more children a chance to be in the limelight.

The interview technique enables children to develop oral language and creative thinking skills, as they must incorporate knowledge of plot structure, story sequence, setting, and character personalities into their questions and responses. As students will both sympathize and identify with major and minor characters, here is the chance to measure affective or emotional response to a work of literature, in addition to the more straightforward cognitive or factual response.

As you conduct the interviews, keep in mind the different types of questions that can be asked of such diverse personalities as those in *The Monster Garden*. The following list covers some of the literal, interpretive, critical, and creative questions that you might pose during a class interview with the characters from that book.

Character	Questions to Ask
Frankie Stein:	How old are you? Tell us about your family. What does your father do for a living? Why did your father's job cause you problems at school? How did you react when children called you "Frankenstein?" Tell us what Monnie was like.
Frankie's brother, David:	Why did you steal the dish of goo from your father's lab? What did you do with it when you brought it home? Why did you give Frankie half of it?
Julia Hobson:	Is Frankie a friend of yours? How did you react when you saw her creature for the first time? Why were you so against Frankie keeping Monnie?
John Hobson:	Describe what Monnie looked like the first time you saw him. Did you think he was dangerous? Why? Why were you so willing to help Frankie hide her monster, even though your sister Julia was against it?
Alf, the gardener:	What is your job? Why did you agree to build a hutch for Frankie's pet? What kind of pet was Monnie?

Any memorable story with diverse and potentially complex main characters is fair game for the interviewing technique. Fairy tales are a good source; although little detail is given about each character, children will make remarkable inferences about each one. Look for stories that boast a large cast so different points of view can be explored, and a serious or semi-serious theme with a compelling message.

Good choices for first- and second-graders include well-known favorites like *Cinderella* and *The Three Little Pigs*, and memorable sagas like Beatrice Schenk de Regniers's *Little Sister and the Month Brothers* or Robert D. San Souci's *The Talking Eggs*. What a field day you could have with Verna Aardema's African tale *Bimwilli and the Zimwi*, where a little girl is captured by an opportunistic monster who stuffs her into a drum, forces her to sing at each village, and collects the benefits from townspeople willing to pay for the treat of hearing a singing drum.

Fiction works well with younger children, though one should select stories with ample grist for discussion. Be wary of sequence stories or some adventures where mostly stock responses are likely. Instead, interview the chickens, Mr. Johnson the fox, and the townscritters in James Marshall's *Wings: A Tale of Two Chickens*, or the inhabitants of Bill Peet's books.

With Evaline Ness's *Sam, Bangs and Moonshine*, children could explore how exaggeration led to danger when Sam convinced her gullible friend Thomas to search for a nonexistent creature. Though there are only three characters with speaking parts—Sam, her father, and Thomas—there's no reason why Sam's cat Bangs couldn't add his opinions.

Bernard Waber's "Lyle" books are populated with unusual characters. In *Lyle, Lyle Crocodile*, aside from the large friendly reptile of the title, there are the uncomplicated Primm family, hostile next-door neighbor Mr. Grumps and his terrified cat Loretta, assorted neighborhood kids, and the flamboyant Hector P. Valenti, star of stage and screen.

Just for a start, grades 2 to 4 would have fun with the following folktales: P. C. Asbjørnsen's *The Squire's Bride*, *Jack and the Beanstalk* or any of its variants, *Hansel*

65

and Gretel, and Harve Zemach's Cornish *Rumpelstiltskin* variant, *Duffy and the Devil.* Move into fiction with Anna Elizabeth Bennett's *Little Witch,* Dr. Seuss's weather classic *Bartholomew and the Oobleck,* and E. B. White's *Charlotte's Web.*

Grades 4 to 6, where the responses will be most complex, would enjoy meeting the principals from George Webbe Dasent's Norwegian folktale, *East of the Sun, West of the Moon,* William Hooks's U.S. *Cinderella* variant, *Moss Gown,* Walter McVitty's retelling of *Ali Baba and the Forty Thieves,* and John Steptoe's graceful African tale *Mufaro's Beautiful Daughters.* Fiction that will hit the spot includes Bill Brittain's *Dr. Dredd's Wagon of Wonders,* Roald Dahl's *Matilda* and *The Witches,* Sid Fleischman's *The Whipping Boy,* Brian Jacques's mouse epic *Redwall,* and Christine Nostlinger's canned kid *Konrad.*

Characters on Trial

Another way to get your students pondering the intricacies of a character's personality is to hold a mock trial. *The Rise and Fall of Ben Gizzard* by Richard Kennedy is an ideal choice for grades 3 to 6. According to an old Indian's prophecy, Ben would die on the day he saw a white mountain upside down and a blackbird spoke to him. Mindful of this prediction, he became the villainous sheriff of Depression Gulch, a silver mining town bereft of trees, birds, and mountains, and ultimately met his fate in the form of an innocent young painter.

After a discussion of how your court will operate, appoint counsel for the defense and prosecution of this evil man and permit each side to discuss the case and develop questions. Lawyers may call main and minor characters as witnesses. Questions should require a range of responses from simple one-word answers to those that entail thought and ingenuity. As the judge, your role is to supervise the proceedings and ask questions when clarification is necessary. You may want to select jurors and run your courtroom according to protocol, which means offering your group a crash course in the judicial process. Upper grades studying the judicial system will want to go into more detail, though all will thrive on knowing how to throw around terms like "Your witness," or "I object, your honor!"

The thundering headmistress Miss Trunchbull in Roald Dahl's *Matilda* and his Grand High Witch in *The Witches* would make fascinating defendants, as would the disguised alien Great Aunt Emma in Nicholas Fisk's *Grinny;* Gast, the Pied Piper in Gloria Skurzynski's *What Happened in Hamelin;* and A. Wolf from John Scieszka's *The True Story of the 3 Little Pigs.*

First- and second-graders can get to the bottom of the mystery in *The Big Yellow Balloon* by Edward Fenton with a range of activities culminating in a simple trial where you ask the questions. After reading aloud, assign parts and act out in narrative pantomime to set the sequence the first time through. Now run through the story again, this time encouraging students to improvise their own dialogue to personalize each of the chasers and chased. Afterward, hold a trial where you call each witness in reverse sequence—policeman, thief, old lady, dog catcher, dog— and allow them to flesh out their various motives. When you finally call the cat to the witness stand, you will discover the culprit at the bottom of the whole affair, as the cat mistook Roger's balloon for the sun and planned to kill it so the ensuing darkness would provide him with risk-free hunting.

Two-Character Dialogues

In many stories, two conflicting characters must resolve a problem, and children can pair up to hammer out the solution. The purpose of this exercise is to argue out a problem where each person must listen and respond to the other partner. For younger grades, a heated discussion will ensue as heroine Minneapolis Simpkin, alias Minn, tries to convince her mother to let her have a pet in Peggy Parish's *No More Monsters for Me*. After the children choose partners, allow them five minutes to conduct their arguments and settlements. Remind both sides to employ good reasons for their cases and listen to each other without screaming. Once they begin, walk around the room and eavesdrop a bit. After five minutes, call the group back together and discuss how each pair ironed out its difficulties.

For grades 2 and 3, *Melvil and Dewey in the Chips* by Pamela Curtis Swallow is one of those library-oriented books no collection should be without. Two cage-bound library gerbils, named after the decimal system inventor, live the soft life until impulsive, adventurous Dewey decides they should bust out of the cage and see the sights. Poor nervous Melvil wants no part of the unknown, but his brother talks him into it. Pairs can become the long-tailed duo where one convinces the other to take a chance on the world outside the school library.

Third- and fourth-graders can portray the intelligent Maine porcupine, Janwillem Van de Wetering's *Hugh Pine*, and the delegation of his less-talented fellow quill-rattlers who convince him to help their cause. Hugh is the only porcupine who has figured out how to walk upright and wear a hat and coat. At the same time, so many of his slow-moving relatives are being run down and killed by fast-moving cars on the road that the delegation decides to ask antisocial Hugh to come up with a safety plan. In pairs, one tenacious porcupine can struggle to convince Hugh where his loyalties lie.

Third- through fifth-graders can double up to become Ellen Toliver and her grandfather who convinces her to take a message through British troops to General Washington. In this gripping historical fiction, *Toliver's Secret* by Esther Wood Brady, Ellen, a meek scaredy-cat, is horrified when her grandfather elects her to undertake the dangerous mission. In a second pairs dialogue, Ellen must convince a hungry British soldier not to take her loaf of bread. At the time, Ellen is disguised as a boy, and the loaf contains a snuff box with the secret message. What the soldier considers a mere argument over bread is a matter of life and death for Ellen, who is terrified of being found out.

Near the end of Mildred Ames's unsettling *Is There Life on a Plastic Planet?*, Hollis meets and argues with the life-size doll twin with whom she has traded her public existence. Fifth- and sixth-graders can partner up to re-enact and try to resolve that conflict, as the doll claims to be Hollis and refuses to leave the house until Hollis can convince her otherwise.

Improvised Dialogue

Understated and exaggerated humor often passes right over children's heads. They know they're supposed to laugh but aren't always sure why. After reading aloud to a fifth-grade class *Mr. Yowder and the Train Robbers* by Glen Rounds, I wondered if they understood the irony of the ending, so we undertook to act out the last scene.

The story concerns mild-mannered peripatetic sign painter Mr. Yowder who, with the ingenious assistance of several dozen local rattlesnakes, plots the capture of train robbers so he can gain the reward. But after the robbers are herded out to the road, a posse appears, also looking for the robbers, who escape, and Mr. Yowder is back where he started.

We blocked out the scene with two children playing Mr. Yowder, six outlaws, twelve snakes, and four posse members, and discussed the importance of listening so everyone would not talk at the same time. Each group took a few minutes to talk over the scope and sequence of their movements and designate dialogue. The snakes practiced their rattling and threatening looks.

The play began. The two Misters Yowder had worked out a signal to summon the snakes, and the robbers acted truly surprised and scared when they found themselves encircled and outnumbered. The actors had no trouble talking tough and creating believable dialogue, and when the posse thundered in, snakes and outlaws fled to safety, leaving the poor Yowders in dismay.

After a good laugh and a discussion of how to make the next run-through even better, we recast those who wanted to change parts and went through the scene again. This time, the dialogue was smoother, the snakes more quietly menacing, and there was an aura of tension and fear until the posse arrived. Everyone especially adored diving out of the way of the thundering hooves, and all would have opted for a third run if we had had more time.

After dramatizing this rowdy story, I made a discovery. The fifth-grade teacher, on entering the library and observing her children strutting, rattling, and galloping, shook her head, rolled her eyes and said, semiseriously, "Thanks a heap. I'll never get them down to earth now, after all this excitement." And yet, after we finished, the children became noticeably relaxed and content with themselves as they browsed for books, and were not in the least bit rowdy or wound up. After noting the same result with most of the other classes that undertook improvised dramas, I've concluded that these activities actually have a calming effect on children, leaving them exhilarated and feeling very positive about themselves.

To reap the benefits of improvised drama, teachers must be willing to allow time for the discussion and planning that come before any actual acting. You must also spend sufficient time on the drama itself, replaying a scene as needed, working out rough spots, and developing characterization.

Children will not respond well if you thrust them into an improvised drama without any prior experience to warm them up. Unlike narrative pantomime, which is basically intuitive, improvising dialogue to reconstruct a story or scene is risky for children. They must use reasoning skills, cooperate and interact intimately with their peers, respond to cues, recall a specific sequence, and make the scene become real using their ingenuity. Improvised dialogue is looser and less structured than a scripted play, which stays the same each time.

Other Good Books for Improvised Drama

For primary grade children, cumulative tales with some improvised drama provide a good starting place. "The Travels of a Fox" from Anne Rockwell's *The Old Woman and Her Pig and 10 Other Stories* is a satisfying story, as the sequence is easy to recall, there are enough characters for everyone to have a part, and the dialogue is simple enough to either remember or invent. Other retellings of the same tale include Paul Galdone's *What's in Fox's Sack* and Jennifer Westwood's *Going to Squintums*. After casting the fox, the various mistresses of each house, a bumblebee, and all the other assorted animals, seat the cast in one long row in the order of each character's appearance. Students will now have no trouble moving in and out of each scene as needed. You may need to do some side-coaching, or narrating of the story line, in between the dialogue. Side-coaching helps you keep the action flowing smoothly. Use a long narrow piece of cloth to simulate the fox's sack, which can be tied loosely around the necks of the successive characters the fox abducts. Sometimes the use of a simple prop makes the story more believable.

Other good cumulative tales include "Sody Saleratus" from Richard Chase's *Grandfather Tales*, Paul Galdone's *The Greedy Old Fat Man*, "The Cat and the Parrot" from Virginia Haviland's *Favorite Fairy Tales Told in India*, and *The Fat Cat* by Jack Kent. All four are similar and would be interesting to tell, act out, and compare.

Folktales often provide enough parts for everyone to jump in. A fine example is *Could Anything Be Worse?*, a Jewish folktale retold by Marilyn Hirsch. Before acting out this one, discuss with your students the necessity of staying in character so the play does not turn into a barnyard free-for-all. It might be wise to bang a hand drum to freeze the action as needed, as the story of a poor man who seeks peace and tranquillity in his crowded house is noisy although deliriously funny.

Children are fascinated with the plot and realistic pencil illustrations in the Caldecott winner *Jumanji* by Chris Van Allsburg. Enhance the story by actually playing that dangerous game. Find or make one large die and ask each student to dream up one new move for the game board, such as, "Caught in a tornado. Lose one turn." Up to four players at a time can compete to reach the golden city of Jumanji, while the rest of the class comprises a human game board, lined up around the room. One at a time, each player rolls and counts off the number of "squares" by touching the hand of each corresponding child in the game board line. When the player lands, the "square" comes to life, reciting its consequences and acting them out. (The tornado, for instance, would twist and howl.) This activity is great fun, and you may want to go even further by requesting that your students dream up and design their own games, replete with rules and game board, for others in the class to play.

Not every story has enough characters to go around, so don't be afraid to assign two or more children to the same part or to have some children as spectators. Another alternative is to divide the class into groups so that each group can work on a different scene from one or more stories. Aesop's fables work wonderfully for all ages, as do Arnold Lobel's *Fables* for older students. They're short, easy to recall, and entertaining. Select and read aloud an assortment; then assign each group of from two to six children one story to dramatize. Walk around the room, dispensing advice and encouragement, and then have each group present its skit.

Fourth- and fifth-graders can dramatize a trio of scenes such as Billy's encounter with the first worm in Thomas Rockwell's *How to Eat Fried Worms*, the classroom chapter in Daniel Pinkwater's *Fat Men from Space* when teacher Mr. Wendell can't figure out who has the hidden radio, and the kidnapping of Polly and Josh by two strangers who claim to be relatives in Barbara Holland's *Prisoners at the Kitchen Table*. Each group will need to ponder how to set up each scene and what to say, a good experience in cooperation for everyone.

Readers Theater

Improvised drama depends on the talents of the actors to make the unscripted production smooth and believable. With Readers Theater, a more structured drama variation, children are given or write their own scripts to act out a scene. You don't need stage sets or props, unless you decide to memorize your scripts and put on a play. Readers Theater stresses reading aloud and, as such, is a boon to the children who are less flamboyant.

If you are reticent about transposing your own scripts, do not despair. Caroline Feller Bauer's *Reader's Theater* provides over 50 scripts derived from children's books, folktales, and poems, and *Plays Magazine* is a gold mine as well.

Many books you read aloud or booktalk have scenes or chapters with multiple characters and an emphasis on dialogue. Transposing those scenes into scripts is fairly straightforward, as you can use the dialogue as written and the descriptions as stage directions when needed. Make copies of the script so each child has one, distribute parts, and have the actors sit in a circle for the first reading. The second time through, block out movement and set your stage area. Children who feel intimidated by the demands of improvised drama will be reassured by the presence of the script.

All of the suggestions of books to use for improvised drama work just as well for Readers Theater, though it means more preparation time for you, either writing the script yourself or supervising your students. As a writing exercise, scripting a scene is challenging and fun for children once you have demonstrated the format and construction. Hand out samples of plays so children can see how to plan dialogue and directions for characters. Do your first script together as a class by handing out copies of the same story and outlining the script on the board. The tedious part is copying down the dialogue verbatim and then typing it up. Still, if you and your students create a couple of new scripts each year, your collection will accrue and you can use each one over and over.

After reading a corker like Arthur Yorink's *Company's Coming*, you get the urge to act it out. Try this story of a spaceship landing in Moe's and Shirley's backyard as improvised drama or write a script with your students, perhaps expanding the dialogue to give everyone bigger parts.

Matilda by Roald Dahl is a book you either adore or find hideously offensive. Brilliant five-year-old Matilda gets revenge on her family and on the outrageous headmistress at her school. In a chapter entitled "The Ghost," she borrows a friend's talking parrot for the evening and convinces her parents that there are robbers in the house. The simple scene is practically all dialogue and would be a cinch to work into a five- or six-person script. Other possibilities abound in the chapters "Bruce Bogtrotter and the Cake" and "The Weekly Test."

A Creative Drama Warning

Don't be surprised when the creative dramatics exercises you try with your students turn out to be wildly successful. They may well end up as the high point of your year. It's up to you to figure out what to say after you finish reading a selection to your class and they clamor, "May we act it out now?" If your answer is yes, you are helping to equip them with the self-esteem needed to survive when called upon to do some public speaking. They will learn social and language interaction skills that would make Miss Manners proud, and you may even provide the impetus for a twenty-first century Meryl Streep or Robin Williams.

If these ideas have primed you for more, search the annotated Read-Aloud Lists—and the Subject Index under the headings Call and Response Stories, Chantable Refrain, Creative Drama, Cumulative Stories, Sequence Stories, Sound Effects, and Stories with Songs—for other creative drama suggestions.

Let yourselves go crazy a bit. A first-grade teacher once implored me to read aloud Harry Allard's then-new *Miss Nelson Has a Field Day*. Not guessing what she was up to, I did. How was I to know she was in cahoots with the nefarious Mrs. Balunis? After I read the book, the library door flew open and in marched Coach Swamp of the story in her black sweatshirt, followed by the Smedley Tornadoes football team in full regalia, uniformed chanting cheer leaders, pom poms flying, and spectators waving banners.

"Wow," my first-graders sighed. "Was that really Miss Swamp?"

Now *that's* creative drama.

Illustration by Lorinda Bryan Cauley reprinted by permission of G. P. Putnam's Sons from GOLDILOCKS AND THE THREE BEARS retold and illustrated by Lorinda Bryan Cauley, © 1981 by Lorinda Bryan Cauley.

STORYTELLING:
A CRASH COURSE

FOLKTALES ARE FAMILIAR FARE TO MOST STUDENTS, AND IN MY school 398.2, the Dewey decimal number representing fairy tales in the nonfiction section of the library, is well known. When you walk in the library and look up, you'll see that number prominently displayed on the fairy tale ceiling mural created by Joyce Houser's third-grade class some years back. Every child knows the 398.2 chant I wrote to help them remember its significance.

LOOK FOR 398.2

by Judy Freeman © 1983

If you want a good story,
Let me tell you what to do:
LOOK FOR 398.2, LOOK FOR 398.2

If dragons are your fancy,
Shiny tails of green and blue:
LOOK FOR 398.2, LOOK FOR 398.2

Prince or princess in hot water,
Trouble with a witch's brew:
LOOK FOR 398.2, LOOK FOR 398.2

Ogres, leprechauns, and goblins
All are waiting there for you:
LOOK FOR 398.2, LOOK FOR 398.2

Find a tale from every country,
From Morocco to Peru:
LOOK FOR 398.2, LOOK FOR 398.2

If you have been bemoaning your students' lack of concentration, their poor listening skills, and their inability to relate to you or each other on more than a superficial level, there is one universal balm for your woes. Make storytelling part of your school routine. There is no better way to pull a group together with a common thread, and the stories you share with your children will be remembered long after the other details of the year are forgotten.

The tragedy is that most children have never heard stories told. Parents, teachers, and even librarians are afraid to tell stories for fear of somehow doing it "wrong." It's true that some people are born storytellers and seem to master each new yarn effortlessly. Still, all of us are capable of telling stories well. Once you decide it is a worthwhile endeavor and give it a try, you will understand what you and your students have been missing and go from there. Children love stories, but few have ever heard them live, with no text, no illustrations, and no commercial breaks or probing questions in midplot.

As a young librarian I used to tell Pete Seeger's "Abiyoyo," which I first heard told by the folksinger at a concert when I was eight years old. For the longest time, I never realized that when I told "Abiyoyo" and Seeger's other masterpiece, "The Foolish Frog," I was a storyteller. I thought of them as story-songs. I recognized that children were enamored of these tales, as they would walk around school humming and sometimes break into song when they saw me outside the library.

Several years before the book version of "Abiyoyo" came out, a second-grade boy said to me, "Could I have the book you read to us that time—the one about Abiyoyo?"

"There is no book," I reminded him. "It was a story I told you, remember?"

"Yes, it is too a book. I remember the pictures," he insisted, and I had a hard time convincing him otherwise.

The mind's eye is a powerful artist, and if we do our part, children will see more of the "pictures" that make stories so real to them. Teachers can compensate children for the affection, emotion, and personal contact that the electronic age does not provide. When television tells a story, it offers the viewer no eye contact, no response, and no reason to become emotionally enticed. Storytelling, however, provides us with the drama and emotion that speaks to each individual and allows our imaginations to flourish.

FOLKLORE VERSUS FICTION

As adults, we often assume that children are familiar with what are, to us, obvious folk and fairy tales. When I told a third-grade class *Rumpelstiltskin*, I was appalled to discover that many of them had never heard it or many other basic and well-known tales. Most of the students in my kindergarten classes had seen the bowdlerized, Disney-fied version of *Little Red Riding Hood*, and when I told them the story, they were shocked. "You mean Little Red Riding Hood and her grandmother really got *eaten*? I saw that story on TV, but the wolf just locked the grandmother in the closet and chased Little Red Riding Hood around the bed until the hunter came."

As a librarian, I had always assumed that children still heard the old familiar folktales told or read at home, but it seems that this is no longer the case. Folktales, the world's earliest form of communication and literature, handed down from parent to child for generations, should become a standard part of the school curriculum. Basal readers usually include folktales, but these are often watered down and lose the effect of live presentation. The study of folktales not only enriches any basic curriculum, helping children discover the universal qualities of humankind, but also lays the groundwork for understanding all of literature. From kindergarten on up, storytelling can be used as a tool to reinforce comprehension skills, encourage creativity, foster respect for other cultures, and stimulate interest in independent reading and writing.

Folktales read aloud or told have universal appeal. They are usually short, have fast-moving plots, are often humorous, and almost always end happily. Wishes do come true and enchantments are lifted or reversed, but not without the sacrifices of the hero, most often the youngest, weakest child who overcomes the label of nitwit or fool. Many of the tales contain a fair amount of violence, but it is violence resolved, with good triumphing over evil, the powerless fighting for deserved recognition, and the tyrannical wrongdoers punished. Folktales instill values of humility, kindness, patience, courage, and hard work without preaching or condescending, and provide a way out through fantasy for children who are looking to resolve life's problems. Certainly, these tales would never have lingered so long if they were inconsequential or meaningless.

Storytelling and reading aloud go hand in hand. Check the folklore Read-Aloud Lists in this book and you will find an array of single-story picture books, as well as fascinating longer collections, usually not illustrated so sumptuously. In the past decade, the proliferation of elaborately illustrated picture books of well-known folktales has resulted in multiple versions of such classics as *The Three Little Pigs*, *Snow White*, *Cinderella*, *The Three Bears*, and more. When reading one of these tales aloud, show the other versions as well and compare the artists' interpretations along with the texts. If there is more than one version or variant of a tale listed here, I cross-referenced each one within the annotations, so you can gather them easily.

Sometimes, perhaps, illustrators show us *too* much, and that is why interspersing reading of the illustrated tales with those you tell allows your children to maintain their own interpretations. Try telling one story and then reading aloud other variants to compare and contrast their similarities and differences. For instance, *Bony Legs* by Joanna Cole is easy to learn to tell, and Ernest Small's *Baba Yaga* and Maida Silverman's *Anna and the Seven Swans* are two more Russian tales about the witch with the iron teeth who lives in a hut on chicken legs.

In the space of three class sessions, I tell a dark version of the southern U.S. story "Barney McCabe," in which three hound dogs come to the rescue of a brother and sister trapped by a butcher knife-wielding witch; read aloud and show the illustrated versions of Grimm's *Hansel and Gretel*; and then show the terrifying filmstrip of Barbara Walker's Turkish variant, "Teeny Tiny and the Witch Woman," about three brothers lost in the woods. Afterward, we have a spirited discussion of how the stories are similar and different. Invariably, the story they request the most is "Barney McCabe," which, alas, does not exist in book form, though a cheerier version is on storyteller David Holt's record "The Hairy Man and Other Wild Tales," recorded on the High Windy Productions label.

We assume that children know intuitively just what a folk or fairy tale is, but they most emphatically do not. Often, teachers will assign fairy tale book reports to, say, a fourth-grade class, and the librarian will be besieged by children waving copies of *The Lion, the Witch and the Wardrobe* or *Charlotte's Web*, and asking frantically, "Is this a fairy tale?" To children, all cartoons are fairy tales, as are all fantasies. If the book is old or famous or includes magic, they reason it must be a fairy tale.

When showcasing folktales, talk about the difference between stories in the fiction section of the library and those in folklore. Talk about the days before VCRs or radios or even electric lights, when stories were a means of entertainment and a way to explain all the scary or perplexing mysteries of life. Explain that people would make up stories and pass them around without ever writing them down.

Stories would travel, from one village to another or one country to another, via travelers and traders. Every time we tell a story, it changes a bit, and that's one reason that stories like *Cinderella* made the rounds the world over.

Nowadays, when someone makes up a story, he or she writes it down and tries to get it published. We call that fiction. The stories in 398.2 are old stories, and we don't know who made them up the first time. They were passed down from one generation to the next until someone—a reteller—decided to write them down in his or her own words. Famous retellers of old like Jacob and Wilhelm Grimm from Germany, Joseph Jacobs from England, Charles Perrault from France, and P. C. Asbjørnsen and Jørgen Moe from Norway brought us so many of the tales we now take for granted. Modern collectors such as Richard Chase, Harold Courlander, and Diane Wolkstein have continued the folklorist tradition.

Unless children are familiar with the 398.2 section of the library, those books often go untouched until a teacher or librarian with discriminating taste introduces them to students and explains that they are shelved in nonfiction with the social sciences books, as stories that explain customs and stories of world cultures, instead of in fiction, where they would seem to belong. Many libraries intermingle folk and fairy tales in the picture book sections, where they will find a greater readership.

There is a certain stigma attached to fairy tales for upper-grade children. "Those stories are for little kids," they proclaim. Once you read aloud and tell some of these stories, they will change their tune. Invariably, teachers are startled to discover how much their students love and clamor for good folklore once they have sampled some of it. Fiction brings us into today's imaginations; folk and fairy tales connect us to our past. Both are essential forms of literature for children to discover.

TELLING STORIES YOU ALREADY KNOW

Without ever formally sitting down to learn a story, you probably already know half a dozen stories that you could tell right now. Some are bedtime stories you made up to entertain your children at home. Others are old folktales you know from childhood. Still others are picture books you've read aloud so many times that you could tell them with your eyes closed.

I read Jill Murphy's *Peace at Last* to many first grades over a three-year span. But one day when the book wasn't in, I realized that the story tells every bit as well as it reads and that I already knew it by heart without ever attempting to "learn" it.

Think back to all the stories you love, and try telling one to yourself. Chances are, you could tell it to children right now and they would be thrilled to hear it. Don't worry about being perfect. You only have to remember the basic sequence.

FINDING NEW STORIES TO TELL

The first step in learning a new story is to find one that you love madly. Pick just any old tale, and you'll end up loathing it before you ever tell it. The story must touch or tickle or intrigue you in an unforgettable way. You will be spending hours together with your story over the years, as you first learn it and then tell it, so be sure that you and the story are compatible for the long haul. Some stories you'll learn because you need a quick filler. These you will forget after the need has passed. The best stories are the ones that reach out and grab you for good, keeping you as fascinated the fiftieth time told as the first.

As I was brushing my teeth one bland morning, while reading Yoshiko Uchida's *The Sea of Gold*, a superb collection of Japanese folktales, I was jarred into wakefulness by one story, "The Terrible Black Snake's Revenge." I fell in love—and six years later, still feel that way—with the story about a timid man named Badger who unwittingly outsmarts the terrible villager-eating black snake of the mountains and becomes a rich man in the bargain. I began learning it the same week.

The search for a tellable tale can be an elusive one, and there is no substitute for the groundwork you must do. Start by reading folktales from the Read-Aloud Lists in this book. This will give you a background in national tale characteristics, plot similarities, common motifs used, variants from all over the globe, and the narrator's voice. Read your favorites aloud to your students to see what they think. Every so often, a folk or fairy tale will leap out and leave you breathless. Photocopy that story, including the book's title and author, for your files right away, or you will undoubtedly forget where you read it when you find yourself all set to learn it.

I keep one file of stories already learned, which I use to dust off my memory when I haven't told a certain tale in a long time, and another file of stories I'd like to learn. When the urge hits me to dig into a new one, I rummage through that file and pick the one that best fits my mood and the occasion. If you make the effort to learn but one or two stories a year, your repertoire will grow almost effortlessly.

Starting out, select short, funny folktales, so you can learn them quickly without being overwhelmed. Short means they take less than five minutes or so to tell. If you decide to start with a long, involved epic, chances are you will become overwhelmed and discouraged.

For expert guidance in telling simple stories, see the Professional Bibliography at the end of this book. Particularly helpful for general advice and style are Augusta Baker and Ellin Greene's *Storytelling: Art and Technique*, Caroline Feller Bauer's *Handbook for Storytellers*, and Norma J. Livo and Sandra A. Rietz's comprehensive *Storytelling: Process and Practice*. For a step-by-step walk-through of easy-to-tell tales, don't miss the following gold mines: Margaret Read MacDonald's *Twenty Tellable Tales: Audience Participation for the Beginning Storyteller* and *When the Lights Go Out: Twenty Scary Tales to Tell*, and Anne Pellowski's *The Family Storytelling Handbook* and *The Story Vine*. Each of these four indispensable books is filled with stories one can pick up and tell immediately.

Kindergarten through second grades are ideal for telling brief, whimsical, cumulative, or repetitive tales, where children can join in as co-tellers. In upper elementary grades, stories should reflect the variety of world cultures, styles, and genres such as myths, legends, fairy tales, and fables, along with some ghost stories to scare your students' socks off. Picture books and other easy fiction stories are often delightful when told instead of read. In the Subject Index, look under the entry Stories to Tell, where I have listed some of my favorites.

Other sources for great stories include records, cassettes, and videotapes of well-known storytellers, live concerts and storytelling workshops, local storytelling groups, and friends who don't mind sharing. Often I'll read a story in a book and think that it does nothing for me; then, I hear someone tell the same story and make it hum with life. Feel free to borrow such tales for your own collection, and, while paying homage to your source, take steps to make the story your own. Every person has his or her own style of telling, which evolves from practice.

Recorded stories are a boon to tellers who want to hear how voice, pause, and pacing work, but they are not substitutes for the real thing—a live performance. Don't be daunted by the "pros." Unless you intend to take your show on the road, your own comfortable style will suit your students just fine, though you'll learn plenty from watching a top-notch longtime storyteller at work.

LEARNING STORIES TO TELL

Storyteller Laura Simms lists five basic steps to learning a new story:
READ (or hear it told) / OUTLINE / DISCUSS / CONTEMPLATE / TELL.
You will notice that memorization is not one of the steps. Unless you are learning a literary folktale that requires the precise language, such as a "Just-So" story by Rudyard Kipling, you will not need or want to memorize the bulk of your stories. What you aim for is to internalize each saga so you remain faithful to the story source while making it come alive in your own imagination. Memorize only those sections that are essential to the story: the beginning and ending paragraphs, if the precise wording is desirable, and any refrains or repeated phrases that capture the flavor of the tale.

Once you've decided on a story, reread it several times until you can outline the sequence either in written or mental form. This helps clarify the sequence and lets you know if you've selected a story you find special. If you learn best by listening, read the story onto a tape and listen to it.

Discuss the plot with an interested friend to flesh out the story and clarify form and details. Contemplate the layers of meanings, the motivation of each character, the way you see and hear each one, and bring the tale to life in your imagination. Allow yourself into the story to visualize the setting and every scene. What kind of voice will you use? Should you sit or stand? What, if any, hand motions should you use? The answers depend on the story being told. A rule of thumb: Less is more effective than more. Too much leaping about when changing characters can leave your audience baffled and exhausted from all the activity.

Avoid being too flamboyant when you tell, or the focus will be on you and not the story. Your use of voice must come from your own personality. You are but the messenger and can spellbind your listeners with the power of your message. Better to let a story tell itself simply, with no adornment, than to dress it up in ill-fitting garb. The classic New York Public Library style of storytelling, where the teller lights a story candle and tells with few if any hand motions and with well-modulated voice, is usually effective, though I tend to be a bit more worked up than that.

Sit or stand? It's fine to sit for a small group, though you feel the story more if you stand. Sitting allows you to hide behind the story and feel less personally vulnerable; standing is more satisfying. Try both and vary them according to your audience.

Figuring out all of the above takes time. Some quick-study types can read a story once and tell it the next day. Most of us take a bit longer. At first, when I learned a new story, I would make a copy to take along with me. Then I bought a car with a tape deck. Now I read the story onto a tape, and while driving, tell the story aloud along with the recording. Take care, however, that you don't become a road hazard, although you can make great use of your driving time to learn those stories that you feared would take too long to master. Spend 15 minutes a day working on a story, and at the end of two weeks, you have another treat for your students.

Once the story is in your memory, practice telling it aloud every chance you get, first to yourself, then to a patient friend, child, or spouse. Strut your stuff in front of the mirror, the cat, or even the portulaca before you try a larger audience. That spontaneous-seeming delivery takes time to master, without all the "uhs" and "ums" that plague an unprepared teller. Wipe out all instances of "she goes" or "like" or "so he says" from your delivery. We tell jokes in the present tense, but folk and fairy tales happened once upon a time, so stick to the past tense when you tell them.

TELLING STORIES: THE FINAL FRONTIER

When you feel ready, do not delay. Sit your children down and *tell that tale*. The first time will be shaky, though your audience is usually the last to notice or care. The second time will be better, the third is satisfying, and by the fourth, you'll feel as comfortable as a broken-in running shoe.

The first time you tell a story to children, let them know what you expect of them. Discuss the difference between telling and reading stories aloud. When you read, the words are in front of you, and so are the pictures for all to see. A story told allows the listeners to make up their own pictures using their imagination. They must concentrate very hard on the story so it can come alive for them inside their heads.

Children who have never heard stories told often do not know how to react. They will interrupt you, raising their hands to describe to you in great detail how they once went into the woods, too, or heckle you in an affectionate way, not realizing how rattling this is for you. Don't expect an intuitively respectful response, though you may well get one, but prepare them for the experience. Once you start a story, it is difficult to stop and say, "Steven, leave Sharron alone," or "Amy, sit up straight and stop playing with Myra's baseball cards." By the time you get the group straightened out, you'll have lost their attention.

Often, storytelling warm-up exercises will help the children unwind and focus their energy on the teller, just as aerobic dancing warm-ups prepare us for exercising. Here is a sampling of storytelling warm-ups that can be used before you start, between stories, or afterward, as you see fit.

1. Slowly look left for three seconds or so. Look right. Tilt head to left. Tilt head to right. Tilt chin to chest. Repeat the sequence twice.
2. Slowly rotate one shoulder forward, then the other. Reverse directions. Repeat the sequence twice.
3. Open eyes and mouth as wide as you can, then close. Repeat twice.
4. Shake hands in front of you. Shake high; shake low.
5. "Now mush your face," you say, as you proceed to massage your cheeks in concentric circles. "You look ridiculous!" I tell the group, who rush to assure me that I do, too.
6. Massage head with fingertips to make sure the brain is working.

7. Take the deepest breath you can and exhale loudly with your tongue sticking out. We call this "Monster Breath." Do it again. Now, once more with feeling!

8. Now that your face and hands and shoulders and brain are ready, don't forget to prepare the room for the story. Sometimes the walls are not high enough for the story you want to tell. Push out the walls by extending your arms out to the sides. Now push both arms straight up to raise the ceiling. And finally, push both arms down to lower the floor.

These exercises may seem flip, but they do get the wiggles out and prepare students for listening. They also feel wonderful when you are tense or tired.

Now, set the stage. Tell them, as Laura Simms does, "When I tell you a story instead of reading it, the words are in my brain. You must listen extra carefully, and except when I need your help in telling the story, never interrupt. If you start to poke someone or talk to someone or tell me something interesting, I'll forget where I am in the story. In fact, the story could fly right out of my head, and then you and I will never find out how it comes out in the end! That would be a terrible thing!"

Eye contact usually does the trick in keeping everyone focused on you. This is not the Miss Viola Swamp evil eyeball kind of eye contact, though you may revert to that in a tight spot. Rather, you tell the story to each person, watching their reactions, and holding their attention through the power of your words. Avoid sweeping the faces with your eyes; linger on each person for a sentence or so before moving on.

Regardless of how prepared you are, disaster will strike from time to time. The fire drill bell will go off, your principal will ask you a question over the intercom, or three children will come barreling into your room at the most dramatic part of the narrative. Relax. Resume as soon as you can, and if it bombs, worse things could happen. The next time will be better, unless someone in the group breaks wind and the class falls apart, laughing wildly and moving away from the designated suspect. I still haven't figured a way to settle a group effectively after that one, and yes, it does happen every so often.

The main rule of thumb is: Don't panic. There you are in the middle of a story and you realize with a jolt that you've left out a major section upon which the whole rest of the story hinges. You could stop and say, "Oh, I made a mistake. Let me start over." Don't do that. You'll break the spell and lose credibility. Since you are usually the only person in the world who is aware of the omission, you can easily put it right again. Simply say, "Now you may not know this, but . . ." and weave that missing piece right into your narrative, like a flashback, as though it belonged there in the first place. Losing track or omitting something happens more often if you start thinking about lunch or your meeting with your boss instead of concentrating on the story. As you tell the story, you must visualize it yourself, or risk blanking out in mid-image. Think fast, and you can save any story.

FAMILY STORIES

Stories connect us to the past and to each other. When my friend and fellow librarian Lois Schochet brought me back a set of painted, wooden nesting dolls or Matrioska, from Russia, it occurred to me that they could be used to explain the concept of stories being passed down from generation to generation. I now tell my students, "It could be that your parents and your grandparents know lots of stories that they've never told you, either because they've forgotten them or because they never knew you were interested. When you go home tonight, ask your family to tell you stories—either made-up stories like folktales, or family stories of what life was like when they were little, and all the crazy things that happened back then. You may be astonished at what they can remember, once you've reminded them.

"If you ask your mother to tell a story, perhaps she'll remember one that she heard, when she was growing up, from her mother—your grandmother." (Here I open the first layer of wooden dolls and take out the slightly smaller "grand-mother" and hold it up.)

"It could be that your grandmother heard the same story, told night after night, until she knew it by heart, from her mother—your great-grandmother." Each time I discuss another mother, I uncap another doll and hold it up, until, at the end, when we get to their great-great-great-great-great grandmothers, there is only one tiny fingernail-size doll left.

Then we assemble the dolls in sequence, as the children say with me, "If your great-great-great-great-great grandmother told a story to your great-great-great-great grandmother, and she told that story to your great-great-great grandmother, and she told that story to your great-great grandmother, and she told that story to your great grandmother, and she told that story to your grandmother, and she told that story to your mother, maybe tonight, your mother will tell that story to you, and when you grow up you can tell it to your children, and when they grow up, they can tell it to their children, and the story will live on, forever, passed on from one generation to the next, from now until the end of time."

Family stories can be just as entertaining as folktales, and you may want to start a family storytelling project, where the children tape record their family members telling stories, or the children themselves tape the stories they've heard. Tapes can become part of the classroom oral history collection, with duplicate copies made so each child can keep a record of his or her own contributions. Parents often don't realize that keeping these stories alive connects their children to a piece of the past that will otherwise become lost or disregarded.

Realistic or autobiographical family-centered picture books such as Deborah Hartley's *Up North in Winter*, Marisabina Russo's *Waiting for Hannah*, or Mary Stolz's *Storm in the Night* will get students thinking about their own families. After reading aloud Ina R. Friedman's *How My Parents Learned to Eat*, about a half-American, half-Japanese child who recalls how her parents, an American sailor and a Japanese schoolgirl, met and fell in love, I encourage my second-graders to find out how their parents got together. "It was the first step to your being alive today. If your parents never met, you wouldn't be sitting here right now. You wouldn't exist," I tell them, and this small truth stuns them. When next we meet, they are bursting with family tales, some unusual, some very funny. Recording these tales, either through writing or taping, ensures they won't be forgotten. (Caution: If many children from the group come from single-parent homes, this activity may not be appropriate, so use discretion.)

After giving a storytelling program in a New Jersey elementary school, during which I suggested the children sound out their families, I was thrilled to receive letters from one class, telling me which stories they had liked and why. One letter was unforgettable in its poignancy. It read in full: "Dear Miss Freeman, I liked the storys you told us. I have two grandmothers. They don't tell me storys." It was signed "Love, Amanda."

KIDS TELL STORIES

Storytelling adds a refreshing slant to the teaching of listening, comprehension, and critical thinking skills, not to mention the huge benefits it offers in terms of vocabulary and language development, a sharpened sense of humor, and a working understanding of the basic components of all literature. Children can easily learn to tell stories, most likely with far less effort than it takes us grown-ups.

In a library project that I have developed and conducted with fourth- and fifth-grade classes, the children spent 10 weeks learning to be storytellers. My general goals in the "Kids Tell Stories" project were as follows:

1. To familiarize students and teachers with the background and traditions of oral literature,
2. to introduce children to a body of written literature (i.e., folktales),
3. to acquaint students with the skills of storytelling and oral expression,
4. to develop the ability of students to conceptualize, using the "mind's eye" to visualize a complete story,
5. to develop reading and writing skills as an outgrowth of storytelling, and
6. to enhance students' self-esteem, poise, and ease in speaking before a group.

During our once-a-week, one-hour sessions, we explored the origins of storytelling and read folk and fairy tales from all over the world, noting the characteristics of tales from Japan, Africa, Germany, England, China, the United States, and other countries. We charted the types and themes of stories and examined the characteristics of main characters.

Each week I told them at least one new story, and they dramatized some, outlined the plots, drew vivid portraits of main characters, and constructed detailed maps of the settings. Even after a week had passed, a class, sitting in a circle, could collectively retell an entire story round-robin, almost line for line. When one child forgot a section, someone else was sure to recall it and fill in the missing details.

We read and contrasted variants of well-known stories, such as a French versus a German version of *Cinderella*, Dang Manh Kha's Vietnamese *In the Land of Small Dragon*, Ai-Ling Louie's *Yeh Shen* from China, and "Cenerentola" from Virginia Haviland's *Favorite Fairy Tales Told in Italy*.

Students performed exercises to hone their storytelling skills by using their bodies to fit the tone and point of view of each character, and by learning to breathe properly from the diaphragm and to project their voices. They drew up large charts listing and comparing folktale characters, story beginnings and endings, and common folktale motifs, such as the use of magical numbers 3, 7, and 12 (i.e., 3 wishes, 3 little pigs, 7 dwarfs, 12 dancing princesses), and the occurrence of transformations and magical objects.

Back in the classroom each week, the classroom teacher supplemented my lesson by reading aloud a sampling of additional folktales and using the stories as a kickoff to writing. For instance, after hearing "Why Dogs Hate Cats" from Julius

Lester's *The Knee-High Man*, students made up new stories to explain the ongoing rivalry between mutt and feline.

Reading and creating folktale parodies works here, once children know and respect the original stories on which the spoofs are based. After everyone has heard a sampling of *Cinderella* stories, Bernice Myers's *Sidney Rella and the Glass Sneakers* is a gas, and you can discuss how the author constructed her spoof based on the original. Many teachers expect their students to write folktale satire without understanding its underlying structure, which misses the point. In *The True Story of the 3 Little Pigs*, Jon Scieszka's A. Wolf explains that he was an innocent victim framed by the media. Students can retell other stories from another character's point of view.

After all this background, which is in and of itself a valid and lasting way to extend the language arts, social studies, and science curriculums, each child selected and learned a story to tell. All stories had to be approved by the teacher or me, as some children wanted to try long, involved dissertations, and we offered guidance in selecting good, tellable folk and fairy tales.

Once the stories were selected, students outlined their stories, drew main character portraits and story maps—as they had already done with one of the stories I told—discussed them first with a partner and then a small group, and next, told them to their groups. Classroom teachers allowed their tellers to adjourn to the hallway with partners to practice their stories as time allowed.

As a final rehearsal, they told their now-learned tales to the rest of the class seated on the floor on the library Story Rug. After each person finished, the class offered positive encouragement and suggestions for improvement. Children in this situation will be helpful and supportive as long as you lay the ground rules for what constitutes a helpful critique. After telling stories themselves, students are far more courteous, sympathetic, and encouraging when listening to their peers.

Since a storyteller is not fulfilled until an audience is enthralled, the final goal of the 10 weeks was for each "trainee" to tell his or her story to other classes. We used kindergarten, first-, and second-graders as our willing guinea pigs. For each library class, I asked three or four different tellers to be the guest storytellers, until each student had told his or her story at least twice, and usually three times. The younger classes were wonderfully receptive audiences, as the performers discovered once they got over their initial jitters. "I'm so nervous. My knees are knocking!" was a typical "before" comment. Afterward, most children said, "When can we do that again?"

Some of the tellers were terrible, at least the first time. Many were brilliant, and some were great surprises to us all. I'll never forget one girl who rarely spoke aloud, especially when adults were in earshot. Her teacher and I were sure she would never learn her story, as during rehearsals, she would not participate, and she seemed overwhelmed by what to her must have seemed an ordeal. Imagine our shock when, during the final rehearsal for the entire class, she stood up and knocked us all down with the best-told story in the entire class. Something clicked for her, and she was radiant with her success.

The program's results can be measured in part by the number of students who still remember their stories the following year, and the de-mystification of the folktale section of the library, made obvious by the number of books children of all grades check out.

In 1942 famed storyteller Ruth Sawyer wrote in her book *The Way of the Storyteller* (p. 167): "Insecurity, disturbance, apathy, national distrust are everywhere today. If we can make the art of storytelling an applied art, by which we may bring the rich heritage of good books into the lives of children throughout our country, that they may find a universal eagerness toward life and an abiding trust, then I think we may truly help build for the future."

Children never tire of the magical stories that make them laugh or let them linger in an enchanted world. By giving them the chance to hear stories told and to become storytellers themselves, we are indeed providing for the next generation, continuing an age-old tradition that must not become a victim of progress.

Illustration by Tomie dePaola reprinted by permission of G. P. Putnam's Sons from TOMIE DEPAOLA'S MOTHER GOOSE, copyright © 1985 by Tomie dePaola.

USING POETRY, NONSENSE, AND LANGUAGE-ORIENTED NONFICTION

THE NONFICTION SECTION OF THE LIBRARY COMES JAMMED WITH surprises. We tend to tell our children that fiction books are made up in an author's brain, whereas nonfiction books are true. This is not really so in terms of library arrangement. According to Dewey Decimal Classification standards, nonfiction is everything that is not considered fiction. On the one hand, *most* nonfiction books are full of facts, but there are plenty of exceptions to the rule. These include folk and fairy tales, jokes and riddles, drawing books, poetry, songs, and nonsensical topics that do not fit in with children's rigid notions of what is fact.

One thing is clear: In the nonfiction section there is enough material to enrich and expand our grasp on the world's knowledge. Look around your library and you see a vast storehouse of information and entertainment. We are crazy not to build our curricula around that wealth. The room is crammed with books that can light our lives, and it is our mission to expose our kids to as many as possible in the time they spend with us.

USING NONSENSE

Children's poetry is hard to resist, especially when you start by reading such zanies as Jack Prelutsky, Shel Silverstein, Kaye Starbird, and Judith Viorst. Yet many teachers and librarians avoid poetry like the chicken pox; we know it's there, but if we don't encourage it, perhaps we can get away with using only what's in the basals. Otherwise learned adults are under the grand delusion that children hate poetry and would rather avoid it, but those children who avoid it just haven't heard any lately. Who could resist the passion of:

> Homework! Oh, homework!
> I hate you! You stink!
> I wish I could wash you
> away in the sink,
> if only a bomb
> would explode you to bits.
> Homework! Oh, homework!
> You're giving me fits.

I'd rather take baths
with a man-eating shark,
or wrestle a lion
alone in the dark,
eat spinach and liver,
pet ten porcupines,
than tackle the homework
my teacher assigns.

Homework! Oh, homework!
You're last on my list,
I simply can't see
why you even exist,
if you just disappeared
it would tickle me pink.
Homework! Oh, homework!
I hate you! You stink!

>   ("Homework! Oh, Homework!"
>   from *The New Kid on the Block* by Jack Prelutsky)

Listen to children jumping rope and bouncing balls, and you'll hear the traces of the chants from your own childhood being passed down to this new generation. Books like Alvin Schwartz's *Tomfoolery* or *Witcracks* and Duncan Emrich's *The Whim-Wham Book, The Hodgepodge Book,* and *The Nonsense Book* are compilations of the rhythms, superstitions, sayings, and riddles of childhood, and children devour these collections. They love the sound and cadence of nonsense, even if they don't understand all of it.

Just as too many children are not hearing folk and fairy tales at home, many are missing out on the foundations of poetry as well: Mother Goose rhymes. While bouncing on a parent's knee to the beat of a nursery rhyme, the child figures that this thing we call language is full of silly surprises. How are these rhymes relevant to modern life, parents ponder. In the first place, they prepare our imaginations for life-long duty. Without the ability to fool around with words and thoughts, we are dull indeed.

If we wish to consider ourselves well-rounded, part of our foundation of that circle stems from the rhymes and poems we hear growing up. There are scores of Mother Goose books on the market, and more are published yearly. The old dame never goes out of style. With so many collections available, it can become baffling to know which ones to use. The ones on the poetry lists, listed under MOTHER GOOSE, are all highly recommended. Use several collections at a time, comparing illustrations, dipping into each volume for a sampling of whimsy, reciting well-known versions in unison, and digging up lesser-known ones to learn and repeat.

In addition to the old nursery rhymes we remember with affection, there are others worth introducing, whether they're traditional ones from other countries, like N. M. Bodecker's Danish collection *"It's Raining," Said John Twaining* and Demi's Chinese *Dragon Kites and Fireflies,* or modern-day nonsense from Dennis Lee's *Jelly Belly* to Arnold Lobel's *Whiskers and Rhymes.* Iona Opie's magnificent *Tail Feathers from Mother Goose* gives us a look at less familiar rhymes, some of them obscure variants of ones we know. Each page is illustrated by a different well-known artist, most but not all English, and the results are glorious to behold. As a reference tool for adults, William and Cecil Baring-Gould's *The Annotated Mother*

Goose is a fascinating source of the origins of rhymes, many of which date back centuries.

It is never too late to fill in the Mother Goose gaps. Just because older children do not ordinarily dwell in the realm of nursery rhymes is no reason they can't visit every so often. My fifth-graders were intrigued when I sang them the following faintly familiar song, which can be found in Marie Winn's indispensable *The Fireside Book of Fun and Game Songs*.

> Three myopic rodents, three myopic rodents,
> Observe how they perambulate, observe how they perambulate.
> They all circumnavigated the agriculturalist's spouse;
> She excised their extremities with a carving utensil,
> Did you ever observe such an occurrence in your existence
> As three myopic rodents.

Next I added a verse of my own:

> Now take your thesaurus, now take your thesaurus,
> Find a dictionary, find a dictionary;
> Pick a nursery rhyme that appeals to you,
> Take out all the words, put in synonyms, do
> Set Mother Goose on her beak, and you'll
> Have written an erudite poem.

That's just what we did. First we rooted through all of the nursery rhyme books in the library and, working as partners, each pair selected a favorite one to rewrite, with the able help of the reference tools suggested in my song. When the new versions were composed, students lettered and illustrated a good copy, which they read aloud. The rest of the class tried to unmask each rhyme by quoting the answer in its original form.

Their creations included such gems as "Minute Miss Muffet, perched upon a hassock, Devouring her coagulated milk and lactalbumin"; and "Moisture, moisture, frolic away, Follow again another morning; Bantam Johnny desires to dally."

I can't resist adding a proverb my York, Pennsylvania, pal Marta Smith told me: "A specimen of ornithology in the gripith of the metacarpals has more intrinsic value than dual specimens in the uncultivated shrubbery." (For those unfamiliar with proverbs in fancy dress: "A bird in the hand. . . . ")

When people know you are on the lookout for nonsense and nursery rhymes, they will take pains to share with you. Teacher Carol Shields told me one she remembered from her childhood in Lowell, Massachusetts. I've never seen it in print before.

> Help! Murder! Police!
> My mother fell in the grease.
> I laughed so hard, I fell in the lard.
> Help! Murder! Police!

Sara Vesuvio, a student, sang me a song her grandfather taught her. I don't know if he made it up or it's an oldie.

> Rockabye baby upon the moon,
> Eating her cornflakes with a big spoon;
> When the wind blows, the moon it will break,
> And down will come baby on a cornflake.

Nursery rhymes are supplanted with tongue twisters, jump rope chants, autograph verse, and plenty of silly jokes by older children. Tell one simple knock-knock joke to a group, and like coat hangers in the back closet, 10 more jokes will arise out of nowhere. After telling a knock-knock joke, ask "Do you want to hear my other knock-knock joke? I'm crazy about it. You do? Okay. You start it." Eagerly, they say, "Knock knock." "Who's there?" you ask, and pause. It takes some children a minute to catch on. Others will laugh immediately, realizing you've turned the tables on them. Still others will look bewildered.

Children often don't "get" jokes and riddles, especially those depending on more sophisticated plays on language. If a child is still blank after a minute or so, don't hesitate to explain a punch line. Some children need this crutch, and you will be enhancing their joke comprehension skills, a subject not covered in the regular course of study, but so useful in real life. Invariably, as the light dawns, that child then turns around and tells the riddle to someone else, saying, "Don't you get it?" as if he knew it all along.

"Why did the projector blush? Because he saw the filmstrip." After several fifth-graders cracked up the class and me with that and other choice selections from the Joseph Rosenbloom riddle books they had just discovered, I decided to spend one whole class period on jokes and riddles. All you do is litter the tables with joke books and construction paper bookmarks, give your children 10 minutes to read, and mark the funniest ones, and then go around the circle so each person can read one aloud. Keep going until you run out of time or you hurt too much from laughing. Discuss the difference between kinds of jokes—riddles, knock-knocks, word plays, and so on—and demonstrate the art of reading a joke aloud so all can hear and understand it.

As they mature, those children who can play with language will put their creative bursts to use in ways that may benefit the world. It is now recognized that play and daydreaming are essential components to developing new ideas, whether in the arts or sciences. In John Reynolds Gardiner's *Top Secret*, about a boy who turns into a plant as part of his science project on photosynthesis, everyone tells Allen his idea is preposterous and impossible. Only his Grandpop believes in his scheme, and advises him to "think crazy." "Let your mind go," he tells his grandson. "Don't be afraid to think of silly things, things so ridiculous that you burst out laughing at the mere thought of them. That's the power of the sixth tool, Allen. To think of things that no one else has ever thought of before." Using our "sixth tools"—our brains—and thinking crazy allows discoveries to be made, and even if *we* really can't turn into plants, we can enjoy ourselves in the process.

TAKING POETIC LICENSE: USING POETRY WITH CHILDREN

Children's poetry has become publicly respectable in the past 10 years or so. Shel Silverstein got the ball rolling with his *Where the Sidewalk Ends* and *A Light in the Attic*, which hit the *New York Times* Best Seller list. With both books, children started, quite unassigned by parents or teachers, to memorize poems about a baby-sitter who sat on the baby, a sharp-toothed snail ready to bite off the fingers of nose-pickers, a girl who refused to take out the garbage, and one who feigned illness to stay home from school. They took great glee in reciting these poems to their peers, and in some libraries, Silverstein's book was the only book of poems that ever made it off the 800s shelves.

There have always been wonderful children's poets, but until fairly recently the formats of standard poetry books were often drab. Either large print-filled anthologies with yellowing pages and no pictures or skinny picture books with serious line drawings, these types of books were and are unattractive to children. Silverstein's books are fat and riotous; they make fun of grown-ups, and each poem is more fun to read than the last one.

Poetry does not have to be funny any more than it has to rhyme, but for children to pick up a poetry book unassigned, it helps if it is attractive, with a good clear layout and interesting illustrations. You are the one who can make poetry appealing by reading it aloud often and with vigor. Punt between rhyming and unrhyming ones, funny and thoughtful ones, short ones and narrative ones. There are well over 100 listings in the Subject Index within for Stories in Rhyme, and a goodly assortment under Narrative Poetry. Intersperse these with individual poems by a wide array of poets. Some of the greats worth introducing, in addition to those already mentioned, include Lewis Carroll, John Ciardi, Lucille Clifton, Beatrice Schenk de Regniers, Eloise Greenfield, Mary Ann Hoberman, X. J. Kennedy, Maxine W. Kumin, Karla Kuskin, Edward Lear, Dennis Lee, Myra Cohn Livingston, Arnold Lobel, David McCord, Eve Merriam, A. A. Milne, Ogden Nash, Valerie Worth, and Charlotte Zolotow.

In some books the poems are sequential, meant to be read straight through, without skipping. Jack Prelutsky's 15 poems that comprise *Rolling Harvey Down the Hill* tell the story of five best pals who do everything together. The other four finally get fed up with Harvey's bossy ways, and in the final poem, they teach him a well-deserved lesson. In *Secrets of a Small Brother* by Richard J. Margolis, the younger sibling gets his say in 22 short poems about his relationship with a brother he alternately loves and envies. Cynthia Rylant's *Waiting to Waltz: A Childhood* is poignantly autobiographical, about growing up in a country town and the people she remembered.

Good poetry anthologists are a breed to be admired. They have a sense of the silly, a feel for what children find fanciful, and the confident foresight to select poems that might be atypical or broadening. William Cole, Lee Bennett Hopkins, Myra Cohn Livingston, and Jack Prelutsky have all done their part in collecting both the familiar and the obscure. Their books are indispensable to poetry collections.

When a first-rate collection is matched to a superb illustrator, the result is a book children will treasure. Memorable matches include Nancy Larrick and Ed Young in *Cats Are Cats* and Laura Whipple and Eric Carle in *Animals, Animals*. Jack Prelutsky has produced two eye-catching anthologies: *The Random House Book of Poetry for Children* illustrated by Arnold Lobel and *Read-Aloud Rhymes for the Very Young* illustrated by Marc Brown. *Sing a Song of Popcorn: Every Child's Book of Poems*, compiled by Beatrice Schenk de Regniers and others, is a stellar collection with sublime illustrations by nine Caldecott Medal artists.

READING POETRY ALOUD

In most poetry collections, whether by a single poet or contained in an anthology, we dabble, reading aloud those poems that appeal to our sense of rhythm and word fun. Allow yourself to be eclectic; poems are personal, and some will speak to you right off, but choose others because they are so unlike you. Read each poem aloud to yourself first to see how it's structured and how it sounds.

Before sharing Robert Service's macabre narrative poem *The Cremation of Sam McGee* with fifth-graders, I practiced it several times, as the pacing is tricky. Trying it aloud was a treat, as the rhythm and humor work so wonderfully together. Narrative poems like this are fun to memorize. While studying the American Revolution, one third-grade teacher had her class recite "Paul Revere's Ride" by Henry Wadsworth Longfellow, with each child responsible for memorizing one stanza, just like in the old days. They loved every line, come recitation day.

Memorizing poems can be fun and is a tested memory enhancer for later on. Before assigning your students, learn one yourself to see how difficult it is, and recite it for them as an example. When I heard Dennis Lee's manic and gory rendition of "Bloody Bill" on his Caedmon record, *Alligator Pie*, I painstakingly transcribed it from the record and set about learning it. Once you've mastered a poem, practice it every so often to make sure you haven't forgotten any stanzas, and you'll have it for life.

Many adults recoil in horror when recalling poetry memorization assignments from their youths. Some decide to foist those bad experiences back onto children. This is, of course, a proven way to develop poetry-haters. Yet, the experience can be a delightful one if you make it so, and should be entertaining for all involved.

Former fourth-grade teacher Dot Leef used a variation of the cloze reading technique to help her whole class memorize poems in a simple way: "First, I would write the whole poem or song on the board and we would read it aloud together. Then the children would close their eyes and I would erase a few words. We read the poem again, filling in from memory the missing words. We repeated these steps several times, till the board was empty and Eureka! We had memorized the whole thing and had fun doing it."

With poetry, every word is important. Read poems aloud more than once. The first time, ask your audience to listen to the sounds; the second time, to observe how they all fit together. Even poem titles are vital, none more so than Judith Viorst's wicked little gem that third- and fourth-graders find hilarious, from *If I Were in Charge of the World and Other Worries*: "Thoughts on Getting Out of a Nice Warm Bed in an Ice-Cold House to Go to the Bathroom at Three O'Clock in the Morning."

> Maybe life was better
> When I used to be a wetter.

Lilian Moore's *Go with the Poem* sports no illustrations, and few of the 90 poems in the collection rhyme. There is a vibrancy about the book that grabs me every time I open it to read aloud to older students, and I always find something new I overlooked last time. Good poetry books are like that. They draw you back over and over, daze you with the way they catch thoughts and feelings.

After being turned off of poetry in college, I learned to like it again after I became a librarian, because children's poetry wasn't afraid of being ridiculous. Poems from Lilian Moore's thoughtful book help me keep my perspective.

Read a few poems from Valerie Worth's "Small Poems" books, collections of sparsely worded, mostly unrhyming descriptions of common objects, and you will jump as if someone had tweaked you on the head. Her eye is so steady, you will be startled by what you missed all your life when looking at flowers, animals, and household stuff.

When reading these poems aloud, have at hand some of the objects you're planning to read about for children to examine before your third reading. Make available a collection of additional unextraordinary objects: a paper clip, a piece of chalk, a spoon, a sprig of dill. Paired up to examine these treasures, the children can then write and draw their observations.

Eats: Poems, Arnold Adoff's love affair with good food, is not one children will read alone without a reason. The cover is attractive but words dance all over the pages. Children who have never seen poetry like this think the book is defective. All those strange food recipes, with the text darting to every side, make children wonder what kind of cookbook looks so jumpy. Start reading from the beginning, and they'll soon get hungry, too.

Every year, I give several Poetry Talks, where I collect objects to accompany the poems I select to read aloud. To prepare, I go through a dozen or so books, pick out and mark 20 or so poems that seem ripe and fit my and the class mood, and then run around the library rooting for a tiny prop to coincide with each one. Chopsticks, rubber earthworms, stuffed animals, wind-up chickens; my collection of useless junk is precious at times like these. When reading aloud, always use the book and not a copied sheet. You want to be able to show off and give away the book after reading from it.

Fiction books about poetry like Betsy Byars's *Beans on the Roof*, Scott Corbett's *The Limerick Trick*, or Lilian Moore's *I'll Meet You at the Cucumbers* are obvious candidates for poetry tie-ins. Don't restrict yourself to the obvious. There are poems about every possible subject, and whenever you stumble on one that fits perfectly with a folktale or story, make a copy of it and record where you found it. *Roald Dahl's Revolting Rhymes* retell well-known fairy tales, but his versified "Cinderella" has her slipper flushed down the loo, a prince who cuts off her sister's heads and calls Cindy a slut, and a fairy godmother who comes up with a more suitable match. No doubt about it, Dahl's version is too caustic for some, but kids will howl.

To love poetry, it helps to hear it sing. Choral reciting and choral reading involve listeners and get them into the rhythm of the piece. Hand out copies of a poem for choral reading and have readers join you in unison, solo, or in groups.

Paul Fleischman's *Joyful Noise*, the Newbery Award-winning book of insect poems, was designed so two people or groups would read aloud each poetic duet. Although some of the 14 poems will be over the heads of the elementary crowd, most are accessible and affecting, running the gamut from funny and clever to tragic.

Even unwilling readers enjoy choral reading where everyone reads aloud simultaneously. Not only can you stress enunciation and reading aloud with feeling, but the poor readers can be just as successful as the others. Song lyrics are especially popular. Reading the words to a song as you sing it is not construed as work by most children. Often a song will beg to be extended, and readers become lyricists in short order.

Raffi's *Down by the Bay*, a nonsense song if ever there was one, cries out for new verses. The song is easy to learn and sing indefinitely, and kids double over laughing at stanzas like this one:

> Down by the bay, where the watermelons grow,
> Back to my home I dare not go.
> For if I do my mother will say,
> "Did you ever see a whale with a polka dot tail,
> Down by the bay?"

After teaching it to first-, second-, and third-graders, I asked them to make up some new verses. Most were composed by the group on the spot, and we sang them as fast as we thought of them. "If you dream up any new ones tonight, write them down and leave them in the box on my desk," I suggested. By the end of the week, there were well over 50 new verses, scratched out on little strips of notebook paper, stuffed into the box, and I typed up a song sheet that included over 40. Some of their tag lines included:

> Did you ever see a worm getting a perm
> Did you ever see a mosquito eating a dorito
> Did you ever see a turtle wearing a girdle
> Did you ever see a gorilla sailing a flotilla

Canadian poet Dennis Lee's three-verse title poem from the book *Alligator Pie* sang to me the first time I read it, so I put it to music. It's easier to write new verses for a song than a poem, as the music tends to keep you in sync with the rhythm of the words. "Alligator Pie" is so goopily disgusting that it goes over with all grades, whether you've just read Thacher Hurd's *Mama Don't Allow* to kindergartners or booktalked Daniel Pinkwater's *Lizard Music* to fourth-graders.

> Alligator pie, alligator pie,
> If I don't get some I think I'm gonna die.
> Give away the green grass, give away the sky,
> But don't give away my alligator pie.

After singing or chanting the delectable verses, all ages will come up with tasty new food delights. Some we've enjoyed included alligator cookies, steak, ice cream, mousse, juice, milk, shakes, and bread. Here is one typical verse composed on the spot by a second-grade class:

> Alligator bread, alligator bread,
> If I don't get some I think I'll lose my head.
> Give away my ice skates, give away my sled,
> But don't give away my alligator bread.

Linda Forte was reading limericks to her third-graders and began a writing exercise where they were each to write one about themselves or a friend. They were having a hard time making their poems scan until they learned "The Limerick Song," which is to the tune of "Celito Lindo" and can be found in Marie Winn's *The Fireside Book of Fun and Game Songs*. After singing all their newly composed verses, they had no trouble understanding how to improve each one. Their official class rhyme reads:

There was a nice teacher named Forte
Whose class made a very big snort.
She often yelled out,
"Oh, please do not shout,
Or I'll have to send you to court."

As a rule, children do not check out scores of poetry books to read. This will change during those periods when you ask children to pick their favorite funny poems to share in class the next week during a Poetry Round Table, or when you read aloud a few perfect picks. You might even throw a Poetry Gala where each child recites a poem, after which you serve Alligator Pie, Poem Stew, Doodle Soup, or other rhyme-based tidbits. What you do when you read poetry aloud is take away the stigma, so when a child finds she enjoys reading poetry, the others won't chime in derisive tones. "What are you reading *that* for?" When students start asking you to find another fun book like X. J. Kennedy's grandly funny and grizzly *Brats!* or Lois Simmie's dotty *Auntie's Knitting a Baby,* you will know you have made an impact.

From TOP SECRET by John Reynolds Gardiner with illustrations by Marc Simont. Illustrations copyright © 1984 by Marc Simont. By permission of Little, Brown and Company.

USING NONFICTION
AND BIOGRAPHY

WHAT SHORT SHRIFT WE GIVE THOSE BOOKS THAT HAVE THE AUDACITY to be true. "This isn't actually *literature*," we reason, "it's just facts with pictures." So teachers assign the obligatory nonfiction book report once a year where students dutifully write down information about what aardvarks eat or how magnets work, and that's the end of it.

As I began assembling a bibliography of recommended nonfiction books, I searched out some new titles lurking in an ever-bulging consideration file, and added to my growing stack an attractive, color-photo-crammed book from the "Lerner Natural Science Book" series *Mantises*, edited by Sylvia Johnson (Lerner, 1984). Like a listener drawn in by a master storyteller, for a half hour I moved in with my favorite garden insect, with its spiky body all arms and legs. Reading that book, I was aware of the author's choice of words, information, and organization, and I read it like an adventure novel. I wouldn't chose it to read aloud, as it is a bit too technical, but this is the kind of nonfiction children would read from end to end.

Nonfiction has been reinvented in the last decade, thanks to outstanding writers like Jean Fritz, Seymour Simon, Millicent Selsam, Russell Freedman, and Rhoda Blumberg. This is not to say that all nonfiction is wonderful today. Too much of it still sports tiny, dark photographs or dull sketches, small print, and turgid, snooty prose. The reviewers may rave about it; children will pass it by in droves. What excites children is a book with large color photographs or illustrations, readable print, and a text that fills them with wonder.

The National Geographic Society's "Books for Young Explorers" series started that trend in the early 1970s, followed by their longer and more complex "Books for World Explorers" series. Reasonably priced and covering every topic imaginable in the sciences and social sciences, with a heavy concentration on animals, they continue to be in constant demand. Knopf's superb "Eyewitness" series is making true believers of my students, with a dozen or more finely detailed color, captioned photographs laid tantalizingly across each double-page spread.

Seymour Simon's books on planets, volcanoes, icebergs, and the like are greatly appreciated by children. When readers seek out books on volcanoes, they want to see lava in living color and fiery explosions. Simon's huge color photographs deliver the goods, and his texts are so elegant and absorbing, readers finish each book yearning to find out more. Great nonfiction writers find ways to phrase facts in a clear, familiar, unintimidating tone so that even complex subjects are understandable and engrossing.

In selecting nonfiction books to read aloud, I looked for ones that had staying power from start to finish, as well as aesthetic merits. Those that were too long or technical, I passed over. When you are reading to a group, you must not just catch their interest and imagination, but sustain it. More involved, detailed nonfiction is better for booktalking, after which readers interested in the subject can pursue it on their own. When reading aloud fiction, make a point of tying in a variety of nonfiction titles as well to strengthen children's knowledge base and expand their interests. Whether you lead off with a fiction or a nonfiction book, make it clear that they are interdependent and equally relevant. If you think of each book you read as part of a package deal, you can introduce far more literature with the same basic effort.

One good read-aloud can start a chain reaction. Share Francine Patterson's *Koko's Kitten* or *Koko's Story* with your group, and related books that you just happen to have handy on simians or sign language will be snapped up, too. Pull in everything you can find, including fiction like Sandy Landsman's *Castaways on Chimp Island* and Ron Roy's *The Chimpanzee Kid*, put it in a box or basket, and show them all off.

BIOGRAPHY

Jean Fritz's biographies of American revolutionary heroes proved that biographies do not have to be fictionalized to be worth reading. She digs up facts with child appeal, such as those about Paul Revere's big ride when he forgot his spurs and had to send his dog home to fetch them. *And Then What Happened, Paul Revere?* does not rely on invented dialogues and puffed up attributes of its hero. Growing up when children read the silhouette-illustrated "Childhood of Famous Americans" series, still selling today, I thought that all famous people were destined for greatness from a young age, so good and kind and perfect they seemed. Jean Fritz allows children to see that eccentricities are what make us interesting, and her tightly paced, snappy toned, intimate biographies allow us to identify with real people, not icons.

In the next decade, the art of writing biographies for children should become a more respected one, due in large part to Russell Freedman's Newbery Award for his masterful *Lincoln: A Photobiography*. Freedman surpassed all the requirements for writing a biography children might read and enjoy. There are illuminating photographs of the president, original daguerreotypes in which we can discern the burdens the Civil War placed upon him. Anecdotes reveal his sense of humor and irony, while allowing us to discern flaws as well. That Lincoln and his wife were given to great depressions is not hidden, and we are allowed to live through that terrible night at Ford's Theater and grieve after the assassination. One perceptive student showed me her favorite photograph in the book, saying with great feeling, "I just love to look at his face here. He seems like someone I would want to know, he's so human and real. When I read about the shooting, I already knew what was going to happen, but I kept hoping it could somehow turn out differently in the book. I didn't want him to die."

When reading a new biography, there are certain criteria I seek. Like my students, I want to see what the person looked like. Naturally, if the subject died 500 years ago, this proves tricky, though prints and maps and other such reproductions are always appreciated when possible. Most elementary school children have a limited sense of time as to when events occurred in history and need to be able to put them in perspective. When one third-grade teacher described the Boston Tea Party to her class, they were greatly attentive and asked her what else she remembered from back then.

After finishing a biography, the reader should still be curious about the famous person, and want to know more about his or her chosen field. Reading Patricia Lauber's *Lost Star: The Story of Amelia Earhart*, one is shaken by the danger of each flight she took and the mystery of her disappearance at the age of 39 in 1937. Lauber not only provides anecdotes of Earhart's childhood, some of it not cheerful, but sprinkles the text with photographs, interests us in flight, provides us with a sensible bibliography for further reading, and includes a good index.

Rhoda Blumberg assembled a truly wondrous collection of paintings and illustrations, charts, sketches, portraits, and maps of the American West, expedition participants, and Native Americans in *The Incredible Journey of Lewis and Clark*, a most outstanding example of exquisite book design combined with a dazzling narrative. If all history could be taught with this level of interest and verve, perhaps our children would not come up so short on geography and history assessments.

Much of the time, publishers do not consider what children require. Of what use is a biography about Beatrix Potter, watercolorist and author/illustrator of *The Tale of Peter Rabbit* and other beloved animal classics, when the book includes either no examples of her work or photographs of her, but instead relies on a modern-day illustrator's lackluster pen and inks? The narrative may be first rate, but if we wish children to relate to the person, they must be allowed to gaze at photographs and study every detail, tying the past to the present. In this era of video-current images, anything less smacks of poor design and lack of concern for the audience.

The biography section is usually the weakest in the library. Librarians die a thousand deaths every time a fourth-grade teacher sends her class in with the pronouncement, "We each need an autobiography for a book report." Just how many famous adults have decided to sit down and write the stories of their illustrious lives for nine-year-olds? Thank heavens for Roald Dahl and his gleefully grizzly *Boy*, which is as good as his fiction (and better in places).

Very few unforgettable biographies are written every year. Even fewer are well written enough or interesting enough to read aloud all the way through, though booktalkers will find ample anecdotes and chapters to suit their purposes. If you can slip but one or two worthy biographies a year into your read-aloud schedule, and booktalk an assortment of others, your students will be adequately served as you await a stellar new crop to burst upon the scene.

SELF-EDUCATION: THE LIBRARY'S ROLE

Some children gravitate to nonfiction and refuse to read fiction. Others do just the opposite. Both groups need to be stimulated enough to reach for both rings. Several years ago, I thought up a nonfiction lesson for fourth-graders that was so basic I was almost embarrassed to try it. Since then, I have repeated this lesson every year, and it always gets an enthusiastic response. My premise was that children who don't read nonfiction have never had the chance to see what is available. They are rarely given enough time in the library to relax, explore, and read at leisure without any other imposed requirements. Thus, the "Dewey Browse" originated.

First I made a list of well over 200 Dewey Decimal numbers and subjects that were representative of our collection and interesting to pursue. The list was in number order by each of the 10 Dewey categories, single spaced but nicely typed, and illustrated. An abridged representative section of one category is as follows:

700–799 Fine Arts and Recreation

737.4	Coins and coin collecting	792	Acting
741–743	Drawing books	792.8	Ballet
745	Arts and crafts	793.7	Jokes and riddles
759	Painting	793.8	Magic
769	Stamp collecting	794.1	Chess
770	Photography	796	Sports
784.6	Folk songs	798	Horseback riding
791.3	Circus	799.1	Fishing
791.5	Puppets		

After handing out a copy of the complete list for each student to keep, I ask them to spend several minutes looking at the subjects included and star the ones that sound unusual or worth investigating. Next, they are to go to the nonfiction shelves and spend the remaining half hour browsing, looking at as many books on these subjects as they like, thumbing through, reading bits, and just generally losing themselves in a topic or two. I specify that this time they are to avoid all sections with which they are already familiar, like 567.9 (dinosaurs), 636.7 (dogs), 793.7 (jokes and riddles), or 940.54 (World War II), so as to have time to be exotic and untypical for a while.

I tell them: "What if you find a new subject you never realized we had, and on a whim, discover a new field that intrigues you so that it changes your entire life. What if you never saw our books on ancient Egypt before, and you find them so extraordinary, you decide to become an archaeologist when you grow up. In 20 years, when you are accepting an award for your latest find—the ancient, lost City of Pinkwater—you can say 'It all began when I was a fourth-grade student and stumbled onto the 900s in my library.'" That is my standard speech, and although the kids snicker, they nod their heads in agreement and rush to the shelves with gusto, eager to discover a new line of thought heretofore unknown to them.

After 10 minutes, I call, "Freeze," and ask each person to yell out, one at a time, the subject he or she is investigating. The array is gratifying. At book checkout time, I allow everyone who has found something new to check out several extra books if they so desire. They always do. The following week, children can display the books they uncovered, all can walk around and browse through them for a brief time, and then spend the rest of the time discussing what they found out that they never knew before.

As an additional or alternative nonfiction list of subjects, a handy new one has come out, published by elementary school librarian Ellen J. Dibner and teacher Ronald Gustafson, called *Book Finders for Kids*. This is a simple, attractive, 16-page illustrated booklet listing over 400 nonfiction subjects in alphabetical order, along with their corresponding call numbers. At under $3 per booklet, you could hand out one per child as a keepsake to help them locate the books they want in a painless and entertaining way. (Write or call: Point Publications, P.O. Box 145, Point Lookout, NY 11569. 516-889-3526.)

Trivia is a powerful motivator. At the beginning of each lesson, throw out a fact or ask a question that is tied in with the book you happen to be holding: "What is the largest mammal that ever lived? How old was Pocahontas when she died? Watch carefully; with this string, I will now make a cup and saucer. Did you know the largest iceberg ever measured was bigger than the state of Vermont? It was 200 miles long and 60 miles wide." Like the jokes, riddles, poems, and nonsense you spout, your trivia will be returned to you 20-fold as students attempt to stump you with outlandish facts.

Children are naturally inquisitive. We need to channel their fascination with the unknown into the desire to instruct themselves, for school constitutes but a small part of what they need to know. Students are in large part responsible for their own educations, a fact of which they may be unaware. The child's inner drive and innate curiosity are essential factors, both of which can be stirred up or stymied by parents and teachers. The library is a powerful place, providing the resource to investigate every angle of intrigue and every type of literature. Children primed for exploration will grow into stimulated, stimulating adults, with an ever-increasing passion for knowledge, as poet Valerie Worth, in her book *Small Poems Again*, understands:

library

No need even
To take out
A book: only
Go inside
And savor
The heady
Dry breath of
Ink and paper,
Or stand and
Listen to the
Silent twitter
Of a billion
Tiny busy
Black words.

Illustration from MISS NELSON HAS A FIELD DAY by Harry Allard, illustrated by James Marshall. Copyright © 1985 by Harry Allard. Copyright © 1985 by James Marshall. All rights reserved. Reprinted by permission of Houghton Mifflin Company and James Marshall.

101 WAYS TO
CELEBRATE BOOKS

AS YOU PLOW THROUGH THE READ-ALOUD LISTS, CONSIDER incorporating into your lesson plans some of the following book-related activities, designed to give a boost to any reading program. Add your own ideas to the ones below and go to town.

Book reports can range from the casual to the formal, but their primary use should not be as a means for checking up on your students and grading them. Instead your goal should be to get children to immerse themselves in books and plead for more. Books need to be part of the everyday classroom conversation, and not relegated to the reading group table.

A well-balanced school library program must consist of literature-based activities in addition to and as part of traditional library skills and instruction. In my experience, anything that excites students about books is worth the time, effort, and even the mess. Following are 101 ideas for fooling around with books. May they spark you to come up with countless more.

READING BOOKS

1. Allow children ample time for DEAR (Drop Everything and Read). Other schools call it USSR (Uninterrupted, Sustained Silent Reading) or SQUIRT (Special Quiet Uninterrupted Individual Reading Time).
2. If your library is carpeted, hold DEAR, but require children to sit anywhere they like except on chairs at tables. Sprawling under tables and lying on the floor are to be encouraged.
3. After library period, the class can make a Book Train in the hallway where each child snuggles up against the hall wall as part of a great long line, and reads silently. Our All-School Book Train for National Library Week was a huge success. For 20 minutes, the line of silent, reading children and adults stretched throughout the corridors of the school. The only sound was the turning of pages. The only complaint? "Why couldn't it have been longer?"

SELECTING BOOKS

4. Children always want to know your favorite books. Make an oversized, large-print list of your top 10 or 25 or 100, with authors included. Post it so browsers can consult it and try out your recommendations.

5. Bring in copies of spring and fall book announcements from *Publishers Weekly, Booklist, School Library Journal,* and the *New York Times Book Review* for children to peruse and decide which sound good. Have them each make up a wish list of the 10 books that interest them most.

6. Produce a library or classroom newsletter for kids and parents. Include student book reviews, the top 10 books of the month (or semester), and suggestions of books for parents to read aloud. (Borrow freely from the Read-Aloud Lists as needed.)

7. For students in first through third grades, teach them the Fist Test so they will always be able to tell in advance if the book is too easy, too hard, or just right. Explain the following: To take the Fist Test, open to the first long page of text (the first page usually being too short), make a fist, and read the page to yourself. Every time you don't know a word, put out a finger from your fist. If you run out of fingers, the book is most likely to be too hard. With five fingers, it may be challenging, but if you liked and understood what you read, keep going. If not, put it away for another time. No fingers? It's either too easy, or you're a very good reader and it's just right. Children become more independent and self-confident if they know in advance that the books they have picked will suit their reading abilities.

8. Discover everything on one typical library shelf. With younger children, have them help you take off every single book from, say, picture book shelf W–Z, and spread them out across the library tables so all can browse through what is there. (Select a bottom shelf that is packed with books. We tend to ignore these, and there are always loads of treasures.) For older students, choose a fiction shelf. Once the books are all spread out, many children will be thrilled to discover great books they've never seen or noticed before.

9. In the library, assign an interesting nonfiction Dewey Decimal number to each pair of children, grades 2 and up, to find and further investigate. They must browse through and select the best books on that subject (such as 523.4 Planets, 641.5 Cookery, and 796.357 Baseball), and share their findings with the class.

SHARING BOOKS

10. Hold a paperback Book Swap for one or more classes. Make sure parents approve the books their children are bringing in and spread everything out onto tables so all can browse.

11. Find a dozen or so good fiction books that the library has in duplicate copies. Assign or let the children choose reading partners and books. Each pair will read the book aloud in alternating chapters, to each other. While one partner reads, the other follows along in his or her copy.

12. From a hat or basket, each child selects the name of a class member who will become his secret reading pal and whose reading interests and favorite titles he must discover without giving himself away. Each person can write his pal a letter disclosing what he or she has found out and recommending titles to read. Both teacher and librarian should be heavily involved in suggesting good titles. If this is done around holiday time, perhaps children could buy their secret pals a paperback book as a present instead of the usual class grab bag.

13. Set up parent-child contracts where children promise to read to their parents for 10 minutes every other night, and vice versa on alternate nights. Families can keep a reading log.

14. Librarians: When the new books come in at the beginning of the school year, set up an attractive book display for staff and parents. Arrange books by subject, bake goodies to draw in the crowd, and find something new and interesting to grab each teacher. Encourage teachers to insert request slips into all materials desired right away so you can route the books to them at the end of the day.

15. Librarians again: Leave the new books on display so children can also browse through and check them out.

16. Librarians yet again: When new books come in during the year, allow several upper-grade classes to assist you in unpacking, checking for damage, putting them in whatever order you need, and looking through what's there to stimulate student interest. In exchange, promise them first dibs when possible.

17. Every so often, someone does a survey on what books famous people— such as governors or sports stars—remember and value most from their youth. Students can survey the staff and/or their parents, and put up a bulletin board advertising the results for all to see. If you're stressing letter writing, children can write to admired heroes and pose the question to them.

READING ALOUD FROM BOOKS

18. Compile a list of classic picture books you feel all children should know. Assign older students to read these books aloud, first to each other, and then to younger children. This serves a dual purpose, by exposing both older and younger children to the classics they may have missed.

19. A variation: Ask older children to search the picture book shelves, first to find books they loved when they were younger, and then to read them aloud to others.

20. Invite parents, grandparents, and community leaders to read aloud to your classes.

21. Hold DEARA (Drop Everything And Read Aloud) in your room. Assign responsibility to children as well as yourself for making selections and reading them to the group.

22. Hold DEARA over the loudspeaker for Book Week, National Library Week, or Any Old Week. Select short, one-to-three-minute excerpts of stories and poems, and be sure those books are then put on display in the

library for the children who request them. Ask a variety of staff members and students to read aloud. Sometimes, ask the children to guess who read aloud instead of announcing it beforehand.

23. Children can each select and read aloud a favorite passage, stopping at a strategic point to stimulate borrower interest.
24. Play Name That Paragraph. Each student finds one paragraph that typifies a favorite book and reads it aloud for the rest of the group to identify.
25. Have children look for favorite lines from books and read them aloud. Some memorable ones: " 'It was so dark in there, I couldn't read a *word*,' said Granny" (*Red Riding Hood* by James Marshall). " 'Momma, it's a very big chicken!' Arthur shouted" (*The Hoboken Chicken Emergency* by Daniel Pinkwater).
26. Hand out a joke or riddle book to each person in the class. Going round the circle, read the best ones aloud until everyone's sides hurt from laughing.
27. Duplicate and hand out the words of silly songs from your favorite song books and hold a songfest. If you play an instrument, that's a plus, but kids usually don't care if you sing off-key, as long as it's fun.
28. When reading fairy tales, have the children pore over books in 398.2 to find unusual first and last lines that deviate from or expand on "once upon a time" and "happily ever after."
29. Librarian Louise Sherman has established a Story Lunch Read-Aloud Program for the students in her school in Leonia, New Jersey. Children who have signed up for this popular activity spend the first 30 minutes of their lunch hour eating and listening as an adult volunteer reader enthralls them with the next installment of the book chosen for that session. Eight different books are offered to each grade level each year.

SELLING BOOKS

30. Students can write and videotape commercials for their books. To ensure diversity, discuss the many ways products are sold on the tube. These include the hard sell, the humorous spot, the slice-of-life approach, and the singing jingle.
31. Discuss the prevalence of door-to-door salespeople in the past. (Dagwood Bumstead still meets a lot of them.) Children can pair up and develop door-to-door bookselling skits to market their latest favorite titles to the rest of the class.
32. Everyone loves to get mail. Strike up a correspondence with another class. Children can write to recommend books they love.
33. Using the *New York Times Sunday Book Review* section as an example, write publishers' blurbs and reviewer quotations to sell your favorite books.
34. Children can share, by telling about or reading aloud, the most humorous incidents, the most exciting events, or their favorite sections of the books they have just finished reading. Then they can raffle them off. (If these are library books, the raffler and the rafflee should go together to the library to check the book in and out again.)
35. Compose telegrams, condensing the essence of each book in 15 words.

Also try 100-word overnight telegrams, or even singing ones. (First, you'll need to design a mailgram form that everyone can use.)

36. LOVE YOUR LIBRARY! Start an Ugly Book Beautification Program. Pull together a batch of good reads that are hampered by awful covers or missing dust jackets. After reading one of these books, each artist can create a new jacket to jazz up the cover and give the book a second chance. Newly designed book jackets, replete with title, author, illustrator, typed spine label, book blurb on the front flap, and author information on the back flap, can then be covered with new clear plastic dust jacket covers by you and/or the librarian. First, hold a kick-off session where you present examples of good cover design.

37. Children can write and submit book reviews for a local newspaper or children's magazine. *Cricket* and *Stone Soup* publish children's work. Two excellent magazines that publish children's writings exclusively are *Creative Kids* (P.O. Box 6448, Mobile, AL 36660) and *Shoe Tree: The Literary Magazine by and for Young Writers* (National Association for Young Writers, Membership Service, P.O. Box 3000, Dept. YW, Denville, NJ 07834).

38. Students can write radio announcements advertising books to be broadcast over the school P.A. system.

39. Artists should delight in creating new posters to advertise loved books.

40. Join the Trumpet Club, a top-notch book club that is run by Bantam Doubleday Dell (P.O. Box 604, Holmes, PA 19043. 1-800-826-0110) and send in an order each month. Teachers, when titles on the order form are unfamiliar, check with your librarian, as Trumpet appeals to a wide age range, and some titles will be inappropriate for your children. Promotionals in free books and author interview tapes are just the thing to perk up classroom collections or to put aside book prizes for deserving readers.

41. Hold a school Book Fair. Search around for a company or bookstore that will let you request specific titles, as many book fairs are stocked with books of less than dubious quality. This makes more work for you but ensures better quality, which translates into higher profits for your library.

GETTING TO KNOW AUTHORS AND ILLUSTRATORS OF BOOKS

42. Students can research the lives of popular authors and learn about their other works. *Something about the Author*, a multivolume reference set edited by Anne Commire and published by Gale, is a fine place to start.

43. In a more cloak-and-dagger approach, try the Secret Author project. Each child selects an author approved by you, reads at least three of that person's books, and researches interesting tidbits about her life. During Author's Day (or Week or Month), each child regales the class with anecdotes about the writer's life and work while listeners attempt to guess her identity.

44. Compose a class letter to a favorite author describing your reactions to his or her books. Be flamboyant and original to ensure a response. Record a class tape, write about and illustrate reactions to stories, or send photos. Authors like some excitement in the mail.

45. Invite a favorite author or illustrator to speak at your school or library. This costs money—sometimes quite a bit—but is usually well worth the expense. If your institution is broke, you might sell copies of the author's book to parents and use the profits to pay some, if not all, of your expenses. Treat your guest like royalty, wine and dine him, and prepare well for the visit so children know all about his books before he sets foot in your school. To get started, read David Melton's *How to Capture Live Authors and Bring Them to Your Schools: Practical and Innovative Ways to Schedule Authors for Author-in-Residence Programs, Children's Literature Festivals and Young Authors' Days* (Landmark Editions, Inc., 1986), and plan accordingly.

46. Hold a yearly election with students in one or more grades to select their top three favorite authors. (Design a ballot for voters to submit.) Ask student help in compiling and recording the results. Celebrate the winning authors by holding a reading of selected works.

47. When studying the United States, each student can search out and read a fiction book that is either written by an author who comes from or lives in the state that child is studying, or takes place there. This is a tricky assignment, as some states are difficult to match, but if you start compiling a bibliography, each year it will get easier. Put up a U.S. map and have children flag their states with mini-replicas of their book covers. Librarian Joan Brody had her students read across America. For every page they read, they received that number of miles in "Frequent Flyer" coupons. Each time a child finished a book, he received a bonus of 100 miles. At 1,000 miles, qualifying readers were invited to a Make-Your-Own-Sundae Party.

48. KIDSTAMPS, a business started by two librarians, sells rubber stamps designed by well-known children's book illustrators. (Call them at 1-800-727-5437 for their delightful catalogue.) Use these stamps to make stickers, bookmarks, commemorative library bookplates, or handouts advertising a given illustrator's work. Aliki, Trina Schart Hyman, James Marshall, Bill Peet, and James Stevenson are just a few of the artists represented.

DISCUSSING AND EVALUATING BOOKS

49. When students have read the same book or a group of similar ones, hold a panel discussion.

50. Organize a pro and con debate panel, made up of those who will defend a book versus those who will criticize it. Include the author, illustrator, and publisher as characters on the panel.

51. Monitor a class discussion comparing and contrasting a well-known book (such as *The Lion, the Witch and the Wardrobe, Charlotte's Web,* or *Charlie and the Chocolate Factory*) with the movie or TV version.

52. Call individual conferences during which students talk to you about books they are reading.

53. Have students tell the class or write about the book characters they would choose as best friends and why.

54. Videotape individual spoken reactions to a book you are reading aloud, and play it back for all to hear.

55. Children can write book reviews of new library books and then compare their opinions with those in published reviews from *Booklist*, *School Library Journal*, or *Hornbook*.

56. Form an eight-week Winners and Losers Club for those who want to read and discuss new books. Using the past year's "Best of" lists in *Booklist*, *Hornbook*, and *School Library Journal*, assemble a shelf of 20 to 50 books, from which members must read a minimum of one title a week and record their opinions about it as preparation for your once-a-week free-wheeling discussion session.

57. Read aloud five to ten of the year's best picture books and ask children to discuss and vote on their choices for the Caldecott Medal. After the voting, reveal which book the American Library Association's Caldecott Committee chose.

58. Design and reproduce a Newbery-type medal that can be awarded to the year's favorite titles. Name your award Fifth's Favorites or Sixth's Superlatives or something equally pithy for which children can cast their ballots. If you narrow it down to a finalist list of 10 titles, children can booktalk and speak up for their candidates before election day. Affix the award to the dust jacket for posterity, and keep a year-by-year list of the winners for new readers to consult.

VISUALIZING BOOKS

59. For books they have read, children can design maps of places where different characters lived or events occurred. (See the endpapers of *Winnie-the-Pooh* for an example.)

60. To help visualize a book's setting, students can build miniature stage setting dioramas for climactic scenes. This is particularly effective with science fiction books, where the settings are often out of this world.

61. Draw portraits of main characters and make construction paper picture frames for display.

62. Sculpt clay figures of book characters.

63. Compile a character's scrapbook suggested by information or events in a book you are reading aloud.

64. What if your students' book characters needed to go on a trip? Each child can bring to school a suitcase packed with everything his or her character might take along, and explain what's inside to the rest of the class.

65. Make filmstrips illustrating key scenes from a story, with the accompanying narration also written and recorded by the children.

WRITING ABOUT BOOKS

66. Many books have sequels and, occasionally, even prequels. For books that have neither, children can write possible plot descriptions.

67. Readers can assume a character's point of view and write his or her diary, detailing memorable points from the book.

68. Compose letters that characters from one book might have written to each other.

69. Compose letters that characters in different books would write to each other.

70. Pupils can write down questions for others to answer after reading a book, to check their comprehension, and gauge reactions.

71. Each student first selects a favorite book character, searches the book's text for physical and other descriptive details, and writes a paragraph about that character's personality, interests, and appearance. They then read their sketches aloud for others to identify.

72. Have your budding lyricists compose poems or songs inspired by books they have read. (One fourth-grade class, inspired by Daniel Pinkwater's *Lizard Music*, wrote a song with the following chorus: "Here come the lizards on TV, / Singing 'Neeble Neeble' to me. / We're watching lizards on TV / They're watching you and watching me.")

73. After reading tall tales, inspire your children to exaggerate their own. Compile a class book of tall tales to share with other classes. For good copies, use a scroll or several long sheets taped together so the end product will indeed be TALL.

74. Gather together a gaggle of wordless books and assign them to pairs who will then write the story the pictures tell, including dialogue. Younger children can talk the story through and "read" it to the rest of the group.

75. After reading aloud various authors' book dedications, have students search the library shelves for more to share aloud. They can then compose their own, either for Young Authors books they are writing or for the future books they might write someday when they become famous authors themselves.

DRAMATIZING BOOKS

76. Using a flannel board, children can retell a story using felt cutouts they have designed.

77. Construct paper bag or popsicle stick puppets to use when dramatizing a story.

78. Break the class into groups to write skits based on episodes in books they are reading. Rehearse these one-act plays and then perform them for other classes.

79. Children love to read about other kids in school. Spend time as another teacher (i.e., Mr. Smeal from *That Dreadful Day*, the new schoolmaster from *Farmer Boy*, or Mr. Wendell from *Fat Men from Space*) and transform your class accordingly.

80. Each student can relate a dramatic incident from the point of view of a major or minor character in a book.

81. Demonstrate how to tape record a story for others to play back. Stress reading slowly, clearly, and with expression. Each week, one or more children can tape a read-along story, ringing a bell for each page turn. Select a variety of books, including nonfiction and poetry.

CREATING PROJECTS WITH BOOKS

82. Everybody loves to eat. Students can devise menus for their favorite fiction book characters and give reasons for their selections. Hold a Book Character Food Fest.

83. Make some book mobiles to jangle the upper spaces in your classroom or library. Each child can design one section. Using fiction genres as the theme, make separate mobiles for mystery, historical fiction, sci-fi, fantasy, humor, animals, sports, suspense, and then some.

84. Make author mobiles, with each mobile representing the different works by one author.

85. Herald the artistic talents of your young Rembrandts when they create original illustrations to accompany the stories they have just read or heard.

86. For a "How To" book, children can make something following the directions in the book.

87. Kids love T-shirts, so why not have them design originals to flaunt their books?

88. Make a group mural to illustrate a book or books. If your ceiling is covered with acoustical tiles, decorate them with panels you've designed on paper cut to size. When the illustration is ready, take down the tile and rubber cement your instant Sistine ceiling to it. Teacher Joyce Houser started the ceiling art craze in our district over 15 years ago, and the results have been spectacular.

PLAYING GAMES WITH BOOKS

89. For teachers and librarians who really know their onions, play Fiction Stump. Each pair of students brings one card catalog drawer back to their seats and at the signal, has 60 seconds to select a card for any fiction book they choose. As you call on each pair, they will tell you the title of the book, and you must supply them with the author. If you can do so, chalk up one point for yourself on the scoreboard; if not, the point goes to the class. If you are conversant with the fiction books in your library's collection, your students will be astonished at your knowledge and gain respect for your skills at picking out good books for them to read.

90. If you dare, play Nonfiction Stump as well. The same rules apply as in Fiction Stump, but instead of titles, players will select a nonfiction Subject Card and attempt to stump you with Dewey Decimal numbers, for which you must supply the correct subject, or vice versa.

91. The card catalog, what we call The Brains of the Library, is not the best place to look for good books to read. Tell students that it offers information on where everything is located, but gives no opinions. (For opinions, ask The Brain's Chief Assistant, the librarian.) However, fooling around with the card catalog is a necessary skill for all book users. Play One Minute Warning with third through sixth grade for a quick way to locate a book that sounds promising. Each child brings a catalog drawer to her seat and fingerwalks through the cards, reading titles and annotations until she

locates one fiction (or nonfiction, if you like) book that she has never seen and that appeals to her in some way. Before you start the stopwatch, check each card to make sure the student has picked an acceptable book. (When everyone's looking for fiction, you might not want someone wallowing in the biographies.) At the signal, they have one minute to find that book on the shelf and bring it back to the table. After time's up, match up their books with the catalog cards, and then ask the class to show and discuss the books they found.

92. Play the Book Character Guessing Game with grades 3 and up. Pin 3-by-5-inch cards, each with the name of a different, easily recognizable book character written on it, on the backs of half your group. The rest of the children form the Panel of Experts. Tagged students have up to five minutes to ask yes/no questions of the panel, and thus discover their characters' identities. (This type of questioning is difficult for children to master, so demonstrate to them the types of questions they might ask and show how one accumulates details to come up with a reasonable guess, as in the game "Twenty Questions.") After the five minutes are up, contestants can tell everyone who they are. For those who are still in the dark, have the group give three more broad clues and then reveal their characters' names.

93. Play the In What Book Game, which I developed after being inspired by the over 400 questions about children's books in Ruth Harshaw and Hope Harshaw Evans's *In What Book* (Macmillan, 1970). Third- through sixth-graders can play this one. Using fiction books the library owns and that they have read, students each write two or three plot statement questions, beginning with the words, "In what book."

Try these: (a) In what book do Bran and Fiona travel back in time to ancient Ireland with a boy who can transform himself into a fish? (b) In what book do Marv the Magnificent and Raymond the Rat search through a cash register to find who bought a doll baby carriage with their friend Fats still inside it? (c) In what book do a brother and sister run away from home and spend a week hiding out at the Metropolitan Museum of Art in New York City?

Answers: (a) *The Wizard Children of Finn* by Mary Tannen; (b) *The Great Rescue Operation* by Jean Van Leeuwen; (c) *From the Mixed-Up Files of Mrs. Basil E. Frankweiler* by E. L. Konigsburg.

Once the children have written their questions and answers, submitted them to you for approval and comments, and rewritten them as needed, hold a class practice session. Players need to read each question clearly and slowly. Two classes can compete against each other, with one-, two-, and three-point rounds. (If the classes are large, we only play two rounds so there's time to finish.) Teams alternate reading their own questions aloud, and points are given when any player on the opposite team correctly volunteers a title. Give a bonus point for each author identified.

CELEBRATING WITH BOOKS

94. Hold a Booktalk Party with popcorn and lemonade and give "Coming Attraction" booktalks. Raffle off your titles.

95. Hold a Poetry Party where students read aloud and recite favorite poems they have discovered.

96. Throw a Costume Ball where readers come dressed as characters from their books. Give prizes, of course.

97. After each person selects and learns a folktale, hold a Storytelling Festival in your room. Invite neighboring classes to listen.

98. Invite grandparents to visit and tell stories to children.

99. Dress up as characters from well-known folktales and hold a Once Upon a Time Parade. (Two teachers from my school came to one dressed as a severed head on a platter, from a story in Andrew Lang's *The Brown Fairy Book*. They looked sensational.)

100. Librarian Lois Schochet holds a reading reception each year for all students who have read a designated number of books. She hands out certificates of achievement and makes a flowery speech. Those who have read even more are invited to a Pizza Party.

101. Invite parents to your school or library for a Book Workshop where you display, talk about, and read from new titles, and give book-sharing ideas of ways to get children reading at home. Serve refreshments and encourage parents to check out an armload of good titles. This is best held at night so more working parents have the chance to attend.

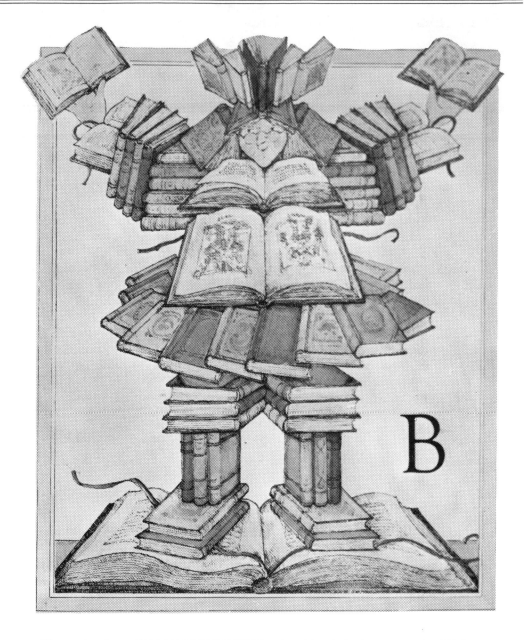

Illustration from ON MARKET STREET by Arnold Lobel. Illustration © 1981 by Anita Lobel. By permission of Greenwillow Books, William Morrow & Co.

Annotated
Read-Aloud Lists

FICTION FOR PRESCHOOL–KINDERGARTEN

1   **Adams, Adrienne.** *A Woggle of Witches.* **Illus. by the author. Scribner, 1971. ISBN 0-684-12506-4**

Spooky Halloween mood piece. Students can pantomime witches' flight, then zoom in closer with Tony Johnston's *The Witch's Hat.* CREATIVE DRAMA. FLIGHT. HALLOWEEN. WITCHES.

2   **Alexander, Martha.** *The Story Grandmother Told.* **Illus. by the author. Dial, 1969.**

Lisa wants her grandmother to tell her again about the fine green humming cat balloon and how it broke. A small-sized jewel that should make your listeners want to tell their stories too. CATS. GRANDMOTHERS. JEALOUSY. STORYTELLING.

3   **Alexander, Sue.** *There's More . . . Much More.* **Illus. by Patience Brewster. Harcourt, 1987. ISBN 0-15-200605-2**

A talking squirrel guides young Sherri through a tour of spring, from leaves and flowers to smells and feelings. Take your children on a spring fling outside to see what they can find. Bethany Roberts's *Waiting for Spring Stories* will also help pull them into the season, while Else Holmelund Minarik's *It's Spring!* will start a celebration. SEASONS. SPRING.

4   **Aliki.** *At Mary Bloom's.* **Illus. by the author. Greenwillow, 1983. ISBN 0-688-02481-5**

Afraid of all Mary Bloom's animals creating a racket, a little girl debates whether or not to phone her grown-up friend to tell her some good news. Not only is the repetition useful for recalling sequence, it is irresistible for making sound effects and acting out the various animal noise-makers. CREATIVE DRAMA. PETS. SOUND EFFECTS.

5   **Aliki.** *Keep Your Mouth Closed, Dear.* **Illus. by the author. Dial, 1966. ISBN 0-8037-4418-8**

Alligator swallows everything from a clock to the zipper his mother puts on his mouth to cure him. Contrast with Mitchell Sharmat's *Gregory the Terrible Eater* who has no appetite for such junk food. ALLIGATORS.

6   **Aliki.** *We Are Best Friends.* **Illus. by the author. Greenwillow, 1982. ISBN 0-688-00823-2**

The boy left behind when his friend moves befriends a new boy. Good discussion starter on how to make friends, as is Yoriko Tsutsui's *Anna's Secret Friend*. FRIEND-SHIP. MOVING, HOUSEHOLD.

7   **Allen, Pamela.** *Bertie and the Bear.* **Illus. by the author. Coward, 1984. ISBN 0-698-20600-2**

Because a bear was chasing Bertie, the Queen, King, Admiral, Captain, General, Sergeant, and a little dog ran to the rescue, with their loud instruments making an *incredible* noise. The first time, have everyone make all of the sound effects. Then divide your class into groups of characters so each group can make its own racket in turn. Fun to act out with percussion instruments such as drum, triangle, bells, and cymbals. BEARS. CREATIVE DRAMA. SOUND EFFECTS.

8   **Armitage, Ronda, and David Armitage.** *The Bossing of Josie.* **Illus. by the authors. Deutsch, 1980.**

A witch outfit for a birthday present gives Josie the chance to do some of her own bossing of her family for a satisfying change. BIRTHDAYS. COSTUMES. FAMILY LIFE.

9   **Artis, Vicki K.** *Gray Duck Catches a Friend.* **Illus. by Giulio Maestro. Putnam, 1974.**

Figuring the best way to find a new friend, she builds a trap with box string and stick and catches something that *flashes*. Bring in a box big enough for a child to hide under with a flashlight and act it all out. CREATIVE DRAMA. DUCKS. FRIENDSHIP.

10   **Asch, Frank.** *Bear Shadow.* **Illus. by the author. Simon & Schuster, 1988. ISBN 0-671-66866-8**

When Bear's shadow scares a big fish away, Bear tries to get rid of it by running away, nailing it to the ground, and even burying it in a hole. Other good shadow-y titles include Asch's *Just Like Daddy*, Edward Frascino's *My Cousin the King*, John Himmelman's *Talester the Lizard*, Jack Kent's mirror reflection story *Jim Jimmy James*, and Keiko Narahashi's *I Have a Shadow*. BEARS. SHADOWS.

11   **Asch, Frank.** *Goodbye House.* **Illus. by the author. Prentice Hall, 1986. ISBN 0-13-360272-9**

After their moving van is loaded, Baby Bear and his parents take one last look at their empty house, remember how it looked before, and say goodbye to each room. Other aspects of moving are dealt with in Aliki's *We Are Best Friends*, Elizabeth O'Donnell's *Maggie Doesn't Want to Move*, Yoriko Tsutsui's *Anna's Secret Friend*, and Bernard Waber's *Ira Says Goodbye*. BEARS. HOUSES. MOVING, HOUSEHOLD.

12   **Asch, Frank.** *Happy Birthday, Moon.* **Illus. by the author. Simon & Schuster, 1988. ISBN 0-671-67145-6**

Convinced the moon is talking to him when all he really hears is his own echo, Bear buys the moon a birthday hat. Act this out with echoed dialogue. BEARS. BIRTH-DAYS. CREATIVE DRAMA. GIFTS. MOON.

13   **Asch, Frank.** *Just Like Daddy.* **Illus. by the author. Prentice Hall, 1981.**

Young bear gets up, dresses, eats, goes fishing, and baits his hook just like Daddy, but then catches a fish—just like Mommy! Children can repeat the title refrain until the surprise ending. Then pair up and act out the book in mirror pantomime with one of each pair as the father and the other the child. BEARS. CHANTABLE REFRAIN. CREATIVE DRAMA. FATHERS AND DAUGHTERS.

14   **Asch, Frank.** *Moongame.* **Illus. by the author. Prentice Hall, 1984.**

Bear plays hide-and-seek with the moon. Use alone or with other Asch "Moon" books like *Happy Birthday, Moon,* as an introduction to a unit on the night sky. Also don't miss Eric Carle's *Papa, Please Get the Moon for Me.* BEARS. GAMES. MOON.

15   **Asch, Frank.** *Popcorn.* **Illus. by the author. Parents, 1979. ISBN 0-686-86568-5**

Bear gets a houseful when he pops too much at his Halloween party. Bring out the popper and make a snack. Also try Jane Thayer's *The Popcorn Dragon* and search out the facts in Tomie dePaola's *The Popcorn Book.* BEARS. FOOD. HALLOWEEN. PARTIES. POPCORN.

16   **Asch, Frank.** *Turtle Tale.* **Illus. by the author. Dial, 1980. ISBN 0-8037-8785-5**

Turtle learns the hard way when to pull his head into his shell and when to stick it out, as any wise turtle should. Bring a real or fake turtle, and try some other turtle books like Ellen MacGregor's *Theodore Turtle* and Barbara Williams's *Albert's Toothache.* TURTLES.

17   **Aylesworth, Jim.** *One Crow: A Counting Rhyme.* **Illus. by Ruth Young. Lippincott, 1988. ISBN 0-397-32175-9**

Rhyming couplets of one to ten farm animals shown first in summer and then repeated with a winter slant. Children can count the animals, compare summer and winter vistas, and repeat each rhyme after you, call-and-response style. Other counting rhymes about animals include Fritz Eichenberg's *Dancing with the Moon* and both Paul Galdone's and John Langstaff's versions of *Over in the Meadow,* while Mary Serfozo's *Who Wants One?* stays on the farm. COUNTING BOOKS. DOMESTIC ANIMALS. FARM LIFE. SEASONS. STORIES IN RHYME.

18   **Aylesworth, Jim.** *Two Terrible Frights.* **Illus. by Eileen Christelow. Atheneum, 1987. ISBN 0-689-31327-6**

Cozy tale of a girl and mouse who scare each other silly when they both go to the kitchen for a bedtime snack. Divide the class into children versus mice and act out either the whole story (with you as double-mothers) or the scene where mouse and girl tiptoe to the kitchen and find each other. Ambitious types: break the group into fours and have them act out the whole story, dialogue and all. BEDTIME STORIES. FEAR. MICE.

19   **Balian, Lorna.** *Amelia's Nine Lives.* **Illus. by the author. Abingdon, 1986. ISBN 0-687-37096-5**

When Nora's black cat disappears for a week, all of her friends and relatives think they have found her. Along with Tony Blundell's *Joe on Sunday,* use this cat-filled saga to review the days of the week. CATS. DAYS OF THE WEEK.

20   **Balian, Lorna.** *Humbug Witch.* **Illus. by the author. Abingdon, 1965. ISBN 0-687-37105-8**

Big-nosed little witch with two crooked teeth, long stringy red hair, witchily appropriate clothing, and a black cat named Fred realizes her spells won't work, so she sheds her disguise and becomes a little girl again. This makes a terrific flannel board story if you're the crafty type. CLOTHING AND DRESS. COSTUMES. WITCHES.

21   **Barton, Byron.** *Buzz Buzz Buzz.* **Illus. by the author. Macmillan, 1973.**

A cause-and-effect story of what happened on the farm when the bee stung the bull. Similar in theme to *Toby's Toe* by Jane Goodsell, Jim Aylesworth's *Hush Up!*, and Charlotte Zolotow's *The Quarreling Book*. CAUSE AND EFFECT. FARM LIFE. SEQUENCE STORIES.

22   **Benjamin, Alan.** *Rat-a-Tat, Pitter Pat.* **Photos by Margaret Miller. Crowell, 1987. ISBN 0-690-04611-1**

Eighteen pairs of large black-and-white photographs illustrate the sounds of the simple, rhyming onomatopoeic captions. Starting with "knock-knock, tick-tock," showing a boy and a door and a sleeping child next to an alarm clock, children will want to make noises too. Other noisy/quiet books include Benjamin Elkin's *The Loudest Noise in the World*, Lou Ann Gaeddert's *Noisy Nancy Norris*, and Suzy Kline's *SHHHH!* NOISE. SOUND EFFECTS.

23   **Bonsall, Crosby.** *Tell Me Some More.* **Illus. by Fritz Siebel. Harper & Row, 1961. ISBN 0-06-020601-2**

The magic of books and libraries, as described by one small boy to another. Set aside books on lions, camels, rockets, giraffes, and elephants to show as they come up in the story. BOOKS AND READING. LIBRARIES.

24   **Borden, Louise.** *Caps, Hats, Socks, and Mittens: A Book about the Four Seasons.* **Illus. by Lillian Hoban. Scholastic, 1989. ISBN 0-590-41257-4**

With Hoban's typically cheerful big-headed children and few words, we find out what each season means when you are young. Your season-lovers can dictate and illustrate four pages of what each season means to them, resulting in a class book. CLOTHING AND DRESS. SEASONS.

25   **Bozzo, Maxine.** *Toby in the Country, Toby in the City.* **Illus. by Frank Modell. Greenwillow, 1982. ISBN 0-688-00917-4**

Two children show the differences between their environments. Fine for a social studies discussion, along with Virginia Lee Burton's *The Little House*. CITIES AND TOWNS. COUNTRY LIFE.

26   **Brandenberg, Franz.** *I Wish I Was Sick, Too.* **Illus. by Aliki. Greenwillow, 1976. ISBN 0-688-84047-7**

Cat sister is envious of her brother's illness until she catches it herself. Other "sickly" titles include Lynne Cherry's rhyming *Who's Sick Today?*, Dick Gackenbach's *What's Claude Doing?*, and Ursula K. Le Guin's *A Visit from Dr. Katz*. BROTHERS AND SISTERS. CATS. JEALOUSY. SICK.

27   **Brimner, Larry Dane.** *Country Bear's Good Neighbor.* **Illus. by Ruth Tietjen Councell. Orchard, 1988. ISBN 0-531-08308-X**

Related in simple one-sided dialogue, a girl lends her large, overalled bear neighbor first apples, then a series of other ingredients, which he uses to make her a cake. The recipe is appended in case you want to prepare it with your hungry listeners. BEARS. COOKERY. FOOD. FRUIT. NEIGHBORS.

28   **Brown, Marcia.** *How, Hippo!* **Illus. by the author. Scribner, 1969.**

Little Hippo is caught unawares by a crocodile. Muted river woodcuts complement Margaret Mahy's batik-illustrated jungle poem, *17 Kings and 42 Elephants*. CROCODILES. HIPPOPOTAMUS.

29   **Brown, Margaret Wise.** *The Runaway Bunny.* **Illus. by Clement Hurd. Harper & Row, 1972. ISBN 0-06-020766-3**

How a loving rabbit mother talks her rebellious son into staying home. More leaving-home tales include Natalie Savage Carlson's *Runaway Marie Louise* and Jack Kent's *Joey Runs Away.* MOTHERS AND SONS. RABBITS. RUNAWAYS.

30   **Browne, Anthony.** *Bear Hunt.* **Illus. by the author. Atheneum, 1979.**

Out for a walk in the forest, Bear foils two pith-helmeted hunters when he draws escape routes with his trusty pencil. Children can predict what Bear is drawing each time, and then draw their own solutions. See also Crockett Johnson's *Harold and the Purple Crayon.* BEARS. DRAWING. HUNTERS AND HUNTING.

31   **Bucknall, Caroline.** *One Bear in the Picture.* **Illus. by the author. Dial, 1988. ISBN 0-8037-0463-1**

The rhyming text explains how Ted, a bear, tried to stay clean for his class picture but failed. Use with David McPhail's *Pig Pig and the Magic Photo Album*, bring in a camera, and take a group portrait. Barbara Bottner's *Messy* also applies here. BEARS. CLEANLINESS. PHOTOGRAPHY. TEDDY BEARS.

32   **Bunting, Eve.** *The Mother's Day Mice.* **Illus. by Jan Brett. Clarion, 1986. ISBN 0-89919-387-0**

Three young mice brave the dangers of the field to bring a strawberry, a fluff ball, and a song home to their mother for her Mother's Day gifts. Read before the holiday and mull over other ways to show Mom we love her. GIFTS. MICE. MOTHERS. MOTHER'S DAY.

33   **Burningham, John.** *Mr. Gumpy's Outing.* **Illus. by the author. Henry Holt, 1971. ISBN 0-8050-0708-3**

Although Mr. Gumpy cautions his many boat passengers to behave, the children squabble, the rabbit hops, the cat chases the rabbit, and the rest of the animals follow suit till the boat capsizes. Make animal sound effects, of course; and then assign parts, place a large sheet of kraft paper on the floor to act as your boat, and act the whole thing out. ANIMALS. BOATS AND BOATING. CREATIVE DRAMA. SOUND EFFECTS.

34   **Burton, Marilee Robin.** *Tails, Toes, Eyes, Ears, Nose.* **Illus. by the author. Harper & Row, 1988. ISBN 0-06-020874-0**

A bright-colored, simple, animal guessing game. Children must identify the animal when only tail, toes, eyes, ears, and nose are shown on one page, with the put-together answer illustrated on the other side. Summary pages with all tails or toes or eyes, and so on, challenge the guesser to identify each animal, from horse, pig, cat, mouse, and dog to rabbit, elephant, bird, and boy. Keep them guessing with Beatrice Schenk de Regniers's *It Does Not Say Meow and Other Animal Riddle Rhymes*, Beau Gardner's *Guess What*, Deborah Guarino's *Is Your Mama a Llama?* and Tana Hoban's *Look Again!* and *Take Another Look* (Greenwillow, 1981). ANIMALS.

35   **Burton, Virginia Lee.** *Katy and the Big Snow.* **Illus. by the author. Houghton Mifflin, 1973. ISBN 0-395-18155-0**

Tractor plows out town. Good for a snowy day or a social studies lesson on communities. Other snowy books include Ezra Jack Keats's *The Snowy Day*, Florence Slobodkin's *Too Many Mittens*, Harriet Ziefert's *Snow Magic*, and Charlotte Zolotow's *Something Is Going to Happen*. Also try a dusting of poetry with Jack Prelutsky's *It's Snowing! It's Snowing!* CITIES AND TOWNS. MACHINES. SEASONS. SNOW. WINTER.

36   **Burton, Virginia Lee.** *Mike Mulligan and His Steam Shovel.* **Illus. by the author. Houghton Mifflin, 1939. ISBN 0-395-06681-6**

Together they dig the new Town Hall cellar in only one day. Follow up with Julia Lina Sauer's *Mike's House*, about a boy whose favorite book character is Mike Mulligan himself. MACHINES.

37   **Carle, Eric.** *The Grouchy Ladybug.* **Illus. by the author. Harper & Row, 1977. ISBN 0-690-01392-2**

Unwilling to share aphids with a friendly ladybug, the grouchy one looks from 6:00 A.M. to 6:00 P.M. for someone bigger, all the while repeating her chantable refrain, "Hey you. Want to fight?" Split pages increase in width with each hour as she finds ever-larger animals. After eight massive pages worth of whale, she ends up back where she began, chaste and hungry. This one makes a splendid flannel board story with the addition of a practice clock face. Use as an introduction to telling time, along with Jeffrey Allen's "Mary Alice" books and Pat Hutchins's *Clocks and More Clocks*. ANIMALS. CHANTABLE REFRAIN. INSECTS. TIME.

38   **Carle, Eric.** *The Mixed-Up Chameleon.* **Illus. by the author. Harper & Row, 1984. ISBN 0-690-04397-X**

As Chameleon's wishes come true, he becomes a composite of the ten creatures he most envies. Children can predict what part of each animal and what color will be used before you show each illustration. In the same vein, see also Theo LeSieg's *I Wish That I Had Duck Feet*, James Howe's *I Wish I Were a Butterfly*, Bernard Waber's *"You Look Ridiculous," Said the Rhinoceros to the Hippopotamus*, and Pauline Watson's *Wriggles the Little Wishing Pig*. For more animal and color silliness, don't miss Bill Martin, Jr.'s *Brown Bear, Brown Bear, What Do You See?*, also illustrated by Carle, and Merle Peek's *Mary Wore Her Red Dress*. CHAMELEONS. COLOR. REPTILES. SELF-CONCEPT. WISHES.

39   **Carle, Eric.** *Papa, Please Get the Moon for Me.* **Illus. by the author. Picture Book Studio, 1986. ISBN 0-88708-026-X**

When Monica asks for the moon, her father takes along a ladder and fetches it. Children will be entranced by the large folded pages that open up and out to extend the moon's range as it goes through its phases. See also the Frank Asch "Moon" series, such as *Moongame* and *Happy Birthday, Moon*. FATHERS AND DAUGHTERS. MOON. NIGHT.

40   **Carle, Eric.** *The Secret Birthday Message.* **Illus. by the author. Crowell, 1972. ISBN 0-690-72348-2**

Tim receives a secret message with rebus shape clues that leads him on a treasure hunt to find his birthday present—a puppy. Large, garish pages with cutouts corresponding to their shape clues will be a magnet for exploring fingers. Using basic shapes, why not design your own class message, with clues leading to a "treasure"—cookies cut into various shapes. BIRTHDAYS. CODES AND CIPHERS. GIFTS. SHAPES.

41   Carle, Eric. *The Very Busy Spider*. Illus. by the author. Philomel, 1984. ISBN 0-399-21166-7

Each barnyard animal tries to divert the attention of the unperturbable spider who is busily spinning her web. Animal noises, bold illustrations, and a repeated refrain make this ideal for audience participation. DOMESTIC ANIMALS. SOUND EFFECTS. SPIDERS.

42   Carle, Eric. *The Very Hungry Caterpillar*. Illus. by the author. Putnam, 1981. ISBN 0-399-20853-4

Caterpillar munches holes through a succession of fruits and other foods before becoming a butterfly. Makes a swell flannel board or sock puppet story to tell. BUTTERFLIES. CATERPILLARS. FOOD. INSECTS.

43   Carlson, Natalie Savage. *Runaway Marie Louise*. Illus. by Jose Aruego and Ariane Dewey. Scribner, 1977.

Mongoose, who feels unloved after her mama gives her a spanking, takes her peanut butter and jellyfish sandwich and sets out to look for a new mama. For a kangaroo's perspective on leaving home, see Jack Kent's *Joey Runs Away*. BEHAVIOR. MOTHERS AND DAUGHTERS. RUNAWAYS.

44   Caseley, Judith. *Silly Baby*. Illus. by the author. Greenwillow, 1988. ISBN 0-688-07356-5

Even though only-child Lindsay tells mama "No, thank you," her mother has the new baby anyway. Lindsay is none too pleased with baby Callie's constant crying, till her parents show her photos proving she was just as silly a baby as her new sister. For more family album snapshots, see also Marc Brown's *Arthur's New Baby*. BABIES. FAMILY LIFE. SIBLING RIVALRY.

45   Cauley, Lorinda Bryan. *The Three Little Kittens*. Illus. by the author. Putnam, 1982. ISBN 0-399-20855-0

The old rhyme of mittens lost, found, soiled, and washed combines well with other mitten tales including Jean Rogers's *Runaway Mittens*, Florence Slobodkin's *Too Many Mittens*, and Alvin Tresselt's *The Mitten*. CATS. CLOTHING AND DRESS. NURSERY RHYMES. SONGS. STORIES IN RHYME.

46   Causley, Charles. *"Quack!" Said the Billy-Goat*. Illus. by Barbara Firth. Lippincott, 1986. ISBN 0-397-32192-9

Because Farmer Brown has laid an egg, all of the barnyard animals make the wrong noises. On the second reading of this brief, silly rhyme, try out the mixed-up sound effects, and then read or tell Victoria Forrester's *The Magnificent Moo*. DOMESTIC ANIMALS. SOUND EFFECTS. STORIES IN RHYME.

47   Cherry, Lynne. *Who's Sick Today?* Illus. by the author. Dutton, 1988. ISBN 0-525-44380-0

Captivating colorful illustrations of animals with ailments, from beavers with fevers to cranes with pains. Simpler to read than Raffi's similarly patterned *Down by the Bay*, and more specific than Fritz Eichenberg's animal alphabet *Ape in a Cape*, and counting rhyme book *Dancing in the Moon*. Other ailment books to make you feel better include Fritz Brandenberg's *I Wish I Was Sick, Too*, Dick Gackenbach's

What's Claude Doing? and Ursula K. Le Guin's *A Visit from Dr. Katz.* ANIMALS. CREATIVE WRITING. SICK. STORIES IN RHYME.

48   **Christelow, Eileen.** *Five Little Monkeys Jumping on the Bed.* **Illus. by the author. Clarion, 1989. ISBN 0-89919-769-8**

One fell off and bumped his head; the old rhyme that children can recite along with you. More trouble abounds in Nadine Bernard Westcott's updated chanting verse *The Lady with the Alligator Purse.* BEDTIME STORIES. CHANTABLE REFRAIN. COUNTING BOOKS. MONKEYS.

49   **Christelow, Eileen.** *Henry and the Dragon.* **Illus. by the author. Clarion, 1984. ISBN 0-89919-220-3**

Afraid of a dragonlike shadow on his wall, rabbit Henry wants his parents to check out his surroundings before bed. Tie this in either to bedtime stories such as Russell Hoban's *Bedtime for Frances,* Katherine Holabird's *Alexander and the Dragon,* Felicia Bond's *Poinsettia and the Firefighters,* Joan Lowery Nixon's *The Alligator under the Bed,* and Elaine Willoughby's *Boris and the Monsters,* or ones about shadows, like Keiko Narahashi's *I Have a Friend* and Frank Asch's *Bear Shadow.* BEDTIME STORIES. FEAR. NIGHT. RABBITS. SHADOWS.

50   **Cleary, Beverly.** *The Growing-Up Feet.* **Illus. by DyAnne DiSalvo-Ryan. Morrow, 1987. ISBN 0-688-06620-8**

Twins Jimmy and Janet get beautiful new red boots, perfect for puddle splashing. Have your children wear or draw their favorite shoes, and/or pair up stories with Niki Daly's *Not So Fast, Songololo,* Shirley Hughes's *Alfie's Feet,* Tomi Ungerer's *One, Two, Where's My Shoe,* and Elizabeth Winthrop's *Shoes.* BROTHERS AND SISTERS. FOOT. SHOES. TWINS.

51   **Cohn, Janice.** *I Had a Friend Named Peter: Talking to Children about the Death of a Friend.* **Illus. by Gail Owens. Morrow, 1987. ISBN 0-688-06686-0**

Betsy's parents and teachers help her deal with her best friend's death in a car accident. Including a detailed introduction of questions and answers for adults on how to explain death to young children, this is sensitively written and illustrated and a superb treatment of a difficult subject. DEATH.

52   **Cole, Brock.** *No More Baths.* **Illus. by the author. Farrar, 1989. ISBN 0-374-45514-7**

A dirty little girl runs away in disgust when her mother wants to give her a bath in the middle of the day. Fun to act out as you read. For a pig's view of bathing, try *The Piggy in the Puddle* by Charlotte Pomerantz. Woody Guthrie's song "Cleano" fits right in here. BATHS. CREATIVE DRAMA. DOMESTIC ANIMALS. RUNAWAYS.

53   **Cole, William.** *Frances Face-Maker: A Going to Bed Book.* **Illus. by Tomi Ungerer. World, 1963.**

Every night, Frances plays a face-making game with her dad, who instructs her to look angry, ninnylike, happy, proud, ill, surpised, stubborn, and more, and expects us, the listeners, to do the same. Pair the funny, rhyming text with Marie Hall Ets's *Talking without Words* or Robert Kraus's *Owliver,* and finish up with Eloise Greenfield's affecting *Grandpa's Face.* BEDTIME STORIES. CREATIVE DRAMA. EMOTIONS. STORIES IN RHYME.

54   Coleridge, Sara. *January Brings the Snow: A Book of Months.* Illus. by Jenni Oliver. Dial, 1986. ISBN 0-8037-0314-7

Large expressive watercolors detail this 1834 nursery rhyme of the months and seasons in the country. Also don't forget Shirley Hughes's *Out and About* and Maurice Sendak's *Chicken Soup with Rice* for a tasty view of each month. MONTHS. NURSERY RHYMES. SEASONS. STORIES IN RHYME.

55   Cooney, Nancy Evans. *The Blanket That Had to Go.* Illus. by Diane Dawson. Putnam, 1981.

Susie dreads leaving her blanket behind when kindergarten starts. Other stories that confront "blanket withdrawal" include Holly Keller's *Geraldine's Blanket* and Deborah Robison's *Bye-Bye, Old Buddy.* Another related treasure is Nicky Weiss's *Hank and Oogie.* Tell this in September while displaying, one at a time, a series of blanket squares, cut in decreasing sizes, so each time you show one, the blanket magically appears to be shrinking. BLANKETS. HABITS.

56   Cooney, Nancy Evans. *Donald Says Thumbs Down.* Illus. by Maxie Chambliss. Putnam, 1987. ISBN 0-399-21373-2

Preschool boy kicks his thumb-sucking habit when he's finally ready. Use with Cooney's and other blanket-weaning stories listed above. HABITS.

57   Cooney, Nancy Evans. *The Umbrella Day.* Illus. by Melissa Bay Mathis. Philomel, 1989. ISBN 0-399-21523-9

With a big, old, dusty umbrella at her side, Missy finds excitement when she wishes it into a toadstool, a wild animal tent, and a boat. Open up such an umbrella and encourage your children to dream up new, imaginative possibilities for its use. Prolong the adventure with Don Freeman's *A Rainbow of My Own.* Other shelters from the rain can be found in Mirra Ginsburg's *Mushroom in the Rain* and Audrey Wood's *The Napping House.* CREATIVE DRAMA. IMAGINATION. RAIN AND RAINFALL. WEATHER.

58   Crews, Donald. *Freight Train.* Illus. by the author. Greenwillow, 1978. ISBN 0-688-80165-X

Brightly colored eight-car train moves through tunnels, goes by cities, crosses trestles, and is gone in a blur of color. Get into the train rhythm of this briefest of narratives and read several times. Listeners can provide train sound effects and repeat each phrase in call and response. If you know the song "Freight Train," now is the time to sing it. CALL AND RESPONSE STORIES. COLOR. TRAINS.

59   Crews, Donald. *Ten Black Dots.* Illus. by the author. Greenwillow, 1986. ISBN 0-688-06067-6

A counting rhyme, from one to ten, that shows what simple black dots can become. Hand out up to ten black dots to your children and have them draw a picture incorporating them. COUNTING BOOKS. SHAPES. STORIES IN RHYME.

60   Crowe, Robert L. *Clyde Monster.* Illus. by Kay Chorao. Dutton, 1976. ISBN 0-525-28025-1

Young Monster boy, afraid to go to bed in his dark cave, confides his fear of people to his parents who reassure him that we're quite harmless. Similar bedtime-fears stories include Mercer Mayer's *There's a Monster in My Closet* and Jeanne Willis's *The Monster Bed.* BEDTIME STORIES. FEAR. MONSTERS. NIGHT.

61   Cuyler, Margery. *Shadow's Baby*. Illus. by Ellen Weiss. Clarion, 1989. ISBN 0-89919-831-7

The Parker's dog Shadow takes wonderful care of new baby girl Samantha, even though she is not a puppy. Siam the cat and the other household pets are not so understanding about the arrival of a human baby in Alane Ferguson's *That New Pet*. BABIES. DOGS.

62   Daly, Niki. *Not So Fast, Songololo*. Illus. by the author. Atheneum, 1986. ISBN 0-14-050715-9

Young Malusi accompanies his large, old, slow-moving granny GoGo to the city, where she buys him beautiful new red-and-white sneakers, or tackies, as they are called in South Africa. Racial comment or controversy goes unmentioned in this warm, understated gem. If you're doing "footwear" or clothing stories, size this up with Beverly Cleary's *The Growing-Up Feet*, Shirley Hughes's *Alfie's Feet*, Tomi Ungerer's *One, Two, Where's My Shoe?* and Elizabeth Winthrop's *Shoes*. AFRICA. GRANDMOTHERS. SHOES. SHOPPING.

63   Davis, Gibbs. *Katy's First Haircut*. Illus. by Linda Shute. Houghton Mifflin, 1985. ISBN 0-395-38942-9

Shorn of her long tresses, Katy must get used to having short hair. Pair with Don Freeman's *Mop Top* and read on a day when you or a student have just had your locks noticeably clipped. HAIR. SCHOOLS.

64   Degen, Bruce. *Jamberry*. Illus. by the author. Harper & Row, 1983. ISBN 0-694-00157-0

Berryland fruit pickers go on an unforgettable rhyming jam jamboree. It's the berries! Read with Russell Hoban's *Bread and Jam for Frances*, Robert McCloskey's *Blueberries for Sal*, and, of course, Nadine Bernard Westcott's *Peanut Butter and Jelly* and bring in jam jars and fresh berries to taste and compare. FOOD. FRUIT. STORIES IN RHYME.

65   Delton, Judy. *I'm Telling You Now*. Illus. by Lillian Hoban. Dutton, 1983. ISBN 0-525-44037-2

Artie climbs onto the roof, attends a birthday party uninvited, and takes a strange dog for a walk before his mother tells him not to. Delve into what children are and are not allowed to do at home and at school. BEHAVIOR. MOTHERS AND SONS.

66   Delton, Judy. *Two Good Friends*. Illus. by Giulio Maestro. Crown, 1974. ISBN 0-517-55949-8

As a surprise, messy Bear bakes muffins for Duck, and while he's delivering the goodies, neat Duck sneaks in and cleans Bear's sticky house. Along with reading Arnold Lobel's "Frog and Toad" series and James Marshall's "George and Martha" books, share experiences of what unsung heroes friends can be to each other. BEARS. COOKERY. DUCKS. FRIENDSHIP.

67   Demarest, Chris L. *Morton and Sidney*. Illus. by the author. Macmillan, 1987. ISBN 0-02-728450-6

Morton, a boy, helps Sidney, his monster, regain his rightful place in the monster-filled closet. Read as an unthreatening alternative to Mercer Mayer's *There's a Nightmare in My Closet* and *There's an Alligator under My Bed*. MONSTERS.

68 **Demarest, Chris L.** *No Peas for Nellie.* **Illus. by the author. Macmillan, 1988. ISBN 0-02-728460-3**

Nellie would rather eat a spider, salamander, wart hog, a pair of aardvarks, or a python than the peas on her dinner plate. Nellie's open-ended last line—"There are other things I'd rather drink"—should lead to a whole new story, written and illustrated by your students, plus a spirited "yuck" session recounting foods they love and loathe. Meet other picky eaters in Dr. Seuss's *Green Eggs and Ham* and Mitchell Sharmat's *Gregory, the Terrible Eater.* FOOD.

69 **De Regniers, Beatrice Schenk.** *May I Bring a Friend?* **Illus. by Beni Montresor. Atheneum, 1964. ISBN 0-689-20615-1**

Invited for refreshments by the king and queen, the boy narrator arrives each time with a different assortment of zoo pals. Charmingly set out in rhyme, and children can chant "So I brought my friend," and predict which animal will appear next. ANIMALS. CALDECOTT MEDAL. KINGS AND RULERS. STORIES IN RHYME. ZOOS.

70 **Dillon, Barbara.** *The Beast in the Bed.* **Illus. by Chris Conover. Morrow, 1981.**

The small, affable green beast is Marcia's faithful companion until she starts kindergarten, when the beast sets out to find another preschool child for a new temporary friend. Janell's imaginary friend deserts her the same way in Eloise Greenfield's *Me and Neesie.* MONSTERS.

71 **Dobbs, Dayle-Ann.** *Wheel Away!* **Illus. by Thacher Hurd. Harper & Row, 1989. ISBN 0-06-021689-1**

Pa-da-rump pa-da-rump pa-da-rump-pump-pump, the boy's bicycle wheel rolls loose down the hill, through the mill, in the lake, over the cake, and on, until it reverses direction and retraces its "steps." Full-page action graphics and a bouncing array of sound effects make this sheer bliss to chant with a group, in the same style as "We're Going on a Bear Hunt." CHANTABLE REFRAIN. SOUND EFFECTS. STORIES IN RHYME.

72 **Douglass, Barbara.** *Good As New.* **Illus. by Patience Brewster. Lothrop, 1982. ISBN 0-688-51983-0**

Grandpa fixes up Grady's damaged stuffed bear after cousin K. C. wrecks it. A good companion to Don Freeman's *Corduroy* and Richard Galbraith's *Reuben Runs Away*; all three can stimulate desire for a bear party in your room. GRANDFATHERS. TEDDY BEARS.

73 **Douglass, Barbara.** *The Great Town and Country Bicycle Balloon Chase.* **Illus. by Carol Newsom. Lothrop, 1984.**

With the first two bikers to touch the balloon after it lands to receive a free ride, Gina and Grandpa chase first the hot air balloon, and then the aeronaut's escaped parrot. Compare balloons with the one that gets away in Nigel Gray's *A Balloon for Grandad.* BALLOONS. BICYCLES. GRANDFATHERS. PARROTS. TRANSPORTATION.

74 **Drummond, V. H.** *Phewtus the Squirrel.* **Illus. by the author. Lothrop, 1987. ISBN 0-688-07013-2**

A knitted orange-wool squirrel becomes real and then a toy again in this mix-up yarn of a boy who loses his favorite toy animal. Compare with other lost stuffed animal tales such as James Flora's *Sherwood Walks Home,* Sarah Hayes's *This Is the Bear,* and Shirley Hughes's *Dogger.* LOST. SQUIRRELS. STUFFED ANIMALS.

75 **Duke, Kate.** *Guinea Pigs Far and Near.* **Illus. by the author. Dutton, 1984. ISBN 0-525-44480-7**

Large, colorful watercolors clearly depict guinea pigs acting out over two dozen basic concept words including *above, below, over, under, behind, beside,* and *between.* Children can guess the words depicted, and then pair up to act them out. Also see Colleen Stanley Bare's *Guinea Pigs Don't Read Books* and Tricia Springstubb's *The Magic Guinea Pig.* CREATIVE DRAMA. GUINEA PIGS. VOCABULARY.

76 **Ehlert, Lois.** *Color Zoo.* **Illus. by the author. Lippincott, 1989. ISBN 0-397-32260-7**

Cutout basic shapes, layered in startlingly bold colors, compose the faces of nine wild animals. No child will be able to resist the unpretentious charm of this Caldecott honor book. Other children may want to assemble new animal faces using the same format. ANIMALS. COLOR. PICTURE BOOKS FOR ALL AGES. SHAPES.

77 **Ehlert, Lois.** *Eating the Alphabet: Fruits and Vegetables from A to Z.* **Illus. by the author. Harcourt, 1989. ISBN 0-15-224435-2**

What a smashing way to introduce and mesh fruits, vegetables, and the alphabet! Ehlert spent a year drawing and eating the 75 bright, luscious edibles, from apples to zucchini. Her *Growing Vegetable Soup* and Bruce McMillan's *Growing Colors* go along nicely here. Bring in an assortment of fruits and vegetables for children to categorize. The fruits can go into fruit salad—read Charlotte Zolotow's *Mr. Rabbit and the Lovely Present* first—while the veggies can go into soup. Also introduce several varieties of specific fruits or vegetables from apples and plums to lettuce or beans. ALPHABET BOOKS. FRUIT. VEGETABLES.

78 **Ehlert, Lois.** *Growing Vegetable Soup.* **Illus. by the author. Harcourt, 1987. ISBN 0-15-232575-1**

An activity book to use in the spring (bring in seeds, tools, and soil and make a garden) or the fall (have each child bring in a vegetable and make soup). Garishly colored vegetables and tools in each large, simple illustration are labeled, and there's a simple soup recipe on the back flap. Another tasty soup story is James Stevenson's *Yuck.* If you want to do a bit of gardening, also read Ruth Krauss's *The Carrot Seed* and Bruce McMillan's *Growing Colors.* Extend the lot with Ehlert's *Eating the Alphabet* to identify dozens of fruits and vegetables. COOKERY. FOOD. GARDENING. SOUP. VEGETABLES.

79 **Eichenberg, Fritz.** *Ape in a Cape: An Alphabet of Odd Animals.* **Illus. by the author. Harcourt, 1952. ISBN 0-15-607830-9**

Large, colorful, good-natured animals are involved in often-unusual rhyming activities, like carp with a harp and a vulture with culture. Also see the companion volume of counting rhymes *Dancing in the Moon,* as well as Lynne Cherry's *Who's Sick Today?* and Raffi's *Down by the Bay,* to give children rhyming examples so they can dictate and illustrate their own. ALPHABET BOOKS. ANIMALS. CREATIVE WRITING. STORIES IN RHYME.

80 **Emberley, Barbara.** *Drummer Hoff.* **Illus. by Ed Emberley. Prentice Hall, 1967.**

How General Border, Major Scott, Captain Bammer, Corporal Farrell, Private Parriage, and Drummer Hoff loaded the cannon and fired it off. These simplest of rhyming couplets delineate army rank and should be chanted by all, including the ear-shattering *kahbah bloom!* at the end. If you can find a toy cannon, a pipe cleaner, and a drum, you can reenact the whole procedure with props; if not, pantomime it. CALDECOTT MEDAL. CREATIVE DRAMA. CUMULATIVE STORIES. SEQUENCE STORIES. STORIES IN RHYME.

81   Emberley, Ed. *The Wing on a Flea.* Illus. by the author. Little, Brown, 1961. ISBN 0-316-23600-4

A rhyming book about shapes. Follow up with Eric Carle's shape-based *The Secret Birthday Message.* SHAPES. STORIES IN RHYME.

82   Ets, Marie Hall. *Talking without Words.* Illus. by the author. Viking, 1968.

About nonverbal communication and when we use it. Children can pantomime each emotion presented, as in William Cole's *Frances Face-Maker.* To show how someone's expressions can influence others, read Eloise Greenfield's *Grandpa's Face.* ACTING. COMMUNICATION. EMOTIONS.

83   Felt, Sue. *Rosa-Too-Little.* Illus. by the author. Doubleday, 1950.

Rosa can't have her own library card until she can print her whole name. Encourage every child to seek out a public library card. BOOKS AND READING. LIBRARIES.

84   Flack, Marjorie. *Angus and the Cat.* Illus. by the author. Doubleday, 1931. ISBN 0-385-07212-0

The curious Scotty dog chases the feisty new feline all over the house until they become friends. Read all three "Angus" books together for an affectionate portrait of a classic pup. CATS. DOGS.

85   Flack, Marjorie. *Angus and the Ducks.* Illus. by the author. Doubleday, 1930. ISBN 0-385-07213-9

Scotty dog loses his curiosity, thanks to the hissing ducks next door. Good sound effects possibilities here. DOGS. DUCKS. SOUND EFFECTS.

86   Flack, Marjorie. *Angus Lost.* Illus. by the author. Doubleday, 1932. ISBN 0-385-07214-7

Scotty dog gets out of his yard. Make a sound effects tape with your students of the book's many noises. DOGS. LOST. SOUND EFFECTS.

87   Flack, Marjorie. *Ask Mr. Bear.* Illus. by the author. Macmillan, 1932. ISBN 0-02-043090-6

Animals advise a young boy on his mother's birthday present. This makes a fine flannel board story to tell, and classes love to act this out. On the same topic are George Shannon's *The Surprise* and Charlotte Zolotow's *Mr. Rabbit and the Lovely Present.* ANIMALS. BIRTHDAYS. CREATIVE DRAMA. GIFTS. STORIES TO TELL.

88   Flora, James. *Sherwood Walks Home.* Illus. by the author. Harcourt, 1966.

Robert's wind-up bear, left behind in the rain, sets out for home, followed by a fish, cat, dog, girl, policeman, drum major, and parade. Similar to *The Big Yellow Balloon* by Edward Fenton, Sarah Hayes's *This Is the Bear,* and V. H. Drummond's *Phewtus the Squirrel,* and a fantasy-based companion to Shirley Hughes's *Dogger.* For another wind-up bear, see also Don Freeman's *Beady Bear.* LOST. SEQUENCE STORIES. STUFFED ANIMALS. TEDDY BEARS.

89   Forrester, Victoria. *The Magnificent Moo*. Illus. by the author. Atheneum, 1983.

Overcome with fright at the sound of her own moo, a cow trades it for a cat's meow. A cumulative tale ripe for telling, with animal sound effects for all to try. Two melodious matches are Charles Causley's *"Quack!" Said the Billy-Goat* and Lisa Campbell Ernst's *When Bluebell Sang*. ANIMALS. COWS. SOUND EFFECTS. STORIES TO TELL.

90   Fowler, Susi Gregg. *When Summer Ends*. Illus. by Marisabina Russo. Greenwillow, 1989. ISBN 0-688-07605-X

Convinced that everything good happens in summer, a little girl is reminded by her mother of the joys of the other three seasons. Children can paint their favorite memories, one for each season. Louise Borden's *Cats, Hats, Socks, and Mittens*, Sara Coleridge's poem *January Brings the Snow*, Shirley Hughes's poems *Out and About*, Maurice Sendak's *Chicken Soup with Rice*, and Janice May Udry's *A Tree is Nice* give more reasons to appreciate the whole year. SEASONS.

91   Fox, Mem. *Hattie and the Fox*. Illus. by Patricia Mullins. Bradbury, 1987. ISBN 0-02-735471-7

An observant chicken spies a nose, two eyes, two ears, a body, four legs, and a tail in the bushes. The other barnyard animals remain unconcerned until they realize it's a fox. Good repetitive dialogue and creative drama possibilities abound, as each animal makes its own comment and the ending is nicely noisy. For another cunning fox thwarted by a chicken, read Pat Hutchins's *Rosie's Walk* or Denys Cazet's *Lucky Me*. CHICKENS. DOMESTIC ANIMALS. FOXES. SOUND EFFECTS. STORIES TO TELL.

92   Freeman, Don. *Beady Bear*. Illus. by the author. Viking, 1954. ISBN 0-670-15056-8

Even with a pillow, a flashlight, and the evening papers, Thayer's wind-up teddy bear finds life in a cave to be lacking something essential: Thayer. Bring in the aforementioned props to use as you read, and have a Bear Fest with James Flora's lost wind-up bear tale, *Sherwood Walks Home*, Richard Galbraith's *Reuben Runs Away*, and Sarah Hayes's nursery-rhymish *This Is the Bear*. TEDDY BEARS.

93   Freeman, Don. *Corduroy*. Illus. by the author. Viking, 1968. ISBN 0-14-050173-8

The well-known and beloved department store stuffed bear searches for his lost button and finds a friend. Also read the sequel, *A Pocket for Corduroy*. TEDDY BEARS.

94   Freeman, Don. *Mop Top*. Illus. by the author. Viking, 1955. ISBN 0-670-48882-8

Sent by his mother to the barber, red-haired Moppy hides in the grocery store instead. Pair with Gibbs Davis's *Katy's First Haircut*. HAIR.

95   Freeman, Don. *A Pocket for Corduroy*. Illus. by the author. Viking, 1978. ISBN 0-670-56172-X

In the sequel to *Corduroy*, Lisa loses her bear in the laundromat overnight when he wanders off while searching for a pocket. For another pocket-seeker, meet Emmy Payne's handicapped kangaroo, *Katie-No-Pocket*. CLOTHING AND DRESS. TEDDY BEARS.

96   Freeman, Don. *Quiet! There's a Canary in the Library*. Illus. by the author. Golden Gate, 1969. ISBN 0-516-08737-1

A little girl imagines all the animals she would invite to the library if she were in charge. Assign parts and act out with all appropriate sound effects. ANIMALS. CREATIVE DRAMA. LIBRARIES. SOUND EFFECTS.

97   Freeman, Don. *A Rainbow of My Own*. Illus. by the author. Viking, 1966. ISBN 0-670-58928-4

A yellow-slickered, rain-hatted boy describes his real and imaginary search for a rainbow. First, pantomime the boy's antics with his rainbow; then, show everyone how a glass prism can make a rainbow; and finally, dig into the crayons or watercolors so everyone can make a rainbow of his or her own. Stay out in the wet for a while with Nancy Evans Cooney's *The Umbrella Day*. CREATIVE DRAMA. IMAGINATION.

98   Gackenbach, Dick. *Harry and the Terrible Whatzit*. Illus. by the author. Seabury, 1977. ISBN 0-395-28795-2

There's a double-headed, three-clawed, six-toed, long-horned monster lurking in the cellar, and Harry gets rid of it. Children can draw pictures of their houses with each room displayed, and the accompanying creatures, if any, within. Pair this with Mercer Mayer's *There's a Nightmare in My Closet* and *There's Something in My Attic*, Tony Ross's *I'm Coming to Get You*, and Elizabeth Winthrop's *Maggie and the Monster*. COURAGE. MONSTERS. MOTHERS AND SONS.

99   Gackenbach, Dick. *Hurray for Hattie Rabbit*. Illus. by the author. Harper & Row, 1986. ISBN 0-06-021960-2

Two brief but perfect episodes: It's too bright for Hattie to fall asleep, so her mother paints a night scene on the window shade; and Hattie and her friend Rosie Pig try to get Rosie's mom to say "yes" for once. Give out gumdrops after reading, and then, if you're tooth-wise, teach everyone how to brush with a finger. BEDTIME STORIES. MOTHERS AND DAUGHTERS. RABBITS.

100   Gackenbach, Dick. *Poppy, the Panda*. Illus. by the author. Clarion, 1984. ISBN 0-89919-276-9

Katie's stuffed panda refuses to sleep until he gets something nice to wear. Have a stuffed toy dress-up and read Don Freeman's *A Pocket for Corduroy*, Jane Hissey's *Little Bear's Trousers*, and Nancy Willard's *Papa's Panda*. CLOTHING AND DRESS. PANDAS. STUFFED ANIMALS.

101   Gackenbach, Dick. *What's Claude Doing?* Illus. by the author. Clarion, 1984. ISBN 0-89919-464-8

Loyal hound won't leave the house, even when tempted by other dog and cat friends with a trip to the butcher, meeting the school bus, ice skating, and cat chasing. Children can predict what's keeping him home and relate times their pets have stayed by them through sickness and health. For a feline view, also read Franz Brandenberg's *I Wish I Was Sick Too!* and Ursula K. Le Guin's *A Visit From Dr. Katz*, and heal everyone with Lynne Cherry's couplets in *Who's Sick Today?* DOGS. FRIENDSHIP. SICK.

102   Gaeddert, Lou Ann. *Noisy Nancy Norris*. Illus. by Gioia Fiammenghi. Doubleday, 1965.

When downstairs apartment owner Mrs. Muffle insists on complete peace and quiet or else, young Nancy clams up. Your own rambunctious crew can do the sound effects, and afterward, can try being as quiet as Nancy was. Also see Alan Benjamin's *Rat-a-Tat, Pitter Pat*, Benjamin Elkin's *The Loudest Noise in the World*, and Suzy Kline's *SHHHH!* APARTMENT HOUSES. NOISE. SOUND EFFECTS.

103   **Gag, Wanda. *The Funny Thing*. Illus. by the author. Coward, 1929. ISBN 0-698-30097-1**

A doll-eating dragon reforms thanks to Bobo, the good little man of the mountains, who feeds him jum-jills. Make your own follow-up treat of all-cheese jum-jill balls for everyone. A good introduction or sequel to Lorna Balian's *The Aminal*. DRAGONS.

104   **Gag, Wanda. *Millions of Cats*. Illus. by the author. Coward, 1928. ISBN 0-698-20091-8**

Classic of an old man who can't pick just one. Children love to chant the refrain, and you can use this to introduce the concept of hundreds, thousands, millions, billions, and trillions. If each child draws and cuts out ten cats and you paste them onto a scroll of paper, you'll have hundreds of cats to count too. For only one feline, but many more pets, also read Mona Rabun Reeves's *I Had a Cat*. CATS. CHANTABLE REFRAIN. STORIES IN RHYME. STORIES TO TELL.

105   **Galbraith, Kathryn O. *Laura Charlotte*. Illus. by Floyd Cooper. Philomel, 1990. ISBN 0-399-21613-8**

Not sleepy at bedtime, Laura entreats her mother to tell her once again the story of Charlotte, the beautiful gray flannel elephant her mother received on her fifth birthday. Charlotte Pomerantz's *The Chalk Doll* is another warm, lovingly told story of a mother's childhood, as related to her daughter. FAMILY STORIES. MOTHERS AND DAUGHTERS. STUFFED ANIMALS. TOYS.

106   **Galbraith, Richard. *Reuben Runs Away*. Illus. by the author. Orchard, 1989. ISBN 0-531-05790-9**

Fed up with Anna's careless treatment and lack of respect, her teddy bear Reuben runs away to the big city where he ends up in a secondhand shop, only to be bought and brought back home by Anna's own grandfather. Other briefly unappreciated bears include Barbara Douglas's *Good As New*, Don Freeman's *Beady Bear* and *Corduroy*, and Rosemary Wells's *Peabody*. RUNAWAYS. TEDDY BEARS.

107   **Galdone, Joanna, and Paul Galdone. *Gertrude the Goose Who Forgot*. Illus. by Paul Galdone. Franklin Watts, 1975.**

On her way out of the house to go shopping, an absent-minded goose searches for her key, back-tracking through the farmyard and picking up the hat, shawl, socks, shoes, bag, and fan she has left with various animal friends on recent visits. All can chant the refrain, "Oh ginder, oh gander, how silly of me. Have you seen what I did with my rusty old key?" If you're ambitious, turn this into a flannel board story and read, adding each item of clothing as Gertrude retrieves it. Ellen MacGregor's *Theodore Turtle* displays comparable memory skills. CHANTABLE REFRAIN. GEESE. MEMORY. STORIES IN RHYME.

108   **Galdone, Paul. *Over in the Meadow: An Old Nursery Counting Rhyme*. Illus. by the author. Prentice Hall, 1986. ISBN 0-671-67837-X**

I can still remember reciting this one with my parents when I was small. Do it over and over again until your children can say it with you. This one gives different verses from the John Langstaff version. CALL-AND-RESPONSE STORIES. COUNTING BOOKS. NURSERY RHYMES. SONGS. STORIES IN RHYME.

109   **Gantos, Jack.** *Greedy Greeny.* **Illus. by Nicole Rubel. Doubleday, 1979.**

Monster has a watermelon nightmare caused by guilt and overeating. Fun to act out, followed by a watermelon treat. CREATIVE DRAMA. FRUIT. GREED. MONSTERS.

110   **Gardner, Beau.** *Guess What?* **Illus. by the author. Lothrop, 1985. ISBN 0-688-04982-6**

A bold-colored graphic guessing game of animals, similar in theme to Marilee Robin Burton's *Tails, Toes, Eyes, Ears, Nose,* Tana Hoban's *Look Again!* and *Take Another Look,* and Suse MacDonald's *Alphabatics.* Each page showcases one part of an animal, with the whole animal in gray on the reverse side. For aural as well as visual clues, see Beatrice Schenk de Regniers's *It Does Not Say Meow and Other Animal Riddle Rhymes* and Deborah Guarino's *Is Your Mama a Llama?* ANIMALS. VISUAL PERCEPTION.

111   **Geringer, Laura.** *A Three Hat Day.* **Illus. by Arnold Lobel. Harper & Row, 1985. ISBN 0-06-021988-2**

R. R. Pottle, hat collector, meets and weds Isabel, who appreciates his fetish. Schedule a hat parade and make your own chapeaux to wear. A witty compatriot to John Dyke's *Pigwig* as well as Ezra Jack Keats's *Jennie's Hat,* Margaret Miller's photo-guesser *Whose Hat?* and Esphyr Slobokina's *Caps for Sale.* HATS. LOVE.

112   **Gerstein, Mordicai.** *Follow Me!* **Illus. by the author. Morrow, 1983.**

Seven ducks and a goose, each a different color, lose their way home until the duckherd leads them back. Make birds from colored construction paper and act this out. COLOR. CREATIVE DRAMA. DUCKS. GEESE. LOST.

113   **Gerstein, Mordicai.** *William, Where Are You?* **Illus. by the author. Crown, 1985. ISBN 0-517-55644-8**

As William's parents search for him, you fold out the flaps to find everyone but. Tiny format, a chantable reply, and a surprise ending help present concept words *up, out, in, back,* and *under.* BEDTIME STORIES. PETS.

114   **Ginsburg, Mirra.** *The Chick and the Duckling.* **Illus. by Jose Aruego and Ariane Dewey. Macmillan, 1972. ISBN 0-689-71226-X**

Chick is successful at imitating everything the duckling does until he tries swimming. A simple tale for children to act out in pairs. CHICKENS. CREATIVE DRAMA. DUCKS.

115   **Ginsburg, Mirra.** *Mushroom in the Rain.* **Illus. by Jose Aruego and Ariane Dewey. Macmillan, 1974. ISBN 0-02-736241-8**

Animals under an ever-expanding mushroom hide from weather and a hungry fox. Fun to act out as a group using improvised dialogue. Compare with Alvin Tresselt's folktale *The Mitten* and Nancy Evans Cooney's fantasy *The Umbrella Day.* ANIMALS. CREATIVE DRAMA. RAIN AND RAINFALL. WEATHER.

116   **Goodspeed, Peter.** *A Rhinoceros Wakes Me Up in the Morning.* **Illus. by Dennis Panek. Bradbury, 1982. ISBN 0-14-050455-9**

In rhyme, a red-haired boy describes all of the 200 animals who help him through his day, from wake-up to bedtime, where we find the animals as toys surrounding him on the covers. On the second reading, have children identify each animal before you read the rest of the line. ANIMALS. BEDTIME STORIES. STORIES IN RHYME. STUFFED ANIMALS.

117   **Gould, Deborah.** *Aaron's Shirt.* **Illus. by Cheryl Harness. Bradbury, 1989. ISBN 0-02-736351-1**

For two years, Aaron wears his favorite red-and-white striped shirt at every opportunity, and when even he must admit it's too small, hands it down to his favorite teddy bear. Read along with Leone Castell Anderson's *The Wonderful Shrinking Shirt* and have everyone wear his or her favorite shirt to school the next day to draw and tell about it. CLOTHING AND DRESS.

118   **Graham, Margaret Bloy.** *Benjy and the Barking Bird.* **Illus. by the author. Harper & Row, 1971. ISBN 0-06-022079-1**

Dog is so jealous of visiting Aunt Sarah's parrot, Tilly, he sets her free. Talk about how we make amends when we do something wrong. BIRDS. DOGS. JEALOUSY. PARROTS.

119   **Graham, Thomas.** *Mr. Bear's Chair.* **Illus. by the author. Dutton, 1987. ISBN 0-525-44300-2**

After Mrs. Bear's chair breaks, Mr. Bear cuts down a hickory tree and makes a new one. An attractive lesson in how things are made, in the vein of Elsa Beskow's *Pelle's New Suit* and Tomie dePaola's *Charlie Needs a Cloak.* BEARS. CHAIRS.

120   **Gramatky, Hardie.** *Hercules.* **Illus. by the author. Putnam, 1940. ISBN 0-399-60240-2**

"The story of an old-fashioned fire engine." A classic, along with *Mike Mulligan and His Steam Shovel* and *Katy and the Big Snow*, both by Virginia Lee Burton. FIRE. MACHINES.

121   **Gray, Nigel.** *A Balloon for Grandad.* **Illus. by Jane Ray. Orchard, 1988. ISBN 0-531-05755-0**

When Sam's beautiful, silver-starred red balloon blows away, his father comforts him by describing how it will float far away across mountains, sea, desert, river, and island to where his grandad Abdulla lives, tending his goats and date trees. Hand out balloons and encourage children to ask parents for help in mailing them, along with a tape, a picture or a letter, to a favorite grandparent. BALLOONS. FAMILY STORIES. GRANDFATHERS.

122   **Griffith, Helen V.** *Plunk's Dreams.* **Illus. by Susan Condie Lamb. Greenwillow, 1990. ISBN 0-688-08813-9**

It's not chasing rabbits and getting dinner that John thinks his snoozing dog Plunk dreams about; it's paddling an Indian canoe, and meeting dog aliens from space, and being chased by a cat grown huge. Ask all pet owners and lovers to observe and then draw a double picture of their sleeping animals, with one side detailing what they might be dreaming. DOGS. DREAMS. IMAGINATION.

123   **Guarino, Deborah.** *Is Your Mama a Llama?* **Illus. by Steven Kellogg. Scholastic, 1989. ISBN 0-590-41387-2**

A young llama asks all its animal friends that question, but then figures out the answers from their rhyming descriptions, which listeners can do as well. Keep the guessing game going with Beatrice Schenk de Regniers's *It Does Not Say Meow and Other Animal Riddle Rhymes.* ANIMALS. STORIES IN RHYME.

124   **Hadithi, Mwenye.** *Crafty Chameleon.* **Illus. by Adrienne Kennaway. Little, Brown, 1984. ISBN 0-316-33721-8**

Chameleon tricks Leopard and Crocodile into never bothering him again by setting up a tug of war that he appears to win. Julius Lester retells a variant of this story in his folktale collection *How Many Spots Does a Leopard Have?* On the theme of small animals outsmarting big ones, also read Aesop's *The Tortoise and the Hare* or Brian Wildsmith's *The Hare and the Tortoise* and Mwenye Hadithi's *Tricky Tortoise*. ANIMALS. BULLIES. CHAMELEONS. SIZE.

125 **Hadithi, Mwenye.** *Greedy Zebra.* **Illus. by Adrienne Kennaway. Little, Brown, 1984. ISBN 0-316-33721-8**

An original pourquoi story of how the ever-hungry zebra ended up with stripes while all the other African animals made themselves fine colorful coats. Pair with how-and-why folktales such as Verna Aardema's *Why Mosquitoes Buzz in People's Ears*, Shirley Climo's *King of the Birds*, and Joanna Troughton's *How the Birds Changed Their Feathers*. ANIMALS. POURQUOI TALES. ZEBRAS.

126 **Hadithi, Mwenye.** *Tricky Tortoise.* **Illus. by Adrienne Kennaway. Little, Brown, 1988. ISBN 0-316-33724-2**

Tired of Elephant stepping on him all the time, Tortoise bets that he can jump over Elephant's head, which, with the help of a look-alike brother, he seems to do. Use with *Crafty Chameleon* above, to prove that brains, not brawn, can win, and, of course, *The Hare and the Tortoise* by Brian Wildsmith, or any other Aesop version. AFRICA. ELEPHANTS. SIZE. TURTLES.

127 **Hale, Sarah Josepha Buell.** *Mary Had a Little Lamb.* **Illus. by Tomie dePaola. Holiday House, 1984. ISBN 0-87499-125-0**

The complete 1830 text and score of the famous be-kind-to-animals nursery rhyme. Other nursery rhymes in picture book form include Lorinda Bryan Cauley's version of *The Three Little Kittens*, Tomie dePaola or Paul Galdone's *Old Mother Hubbard and Her Dog*, and John Ivimey's *The Complete Story of the Three Blind Mice*. NURSERY RHYMES. SHEEP. STORIES IN RHYME.

128 **Hayes, Sarah.** *This Is the Bear.* **Illus. by Helen Craig. Lippincott, 1986. ISBN 0-397-32171-6**

Dumped into the trash can by the dog, teddy bear Fred lands at the dump, where his devoted boy searches for him. Treat the rhyming text as a call-and-response activity. Other lost stuffed toy books you won't want to miss include James Flora's *Sherwood Walks Home*, Shirley Hughes's *Dogger*, V. H. Drummond's *Phewtus the Squirrel*, and Don Freeman's *Beady Bear*. DOGS. LOST. STORIES IN RHYME. TEDDY BEARS.

129 **Heine, Helme.** *The Most Wonderful Egg in the World.* **Illus. by the author. Atheneum, 1983. ISBN 0-689-50280-X**

When a king tell his three competing hens that what they do is more important then how they look, each lays an extraordinary egg. Making egg salad may seem callous after this, but an egg-decorating activity might not be amiss. CHICKENS. EGGS. KINGS AND RULERS.

130 **Hellsing, Lennart.** *Old Mother Hubbard and Her Dog.* **Trans. by Virginia Allen Jensen. Illus. by Ib Spang Olsen. Coward, 1976.**

While the verses start out with the familiar couplets, this version sports a spate of new rhymes by a Swedish poet. Contrast verses with those in the Tomie dePaola and Paul Galdone editions. CREATIVE DRAMA. DOGS–POETRY. NURSERY RHYMES. STORIES IN RHYME.

131 **Henkes, Kevin.** *Bailey Goes Camping.* **Illus. by the author. Greenwillow, 1985. ISBN 0-688-05701-2**

Thanks to his understanding parents, the youngest bunny makes the most of being home alone when his brother and sister go on a camping trip. Similar in feel to P. K. Roche's *Goodbye, Arnold*; also read David McPhail's *Pig Pig Goes to Camp*. BROTHERS AND SISTERS. CAMPING. JEALOUSY. RABBITS.

132 **Henkes, Kevin.** *Sheila Rae, the Brave.* **Illus. by the author. Greenwillow, 1987. ISBN 0-317-60820-7**

Mouse girl, afraid of nothing, gets lost and depends on her little sister Louise to lead the way home. The refrain, "I am brave, I am fearless," is a good one for children to chant whenever they're feeling timid. COURAGE. LOST. MICE. SISTERS.

133 **Hennessy, B. G.** *The Missing Tarts.* **Illus. by Tracey Campbell Pearson. Viking, 1989. ISBN 0-670-82039-3**

When the Queen of Hearts searches for the Knave who has stolen her strawberry tarts, she is joined in her search by other nursery-rhyming characters, from Jack and Jill to Little Boy Blue, who give her encouragement through rhyming couplets such as, " 'Follow that sheep,' said Little Bo Peep." Friends of nursery rhymes can supply the last word for each couplet. Similar in scheme to Polly Cameron's *"I Can't," Said the Ant.* NURSERY RHYMES. KINGS AND RULERS. STORIES IN RHYME.

134 **Himmelman, John.** *Talester the Lizard.* **Illus. by the author. Dial, 1982. ISBN 0-8037-8788-X**

Lizard befriends his own reflection. Pair up for a mirror pantomime along with other titles like Frank Asch's *Bear Shadow* and *Just Like Daddy*, Jack Kent's *Jim Jimmy James* and Keiko Narahashi's *I Have a Friend*. CREATIVE DRAMA. LIZARDS. REPTILES.

135 **Hissey, Jane.** *Little Bear's Trousers.* **Illus. by the author. Philomel, 1987. ISBN 0-399-21493-3**

Stuffed bear tracks them down after consulting with Old Bear, camel, sailor, dog, and all the other toys, who used the trousers for hump warmers, sails, two-bone bone-holders, and other such useful functions. For a prop, borrow a pair of doll trousers. Ask kids what else they could be used for, other than the obvious, and expand on the theme with Joan L. Nodset's *Who Took the Farmer's Hat?* BEARS. CLOTHING AND DRESS. TEDDY BEARS. TOYS.

136 **Hoban, Lillian.** *Arthur's Honey Bear.* **Illus. by the author. Harper & Row, 1974. ISBN 0-06-022369-3**

On spring-cleaning day, chimp Arthur cleans out his toy chest for a Tag Sale, but is reluctant to give up his stuffed bear. On a similar theme, see Shirley Hughes's *Dogger* and Nicki Weiss's *Hank and Oogie*. CHIMPANZEES. TEDDY BEARS. TOYS.

137 **Hoban, Russell.** *A Baby Sister for Frances.* **Illus. by Lillian Hoban. Harper & Row, 1964. ISBN 0-06-022335-9**

Feeling unloved with the new baby in the house, the badger girl runs away under the dining room table. Read with all the others in the "Frances" series on the K–1 list. Judith Caseley's *Silly Baby*, Alane Ferguson's *That New Pet*, and Ezra Jack

Keats's *Peter's Chair* also confront ambivalent feelings of the first born, as does Roslyn Banish's first-rate photo essay, *Let Me Tell You about My Baby*. BABIES. BADGERS. FAMILY LIFE. JEALOUSY. STORIES WITH SONGS.

138   **Hoban, Tana. *Push, Pull, Empty, Full*. Photos by author. Macmillan, 1972. ISBN 0-02-744810-X**

By examining the full-page black-and-white photographs of opposites, children can figure out each pair of words. OPPOSITES.

139   **Hoff, Syd. *Lengthy*. Illus. by the author. Putnam, 1964. ISBN 0-399-20704-X**

Preposterously long dachshund feels so guilty when his beloved poor old lady owner spends money on him that he runs away to a rich neighborhood. Have the class come up with more absurd ways he could be useful around the house. DOGS.

140   **Holabird, Katharine. *Alexander and the Dragon*. Illus. by Helen Craig. Clarkson N. Potter, 1988. ISBN 0-517-56996-5**

Afraid of the dragon under his bed, a young boy armed with helmet, shield, and sword is prepared to bash it until he realizes it's friendly. A common theme which fits in with Eileen Christelow's *Henry and the Dragon*, Mercer Mayer's *There's an Alligator under My Bed*, Susan Meddaugh's *Beast*, Deborah Robison's *No Elephants Allowed*, and Elizabeth Winthrop's *Maggie and the Monster*. BEDTIME STORIES. DRAGONS. FEAR.

141   **Howard, Jane R. *When I'm Sleepy*. Illus. by Lynne Cherry. Dutton, 1985. ISBN 0-525-44204-9**

A sleep-dazed little girl imagines what it would be like to sleep with the animals in a nest, swamp, log, cave, and other habitats, from cold to wet. Not just an elegant bedtime calmer, this is also a unique way to open a discussion of animal homes and sleep customs. ANIMALS. SLEEP.

142   **Howe, James. *The Day the Teacher Went Bananas*. Illus. by Lillian Hoban. Dutton, 1984. ISBN 0-525-44107-7**

The class's new teacher is a gorilla! Children can describe and pantomime the simian styles of counting, writing, painting, and eating, as pictured in the story. GORILLAS. SCHOOLS. TEACHERS.

143   **Hughes, Shirley. *Alfie Gets in First*. Illus. by the author. Lothrop, 1981. ISBN 0-688-00848-8**

Little boy accidentally locks his mother out of the house and is then unable to open the door. Read together with the other "Alfie" books for an introduction to a new friend. ENGLAND. MOTHERS AND SONS. SELF-RELIANCE.

144   **Hughes, Shirley. *Alfie Gives a Hand*. Illus. by the author. Lothrop, 1983. ISBN 0-688-02386-X**

Alfie brings his blanket to a birthday party, where he learns how to be without it. Melds with Nancy Evans Cooney's *The Blanket That Had to Go*, Holly Keller's *Geraldine's Blanket*, and Nick Weiss's *Hank and Oogie*. BIRTHDAYS. BLANKETS. ENGLAND. HABITS.

145   **Hughes, Shirley. *Alfie's Feet*. Illus. by the author. Lothrop, 1982. ISBN 0-688-01658-8**

His new yellow puddle-splashing boots end up on the wrong feet. More shoe-filled books include Beverly Cleary's *The Growing Up Feet*, Niki Daly's *Not So Fast, Songololo*, Tomi Ungerer's *One Two, Where's My Shoe?* and Elizabeth Winthrop's *Shoes*. BROTHERS AND SISTERS. ENGLAND. FOOT. SHOES.

146   **Hughes, Shirley. *Dogger*. Illus. by the author. Lothrop, 1988. ISBN 0-688-07980-6**

David is heartsick when he loses his favorite stuffed animal. You may recognize this under its American title, *David and Dog* (Prentice Hall, 1977). Pair up with V. H. Drummond's *Phewtus the Squirrel*, James Flora's *Sherwood Walks Home*, Sarah Hayes's *This Is the Bear*, and Lillian Hoban's *Arthur's Honey Bear*. ENGLAND. LOST. STUFFED ANIMALS.

147   **Hughes, Shirley. *An Evening at Alfie's*. Illus. by the author. Lothrop, 1984. ISBN 0-688-04122-1**

The night Alfie's baby-sitter reads to him about Noah's Ark, a pipe bursts in the ceiling, making puddles all over the floor. For a large-scale flood, try Elphinstone Dayrell's *Why the Sun and Moon Live in the Sky*. BABY-SITTERS. ENGLAND. FAMILY LIFE. WATER.

148   **Hutchins, Pat. *Good-Night, Owl*. Illus. by the author. Macmillan, 1972. ISBN 0-02-745900-4**

Owl can't sleep due to the rackets made by bees, squirrel, crows, woodpecker, starlings, jays, cuckoo, robin, sparrows, and doves. Simple repetition includes dandy sound effects for listeners to make. For a realistic approach to owls at night, read Tejima's *Owl Lake* and Jane Yolen's *Owl Moon*. BIRDS. OWLS. SOUND EFFECTS.

149   **Hutchins, Pat. *Rosie's Walk*. Illus. by the author. Macmillan, 1968. ISBN 0-02-745850-4**

A farmyard hen inadvertently escapes the fox's trail each time in this amusing one-sentence sequence story, similar to Ron Roy's *Three Ducks Went Wandering*. Children will vie to predict the outcome of each fox predicament, and can then retell the story in sequence and work in a pairs pantomime, with the action narrated by you. For more chicken/fox nonsense, see Denys Cazet's *Lucky Me*. CHICKENS. CREATIVE DRAMA. FARM LIFE. FOXES. SEQUENCE STORIES.

150   **Hutchins, Pat. *The Very Worst Monster*. Illus. by the author. Greenwillow, 1985. ISBN 0-688-04010-1**

Monster sister Hazel sets out to prove she's much worse behaved than baby brother Billy, so she gives him away. Also read the madcap rhyming sequel, *Where's the Baby?* BEHAVIOR. BROTHERS AND SISTERS. MONSTERS.

151   **Ivimey, John W. *The Complete Story of the Three Blind Mice*. Illus. by Paul Galdone. Clarion, 1987. ISBN 0-89919-481-8**

Being the whole riotous account of how they lost their tails and got them back again. Compare this very slightly revised, newly illustrated version with the original 1904 poem illustrated by Walton Corbould. MICE. NURSERY RHYMES. SONGS. STORIES IN RHYME.

152   **Ivimey, John W. *Complete Version of Ye Three Blind Mice*. Illus. by Walton Corbould. Warne, 1979.**

Story-song of what happened after the farmer's wife caught up with them. Sing and compare with Paul Galdone's illustrations above. MICE. NURSERY RHYMES. SONGS. STORIES IN RHYME.

153   **Johnson, Crockett.** *Harold and the Purple Crayon.* **Illus. by the author. Harper & Row, 1955. ISBN 0-06-443022-7**

First of a series of wonderful, tiny drawing stories about a little boy who draws each adventure as he goes. Children can act out or draw new episodes with their own "magic" purple crayons. If you're artistic, this is a good one to tell as you draw it on a large board. Related stories include Anthony Browne's *Bear Hunt*, Susan Jeschke's *Angela and Bear*, and Dick Gackenbach's *Mag the Magnificent*. DRAWING.

154   **Johnson, Jane.** *Today I Thought I'd Run Away.* **Illus. by the author. Dutton, 1986. ISBN 0-525-44193-X**

His carpet bag, packed with special things, saves a young boy when he meets an ogre, goblin, dragon, demon, and monster and is able to dispatch them with his magic comb, egg-cup, belt, scarf, and hat. Repetitive dialogue makes this a joy for audience participation. Assemble the above props in your own bag, divide your group in half (monster versus boy), and act out the story, pulling out objects as you go. Children can bring in their own magic objects to show or illustrate, and decide what magical properties each has. Maurice Jones's *I'm Going on a Dragon Hunt* would be a logical companion read with this one. Joanna Cole's Russian folktale *Bony Legs* and Maida Silverman's *Anna and the Seven Swans* are but two with the same type of magic object motifs. CREATIVE DRAMA. MONSTERS. RUNAWAYS. STORIES TO TELL.

155   **Johnston, Johanna.** *Edie Changes Her Mind.* **Illus. by Paul Galdone. Putnam, 1964.**

When bedtime-hating Edie throws her evening tantrum once too often, her parents dismantle her bed and give her their blessing to stay up all night. Mr. Bear spends the night up as well, though involuntarily, in Jill Murphy's *Peace at Last*. BEDTIME STORIES. NIGHT. SLEEP.

156   **Johnston, Tony.** *The Witch's Hat.* **Illus. by Margot Tomes. Putnam, 1984. ISBN 0-399-21010-5**

A witch's hat falls into her big, fat, magic brew and turns into a bat, a rat, and a cat. With you as the witch and your students as hat, bat, rat, and cat, act out this story as you tell it for the second time. Alternate hat transformations take a place in Joan L. Nodset's *Who Took the Farmer's Hat?* Also take off with Adrienne Adams's *A Woggle of Witches*. CREATIVE DRAMA. WITCHES.

157   **Jones, Carol.** *Old MacDonald Had a Farm.* **Illus. by the author. Houghton Mifflin, 1989. ISBN 0-395-49212-2**

For each new verse, singers can first guess the animal being chorused by looking through the peephole in the page. Sing a second time using Tracey Campbell Pearson's rendition, and then show Stephen Gammell's mixed-up farmer in *Once upon MacDonald's Farm*. As encores, also sing Kathy Parkinson or Mary Maki Rae's *The Farmer in the Dell* and Nadine Bernard Westcott's *Skip to My Lou*. FARM LIFE. SONGS. SOUND EFFECTS.

158   Jones, Maurice. *I'm Going on a Dragon Hunt*. Illus. by Charlotte Firmin. Four Winds, 1987. ISBN 0-02-748000-3

A good ready-to-chant-and-act-out variation "We're Going on a Bear Hunt," fraught with danger and fun. Also don't miss Jane Johnson's *Today I Thought I'd Run Away*, which is similar in feel, Michael Rosen's *We're Going on a Bear Hunt*, and Sandra Stroner Sivulich's *I'm Going on a Bear Hunt*. CALL-AND-RESPONSE STORIES. CREATIVE DRAMA. DRAGONS. SOUND EFFECTS. STORIES TO TELL.

159   Jorgensen, Gail. *Crocodile Beat*. Illus. by Patricia Mullins. Bradbury, 1989. ISBN 0-02-748010-0

As the jungle animals fill the air with a boom, chitter-chatter, roar, growl, and hisssssss, they awaken the mean croc who comes after them for dinner. Lots of noises, the simplest of texts, and large, expressive, tissue paper collages make this perfect for the youngest listeners. Marcia Brown's *How, Hippo* also meets up with a hungry crocodile, while the possum in Thacher Hurd's *Mama Don't Allow* outsmarts a batch of alligators. ANIMALS. CROCODILES. SOUND EFFECTS.

160   Kalan, Robert. *Jump, Frog, Jump*. Illus. by Byron Barton. Greenwillow, 1981. ISBN 0-688-80271-0

Cumulative sequence story of a frog's narrow escapes from a fish, snake, turtle, and kids. Students can chant the title refrain each time there's danger. CHANTABLE REFRAIN. CUMULATIVE STORIES. FROGS.

161   Kasza, Keiko. *The Pigs' Picnic*. Illus. by the author. Putnam, 1988. ISBN 0-399-21543-3

On a perfect day for a picnic, Mr. Pig borrows Mr. Fox's tail, Mr. Lion's mane, and Mr. Zebra's stripes in order to impress Miss Pig, who is terrified by the "monster" that shows up at her door. This would make an arresting flannel board story. Other mixed-up animals who learn their lessons can be found in Eric Carle's *The Mixed-Up Chameleon*, Don Freeman's *Dandelion*, James Howe's *I Wish I Were a Butterfly*, Pauline Watson's *Wriggles the Little Wishing Pig*, and Bernard Waber's *"You Look Ridiculous," Said the Rhinoceros to the Hippopotamus*. PICNICS. PIGS. SELF-CONCEPT.

162   Kasza, Keiko. *The Wolf's Chicken Stew*. Illus. by the author. Putnam, 1987. ISBN 0-399-21400-3

Before grabbing a blue-bonneted chicken for his stewpot, a ravenous wolf decides first to fatten her up with his own homemade pancakes, doughnuts, and cake. Read along with Harry Allard's *It's So Nice to Have a Wolf around the House* and Betsy and Giulio Maestro's *Lambs for Dinner* to counter the usual stereotype of the all-bad wolf. CHICKENS. FOOD. WOLVES.

163   Keats, Ezra Jack. *Pet Show!* Illus. by the author. Macmillan, 1972. ISBN 0-689-71159-X

When Archie can't find the neighborhood stray cat in time, he brings a germ in a jar as his entry for the pet contest. Demonstrate with a magnifying glass how we can make small things look larger, and have everyone draw an enlarged portrait of Archie's germ. AFRICAN AMERICANS. CATS. PETS.

164   Keats, Ezra Jack. *Peter's Chair*. Illus. by the author. Harper & Row, 1967. ISBN 0-06-023111-4

A new baby sister makes him jealous and possessive of his old baby furniture. Work out the new-baby blues with Judith Caseley's *Silly Baby*, Alane Ferguson's *That*

New Pet!, and Russell Hoban's *A Baby Sister for Frances*. AFRICAN AMERICANS. BABIES. JEALOUSY.

165   Keats, Ezra Jack. *The Snowy Day*. Illus. by the author. Viking, 1962. ISBN 0-670-65400-0

Peter spends a typical, idyllic day outside in this classic winter story, perfect for sharing and acting out in pantomime or outside in the snow, if you can. Read with Virginia Lee Burton's *Katy and the Big Snow*, Mark Taylor's *Henry the Explorer*, Harriet Ziefert's *Snow Magic*, and Charlotte Zolotow's *Something Is Going to Happen*. Also throw in some poems from Jack Prelutsky's *It's Snowing! It's Snowing!* AFRICAN AMERICANS. CALDECOTT MEDAL. SNOW. WEATHER. WINTER.

166   Keats, Ezra Jack. *Whistle for Willie*. Illus. by the author. Viking, 1964. ISBN 0-670-76240-7

Peter yearns to be able to whistle so that he can summon his dachshund Willie. Over the course of a week, read with the others in the series, including *Goggles*; *A Letter to Amy*; *Peter's Chair*; and *The Snowy Day*. AFRICAN AMERICANS. DOGS.

167   Keller, Holly. *A Bear for Christmas*. Illus. by the author. Greenwillow, 1986. ISBN 0-688-05988-0

When his mother hides Joey's present, he finds it, sneaks a peek, and accidentally damages it. This might be a good time to talk about guilt and how to assuage it. CHRISTMAS. GIFTS. TEDDY BEARS.

168   Keller, Holly. *Geraldine's Blanket*. Illus. by the author. Greenwillow, 1984. ISBN 0-688-02539-0

A young pig, not willing to give up her old security blanket, makes it into a dress for her new baby pig doll. Several more good ones are Nancy Evans Cooney's *The Blanket That Had to Go*, Shirley Hughes's *Alfie Gives a Hand*, and Deborah Robison's *Bye-Bye, Old Buddy*. BLANKETS. HABITS. PIGS.

169   Kent, Jack. *Joey Runs Away*. Illus. by the author. Prentice Hall, 1985. ISBN 0-671-67936-8

Kangaroo boy figures it's easier to leave home than clean his room. Also see Margaret Wise Brown's *The Runaway Bunny*, Natalie Savage Carlson's *Runaway Marie Louise*, and Emmy Payne's kangaroo classic *Katy-No-Pocket*. KANGAROOS. MOTHERS AND SONS. RUNAWAYS.

170   Kline, Suzy. *Don't Touch!* Illus. by Dora Leder. Albert Whitman, 1985. ISBN 0-8075-1707-0

A young boy deals with everyone who says "don't touch" by retreating to the basement where he can punch, poke, pound, and mash clay to his heart's content. A simple, cheerful means of letting your children know when they need to keep their hands to themselves; afterward, bring out the modeling clay and say, "Now *touch*." BEHAVIOR.

171   Kline, Suzy. *SHHHH!* Illus. by Dora Leder. Albert Whitman, 1984. ISBN 0-8075-7321-3

No matter what she does, the young narrator gets shushed by parents, grandparents, siblings, and more. Not until she whoops it up in the backyard does she feel able to cope with all that quiet. A perfect prelude, with noises included, to "Quiet Time" in your room. For a more global view, try Benjamin Elkin's *The Loudest Noise in the World*, and then do some sound effects with Alan Benjamin's *Rat-a-Tat, Pitter Pat* and Lou Ann Gaeddert's *Noisy Nancy Norris*. NOISE.

172   **Koide, Tan.** *May We Sleep Here Tonight?* **Illus. by Yasuko Koide. Athenuem, 1983. ISBN 0-689-50261-3**

Three gophers, two rabbits, and three raccoons, all lost in the fog, seek refuge in a cozy house and get a scare when the bear who lives there comes home. The unexpectedly gentle ending, reminiscent of Betsy and Giulio Maestro's *Lambs for Dinner*, caps off a series of sound effects and a chantable refrain. Act this one out with you as the bear, and all of your children as animals in the bed. ANIMALS. CHANTABLE REFRAIN. CREATIVE DRAMA. SLEEP. SOUND EFFECTS.

173   **Kovalski, Maryann.** *The Wheels on the Bus.* **Illus. by the author. Little, Brown, 1987. ISBN 0-316-50256-1**

While Grandma, Jenny, and Joanna wait for the bus to come, they sing the title song, getting so involved that they miss the bus (and have to take a taxi). You'll want to sing this exuberant book over and over, with motions and new words as your kids compose them. Extend the bus theme by also reading Rodney Peppé's *The Mice and the Clockwork Bus* and Dyan Sheldon's *A Witch Got on at Paddinton Station*. Raffi's *Wheels on the Bus* is another version of the same song. BUSES. SONGS. STORIES WITH SONGS. TRANSPORTATION.

174   **Kraus, Robert.** *Milton the Early Riser.* **Illus. by Jose Aruego and Ariane Dewey. Windmill, 1972. ISBN 0-13-583162-8**

Panda looks for playmates and finds every family, from the Creeps to the Whippersnappers, still snoozing. Fun to act out as narrative pantomime. CREATIVE DRAMA. PANDAS. SLEEP.

175   **Kraus, Robert.** *Noel the Coward.* **Illus. by Jose Aruego and Ariane Dewey. Dutton, 1977. ISBN 0-671-66845-5**

Plagued by bullies, a nonviolent kangaroo father and son attend Charlie's School of Self-Defense, where they learn how to fight and when it's not necessary. Also try Anthony Browne's *Willy the Wimp* and dare to be different with Munro Leaf's pacifist bull, *Ferdinand*. BULLIES. COURAGE. FIGHTING. KANGAROOS.

176   **Kraus, Robert.** *Phil the Ventriloquist.* **Illus. by the author. Greenwillow, 1989. ISBN 0-688-07987-3**

A voice-throwing bunny frightens away a burglar by making the furniture appear to say, "Cheeze it, the cops," and other discouraging words. Burglars are just as speedily dispatched by the dog in Steven Kellogg's *Pinkerton, Behave* and Patricia Lauber's *Clarence and the Burglar*, and the pet snake in Tomi Ungerer's *Crictor*. Children can make up conversations between other inanimate objects like pencil sharpeners and pencils. RABBITS. ROBBERS AND OUTLAWS. VOICE.

177   **Kraus, Robert.** *Whose Mouse Are You?* **Illus. by Jose Aruego. Macmillan, 1970. ISBN 0-689-71142-5**

Young mouse saves his mother from the cat, frees his father from the trap, brings his sister home, and welcomes his new baby brother. This briefest of texts, in question-and-answer format, is worth reading several times, until children pick up the responses. FAMILY LIFE. MICE.

178   **Krauss, Ruth.** *The Carrot Seed.* **Illus. by Crockett Johnson. Harper & Row, 1945. ISBN 0-06-443210-6**

Little boy has faith that the seed he planted will come up, in spite of his doubting parents and brother. Hand out tiny carrots or carrot sticks for munching. Use with either Janina Domanska's folktale *The Turnip*, Lois Ehlert's *Planting Vegetable Soup*, and Bruce McMillan's *Growing Colors* as part of a gardening lesson, or Alexei Tolstoi's *The Great Big Enormous Turnip*. Plant seeds or just cut carrot tops and grow the greens. GARDENING. PLANTS. VEGETABLES.

179   **Langstaff, John.** *Frog Went a-Courtin'.* **Illus. by Feodor Rojankovsky. Harcourt, 1955. ISBN 0-15-230214-X**

Sword and pistol by his side, Frog woos Mistress Mouse, and the wedding feast begins, interrupted by an uninvited guest, the old tom cat. Music to the traditional song is appended so you can sing the story. Edward Lear's *The Owl and the Pussycat* also has a merry nonsense wedding. FROGS. MICE. SONGS. STORIES IN RHYME.

180   **Langstaff, John.** *Over in the Meadow.* **Illus. by Feodor Rojankovsky. Harcourt, 1957. ISBN 0-15-258854-X**

Old counting animal song, with music appended. Compare with the Paul Galdone version, which incorporates completely different creatures, and Jim Aylesworth's *One Crow: A Counting Rhyme*. ANIMALS. COUNTING BOOKS. SONGS. STORIES IN RHYME.

181   **Lear, Edward.** *The Owl and the Pussycat.* **Illus. by Paul Galdone. Clarion, 1987. ISBN 0-89919-505-9**

The classic rhyming nonsense ditty about two sweethearts who set sail in a pea-green boat to the land where the Bong-tree grows, where they marry and dance by the light of the moon. Lorinda Bryan Cauley's illustrated version (Putnam, 1986) provides a complementary comparison. Another mixed-marriage occurs in John Langstaff's ballad *Frog Went a-Courtin'*. BOATS AND BOATING. CATS. NONSENSE VERSES. OWLS. STORIES IN RHYME.

182   **Leedy, Loreen.** *A Number of Dragons.* **Illus. by the author. Holiday House, 1985. ISBN 0-8234-0568-0**

A rhyming ten-to-one-and-back-again dragon counting book, fun for call-and-response reading and group narrative pantomime. CALL-AND-RESPONSE STORIES. COUNTING BOOKS. CREATIVE DRAMA. DRAGONS. STORIES IN RHYME.

183   **Le Guin, Ursula K.** *A Visit from Dr. Katz.* **Illus. by Ann Barrow. Atheneum, 1988. ISBN 0-689-31332-2**

When Marianne gets the flu and has to stay in bed, cat brothers Philip and The Bean, known together as "Dr. Katz," keep her company and make her feel better. Pair with Franz Brandenberg's cat siblings in *I Wish I Was Sick, Too!* and Dick Gackenbach's *What's Claude Doing?* for the canine set, and then top it off with Lynn Cherry's rhyming *Who's Sick Today?* CATS. SICK.

184   **Lemieux, Michele.** *What's That Noise?* **Illus. by the author. Morrow, 1985. ISBN 0-688-04139-6**

Before falling asleep for the winter, Brown Bear finally identifies the thump-bump noise he hears as his own heart. Filled with animal and nature noises for listeners to imitate. To carry on the hibernating theme, also read Don Freeman's *Bearymore* and Joanne Ryder's *Chipmunk Song*. BEARS. HIBERNATION. SEASONS. SLEEP.

185   **Lester, Helen.** *The Wizard, the Fairy and the Magic Chicken.* **Illus. by Lynn Munsinger. Houghton Mifflin, 1983. ISBN 0-395-47945-2**

Three dippy magicians, boastful of their own talents and jealous of each others', find they must cooperate to save their skins when their showing off results in the creation of three threatening monsters. Bring in a magic wand for pretend spells, and a few "magic" pickles for eating. CHICKENS. FAIRIES. FRIENDSHIP. MAGIC. MONSTERS.

186   **Leverich, Kathleen.** *The Hungry Fox and the Foxy Duck.* **Illus. by Paul Galdone. Parents, 1978. ISBN 0-8193-0987-7**

In the spirit of *The Three Little Pigs*, Fox plans on a duck dinner, but the duck is too clever for him. Also see Edna Mitchell Preston's *Squawk to the Moon, Little Goose.* DUCKS. FOXES.

187   **Lexau, Joan.** *That's Good, That's Bad.* **Illus. by Aliki. Dial, 1963.**

Sequence story of a boy being chased by an angry rhino. Fine to retell and act out, along with Remy Charlip's *Fortunately.* CAUSE AND EFFECT. RHINOCEROS. SEQUENCE STORIES.

188   **Leydenfrost, Robert.** *The Snake That Sneezed.* **Illus. by the author. Putnam, 1970.**

Forgetting his father's advice, a young snake bites off more than he can chew, swallowing every animal that crosses his path. Fun to act out; as each "animal" is swallowed, actors can line up under a sheet behind the child playing the snake. For an additional mouthful, try also Paul Galdone's folktale *The Greedy Old Fat Man* and Jack Kent's *The Fat Cat.* ANIMALS. CREATIVE DRAMA. SNAKES.

189   **Lindgren, Astrid.** *I Want a Brother or Sister.* **Illus. by Ilon Wikland. Harcourt, 1978. ISBN 9-12-958778-6**

Peter is jealous of his new baby sister until he starts to help care for her. Also see Judith Caseley's *Silly Baby* and Alane Ferguson's *That New Pet!* BABIES. BROTHERS AND SISTERS. JEALOUSY.

190   **Lionni, Leo.** *It's Mine!* **Illus. by the author. Knopf, 1986. ISBN 0-394-87000-X**

Three frogs learn the necessity and pleasure of sharing when a flood almost wipes them out. Good for crisis mediation when your group comes down with a case of selfishness. Pettiness vanishing in the face of adversity can be found as well in Barbara Brenner's *Mr. Tall and Mr. Small.* FROGS.

191   **Lionni, Leo.** *Little Blue and Little Yellow.* **Illus. by the author. Obolensky, 1959. ISBN 0-8392-3018-4**

Blue + yellow = green. A scrap-paper story of two good friends. Children can invent adventures using torn paper, and mix primary watercolors to make new ones. COLOR. FRIENDSHIP.

192   **Lobel, Arnold.** *How the Rooster Saved the Day.* **Illus. by Anita Lobel. Greenwillow, 1977.**

A fast-thinking rooster tricks a thief into calling up the sun. Compound your crowing with Charles Causley's *"Quack!" Said the Billy-Goat* and Jack Kent's *Little Peep,* and try some creative drama with Cheli Duran Ryan's *Hildilid's Night.* FARM LIFE. ROBBERS AND OUTLAWS. ROOSTERS. SUN.

193   **Lyon, David.** *The Biggest Truck.* **Illus. by the author. Lothrop, 1988. ISBN 0-688-05514-1**

After everyone else goes to sleep, Jim awakens, eats breakfast, and hits the road with his truck and 20 tons of strawberries, to reach the town of Woosterville before morning. Vrooommm through the night with the mechanical sound effects, and don't forget to pair this with Dave Siebert's rhyming *Truck Song* and take Bernie Karlin's *Night Ride* by car for another look at the scenery. SOUND EFFECTS. TRUCKS.

194   **McCloskey, Robert.** *Blueberries for Sal.* **Illus. by the author. Viking, 1948. ISBN 0-670-17591-9**

A little girl and a bear cub cross paths while out berrying with their mothers. More berry-filled titles include Bruce Degen's *Jamberry*, Russell Hoban's *Bread and Jam for Frances*, and Nadine Bernard Westcott's *Peanut Butter and Jelly*. Bring in blueberries for all to taste. BEARS. FOOD. FRUIT.

195   **McCully, Emily Arnold.** *The Christmas Gift.* **Illus. by the author. Harper & Row, 1988. ISBN 0-06-024212-4**

A wordless celebration of a close-knit mouse family's holiday, from baking cookies and trimming the tree to the trauma of breaking a favorite present. As with *Picnic*, bring your children up close to examine the pictures; then have them imagine what the mice are saying on each page and become the "sound track" as they speak their own invented dialogue for each "scene." CHRISTMAS. GIFTS. GRANDFATHERS. MICE. STORIES WITHOUT WORDS.

196   **McCully, Emily Arnold.** *Picnic.* **Illus. by the author. Harper & Row, 1984. ISBN 0-06-443199-1**

Baby Mouse's accidental exit off the back of the family truck goes unnoticed until the family picnic is in full swing. Children should supply the missing dialogue on each page as they narrate this wordless treasure. Afterward, sponsor a mouse-picnic of tiny foods for your hungry nibblers. First in a series about this extended mouse family. FAMILY LIFE. LOST. MICE. PICNICS. STORIES WITHOUT WORDS.

197   **McMillan, Bruce.** *Growing Colors.* **Photos by author. Lothrop, 1988. ISBN 0-688-07845-1**

Glistening color photographs of fruits and vegetables on the vine, plant, or tree are ripe for children to discuss and identify. If you intend to sow a few seeds, then also read Leslie Conger's folktale *Tops and Bottoms*, Janina Domanska's folktale *The Turnip*, Lois Ehlert's *Planting Vegetable Soup*, Ruth Krauss's *The Carrot Seed*, and Alexei Tolstoi's *The Great Big Enormous Turnip*. For colors, read Sheila White Samton's *Beside the Bay* and Charlotte Zolotow's fruit-filled *Mr. Rabbit and the Lovely Present*. To identify almost every fruit or vegetable you could name, don't miss Lois Ehlert's *Eating the Alphabet*. COLOR. FRUIT. VEGETABLES.

198   **McMillan, Bruce.** *Kitten Can.* **Photos by author. Lothrop, 1984. ISBN 0-688-02668-0**

Full-page color photographs and brief, large-print, verb-filled text show how one kitten stares, squeezes, stretches, scratches, and more. Children can describe the kitten's actions sans text, and, in narrative pantomime, act it all out. You may want to extend the same verb treatment to dogs, birds, fish, or even children, and have your students illustrate their own sentences to be shared in class. Ruth Brown's *Our Cat Flossie* fits in here. CATS. CREATIVE DRAMA. ENGLISH LANGUAGE–GRAMMAR.

199 **McMillan, Bruce.** *Super Super Superwords.* **Photos by author. Lothrop, 1989. ISBN 0-688-08098-7**

For each double-page spread, a small, medium, and large color photograph illustrate degrees of comparison—i.e., heavy, heavier, heaviest, or low, lower, lowest—that take us through a typical day at kindergarten. Children can examine each trio of photos and surmise each word being depicted. As an extension, act out or demonstrate other comparison words such as cold, thin, sloppy, soft, or happy. VOCABULARY.

200 **McPhail, David.** *Emma's Pet.* **Illus. by the author. Dutton, 1985. ISBN 0-525-44210-3**

After rejecting bug, mouse, bird, frog, snake, fish, and dog, a young bear child finds a big, soft, cuddly, "pet"—her own father. Read when preparing for Father's Day, along with Janice May Udry's *What Mary Jo Shared.* BEARS. FATHERS AND DAUGHTERS. PETS.

201 **McPhail, David.** *Emma's Vacation.* **Illus. by the author. Dutton, 1987. ISBN 0-525-44315-0**

Her parents show her all the glittery sights, but bear Emma would prefer to wade, catch fish, pick berries, and enjoy the outdoor life. A "What I did on my summer vacation" discussion starter. BEARS. COUNTRY LIFE. FAMILY LIFE.

202 **McPhail, David.** *Pig Pig Grows Up.* **Illus. by the author. Dutton, 1980. ISBN 0-525-37027-7**

Pig Pig enjoys being babied until he sees the advantage of acting his age. An effective and beloved beginning-of-the-school-year story to help children adjust to change, along with Robert Kraus's *Leo the Late Bloomer.* MATURITY. PIGS.

203 **Marshall, James.** *The Guest.* **Illus. by the author. Houghton Mifflin, 1975. ISBN 0-395-31127-6**

Moose Mona is heartbroken when her house guest and dear friend, snail Maurice, leaves her unexpectedly. Find out more about snails in Joanne Ryder's *The Snail's Spell.* FRIENDSHIP. MOOSE. SNAILS.

204 **Martin, Bill, Jr.** *Brown Bear, Brown Bear, What Do You See?* **Illus. by Eric Carle. Henry Holt, 1983. ISBN 0-8050-0201-4**

"I see a redbird looking at me," replies the large double-paged bear, starting a call-and-reponse chant involving a yellow duck, blue horse, green frog, purple cat, white dog, black sheep, goldfish, and finally, a mother (in the 1967 edition, it was a teacher), and children, all looking back at them. Read and recalled several times, it reinforces colors, tickles sequential memory skills, and enthralls all listeners. Cut out large oaktag animals, hand them out and recite the story. Also read Eric Carle's *The Mixed-Up Chameleon,* Merle Peek's *Mary Wore Her Red Dress and Henry Wore His Green Sneakers,* and Mary Serfozo's *Who Said Red?* ANIMALS. CALL-AND-RESPONSE STORIES. CHANTABLE REFRAIN. COLOR.

205 **Martin, Bill, Jr., and John Archambault.** *Chicka Chicka Boom Boom.* **Illus. by Lois Ehlert. Simon & Schuster, 1989. ISBN 0-671-67949-X**

One by one, all the lower case alphabet letters climb to the top of the coconut tree until they overload it, and fall down wounded. In rhyme, this is fun to chant, and Ehlert's assertive graphics will lead you to pull out a set of those old refrigerator magnet letters to act it out on a metallic board. Suse MacDonald's *Alphabetics* is another energetic introduction to the band of 26 letters. ALPHABET BOOKS. STORIES IN RHYME.

206   **Martin, Jacqueline Briggs.** *Bizzy Bones and the Lost Quilt.* **Illus. by the author. Lothrop, 1988. ISBN 0-688-07407-3**

When Bizzy accidentally loses his treasured good-dreams quilt, the young mouse feels cold and lonely without it until his Uncle Ezra and the orchard mice start a new one. Ask the children about their good dreams, and put together an illustrated "good dreams" book of their recollections. MICE. QUILTS. UNCLES.

207   **Mayer, Mercer.** *There's a Nightmare in My Closet.* **Illus. by the author. Dial, 1968. ISBN 0-8037-8682-4**

Boy overcomes his fear and tames a bedtime monster. In addition to using the alligator sequel *There's an Alligator under My Bed,* meet his female counterpart in *There's Something in My Attic.* Follow up with Dick Gackenbach's *Harry and the Terrible Whatzit,* Deborah Robison's *No Elephants Allowed,* Elaine Willoughby's *Boris and the Monsters,* and Elizabeth Winthrop's *Maggie and the Monster.* Children can draw portraits of the critters lurking in their houses and discuss how they deal with them. BEDTIME STORIES. FEAR. MONSTERS. NIGHT.

208   **Mayer, Mercer.** *There's an Alligator under My Bed.* **Illus. by the author. Dutton, 1987. ISBN 0-8037-0374-0**

Once the boy has dealt with the nightmare in his closet, he must lure out an alligator he knows is there. See also Mayer's *There's Something in My Attic* for a female hero, Joan Lowery Nixon's *The Alligator under the Bed,* and Deborah Robison's *No Elephants Allowed.* ALLIGATORS. BEDTIME STORIES. FEAR. REPTILES.

209   **Mayer, Mercer.** *There's Something in My Attic.* **Illus. by the author. Dial, 1988. ISBN 0-8037-0414-3**

When the city girl narrator moves out to a farm, she's afraid every night of the nightmare lurking in her attic. Like the boy in Mayer's *There's A Nightmare in My Closet* and *There's an Alligator under My Bed,* or Dick Gackenbach's *Harry and the Terrible Whatzit* and Elizabeth Winthrop's *Maggie and the Monster,* she pursues her creature. BEDTIME STORIES. FEAR. MONSTERS.

210   **Meddaugh, Susan.** *Beast.* **Illus. by the author. Houghton Mifflin, 1981. ISBN 0-395-30349-4**

Anna finds for herself that the feared beast in the family barn is neither ferocious nor fearless, but timid, as is the creature in Katherine Holabird's *Alexander and the Dragon.* Apply these lessons of the perils of preconceptions to everyday life. MONSTERS.

211   **Mendoza, George.** *The Sesame Street Book of Opposites.* **Photos by author. Platt & Munk, 1974.**

A long out-of-print gem featuring zany full-color photos of a diapered Zero Mostel. Cover the two words at the bottom of each double-paged spread so children can identify them from the photos. Also see *King Wacky* by Dick Gackenbach and *Push-Pull, Empty-Full* by Tana Hoban. OPPOSITES.

212   **Miller, Margaret.** *Whose Hat?* **Illus. by the author. Greenwillow, 1988. ISBN 0-688-06906-1**

145

For each large color photo of hats belonging to a chef, fire fighter, pirate, nurse, cow hand, or magician, on the next double-paged spread is a photo of one adult and a child dressed for that occupation. This simple nonstereotyped concept book will promote career discussion and may even lead to a hat parade. Related titles include John Dyke's *Pigwig*, Ezra Jack Keats's *Jennie's Hat*, Laura Geringer's *A Three Hat Day*, Joan L. Nodset's *Who Took the Farmer's Hat?* and Esphyr Slobodkina's *Caps for Sale*. HATS. OCCUPATIONS.

213   **Minarik, Else Holmelund.** *It's Spring!* **Illus. by Margaret Bloy Graham. Greenwillow, 1989. ISBN 0-688-07619-X**

Giddy with joy over the new season, orange and gray tabbies Pit and Pat each declare they could jump over a tulip, bush, tree, house, island, mountain, moon, sun, and each other. The growing succession of objects named can be compared with those in Daniel M. Pinkwater's *The Wuggie Norple Story* or Nadine Bernard Westcott's *I Know an Old Lady Who Swallowed a Fly*. CATS. SEASONS. SPRING.

214   **Murphy, Jill.** *Peace at Last.* **Illus. by the author. Dial, 1980. ISBN 0-8037-6757-9**

Mr. Bear can't sleep. A perfect story to act out, retell and/or join in on sound effects and refrain. Tape record the sound effects your children make and use as the audio part in the dramatization. BEARS. CREATIVE DRAMA. NIGHT. SLEEP. SOUND EFFECTS.

215   **Narahashi, Keiko.** *I Have a Friend.* **Illus. by the author. Macmillan, 1987. ISBN 0-689-50432-2**

Poetic description by a young boy who likes his shadow, as opposed to Bear in Frank Asch's *Bear Shadow* who tries to get rid of his. Go shadow stalking outside in the sun, and have the children pair up for pantomime, as in Jack Kent's *Jim Jimmy James*, and John Himmelman's *Talester the Lizard*, where they can mirror each other's actions. SHADOWS.

216   **Naylor, Phyllis Reynolds.** *Keeping a Christmas Secret.* **Illus. by Lena Shiffman. Atheneum, 1989. ISBN 0-689-31447-7**

Horrified when he inadvertently lets slip to his father that the family present to him is a new sled, youngest sibling Michael thinks of another secret gift—a rope to pull the sled—that more than makes up for his ruining the first surprise. In *A Bear for Christmas* by Holly Keller, Joey feels guilty when he opens up a surprise gift meant for him. CHRISTMAS. FAMILY LIFE. GIFTS.

217   **Nietzel, Shirley.** *The Jacket I Wear in the Snow.* **Illus. by Nancy Winslow Parker. Greenwillow, 1989. ISBN 0-688-08030-8**

The rhyming, rebus-filled, cumulative verse, told "This is the House That Jack Built" style, chronicles the winter woes of a child whose scarf is stuck in her jacket zipper. In Eve Rice's *Oh, Lewis!* the hero has an equally vexing problem keeping his heavy clothing fastened. Other same-styled books include Arnold Lobel's summer rhyme, *The Rose in My Garden*, Rose Robart's *The Cake That Mack Ate*, and Colin West's *The King of Kennelwick Castle*. CLOTHING AND DRESS. CUMULATIVE STORIES. SNOW. STORIES IN RHYME. WINTER.

218   **Nixon, Joan Lowery.** *The Alligator under the Bed.* **Illus. by Jan Hughes. Putnam, 1974.**

Not until Uncle Harry comes in to pull the reptile out can Jill relax and go to bed. One of a myriad bedtime stories about kids who can't sleep due to critters in the room like Mercer Mayer's *There's a Nightmare in My Closet* and *There's an Alligator under My Bed* or Eileen Christelow's *Henry and the Dragon*. ALLIGATORS. BEDTIME STORIES. FEAR. REPTILES.

219   **Nodset, Joan L.** *Who Took the Farmer's Hat?* **Illus. by Fritz Siebel. Harper & Row, 1963. ISBN 0-06-024566-2**

Searching for his old brown hat after the wind whisks it away, a farmer questions a squirrel, mouse, fly, goat, duck, and bird, all of whom mistook the hat for something else. Bring in a hat so children can describe what other uses it might have. Then, using a pattern, have them cut out brown construction paper hats that they can incorporate into their own illustrations. Follow-ups include Tony Johnston's *The Witch's Hat*, Ezra Jack Keats's *Jennie's Hat*, Laura Geringer's *A Three Hat Day*, Margaret Miller's *Whose Hat?* and Esphyr Slobodkina's *Caps for Sale*. In the "alternative uses for common objects" department, also read Jane Hissey's *Little Bear's Trousers*. ANIMALS. FARM LIFE. HATS.

220   **Olson, Arielle North.** *Hurry Home, Grandma!* **Illus. by Lydia Dabcovich. Dutton, 1984. ISBN 0-525-44113-1**

Grandma hurries through the jungle, paddles down croc-infested waters and flies her own plane to get home to grandkids Timothy and Melinda in time for Christmas. Get into the jungle frame of mind with Margaret Mahy's *17 Kings and 42 Elephants*, brainstorm to come up with additional perils Grandma could have faced, then act them out in pantomime as you describe them in steamy detail. BROTHERS AND SISTERS. CHRISTMAS. GRANDMOTHERS.

221   **Palmer, Helen.** *A Fish Out of Water.* **Illus. by P. D. Eastman. Random House, 1961. ISBN 0-394-80023-0**

Overfed fish Otto *grows.* Ample proof that a controlled vocabulary does not need to be dull. The Random House filmstrip is a stitch! FISHES.

222   **Panek, Dennis.** *Catastrophe Cat.* **Illus. by the author. Bradbury, 1978.**

This almost wordless action-filled tale of a crazy cat's misadventures is a must for narrative pantomime, along with the sequel, *Catastrophe Cat at the Zoo* (1979). Children can first provide a running newscasterlike description of the action as you show each page. CATS. CREATIVE DRAMA.

223   **Parkinson, Kathy.** *The Farmer in the Dell.* **Illus. by the author. Albert Whitman, 1988. ISBN 0-8075-2271-6**

Sing and play this one after you read it, along with Mary Maki Rae's rendition, Tracey Campbell Pearson's *Old MacDonald Had a Farm*, and Nadine Bernard Wescott's merry *Skip to My Lou*. DOMESTIC ANIMALS. FARM LIFE. GAMES. SONGS.

224   **Paxton, Tom.** *Jennifer's Rabbit.* **Illus. by Donna Ayers. Morrow, 1988. ISBN 0-688-07431-6**

Paxton's old lullaby of Jennifer's nighttime trip to sea with her animal friends works wonders as a bedtime poem, especially with the marvelous midnight illustrations. Other traveling, late night adventures include Anthony Browne's *Gorilla*, Phyllis Root's *Moon Tiger*, and Joanne Ryder's *The Night Flight*. ANIMALS. BEDTIME STORIES. OCEAN. SAILING. STORIES IN RHYME.

225   **Payne, Emmy.** *Katy-No-Pocket.* **Illus. by H. A. Rey. Houghton Mifflin, 1944. ISBN 0-395-17104-0**

Pouchless kangaroo searches for a suitable pocket. Pair with Don Freeman's bear in *A Pocket for Corduroy* or Jack Kent's kangaroo in *Joey Runs Away*. KANGAROOS. LETTER WRITING.

226 **Pearson, Tracey Campbell.** *Old MacDonald Had a Farm.* **Illus. by the author. Dial, 1984. ISBN 0-8037-0068-7**

Comical illustrations of a day on the farm accompany the animal noises-filled song. While you're making music, see also Carol Jones's pleasing version, and give Kathy Parkinson's or Mary Maki Rae's *The Farmer in the Dell* a try too. Also don't miss Stephen Gammell's laid-back spoof *Once upon MacDonald's Farm* and Nadine Bernard Westcott's *Skip to My Lou*. FARM LIFE. SONGS. SOUND EFFECTS.

227 **Peek, Merle.** *Mary Wore Her Red Dress and Henry Wore His Green Sneakers.* **Illus. by the author. Clarion, 1985. ISBN 0-89919-324-2**

Adapted from an old folk song, the simple, singable, color-coded verses follow eight animals on their way to Katy Bear's birthday party. Your children can make up new verses to match the colors and clothing they are wearing. Additional animal and color-themed books include Eric Carle's *The Mixed-Up Chameleon*, Bill Martin, Jr.'s *Brown Bear, Brown Bear, What Do You See?* and Mary Serfozo's *Who Said Red?* ANIMALS. COLOR. PARTIES. SONGS.

228 **Perkins, Al.** *Hand, Hand, Fingers, Thumb.* **Illus. by Eric Gurney. Random House, 1969. ISBN 0-394-81076-7**

The simplest and silliest story of monkeys drumming on a drum, dum ditty dum ditty dum dum dum. I never realized what a prize this was till my then five-year-old nephew Josh followed me around his house chanting the whole book. Completely infectious and satisfying, this needs to be chanted, pantomimed, and laughed over many times. Bring out percussion instruments and drum, blow, shake, and wave till you can't take any more. CHANTABLE REFRAIN. CREATIVE DRAMA. MONKEYS. MUSIC. STORIES IN RHYME.

229 **Pinkwater, Daniel.** *Three Big Hogs.* **Illus. by the author. Seabury, 1975.**

Porkers look for a new home and learn to fend for themselves in the woods when their farmer leaves them behind, not unlike the way the animals did once upon a time in Jacob Grimm's *The Bremen Town Musicians*. PIGS.

230 **Polushkin, Maria.** *Mother, Mother, I Want Another.* **Illus. by Diane Dawson. Crown, 1978. ISBN 0-517-53401-0**

Baby mouse just wants another good night kiss, but his mother thinks he wants another mother. Children can chant the title refrain. BEDTIME STORIES. CHANTABLE REFRAIN. MICE. MOTHERS AND SONS.

231 **Pomerantz, Charlotte.** *The Piggy in the Puddle.* **Illus. by James Marshall. Macmillan, 1974. ISBN 0-02-774900-2**

Delicious oofy-poofy nonsense rhyme of a dirty pig and her worried family's insistence on soap. Also read Brock Cole's *No More Baths* and Brenda Nelson's *Mud fore Sale*. Blither a bit more with Edna Preston Mitchell's *Pop Corn and Ma Goodness*. BATHS. PIGS.

232   **Pomerantz, Charlotte.** *Posy.* **Illus. by Catherine Stock. Greenwillow, 1983.**

At bedtime, Posy's father tells her three stories about her when she was little. Encourage your students to ask their parents to do the same, and share the resulting memories in a group. Children can also recall their own earliest memories. Make a tape recording of these stories as an oral history of the class. BEDTIME STORIES. FATHERS AND DAUGHTERS.

233   **Preston, Edna Mitchell.** *Squawk to the Moon, Little Goose.* **Illus. by Barbara Cooney. Viking, 1974. ISBN 0-14-050546-6**

Disobeying his mother's instructions, Little Goose heads down to the pond one night and worries needlessly about the moon's safety until a fox catches him unaware. Frank Asch's Bear is also moonstruck in *Happy Birthday, Moon,* and *Moongame.* Compare Little Goose's cleverness with the duck's in Kathleen Leverich's *The Hungry Fox and the Foxy Duck.* FARM LIFE. FOXES. GEESE. MOON. SOUND EFFECTS.

234   **Rae, Mary Maki.** *The Farmer in the Dell: A Singing Game.* **Illus. by the author. Viking, 1988. ISBN 0-670-81853-4**

A pleasant introduction to an old favorite. After singing the book, play the game in a circle. Compare this book with Kathy Parkinson's version; both go well with Tracey Campbell Pearson's *Old MacDonald Had a Farm* and Nadine Bernard Westcott's *Skip to My Lou.* DOMESTIC ANIMALS. FARM LIFE. GAMES. SONGS.

235   **Raffi.** *Wheels on the Bus.* **Illus. by Sylvie Kantrovitz Wickstrom. Crown, 1988. ISBN 0-517-56784-9**

A cheerfully illustrated version of the song, with music appended. If you don't sing, be sure to play Raffi's recording. Other bus titles too good to miss are Maryann Kovalski's *The Wheels on the Bus,* Rodney Peppés *The Mice and the Clockwork Bus,* and Dyan Sheldon's *A Witch Got on at Paddington Station.* BUSES. SONGS.

236   **Ravilious, Robin.** *The Runaway Chick.* **Illus. by the author. Macmillan, 1987. ISBN 0-02-775640-8**

A cheeky little barnyard chick finds himself in the farmhouse with a cat on his trail. Do a medley of chicken tales with Marjorie Flack's *The Story about Ping,* Mem Fox's *Hattie and the Fox,* Helme Heine's *The Most Wonderful Egg in the World,* Keiko Kasza's *The Wolf's Chicken Stew,* and Mirra Ginsburg's *The Chick and the Duckling.* CATS. CHICKENS.

237   **Reeves, Mona Rabun.** *I Had a Cat.* **Illus. by Julie Downing. Bradbury, 1989. ISBN 0-02-775731-5**

Rhyming girl narrator with a menagerie of 36 animals gives them away to the zoo, Farmer Brown, and a boy, leaving only her pet cat. Pair this with Wanda Gag's *Millions of Cats.* ANIMALS. CATS. STORIES IN RHYME.

238   **Rey, H. A.** *Curious George.* **Illus. by the author. Houghton Mifflin, 1941. ISBN 0-395-15993-8**

Children love this everlasting trouble-making monkey. Continue with the sequels *Curious George Takes a Job* (1947) and *Curious George Rides a Bike* (1952), after which you might make your children newspaper boats. For more monkey mischief, tell and act out Esphyr Slobodkina's *Caps for Sale.* BEHAVIOR. CURIOSITY. MONKEYS.

239   **Rice, Eve.** *Oh, Lewis!* **Illus. by the author. Macmillan, 1987. ISBN 0-02-775990-3**

On a winter's day shopping trip with his mother and little sister, Lewis's boots, jacket, mittens, and hood come undone. Read this on one of those cold snowy days before everyone gets bundled up to go outside. CLOTHING AND DRESS. WINTER.

240   **Riddell, Chris.** *The Trouble with Elephants.* **Illus. by the author. Harper & Row, 1988. ISBN 0-397-32273-9**

According to the young girl narrator, who loves them nevertheless, elephants spill the bath water, take all the covers, and drink your lemonade, among other complaints. Your elephant-lovers may come up with new problems. You might also read aloud some ridiculous elephant riddles from Polly Cameron's *The Two-Ton Canary and Other Nonsense Riddles* and top it all off with Nancy Patz's *Pumpernickel Tickle and Mean Green Cheese*, Marilyn Sadler's hilariously understated *Alistair's Elephant*, and Shel Silverstein's *Who Wants a Cheap Rhinoceros?* ELEPHANTS.

241   **Robart, Rose.** *The Cake That Mack Ate.* **Illus. by the author. Little, Brown, 1987. ISBN 0-316-74890-0**

Mack's a dog, and the storyline, meant to be chanted, is a cake version of *The House That Jack Built*. Use with Janet Stevens's original version, Verna Aardema's *Bringing the Rain to Kapiti Plain*, Arnold Lobel's *The Rose in My Garden,* and Colin West's *The King of Kennelwick Castle.* COOKERY. CUMULATIVE STORIES. DOGS. FOOD.

242   **Robbins, Ken.** *Beach Days.* **Illus. by the author. Viking, 1987. ISBN 0-670-80138-0**

Large, striking, hand-tinted photos grace a simple narrative about what people do at the beach on a typical day. Teamed with sand, shells, and salt water, this would make an appealing start or finish to a science lesson along with Susan Russo's bright collection of sea poems in *The Ice Cream Ocean,* Sheila White Samton's *Beside the Bay,* and James Stevenson's noisy *Clams Can't Sing.* SEASHORE. SUMMER.

243   **Robison, Deborah.** *No Elephants Allowed.* **Illus. by the author. Houghton Mifflin, 1981. ISBN 0-395-30078-9**

Justin tries to chase the elephants out of his room so he can sleep. At the end, have children guess what picture he hung on his wall to scare them off. More titles with this well-covered theme include Russell Hoban's *Bedtime for Frances,* Katharine Holabird's *Alexander and the Dragon,* Mercer Mayer's *There's a Nightmare in My Closet* and *There's an Alligator under My Bed,* Joan Lowery Nixon's *The Alligator under the Bed,* Elaine Willoughby's *Boris and the Monsters,* and Elizabeth Winthrop's *Maggie and the Monster.* Chris Riddell's *The Trouble with Elephants* details the pros and cons of pachyderms. BEDTIME STORIES. ELEPHANTS. FEAR. NIGHT.

244   **Rogers, Jean.** *Runaway Mittens.* **Illus. by the author. Greenwillow, 1988. ISBN 0-688-07053-1**

Inuit boy loves the mittens his grandmother knit him, even though he constantly misplaces them. This slice of Eskimo village life in winter will contrast nicely with Florence Slobodkin's *Too Many Mittens* and Alvin Tresselt's *The Mitten,* as well as compare with Jan Andrews's stunning *Very Last First Time.* ALASKA. CLOTHING AND DRESS. MITTENS. WINTER.

245   **Rosen, Michael.** *We're Going on a Bear Hunt.* **Illus. by Helen Oxenbury. Macmillan, 1989. ISBN 0-689-50476-4**

Dad, four kids, and the dog all head out through the tall grass (swishy swashy!), through the deep, cold river (splash splosh!), the thick, oozy mud (squelch squerch!), the big dark forest (stumble trip!), and the like, till they tiptoe into the gloomy cave and find *a bear!!!!* As children will want to help tell this again and again, alternate with Jane Johnson's *Today I Thought I'd Run Away*, Maurice Jones's *I'm Going on a Dragon Hunt*, and Sandra Stroner Sivulich's *I'm Going on a Bear Hunt*. BEARS. CALL-AND-RESPONSE STORIES. CREATIVE DRAMA. STORIES TO TELL.

246 **Roy, Ron.** *Three Ducks Went Wandering.* **Illus. by Paul Galdone. Seabury, 1979. ISBN 0-395-28954-8**

In their innocence, the ducks inadvertently avoid a dangerous bull, fox, hawk, and snake in this clever sequence story, similar to Pat Hutchins's *Rosie's Walk*. DUCKS. SEQUENCE STORIES.

247 **Russo, Marisabina.** *The Line Up Book.* **Illus. by the author. Greenwillow, 1986. ISBN 0-688-06204-0**

When his mother calls him for lunch, Sam first stretches out all his blocks, books, toys, shoes, cars, and himself to reach the kitchen in one continuous line. Good lead-in to a measuring activity. MEASUREMENT. MOTHERS AND SONS.

248 **Russo, Marisabina.** *Only Six More Days.* **Illus. by the author. Greenwillow, 1988. ISBN 0-688-07071-X**

"Only six more days!" Ben says excitedly, starting the daily countdown to his fifth birthday. "Who cares?" says older sister Molly, until she realizes there are only 47 days left to hers. Outstanding gouache illustrations light up this wry look at sibling jealousy. Ask everyone to find out the day, month, and year of their own births. BIRTHDAYS. BROTHERS AND SISTERS. SIBLING RIVALRY.

249 **Ryder, Joanne.** *The Snail's Spell.* **Illus. by Lynne Cherry. Frederick Warne, 1982. ISBN 0-14-050891-0**

Like her *Chipmunk Song*, you the reader assume the role of an animal, in this case a two-inch, soft gray snail in a vegetable garden. After reading aloud once, act out the story again in narrative pantomime, and, if you have access to one, bring in a snail or a slug from your garden. Introduce other invertebrates through fiction with Eric Carle's *The Very Hungry Caterpillar*, James Howe's *I Wish I Were a Butterfly*, and Joanne Oppenheim's *You Can't Catch Me*. CREATIVE DRAMA. SNAILS.

250 **Samton, Sheila White.** *Beside the Bay.* **Illus. by the author. Philomel, 1987. ISBN 0-399-21420-8**

Bright seashore colors and creatures are introduced one at a time in a simple rhyming walk along a white stone wall. Extend the experience with Ken Robbins's *Beach Days* and James Stevenson's *Clams Can't Sing*. For a farm version, see Mary Serfozo's *Who Said Red?* and, in the woods, Charlotte Zolotow's *Mr. Rabbit and the Lovely Present*. BAYS. COLOR. SEASHORE. STORIES IN RHYME.

251 **Samuels, Barbara.** *Duncan & Dolores.* **Illus. by the author. Macmillan, 1986. ISBN 0-689-71294-4**

A young girl can't help overwhelming her new cat with attention. The same idea as Alma Whitney's *Leave Herbert Alone*; use both as an opportunity to discuss how to treat pets. CATS. SISTERS.

252   **Sauer, Julia L.** *Mike's House.* **Illus. by Don Freeman. Viking, 1954.**

Four-year-old Robert considers the main character from *Mike Mulligan and His Steam Shovel* to be his best friend, and insists on going to visit him at the library even though it's snowing hard outside. Read in tandem with the Virginia Lee Burton classic. BOOKS AND READING. LIBRARIES. LOST. POLICE. SNOW.

253   **Segal, Lore.** *All the Way Home.* **Illus. by James Marshall. Farrar, 1973. ISBN 0-374-30215-4**

On a trip to the park with her mother and baby brother, George, Juliet falls down and refuses to be comforted. A cumulative crying, barking, meowing, squawking, and grinning story, great for class participation, retelling, and acting out. NOISE. SOUND EFFECTS. STORIES TO TELL.

254   **Sendak, Maurice.** *One Was Johnny: A Counting Book.* **Illus. by the author. Harper & Row, 1962. ISBN 0-06-025540-4**

A counting rhyme to act out in sequence, about Johnny and all the intruders who destroy his peace and quiet until he issues an ultimatum. For kindergartners, you might want to read also the three remaining titles from "The Nutshell Library" including *Alligators All Around, Chicken Soup with Rice,* and *Pierre,* and show the knockout video or play the Carol King soundtrack record for "Really Rosie." COUNTING BOOKS. CREATIVE DRAMA. STORIES IN RHYME.

255   **Sendak, Maurice.** *Where the Wild Things Are.* **Illus. by the author. Harper & Row, 1963. ISBN 0-694-00096-5**

World's best monster tale; students will need to don their imaginary wolf suits beforehand and join Max on all the teeth-gnashing and eye-rolling. CALDECOTT MEDAL. MONSTERS.

256   **Serfozo, Mary.** *Who Said Red?* **Illus. by Keiko Narahashi. Macmillan, 1988. ISBN 0-689-50455-1**

Blue, green, and yellow are described as well in a simple rhyming exposition of colors by a farm girl and her red-kite-flying brother. More color-filled titles include Bill Martin, Jr.'s *Brown Bear, Brown Bear, What Do You See?*, Merle Peek's *Mary Wore Her Red Dress and Henry Wore His Green Sneakers*, Sheila White Sampton's *Beside the Bay,* and Charlotte Zolotow's *Mr. Rabbit and the Lovely Present.* COLOR. FARM LIFE. STORIES IN RHYME.

257   **Serfozo, Mary.** *Who Wants One?* **Illus. by Keiko Narahashi. Macmillan, 1989. ISBN 0-689-50474-8**

As in *Who Likes Red?*, a big sister offers her stubborn little brother a panoply of rhyming animals and objects, from one to ten. Children can bellow his response, "No, I want one!" Still on the farm, see also Jim Aylesworth's *One Crow: A Counting Rhyme.* COUNTING BOOKS.

258   **Seuss, Dr.** *The Cat in the Hat.* **Illus. by the author. Random House, 1966. ISBN 0-394-90001-4**

When the cat visits two children on a rainy day, trouble follows. A deserved favorite. CATS. STORIES IN RHYME.

259   Seuss, Dr. *Green Eggs and Ham*. Illus. by the author. Random House, 1960. ISBN 0-394-90016-2

This off-the-wall rhyming declaration of the ways Sam-I-Am tries to get his friend to sample a tasty dish was written as a read-alone. The sheer nuttiness of the narration is infectious when read aloud, and may even convince your fussy eaters to try something new, along with Chris L. Demarest's *No Peas for Nellie* and Marjorie Weinman Sharmat's *Gregory the Terrible Eater*. EGGS. FOOD. STORIES IN RHYME.

260   Shannon, George. *Dance Away*. Illus. by Jose Aruego and Ariane Dewey. Greenwillow, 1982. ISBN 0-688-00838-0

With a left two three kick, right two three kick, left skip, right skip, turn around, Rabbit saves his friends from Fox. Great to act out with the dance and chant. DANCING. FOXES. RABBITS.

261   Shannon, George. *Lizard's Song*. Illus. by Jose Aruego and Ariane Dewey. Greenwillow, 1981. ISBN 0-688-80310-5

When Bear can't remember Lizard's song, he puts him in a sack to take home with him. Act out this one—music is included—and the "Zoli, Zoli, Zoli" refrain is positively addicting. BEARS. CREATIVE DRAMA. HOUSES. REPTILES. STORIES WITH SONGS.

262   Shannon, George. *The Surprise*. Illus. by Jose Aruego and Ariane Dewey. Greenwillow, 1983. ISBN 0-688-02313-4

Unable to think of an original birthday present for his mother, Squirrel gives her a box within a box within other boxes, the last of which contains . . . him! As a warm-up, put a tiny book in a small box, and wrap in a succession of larger ones, with plenty of ribbons and bows so the children can open it, one box at a time. The message you can pass on is, "There's no present I can give you that's better than a good book!" Other special moms' gift books include Marjorie Flack's *Ask Mr. Bear* and Charlotte Zolotow's *Mr. Rabbit and the Lovely Present*. BIRTHDAYS. GIFTS. MOTHERS AND SONS. SQUIRRELS.

263   Sharmat, Marjorie Weinman. *Go to Sleep, Nicholas Joe*. Illus. by John Himmelman. Harper & Row, 1988. ISBN 0-06-025496-3

Using his sheet as a magic carpet, a young boy flies around the world and puts everyone to bed. Ask your wide-awake listeners what rituals they follow before they can fall asleep every night. For dream-starters, read Jacqueline Briggs Martin's *Bizzy Bones and the Lost Quilt*. Also try Anthony Browne's *Gorilla*, Russell Hoban's *Bedtime for Frances*, Ellen Kandoian's *Under the Sun*, Bernie and Mati Karlin's realistic *Night Ride*, Jack Prelutsky's poems in *My Parents Think I'm Sleeping*, and Joanne Ryder's *The Night Flight*. BEDTIME STORIES. NIGHT. SLEEP.

264   Shaw, Charles G. *It Looked Like Spilt Milk*. Illus. by the author. Harper & Row, 1947. ISBN 0-06-443159-2

Cloud-gazing is an obvious follow-up to this simple white-on-dark-blue depiction of what a cloud resembled, including a rabbit, bird, tree, ice cream cone, flower, and then some. Also good for simple pantomime where the children assume each identity. Extend their imagination with Beau Gardner's inventive *The Look Again . . . and Again, and Again, and Again Book* and *The Turn About, Think About, Look*

About Book. Continue guessing with Arnold Sundgaard's rain-stained story, *Meet Jack Appleknocker.* CLOUDS. CREATIVE DRAMA. IMAGINATION. SKY. VISUAL PERCEPTION.

265   **Sheldon, Dyan.** *A Witch Got on at Paddington Station.* **Illus. by Wendy Smith. Dutton, 1987. ISBN 0-525-44352-5**

Annoyed with the good-natured witch's loud singing on the London bus, a bad-tempered conductor tries to throw her off, and tugs at her large handbag until the magic spills out, making the rest of the ride a delight for all the passengers. Good for a grumpy day when you can also sing and read Maryann Kovalski's *The Wheels on the Bus.* BUSES. ENGLAND. WITCHES.

266   **Siebert, Diane.** *Truck Song.* **Illus. by Byron Barton. Crowell, 1984. ISBN 0-690-04411-9**

Rhyming realistic description of a trucker's run, on the road with the rest of the rigs. Rev it up with David Lyon's sound-effect-filled *The Biggest Truck.* STORIES IN RHYME. TRANSPORTATION. TRUCKS.

267   **Sivulich, Sandra Stroner.** *I'm Going on a Bear Hunt.* **Illus. by Glen Rounds. Dutton, 1973.**

A call-and-response story where children pattern your motions and repeat each sentence as you go through the grass, up the tree, across the lake, through the swamp, and into a dark cave where you find *a bear!* and then quickly retreat, repeating all in reverse sequence. See also Maurice Jones's *I'm Going on a Dragon Hunt* and Michael Rosen's *We're Going on a Bear Hunt.* BEARS. CALL-AND-RESPONSE STORIES. CREATIVE DRAMA. SOUND EFFECTS. STORIES TO TELL.

268   **Slobodkin, Florence.** *Too Many Mittens.* **Illus. by the author. Hale, 1963.**

Twins lose one red mitten, but end up with many. Extend the mitten theme with Jean Rogers's *Runaway Mittens,* Alvin Tresselt's *The Mitten,* and Lorinda Bryan Cauley's version of *The Three Little Kittens.* CLOTHING AND DRESS. MITTENS. SNOW. TWINS. WINTER.

269   **Slobodkina, Esphyr.** *Caps for Sale.* **Illus. by the author. W. R. Scott, 1947. ISBN 0-06-443143-6**

Monkeys tease a peddler by stealing all his caps as he naps. Divide the class so that one half play the monkeys and the other half are peddlers; act out and then switch parts. More hat-minded books include Laura Geringer's *A Three Hat Day,* Ezra Jack Keats's *Jennie's Hat,* and Margaret Miller's *Whose Hat?* H. A. Rey's *Curious George* is another mischief-minded monkey. CREATIVE DRAMA. HATS. MONKEYS. PEDDLERS AND PEDDLING.

270   **Springstubb, Tricia.** *The Magic Guinea Pig.* **Illus. by Bari Weissman. Morrow, 1982.**

Upset when he can't do anything right in his family's eyes, Mark helps out a bumbling witch who gives him an unexpected pet. Find out more about guinea pigs in Colleen Stanley Bare's simple nonfiction tribute, *Guinea Pigs Don't Read Books,* and expand basic concept knowledge with Kate Duke's *Guinea Pigs Far and Near.* AFRICAN AMERICANS. GUINEA PIGS. PETS. SELF-CONCEPT. WITCHES.

271   **Stevens, Janet.** *The House That Jack Built: A Mother Goose Nursery Rhyme.* **Illus. by the author. Holiday House, 1985. ISBN 0-8234-0548-6**

The traditional cumulative chant, with appealingly chunky illustrations. Follow this one up with similarly formatted tales such as Verna Aardema's *Bringing the*

Rain to Kapiti Plain, Arnold Lobel's *The Rose in My Garden,* Rose Robart's *The Cake That Mack Ate,* and Colin West's *The King of Kennelwick Castle.* CHANTABLE RE-FRAIN. CUMULATIVE STORIES. HOUSES. NURSERY RHYMES.

272   **Sundgaard, Arnold.** *Meet Jack Appleknocker.* **Illus. by Sheila White Samton. Philomel, 1988. ISBN 0-399-21472-0**

Each morning of the week, the Woodsman looks at the stain made by the rain on the ceiling and, Rorschach-like, concludes from its shape what he needs to do that day, such as make pancakes, dig potatoes, and play his fiddle. Bright, primary colors on large double pages will make you want to open the watercolor boxes. Children can paint "stain" pictures for others to guess while they review the days of the week, Jack-style. For cloud-suggested images, also read Charles G. Shaw's *It Looked Like Spilt Milk.* ANIMALS. COUNTRY LIFE. DAYS OF THE WEEK. SHAPES.

273   **Thayer, Jane.** *The Popcorn Dragon.* **Illus. by Jay Hyde Barnum. Morrow, 1953. ISBN 0-688-08340-4**

A lonely dragon learns to put his fire to good use and makes new friends in the process. After reading this and Frank Asch's *Popcorn,* pop up a batch and talk about friendship. BEHAVIOR. DRAGONS. FOOD. FRIENDSHIP. POPCORN.

274   **Titherington, Jeanne.** *A Place for Ben.* **Illus. by the author. Greenwillow, 1987. ISBN 0-688-06493-0**

Needing some privacy from his baby brother, Ben marks off a spot for himself in the back corner of the garage. Large, softly shaded colored-pencil illustrations gently reveal Ben's conflicting feelings of annoyance and love toward his brother, which children can relate to their own families. BABIES. BROTHERS. FAMILY LIFE.

275   **Tsutsui, Yoriko.** *Anna's Secret Friend.* **Illus. by Akiko Hayashi. Viking, 1987. ISBN 0-670-81670-1**

When Anna, a little Japanese girl, moves to a new house, she receives flowers, a paper doll, and a letter from a mysterious someone who wants to be friends. Utterly simple but affecting, read after Frank Asch's *Goodbye House* and along with Aliki's *We Are Best Friends.* FRIENDSHIP. LETTER WRITING. MOVING, HOUSEHOLD.

276   **Tyler, Linda Wagner.** *Waiting for Mom.* **Illus. by the author. Viking, 1987. ISBN 0-670-81408-3**

After the 3:00 P.M. bell rings, a young hippo child keeps busy at school when mom is unexpectedly an hour late. Reassuring for all kids whose parents run behind schedule from time to time. HIPPOPOTAMUS. MOTHERS AND DAUGHTERS. SCHOOLS.

277   **Udry, Janice May.** *Thump and Plunk.* **Illus. by Ann Schweninger. Harper & Row, 1981. ISBN 0-06-026149-8**

Mother mouse wants Thump to stop plunking Plunk's plunkit, and vice versa. A real tongue twister which you can use to introduce others like Alvin Schwartz's *Busy Buzzing Bumblebees.* BROTHERS AND SISTERS. FIGHTING. MICE.

278   **Udry, Janice May.** *A Tree Is Nice.* **Illus. by Marc Simont. Harper & Row, 1956. ISBN 0-06-443147-9**

Gives reasons why. Read for Arbor Day and plant seedlings for all to take home. Children can also draw pictures of their favorite trees and identify the types with the help of George Ella Lyon's handsome tree alphabet book, *A B Cedar.* For a

155

gardening unit, use with Janina Domanska's folktale *The Turnip*, Lois Ehlert's *Planting Vegetable Soup*, Ruth Krauss's *The Carrot Seed*, and Bruce McMillan's *Growing Colors*. CALDECOTT MEDAL. NATURE. SEASONS. TREES.

279   **Udry, Janice May. *What Mary Jo Shared*. Illus. by Eleanor Mill. Albert Whitman, 1966. ISBN 0-590-40731-7**

A shy little girl thinks of the perfect thing to share for show-and-tell: her own father. Children can share stories about their fathers. Also see David McPhail's *Emma's Pet*. AFRICAN AMERICANS. FATHERS AND DAUGHTERS. SCHOOLS. SELF-CONCEPT.

280   **Ueno, Noriko. *Elephant Buttons*. Illus. by the author. Harper & Row, 1973. ISBN 0-06-026161-7**

Out from beneath the buttons on the elephant's belly springs a buttoned horse who begets a lion, then a seal, monkey, duck, and mouse. Black and white and wordless, with an absurd surprise ending that should tickle watchers who have been predicting each new animal along the way. Do a simple creative dramatics sound-effects exercise where children "unbutton" and pop out as each of the animals you summon. ANIMALS. CREATIVE DRAMA. STORIES WITHOUT WORDS.

281   **Ungerer, Tomi. *One, Two, Where's My Shoe?* Illus. by the author. Harper & Row, 1964.**

On each page of this practically wordless book, children must examine the illustration to find the disguised shoe, boot, loafer, or pump cleverly but blatantly hidden within. Instead of allowing children to point, have them verbally describe how and where each shoe is incorporated into the picture to reinforce vocabulary and directional concepts. Then trace and cut out construction paper shoes and draw new hidden-shoes pictures in the same vein. Other lasting titles include Beverly Cleary's *The Growing-Up Feet*, Niki Daly's *Not So Fast, Songololo*, Shirley Hughes's *Alfie's Feet*, and Elizabeth Winthrop's *Shoes*. SHOES. VISUAL PERCEPTION.

282   **Van Laan, Nancy. *The Big Fat Worm*. Illus. by Marisabina Russo. Knopf, 1987. ISBN 0-394-88763-8**

Eye-catching cyclical story of a worm and a hungry bird, cat, and dog, told in rhythm, with a refrain your audience will pick up quickly. Act this one out several times using puppets for each animal. ANIMALS. BIRDS. CREATIVE DRAMA. STORIES TO TELL. WORMS.

283   **Vipont, Elfrida. *The Elephant & the Bad Baby*. Illus. by Raymond Briggs. Putnam, 1986. ISBN 0-698-20039-X**

In which the bad baby learns to say please, after the Elephant takes an ice cream, a pie, a bun, some gingersnaps, and more. Originally published by Coward in 1969, this whimsical nonsense cumulative story is made for telling and creative drama, with its chant-along refrain. BABIES. CREATIVE DRAMA. ELEPHANTS. STORIES TO TELL.

284   **Wade, Barrie. *Little Monster*. Illus. by Katinka Kew. Lothrop, 1990. ISBN 0-688-09597-6**

Tired of being the perfect child, Mandy misbehaves for one whole day, but finds her mother still loves her, even when she's naughty. Mem Fox's *Koala Lou* finds her mom loves her even when she doesn't win a game. BEHAVIOR. LOVE.

285   **Wells, Rosemary.** *Good Night, Fred.* **Illus. by the author. Dial, 1981. ISBN 0-8037-0059-8**

A little boy's Grandma pops out of the telephone to keep him company late one night. Bring in an old telephone or two so children can have pretend conversations with grandparents and each other.   BEDTIME STORIES. GRANDMOTHERS. TELEPHONE.

286   **Wells, Rosemary.** *Max's Chocolate Chicken.* **Illus. by the author. Dial, 1989. ISBN 0-8037-0585-9**

Even though he hasn't made an effort to find a single Easter egg, unlike efficient sister Ruby, Max takes the chocolate chicken prize from the birdbath and eats it all. Compare the Easter Bunny character with the ones in DuBose Heyward's *The Country Bunny and the Little Gold Shoes* and Priscilla and Otto Friedrich's *The Easter Bunny That Overslept.*   BROTHERS AND SISTERS. CANDY. EASTER. PICTURE BOOKS FOR ALL AGES. RABBITS.

287   **Wells, Rosemary.** *Max's Christmas.* **Illus. by the author. Dial, 1986. ISBN 0-8037-0289-2**

In spite of know-it-all sister Ruby's warning not to, rabbit Max peeks when Santa comes. Side-splitting in its simplicity, especially the use of who, what, where, why, and when. Adorable for all ages, especially as a "5 W's" lesson for upper-grade students. For Santa skeptics, follow up with Lorna Balian's *Bah! Humbug?* and Carolyn Haywood's *A Christmas Fantasy.*   CHRISTMAS. PICTURE BOOKS FOR ALL AGES. RABBITS. SANTA CLAUS.

288   **Wells, Rosemary.** *Peabody.* **Illus. by the author. Dial, 1973. ISBN 0-8037-0005-9**

Peabody, Annie's new bear, goes everywhere with her—skiing, to the beach, to tea parties—until his first birthday, when talking doll Rita takes his place. Bring in your stuffed bears to listen for a day of once-rejected teddy stories such as Barbara Douglass's *Good As New,* Don Freeman's *Corduroy,* and Richard Galbraith's *Reuben Runs Away.* Owners can supply the bears' voices to tell their adventures.   DOLLS. TEDDY BEARS.

289   **West, Colin.** *The King of Kennelwick Castle.* **Illus. by the author. Harper & Row, 1987. ISBN 0-397-32197-X**

A cumulative chant (à la *The House That Jack Built*—try the Janet Stevens version) that comes full circle from the boy who carries a birthday bundle, to the king who receives it. A treasure to be chanted over and over, along with Arnold Lobel's *The Rose in My Garden,* Verna Aardema's *Bringing the Rain to Kapiti Plain,* and Rose Robart's *The Cake That Mack Ate.*   BIRTHDAYS. CHANTABLE REFRAIN. CUMULATIVE STORIES. KINGS AND RULERS.

290   **Westcott, Nadine Bernard.** *The Lady with the Alligator Purse.* **Illus. by the author. Little, Brown, 1988. ISBN 0-316-93135-7**

A chantable, frenetic, revised version of the nonsense rhyme "Tiny Tim." Instead of dying with a bubble in his throat, this tot ends up with a pizza. Compare this one with the title poem in Jill Bennett's *Tiny Tim: Verses for Children.*   CHANTABLE REFRAIN. NONSENSE VERSES. STORIES IN RHYME.

291   **Westcott, Nadine Bernard.** *Peanut Butter and Jelly: A Play Rhyme.* **Illus. by the author. Dutton, 1987. ISBN 0-525-44317-7**

An illustrated chant of the real way to make a PB&J sandwich, including mashing the peanuts and squashing the grapes. Includes directions for hand and body actions. Bring in the works for a snack, and also read Bruce Degen's *Jamberry*, Russell Hoban's *Bread and Jam for Frances*, and Robert McCloskey's *Blueberries for Sal*. Grades 1–2 will also love doing this, along with titles like John Vernon Lord's *The Giant Jam Sandwich*, Margaret Mahy's *Jam: A True Story*, and then, if you're still starved, sing Tom Glazer's *On Top of Spaghetti*. CHANTABLE REFRAIN. ELEPHANTS. FINGERPLAYS. FOOD.

292   **Westcott, Nadine Bernard.** *Skip to My Lou.* **Illus. by the author. Little, Brown, 1989. ISBN 0-316-93137-3**

Left to care for the farm till two o'clock, a young boy has a mess of a time, what with all the flies in the sugarbowl—shoo fly shoo—, cats in the buttermilk, and pigs in the parlor. You'll want to join in with the joyous singing farm animals and pantomime their frantic actions to clean up in time. More farm-set-sing-alongs include Kathy Parkinson's or Mary Maki Rae's *The Farmer in the Dell* and Tracy Campbell Pearson's *Old MacDonald Had a Farm*. CREATIVE DRAMA. DOMESTIC ANIMALS. FARM LIFE. SONGS. STORIES IN RHYME.

293   **Whitney, Alma Marshak.** *Just Awful.* **Illus. by Lillian Hoban. Harper & Row, 1985. ISBN 0-201-08625-5**

When he cuts his finger, James is afraid to go to the school nurse for fear of what she might do, in this reprint of the 1971 edition. Perhaps your school nurse would read this story aloud for you, and then give a tour of her office to allay apprehensions. FEAR. SCHOOLS.

294   **Whitney, Alma Marshak.** *Leave Herbert Alone.* **Illus. by David McPhail. Addison-Wesley, 1972. ISBN 0-201-08623-9**

Jennifer wants the next door cat to like her. Good for pairs pantomime. On the same subject, see Barbara Samuels's *Duncan & Dolores*. CATS. CREATIVE DRAMA.

295   **Willard, Nancy.** *Papa's Panda.* **Illus. by Lillian Hoban. Harcourt, 1979. ISBN 0-15-259462-0**

On James's birthday, his father spins a yarn about what would happen if a live panda came to visit, culminating in a present of a stuffed panda. Meet another stuffed panda in Dick Gackenbach's *Poppy the Panda*. BIRTHDAYS. FATHERS AND SONS. PANDAS. STUFFED ANIMALS.

296   **Williams, Barbara.** *Albert's Toothache.* **Illus. by Kay Chorao. Dutton, 1974. ISBN 0-525-44363-0**

No one in his toothless turtle family believes him when he complains of a toothache and wants to stay in bed all day, though he's actually telling the truth. Check out other animal complaints in *Who's Sick Today?* by Lynne Cherry. More turtle stories include Frank Asch's *Turtle Tale* and Ellen MacGregor's *Theodore Turtle*. FAMILY LIFE. GRANDMOTHERS. SICK. TURTLES.

297   **Willoughby, Elaine.** *Boris and the Monsters.* **Illus. by Lynn Munsinger. Houghton Mifflin, 1980. ISBN 0-395-29067-8**

A little boy is afraid of the dark until he gets Ivan the Terrible, a puppy who needs protecting. Group with Eve Bunting's *Ghost Hour, Spook's Hour*, and other bedtime fears books like Eileen Christelow's *Henry and the Dragon*, Russell Hoban's *Bedtime for Frances*, or Tobi Tobias's *Chasing the Goblins Away*. BEDTIME STORIES. DOGS. FEAR. MONSTERS.

298   Winthrop, Elizabeth. *Bear and Mrs. Duck.* Illus. by Patience Brewster. Holiday House, 1988. ISBN 0-8234-0687-3

Nora's bear is chagrined when Mrs. Duck comes to sit for him while Nora goes to the store, but she wins him over with crayons, flying skills, hide-and-seek, and her kind attention. Comforting and anxiety-easing for children nervous about sitters or substitute teachers, along with Shirley Hughes's *An Evening at Alfie's* and Rosemary Wells's *Shy Charles.*   BABY-SITTERS. BEARS. DUCKS.

299   Winthrop, Elizabeth. *Maggie & the Monster.* Illus. by Tomie dePaola. Holiday House, 1987. ISBN 0-8234-0639-3

When a monster clomps into spunky Maggie's room each night, she's annoyed, not scared. A novel way to deal with nighttime fears: confront them head on. For other children undaunted by monsters, read Chris Demarest's *Morton and Sidney*, Dick Gackenbach's *Harry and the Terrible Whatzit*, Katharine Holabird's *Alexander and the Dragon*, Mercer Mayer's *There's a Nightmare in My Closet* and *There's Something in My Attic*, and Deborah Robison's *No Elephants Allowed.*   BEDTIME STORIES. FEAR. MONSTERS. NIGHT.

300   Winthrop, Elizabeth. *Shoes.* Illus. by William Joyce. Harper & Row, 1986. ISBN 0-06-026592-2

A simple, giggling rhyme about the uses of shoes for kids. A "soleful" companion to "The Journey" from Arnold Lobel's *Mouse Tales*, Beverly Cleary's *The Growing-Up Feet*, Shirley Hughes's *Alfie's Feet*, Niki Daly's *Not So Fast, Songololo*, and Tomi Ungerer's *One, Two, Where's My Shoe?*   FOOT. SHOES. STORIES IN RHYME.

301   Wood, Audrey. *The Napping House.* Illus. by Don Wood. Harcourt, 1984. ISBN 0-15-256708-9

On a rainy day, a granny, boy, dog, cat, and mouse snooze together on a cozy bed until a wakeful flea bites the mouse, starting a chain reaction that gets everyone up. A whimsical cumulative tale for children to chant in all weather. Sample some of Jack Prelutsky's wet poems from *Rainy Rainy Saturday.*   CUMULATIVE STORIES. RAIN AND RAINFALL. SLEEP. WEATHER.

302   Yektai, Niki. *Bears in Pairs.* Illus. by Diane de Groat. Bradbury, 1987. ISBN 0-02-793691-0

A profusion of irrepressible bears, four per page of rhyming couplets, all hurry to Mary's tea party. Listeners can fill in the last word of each rhyme using context clues for opposites, colors, and more. What a perfect time for an in-class teddy bear celebration! BEARS. COLOR. OPPOSITES. PARTIES. STORIES IN RHYME.

303   Yektai, Niki. *What's Missing?* Illus. by Susannah Ryan. Clarion, 1987. ISBN 0-89919-510-5

In every other illustration of a girl and her parents, something major—bicycle, clothes, house, bed—is missing, and viewers must identify it. Children can draw their own pictures with something missing for the rest of the class to guess. Turn this into a pantomime lesson; make picture cards of common items—ice cream cone, jump rope, fork, book, and so on—and hand them out. One at a time, children can pantomime using these objects. Each time the audience is correct, bring out the real object for the actor to demonstrate. CREATIVE DRAMA. VISUAL PERCEPTION.

304   **Yektai, Niki.** *What's Silly?* **Illus. by Susannah Ryan. Clarion, 1989. ISBN 0-89919-746-9**

Like *What's Missing?*, the audience must state what's wrong with every other picture, which often reverses the location of two common objects like bird's nest and lady's hat with incongruous results. Children can draw their own "silly" pictures for others to set right. VISUAL PERCEPTION.

305   **Zemach, Harve.** *Mommy, Buy Me a China Doll.* **Illus. by Margot Zemach. Follett, 1966. ISBN 0-374-35005-1**

Although the music is not appended, you can hear it in the Weston Woods filmstrip of this cumulative song about a little girl eager to move everyone on the farm from his bed in order to trade Daddy's feather bed for a much-coveted china doll. William also wants a doll in Charlotte Zolotow's stereotype-breaking *William's Doll*. BEDTIME STORIES. CUMULATIVE STORIES. DOLLS. FAMILY LIFE. SONGS.

306   **Ziefert, Harriet.** *Snow Magic.* **Illus. by Claire Schumacher. Viking, 1988. ISBN 0-670-82423-2**

When the year's first snow falls on the first day of winter, the snow people gather for a snow party. Read this on a snowy day when you can take your children outside to make miniature snow folk, or stay warm indoors and make nonmelting ones out of styrofoam balls and fabric. Read after Ezra Jack Keats's realistic *The Snowy Day* and Charlotte Zolotow's *Something Is Going to Happen*, and wax poetic with Jack Prelutsky's *It's Snowing! It's Snowing!* WINTER. SNOW.

307   **Zion, Gene.** *Harry by the Sea.* **Illus. by Margaret Bloy Graham. Harper & Row, 1965. ISBN 0-06-026855-7**

The family's pet dog causes an uproar at the beach when a sudden wave leaves him covered in seaweed and looking like a giant sea slug. Read with the others in the series, listed below, and with Ken Robbins's photo-realistic *Beach Days*. DOGS. LOST. SEASHORE.

308   **Zion, Gene.** *Harry the Dirty Dog.* **Illus. by Margaret Bloy Graham. Harper & Row, 1956. ISBN 0-06-026865-4**

He gets so dirty, even his own family doesn't recognize him. For another series about a small pup with personality, introduce Marjorie Flack's "Angus" books. BATHS. DOGS.

309   **Zion, Gene.** *No Roses for Harry.* **Illus. by Margaret Bloy Graham. Harper & Row, 1958. ISBN 0-06-026890-5**

Dog Harry hates his new sweater and sets out to lose it. Have an "I hate my clothes" day where everyone wears something he or she loathes and tells why. CLOTHING. DOGS.

310   **Zolotow, Charlotte.** *Mr. Rabbit and the Lovely Present.* **Illus. by Maurice Sendak. Harper & Row, 1962. ISBN 0-06-026945-6**

With the help of a Harvey-sized rabbit, a young girl puts together the perfect present for her mother: a basket of red apples, green pears, yellow bananas, and blue grapes. As you read about each fruit, place a piece of it in a bowl or basket; afterward, make fruit salad. Other color-themed titles include Bruce McMillan's *Growing Colors*, Sheila White Samton's *Beside the Bay*, and Mary Serfozo's *Who Said Red?* More moms' birthday books include Marjorie Flack's *Ask Mr. Bear* and George

Shannon's *The Surprise*. Finally, take a taste of Lois Ehlert's *Eating the Alphabet*. COLOR. FRUIT. GIFTS. MOTHERS AND DAUGHTERS. RABBITS.

311   **Zolotow, Charlotte.** *Something Is Going to Happen.* **Illus. by Catherine Stock. Harper & Row, 1988. ISBN 0-06-027028-4**

The members of a family—mother, father, two children and dog—awake one cold November Monday with an inexplicable feeling of anticipation; opening the front door, they find it's snowing. More snowy day tales include Virginia Lee Burton's *Katy and the Big Snow*, Ezra Jack Keats's *The Snowy Day* (of course), Florence Slobodkin's *Too Many Mittens*, and Harriet Ziefert's *Snow Magic*. Stay in the mood with Jack Prelutsky's poems in *It's Snowing! It's Snowing!* FAMILY LIFE. SNOW. WINTER.

312   **Zolotow, Charlotte.** *William's Doll.* **Illus. by William Pène du Bois. Harper & Row, 1972. ISBN 0-06-027047-0**

A boy wants his own baby doll, much to his father's chagrin. This contains tiny illustrations (so sit close), and a message not to be missed: that a boy can be nurturing without being considered a "sissy." DOLLS. FATHERS AND SONS.

Illustration from IT WASN'T MY FAULT by Helen Lester, illustrated by Lynn Munsinger. Text copyright © 1985 by Helen Lester. Illustrations copyright © 1985 by Lynn Munsinger. Reprinted by permission of Houghton Mifflin Company.

FICTION FOR KINDERGARTEN – GRADE 1

313 Adler, David A. *My Dog and the Birthday Mystery*. Illus. by Dick Gackenbach. Holiday House, 1987. ISBN 0-8234-0632-6

On her birthday, Jenny and her big mystery-solving mutt My Dog search for clues when Ken reports a missing bicycle, and end up at a surprise party. An introduction to the mystery genre with obvious clues and cheerful illustrations, this is the first of a series. BIRTHDAYS. DOGS. MYSTERY AND DETECTIVE STORIES.

314 Ahlberg, Janet, and Allan Ahlberg. *Funnybones*. Illus. by the authors. Greenwillow, 1980. ISBN 0-688-84238-0

One dark, dark night, a big and a little skeleton take their dog skeleton for a walk through town and look for someone to frighten. Starting out like Ruth Brown's *A Dark Dark Tale*, and including a bit of the song "Dem Bones" to chant and pantomime, this is ready-made for Halloween and other chillingly funny times. BONES. HALLOWEEN.

315 Alexander, Martha. *Move Over, Twerp*. Illus. by the author. Dial, 1989. ISBN 0-8037-6139-2

Now that Jeffrey is old enough to take the school bus, he has to figure out a way to keep the big kids from taking over his seat every day. His simple, witty solution should encourage a problem-solving discussion of how to deal with similar situations as demonstrated in Carol Chapman's *Herbie's Troubles* and Hans Wilhelm's *Tyrone the Horrible*. BULLIES. BUSES. SCHOOLS.

316 Allard, Harry. *I Will Not Go to Market Today*. Illus. by James Marshall. Dial, 1981. ISBN 0-8037-4178-2

Fenimore B. Buttercrunch, a rooster with bad luck, keeps getting delayed en route to the store. With editing, a nifty pantomime. Tie in to Denys Cazet's *Lucky Me*, where the chicken has better fortune. CHICKENS. CREATIVE DRAMA. LUCK. SHOPPING.

317 Allard, Harry. *It's So Nice to Have a Wolf around the House*. Illus. by James Marshall. Houghton Mifflin, 1978.

Cuthbert Q. Devine proves that even a wolf with a wicked past can reform. Use this, Keiko Kasza's *The Wolf's Chicken Stew*, and Betsy Maestro's *Lambs for Dinner* to deal with the evils of wolf stereotyping. WOLVES.

318   **Allard, Harry.** *The Stupids Die.* **Illus. by James Marshall. Houghton Mifflin, 1981. ISBN 0-395-30347-8**

Wacky family gets confused when the lights go out, and concludes they have died. In *The Stupids Have a Ball* (1978), they throw a costume party, and in *The Stupids Step Out* (1978), they go visiting. Students can make up new "Stupid" stories and design new rooms for the household. For aghast parents who don't approve of calling anything "stupid," here is one way for them to allow their children a healthy way to circumvent the rule without harming anyone, as the Stupids fit their name to a "T." Other lamebrains can be found in Joanna and Philip Cole's *Big Goof and Little Goof*, Anne Rose's *The Triumphs of Fuzzy Fogtop*, and Larry Weinberg's *The Forgetful Bears Meet Mr. Memory.*   FAMILY LIFE. PARTIES. SLAPSTICK.

319   **Allard, Harry.** *There's a Party at Mona's Tonight.* **Illus. by James Marshall. Doubleday, 1981.**

When Potter Pig is kicked out of Mona's party, he tries disguising himself as a statue, a bagpiper, and even Santa Claus to get in. Absurdly silly. Don Freeman's *Dandelion* has party trouble, too.   CLOTHING AND DRESS. COSTUMES. PARTIES. PIGS.

320   **Allen, Jeffrey.** *Mary Alice, Operator Number Nine.* **Illus. by James Marshall. Little, Brown, 1975. ISBN 0-316-03425-8**

"At the sound of the tone, the time will be eight-fifteen and ten seconds exactly. Quack!" When this efficient duck gets sick, it's impossible to find a competent replacement. Use to introduce the concept of telling time along with the sequel *Mary Alice Returns* (1986), Eric Carle's *The Grouchy Ladybug*, and Pat Hutchins's *Clocks and More Clocks.*   DUCKS. TELEPHONE. TIME.

321   **Allen, Marjorie N.** *One, Two, Three—Ah-Choo!* **Illus. by Dick Gackenbach. Coward, 1980.**

An allergic boy who needs a furless, featherless pet gets a hermit crab. It's the father who's allergic in Barbara Ann Porte's *Harry's Dog.*   ALLERGIES. PETS.

322   **Andersen, Hans Christian.** *The Princess and the Pea.* **Illus. by Paul Galdone. Houghton Mifflin, 1979. ISBN 0-395-28807-X**

Even 20 mattresses can't lie in the way of a true princess. A classic literary folktale. PRINCES AND PRINCESSES–FOLKLORE.

323   **Aylesworth, Jim.** *Hush Up!* **Illus. by Glen Rounds. Holt, 1980.**

When the biggest, nastiest, meanest horsefly you ever saw bites old Jasper's horse, it sets off a chain reaction that wakes all the animals. A cyclical tale, fun for tellers, that ends as it started and would mesh well with Verna Aardema's *Why Mosquitoes Buzz in People's Ears*, Byron Barton's *Buzz Buzz Buzz*, or Joanne Oppenheimer's *You Can't Catch Me.*   DOMESTIC ANIMALS. CAUSE AND EFFECT. INSECTS. STORIES TO TELL.

324   **Baer, Edith.** *Words Are Like Faces.* **Illus. by Karen Gundersheimer. Pantheon, 1980.**

A tiny-sized book of a lovely poem about words and what they do for us. Children can decide on and illustrate their own favorite words.   STORIES IN RHYME. VOCABULARY.

325   **Baker, Alan.** *Benjamin's Book.* **Illus. by the author. Lothrop, 1982.**

A hamster tries unsuccessfully to remove his paw print from a blank book page. Use this as an effortless way to introduce proper book care. BOOKS AND READING. HAMSTERS.

326   **Baker, Alan.** *Benjamin's Portrait.* **Illus. by the author. Lothrop, 1987. ISBN 0-688-06878-2**

It can't be that hard to do a self-portrait, can it? Hamster sketches and then paints himself on canvas, with amusing and messy results. Simple, charming life-sized illustrations will inspire your artists to try their own hands at paint or crayons. (Supply them with mirrors.) As a grand finale, have them snap each other's photos. Also use with Cynthia Rylant's *All I See* and Paul O. Zelinsky's *The Lion and the Stoat* to discuss the role of an illustrator. ARTISTS. HAMSTERS. PAINTINGS.

327   **Balian, Lorna.** *The Aminal.* **Illus. by the author. Abingdon, 1972. ISBN 0-687-37101-5**

Patrick finds a round, green, blinky-eyed, pricky-toenailed, waggy-tailed creature which, as his friends describe it to each other, grows in their imaginations. Follow up with either Wanda Gag's *The Funny Thing* about a "real" fantasy animal, or some more turtle stories, such as Frank Asch's *Turtle Tale,* Ellen MacGregor's *Theodore Turtle,* and Barbara Williams's *Albert's Toothache.* IMAGINATION. TURTLES.

328   **Balian, Lorna.** *Bah! Humbug?* **Illus. by the author. Abingdon, 1977. ISBN 0-687-37107-4**

Santa is real!? Faithful little girl and her skeptical brother find out when they set a trap in the living room. Also see Rosemary Wells's *Max's Christmas.* BROTHERS AND SISTERS. CHRISTMAS. SANTA CLAUS.

329   **Balian, Lorna.** *The Sweet Touch.* **Illus. by the author. Abingdon, 1976. ISBN 0-687-40774-5**

Tiny Genie's spell causes everything Peggy touches to turn into candy. Have your listeners try saying the alphabet backward to complete the spell. CANDY. GENIES. MAGIC.

330   **Barrett, Judi.** *Benjamin's 365 Birthdays.* **Illus. by Ron Barrett. Macmillan, 1978. ISBN 0-689-70443-7**

Bear finds a way to get gifts all year long by wrapping up everything he owns, including his house. Prepare a surprise: Wrap this book, put it in a box, wrap the box, put it in a bigger box with plenty of ribbons and bows so the children can open it, one box at a time, and guess what's inside. The message you can pass on is, "There's no present I can give you that's better than a good book!" BEARS. BIRTHDAYS. GIFTS.

331   **Barton, Byron.** *Applebet Story.* **Illus. by the author. Viking, 1973.**

In this alphabet sequence story, children can guess the word that goes with each letter and then tell the story with great elaboration. Hand out apple chunks afterward and follow up with Susan Hoguet's *I Unpacked My Grandmother's Trunk,* Arnold Lobel's *On Market Street,* and Suse MacDonald's *Alphabatics.* ALPHABET BOOKS. FRUIT.

332   **Bate, Lucy.** *Little Rabbit's Loose Tooth.* **Illus. by Diane de Groat. Crown, 1975. ISBN 0-517-52240-3**

It falls out, finally, in a dish of chocolate ice cream. Also try Marc Brown's *Arthur's Tooth,* Nancy Evans Cooney's *The Wobbly Tooth,* Lillian Hoban's *Arthur's Loose Tooth,* and Nurit Karlin's *The Tooth Witch.* RABBITS. TEETH.

333   **Bauer, Caroline Feller.** *Too Many Books!* **Illus. by Diane Paterson. Viking, 1986. ISBN 0-670-81130-0**

One girl's passion inspires the town when her house becomes so book-crammed that she starts giving away volumes. A simple but effective reading motivator for Book Week or any old time; you may want to use this to kick off a used-paperback book swap. BOOKS AND READING.

334   **Bayer, Jane.** *A My Name Is Alice.* **Illus. by Steven Kellogg. Dial, 1984. ISBN 0-8037-0124-1**

Another amusing alphabet book based on the bouncing ball chant from childhood. Children can make up new verses based on their own names and bounce balls as they recite them. Companion alphabet books include Suse MacDonald's *Alphabatics,* Maurice Sendak's *Alligators All Around,* and Sandra Boynton's *A Is for Angry.* An imaginary creature variant is *Zoophabets* by Robert Tallon. ALLITERATION. ALPHABET BOOKS.

335   **Bemelmans, Ludwig.** *Madeline's Rescue.* **Illus. by the author. Viking, 1953. ISBN 0-670-44716-1**

When a dog saves her from drowning in the Seine, Madeline and the 11 other convent school little girls take it back to their dormitory as a pet. Second in the classic rhymed series, the first being *Madeline* (1939), where she gets appendicitis and needs an operation; this one provides a splendid tour of Paris. CALDECOTT MEDAL. DOGS. SCHOOLS. STORIES IN RHYME.

336   **Beskow, Elsa.** *Pelle's New Suit.* **Illus. by the author. Harper & Row, 1929. ISBN 0-06-020496-6**

Swedish story of a boy whose enterprising ways earn him new wool clothes made step by step, starting with the sheep. Also see Tomie dePaola's *Charlie Needs a Cloak* and Harriet Ziefert's *A New Coat for Anna.* CLOTHING AND DRESS. SHEEP.

337   **Blundell, Tony.** *Joe on Sunday.* **Illus. by the author. Dial, 1987. ISBN 0-8037-0446-1**

On each successive day of the week, Joe becomes a piggy, lion, mouse, monkey, monster, king, and himself again. Along with a chantable refrain from Joe's mom, this jovial romp is a sure bet for narrative pantomime and, along with Lorna Balian's *Amelia's Nine Lives,* for reviewing the days of the week. BEHAVIOR. DAYS OF THE WEEK.

338   **Bond, Felicia.** *Poinsettia and the Firefighters.* **Illus. by the author. Harper & Row, 1984. ISBN 0-690-04401-1**

Spending her first night alone in her new attic room, a young piglet is terrified by all the noises she hears until she spots a real fire outside her window. For another dreamy example of night-watching, see Ezra Jack Keats's *Dreams.* BEDTIME STORIES. FEAR. FIRE. NIGHT. PIGS.

339   **Bottner, Barbara.** *Messy.* **Illus. by the author. Delacorte, 1979. ISBN 0-440-05492-3**

Sloppy girl tries to reform. Read this at the end of the day to inspire your own messy crew to clean up the room in a jiffy. HYGIENE.

340   **Boyd, Selma, and Pauline Boyd.** *I Met a Polar Bear.* **Illus. by Patience Brewster. Lothrop, 1983.**

Late for school again, the bespectacled narrator explains to his teacher how he took time on his way to help a polar bear, an earthworm, an ant, and a pony. Pair with

Franz Brandenberg's *No School Today*, where the cats get there *too* early. EXAGGER-ATION. IMAGINATION. SCHOOLS.

341   Boynton, Sandra. *A Is for Angry: An Animal and Adjective Alphabet*. Illus. by the author. Workman, 1987. ISBN 0-89480-507-X

Each large bright alphabet letter interacts with a corresponding animal; cover up each adjective so listeners can guess it. Fun for narrative pantomime, where students act out each adjective. One step up from Suse MacDonald's *Alphabatics*, and a fit companion to Maurice Sendak's *Alligators All Around* and Jane Bayer's *A My Name Is Alice*. ALPHABET BOOKS. CREATIVE DRAMA. ENGLISH LANGUAGE–GRAMMAR.

342   Brandenberg, Franz. *No School Today*. Illus. by Aliki. Macmillan, 1975.

When a cat brother and sister leave home an hour early and get to school first, they jump to conclusions. Moving from early to late, read Selma and Pauline Boyd's *I Met a Polar Bear*. CATS. SCHOOLS.

343   Brenner, Barbara. *Mr. Tall and Mr. Small*. Illus. by Tomi Ungerer. Young Scott, 1966.

What's better—tall or small? A giraffe and his mouse friend can't agree until a forest fire brings out their best qualities. Other titles emphasizing the value of small and large include Brian Wildsmith's *The Lion and the Rat* and Bill Peet's *The Ant and the Elephant*, while Leo Lionni's *It's Mine* shows frogs learning the value of working together when a flood threatens. FIRE. GIRAFFES. MICE. SIZE. STORIES IN RHYME.

344   Brown, Marc. *Arthur's Baby*. Illus. by the author. Little, Brown, 1987. ISBN 0-316-11123-6

Arthur, who doesn't know beans about babies, and sister D. W. the know-it-all, get a new sister, Kate. Ask everyone to bring in their baby pictures for a "Who am I?" bulletin board. For another apprehensive sibling, see also Judith Caseley's *Silly Baby*. BABIES. BROTHERS AND SISTERS.

345   Brown, Marc. *Arthur's Eyes*. Illus. by the author. Little, Brown, 1979. ISBN 0-316-11063-9

Embarrassed by his new glasses, aardvark Arthur tries to lose them. Peter and Archie are thrilled with the specs they find in *Goggles!* by Ezra Jack Keats. Raffi's song "The Corner Grocery Store" would be fun here. EYEGLASSES.

346   Brown, Margaret Wise. *The Steamroller*. Illus. by Evaline Ness. Walker, 1974.

Daisy's unique Christmas present runs amok and squashes everything and everybody flat. Great to act out, with children all playing the steamrollers. CHRISTMAS. CREATIVE DRAMA. MACHINES.

347   Brown, Ruth. *A Dark, Dark Tale*. Illus. by the author. Dial, 1981. ISBN 0-8037-1673-7

A cat's variant of the old chant "In a dark dark woods," this time ending not with a ghost, but a frightened mouse in the box. Children can chant each line after you, and then retell the story in sequence in suitably chilling voices. See also Janet and Allan Ahlberg's *Funnybones* for another version of the chant. CATS. CHANTABLE REFRAIN. STORIES TO TELL.

348   Brown, Ruth. *If at First You Do Not See*. Illus. by the author. Henry Holt, 1983. ISBN 0-8050-1053-X

A caterpillar sets out on an eating journey around each double-page spread. Similar to Ann Jonas's *Round Trip* and *Reflections*, each remarkable illustration turns into something else when turned upside down. For another real eye-opener, see Beau

Gardner's *The Look Again ... and Again, and Again, and Again Book* and *The Turn About, Think About, Look About Book*. BUTTERFLIES. CATERPILLARS. FOOD. ILLUSTRATION OF BOOKS. VISUAL PERCEPTION.

349   **Browne, Anthony.** *Gorilla.* **Illus. by the author. Knopf, 1985. ISBN 0-394-97525-1**

On Hannah's birthday, her busy father gives her a toy gorilla that turns real and takes her on the town. Now's the time to round up all those good simian stories to try in tandem, for example, Browne's *Willy the Wimp*, Al Perkins's *Hand, Hand, Fingers, Thumb*, Esphyr Slobodkina's *Caps for Sale*, and Giulio Maestro's *A Wise Monkey Tale* for starters. Or focus on bedtime travels with Phyllis Root's *Moon Tiger* and Joanne Ryder's *The Night Flight*. BEDTIME STORIES. FATHERS AND DAUGHTERS. GORILLAS.

350   **Browne, Anthony.** *Willy the Wimp.* **Illus. by the author. Knopf, 1985. ISBN 0-394-97061-6**

Exercises, jogging, a special banana diet, aerobics classes, and body building turn Willy from scrawny weakling chimp to a hero. See also Robert Kraus's *Noel the Coward* and read both before gym class. BULLIES. CHIMPANZEES.

351   **Bunting, Eve.** *Ghost's Hour, Spook's Hour.* **Illus. by Donald Carrick. Clarion, 1987. ISBN 0-89919-484-2**

At midnight, with the wind blowing and the power knocked out, Jake and his dog Biff are scared silly until his parents calm him down. Good interactive sound effects are scattered throughout. Also read Helena Clare Pittman's *Once When I Was Scared*, Mary Stolz's *Storm in the Night*, and Elaine Willoughby's *Boris and the Monsters*. DOGS. FEAR. NIGHT.

352   **Bunting, Eve.** *Scary, Scary Halloween.* **Illus. by Jan Brett. Clarion, 1986. ISBN 0-89919-414-1**

Large spooky illustrations show trick or treaters in their ghoulish disguises, witnessed in rhyme by a cat and her kittens. Students will want to intone the tag word —"Halloween"—at the end of each page. For another cat loose on Halloween eve, read Natalie Savage Carlson's *Spooky Night*. CATS. HALLOWEEN. STORIES IN RHYME.

353   **Bunting, Eve.** *The Valentine Bears.* **Illus. by Jan Brett. Clarion, 1984. ISBN 0-89919-138-X**

Mrs. Bear sets her alarm clock for February 14 so she and Mr. Bear can share their first Valentine's Day ever. For more hearts and flowers, see Nancy L. Carlson's *Louanne Pig in the Mysterious Valentine*, Lillian Hoban's *Arthur's Great Big Valentine*, Frank Modell's *One Zillion Valentines*, Jack Prelutsky's original poetry in *It's Valentine's Day*, Marjorie Weinman Sharmat's *The Best Valentine in the World*, and James Stevenson's *Happy Valentine's Day, Emma*. BEARS. HIBERNATION. VALENTINE'S DAY.

354   **Bunting, Eve.** *The Wall.* **Illus. by Ronald Himler. Clarion, 1990. ISBN 0-395-51588-2**

The young narrator and his father search the wall of the Vietnam Veterans Memorial in Washington, D.C., to find the name of the boy's grandfather who was killed in the war long ago. Told from the child's point of view, this is a poignant, somber tribute to all who died, and a fine way to commemorate Memorial Day. FATHERS AND SONS. MONUMENTS. PICTURE BOOKS FOR ALL AGES. WASHINGTON, D.C.

355   Burningham, John. *Would You Rather . . . .* Illus. by the author. Crowell, 1978. ISBN 0-690-03917-4

In this hilarious big book of unsavory choices, five per double-page spread, listeners must decide which choices they would make and give reasons. Let children compile their own additional circumstances. IMAGINATION.

356   Caple, Kathy. *The Biggest Nose.* Illus. by the author. Houghton Mifflin, 1985. ISBN 0-395-36894-4

Elephant Eleanor is so embarrassed at having the biggest nose in her school, she ties it in a knot. A compassionate, amusing vignette guaranteed to start kids thinking about the way they treat others and how to overcome teasing. ELEPHANTS. NOSES. SELF-CONCEPT.

357   Carlson, Natalie Savage. *Spooky Night.* Illus. by Andrew Glass. Lothrop, 1982. ISBN 0-688-00935-2

Spooky, a black, pussyfooting witch's cat, must capture the moon on Halloween before he is allowed to go back to his human family. Get in the late night mood with Eve Bunting's cats in *Scary, Scary Halloween.* CATS. HALLOWEEN. MOON. WITCHES.

358   Carrick, Carol. *Patrick's Dinosaurs.* Illus. by Donald Carrick. Clarion, 1983. ISBN 0-89919-189-4

As his big brother tries to impress him with his knowledge of dinosaurs, Patrick imagines each one life-sized before him. Use this to fan children's frenzies for nonfiction dinosaur books, along with the sequel *What Happened to Patrick's Dinosaurs?*, Henry Schwartz's *How I Captured a Dinosaur*, Steven Kellogg's *Prehistoric Pinkerton*, and Jane Thayer's *Quiet on Account of Dinosaur.* BROTHERS. DINOSAURS. IMAGINATION.

359   Cazet, Denys. *December 24th.* Illus. by the author. Bradbury, 1986. ISBN 0-02-717950-8

It's Grandpa's day-before-Christmas birthday and grand-rabbits Emily and Louie watch him change costumes as he tries to guess the holiday coming up. A good giggly one for reviewing some major holidays. BIRTHDAYS. CHRISTMAS. GRANDFATHERS. HOLIDAYS. RABBITS.

360   Cazet, Denys. *Lucky Me.* Illus. by the author. Bradbury, 1983. ISBN 0-02-717870-6

Cumulative tale of a chicken being followed by a fox and other animals, all looking for a free meal. Clever to act out with improvised dialogue. Contrast with the unlucky rooster in *I Will Not Go to Market Today* by Harry Allard and the dumb cluck in James Marshall's *Wings: A Tale of Two Chickens*; then compare with pursued Roger in Edward Fenton's *The Big Yellow Balloon* and the unflappable chicken in *Rosie's Walk* by Pat Hutchins. CHICKENS. FOOD.

361   Chapman, Carol. *Herbie's Troubles.* Illus. by Kelly Oechsli. Dutton, 1981. ISBN 0-525-31645-0

Jimmy John, a class bully, only gets worse when Herbie tries being assertive, sharing, and punching back, as advised by three friends. His own solution—ignoring—works best. Compare this one with Martha Alexander's *Move Over, Twerp* and Hans Wilhelm's dinosaur bully in *Tyrone the Horrible.* BULLIES. SCHOOLS.

362   Christelow, Eileen. *Henry and the Red Stripes*. Illus. by the author. Clarion, 1982. ISBN 0-89919-118-5

Rabbit's hand-painted stripes save him from a hungry fox family. For more about Henry, also read *Henry and the Dragon*. FOXES. RABBITS.

363   Christelow, Eileen. *Jerome and the Witchcraft Kids*. Illus. by the author. Clarion, 1988. ISBN 0-89919-742-6

With Jerome Alligator pulling in more baby-sitting jobs after three weeks than his sister gets after three years, Winifred plans a haunted house Halloween baby-sitting surprise to humble him a bit in this sequel to *Jerome the Babysitter*. Duplicate the lunch menu with your own lizard's eyeball, dead worm, and vampire blood sandwiches. ALLIGATORS. BABY-SITTERS. HALLOWEEN.

364   Christelow, Eileen. *Jerome the Babysitter*. Illus. by the author. Clarion, 1985. ISBN 0-89919-331-5

At Jerome Alligator's first baby-sitting job, the 12 Gatorman kids leave him stranded on the roof. Compare with Natalie Savage Carlson's *Marie Louise's Heyday*, contrast with Mary Rayner's *Mr. and Mrs. Pig's Evening Out*, and listen to your children's own baby-sitting sagas. ALLIGATORS. BABY-SITTERS.

365   Christelow, Eileen. *Olive and the Magic Hat*. Illus. by the author. Clarion, 1987. ISBN 0-89919-513-X

After Olive and Otis Opossum accidentally knock their father's birthday present, a fancy dress hat, out the window, they must figure a way to retrieve it from Mr. Foxley who finds it. Speaking of splendid hats, don't miss John Dyke's *Pigwig* or Ezra Jack Keats's *Jennie's Hat*. BIRTHDAYS. CLOTHING AND DRESS. FOXES. HATS. OPOSSUMS.

366   Cleveland, David. *The April Rabbits*. Illus. by Nurit Karlin. Scholastic, 1988. ISBN 0-590-41288-4

The number of rabbits Robert spots corresponds to and increases with each April day. Hilarious for April Fools' Day and narrative pantomime with children being the rabbits. More "following" stories include Margaret Mahy's *The Boy Who Was Followed Home* and Marilyn Sadler's *Alistair's Elephant*. COUNTING BOOKS. RABBITS.

367   Cohen, Miriam. *Jim Meets the Thing*. Illus. by Lillian Hoban. Dell, 1989. ISBN 0-440-40149-6

Scared after seeing "The Thing" on television, a first-grader faces his fears. Good discussion starter. Over a week, read the four following "First Grade" series books by Cohen to compare their classroom experiences with yours. FEAR. SCHOOLS. TELEVISION.

368   Cohen, Miriam. *Jim's Dog Muffins*. Illus. by Lillian Hoban. Greenwillow, 1984. ISBN 0-688-02565-X

First-grader Jim takes time to grieve when his dog is run over. See also Holly Keller's *Goodbye, Max* and Judith Viorst's *The Tenth Good Thing about Barney*. DEATH. DOGS.

369   Cohen, Miriam. *Lost in the Museum*. Illus. by Lillian Hoban. Greenwillow, 1979. ISBN 0-688-80187-0

Jim and half of his first-grade classmates wander off at the Natural History Museum. Read before your next class trip! At the same museum, you'll also find that lovable teething Great Dane in Steven Kellogg's *Prehistoric Pinkerton*. LOST. MUSEUMS.

370 **Cohen, Miriam.** *No Good in Art*. **Illus. by Lillian Hoban. Greenwillow, 1980. ISBN 0-688-84234-8**

First-grader Jim lacks confidence in his drawing abilities. Break out the paints and have your budding artists paint what they'd like to be someday. DRAWING. SCHOOLS. SELF-CONCEPT.

371 **Cohen, Miriam.** *Starring First Grade*. **Illus. by Lillian Hoban. Greenwillow, 1985. ISBN 0-688-04030-6**

During the first-grade play of "The Three Billy Goats Gruff," Jim saves the day when the troll gets stage fright. Read this with the Galdone or Brown version of *The Three Billy Goats Gruff*, which your students can then act out. Other class plays raise the curtain in Joan Lowery Nixon's *Gloria Chipmunk, Star* and Joanne Oppenheim's *Mrs. Peloki's Class Play*. ACTING. PLAYS. SCHOOLS.

372 **Cole, Joanna.** *Golly Gump Swallowed a Fly*. **Illus. by Bari Weissman. Parents, 1982. ISBN 0-8193-1069-7**

A new prose variant of the song "I Know an Old Lady Who Swallowed a Fly" that's also fun to tell. Use with Nadine Bernard Westcott's book of the same song. ANIMALS. CUMULATIVE STORIES. STORIES TO TELL.

373 **Cole, Joanna, and Philip Cole.** *Big Goof and Little Goof*. **Illus. by M. K. Brown. Scholastic, 1989. ISBN 0-590-41591-3**

Two nitwit friends think their new pet turtle is a dog, go out to ice skate in the summer, and panic when they have a clothing mix-up, with Big Goof sure he is shrinking. This is the dippiest duo to come along since Harry Allard's "Stupids" family and Anne Rose's *The Triumphs of Fuzzy Fogtop*. FOOLS. FRIENDSHIP.

374 **Cooney, Nancy Evans.** *The Wobbly Tooth*. **Illus. by Marylin Hafner. Putnam, 1981. ISBN 0-399-20776-7**

Elizabeth's loose tooth refuses to come out. Also don't miss Lucy Bate's *Little Rabbit's Loose Tooth*, Nurit Karlin's *The Tooth Witch*, Marc Brown's *Arthur's Tooth*, and Lillian Hoban's *Arthur's Loose Tooth*. BASEBALL. TEETH.

375 **Craig, M. Jean.** *The Dragon in the Clock Box*. **Illus. by Kelly Oechsli. Norton, 1962.**

Joshua's imaginary dragon egg hatches. Hand out invisible dragon eggs for your children to incubate and have them write about and draw them. In Val Willis's *The Secret in the Matchbox*, the dragon isn't nearly so friendly. DRAGONS. EGGS. IMAGINATION.

376 **dePaola, Tomie.** *Charlie Needs a Cloak*. **Illus. by the author. Prentice Hall, 1973.**

This story details all the steps a shepherd boy takes to get a new cloak: shearing the sheep, washing, carding, spinning, dying and wearing the wool, and sewing the cloth, kept company all the while by an endearing and frisky pet sheep. Students will enjoy acting out the process. Also see Elsa Beskow's classic Swedish counterpart, *Pelle's New Suit*, and Harriet Ziefert's *A New Coat for Anna*. CLOTHING AND DRESS. CREATIVE DRAMA. SHEEP.

377 Duke, Kate. *Seven Froggies Went to School*. Illus. by the author. Dutton, 1985. ISBN 0-525-44160-3

Based on an old song the illustrator learned as a tadpole, this frolicking rhyme is a hopping good back-to-school read aloud and a bouncy call-and-response activity, giving listeners time to examine the illustrations and join in the merriment. CALL-AND-RESPONSE STORIES. FROGS. SONGS.

378 Duvoisin, Roger. *Petunia*. Illus. by the author. Knopf, 1989. ISBN 0-394-82589-6

Silly goose who can't read finds a book that she thinks will make her wise, and because of her arrogance, blows up the barnyard. This classic, originally published in 1950, effectively promotes the idea that knowing how to read is important. Also have a gander at *Petunia the Silly Goose Stories* (Knopf, 1987), an anthology of five well-loved stories about Petunia and her barnyard chums. BIRDS. BOOKS AND READING. GEESE.

379 Dyke, John. *Pigwig*. Illus. by the author. Methuen, 1978.

Acting with unrequited love for Matilda, a young pig sets out to make a hat grand enough to impress her. Children can design new ridiculous, outrageous hats for a silly hat parade inspired by this and other hat tales such as Laura Geringer's *A Three Hat Day* and Ezra Jack Keats's *Jennie's Hat*. For another love-besotted pig, read Keiko Kasza's *The Pigs' Picnic*. FARM LIFE. HATS. PIGS. ROBBERS AND OUTLAWS.

380 Eichenberg, Fritz. *Dancing in the Moon: Counting Rhymes*. Illus. by the author. Harcourt, 1975. ISBN 0-15-623811-X

Numbers one through twenty are represented poetically by a variety of cavorting animals, from the one raccoon of the title to twenty fishes juggling dishes in this partner to the alphabet book *Ape in a Cape*. Aside from composing new animals in rhyming positions, your math group can act out each number starting with one child—the dancing raccoon—and adding on until twenty are juggling; then go backward and subtract. Other rhyming animal books include Lynne Cherry's *Who's Sick Today?* and Raffi's song *Down by the Bay*. ANIMALS. COUNTING BOOKS. CREATIVE DRAMA. CREATIVE WRITING. STORIES IN RHYME.

381 Elkin, Benjamin. *The Loudest Noise in the World*. Illus. by James Daugherty. Viking, 1954.

The young prince of Hub-Bub wants to hear the loudest noise in the world. Follow up with a listening walk and then try Alan Benjamin's *Rat-a-Tat, Pitter Pat*, Suzy Kline's *SHHHH!* and Dr. Seuss's *Horton Hears a Who*. NOISE. PRINCES AND PRINCESSES.

382 Ellis, Anne. *Dabble Duck*. Illus. by Sue Truesdale. Harper & Row, 1984. ISBN 0-06-021818-5

City apartment living isn't lonely any more for Jason's pet duck when the family befriends and adopts Dabble, the stray little black dog they found in the park. A contrasting story where the two animals don't hit it off is Marjorie Flack's *Angus and the Ducks* (Doubleday, 1930). APARTMENT HOUSES. CITIES AND TOWNS. DOGS. DUCKS. FRIENDSHIP.

383 Ernst, Lisa Campbell. *When Bluebell Sang*. Illus. by the author. Bradbury, 1989. ISBN 0-02-733561-5

When the unscrupulous talent agent Big Eddie hears the dulcet tones of Swenson's lovely cow, Bluebell, he masterminds her career, booking her into concert halls and fairs coast to coast, heedless of her wishes. Unlike Susan Jeschke's *Perfect the Pig*, Bluebell devises her own scheme to get back to the farm. Stay in the mood with Victoria Forrester's tellable tale, *The Magnificent Moo*. COWS. MUSIC.

384 **Everitt, Betsy. *Frida the Wondercat*. Illus. by the author. Harcourt, 1990. ISBN 0-15-229540-2**

The beautiful ruffled collar Louise finds in a box on the doorstep not only fits her pet cat but changes Frida into an extraordinary creature, able to cook bean soup, dance a waltz, and even drive a bus. Encourage children to compose the sequel, describing newfound talents of the subsequent collar recipient, the dog next door. CATS. MAGIC.

385 **Fatio, Louise. *The Happy Lion*. Illus. by Roger Duvoisin. Scholastic, 1986. ISBN 0-590-41936-6**

A French zoo lion gets out for a stroll around town to say "bonjour" to his friends in this reprint of the 1954 edition. Other charming French animals include Eve Titus's cheese-tasting mouse *Anatole* and Tomi Ungerer's boa constrictor hero *Crictor*. Zut alors! You can throw in some basic French vocabulary just for fun, and end up with a tour of Paris in Ludwig Bemelmans's *Madeline's Rescue*. FRANCE. LIONS.

386 **Ferguson, Alane. *That New Pet!* Illus. by Catherine Stock. Lothrop, 1986. ISBN 0-688-05516-8**

Children will readily identify with Siam the cat's narration of pet jealousy over the new baby in the household. Another pet in a huff over sharing parental affection is the dog in Jenny Wagner's *John Brown, Rose and the Midnight Cat*. BABIES. CATS. FAMILY LIFE. JEALOUSY. PETS.

387 **Flack, Marjorie. *The Story about Ping*. Illus. by Kurt Wiese. Viking, 1933. ISBN 0-670-67223-8**

The classic about a Yangtze River duckling who hides to avoid a spank from the master of his boat. Halfway around the world, on the Charles River in Boston, meet Ping's American counterparts in Robert McCloskey's *Make Way for Ducklings*. BIRDS. BOATS AND BOATING. CHINA. DUCKS. RIVERS.

388 **Foreman, Michael. *Cat and Canary*. Illus. by the author. Dial, 1985. ISBN 0-8037-0137-3**

While their human master is at work, Cat and his friend Canary sneak up to the apartment building roof, where an entanglement with a kite sends Cat soaring through the New York City skyline, giving us a breathtaking aerial view. Next, read Susan Seligson and Howie Schneider's *Amos: The Story of an Old Dog and His Couch*. Start your children wondering what strange things their pets do when they are left home alone. BIRDS. CATS. FLIGHT. NEW YORK CITY.

389 **Fox, Mem. *Koala Lou*. Illus. by Pamela Lofts. Harcourt, 1989. ISBN 0-15-200502-1**

Longing to hear her busy mother tell her, "Koala Lou, I *do* love you!" the young marsupial prepares to compete in the gum tree climbing event at the Bush Olympics to ensure her mother's love. The message that parents love you even if you don't win is an important one, and parents reading this endearing Australian tale will be reminded of the value of a hug and a tender word. Continue your introduction to Australian wildlife with the wicked *Wombat Stew* by Marcia K. Vaughn, also illustrated by Pamela Lofts. ANIMALS. AUSTRALIA. KOALAS. LOVE. MOTHERS AND DAUGHTERS.

390   Frascino, Edward. *My Cousin the King.* **Illus. by the author. Prentice Hall, 1985.**

A barnyard cat, believing he is related to royalty, lets out the Travelling Circus lion, who repays him by terrorizing the countryside. Since the cat uses his shadow to scare the lion, this story would work well with Frank Asch's *Bear Shadow* and Ezra Jack Keats's *Dreams.* Both Cat and Lion get their comeuppance in Joseph Low's *Mice Twice.* CATS. DOMESTIC ANIMALS. LIONS. SHADOWS.

391   Freeman, Don. *Bearymore.* **Illus. by the author. Viking, 1976.**

A circus bear has trouble hibernating when he must think up a new act to keep his job. Other titles involving hibernation include Michele Lemieux's *What's That Noise?* and Joanne Ryder's *Chipmunk Song.* BEARS. CIRCUS. HIBERNATION.

392   Freeman, Don. *Dandelion.* **Illus. by the author. Viking, 1964. ISBN 0-670-15174-2**

An overly gussied-up lion is shut out of a party when the hostess doesn't recognize him. Also see Harry Allard's *There's a Party at Mona's Tonight* and Keiko Kasza's *The Pigs' Picnic,* all of which are good discussion starters on being yourself. LIONS. PARTIES.

393   Freeman, Don. *Hattie the Backstage Bat.* **Illus. by the author. Viking, 1988. ISBN 0-14-050893-7**

Thanks to a theater bat with a sense of timing, the new mystery play is a hit. Read a medley of Don Freeman's titles, making sure to include *Norman the Doorman* for a mouse who makes his mark in the museum world. BATS. PLAYS.

394   Friedrich, Priscilla, and Otto Friedrich. *The Easter Bunny That Overslept.* **Illus. by Adrienne Adams. Macmillan, 1987. ISBN 0-688-07038-8**

Attempting late deliveries on Mother's Day, the Fourth of July, and Halloween, the tardy rabbit finds no one wants eggs until he meets up with Santa. For a more efficient messenger, also read DuBose Heyward's *The Country Bunny and the Little Gold Shoes,* and just for laughs, Rosemary Wells's *Max's Chocolate Chicken.* EASTER. RABBITS. SANTA CLAUS.

395   Gackenbach, Dick. *Beauty, Brave and Beautiful.* **Illus. by the author. Clarion, 1990. ISBN 0-395-52000-2**

[1–2 sittings, 4 chapters, 48p.] To Jacob and his little sister Kate, the cross-eyed, sorry-looking little pup they befriend in the woods is beautiful, especially when she saves their lives defending them from a bear. That beauty is in the eye of the beholder is a fine lesson for children to learn. DOGS.

396   Gackenbach, Dick. *Dog for a Day.* **Illus. by the author. Clarion, 1987. ISBN 0-89919-452-4**

Sidney's new invention, a changing box, allows him to switch places with his dog for the day. Pair with Eileen Christelow's *Mr. Murphy's Marvelous Invention.* DOGS. INVENTIONS.

397   Gackenbach, Dick. *Harvey the Foolish Pig.* **Illus. by the author. Clarion, 1988. ISBN 0-89919-540-7**

Too short-sighted to recognize good luck when he sees it, a riches-seeking pig ends up a wolf's supper. Loosely based on an Armenian folktale. Other pigs who don't know what's good for them include Brock Cole's *Nothing But a Pig*, Arthur Getz's *Humphrey the Dancing Pig*, and Pauline Watson's *Wriggles the Little Wishing Pig*. LUCK. MONEY. PIGS.

398   **Gackenbach, Dick.** *Mag the Magnificent.* **Illus. by the author. Clarion, 1985. ISBN 0-89919-339-0**

On the day the young narrator wears his Indian suit, he draws a monster on his wall who comes to life and fulfills his fantasies. Ask your children what special tasks Mag might do for them and hand out drawing material for all to create their come-to-life creatures. More drawn pictures materialize in Susan Jeschke's *Angela and Bear* and David McPhail's *The Magical Drawings of Mooney B. Finch*. DRAWING. MAGIC. MONSTERS.

399   **Gage, Wilson.** *Cully Cully and the Bear.* **Illus. by James Stevenson. Greenwillow, 1983. ISBN 0-688-01769-X**

A confused old codger and an angry bear chase each other around and around a tree. This would make a hilarious pairs pantomime, although you'll need lots of space—outside perhaps—for each pair to run around its own imaginary tree. BEARS. CREATIVE DRAMA.

400   **Galbraith, Kathryn O.** *Waiting for Jennifer.* **Illus. by Irene Trivas. Macmillan, 1987. ISBN 0-689-50430-6**

How long six months takes while Nan and Thea wait for their new baby sister to be born! (Except it turns out to be a brother.) From anticipation to jealousy, Roslyn Banish's photo essay *Let Me Tell You about My Baby* also hits the spot. BABIES. SISTERS.

401   **Gammell, Stephen.** *Once upon MacDonald's Farm.* **Illus. by the author. Four Winds, 1985. ISBN 0-02-737210-3**

The befuddled farmer gets zoo animals for his farm and attempts to plow with an elephant and milk a lion. Try reading this brief understated spoof straight-faced, if you can. For all ages, though only the younger ones will need Tracey Campbell Pearson's *Old MacDonald Had a Farm* as a warm up. ANIMALS. FARM LIFE. PICTURE BOOKS FOR ALL AGES.

402   **Gantos, Jack.** *Rotten Ralph.* **Illus. by Nicole Rubel. Houghton Mifflin, 1976. ISBN 0-395-24276-2**

When Sara's red cat misbehaves one time too many, she leaves him at the circus to learn his lesson. Have students pantomime the cat's naughtiness as you read. First in a series. BEHAVIOR. CATS.

403   **Gardner, Beau.** *Have You Ever Seen . . . ? An ABC Book.* **Illus. by the author. Dodd, Mead, 1986. ISBN 0-396-08825-2**

Vibrant graphics make this odd inventive alphabet vibrate with whimsical combinations that ordinarily don't go together. Have you ever seen . . . an alligator with antlers?. . . a banana with buttons? Cover up the text and have your pre-readers guess it from each picture. Readers can create new captions and illustrations. One step up from Suse MacDonald's *Alphabatics*, this is on par with Fritz Eichenberg's *Ape in a Cape* and Eve Merriam's *Where Is Everybody? An Animal Alphabet*. ALPHABET BOOKS.

404   Gay, Michel. *The Christmas Wolf*. Illus. by the author. Greenwillow, 1983. ISBN 0-688-02291-X

Father Wolf disguises himself in a trench coat and shades to find his children Christmas presents in the local department store. Oinky's lack of manners give him away as well in Boris Zakhoder's *How a Pig Crashed the Christmas Party*. CHRIST-MAS. GIFTS. WOLVES.

405   Getz, Arthur. *Humphrey, the Dancing Pig*. Illus. by the author. Dial, 1980. ISBN 0-8037-4497-8

A jealous barnyard pig thins down like the cat, so the farmer assigns him the new job of mouser. Children of all ages love to pantomime the various dances Humphrey tries to make himself svelte. DANCING. FARM LIFE. PIGS.

406   Giff, Patricia Reilly. *Happy Birthday, Ronald Morgan!* Illus. by Susanna Natti. Viking, 1986. ISBN 0-670-80741-9

Since Ronald's birthday is Friday, and the last day of school is Thursday, he figures he'll miss out on a class celebration, never guessing there's a surprise party being planned for him. This is a first-person school story of strained and mended friendship with illustrations that aptly capture children's expressions and unspoken emotions. Introduce the other books in the "Ronald Morgan" series, including *Today Was a Terrible Day*. BIRTHDAYS. PARTIES. SCHOOLS.

407   Goodsell, Jane. *Toby's Toe*. Illus. by Gioia Fiammenghi. Morrow, 1986. ISBN 0-688-06162-1

Toby's stubbed toe sets off a chain of events that make everyone he encounters grumpy all day until he sets things right again. A sequence story in the same vein as Byron Barton's *Buzz, Buzz, Buzz* and Charlotte Zolotow's *The Quarreling Book*, full of sound effects, ripe for retelling and acting out. For a grand finale and treat, make popcorn balls. CAUSE AND EFFECT. CREATIVE DRAMA. SEQUENCE STORIES. SOUND EFFECTS.

408   Green, John F. *Alice and the Birthday Giant*. Illus. by Maryann Kovalski. Scholastic, 1989. ISBN 0-590-43428-4

On the morning of her birthday party, Alice can feel it will be an extraordinary day, but who could predict a messy, one-eyed giant sleeping in her bed? Librarians everywhere will breathe a sigh of relief when ace librarian Ms. McKracken researches the spell to send him back from whence he came. Adam's magical cat puts on an enchanted birthday show as well in *Abracatabby* by Catherine Hiller. BIRTHDAYS. GIANTS. LIBRARIES. MAGIC.

409   Green, Norma B. *The Hole in the Dike*. Illus. by Eric Carle. Crowell, 1974. ISBN 0-690-00676-4

Adapted from a chapter in Mary Mapes Dodge's *Hans Brinker* where a brave Dutch boy stopped up the leak with his finger, this never actually took place, but has become legendary nevertheless. William Steig's *Brave Irene* is another courageous fictional hero who ignores personal discomfort to help another. Ask for examples of real children who have performed selfless deeds. COURAGE.

410   Greenfield, Eloise. *Grandpa's Face*. Illus. by Floyd Cooper. Philomel, 1988. ISBN 0-399-21525-5

When Tamika sees her grandfather's usually loving, kind face turn cold and mean while he's practicing for a play, she becomes frightened that he might look at her like that someday. Have your children practice making their own faces based on a variety of emotions by means of a guessing game. William Cole's *Frances Face-Maker*, Marie Hall Ets's *Talking without Words*, and Robert Kraus's *Owliver* will help you get started. ACTING. AFRICAN AMERICANS. EMOTIONS. GRANDFATHERS.

411 **Greenfield, Eloise.** *Me and Neesie.* **Illus. by Moneta Barnett. Crowell, 1975. ISBN 0-690-00715-9**

Janell's high-spirited, imaginary best friend leaves for good on the first day of school, just as the green beast does to Marcia in Barbara Dillon's *The Beast in the Bed.* AFRICAN AMERICANS. FAMILY LIFE. FRIENDSHIP. IMAGINATION.

412 **Gretz, Susanna.** *It's Your Turn, Roger!* **Illus. by the author. Dial, 1985. ISBN 0-8037-0198-5**

Sure that other families don't make their children set the table, a young resentful pig visits four other apartments in his building to find there's no meal like home. Use this as a pertinent kick-off to a discussion of family chores, responsibilities, and manners. APARTMENT HOUSES. HELPFULNESS. PIGS.

413 **Gretz, Susanna.** *Teddy Bears Cure a Cold.* **Illus. by Alison Sage. Four Winds, 1985. ISBN 0-02-736960-9**

When William feels sick, he takes to his bed and allows the other bears to cater to his every whim. For those winter doldrums when flu is running rampant and half the class is out sick, recover with Lynne Cherry's *Who's Sick Today?* SICK. TEDDY BEARS.

414 **Grossman, Bill.** *Tommy at the Grocery Store.* **Illus. by Victoria Chess. Harper & Row, 1989. ISBN 0-06-022408-8**

Left behind at the grocery store, little Tom, a pig, is mistaken for salami, meat, a potato, soda bottle, banana, ruler, corn, and even a chair until his mother retrieves him. Another rhyming bit of craziness that could have taken place at "The Corner Grocery Store" from Raffi's song. PIGS. SHOPPING. STORIES IN RHYME.

415 **Harris, Dorothy Joan.** *The School Mouse.* **Illus. by Chris Conover. Warne, 1977.**

[2 sittings, unp.] Bringing his verbal jeep-riding mouse to school helps shy, six-year-old Jonathan adjust. Start the year with this one and discuss kids' ongoing school fears and concerns. MICE. SCHOOLS.

416 **Haywood, Carolyn.** *A Christmas Fantasy.* **Illus. by Glenys Ambrus and Victor Ambrus. Morrow, 1972.**

Meet Santa Claus as a boy and discover how he came to tumble down chimneys and get into the present business. Compare this Santa with the depictions in Chris Van Allsburg's *The Polar Express* and Rosemary Wells's *Max's Christmas.* CHRISTMAS. GIFTS. SANTA CLAUS.

417 **Hazen, Barbara Shook.** *Fang.* **Illus. by Leslie Morrill. Atheneum, 1987. ISBN 0-689-31307-1**

A boy with many fears has a huge dog who looks fierce but is scared of everything. A simple first-person narrative, this would work well in tandem with *Boris and the Monsters* by Elaine Willoughby and *Maggie and the Monster* by Elizabeth Winthrop. DOGS. FEAR.

418   **Henkes, Kevin.** *Jessica.* **Illus. by the author. Greenwillow, 1989. ISBN 0-688-07830-3**

"There is no Jessica," Ruthie's parents insist when Ruthie persists in taking her imaginary friend with her everywhere, even to the first day of kindergarten where she meets a new girl named. . . Jessica. Eloise Greenfield's *Me and Neesie* explores some of the same concerns. Have children draw and describe invisible playmates they knew in their younger days. FRIENDSHIP. IMAGINATION.

419   **Henkes, Kevin.** *Margaret & Taylor.* **Illus. by the author. Greenwillow, 1983. ISBN 0-688-01426-7**

[7 chapters, 64p.] During the week of Grandpa's surprise party, superior older sister Margaret almost always gets the best of her gullible little brother, Taylor. Sibling rivalry is a driving force as well in Judy Blume's *The Pain and the Great One.* BROTHERS AND SISTERS. GRANDFATHERS.

420   **Henkes, Kevin.** *A Weekend with Wendell.* **Illus. by the author. Greenwillow, 1986. ISBN 0-688-06326-8**

Until she asserts herself, mouse Sophie can't wait for her obnoxious weekend house guest to go home. Read and show other books by Kevin Henkes, especially *Sheila Rae, the Brave,* about Wendell's equally aggressive classmate. FRIENDSHIP. MICE. PLAY.

421   **Hest, Amy.** *The Mommy Exchange.* **Illus. by DyAnne DiSalvo-Ryan. Four Winds, 1988. ISBN 0-02-743650-0**

Best friends Jessica and Jason switch houses for the weekend so she can get some peace from the twins and he, an only child, can find some action. The same theme can be found in Peter Desbarats's *Gabrielle and Selena.* Pair children up and have them talk over with their partners what daily life would be like—including meals, chores, rules, and bedtime rituals—if they swapped houses. BROTHERS AND SISTERS. FAMILY LIFE. FRIENDSHIP. MOTHERS.

422   **Hest, Amy.** *The Purple Coat.* **Illus. by Amy Schwartz. Four Winds, 1986. ISBN 0-02-743640-3**

Gabby's tailor grandfather agrees to make a color change from the navy blue winter coats he sews for her each year. Contrast with Harriet Ziefert's *A New Coat for Anna.* CLOTHING AND DRESS. COLOR. GRANDFATHERS. MOTHERS AND DAUGHTERS.

423   **Heyward, DuBose.** *The Country Bunny and the Little Gold Shoes.* **Illus. by Marjorie Flack. Houghton Mifflin, 1974. ISBN 0-395-15990-3**

A cottontail with 21 children is chosen by the Grandfather Bunny at the Palace of Easter Eggs to be one of the five Easter Bunnies when she shows herself to be kind, swift, and wise. Originally published in 1939. Compare characters with Priscilla and Otto Friedrich's *The Easter Bunny That Overslept,* and find the Easter Bunny lurking in Rosemary Wells's adorable *Max's Chocolate Chicken.* EASTER. RABBITS.

424   **Hiller, Catherine.** *Abracatabby.* **Illus. by Victoria de Larrea. Coward, 1981.**

To stop his friends' teasing, Adam wishes his magical cat to show its tricks at Adam's birthday party. Talk it over: if your pet could do one magical thing that only you could see, what would it be? BIRTHDAYS. CATS. FRIENDSHIP. MAGIC.

425   Hoban, Lillian. *Arthur's Christmas Cookies*. Illus. by the author. Harper & Row, 1972. ISBN 0-06-022368-5

Chimp botches up the recipe when he mistakes salt for sugar. A good lead-in to a crafts or cooking activity. BROTHERS AND SISTERS. CHIMPANZEES. CHRISTMAS. COOKERY. FOOD.

426   Hoban, Lillian. *Arthur's Great Big Valentine*. Illus. by the author. Harper & Row, 1989. ISBN 0-06-022407-X

Until he figures out how to make up with his ex-best friend Norman, chimp Arthur is friendless, reduced to having snowball fights with himself on Valentine's Day. Your hearts will also go out to Eve Bunting's *The Valentine Bears*, Nancy L. Carlson's *Louanne Pig in the Mysterious Valentine*, Frank Modell's *One Zillion Valentines*, Marjorie Weinman Sharmat's *The Best Valentine in the World*, and James Stevenson's *Happy Valentine's Day, Emma*. Throw in the affectionate rhymes from Jack Prelutsky's *It's Valentine's Day*. BROTHERS AND SISTERS. CHIMPANZEES. FRIENDSHIP. VALENTINE'S DAY.

427   Hoban, Lillian. *Arthur's Loose Tooth*. Illus. by the author. Harper & Row, 1985. ISBN 0-06-022354-5

Arthur and sister Violet test their bravery when she goes outside in the dark alone and he pulls his own tooth. Explore what your children fear and how they've overcome it. Other "tooth" titles include Lucy Bate's *Little Rabbit's Loose Tooth*, Marc Brown's *Arthur's Tooth*, Nancy Cooney's *The Wobbly Tooth*, and Nurit Karlin's *The Tooth Witch*. BABY-SITTERS. BROTHERS AND SISTERS. CHIMPANZEES. COURAGE. TEETH.

428   Hoban, Russell. *Bedtime for Frances*. Illus. by Garth Williams. Harper & Row, 1960. ISBN 0-06-022351-0

A young badger who is simply not sleepy worries about tigers, giants, and ceiling cracks in her bedroom. Also try Eileen Christelow's *Henry and the Dragon*. BADGERS. BEDTIME STORIES. FEAR.

429   Hoban, Russell. *Bread and Jam for Frances*. Illus. by Lillian Hoban. Harper & Row, 1964. ISBN 0-06-022360-X

Frances won't try any new foods, so her mother gives her bread and jam for every meal. Read in tandem with Bruce Degen's *Jamberry*, John Vernon Lord's *The Giant Jam Sandwich*, Margaret Mahy's *Jam: A True Story*, and Nadine Bernard Westcott's *Peanut Butter and Jelly*; then make jam sandwiches with your class. Also similar in theme to Mary Rayner's *Mrs. Pig's Bulk Buy*. BADGERS. COOKERY. FAMILY LIFE. FOOD.

430   Hoban, Tana. *A Children's Zoo*. Photos by author. Greenwillow, 1985. ISBN 0-688-05204-5

On each double-page spread, three descriptive words—*strong, shaggy, roars*—accompany a large color animal photograph: *lion*. There are ten animals in all, ranging from penguin to panda, in a striking format of large white letters against black pages. Read the three descriptions before showing each page so children can guess the animal. Older children can create additions with photos or their own artwork, and new descriptive words. ANIMALS. CREATIVE WRITING. VOCABULARY.

431   Hoberman, Mary Ann. *A House Is a House for Me.* Illus. by Betty Fraser. Viking, 1978. ISBN 0-670-38016-4

A long and attractive rhyming list along with the chantable title refrain of what lives where, from animals to objects. Warm up by showing your students objects such as an egg, a pea pod, a shell, and a glove, and asking what "lives" in each. After reading, brainstorm more examples of houses and ask everyone to bring one from home for show-and-tell guessing. This is one of many titles also obtainable in a "big book" format (in this case from Scholastic), which makes seeing details so much easier, and which children adore. HOUSES. STORIES IN RHYME.

432   Hurd, Thacher. *Mama Don't Allow.* Illus. by the author. Harper & Row, 1984. ISBN 0-06-022690-0

Possum Miles and his swamp band find partying alligators a great audience for wild music until mealtime reveals their true appetites. Music and words are included for the title song, which all can sing with gusto. Musicians tame wild beasts, making this a worthy companion to Pete Seeger's *Abiyoyo.* ALLIGATORS. MUSIC. OPOSSUMS. STORIES WITH SONGS.

433   Hutchins, Pat. *Clocks and More Clocks.* Illus. by the author. Macmillan, 1970.

With the hall, attic, kitchen, and bedroom clocks all one minute apart, Mr. Higgins seeks the clockmaker to ascertain which one gives the correct time. Use with your telling time lessons, along with Jeffrey Allen's "Mary Alice" books and Eric Carle's *The Grouchy Ladybug.* CLOCKS. TIME.

434   Hutchins, Pat. *Don't Forget the Bacon!* Illus. by the author. Greenwillow, 1976. ISBN 0-688-06788-3

Sent on a shopping mission for: "Six farm eggs / A cake for tea / A pound of pears / And don't forget the bacon, " a young boy confuses the order, and, of course, forgets the bacon. First teach your children the above verse so they can better appreciate the humor of the boy's substitutions. See also *Ollie Forgot* by Tedd Arnold and the world-muddled *Pumpernickel Tickle and Mean Green Cheese* by Nancy Patz. CHANTABLE REFRAIN. MEMORY. STORIES IN RHYME.

435   Hutchins, Pat. *Where's the Baby?* Illus. by the author. Greenwillow, 1988. ISBN 0-688-05934-1

Proud Grandma finds merit in each of baby monster's messes as she, mother, and sister Hazel track him from one disastrously overturned room to the next. The sequel to *The Very Worst Monster,* though this one's in rhyme, as is Barbro Lindgren's tale of another troublemaker, *The Wild Baby.* BABIES. BEHAVIOR. GRANDMOTHERS. MONSTERS. STORIES IN RHYME.

436   Isadora, Rachel. *Max.* Illus. by the author. Macmillan, 1976. ISBN 0-02-747450-X

On the way to his baseball game, Max warms up at his sister's ballet class. Lead your young dancers in some leaps and bends and then go outside and play ball. BALLET. BASEBALL. DANCING.

437   Jeschke, Susan. *Angela and Bear.* Illus. by the author. Henry Holt, 1979.

Angela's new magic crayons cause her polar bear drawing to come to life. Team up with Dick Gackenbach's *Mag the Magnificent* or Crockett Johnson's "Harold" series, and then have your artists draw their own come-to-life pictures. For a trouble-making polar bear, see also Robert Benton's *Don't Ever Wish for a 7-Foot Bear*. BEARS. DRAWING. ZOOS.

438   Jeschke, Susan. *Perfect the Pig*. Illus. by the author. Henry Holt, 1981. ISBN 0-8050-0704-0

After being granted wings by a sow he helps, the runt of the litter flies to the city where he is taken in, first by artist Olive, who loves him, and then by a greedy man who exploits him. Contrast this with the tale of another pig who gets his wish, Pauline Watson's *Wriggles the Little Wishing Pig*, and compare performing woes with Lisa Campbell Ernst's mellifluous cow of *When Bluebell Sang*. FLIGHT. PIGS.

439   Johnson, Crockett. *Will Spring Be Early? or Will Spring Be Late?* Illus. by the author. Crowell, 1959. ISBN 0-690-89423-6

A stray plastic flower causes Groundhog to predict spring's arrival in February. If winter is getting you down, also read Bethany Roberts's *Waiting-for-Spring Stories*. HOLIDAYS. SEASONS. SPRING. WINTER.

440   Johnston, Johanna. *Speak Up, Edie*. Illus. by Paul Galdone. Putnam, 1974.

Chatterbox is confident about her big part in the class Thanksgiving play until she faces the audience. Stage fright also looms large in Barbara Williams's *Donna Jean's Disaster*. Read all three "Edie" books, including *Edie Changes Her Mind* and *That's Right, Edie*. FEAR. PLAYS. SCHOOLS. THANKSGIVING.

441   Johnston, Johanna. *That's Right, Edie*. Illus. by Paul Galdone. Putnam, 1966.

Stubborn Edie would rather scribble than learn to write properly until her birthday present is at stake. Bobby Brown learns a similar lesson in Elizabeth Vreeken's *The Boy Who Would Not Say His Name*. BIRTHDAYS. WRITING.

442   Johnston, Tony. *Mole and Troll Trim the Tree*. Illus. by Wallace Tripp. Putnam, 1989. ISBN 0-440-40243-3

Two best friends get into a fracas over the correct way to decorate the Christmas tree. An amusing prelude to decorating the classroom tree, plus a winning object lesson on how to make up after a fight. CHRISTMAS. FRIENDSHIP.

443   Johnston, Tony. *The Vanishing Pumpkin*. Illus. by Tomie dePaola. Putnam, 1983. ISBN 0-399-20991-3

Who would dare snitch a pumpkin from a 700-year-old man and an 800-year-old woman? "Oh, where is that pumpkin? I want my pumpkin pie," everyone can croak. You could pull one out from under your wizard's hat so all can have a sliver and see what the fuss was about. CHANTABLE REFRAIN. HALLOWEEN. PIE. WIZARDS.

444   Joyce, William. *George Shrinks*. Illus. by the author. Harper & Row, 1985. ISBN 0-06-023071-1

Upon waking, George finds his dream of becoming small has come true. Following the instructions in a note his parents left, he makes his now-enormous bed, brushes his teeth with a gargantuan toothbrush, and performs other daily ablutions with ingenuity. What a delight to pantomime! CREATIVE DRAMA. SIZE.

445   Kandoian, Ellen. *Under the Sun*. Illus. by the author. Dodd, Mead, 1987. ISBN 0-396-09059-1

At bedtime Molly asks her mother where the sun goes at night while she sleeps. Her mother's gentle reply takes us around the globe on a multiethnic tour, which you can supplement with a globe and a flashlight. Both science and social studies lessons are well-served by this simple explanation. For a local look, drive through the dark with Billy and his mom in Bernie and Mati Karlin's *Night Ride*. BEDTIME STORIES. NIGHT. SLEEP. SUN.

446   Karlin, Bernie, and Mati Karlin. *Night Ride.* **Illus. by Bernie Karlin. Simon & Schuster, 1988. ISBN 0-671-66733-5**

Billy accompanies his mom on an all-night car ride from home, across a bridge, past airport, ball park, and train crossing, arriving in the country at dawn. Other choices for those who stay up late or who'd like to, include Eve Bunting's *Ghost's Hour, Spooks' Hour*, Ellen Kandoian's *Under the Sun*, David Lyon's after-dark route in *The Biggest Truck*, Jack Prelutsky's poems in *My Parents Think I'm Sleeping*, Joanne Ryder's *The Night Flight*, Cynthia Rylant's *Night in the Country*, and Marjorie Weinman Sharmat's *Go to Sleep, Nicholas Joe*. AUTOMOBILES. NIGHT.

447   Karlin, Nurit. *The Tooth Witch.* **Illus. by the author. Lippincott, 1985. ISBN 0-397-32120-1**

How the Tooth Fairy came to be. Use with Nancy Evans Cooney's *The Wobbly Tooth*, Lucy Bate's *Little Rabbit's Loose Tooth*, Lillian Hoban's *Arthur's Loose Tooth*, or Marc Brown's *Arthur's Tooth*. TEETH. FAIRIES. WITCHES.

448   Keats, Ezra Jack. *Dreams.* **Illus. by the author. Macmillan, 1974. ISBN 0-02-749610-4**

Unable to sleep, Roberto looks out his window to see Archie's cat trapped in a box by a growling dog, and scares it with a shadow. Read about another plucky insomniac in Felicia Bond's *Poinsettia and the Firefighters*, and another shadow scare in Edward Frascino's *My Cousin the King*. NIGHT. SHADOWS. SLEEP.

449   Keats, Ezra Jack. *Goggles!* **Illus. by the author. Macmillan, 1987. ISBN 0-689-71157-3**

Peter and his friend Archie outwit the big boys with the help of Peter's dog, Willie, in this reprint of the 1969 edition. Introduce the author's series about Peter and his friends. AFRICAN AMERICANS. BULLIES. DOGS. EYEGLASSES.

450   Keats, Ezra Jack. *Jennie's Hat.* **Illus. by the author. Harper & Row, 1966. ISBN 0-06-023114-9**

The birds help Jenny decorate her too-plain hat. Bring in a large straw hat and let your students create the finery or declare a homemade hat day topped off with a hat parade. Other hat tales include Laura Geringer's *A Three Hat Day*, Margaret Miller's *Whose Hat?* and Esphyr Slobodkina's *Caps for Sale*. HATS.

451   Keats, Ezra Jack. *A Letter to Amy.* **Illus. by the author. Harper & Row, 1968. ISBN 0-06-023109-2**

Peter worries that his friend Amy won't come to his birthday party. Practice writing your own invitations to a classroom event. BIRTHDAYS. FRIENDSHIP. LETTER WRITING. PARTIES.

452   Keller, Holly. *Goodbye, Max.* **Illus. by the author. Greenwillow, 1987. ISBN 0-688-06562-7**

Ben can't accept a new puppy in his life until he grieves for his dog Max who died of old age a week before. Other sensitive books about a pet's death include Miriam

Cohen's *Jim's Dog Muffins* and Judith Viorst's *The Tenth Good Thing about Barney*. DEATH. DOGS.

453   **Kellogg, Steven.** *Much Bigger than Martin.* **Illus. by the author. Dial, 1976. ISBN 0-8037-5810-3**

Martin's little brother yearns to grow giant size so he can reach the basket hoop, swim to the raft with all the big kids, eat the biggest pieces of cake, and lord it over his sibling. In the sibling rivalry department, see also Judy Blume's *The Pain and the Great One*, Crescent Dragonwagon's *I Hate My Brother Harry*, and Judith Viorst's *I'll Fix Anthony*. BROTHERS. JEALOUSY. SIBLING RIVALRY.

454   **Kent, Jack.** *Jim Jimmy James.* **Illus. by the author. Greenwillow, 1984. ISBN 0-688-02542-0**

A bored boy spends a rainy day with his mirror reflection, James Jimmy Jim. Pair up your children and have them try a "mirror" pantomime. Other "reflection" stories include Frank Asch's *Bear Shadow* and *Just Like Daddy*. CREATIVE DRAMA. PLAY.

455   **Kent, Jack.** *Little Peep.* **Illus. by the author. Prentice Hall, 1981. ISBN 0-13-537746-3**

Newly hatched chick challenges the strutting barnyard rooster by calling up the sun with a "Peep-a-deedle-peep!" Children can practice crowing from the point of view of other farm animals. Also see Arnold Lobel's *How the Rooster Saved the Day*. CHICKENS. FARM LIFE. ROOSTERS. SUN.

456   **Khalsa, Dayal Kaur.** *How Pizza Came to Queens.* **Illus. by the author. Clarkson N. Potter, 1989. ISBN 0-517-57126-9**

May and her three best friends provide the visiting Mrs. Pellegrino with the ingredients for this mysterious, exotic-sounding dish in the old days before pizza parlors were invented. "Pizza," a perfect sing-along, acting-out song that might influence you into cooking up or ordering in the real thing, can be found on singers April and Susan's wonderful audio cassette *Join In!* Tomie dePaola's pasta-making *Strega Nona* and Tom Glazer's *On Top of Spaghetti* extend the Italian food motif. COOKERY. FOOD.

457   **Kherdian, David.** *The Cat's Midsummer Jamboree.* **Illus. by Nonny Hogrogian. Philomel, 1990. ISBN 0-399-22222-7**

Music teachers will be inspired by this cumulative tale of a mandolin-playing cat who invites five other music-loving forest creatures to play their instruments together for the forest to enjoy. Break into song for a bit and hand out some simple hand instruments to jazz it up. ANIMALS. CATS. MUSIC.

458   **King-Smith, Dick.** *Farmer Bungle Forgets.* **Illus. by Martin Honeysett. Atheneum, 1987. ISBN 0-689-31370-5**

An absent-minded farmer even forgets his own name. There's a chantable reply— "I'll remember that or my name's not Bill Bungle"—and lots of silly errors to deduce from the illustrations. This blends well with *Ollie Forgot* by Tedd Arnold and Ellen MacGregor's *Theodore Turtle*. ENGLAND. FARM LIFE. MEMORY.

459   **Kraus, Robert.** *How Spider Saved Christmas.* **Illus. by the author. Simon & Schuster, 1970.**

Invited to Fly and Ladybug's for Christmas dinner, and unsure of what to bring as a gift, Spider decides to wrap up one box of snow and one of icicles. Children who remember Ezra Jack Keats's *The Snowy Day* will appreciate the irony of the melted snow. Ask all to decide what presents they would bring if they were invited to the insects' dinner. CHRISTMAS. GIFTS. INSECTS. SPIDERS.

460   **Kraus, Robert.** *Leo the Late Bloomer.* **Illus. by Jose Aruego. Windmill, 1987. ISBN 0-87807-043-5**

An immature tiger can't do anything right until his own good time allows him to grow up. For all ages, especially overanxious parents. Use with David McPhail's *Pig Pig Grows Up.* MATURITY. PICTURE BOOKS FOR ALL AGES. TIGERS.

461   **Kraus, Robert.** *Owliver.* **Illus. by Jose Aruego and Ariane Dewey. Simon & Schuster, 1987. ISBN 0-671-66523-5**

Dramatic owl's mom wants him to be an actor, his dad prefers a doctor or lawyer, and son surprises them both. As Owliver does, have children act out a wide range of emotions, also using William Cole's *Frances Face-Maker*, Marie Hall Ets's *Talking without Words*, and Eloise Greenfield's *Grandpa's Face*. ACTING. BIRDS. CREATIVE DRAMA. OCCUPATIONS. OWLS.

462   **Kroll, Steven.** *The Candy Witch.* **Illus. by Marylin Hafner. Holiday House, 1979. ISBN 0-8234-0359-9**

When young Maggie the Witch's good deeds go unnoticed by her family, she turns to Halloween mischief to make everyone notice her. See also Kroll's *Amanda and the Giggling Ghost*. CANDY. HALLOWEEN. WITCHES.

463   **Kudrna, C. Imbior.** *To Bathe a Boa.* **Illus. by the author. Carolrhoda, 1986. ISBN 0-87614-306-0**

A rhyming riot of boy narrator versus recalcitrant snake who won't get in the tub. Put on a shower cap, sling a towel over your shoulder and whip out a bar of soap and a scrubbing brush to introduce this one. Use with other snake stories like Trinka Hakes Noble's *The Day Jimmy's Boa Ate the Wash* and Tomi Ungerer's *Crictor*, or focus on the bathing aspect and read varying views of the tub, from Brock Cole's *No More Baths* to Matt Faulkner's *The Amazing Voyage of Jackie Grace*, Charlotte Pomerantz's *The Piggy in the Puddle*, and Audrey Wood's *King Bidgood's in the Bathtub*. BATHS. PETS. SNAKES. STORIES IN RHYME.

464   **Lasker, Joe.** *The Do-Something Day.* **Illus. by the author. Viking, 1982. ISBN 0-670-27503-4**

When no one at home needs his help, Benjie runs away through town and finds friends who do. Each time a shopkeeper gives him a bonus for helping out, you pull out the real thing—salami, sour pickle, rye bread, cookies, plums, and green grapes—and put it into a sack. Afterward, divide up the goodies for a snack. FAMILY LIFE. HELPFULNESS. RUNAWAYS.

465   **Leaf, Munro.** *The Story of Ferdinand.* **Illus. by Robert Lawson. Viking, 1936. ISBN 0-670-67424-9**

Peaceful bull who only likes to sit and smell the flowers ends up doing just that in the bull-fighting ring. A gentle lesson in nonviolence, still welcome after half a century. DOMESTIC ANIMALS. PICTURE BOOKS FOR ALL AGES.

466   **Lear, Edward.** *The Quangle Wangle's Hat.* **Illus. by Janet Stevens. Harcourt, 1988. ISBN 0-15-264450-4**

Originally published in 1876, this goofy nonsense poem has lost none of its gangly sparkle, especially with Stevens's frantic watercolors. While the Quangle Wangle doesn't mind a bit when a horde of odd critters move in with him into his Crumpetty Tree, Dr. Seuss's *Thidwick, the Big-Hearted Moose* has the opposite reaction under like circumstances. Practice the poem before reading aloud as it's a tricky one. ANIMALS, IMAGINARY–POETRY. NONSENSE VERSES. STORIES IN RHYME.

467   **LeSieg, Theo.** *I Wish That I Had Duck Feet.* **Illus. by the author. Random House, 1965. ISBN 0-394-90040-5**

Boy imagines what it would be like to have them, plus two horns, a whale spout, a long, long tail, and a long, long nose, just like his favorite animals do. Have children make illustrations of how they'd like to change if they could. Additional books on the same theme include Eric Carle's *The Mixed-Up Chameleon,* James Howe's *I Wish I Were a Butterfly,* Keiko Kasza's *The Pigs' Picnic,* David Small's *Imogene's Antlers,* Bernard Waber's *"You Look Ridiculous," Said the Rhinoceros to the Hippopotamus,* and Pauline Watson's *Wriggles the Little Wishing Pig.* SELF-CONCEPT. STORIES IN RHYME. WISHES.

468   **Lester, Helen.** *Cora Copycat.* **Illus. by the author. Dutton, 1979. ISBN 0-525-28241-6**

A wild, wooly wurgal, escaped from the zoo, cures Cora of her mimicking ways. Listeners can echo each line along with Cora. BEHAVIOR. MONSTERS. SOUND EFFECTS.

469   **Lester, Helen.** *It Wasn't My Fault.* **Illus. by Lynn Munsinger. Houghton Mifflin, 1985. ISBN 0-395-35629-6**

Poor accident-prone Murdley Gurdson loses a sneaker that sets off a silly chain of events involving a bird, an aardvark, a pygmy hippo, a rabbit, and a broken egg. The klutzes in your classes will appreciate this one. For another trouble-causing sequence story, see Verna Aardema's *Why Mosquitoes Buzz in People's Ears,* and for one that almost happened, see Jack Tworkov's *The Camel Who Took a Walk.* CAUSE AND EFFECT. EGGS. SEQUENCE STORIES.

470   **Lester, Helen.** *Pookins Gets Her Way.* **Illus. by Lynn Munsinger. Houghton Mifflin, 1987. ISBN 0-395-42636-7**

Spoiled, willful Pookins, who makes faces, throws apples, and yells very loud when things don't go her way, meets up with a gnome who grants her three wishes. Another wisher who learns his lesson is *Wriggles the Little Wishing Pig* by Pauline Watson. BEHAVIOR. FAIRIES. WISHES.

471   **Lester, Helen.** *A Porcupine Named Fluffy.* **Illus. by Lynn Munsinger. Houghton Mifflin, 1986. ISBN 0-395-36895-2**

Spiky little critter can't live up to his incongruous monikor. Since lots of kids hate their names, ask them why and what they'd change to if they had their druthers. NAMES. PORCUPINES. RHINOCEROS.

472   **Lexau, Joan.** *Benjie.* **Illus. by Don Bolognese. Dial, 1964.**

A shy boy finds his grandmother's lost earring and gains confidence in the process. Another bashful one who comes through in a crisis is mouse *Shy Charles* by Rosemary Wells. AFRICAN AMERICANS. GRANDMOTHERS. SELF-CONCEPT.

473   **Lindgren, Barbro.** *The Wild Baby.* **Illus. by Eva Eriksson. Greenwillow, 1981. ISBN 0-688-00601-9**

Mischief-making baby boy causes his loving mother her share of grief. For another real monster, read Pat Hutchins's *Where's the Baby?* BABIES. BEHAVIOR. MOTHERS AND SONS. STORIES IN RHYME.

474   **Lionni, Leo.** *Fish Is Fish.* **Illus. by the author. Pantheon, 1970. ISBN 0-394-90440-0**

A curious fish learns about the world through his frog friend's eyes, but envisions birds, cows, and people from a fish point of view. Have children draw and describe a variety of objects and animals from a fish's perspective. In the same vein, try James Howe's *I Wish I Were a Butterfly*. FISHES. FROGS. IMAGINATION. SELF-CONCEPT.

475   **Lionni, Leo.** *Inch by Inch.* **Illus. by the author. Astor-Honor, 1962. ISBN 0-8392-3010-9**

Inchworm measures all the birds. Follow up with a measuring activity and Marisabina Russo's *The Line-Up Book*. BIRDS. MEASUREMENT. WORMS.

476   **Lionni, Leo.** *Swimmy.* **Illus. by the author. Pantheon, 1963. ISBN 0-394-91713-8**

Classic underwater survival story of little fishes who band together to thwart a big one. For more fishy stuff, read Katy Hall and Lisa Eisenberg's *Fishy Riddles* and Susan Russo's poetry collection *The Ice Cream Ocean*. COOPERATION. FISHES.

477   **Lionni, Leo.** *Tillie and the Wall.* **Illus. by the author. Knopf, 1989. ISBN 0-394-92155-0**

A persevering young mouse with vision wants to know what's on the other side of the wall and won't give up until she figures a way to get over there—by digging a tunnel. Good inspiration for not backing down from life's challenges or giving in to defeatism. On a more personal level, see Ellen Conford's *Impossible Possum*. FABLES. MICE. PERSEVERANCE. PICTURE BOOKS FOR ALL AGES.

478   **Little, Jean, and Maggie De Vries.** *Once Upon a Golden Apple.* **Illus. by Phoebe Gilman. Viking, 1990. ISBN 0-670-82963-3**

Though Briar Rose, Prince Valiant, and their Rock-a-bye baby end up living happily ever after, the tale dad tells his two nay-saying children is all mixed up. Children will chime in on the "no no no" refrains each time dad says something silly, and say "yes" each time he gets his story straight. This is an ingenious crash course in folktale and nursery rhyme motif, characters, and plot that all ages will love; fill in the gaps in your listeners' backgrounds by reading the original tales and rhymes aloud as well. CHANTABLE REFRAIN. FAIRY TALES–SATIRE. STORIES TO TELL.

479   **Lobel, Arnold.** *Frog and Toad Are Friends.* **Illus. by the author. Harper & Row, 1970. ISBN 0-06-023958-1**

Each "Frog and Toad" book, including *Frog and Toad Together* (1972), *Frog and Toad All Year* (1976), and *Days with Frog and Toad* (1979), features five perfect "I Can Read" stories of two best friends. Along with James Marshall's "George and Martha" books, these are unforgettable world-class classics all children should know. Act out your favorite episodes in pairs. FRIENDSHIP. FROGS. TOADS.

480   **Lobel, Arnold.** *The Great Blueness and Other Predicaments.* **Illus. by the author. Harper & Row, 1968. ISBN 0-06-023938-7**

How colors came to be, thanks to a zealous Wizard's wondrous potions. Break out the paints and start mixing, punctuating your art warm-up with color poems from Mary O'Neil's *Hailstones and Halibut Bones*. COLOR. WIZARDS.

481   Lobel, Arnold. *Ming Lo Moves the Mountain*. Illus. by the author. Greenwillow, 1982. ISBN 0-688-00611-6

An old couple consult the wise man for advice when they are fed up with the rain, rocks, and shadows the mountain casts upon their beloved house. After reading, line up your children, reenact the dance of the moving mountain, and all together, pantomime the rebuilding of the house. Other advice-dispensing wise men can be found in Marilyn Hirsch's *Could Anything Be Worse?* and Margot Zemach's *It Could Always Be Worse*. For an eye-opening view of a mountain's power, read Gerald McDermott's Japanese folktale *The Stonecutter*. DANCING. HOUSES. MOUNTAINS.

482   Lobel, Arnold. *Mouse Tales*. Illus. by the author. Harper & Row, 1972. ISBN 0-06-023942-5

Papa Mouse tells seven brief bedtime stories, one for each of his seven children. Try acting out "The Journey" for some giggles. For a similar motif, see also Bethany Roberts's rabbity *Waiting-for-Spring Stories*. BEDTIME STORIES. CREATIVE DRAMA. MICE.

483   Lobel, Arnold. *On Market Street*. Illus. by Anita Lobel. Greenwillow, 1981. ISBN 0-688-84309-3

Ingenious ABC of people constructed out of apples, books, clocks, and so on. Older children can design their own letter pictures; younger ones can identify each word from its illustration. A visual feast for all ages. ALPHABET BOOKS. PICTURE BOOKS FOR ALL AGES.

484   Lobel, Arnold. *Owl at Home*. Illus. by the author. Harper & Row, 1975. ISBN 0-06-023949-2

Five short episodes of winter, bumps in the night, tear-water tea, being in two places at the same time, and a moon friend. Listeners can add sad ideas for making more tea. As a tie-in to the moon story, read Jane Yolen's realistic *Owl Moon*. BIRDS. OWLS.

485   Lobel, Arnold. *The Rose in My Garden*. Illus. by Anita Lobel. Greenwillow, 1984. ISBN 0-688-02587-0

A "House That Jack Built" type of rhyming, cumulative tale about garden flowers, a mouse, a cat, and a bee that saves the day. Bring in a fall bouquet of several flowers from the text for a backdrop. In the same format, see also Verna Aardema's *Bringing the Rain to Kapiti Plain*, Rose Robart's *The Cake That Mack Ate*, Janet Stevens's version of *The House That Jack Built*, and Colin West's *The King of Kennelwick Castle*. CHANTABLE REFRAIN. CUMULATIVE STORIES. FLOWERS. GARDENS. STORIES IN RHYME.

486   Lobel, Arnold. *Uncle Elephant*. Illus. by the author. Harper & Row, 1981. ISBN 0-06-023980-8

When a young elephant's parents are temporarily lost at sea, he is taken in by his uncle. Hand out unshelled peanuts to count, make wishes, and take the class outside to trumpet the dawn. ELEPHANTS. UNCLES.

487 **Long, Claudia.** *Albert's Story.* **Illus. by Judy Glasser. Delacorte, 1978.**

One detail at a time, Albert elaborates on his one-sentence story, which starts out as, "He put the thing on his back." Given a starting sentence by you, students can make up new stories in the same way, adding the 5 Ws to build a large, descriptive sentence. DRAGONS. IMAGINATION. STORYTELLING.

488 **Low, Joseph.** *Mice Twice.* **Illus. by the author. Atheneum, 1986. ISBN 0-689-71060-7**

Cat and mouse plot and counterplot to eat and avoid being eaten, in this reprint of the 1980 edition. Good companion tales include Edward Frascino's *My Cousin the King* and Julius Lester's "Why Dogs Hate Cats" from *The Knee-High Man.* CATS. DOGS. MICE.

489 **McCleery, William.** *Wolf Story.* **Illus. by Warren Chappell. Linnet Books, 1988. ISBN 0-208-02191-4**

[10 chapters, 82p.] In installments, Michael's father tells him a story about Jimmy Tractorwheel's pet hen Rainbow and how Waldo the Wolf, with teeth like butcher knives, sets out to abduct him. With your children, make up a new adventure for the hungry wolf, good chicken, and clever farm boy. Read about reformed and reforming wolves as well, in Harry Allard's *It's So Nice to Have a Wolf around the House* and Keiko Kasza's *The Wolf's Chicken Stew.* CHICKENS. FATHERS AND SONS. STORYTELLING. WOLVES.

490 **MacDonald, Suse.** *Alphabatics.* **Illus. by the author. Bradbury, 1986. ISBN 0-02-761520-0**

An ingenious acrobatic alphabet book where letters undergo a four-stage metamorphosis into new objects. Cover the right-hand pictures with a piece of oak tag so children can guess which animal or item each letter is becoming. This is a color variant of Marty Neumeier's *Action Alphabet;* other follow-ups include Beau Gardner's *Guess What?* and Marilee Robin Burton's *Tails, Toes, Eyes, Ears, Nose.* ALPHABET BOOKS. VISUAL PERCEPTION.

491 **MacGregor, Ellen.** *Theodore Turtle.* **Illus. by Paul Galdone. McGraw-Hill, 1955.**

Turtle's absentmindedness causes him trouble when each time he finds one misplaced item, he leaves another one behind. Additional titles for memory-lapsed listeners include Tedd Arnold's *Ollie Forgot,* Joanna and Paul Galdone's *Gertrude the Goose Who Forgot,* Dick King-Smith's *Farmer Bungle Forgets,* and Larry Weinberg's *The Forgetful Bears Meet Mr. Memory.* MEMORY. REPTILES. TURTLES.

492 **McKissack, Patricia C.** *Nettie Jo's Friends.* **Illus. by Scott Cook. Knopf, 1989. ISBN 0-394-99158-3**

Determined to find a sewing needle to make a new dress for her doll, Nettie Jo asks for help from Miz Rabbit, Fox, and Panther, all of whom seem to be too busy running from or chasing each other to oblige her. Hand out needles and thread to practice your rag-doll sewing skills, like in Charlotte Pomerantz's *The Chalk Doll.* AFRICAN AMERICANS. ANIMALS. DOLLS.

493 **McPhail, David.** *The Bear's Toothache.* **Illus. by the author. Little, Brown, 1972. ISBN 0-316-56312-9**

Late at night, a boy helps a large brown bear pull out its aching tooth. Wonderfully understated; try a pantomime in pairs. BEARS. CREATIVE DRAMA. TEETH.

494   **McPhail, David.** *Fix-It.* **Illus. by the author. Dutton, 1984. ISBN 0-525-44093-3**

When the TV won't work, young bear Emma turns to books. Read this at a PTA or staff meeting. BEARS. BOOKS AND READING. PICTURE BOOKS FOR ALL AGES. TELEVISION.

495   **McPhail, David.** *Great Cat.* **Illus. by the author. Dutton, 1982. ISBN 0-525-45102-1**

Toby and Great Cat, the biggest cat that ever lived, rescue storm-stranded children from the ocean. Talk over what future adventures Toby and his pal could have on their island. Compare this larger-than-horse-sized cat with the fast-growing feline in Daniel Pinkwater's *The Wuggie Norple Story.* CATS. SIZE. STORMS. WEATHER.

496   **McPhail, David.** *Pig Pig and the Magic Photo Album.* **Illus. by the author. Dutton, 1986. ISBN 0-525-44238-3**

Each time he says "cheese," he ends up in unfamiliar surroundings, including a church steeple, the wing of an airplane, and atop a chocolate birthday cake. A natural for narrative pantomime; have your listeners dream up and act out other places Pig Pig could appear. Hand out little squares of cheese for everyone to sample and take a class photo while your posers say, "Cheese!" Next, take a trip to Camp Wildhog in *Pig Pig Goes to Camp* (1983), where the frogs find him irresistible. CREATIVE DRAMA. PHOTOGRAPHY. PIGS.

497   **McPhail, David.** *Something Special.* **Illus. by the author. Little, Brown, 1988. ISBN 0-316-56324-2**

Raccoon Sam is dismayed that he can't play piano or ball, work the computer, cook, carve, knit, do magic, or even balance a bone like the rest of his family members, until he discovers his true talent—painting. Children can draw a picture of and explore their own strong points. ARTISTS. FAMILY LIFE. PAINTING.

498   **Maestro, Betsy, and Giulio Maestro.** *Lambs for Dinner.* **Illus. by Giulio Maestro. Crown, 1978.**

A friend-seeking wolf invites four suspicious lamb children to his place for supper. Also don't miss Keiko Kasza's *The Wolf's Chicken Stew* and Tan Koide's *May We Sleep Here Tonight?* FOOD. SHEEP. WOLVES.

499   **Maestro, Giulio.** *A Wise Monkey Tale.* **Illus. by the author. Crown, 1975.**

Monkey tricks her way out of a hole by enticing the other jungle animals to jump in too. Similar to Joanna Troughton's folktale, *Mouse Deer's Market.* ANIMALS. JUNGLES. MONKEYS. STORIES TO TELL.

500   **Mahy, Margaret.** *17 Kings and 42 Elephants.* **Illus. by Patricia MacCarthy. Dial, 1987. ISBN 0-8037-0458-5**

Tongue-twisterly, rhythmic rhyme, festooned with dazzlingly garish batik illustrations, of what the kings see as they ride elephant-back through the wild wet jungle. Read it several times, and have your listeners make up hand motions to go with each new animal. ANIMALS. ELEPHANTS. JUNGLES. KINGS AND RULERS. STORIES IN RHYME.

501   **Marshall, Edward.** *Troll Country.* **Illus. by James Marshall. Dial, 1980. ISBN 0-8037-6211-9**

Elsie Fay tricks the same troll her mother had outwitted when she was a girl. Read after the group is already familiar with trolls via Marcia Brown's or Paul Galdone's

The Three Billy Goats Gruff. Other smart cookies include Mercer Mayer's *Liza Lou and the Yeller Belly Swamp*, Patricia C. McKissack's *Flossie and the Fox*, and Don Arthur Torgersen's *The Girl Who Tricked the Troll.* TROLLS.

502   **Marshall, James.** *George and Martha.* **Illus. by the author. Houghton Mifflin, 1972. ISBN 0-395-16619-5**

Each George and Martha book is filled with five punchy vignettes of two hippo friends who fight, make up, scare, and delight each other. Classics in their field, along with Arnold Lobel's "Frog and Toad" series, and a treat for all ages, are the following, in order of appearance: *George And Martha Encore* (1973); *George and Martha Rise and Shine* (1976); *George and Martha Back in Town* (1984); *George and Martha One Fine Day* (1978); *George and Martha Tons of Fun* (1980); and *George and Martha Round and Round* (1988). Many of the stories are ideal for acting out in pairs. CREATIVE DRAMA. FRIENDSHIP. HIPPOPOTAMUS. PICTURES BOOKS FOR ALL AGES.

503   **Marshall, James.** *Portly McSwine.* **Illus. by the author. Houghton Mifflin, 1979.**

With his National Snout Day party only a day away, a pessimistic pig becomes obsessed over everything that might go wrong. Pair this with Harry Allard's obnoxious Potter Pig character in *There's a Party at Mona's Tonight*, also illustrated by Marshall. PARTIES. PIGS. SELF-CONCEPT.

504   **Marshall, James.** *Three Up a Tree.* **Illus. by the author. Dial, 1986. ISBN 0-8037-0328-7**

Three friends, Lolly, Spider, and Sam, entertain themselves in their tree house by telling stories about cats and rats, monsters and chickens. Sit in a circle and start your own children off in making up new tales. Continue their tale weaving down by the ocean with *Three by the Sea* (1981). FRIENDSHIP. STORYTELLING.

505   **Martin, Bill, Jr., and John Archambault.** *Barn Dance!* **Illus. by Ted Rand. Henry Holt, 1986. ISBN 0-8050-0089-5**

A wild, rollicking, rhythmic rhyme about the skinny kid who sneaked in to see the animals dance late one magical night. Read this aloud twice, then teach your young dancers a turkey trot or two. Read with John Stadler's *Animal Cafe* where a store's resident cat and dog take over each night unbeknownst to the human owner. DANCING. DOMESTIC ANIMALS. FARM LIFE. STORIES IN RHYME.

506   **Matthews, Louise.** *Gator Pie.* **Illus. by Jeni Bassett. Dodd, Mead, 1979.**

When two alligators find a large pie, they must divide it in half, then in fourths, eighths, and finally hundredths so all the other hungry gators can have a piece. Bring in a pie or two so you can demonstrate and give everyone a sliver. Fractured fraction fun is a fine way to introduce a day's math lesson. ALLIGATORS. MATHEMATICS. PIE.

507   **Merriam, Eve.** *The Christmas Box.* **Illus. by David Small. Morrow, 1985. ISBN 0-688-05256-8**

Looking under the tree on Christmas morning, a large family of six children and five grown-ups find only a very long, thin box, inside of which is, connected together, one present per person. Children can draw the one present they would like to receive this year; tack their drawings up, side by side, connected by yarn. CHRISTMAS. FAMILY LIFE. GIFTS.

508 Merriam, Eve. *Where Is Everybody? An Animal Alphabet*. Illus. by Diane de Groat. Simon & Schuster, 1989. ISBN 0-671-64964-7

Cover up the caption for each large illustration so children can guess that Alligator is in the attic, Bear is in the bakery, and so on. Keep up the alliteration with Beau Gardner's *Have You Ever Seen . . .? An ABC Book*. ALPHABET BOOKS. ANIMALS.

509 Modell, Frank. *Goodbye Old Year, Hello New Year*. Illus. by the author. Greenwillow, 1984. ISBN 0-688-03939-1

On New Year's Eve, pals Marvin and Milton set their alarm clocks for midnight but oversleep till 5:30 A.M., when they go outside with pots and pans to welcome in the dawn. Act out both noisy pages, with one half of the class as the two raucous boys, and the other half the irate, sleepy neighbors. Then switch parts and do it again. CREATIVE DRAMA. HOLIDAYS. SOUND EFFECTS.

510 Moskin, Marietta. *Rosie's Birthday Present*. Illus. by David S. Rose. Atheneum, 1981.

[1–2 sittings, 31p.] Starting with a gold button she finds outside, Rosie trades treasures to acquire the perfect present for her mother. Children can retell the story in sequence. Use a gold button as a motivating prop. BIRTHDAYS. GIFTS. MOTHERS AND DAUGHTERS. SEQUENCE STORIES.

511 Myers, Bernice. *Not This Bear!* Illus. by the author. Four Winds, 1967.

Dressed in a fur coat, boy Herman is mistaken for a bear and escorted back to their den where he tries to prove his human identity. Act out a role reversal, where students must convince you, first that they are human, and next, that they are really bears. See also Patricia C. McKissack's *Flossie and the Fox*. BEARS. CREATIVE DRAMA.

512 Naylor, Phyllis Reynolds. *Old Sadie and the Christmas Bear*. Illus. by Patricia Montgomery Newton. Atheneum, 1984. ISBN 0-689-31052-8

Waking with the feeling that something's in the air, Amos heads from his den on Christmas Eve and is fed and made welcome by a nearsighted old woman who never realizes her visitor is a gentle bear. Compare Amos's experience with that of *The Christmas Wolf* by Michel Gay. BEARS. CHRISTMAS.

513 Noll, Sally. *Jiggle Wiggle Prance*. Illus. by the author. Greenwillow, 1987. ISBN 0-688-06761-1

While this clever, simple, brightly illustrated rhyme (consisting only of 33 action verbs) will help you teach that part of speech, it is also a natural for narrative pantomime. Then brainstorm a new list of verbs and create your own rhymes to chant and act out. CREATIVE DRAMA. ENGLISH LANGUAGE–GRAMMAR. STORIES IN RHYME.

514 Numeroff, Laura. *If You Give a Mouse a Cookie*. Illus. by Felicia Bond. Harper & Row, 1985. ISBN 0-06-024587-5

Cyclical cause-and-effect story of a mouse's probable requests stemming from the bestowal of one mere cookie. After reviewing the sequence, start the story again— "Once he eats his cookie, he'll want to wash his hands"—and have your listeners add new events to the narrative, round robin. CAUSE AND EFFECT. MICE.

515 O'Donnell, Elizabeth Lee. *Maggie Doesn't Want to Move*. Illus. by Amy Schwartz. Four Winds, 1987. ISBN 0-02-768830-5

Upset about moving away from his house, playground, and teacher, Simon claims his toddler sister is the one who's unhappy about the change. A trip to the new neighborhood changes his mind. Other related titles include Larry L. King's *Because of Lozo Brown*, Marjorie Weinman Sharmat's *Gila Monsters Meet You at the Airport*, and Bernard Waber's *Ira Says Goodbye*. BROTHERS AND SISTERS. FAMILY LIFE. MOVING, HOUSEHOLD.

516   **Oppenheim, Joanne.** *You Can't Catch Me!* **Illus. by Andrew Shachat. Houghton Mifflin, 1986. ISBN 0-395-41452-0**

A pesky fly, with the help of a rhyming text and a catchy refrain for all to chant, annoys the farm animals no end. Reminiscent of Scott Cook's or Paul Galdone's retellings of *The Gingerbread Boy*. CHANTABLE REFRAIN. INSECTS. STORIES IN RHYME.

517   **Parish, Peggy.** *No More Monsters for Me.* **Illus. by Marc Simont. Harper & Row, 1981. ISBN 0-06-024658-8**

When her mother says, "No pets!" Minn brings a growing baby monster home instead and hides it in the basement. Draw and talk about the pets you all have at home. MONSTERS. MOTHERS AND DAUGHTERS. SIZE.

518   **Parker, Nancy Winslow.** *Love from Uncle Clyde.* **Illus. by the author. Dodd, Mead, 1977.**

As a special gift, Charlie's uncle sends him a crated hippo. Read the first time without showing any illustrations so that children can draw or describe what animal they think the present is. Set the scene by asking them to listen for clues as to its identity. HIPPOPOTAMUS. LETTER WRITING.

519   **Parkin, Rex.** *The Red Carpet.* **Illus. by the author. Macmillan, 1988. ISBN 0-02-770010-0**

When the Bellevue Hotel rolls out its red carpet for the Duke of Sultana, it continues rolling out into the street, down the hill, through town and country, to meet the Duke's ferry at the dock. Originally published in 1948, outrageously rhyming and ridiculous, and a set up for the further silliness of Raffi's song-story *Down by the Bay*. STORIES IN RHYME.

520   **Patz, Nancy.** *Pumpernickel Tickle and Mean Green Cheese.* **Illus. by the author. Franklin Watts, 1978.**

Sent to the store by his mother to buy a loaf of dark brown pumpernickel bread, a half-pound piece of yellow cheese, and a great big, very green, nice dill pickle, Benjamin and his elephant pal spend so much time diddling with the words, they almost forget what to buy. Of course you'll want the above snack after reading this, and for dessert, read Tedd Arnold's *Ollie Forgot*, Pat Hutchins's *Don't Forget the Bacon!* and Chris Riddell's *The Trouble with Elephants*. CHANTABLE REFRAIN. ELEPHANTS. FOOD. MEMORY.

521   **Peet, Bill.** *The Ant and the Elephant.* **Illus. by the author. Houghton Mifflin, 1980. ISBN 0-395-16963-1**

After an elephant is the only animal considerate enough to rescue a stranded ant, the ant returns the favor, proving that even the smallest creatures can be helpful. A new twist on Aesop's *The Lion and the Rat*, as retold by Brian Wildsmith. ANIMALS. ANTS. COOPERATION. ELEPHANTS. HELPFULNESS.

522   Pinkwater, Daniel. *Guys from Space.* **Illus. by the author. Macmillan, 1989. ISBN 0-02-774672-0**

Looking for Chicago, three green-faced, Pinkwater-look-alike aliens land in the boy narrator's back yard and take him for a ride—with his mother's permission, of course—to a planet with talking blue rocks and a nice root beer stand. Children can draw and describe the next planet they might visit, inhabitants included. For a more drastic overreaction to visitors from far away, read Arthur Yorinks's *Company's Coming*, and finish up with Edward Marshall's *Space Case* and Marilyn Sadler's *Alistair in Outer Space.* EXTRATERRESTRIAL LIFE. SPACE FLIGHT.

523   Pinkwater, Daniel. *Tooth-Gnasher Superflash.* **Illus. by the author. Macmillan, 1990. ISBN 0-02-774655-0**

Mr. and Mrs. Popsnorkle and the five little Popsnorkles trade their worn-out green Thunderclap Eight for a nice new car that turns into a dinosaur, elephant, turtle, and flying chicken. A must for narrative pantomime. For another object that doesn't behave as it should, see Susan Seligson and Howie Schneider's *Amos: The Story of an Old Dog and His Couch.* AUTOMOBILES. CREATIVE DRAMA. STORIES TO TELL. TRANSPORTATION.

524   Pinkwater, Daniel. *The Wuggie Norple Story.* **Illus. by Tomie dePaola. Four Winds, 1980. ISBN 0-02-774670-4**

Cat keeps growing. Have fun making up new names to go with absurd characters like Lunchbox Louis, Bigfoot the Chipmunk, and Freckleface Chilibean. Other fast-growing pets include Steven Kellogg's *The Mysterious Tadpole* and fish Otto in Helen Palmer's *A Fish Out of Water.* CATS. NAMES. SIZE.

525   Polacco, Patricia. *Thunder Cake.* **Illus. by the author. Philomel, 1990. ISBN 0-399-22231-6**

The narrator relates how, when she was a child, her Russian grandmother Babushka helped her overcome her fear of thunderstorms by baking a cake before a storm came. Similarly afflicted children will take comfort in a rational approach to dispelling a threatening fear, in harmony with the grandfather in Mary Stolz's *Storm in the Night.* Show and discuss the majestic color photographs in Seymour Simon's *Storms,* and also consider Patricia Coombs's *Dorrie and the Weather Box,* Bill Martin, Jr., and John Archambault's *Listen to the Rain,* Jack Prelutsky's good-natured verse in *Rainy Rainy Saturday,* and Audrey Wood's *The Napping House.* FEAR. GRANDMOTHERS. RAIN AND RAINFALL. STORMS. WEATHER.

526   Polushkin, Maria. *Bubba and Babba.* **Illus. by Diane de Groat. Crown, 1986. ISBN 0-517-55945-5**

To avoid washing the dinner dishes, two lazy bears agree that whoever speaks first in the morning must do the chore. Based on a Russian folktale, this is good for days when no one wants to help out, as is Arnold Lobel's *A Treeful of Pigs.* BEARS. LAZINESS.

527   Porte, Barbara Ann. *Harry in Trouble.* **Illus. by Yossi Abolafia. Greenwillow, 1989. ISBN 0-688-07722-6**

Harry is distraught when he loses his third library card in one year. Introduce the other books about motherless Harry: *Harry's Dog, Harry's Mom* (1985), and *Harry's Visit* (1983). Speaking of libraries, does each of your children have a card for the public library? No childhood is complete without one. James Daugherty's *Andy and the Lion* shows just how important books and libraries can be. LIBRARIES. LOST.

528   Potter, Beatrix. *The Tale of Peter Rabbit*. Illus. by the author. Warne, 1987. ISBN 0-7232-3460-4

The classic tale, originally published in 1902, of the naughty rabbit trapped in Mr. McGregor's garden. Follow with *The Tale of Benjamin Bunny* (1904), set the day after Peter's escapade in Mr. McGregor's garden, when cousin Benjamin entices him back there to rescue his clothes, eat lettuces, and, alas, encounter a cat. BEHAVIOR. GARDENS. RABBITS.

529   Preston, Edna Mitchell. *Pop Corn & Ma Goodness*. Illus. by Robert Andrew Parker. Viking, 1969.

How they meet, marry, and keep the farm a-chippitty choppetty, mippitty moppetty, all "doon the hill." Nonsense alliterations are tongue-twistingly terrific, and everyone can chime in on the refrain. Practice before using with a group, and expect your listeners to demand that you read it more than once. Another dotty ditty is Charlotte Pomerantz's *The Piggy in the Puddle*. CHANTABLE REFRAIN. FARM LIFE. STORIES IN RHYME.

530   Rabe, Berniece. *The Balancing Girl*. Illus. by Lillian Hoban. Dutton, 1981. ISBN 0-525-26160-5

Wheel chair and crutches-bound Margaret proves her balancing talents—even to skeptical Tommy—when she sets up an intricate domino chain that causes a sensation at the school carnival. Set up and knock down your own classroom domino courses, and talk about handicaps and how we can respond to people who have them. HANDICAPS. SCHOOLS.

531   Roberts, Bethany. *Waiting-for-Spring Stories*. Illus. by William Joyce. Harper & Row, 1984. ISBN 0-06-025062-3

Seven short rabbit stories are told by Papa Rabbit to pass the winter in this hare equivalent to Arnold Lobel's *Mouse Tales*. Also read Crockett Johnson's groundhog story, *Will Spring Be Early? or Will Spring Be Late?* and, as the season progresses, Sue Alexander's *There's More . . . Much More*. RABBITS. SPRING.

532   Robison, Deborah. *Bye-Bye, Old Buddy*. Illus. by the author. Clarion, 1983. ISBN 0-89919-185-1

Jenny doesn't know how to give up her worn out, fuzzy baby blanket until she decides to mail it to a stranger picked from the phone book. Other "blanket" stories include Nancy Evans Cooney's *The Blanket That Had to Go* and Holly Keller's *Geraldine's Blanket*. BLANKETS. HABITS.

533   Roche, P. K. *Good-Bye, Arnold*. Illus. by the author. Dial, 1979.

The younger mouse finds the lack of sibling rivalry is both a pleasure and a bore when his big brother goes away for a week. Also don't miss Kevin Henkes's *Bailey Goes Camping*. BROTHERS AND SISTERS. MICE. SIBLING RIVALRY.

534   Rockwell, Anne. *The Gollywhopper Egg*. Illus. by the author. Macmillan, 1986. ISBN 0-689-71072-0

Expounding on the wondrous qualities of the fictitious rare bird within, a city-smart peddler sells a coconut to a gullible farmer who tries to hatch it. Bring a real coconut to crack, and while munching, talk over the additional attributes the astonishing Gollywhopper might possess. EGGS. FARM LIFE. PEDDLERS AND PEDDLING.

535   **Root, Phyllis.** *Moon Tiger.* **Illus. by Ed Young. Henry Holt, 1985. ISBN 0-8050-0896-9**

When Jessica Ellen is sent to bed early for not reading to her younger brother, she imagines what would happen if a tiger took her on a world-wide ride. Ed Young's illustrations are extraordinary, especially from afar, where views of the tiger will make your listeners gasp. For another night ride, also read Joanne Ryder's *The Night Flight.* BEDTIME STORIES. BROTHERS AND SISTERS. NIGHT. SIBLING RIVALRY. TIGERS.

536   **Ross, Tony.** *I'm Coming to Get You!* **Illus. by the author. Dial, 1984. ISBN 0-8037-0119-5**

A malevolent planet-gobbling monster finds Earth boy Tommy Brown on its spaceship radar, and heads for Earth to eat him up. For another monster who ends up harmless, don't forget Dick Gackenbach's *Harry and the Terrible Whatzit.* BEDTIME STORIES. FEAR. MONSTERS. SCIENCE FICTION.

537   **Rounds, Glen.** *I Know an Old Lady Who Swallowed a Fly.* **Illus. by the author. Holiday House, 1990. ISBN 0-8234-0814-0**

If you can't sing, then chant this graphic version of the old song about the old lady who dies from overeating a horse, goat, dog, cat, bird, spider, and a fly, of course. Nadine Bernard Westcott's version of the same name is also frantic, and Joanna Cole's *Golly Gump Swallowed a Fly* is a prose retelling with a new main character. ANIMALS. CUMULATIVE STORIES. NONSENSE VERSES. SONGS. STORIES IN RHYME.

538   **Russo, Marisabina.** *Waiting for Hannah.* **Illus. by the author. Greenwillow, 1989. ISBN 0-688-08016-2**

Seeing a large pregnant woman in line ahead of them at the store inspires Hannah's mother to relate her memories of the summer before Hannah's birth. Children can ask their parents to recall their pre-histories as well, and share any photographs of the family before they came along. This is the next stage after Ina R. Friedman's *How My Parents Learned to Eat,* where a girl explains her parents' courtship. BABIES. FAMILY STORIES. MOTHERS AND DAUGHTERS.

539   **Ryan, Cheli Druan.** *Hildilid's Night.* **Illus. by Arnold Lobel. Macmillan, 1986. ISBN 0-02-777260-8**

An old woman who hates the night tries every way imaginable to chase it away so the sun will always shine on her hut. Originally published in 1971. Act out in narrative pantomime. Companion pieces of night and sun include Verna Aardema's folktale *Why Mosquitoes Buzz in People's Ears,* Jack Kent's *Little Peep,* and Arnold Lobel's *How the Rooster Saved the Day.* CREATIVE DRAMA. NIGHT.

540   **Ryder, Joanne.** *The Night Flight.* **Illus. by Amy Schwartz. Four Winds, 1985. ISBN 0-02-778020-1**

In the dark, via lion's back, Anna flies through the city. *Night in the Country* by Cynthia Rylant provides a realistic contrast as does Ellen Kandoian's *Under the Sun* and Bernie and Mati Karlin's *Night Ride.* Other dreamy nighttime titles include Anthony Browne's *Gorilla,* Eric Carle's *Papa, Please Get the Moon for Me,* Phyllis Root's *Moon Tiger,* and Marjorie Weinman Sharmat's *Go to Sleep, Nicholas Joe.* BEDTIME STORIES. DREAMS. NIGHT.

541   **Rylant, Cynthia.** *Night in the Country.* **Illus. by Mary Szilagyi. Bradbury, 1986. ISBN 0-02-777210-1**

Glowing pencil drawings, even more vibrant from a distance, show what's out there to see and hear while we are in bed. Take a nighttime car ride in Bernie and Mati Karlin's *Night Ride* and try Joanne Ryder's *The Night Flight* for a contrasting city view. Have your children listen for night noises where they live and then write and illustrate their own class book of night in the city (or country, or suburbs, or seashore, and so on). BEDTIME STORIES. COUNTRY LIFE. NIGHT.

542   **Rylant, Cynthia.** *The Relatives Came.* **Illus. by Stephen Gammell. Bradbury, 1985. ISBN 0-02-777220-9**

Simple description of an extended family visit full of love and fun. Would that all family get-togethers could bring such a sense of joy and sharing! Elicit your listener's own recountings of family reunions. FAMILY LIFE.

543   **Schatell, Brian.** *Farmer Goff and His Turkey Sam.* **Illus. by the author. Harper & Row, 1982. ISBN 0-397-31983-5**

A pie-loving prize turkey "pigs out" at the Country Fair. Cartoonlike, goofy fun for November; bake a pumpkin pie to celebrate. PIE. THANKSGIVING. TURKEYS.

544   **Schertle, Alice.** *Jeremy Bean's St. Patrick's Day.* **Illus. by Linda Shute. Lothrop, 1987. ISBN 0-688-04814-5**

All his classmates tease him when Jeremy Bean forgets to wear green on March 17, until Mr. Dudley, the principal, helps out. Celebrate the holiday with an extra bit of leprechaun lore in *Leprechauns Never Lie* by Lorna Balian. HOLIDAYS. PRINCIPALS. SCHOOLS.

545   **Schwartz, Amy.** *Oma and Bobo.* **Illus. by the author. Bradbury, 1987. ISBN 0-02-781500-5**

Though Alice's grandmother calls the new dog Trouble, Bother, and Nuisance, she teaches him to fetch in time for the dog show. Pair this with another dog-training epic, *Pinkerton, Behave* by Steven Kellogg. DOGS. GRANDMOTHERS.

546   **Schwartz, Henry.** *How I Captured a Dinosaur.* **Illus. by Amy Schwartz. Orchard, 1989. ISBN 0-531-05770-4**

On vacation with her parents in Baja California, Mexico, Liz tracks down huge three-toed footprints to find a hamburger-loving Albertosaurus, which she brings back home with her to Los Angeles. No message here; just matter-of-fact fun to read aloud with Carol Carrick's *Patrick's Dinosaurs* and *What Happened to Patrick's Dinosaurs*, Steven Kellogg's *Prehistoric Pinkerton*, and Jane Thayer's *Quiet on Account of Dinosaur.* DINOSAURS.

547   **Schwartz, Mary Ada.** *Spiffen: A Tale of a Tidy Pig.* **Illus. by Lynn Munsinger. Albert Whitman, 1988. ISBN 0-8075-7580-1**

With a well-aimed bucket of soapy water, a misfit clean pig in the filthy village of Slobbyville becomes a hero when he saves the king from a hungry, fire-breathing dragon. *Piggy in the Puddle* by Charlotte Pomerantz would be an entertaining partner, as would Pete Seeger's *Abiyoyo*, another tale of an outcast who prevails. DRAGONS. HYGIENE. PIGS.

548   **Seeger, Pete.** *Abiyoyo*. **Illus. by Michael Hays. Macmillan, 1985. ISBN 0-02-781490-4**

Seeger's own story-song is loosely based on a South African lullaby, about a giant and the boy who conquers him with music. Naturally, listeners will join in on the title refrain; then cast and act this one out. For another outcast hero, see Mary Ada Schwartz's *Spiffen: A Tale of a Tidy Pig*. CREATIVE DRAMA. MAGIC. MONSTERS. STORIES TO TELL. STORIES WITH SONGS.

549   **Seligson, Susan, and Howie Schneider.** *Amos: The Story of an Old Dog and His Couch*. **Illus. by Howie Schneider. Little, Brown, 1987. ISBN 0-316-77404-9**

For some odd reason, the couch comes alive—*va room*—and Amos, who has been yearning for a bit of excitement, rides it through town every day as soon as his owners, the Bobsons, go out. Children can draw what they think their pets get up to when no one is home. No less plausible than Daniel Pinkwater's car that turns into a dinosaur, among other animals, in *Tooth-Gnasher Superflash*, and both are appropriately nutty when exploring unusual forms of transportation. The sequel, *The Amazing Amos and the Greatest Couch in the World* (1989) is just as cuckoo, though the illustrations are too small and cluttered to make a comfortable read-aloud. DOGS. PICTURE BOOKS FOR ALL AGES.

550   **Sendak, Maurice.** *Alligators All Around*. **Illus. by the author. Harper & Row, 1962. ISBN 0-06-025530-7**

Reptilian alphabet book, destined for narrative pantomime. Also try Sandra Boynton's *A Is for Angry* and Jane Bayer's *A My Name Is Alice*. Carol King's splendid musical sound track record for Sendak's marvelous movie cartoon, *Really Rosie*, includes this, *One Was Johnny: A Counting Rhyme*, and the next two titles, *Chicken Soup with Rice* and *Pierre*. ALLIGATORS. ALPHABET BOOKS. CREATIVE DRAMA.

551   **Sendak, Maurice.** *Chicken Soup with Rice*. **Illus. by the author. Harper & Row, 1962. ISBN 0-06-025535-8**

Soup-inspired monthly rhymes for children to chant. To reinforce the months and seasons, read also Sara Coleridge's *January Brings the Snow* and Shirley Hughes's *Out and About*. Then cook up a pot of "Jewish penicillin." FOOD. MONTHS. SEASONS. STORIES IN RHYME.

552   **Sendak, Maurice.** *Pierre*. **Illus. by the author. Harper & Row, 1962. ISBN 0-06-025965-5**

This indifferent boy only says, "I don't care," until he is eaten by a hungry lion. The boys in Pat Hutchins's *The Tale of Thomas Mead* and Helen Lester's *Cora Copycat* learn similar lessons. LIONS. STORIES IN RHYME.

553   **Seuss, Dr.** *Dr. Seuss' ABC*. **Illus. by the author. Random House, 1960. ISBN 0-394-90030-8**

From Aunt Annie's alligator to a Zizzer-zazzer-zuzz, students will dream up more absurd alliteratives. ALLITERATION. ALPHABET BOOKS. STORIES IN RHYME.

554   **Seuss, Dr.** *Marvin K. Mooney, Will You Please Go Now*. **Illus. by the author. Random House, 1972. ISBN 0-394-92490-8**

Suggesting unusual ways for him to *leave*, the unseen narrator seems desperate. Allow children to invent and draw their own transportation for him. TRANSPORTATION. STORIES IN RHYME.

555   **Sharmat, Mitchell.** *Gregory, the Terrible Eater.* **Illus. by Jose Aruego and Ariane Dewey. Four Winds, 1984. ISBN 0-02-782250-8**

Concerned goat parents worry when their son refuses to eat junk. Your class can make up a new week-long menu for either Gregory or themselves in this kick-off to good eating. Other finicky eaters include those in Chris L. Demarest's *No Peas for Nellie* and Dr. Seuss's *Green Eggs and Ham.* FOOD. GOATS.

556   **Shaw, Nancy.** *Sheep in a Jeep.* **Illus. by Margot Apple. Houghton Mifflin, 1986. ISBN 0-395-41105-X**

Simple, silly rhyming text, ideal for call-and-response chanting, about jeep-driving sheep in a bind. Hapless sheep have as hard a time sailing as they did driving in *Sheep on a Ship* (1989). Few words, tight rhymes; act these out a couple of times! CREATIVE DRAMA. SHEEP. STORIES IN RHYME. TRANSPORTATION.

557   **Sherrow, Victoria.** *There Goes the Ghost!* **Illus. by Megan Lloyd. Harper & Row, 1985. ISBN 0-06-025510-2**

When a farmer and his family move into their new farmhouse, they encounter a bumping, thumping, rapping, tapping, banging, clanging, crashing, smashing, moaning, groaning ghost! A good telling tale. FARM LIFE. GHOSTS. STORIES TO TELL.

558   **Small, David.** *Imogene's Antlers.* **Illus. by the author. Crown, 1985. ISBN 0-517-55564-6**

A little girl wakes up with huge horns and finds them useful. Each student can dream up a new antler function and then draw himself performing it. Also do not miss Theo LeSieg's *I Wish That I Had Duck Feet.* IMAGINATION.

559   **Spier, Peter.** *Oh, Were They Ever Happy!* **Illus. by the author. Doubleday, 1978. ISBN 0-385-13175-5**

Children take it upon themselves to paint their house, rainbow-style, when their parents go out for the afternoon. Draw a giant house on kraft paper or out of an enormous box, and have the whole class paint it. BROTHERS AND SISTERS. HOUSES. PAINTING.

560   **Stevenson, James.** *Clams Can't Sing.* **Illus. by the author. Greenwillow, 1980.**

Oh, yes they can! Make a sound tape of your own beach concert after trying out all the noises in the story. Also read Leo Lionni's *Swimmy* for an underwater view, Ken Robbins's *Beach Days* for that realistic touch, Susan Russo's poetry collection *The Ice Cream Ocean*, and Sheila White Samton's *Beside the Bay.* ANIMALS. SEASHORE. SOUND EFFECTS.

561   **Stevenson, James.** *Monty.* **Illus. by the author. Greenwillow, 1979. ISBN 0-688-84209-7**

A patient alligator ferries small animals across the water to school until they take him for granted once too often. Children can devise ways to get across without getting wet. Continue the tale with *No Need for Monty* (1987), where the animal grown-ups, concerned that Monty is too slow, think up faster but impractical ways for their children to get to school. ALLIGATORS. ANIMALS. RIVERS.

562   **Stevenson, James.** *Yuck!* **Illus. by the author. Greenwillow, 1984. ISBN 0-688-03830-1**

With the help of her animal friends, sweet young witch Emma brews up a powerful vegetable soup "potion" to get even with nasty old witches, Dolores and Lavinia. Written entirely in ballooned dialogue with sound effects, this would make a dandy play. You may wish to cook up a nice pot of vegetable soup with your hungry players. If you need a recipe, pair this with Louis Ehlert's *Growing Vegetable Soup*. First of a series that includes *Emma* (1985), *Fried Feathers for Thanksgiving* (1986), and *Happy Valentine's Day, Emma*. ANIMALS. CREATIVE DRAMA. FOOD. SOUND EFFECTS. WITCHES.

563   **Stevenson, Robert Louis.** *Block City.* **Illus. by Ashley Wolff. Dutton, 1988. ISBN 0-525-44399-1**

The well-known nineteenth-century poem is brought into the twentieth with grand, water-colored woodcut illustrations. About the joys of blocks, this is told from the point of view of a boy whose block buildings become palace, kirk, mill, and tower in his imagination. Now's a good time to discuss the long-lasting power of the mind's eye, and to construct an all-class block city of your own. IMAGINATION. STORIES IN RHYME. TOYS.

564   **Taylor, Mark.** *Henry the Explorer.* **Illus. by Graham Booth. Little, Brown, 1988. ISBN 0-316-83384-3**

On the day after a blizzard, a boy and his Scotty dog discover a cave, get lost, and find their way home. Other snowy stories include Virginia Lee Burton's *Katie and the Big Snow*, Ezra Jack Keats's *The Snowy Day*, and Charlotte Zolotow's *Something Is Going to Happen*. CAVES. DOGS. LOST. SNOW. WINTER.

565   **Tejima, Keizaburo.** *Fox's Dream.* **Illus. by the author. Philomel, 1987. ISBN 0-399-21455-0**

Bold woodcuts in striking, moonlit hues of brown, black, white, and blue inhabit this winter mood piece of a fox, alone in the snow, who sees shapes in the icy trees that remind him of spring. This is a moving alternative to the usual fox-as-villain stories, along with Irina Korschunow's *The Foundling Fox*. Also impressive is *Owl Lake*, an elegantly pared-down, poetic description of Father Owl catching a fish in a moonlit mountain lake. Both work well with Jane Yolen's *Owl Moon* and Astrid Lindgren's *The Tomten*. FOXES. NIGHT. SEASONS. WINTER.

566   **Thayer, Jane.** *The Puppy Who Wanted a Boy.* **Illus. by Lisa McCue. Morrow, 1986. ISBN 0-688-05945-7**

Out on the streets to find a boy for Christmas, shaggy mutt Petey comes upon the Home for Boys where everyone needs him. This newly illustrated edition of a 1958 title is just the ticket to remind children that Christmas is a time for love, not greed. CHRISTMAS. DOGS.

567   **Thayer, Jane.** *Quiet on Account of Dinosaur.* **Illus. by Seymour Fleischman. Morrow, 1964. ISBN 0-688-31632-8**

Dinosaur-wise Mary Ann finds the world's last brontosaurus alive and takes him to school. Also don't miss Carol Carrick's *Patrick's Dinosaurs* and *What Happened to Patrick's Dinosaurs?*, Steven Kellogg's *Prehistoric Pinkerton*, and Henry Schwartz's *How I Captured a Dinosaur*. DINOSAURS. SCHOOLS.

568   **Thomas, Patricia.** *"Stand Back," Said the Elephant, "I'm Going to Sneeze!"* **Illus. by Wallace Tripp. Lothrop, 1971.**

With the imploring refrain of "Oh *please*, don't sneeze!" children can join the rest of the jungle animals as they rhymingly complain about the last time the elephant did. ANIMALS. CHANTABLE REFRAIN. ELEPHANTS. STORIES IN RHYME.

569   Townson, Hazel. *Terrible Tuesday.* Illus. by Tony Ross. Morrow, 1986. ISBN 0-688-06244-X

After overhearing his mother talking about Terrible Tuesday, son Terry fantasizes about what disasters she might be dreading. Before reading the ending, ask listeners to predict what else could possibly happen, and what the consequences would be. FAMILY LIFE. IMAGINATION.

570   Turkle, Brinton. *Deep in the Forest.* Illus. by the author. Dutton, 1976. ISBN 0-525-28617-9

A wordless switch, whereby three bears visit a forest cabin after a human mama, papa, and young girl leave the house. Compare with any of the "Three Bears" retellings, including those by Jan Brett, Lorinda Bryan Cauley, Armand Eisen, Paul Galdone, James Marshall, or Janet Stevens, and have a nice visit with Jane Yolen's *The Three Bears Rhyme Book.* BEARS. FORESTS AND FORESTRY. STORIES WITHOUT WORDS.

571   Tworkov, Jack. *The Camel Who Took a Walk.* Illus. by Roger Duvoisin. Dutton, 1974. ISBN 0-525-27393-X

A jungle sequence story-with-a-twist that's fun to retell when a lumbering camel sets off a chain of thoughts as a tiger, monkey, squirrel, and bird plan in turn what they will do to each other. Also see Verna Aardema's folktale *Why Mosquitoes Buzz in People's Ears,* Paul Galdone's *The Old Woman and Her Pig,* and Helen Lester's *It Wasn't My Fault.* CAMELS. JUNGLES. SEQUENCE STORIES.

572   Udry, Janice May. *Alfred.* Illus. by Judith Shuman Roth. Whitman, 1960.

Young Henry is terrified of all dogs on his block until the day the biggest one of all, an Irish setter, takes drastic measures to make friends. Discuss how to behave around dogs and read Colleen Stanley Bare's photo essay, *To Love a Dog.* DOGS. FEAR. SCHOOLS.

573   Ungerer, Tomi. *Crictor.* Illus. by the author. Harper & Row, 1958. ISBN 0-06-026181-1

Schoolteacher Madame Bodot's new snake who learns to spell, count, and tie knots, captures a burglar and is awarded a medal for bravery. If you have a stuffed snake, dress him up with a woolen sweater, cap, and baby bottle, as a class pet. Just like Crictor, children can shape letters and numbers with their own bodies. Other boa tales include C. Imbior Kudrna's *To Bathe a Boa* and Trinka Hakes Noble's *The Day Jimmy's Boa Ate the Wash,* as well as Diane L. Burns's riddles in *Snakes Alive!* For another robber-foiling pet, read Patricia Lauber's *Clarence and the Burglar,* and, to prolong the French *joie de vivre,* see Louise Fatio's *The Happy Lion* and Eve Titus's cheese expert, mouse *Anatole.* CREATIVE DRAMA. ROBBERS AND OUTLAWS. SNAKES.

574   Viorst, Judith. *I'll Fix Anthony.* Illus. by Arnold Lobel. Harper & Row, 1969. ISBN 0-06-026307-5

The younger brother plots revenge—as soon as he turns six, that is. Other put-upon younger siblings can be found in Judy Blume's *The Pain and the Great One* and Crescent Dragonwagon's *I Hate My Brother Harry.* BROTHERS AND SISTERS. SIBLING RIVALRY.

575   Viorst, Judith. *The Tenth Good Thing about Barney.* Illus. by Eric Blegvad. Atheneum, 1971. ISBN 0-689-20688-7

To help him deal with his grief over his cat's death, a boy's mother suggests he think of ten good things to tell about the cat at its funeral. This touching story deals gracefully with the concepts of heaven and burial. Miriam Cohen's *Jim's Dog Muffins* and Holly Keller's *Goodbye, Max* are also effective. CATS. DEATH.

576   **Vreeken, Elizabeth.** *The Boy Who Would Not Say His Name.* **Illus. by Leonard Shortall. Follett, 1959.**

Bobby Brown pretends to be assorted story characters until he gets lost in a department store and claims his name is Rumpelstiltskin. The joke will be lost unless you preface the story with the original Grimm fairy tale as a reference. (For this age, try the version by Edith Tarcov.) Afterward, ask children to recite their full addresses and phone numbers. Those who don't know them should learn it for homework. IMAGINATION. LOST.

577   **Waber, Bernard.** *An Anteater Named Arthur.* **Illus. by the author. Houghton Mifflin, 1975. ISBN 0-395-20336-8**

What he is really like, as told by his loving mother. Children can discuss how they think their mothers would describe them. ANIMALS. MOTHERS AND SONS.

578   **Waber, Bernard.** *Lyle, Lyle Crocodile.* **Illus. by the author. Houghton Mifflin, 1965. ISBN 0-395-16995-X**

Mr. Grumps, crocodile-loathing next-door neighbor, has the Primm family's tame New York City crocodile committed to the city zoo for scaring his cat, Loretta. Second in a series, all of which should turn you into crocodile fans. Read-aloud naturals include: *The House on East 88th Street* (1962), which explains how he came to live with the Primm family; *Lovable Lyle* (1969), where an unknown enemy sends his hate mail that saps his self-confidence; and *Lyle Finds His Mother* (1974), where the contented New York City reptile is convinced by his now down-and-out former manager Hector P. Valenti, star of stage and screen, to search for his long-lost crocodile parents. Don't worry; I won't even suggest that you let your children sample Lyle's favorite food—Turkish caviar! CROCODILES. NEW YORK CITY. REPTILES.

579   **Waber, Bernard.** *Rich Cat, Poor Cat.* **Illus. by the author. Houghton Mifflin, 1963.**

The lives of pampered pets are contrasted with the life of a city stray named Scat. Discuss the importance of the proper treatment of cats and other pets, and read Wanda Gag's *Millions of Cats* to show how love makes one beautiful. CATS.

580   **Waber, Bernard.** *"You Look Ridiculous," Said the Rhinoceros to the Hippopotamus.* **Illus. by the author. Houghton Mifflin, 1973. ISBN 0-395-07156-9**

Hippo, who hates her looks, has a nightmare where she turns into a monstrous creature with all the features she values. This makes a wonderful flannel board story. For a similar theme, also try Eric Carle's *The Mixed-Up Chameleon*, James Howe's *I Wish I Were a Butterfly*, Keiko Kasza's *The Pigs' Picnic*, Theo LeSieg's *I Wish That I Had Duck Feet*, and Pauline Watson's *Wriggles the Little Wishing Pig*. ANIMALS. HIPPOPOTAMUS. SELF-CONCEPT. WISHES.

581   **Wagner, Jenny.** *John Brown, Rose and the Midnight Cat.* **Illus. by Ron Brooks. Penguin, 1980. ISBN 0-14-050306-4**

An old woman's jealous sheepdog tries to thwart a stray black cat from staying. For more sibling rivalry, pet-style, see Alane Ferguson's *That New Pet!* CATS. DOGS. JEALOUSY.

582 **Watson, Pauline.** *Wriggles the Little Wishing Pig.* **Illus. by Paul Galdone. Seabury, 1978.**

A rash young pig envies other animals until his wishes come true. For a similar theme, also try Eric Carle's *The Mixed-Up Chameleon,* James Howe's *I Wish I Were a Butterfly,* Keiko Kasza's *The Pigs' Picnic,* Theo LeSieg's *I Wish That I Had Duck Feet,* and Bernard Waber's *"You Look Ridiculous," Said the Rhinoceros to the Hippopotamus.* Compare the treatment of wish-fulfillment with Susan Jeschke's *Perfect the Pig.* PIGS. SELF-CONCEPT. WISHES.

583 **Weinberg, Larry.** *The Forgetful Bears Meet Mr. Memory.* **Illus. by Bruce Degen. Scholastic, 1987. ISBN 0-590-40781-3**

An elephant expert helps an absent-minded bear family locate their lost plane tickets to Hawaii. When you want your students to remember something important, have them sway from side to side in unison and chant, "Now I am an elephant. And an elephant never forgets!" Also read Tedd Arnold's *Ollie Forgets* and Ellen MacGregor's *Theodore Turtle.* BEARS. ELEPHANTS. MEMORY.

584 **Weiss, Nicki.** *Hank and Oogie.* **Illus. by the author. Greenwillow, 1982. ISBN 0-688-00936-0**

What a hard time Hank has, giving up his dependence on Oogie, his stuffed hippo. See also Lillian Hoban's *Arthur's Honey Bear,* and for blanket withdrawal, Nancy Evans Cooney's *The Blanket That Had to Go,* Holly Keller's *Geraldine's Blanket,* and Deborah Robison's *Bye-Bye, Old Buddy.* STUFFED ANIMALS. TOYS.

585 **Wells, Rosemary.** *Hazel's Amazing Mother.* **Illus. by the author. Dial, 1985. ISBN 0-8037-0210-8**

Walking home from town, a raccoon child loses her way and is surrounded by bullies who wreck her doll. Mother miraculously comes to the rescue, proving the power of love in this tribute to moms everywhere. BULLIES. DOLLS. LOST. MOTHERS AND DAUGHTERS.

586 **Wells, Rosemary.** *Shy Charles.* **Illus. by the author. Dial, 1988. ISBN 0-8037-0564-6**

A rhyming recounting of how a young mouse, too shy to say hello or good-bye, bravely comes to the rescue when his baby-sitter falls down the stairs. Get kids talking about their experiences with baby-sitters after reading this and Elizabeth Winthrop's *Bear and Mrs. Duck.* Joan Lexau's *Benjie* also overcomes his shyness to help his grandmother. BABY-SITTERS. MICE. SELF-CONCEPT. STORIES IN RHYME.

587 **Wells, Rosemary.** *Timothy Goes to School.* **Illus. by the author. Dial, 1981. ISBN 0-8037-8949-1**

A frustrated raccoon is ready to quit school until he makes a new friend. Read this the first week of school along with Martha Alexander's *Move Over, Twerp* and Amy Schwartz's *Annabelle Swift, Kindergartner.* FRIENDSHIP. RACCOONS. SCHOOLS.

588 **Westcott, Nadine Bernard.** *I Know an Old Lady Who Swallowed a Fly.* **Illus. by the author. Little, Brown, 1980. ISBN 0-316-93128-4**

An illustrated version of the song about a ravenous old woman who swallows a fly, spider, bird, cat, dog, goat, and horse before she dies, of course. Read it, tell it, sing, or chant it, and act it out. Also see the Rose Bonne version *I Know an Old Lady* (Rand, 1961) and Harve Zemach's cumulative story-song *Mommy, Buy Me a China Doll*. ANIMALS. CUMULATIVE STORIES. NONSENSE VERSES. SONGS. STORIES IN RHYME.

589   **Whelan, Gloria.** *A Week of Raccoons.* **Illus. by Lynn Munsinger. Knopf, 1988. ISBN 0-394-98396-3**

Until put-upon Mr. Twerkle brings the fifth troublesome raccoon in five days to the piney woods, the masked bandits have a hard time figuring how to get back to his cottage by the blue-green pond. Good for recalling simple directions, this can be tied in to a simple map skills lesson. Designate the Twerkles's cottage, the log cabin, apple tree, bridge, schoolhouse, farm, and piney woods in your room and act out the whole story. If you assign inanimate parts—for instance, truck, landmarks, garbage can, ears of corn—to your actors, everyone can have a part. COUNTRY LIFE. RACCOONS.

590   **Wilhelm, Hans.** *Tyrone the Horrible.* **Illus. by the author. Scholastic, 1988. ISBN 0-590-41471-2**

The world's first big bully, a tyrannosaurus, gets his comeuppance when he picks on young Boland one time too many. A useful object lesson in dealing with and finally overcoming bullies by using brain over brawn. Similar in theme to Martha Alexander's *Move Over, Twerp* and Carol Chapman's *Herbie's Troubles*, but with a different solution. BULLIES. DINOSAURS.

591   **Williams, Linda.** *The Little Old Lady Who Was Not Afraid of Anything.* **Illus. by Megan Lloyd. Crowell, 1986. ISBN 0-690-04586-7**

On her way home, she encounters in sequence: two clomping shoes, a wiggling pair of pants, a shaking shirt, two clapping gloves, a nodding hat, and one scary pumpkin head. Repeated sound effects and motions make this an inspired choice for group dramatics and storytelling, with or without props. Also read Paul Galdone's folktale *The Teeny Tiny Woman* for a wee scare. CREATIVE DRAMA. FEAR. HALLOWEEN. SOUND EFFECTS. STORIES TO TELL.

592   **Willis, Jeanne.** *The Monster Bed.* **Illus. by Susan Varley. Lothrop, 1987. ISBN 0-688-06805-7**

Little monster Dennis from Withering Wood / Won't go to bed though he knows that he should. / He's afraid of the humans who might find him there, / Till a human boy comes and they both get a scare. Your listeners can talk about their own "things-that-go-bump-in-the-night" fears. Use with a few other similar bedtime tales like Jim Aylesworth's *Two Terrible Frights*, Eileen Christelow's *Henry and the Dragon*, and Robert L. Crowe's *Clyde Monster*. BEDTIME STORIES. FEAR. MONSTERS. STORIES IN RHYME.

593   **Willis, Val.** *The Secret in the Matchbook.* **Illus. by John Shelley. Farrar, 1988. ISBN 0-374-36603-9**

There's a malevolent dragon in there, and Bobby Bell brings it to school where it gets out and grows. "I knew there'd be trouble," Bobby says, and he's right! A semi-sinister companion to Dick Gackenbach's *Harry and the Terrible Whatzit* or M. Jean Craig's gentle *The Dragon in the Clock Box*. DRAGONS. SCHOOLS.

594 **Winthrop, Elizabeth.** *Lizzie & Harold.* **Illus. by Martha Weston. Lothrop, 1985. ISBN 0-688-02712-1**

Six-year-old Lizzie seeks out a new best friend even though there's already a willing contender for that title: the boy next door. Afterward, be sure to give your listeners the opportunity to try out some of their own cat's cradle string fun, as demonstrated in the book. Camilla Gryski's *Cat's Cradle, Owl's Eyes: A Book of String Games* is an indispensable string bible for when you get hooked. FRIENDSHIP.

595 **Winthrop, Elizabeth.** *Sloppy Kisses.* **Illus. by Anne Burgess. Penguin, 1983. ISBN 0-14-050433-8**

A young pig thinks she's too old for her parents to kiss her anymore. Talk over ways we can show our love, and stress that we are never too old for kisses and hugs. Hand out Hershey's Kisses for an affectionate treat. FAMILY LIFE. PIGS.

596 **Wittman, Sally.** *The Wonderful Mrs. Trumbly.* **Illus. by Margot Apple. Harper & Row, 1982. ISBN 0-06-026512-4**

Martin is crushed when he discovers that his beloved teacher has a boyfriend. Showcase books about various types of teachers, from James Howe's *The Day the Teacher Went Bananas*, where the teacher is a gorilla, to the dreaded Miss Viola Swamp in Harry Allard's *Miss Nelson Is Missing.* SCHOOLS. TEACHERS.

597 **Ziefert, Harriet.** *A New Coat for Anna.* **Illus. by Anita Lobel. Knopf, 1986. ISBN 0-394-97426-3**

With the war just ended, Anna's mother has no money to buy her a promised coat, but instead barters her treasures in return for services to a sheep farmer, spinner, weaver, and tailor, all of whom help provide a beautiful red wool coat for Christmas. Based on a true story, this is a thought-provoking coda to Elsa Beskow's *Pelle's New Suit* and Tomie dePaola's *Charlie Needs a Cloak.* CHRISTMAS. CLOTHING AND DRESS. SHEEP.

598 **Zion, Gene.** *The Plant Sitter.* **Illus. by Margaret Bloy Graham. Harper & Row, 1976. ISBN 0-06-443012-X**

A two cents a plant, Tommy works hard maintaining the hundreds of overgrown plants his neighbors have left in his care while they are away on vacation. A light-hearted introduction to a plant unit where children can plant seeds, carrot tops, sweet potatoes, avocados, and other fast-growing greens; see also Christine Black's *Bean and Plant* for a clear, color-photographed show-and-tell presentation that can be easily duplicated. PLANTS.

FICTION FOR GRADES 1–2

599   Ackerman, Karen. *Song and Dance Man.* Illus. by Stephen Gammell. Knopf, 1988. ISBN 0-394-99330-6

The grandchildren describe how Grandpa, in his prime a vaudeville hoofer, puts on his singing, tap dancing, banjo-playing, joke- and magic-filled act for them in the attic when they visit. Patricia C. McKissack's *Mirandy and Brother Wind*, which won a Caldecott Honor the same year this won the gold, is also about dancing and is loosely based on an image of the author's grandmother as a girl; both are vivid reminders for us to ask our parents and grandparents to tell us the family stories they remember. CALDECOTT MEDAL. DANCING. FAMILY STORIES. GRANDFATHERS.

600   Alexander, Sue. *Dear Phoebe.* Illus. by Eileen Christelow. Little, Brown, 1984.

Phoebe Dormouse moves into her own nest, worried that her mother doesn't miss her enough. Letters carried back and forth by an obliging sparrow establish their warm relationship as the mother prepares her daughter for independent living. Start a letter-writing project between parents and children, you and students, or pen pals. LETTER WRITING. MICE. MOTHERS AND DAUGHTERS.

601   Allard, Harry. *Miss Nelson Is Missing.* Illus. by James Marshall. Houghton Mifflin, 1985. ISBN 0-395-40146-1

With the kids in Room 207 misbehaving (again) for their sweet teacher, she stays home and the wicked substitute Miss Viola Swamp arrives to shape them up. Be sure to read this before you take your first sick day. In *Miss Nelson Is Back* (1982), students lose no time taking advantage of their teacher's absence for a tonsillectomy until The Swamp shows up to restore order. *Miss Nelson Has a Field Day* (1985), with the pitiful Smedley Tornadoes football team in dire need of The Swamp to whip them into shape, includes a real surprise ending for Miss Nelson know-it-alls. James Marshall's *The Cut-Ups* and *The Cut-Ups Cut Loose* are soul mates here. BEHAVIOR. PICTURE BOOKS FOR ALL AGES. SCHOOLS. TEACHERS.

602   Andersen, Hans Christian. *It's Perfectly True.* Illus. by Janet Stevens. Holiday House, 1988. ISBN 0-8234-0672-5

An innocent jesting remark about losing a feather, made by a respectable white hen, is repeated, misconstrued, elaborated upon, distorted, and believed by the other birds who are shocked and titillated by the growing gossip about five dead, featherless, lovesick birds. Play "telephone" with a silly message to see for yourselves how a harmless misheard statement can evolve. BIRDS. CHICKENS. GOSSIP. PICTURE BOOKS FOR ALL AGES. STORYTELLING.

603 **Andersen, Hans Christian.** *The Ugly Duckling.* **Illus. by Lorinda Bryan Cauley. Harcourt, 1979. ISBN 0-15-692528-1**

Compare this appealingly illustrated retelling of the classic story about a swan's miserable childhood with the one illustrated by Adrienne Adams (Scribner, 1985). BIRDS. DUCKS. SELF-CONCEPT.

604 **Anderson, Leone Castell.** *The Wonderful Shrinking Shirt.* **Illus. by Irene Trivas. Albert Whitman, 1983.**

Each time it is washed, Elbert's fine yellow flannel shirt with the purple stripes must be passed down to a smaller family member. All should say the "fine shirt" refrain in character each time around and pantomime the "sousing and dousing." When you learn this one to tell, it makes a winning Christmas story with minimal changes needed. CHANTABLE REFRAIN. CLOTHING AND DRESS. FAMILY LIFE. STORIES TO TELL.

605 **Anderson, Lonzo.** *The Halloween Party.* **Illus. by Adrienne Adams. Scribner, 1974.**

Faraday Folsom, who is on his way to a Halloween party at a nearby farm in a ghost costume, happens upon a forest party for real witches, gremlins, and ogres. Celebrate with other odd holiday creatures in Emily Herman's creepy *Hubknuckles* and Alice Schertle's *Bill and the Google-Eyed Goblins,* or poems from John E. Brewton's *In the Witch's Kitchen,* Jack Prelutsky's amusing *It's Halloween,* and Daisy Wallace's trio, *Ghost Poems, Monster Poems,* and *Witch Poems.* HALLOWEEN. PARTIES. WITCHES.

606 **Anderson, Lonzo.** *Two Hundred Rabbits.* **Illus. by Adrienne Adams. Viking, 1968.**

A poor peasant boy, looking for a novel way to entertain the king at the castle festival, meets an old woman who helps him summon 199 marching rabbits. The narrator remains unidentified until the last page for a surprise ending. Before reading, ask children to try to figure out from whose point of view the story is told. KINGS AND RULERS. RABBITS.

607 **Arnold, Tedd.** *Ollie Forgot.* **Illus. by the author. Dial, 1988. ISBN 0-8037-0488-7**

Sent by his mother for "A joint of beef, a wedge of cheese, a loaf of bread, too, if you please," simpleminded Ollie makes his first mistake when he chants instead, "Rain, rain, go away. Come again another day." A cyclical sequence story to retell and act out, with rhyming couplets for listeners to chant along. More forgetful types can be found in Paul Galdone's *Hans in Luck,* Pat Hutchins's *Don't Forget the Bacon!,* Dick King-Smith's *Farmer Bungle Forgets,* Ellen MacGregor's *Theodore Turtle,* Nancy Patz's *Pumpernickel Tickle and Mean Green Cheese,* Anne Rose's *The Triumphs of Fuzzy Fogtop,* and William Wiesner's *Happy-Go-Lucky.* CHANTABLE REFRAIN. CREATIVE DRAMA. FOOLS. MEMORY. SEQUENCE STORIES.

608 **Balian, Lorna.** *Humbug Potion: An A B Cipher.* **Illus. by the author. Abingdon, 1984. ISBN 0-687-37102-3**

A homely witch discovers an old recipe for a Magic Beauty Potion, written in a secret alphabetical number code. Make up a translation card like the book's endpapers, and as you read, have students first guess each word in context, and then translate each ingredient. This may well lead you to the 652 section of your library to search out other types of codes and ciphers for your 19-12-5-21-20-8-19 to try. ALPHABET BOOKS. CODES AND CIPHERS. WITCHES.

609 **Balian, Lorna.** *Leprechauns Never Lie.* **Illus. by the author. Abingdon, 1980. ISBN 0-687-21371-1**

In hopes of getting his pot of gold, lazy Ninny Nanny captures a wee fairy man. Read on St. Patrick's Day and hide gold nuggets or coins for children to find as they straighten up the room. GRANDMOTHERS. LAZINESS. LEPRECHAUNS.

610 **Bang, Molly.** *The Paper Crane.* **Illus. by the author. Greenwillow, 1985. ISBN 0-688-04109-4**

An unusual tale of a stranger who pays for his restaurant meal with an origami crane that comes to life and dances, bringing the restaurant new prosperity. Listeners will pore over the unusual three-dimensional paper cutout illustrations, and older children might try to emulate the style. Related titles worthy of contrasting include Bang's *Dawn* and *The Crane Wife*, the well-known Japanese folktale, retold by Sumiko Yagawa. BIRDS. DANCING. RESTAURANTS.

611 **Barrett, Judi.** *Pickles Have Pimples: And Other Silly Statements.* **Illus. by Lonni Sue Johnson. Atheneum, 1986. ISBN 0-689-31187-7**

"Pickles have pimples. Cheeks have dimples." Each page contains two otherwise unrelated sentences, rhymed and illustrated together into a semblance of cockeyed sense. Children can write and illustrate more of the same. CREATIVE WRITING. STORIES IN RHYME.

612 **Bauer, Caroline Feller.** *My Mom Travels a Lot.* **Illus. by Nancy Winslow Parker. Penguin, 1985. ISBN 0-14-050545-8**

The pros and cons of mom being away on business, as measured by her daughter, the young narrator. Your children can apply the format and write pairs of sentences —the good thing versus the bad thing about it—incorporating the close-to-home experience of having a substitute teacher for a day. CREATIVE WRITING. MOTHERS AND DAUGHTERS.

613 **Baylor, Byrd.** *Amigo.* **Illus. by Garth Williams. Macmillan, 1989. ISBN 0-689-71299-5**

Narrative poem of desert boy and prairie dog who tame each other, reprinted from the 1963 edition. Use with Diane Siebert's masterful poem, *Mojave*. DESERTS-POETRY. NARRATIVE POETRY. PETS. STORIES IN RHYME.

614 **Benton, Robert.** *Don't Ever Wish for a 7-Foot Bear.* **Illus. by Sally Benton. Knopf, 1972.**

[1–2 sittings, 32p.] The polar bear that appears on Harold's doorstep one rainy Saturday breaks toys, makes a mess in the kitchen while baking a cake, and refuses to leave. A better-behaved wished-for bear can be found in Susan Jeschke's *Angela and Bear*. BEARS. WISHES.

615 **Berger, Terry.** *The Turtle's Picnic: And Other Nonsense Stories.* **Illus. by Erkki Alanen. Crown, 1977.**

Three absurd stories—extended jokes, really—introduce an untrusting baby turtle, a picky dog, and a boastful lion. For more foolishness, also see Anne Rose's *The Triumphs of Fuzzy Fogtop*. DOGS. LIONS. TURTLES.

616 **Birdseye, Tom.** *Air Mail to the Moon.* **Illus. by Stephen Gammell. Holiday House, 1988. ISBN 0-8234-0683-0**

Hopping-mad narrator Ora Mae Cotton, looking for the crook who stole her first loose tooth, blames it on everyone in her family—until she finds it in her own pocket. Crackling, down-home country personality provides a fresh interpretation of the "lost tooth" genre, and her warning, "I'm gonna open up a can of gotcha and send you airmail to the moon," is so satisfying to say! Ask your listeners to offer some of their tooth tales of woe, and then read Marc Brown's *Arthur's Tooth.* FAMILY LIFE. TEETH.

617 **Bishop, Claire.** *The Five Chinese Brothers.* **Illus. by Kurt Wiese. Coward, 1938. ISBN 0-698-20044-6**

Unjustly blamed for a little boy's drowning, one of the look-alike brothers is sentenced to death but saved, thanks to his and his brothers' extraordinary talents. Good to act out with improvised dialogue. The illustrations have been the source of controversy about racial stereotyping, so consider carefully before reading aloud. Compare with Cheng Hou-Tien's similar folktale *The Six Chinese Brothers.* BROTHERS. FOLKLORE—CHINA.

618 **Blume, Judy.** *Freckle Juice.* **Illus. by Sonia O. Lisker. Four Winds, 1971. ISBN 0-02-711690-5**

[5 chapters, 40p.] Andrew will try anything to get freckles, including classmate Sharon's fifty-cent secret recipe that gives him a big bellyache. The message to be yourself hits home in a realistic way, while books like James Howe's *I Wish I Were a Butterfly* and Bill Peet's *The Whingdingdilly* make the same point using fantasy. SCHOOLS. SELF-CONCEPT.

619 **Blume, Judy.** *The Pain and the Great One.* **Illus. by Irene Trivas. Bradbury, 1984. ISBN 0-02-711100-8**

One at a time, a six-year-old brother and his eight-year-old sister narrate their complaints about each other, both sure that the other gets all the advantages and parental favoritism. Also try Crescent Dragonwagon's *I Hate My Brother Harry* and Judith Viorst's *I'll Fix Anthony.* BROTHERS AND SISTERS. SIBLING RIVALRY.

620 **Brady, Irene.** *Doodlebug.* **Illus. by the author. Houghton Mifflin, 1977. ISBN 0-395-25782-4**

[2 sittings, 35p.] Jennifer's seemingly worthless lame new pony turns out to be quite valuable. Follow up with a tale of danger and snow in Iceland with Lonzo Anderson's *The Ponies of Mykillengi.* ANIMALS. HORSES.

621 **Brenner, Barbara.** *A Dog I Know.* **Illus. by Fred Brenner. Harper & Row, 1983. ISBN 0-06-020685-3**

As told by the boy owner, a quiet, insightful description of the qualities that make his dog unique. Children can write or tell about their own pets. Show Ruth Brown's *Our Cat Flossie* for the cat angle. CREATIVE WRITING. DOGS.

622 **Brett, Jan.** *The First Dog.* **Illus. by the author. Harcourt, 1988. ISBN 0-15-227650-5**

In the Pleistocene era, after a hungry Paleowolf warns Kip, a cave boy, of danger from Mighty Mammoth, Cave Bear, and Saber-Toothed Cat, Kip brings the friendly creature home and names him "Dog," meaning "one who wags his tail." Stack the noble Paleowolf against a modern-day protector, Steven Kellogg's gangly Great Dane from *Pinkerton, Behave* and *Prehistoric Pinkerton*. ANIMALS, PREHISTORIC. DOGS.

623 **Briggs, Raymond.** *Jim and the Beanstalk*. **Illus. by the author. Putnam, 1989. ISBN 0-698-20641-X**

After climbing the beanstalk outside his window, Jim finds the now old, toothless, bald son of the giant that Jack had met in the old folktale and helps him acquire specs, teeth, and a wig. An obvious follow-up to Lorinda Bryan Cauley's *Jack and the Beanstalk*, Gail E. Haley's *Jack and the Bean Tree*, and James Still's *Jack and the Wonder Beans*; you might want to undertake a series of fairy tale "sets," using original versions along with parodies such as Bernice Myers's *Sidney Rella and the Glass Sneaker*, A. Vesey's *The Princess and the Frog*, and Jane Yolen's *Sleeping Ugly*. FAIRY TALES—SATIRE. GIANTS. PARODIES.

624 **Brown, Jeff.** *Flat Stanley*. **Illus. by Tomi Ungerer. Harper & Row, 1964. ISBN 0-06-020681-0**

[2 sittings, unp.] Stanley Lambchop awakes one morning to find his bulletin board has flattened him half an inch thick, making sliding under doors and into grates a cinch. Use as a "What if . . . ?" kickoff for creative writing. CREATIVE WRITING. ROBBERS AND OUTLAWS.

625 **Brown, Marc.** *Arthur's April Fool*. **Illus. by the author. Little, Brown, 1985. ISBN 0-316-11196-1**

An insecure aardvark practices his new magic tricks while worrying about the school bully who's threatened to pulverize him. Practice a few simple tricks from *Now You See It: Easy Magic for Beginners* by Ray Broekel and Laurence B. White. BROTHERS AND SISTERS. BULLIES. HOLIDAYS. TRICKS.

626 **Brown, Marc.** *Arthur's Birthday*. **Illus. by the author. Little, Brown, 1989. ISBN 0-316-11073-6**

With his party all set for Saturday, the same day as Muffy's, Arthur thinks up a plan to get all his friends together for a big surprise celebration. Since Arthur's already making merry, why not showcase all of the Arthur books to see how he's grown over the years. First, hand out one book to every pair of students who can search for the copyrights and put them in sequence by date. BIRTHDAYS. FRIENDSHIP. PARTIES.

627 **Brown, Marc.** *Arthur's Halloween*. **Illus. by the author. Little, Brown, 1982. ISBN 0-316-11116-3**

Halloween scares him until he follows his feisty little sister D.W. into the "witch's house" and learns not to be afraid of the unknown. Use this title early in the year to kick off a class love affair with the rest of the Arthur and D.W. books. Creep into another haunted house with Grandpa in James Stevenson's *That Terrible Halloween Night*, and stay in the mood with Marc Brown's *Spooky Riddles*. BROTHERS AND SISTERS. HALLOWEEN. HAUNTED HOUSES.

628 **Brown, Marc.** *Arthur's Teacher Trouble*. **Illus. by the author. Little Brown, 1987. ISBN 0-316-11244-5**

Arthur's new teacher, Mr. Ratburn, is a real grind. Hold your own class "spell-athon" after reading, and compare teachers with Mr. Smeal in *That Dreadful Day* by James Stevenson and Miss Viola Swamp in *Miss Nelson Is Missing* by Harry Allard. SCHOOLS. TEACHERS.

629 **Brown, Marc.** *Arthur's Tooth.* **Illus. by the author. Little, Brown, 1985. ISBN 0-316-11245-3**

Oh, the humiliation of being last in class to lose a tooth! Your own toothless ones can write or describe how they lost their first ones, a subject of which children *never* tire. Also do not miss Tom Birdseye's *Airmail to the Moon.* SCHOOLS. TEETH.

630 **Brown, Margaret Wise.** *The Important Book.* **Illus. by Leonard Weisgard. Harper & Row, 1949. ISBN 0-06-020721-3**

Descriptions of why various objects from spoon, daisy, and rain to sky, shoe, and you are important. A good writing starter, especially when you hand out an object to each child to write about, tell about, draw, and share. CREATIVE WRITING.

631 **Brown, Margaret Wise.** *Wheel on the Chimney.* **Illus. by Tibor Gergely. Lippincott, 1954. ISBN 0-397-30296-7**

A description of the miraculous stork migrations from Africa to Hungary and back each year. Delve into more realistic fiction about birds, such as eagles in Betty Waterton's *A Salmon for Simon* and owls in Jane Yolen's *Owl Moon.* BIRDS. CALDECOTT MEDAL.

632 **Brown, Ruth.** *Our Cat Flossie.* **Illus. by the author. Dutton, 1986. ISBN 0-525-44256-1**

Humorous, lustrous paintings belie the text, which is a demonstration of understatement and irony about what the narrator's cat likes to do. Children should bring in pet photos and stories of the activities their pets favor. Use this with Bruce McMillan's *Kitten Can. . .A Concept Book* to stimulate discussion and develop vocabulary and Barbara Brenner's *A Dog I Know* to give equal time to canines. CATS.

633 **Bunting, Eve.** *The Wednesday Surprise.* **Illus. by Donald Carrick. Clarion, 1989. ISBN 0-89919-721-3**

Young narrator Anna and her grandmother are planning a surprise for Dad's birthday. Anna's taught her grandmother to read, proving you're never too old to learn or too young to teach. This could be a kick-off to "Read Aloud to Your Family" month or a follow-up to Barbara Cooney's *Miss Rumphius,* as another suggestion of how to make the world more beautiful. BOOKS AND READING. GRANDMOTHERS.

634 **Burton, Virginia Lee.** *The Little House.* **Illus. by the author. Houghton Mifflin, 1978. ISBN 0-395-18156-9**

About the growth of a town and the plucky house that survives progress. A natural for a social studies lesson on communities. CALDECOTT MEDAL. CITIES AND TOWNS. COUNTRY LIFE. HOUSES. SEASONS.

635 **Calhoun, Mary.** *Cross-Country Cat.* **Illus. by Erick Ingraham. Morrow, 1979. ISBN 0-688-32186-0**

Henry, a Siamese cat on skis, makes it down the snow-covered mountain after being accidentally left behind by his human family. Such a resourceful cat belongs in the company of other great felines like *Puss in Boots,* as retold by Lorinda Bryan Cauley or Paul Galdone. Beatrice Schenk de Regniers's poems in *This Big Cat and Other Cats I've Known* would be a nice touch here. CATS. SKIING. SNOW. WINTER.

636 **Cameron, Polly.** *"I Can't," Said the Ant.* **Illus. by the author. Coward, 1961.**

When the teapot falls, the ant enlists help from its friends. A crazy rhyming story and a natural poem starter; have children supply the rhyme at the end of each line. In the same vein, see also N. M. Bodecker's *Let's Marry Said the Cherry and Other Nonsense Poems.* ANTS. INSECTS. SPIDERS. STORIES IN RHYME.

637 **Carlson, Nancy L.** *Louanne Pig in the Mysterious Valentine.* **Illus. by the author. Penguin, 1987. ISBN 0-14-050604-7**

She tries to find the guy who sent it. Use as an introduction to the rest of the Louanne Pig, Loudmouth George, and Harriet series for your readers to try on their own. Also use Marjorie Weinman Sharmat's *The Best Valentine in the World,* James Stevenson's *Happy Valentine's Day, Emma,* Eve Bunting's *The Valentine Bears,* Lillian Hoban's *Arthur's Great Big Valentine,* and Frank Modell's *One Zillion Valentines.* Top it all off with the poetry of Jack Prelutsky's *It's Valentine's Day.* FATHERS AND DAUGHTERS. PIGS. VALENTINE'S DAY.

638 **Carlson, Natalie Savage.** *Marie Louise's Heyday.* **Illus. by Jose Aruego and Ariane Dewey. Scribner, 1975.**

A put-upon mongoose reluctantly agrees to baby-sit for five rambunctious opossums, even though she had earmarked the day for her heyday. Compare the baby-sitting experience with Eileen Christelow's *Jerome the Babysitter* and Mary Rayner's *Mr. and Mrs. Pig's Evening Out.* ANIMALS. BABY-SITTERS. OPOSSUMS.

639 **Carlson, Natalie Savage.** *The Night the Scarecrow Walked.* **Illus. by Charles Robinson. Scribner, 1979.**

On Halloween night, Jeff and his sister Libby Lou are petrified when the scarecrow in their field seems to come to life. The open ending allows listeners to express their own conclusions; likewise with Emily Herman's *Hubknuckles.* BROTHERS AND SISTERS. FEAR. HALLOWEEN.

640 **Carrick, Carol.** *Ben and the Porcupine.* **Illus. by Donald Carrick. Houghton Mifflin, 1985. ISBN 0-89919-348-X**

Christopher tries to find a way to protect his dog Ben after the dog tangles with a porcupine and comes home with a nose full of painful quills. Sixth in a series about Christopher and his dogs; read this one as a follow-up to *The Foundling.* DOGS. PORCUPINES.

641 **Carrick, Carol.** *The Foundling.* **Illus. by Donald Carrick. Houghton Mifflin, 1977. ISBN 0-395-28775-8**

Still grieving for his dog Bodger, recently killed by a pickup truck, Christopher can't accept a new dog into his life until he realizes the puppy wandering in his yard has no home. Other affecting realistic accounts of faithful dogs include Dick Gackenbach's *Beauty, Brave and Beautiful* and Frances Ward Weller's *Riptide.* DOGS.

642 **Carrick, Carol.** *What Happened to Patrick's Dinosaurs?* **Illus. by Donald Carrick. Clarion, 1986. ISBN 0-89919-406-0**

Patrick explains to his older brother how he thinks the dinosaurs once built homes, roads, cars, and airplanes for people before leaving earth on a spaceship. Dinosaur-crazed children will come up with additional explanations of how dinosaurs helped prehistoric folks. This sequel to *Patrick's Dinosaurs* will also thrive on contact with

Steven Kellogg's *Prehistoric Pinkerton*, Henry Schwartz's *How I Captured a Dinosaur*, Jane Thayer's *Quiet on Account of Dinosaur*, plus the poetry books *Dinosaur and Beasts of Yore* by William Cole, Lee Bennett Hopkins's *Dinosaurs*, Jack Prelutsky's *Tyrannosaurus Was a Beast*, and Joseph Rosenbloom's riddles in *The Funniest Dinosaur Book Ever!* DINOSAURS. IMAGINATION.

643   **Caudill, Rebecca. *Did You Carry the Flag Today, Charlie?* Illus. by Nancy Grossman. Holt, 1966. ISBN 0-03-089753-X**

[6 chapters, 94p.] A mischievous Kentucky backwoods boy full of curiosity adjusts gradually to kindergarten. Contrast country classrooms and customs with big city life in Johanna Hurwitz's New York–based *Superduper Teddy* and the suburbs in Beverly Cleary's *Ramona the Pest*. BEHAVIOR. COUNTRY LIFE. SCHOOLS.

644   **Chapman, Carol. *Barney Bipple's Magic Dandelions*. Illus. by Steven Kellogg. Dutton, 1988. ISBN 0-525-44449-1**

Barney's wishes—to be eight, for his dog to talk, and for a big, shiny car—all come true, thanks to the old woman next door. Students can draw and tell what they would wish for, being careful not to overdo it as Mary Ann did in *The Good-Luck Pencil* by Diane Stanley. Newly released in full color. DOGS. MAGIC. WISHES.

645   **Charlip, Remy. *Fortunately*. Illus. by the author. Parents, 1964. ISBN 0-02-718100-6**

After a series of misadventures where his plane engine explodes and he must bail out by parachute, Jack makes it to his own surprise birthday party. Using the fortunate versus unfortunate sequence of the story, children can retell it or make up their own individual or whole class tales. Also see Steven Kroll's *The Tyrannosaurus Game* and Joan Lexau's *That's Good, That's Bad*. CAUSE AND EFFECT. LUCK. SEQUENCE STORIES.

646   **Charlip, Remy, and Burton Supree. *Mother, Mother, I Feel Sick, Send for the Doctor Quick, Quick, Quick*. Illus. by Remy Charlip. Four Winds, 1966.**

A shadow play in rhyme about a boy who has swallowed apples, a ball, birthday cake, spaghetti, fish, tea, and cookies, dishes and all, and that's just for starters. Instructions on the title page describe how to hang a bed sheet, shine a strong lamp to cast silhouettes, and act out the whole operation. A kindred spirit to Aliki's *Keep Your Mouth Closed, Dear*. CREATIVE DRAMA. FOOD. PLAYS. SICK.

647   **Cherry, Lynne. *The Great Kapok Tree: A Tale of the Amazon Rain Forest*. Illus. by the author. Harcourt, 1990. ISBN 0-15-200520-X**

Native animals from the Brazilian rain forest plead their case for conservation to the sleeping woodcutter who has come to chop down a tree. The brilliant paintings and impassioned discussion of the importance of preserving our wildlife encourage children to value the environment, as do Dr. Suess's *The Lorax* and Barbara Bash's *Desert Giant: The World of the Saguaro Cactus*. Barbara Cooney's *Miss Rumphius* will start them considering what positive impact they can make on the natural world. ECOLOGY. JUNGLES. PICTURE BOOKS FOR ALL AGES. TREES.

648   **Chess, Victoria. *Alfred's Alphabet Walk*. Illus. by the author. Greenwillow, 1979.**

Ignoring his mother's instructions to stay in the yard and learn his ABCs, Alfred, a gray furry creature, goes for a stroll instead and meets 26 alphabetical animals on his way. An alliterative story starter that inspires imitation, along with Jane Bayer's *A My Name Is Alice*. ALLITERATION. ALPHABET BOOKS. CREATIVE WRITING.

649   Christelow, Eileen. *Mr. Murphy's Marvelous Invention.* Illus. by the author. Clarion, 1983. ISBN 0-89919-141-X

A father pig's new housework machine misdoes all the chores. Read with William Pène du Bois's *Lazy Tommy Pumpkinhead* and George Selden's *Sparrow Socks,* and have your inventors design other choresaving devices. INVENTIONS. PIGS.

650   Clifton, Lucille. *The Boy Who Didn't Believe in Spring.* Illus. by Brinton Turkle. Dutton, 1973. ISBN 0-525-27145-7

An inner-city boy and his best friend—King Shabazz and Tony Polito—search the neighborhood for proof of the season and find it in an empty lot in the guise of a batch of yellow flowers and a nest of robin's eggs. Take a walk outside and observe other signs of spring. AFRICAN AMERICANS. CITIES AND TOWNS. SEASONS. SPRING.

651   Cole, Brock. *Nothing but a Pig.* Illus. by the author. Doubleday, 1981.

A farmer's pig, aspiring to a more dignified life, is taken in by the greedy landlord's fine clothes and wealth. In Boris Zakhoder's *How a Piglet Crashed the Christmas Party,* Oinky's human disguise does him no good either. BEHAVIOR. PIGS.

652   Conford, Ellen. *Impossible Possum.* Illus. by Rosemary Wells. Little, Brown, 1971.

Randolph, a young opossum child, is afraid to hang upside down by his tail until sticky tree sap and a boost of self-confidence help him out. An inspirational lift for those kids who are afraid to keep trying. Meet one mouse who refuses to give up in *Tillie and the Wall* by Leo Lionni. BROTHERS AND SISTERS. OPOSSUMS. PERSEVER-ANCE. SELF-CONCEPT.

653   Coombs, Patricia. *Dorrie and the Weather Box.* Illus. by the author. Lothrop, 1966.

A curious witch child causes a storm inside the house when her spell to stop the rain outside backfires. Introduce the "Dorrie" book series for your students to read alone. CATS. MAGIC. RAIN AND RAINFALL. WEATHER. WITCHES.

654   Cooney, Barbara. *Miss Rumphius.* Illus. by the author. Viking, 1982. ISBN 0-670-47958-6

About the "Lupine Lady" from Maine who did something to make the world more beautiful. Spark a discussion of what we might do to improve the world. Wonderful for all ages, along with Donald Hall's *Ox-Cart Man* and Tony Johnston's *Yonder,* which evoke the same pensive mood. AUNTS. FAMILY STORIES. FLOWERS. PICTURE BOOKS FOR ALL AGES.

655   Cox, David. *Bossyboots.* Illus. by the author. Crown, 1987. ISBN 0-517-56491-2

En route to Narribri by stagecoach, Abigail, the bossiest girl in old Australia, thwarts Flash Fred, the wild outlaw. Tie this in with the American Wild West (which looked similar except for a dearth of kangaroos and ostriches) via Richard Kennedy's *The Contests at Cowlick* or to a study of Australia. Look into the lives of marsupials and other odd Australian wildlife, starting with the nonsensical *Wombat Stew* by Marcia K. Vaughn. AUSTRALIA. FRONTIER AND PIONEER LIFE. ROBBERS AND OUTLAWS.

656   Dahl, Roald. *The Enormous Crocodile.* Illus. by Quentin Blake. Knopf, 1978. ISBN 0-394-83594-8

[1–2 sittings, unp.] Foiled each time by the other jungle animals, an evil crocodile skulks about, thinking up secret plans and clever tricks for catching juicy children to eat. Other brutes just as rotten include Jack Prelutsky's *The Mean Old Mean Hyena* and *The Terrible Tiger*. A kinder view of crocodiles is displayed in Bernard Waber's "Lyle" series. ANIMALS. BULLIES. CROCODILES.

657 **Dalgliesh, Alice.** *The Bears on Hemlock Mountain.* **Illus. by Helen Sewell. Macmillan, 1981. ISBN 0-689-70497-6**

[10 chapters, unp.] After convincing himself there are no bears nearby to worry about, Jonathan meets several on his way home from an errand for his mother. Chant the refrain with your children each time. Also read Helen Clare Pittman's *Once When I Was Scared* and Lynd Ward's *The Biggest Bear*. BEARS. COUNTRY LIFE. FARM LIFE. FEAR. MOUNTAINS.

658 **Daugherty, James.** *Andy and the Lion.* **Illus. by the author. Viking, 1938. ISBN 0-670-12433-8**

A modern companion to the Greek tale of Androcles, who dethorned a lion's paw. Try acting out "Part Two" in pairs pantomime. Andy's adventure begins as he is on his way to the library, as does nerdy Alistair's in Marilyn Sadler's *Alistair in Outer Space*. BOOKS AND READING. LIBRARIES. LIONS.

659 **Desbarats, Peter.** *Gabrielle and Selena.* **Illus. by Nancy Grossman. Harcourt, 1968.**

Tired of their usual routines, two best friends switch houses and identities for a day. See also Amy Hest's *The Mommy Exchange*. FAMILY LIFE. FRIENDSHIP.

660 **Devlin, Harry, and Wende Devlin.** *Cranberry Thanksgiving.* **Illus. by Harry Devlin. Macmillan, 1980. ISBN 0-02-729930-9**

When Maggie's clam-digging friend Mr. Whiskers and the respectable gold cane-carrying Mr. Horace both come for the holiday meal, Grandmother suspects the wrong man of stealing her famous cranberry bread recipe. The recipe is appended if you want to try a few loaves. COOKERY. FOOD. GRANDMOTHERS. STEALING. THANKSGIVING.

661 **Devlin, Harry, and Wende Devlin.** *Old Witch Rescues Halloween.* **Illus. by the authors. Parents, 1972.**

Old Witch teaches the sourpuss town mayor a lesson when he tries to cancel the holiday. Sequel to *Old Black Witch* (1972), where Nicky and his mother run their new Jug and Muffin Tea Room out of the witch's house. Try out a variety of witchy books, such as Margaret Embry's *The Blue-Nosed Witch*, Alice Low's *The Witch Who Was Afraid of Witches*, and Dennis Nolan's *Witch Bazooza*. FROGS. HALLOWEEN. WITCHES.

662 **Dillon, Barbara.** *The Teddy Bear Tree.* **Illus. by David Rose. Morrow, 1982.**

[5 chapters, 80p.] After Bertine buries the eye from her missing teddy bear, a strange tree grows, bearing even stranger "fruits": ten teddy bear-filled pods. Children can draw portraits of their own teddy bears and write paragraphs describing their singular personalities. FAMILY LIFE. TEDDY BEARS.

663 **Dragonwagon, Crescent.** *I Hate My Brother Harry.* **Illus. by Dick Gackenbach. Harper & Row, 1983. ISBN 0-06-021758-8**

Convinced that her older brother hates her, a little girl lists her reasons and thinks of a way to test his true feelings. Listeners will identify with this amusing look at a typical sibling relationship. In the same vein are Judy Blume's *The Pain and the*

Great One and Judith Viorst's *I'll Fix Anthony*. BROTHERS AND SISTERS. SIBLING RIVALRY.

664   Drescher, Henrik. *Simon's Book.* **Illus. by the author. Lothrop, 1983. ISBN 0-688-02086-0**

A young boy goes to bed, leaving on the drawing pad his unfinished story about Simon and the scary monster, who then come to life along with the drawing pens and a bottle of ink. A bizarre introduction to the functions of an author and illustrator, this story claims to have "written itself." Use with Jon Agee's *The Incredible Painting of Felix Clousseau* and Paul O. Zelinsky's *The Lion and the Stoat.* If children wish to write and illustrate their own books, start off with Ruth Krauss's *Is This You?* for beginners and Joan Lowery Nixon's *If You Were a Writer* for grades two and up. BOOKS. DRAWING. ILLUSTRATION OF BOOKS. MONSTERS. WRITING.

665   Erickson, Russell E. *A Toad for Tuesday.* **Illus. by Lawrence di Fiori. Lothrop, 1974. ISBN 0-688-51569-X**

[4–5 sessions, 64p.] While skiing to Aunt Toolia's, toad Warton is captured by an irascible owl who plans to eat him for a birthday dinner. Recommend as read alones others in the series including *Warton and Morton* (1976), *Warton and the King of the Skies* (1978), *Warton and the Traders* (1979), *Warton and the Castaways* (1982), and *Warton and the Contest* (1986). FRIENDSHIP. OWLS. TOADS.

666   Faulkner, Matt. *The Amazing Voyage of Jackie Grace.* **Illus. by the author. Scholastic, 1987. ISBN 0-590-40713-9**

Thrill to hero Jackie's bathtub adventures through the bounding main as he out-smarts a dastardly pirate captain and lives to sail again; bathtime will never be the same. Told entirely in large print exclamatory dialogue. Rev up your mind's eye with Nicholas Heller's *An Adventure at Sea* and continue swashbuckling with Bill Peet's *Cyrus the Unsinkable Sea Serpent.* BATHS. IMAGINATION. OCEAN. PIRATES.

667   Fenton, Edward. *The Big Yellow Balloon.* **Illus. by Ib Ohlsson. Doubleday, 1967.**

A chain reaction occurs when Tom the Cat, thinking he can kill the sun, chases Roger's giant balloon while he is in turn being stalked by a policeman intent on tracking down a thief, lady, dog catcher, and dog. A marvelous choice for creative drama with limited dialogue. See also Denys Cazet's *Lucky Me.* BALLOONS. CATS. CREATIVE DRAMA. SEQUENCE STORIES.

668   Flack, Marjorie. *Walter the Lazy Mouse.* **Illus. by Cyndy Szekeres. Doubleday, 1963.**

[10 chapters, 96p.] An ever-dawdling rodent must learn to fend for himself after his family moves away and forgets about him, providing him with a firsthand object lesson on the importance of school and learning. LOST. MICE. TEACHERS.

669   Flora, James. *Leopold the See-Through Crumbpicker.* **Illus. by the author. Harcourt, 1961.**

Minerva's large, furry new pet is invisible and incorrigibly hungry. Have children draw how they think he looks before you reveal his picture. ANIMALS, IMAGINARY. FOOD. PETS. SCHOOLS.

670   Folsom, Michael, and Marcia Folsom. *Easy as Pie: A Guessing Game of Sayings.* **Illus. by Jack Kent. Clarion, 1985. ISBN 0-89919-303-X**

An alphabet book of simple comparison sayings, one per two-sided page, for children to guess and add on, such as "Straight as an . . . Arrow, Snug as a . . . Bug in a rug." Students can ask their relatives for others, or make up new ones to write down and illustrate in the same format. ALPHABET BOOKS. ENGLISH LANGUAGE–IDIOMS.

671   **Freeman, Don.** *Norman the Doorman.* **Illus. by the author. Viking, 1959. ISBN 0-670-51515-9**

Art museum mouse creates his masterpiece—which he calls Trapeese—and enters it anonymously in a sculpture contest. Students can make their own works of art out of pipe cleaners. Read this along with Laurene Krasny Brown's *Visiting the Art Museum.* For another mouse who holds up his end with the human establishment, read Eve Titus's *Anatole.* ARTISTS. MICE. MUSEUMS. SCULPTORS.

672   **Friedman, Ina R.** *How My Parents Learned to Eat.* **Illus. by Allen Say. Houghton Mifflin, 1984. ISBN 0-395-35379-3**

A young girl relates the story of the courtship of her parents, then an American sailor and a Japanese schoolgirl, to explain why she eats with both chopsticks and silverware. Ask your students to find out how their parents met. Afterward, a pair of chopsticks could make a memorable and inexpensive gift to each child in the class. Also pair with Allen Say's postwar Japanese school story, *The Bicycle Man.* FAMILY STORIES. FOOD. JAPAN. LOVE.

673   **Gackenbach, Dick.** *King Wacky.* **Illus. by the author. Crown, 1984. ISBN 0-517-55265-5**

Born with his head on backwards, the cheerful king's opposite ways almost cause a war with a neighboring kingdom. Your own subjects can think up more backwards laws, sayings, and customs for the land of Woosey. Follow with a visit to *Upside-Down Town* by F. Emerson Andrews. KINGS AND RULERS. OPPOSITES.

674   **Gannett, Ruth Stiles.** *My Father's Dragon.* **Illus. by Ruth Chrisman Gannett. Random House, 1986. ISBN 0-394-91438-4**

[10 chapters, 86p.] The narrator relates how his father, when just a boy, met an alley cat who gave him directions to Wild Island to rescue a captive baby dragon from the animals there. To book-talk this title, bring in a sack of all the supplies the boy takes with him to show as you describe the situation on the island. Creative drama possibilities abound in each confrontation between the boy and the animals he meets. Pick pairs of children to present their improvised scenes, don't forget to discuss sequel possibilities, and display the other titles in the series: *The Dragons of Blueland* and *Elmer & the Dragon* (both Dell, 1980). With 10 short chapters this whole book can easily be read in one tangerine-filled week. ANIMALS, IMAGINARY. CREATIVE DRAMA. DRAGONS. ISLANDS.

675   **Gardner, Beau.** *The Look Again . . . and Again, and Again, and Again Book.* **Illus. by the author. Lothrop, 1982. ISBN 0-688-00932-8**

As you rotate the book to see each picture right side up, sideways, and upside down, each page of bold bright graphics depicts four images that children can interpret in any number of ways. Though Gardner labels each picture as he intended it, perceptive viewers will see myriad meanings, like tame two-color Rorschach blots. Children can design their own "look agains" with two colors of construction paper and scissors. More eye-openers include the companion *The Turn About, Think About, Look About Book* (1980), Ruth Brown's *If at First You Do Not See,* Ann Jonas's *Reflections* and *Round Trip,* Suse MacDonald's more primary

Alphabatics, and Charles G. Shaw's *It Looked Like Spilt Milk.* IMAGINATION. PICTURE BOOKS FOR ALL AGES. VISUAL PERCEPTION.

676   **Garrett, Helen.** *Angelo the Naughty One.* **Illus. by Leo Politi. Viking, 1944.**

[1–2 sittings, 40p.] On his sister's wedding day, a Mexican boy who hates baths runs away to avoid taking one. Contrast with Audrey Wood's *King Bidgood's in the Bathtub,* because he won't get out! BATHS. MEXICO. RUNAWAYS.

677   **Gerstein, Mordicai.** *Arnold of the Ducks.* **Illus. by the author. Harper & Row, 1983. ISBN 0-06-022003-1**

A little boy raised by ducks almost becomes one until chance reunites him with his human family. Act out Arnold's duck training in pantomime with your class. CREATIVE DRAMA. DUCKS. FLIGHT.

678   **Giff, Patricia Reilly.** *Today Was a Terrible Day.* **Illus. by Susanna Natti. Viking, 1980. ISBN 0-670-71830-0**

Everything goes wrong in school for second-grader Ronald Morgan who thinks he can't read. Another charmer in the series is *Happy Birthday, Ronald Morgan;* booktalk the others. For more hard luck stories see Steven Kroll's *Friday the 13th* and Judith Viorst's *Alexander and the Terrible, Horrible, No Good, Very Bad Day.* SCHOOLS. TEACHERS.

679   **Glazer, Tom.** *On Top of Spaghetti.* **Illus. by Tom Garcia. Doubleday, 1982.**

Just for dumb fun, sing this one about the renegade meatball which grows into a tree bearing more meatballs and tomato sauce. Compound the nonsense with Tomie dePaola's overflowing pasta pot in *Strega Nona* and Nadine Bernard Westcott's goofy *Peanut Butter and Jelly.* FOOD. SONGS.

680   **Graves, Robert.** *The Big Green Book.* **Illus. by Maurice Sendak. Macmillan, 1985. ISBN 0-02-736810-6**

The author of *I, Claudius,* Graves indulges himself in a wish fulfillment story, as young Jack finds a book of magic and uses it to make his aunt and uncle seem ridiculous. Originally published in 1962. Use with other wishing or magic spell books like Mercer Mayer's *A Special Trick,* Pauline Watson's *Wriggles the Little Wishing Pig,* or Jay William's *One Big Wish.* MAGIC.

681   **Greene, Carol.** *The Thirteen Days of Halloween.* **Illus. by Tom Dunnington. Childrens Press, 1983. ISBN 0-516-08231-0**

A witch-ified parody of the well-loved Christmas song—see first Jan Brett's gorgeous rendition of *The Twelve Days of Christmas*—with the likes of five cooked worms, four giggling ghosts, three fat toads, two hissing cats, and a vulture in a dead tree instead of all those partridges. Make your own large, illustrated, laminated card for each day, hand out one card per pair of children, and sing the song, with each duo responsible for standing up and singing its own part each time. George Mendoza's *A Wart Snake in a Fig Tree* is similar, but a bit more mischievous. HALLOWEEN. PARODIES. SONGS. WITCHES.

682   **Griffith, Helen V.** *Grandaddy's Place.* **Illus. by James Stevenson. Greenwillow, 1987. ISBN 0-688-06254-7**

Janetta gets to know her grandfather for the first time when she and her mother visit his run-down farm. James Stevenson, who has written about another "Grandpa" in

Could Be Worse and its many gregarious sequels, drew this "Grandaddy" as well. Compare their personalities and ask children to draw and describe their own grandfathers and the stories they tell. FARM LIFE. FISHES. GRANDFATHERS. STORY-TELLING.

683   **Hartley, Deborah.** *Up North in Winter.* **Illus. by Lydia Dabcovich. Dutton, 1986. ISBN 0-525-44268-5**

A young boy retells the story of the freezing winter night in 1911 when his grandfather, heading home across the frozen lake, stumbled upon what he assumed was a dead fox. Pair this with Tejima's *Fox's Dream*, another memorable winter tale. FAMILY STORIES. FOXES. WINTER.

684   **Heide, Florence Parry, and Roxanne Heide.** *A Monster Is Coming! A Monster Is Coming!* **Illus. by Rachi Farrow. Franklin Watts, 1980.**

To brother's frantic warnings, sister responds, "Don't bother me, I'm watching TV." Children will be eager to draw the monster as you read or show the illustrations and join in on the refrain. Also fun to act out in pairs. BROTHERS AND SISTERS. MONSTERS. TELEVISION.

685   **Heller, Nicholas.** *An Adventure at Sea.* **Illus. by the author. Greenwillow, 1988. ISBN 0-688-07847-8**

To Harold, the empty box in his yard is a tall-masted ship with red sails, cannons, and a mermaid carved on the bow, and he is the captain, in charge of his doubting brother and sister who insist the sea monsters, treasure ships, and sharks are only the dog, a plate of cookies, and the neighbor's cat. Matt Faulkner's *The Amazing Voyage of Jackie Grace* and Ezra Jack Keats's *Regards to the Man in the Moon* are more "mind's eye" books where the readers are encouraged to let their imaginations run free. A refrigerator box would be just the thing to encourage new sea escapades. BROTHERS AND SISTERS. IMAGINATION. PLAY.

686   **Herman, Emily.** *Hubknuckles.* **Illus. by Deborah Kogan Ray. Crown, 1985. ISBN 0-517-55646-4**

Thinking the white spirit outside her house is really her father in disguise, Lee ventures into the yard and dances with a Halloween ghost. Like Natalie Savage Carlson's *The Night the Scarecrow Walked*, the open ending will give children a chance to debate whether the spirit was real or not. GHOSTS. HALLOWEEN.

687   **Hill, Elizabeth Starr.** *Evan's Corner.* **Illus. by Nancy Grossman. Holt, 1967.**

In the family's two-room apartment, Evan puts all his effort into refurbishing a space to call his own. The story's gentle message—that happiness comes only when you help others too—is worth pursuing. AFRICAN AMERICANS. APARTMENT HOUSES. FAMILY LIFE.

688   **Hoban, Tana.** *Look Again!* **Photos by Tana Hoban. Macmillan, 1971. ISBN 0-02-744050-8**

A collection of partially hidden photos of objects and animals to identify, along with the companion book *Take Another Look* (Greenwillow, 1981). Children can create their own photo surprises. For more guessing, but on a simpler plane, see Beau Gardner's *Guess What?* and Marilee Robin Burton's *Tails, Toes, Eyes, Ears, Nose.* PHOTOGRAPHY. VISUAL PERCEPTION.

689   Hoguet, Susan. *I Unpacked My Grandmother's Trunk*. Illus. by the author. Dutton, 1983. ISBN 0-525-44069-0

Remember that old alphabet memory game you played on long car trips? Here's an illustrated version with half-page flaps, plenty of clever details, and lots to remember. Immediately after reading the book, open a small trunk, suitcase, or magic box, which you have packed with miniature objects, one per letter, and have each child choose an item or two. Play the game in a circle as children hold up their items each time. In an alternate format, assign students a letter and play the game with the real objects they drum up from home. ALPHABET BOOKS. MEMORY. WORD GAMES.

690   Houseman, Laurence. *Rocking-Horse Land*. Illus. by Kristina Rodanas. Lothrop, 1990. ISBN 0-688-09015-X

On Prince Freedling's fifth birthday, he finds in his room the great black rocking horse, Rollande, who comes to life each night when the prince opens the window to set him free. First published in 1922, the sentimental fairy tale-like story will appeal to all who have wished their toys could come to life. Relate this to two other flying horses: Sally Scott's Arabian Nights tale *The Magic Horse* and Lynd Ward's wordless *The Silver Pony*. BIRTHDAYS. HORSES. LITERARY FAIRY TALES. PRINCES AND PRINCESSES.

691   Houston, Gloria. *The Year of the Perfect Christmas Tree*. Illus. by Barbara Cooney. Dial, 1988. ISBN 0-8037-0300-7

In 1918, with her father away at war and Christmas coming, Ruthie prays for him to come home and wishes for a doll with a beautiful dress the color of cream, all trimmed with ribbons and lace. A holiday pleaser of a mother's sacrifice and love. Also see Trinka Hakes Noble's *Apple Tree Christmas* for another thoughtful story that takes place in the past. CHRISTMAS. FAMILY STORIES. FATHERS AND DAUGHTERS. GIFTS. MOTHERS AND DAUGHTERS.

692   Howe, James. *I Wish I Were a Butterfly*. Illus. by Ed Young. Harcourt, 1987. ISBN 0-15-200470-X

How a young cricket, convinced he is ugly because a frog told him so, learns to find his own beauty. A more serious counterpart to acceptance-of-self stories like Eric Carle's *The Mixed-Up Chameleon*, Theo LeSieg's *I Wish That I Had Duck Feet*, Leo Lionni's *Fish Is Fish*, Bernard Waber's *"You Look Ridiculous," Said the Rhinoceros to the Hippopotamus*, Bill Peet's *The Whingdingdilly*, or Pauline Watson's *Wriggles the Little Wishing Pig*. Apply the lesson in human terms with Judy Blume's *Freckle Juice*. INSECTS. SELF-ACCEPTANCE. WISHES.

693   Howe, James. *Scared Silly: A Halloween Treat*. Illus. by Leslie Morrill. Morrow, 1989. ISBN 0-688-07666-1

The Monroe family pets—narrator and dog Harold, young nervous puppy Howie, cynical punning cat Chester, and the enigmatic pointy-fanged rabbit Bunnicula—get the fright of their lives when the lights go out and a witch stops by on Halloween night. You also won't want to miss the howls in *The Fright before Christmas*. HALLOWEEN. PETS. PICTURE BOOKS FOR ALL AGES. WITCHES.

694   Hurwitz, Johanna. *Busybody Nora*. Illus. by Susan Jeschke. Morrow, 1976. ISBN 0-688-32057-0

[6 chapters, 64p.] Winsome anecdotes about a young girl and her family in their New York City apartment. Intersperse the soup and string beans chapters with the related *Stone Soup* by Marcia Brown and Lorinda Bryan Cauley's *Jack and the Beanstalk*. APARTMENT HOUSES. BROTHERS AND SISTERS. FAMILY LIFE. GRANDPARENTS.

695   **Hurwitz, Johanna. *Russell Sprouts*. Illus. by Lillian Hoban. Morrow, 1987. ISBN 0-688-07166-X**

[6 chapters, 68p.] In six endearing episodes, Russell—Nora and Teddy's six-year-old downstairs neighbor—makes up a new bad word, dresses as a daddy for Halloween, writes a report card for his parents, and grows a potato plant. Third in a series that includes *Rip Roaring Russell* (1983), *Russell Rides Again* (1985), and *Russell and Elisa* (1989). FAMILY LIFE. FRIENDSHIP. SCHOOLS.

696   **Hurwitz, Johanna. *Superduper Teddy*. Illus. by Susan Jeschke. Morrow, 1980. ISBN 0-688-32234-4**

[6 chapters, 80p.] Nora's shy little brother matures in kindergarten. In addition to reading or book-talking the other Nora, Teddy, and Russell books, compare Teddy's school exploits with a "country cousin" from Kentucky in Rebecca Caudill's *Did You Carry the Flag Today, Charlie?* and a suburban one in Beverly Cleary's *Ramona the Pest*. APARTMENT HOUSES. BROTHERS AND SISTERS. FAMILY LIFE. GRANDPARENTS.

697   **Hutchins, Pat. *The Tale of Thomas Mead*. Illus. by the author. Greenwillow, 1980. ISBN 0-688-84282-8**

An inspirational rhyming saga of a boy who refuses to read and ends up in jail before he changes his wanton ways. "Why should I?" your listeners will chant along. BOOKS AND READING. STORIES IN RHYME.

698   **Ivanov, Anatoly. *Ol' Jake's Lucky Day*. Illus. by the author. Lothrop, 1984.**

Before attempting to catch the hare he's spotted, Ol' Jake envisions selling it, buying a pig, building a house, and being the envy of his neighbors in his old age. Like "The Country Maid and The Milk Pail" in Louis Untermeyers's *Aesop's Fables*, he scares off the hare and sees his dream vanish. HUNTERS AND HUNTING.

699   **Jeffers, Susan. *Wild Robin*. Illus. by the author. Dutton, 1976. ISBN 0-525-42787-2**

A headstrong, naughty young farm lad is held captive by the Fairy Queen until his devoted sister breaks his enchantment. Based on the Scottish ballad "Tamlane." Sustain the enchantment with selections from Virginia Haviland's *Favorite Fairy Tales Told in Scotland*. BEHAVIOR. BROTHERS AND SISTERS. FAIRIES.

700   **Jonas, Ann. *Reflections*. Illus. by the author. Greenwillow, 1987. ISBN 0-688-06141-9**

A day at the seaside, with surprising dual-purpose color watercolors. Read from front to back, then turn over to continue the journey upside down. Similar in concept to *Round Trip* below and Ruth Brown's *If at First You Do Not See*; top it off with Beau Gardner's four-way guessing pictures in *The Look Again . . . and Again, and Again, and Again Book* and *The Turn About, Think About, Look About Book*. ILLUSTRATION OF BOOKS. PICTURE BOOKS FOR ALL AGES. SEASHORE. VISUAL PERCEPTION.

701   Jonas, Ann. *Round Trip*. Illus. by the author. Greenwillow, 1983. ISBN 0-688-01781-9

A journey from home, into the city, and back again. The striking black-and-white graphics are all the more remarkable when, halfway through the journey, you turn the book upside down for the return trip. Children may want to design their own two-way drawings. Fascinating for all ages, along with *Reflections* above. ILLUS-TRATION OF BOOKS. PICTURE BOOKS FOR ALL AGES. VISUAL PERCEPTION.

702   Joslin, Sesyle. *What Do You Say, Dear?* Illus. by Maurice Sendak. Scott, 1958. ISBN 0-06-023074-6

Etiquette students can think up, write, and illustrate new situations after acting out these outlandish encounters with outlaws and animals, and the correct social response to each. Miss Manners would approve of the proper etiquette displayed in each example, along with those in the accompanying *What Do You Do, Dear?* (1961). CREATIVE DRAMA. CREATIVE WRITING. ETIQUETTE.

703   Keats, Ezra Jack. *Regards to the Man in the Moon*. Illus. by the author. Four Winds, 1981.

Using junkyard castoffs as their rockets, Louie and his friends travel through space via their imaginations much as Harold does with his backyard box in Nicholas Heller's *An Adventure at Sea*. For free play, bring in large boxes for children to decorate. IMAGINATION. SPACE FLIGHT.

704   Kellogg, Steven. *Chicken Little*. Illus. by the author. Morrow, 1985. ISBN 0-688-05691-1

An alternative version of the old tale, this has Foxy Loxy impersonating a police officer and, thanks to Sergeant Hippo Hefty, justice prevailing. Compare with Paul Galdone's more traditional *Henny Penny* and Rafe Martin's *Foolish Rabbit's Big Mistake*. CHICKENS. FOXES.

705   Kellogg, Steven. *The Mysterious Tadpole*. Illus. by the author. Dial, 1977. ISBN 0-8037-6246-1

Louis's Uncle McAllister from Scotland sends him a rare pet that grows into a hungry but amiable Loch Ness Monster. The Weston Woods filmstrip version is delightful. ANIMALS, MYTHICAL. PETS.

706   Kellogg, Steven. *Pinkerton, Behave*. Illus. by the author. Dial, 1979. ISBN 0-8037-6575-4

The ungainly Great Dane flunks obedience school, but gets the burglar anyway. First in a series, and a blue ribbon match for Jan Brett's *First Dog*, Patricia Lauber's *Clarence and the Burglar*, and Amy Schwartz's *Oma and Bobo*. DOGS. ROBBERS AND OUTLAWS.

707   Kellogg, Steven. *Prehistoric Pinkerton*. Illus. by the author. Dial, 1987. ISBN 0-8037-0323-6

His young owner takes the teething mutt, disguised in a stegosaurus costume, to Dinosaur Day at the museum. Use as a light introduction to your dinosaur unit along with Carol Carrick's *Patrick's Dinosaurs* and *What Happened to Patrick's Dinosaurs?*, Henry Schwartz's *How I Captured a Dinosaur*, and Jane Thayer's *Quiet on Account of Dinosaur*. Poetry books you shouldn't do without include William Cole's *Dinosaurs and Beasts of Yore*, Lee Bennett Hopkins's *Dinosaurs*, and Jack Prelutsky's *Tyrannosaurus Was a Beast*. DINOSAURS. DOGS. MUSEUMS. TEETH.

708   **Kennedy, Richard.** *The Contests at Cowlick.* **Illus. by Marc Simont. Little, Brown, 1975.**

Plucky young Wally outwits Hogbone and his outlaw gang who want to tear up the town while the sheriff and his men are off fishing. David Cox's Australian *Bossyboots* puts a few more lowlifes in their places. CONTESTS. ROBBERS AND OUTLAWS. WEST.

709   **Kessler, Leonard.** *Old Turtle's Baseball Stories.* **Illus. by the author. Greenwillow, 1982. ISBN 0-688-00724-4**

Too cold to play ball in winter, Old Turtle's friends huddle by the wood stove while he tells tall ones about an eight-armed pitcher, a mooseball expert, an all-field outfielder, and a base stealing skunk. Bundle up and go outside for a quick game of catch. ANIMALS. BASEBALL. STORYTELLING.

710   **King, Larry L.** *Because of Lozo Brown.* **Illus. by Amy Schwartz. Viking, 1988. ISBN 0-670-81031-2**

When the nervous narrator finally meets Lozo, his brutish, fearsome next-door neighbor, he is stunned to find a new friend instead of a mean, green-tongued bully. Use this wry rhyming account of shattered preconceived fears with books about other aspects of moving, such as Elizabeth Lee O'Donnell's *Maggie Doesn't Want to Move*, Marjorie Weinman Sharmat's *Gila Monsters Meet You at the Airport*, and Bernard Waber's *Ira Says Goodbye.* FEAR. FRIENDSHIP. MOVING, HOUSEHOLD.

711   **King-Smith, Dick.** *Sophie's Snail.* **Illus. by Claire Minter-Kemp. Delacorte, 1989. ISBN 0-385-29824-2**

[6 chapters, 67p.] Racing a snail with her twin brothers, preparing for life as a farmer, entertaining great-great-aunt Alice, and playing "I Spy" with Daddy to take his mind off his bad back are activities that keep four-year-old Sophie engrossed. Play "I Spy," bring in snails to race, and make a class list of the "Good and Bad Things about Going to School." BROTHERS AND SISTERS. ENGLAND. FAMILY LIFE. HUMOROUS FICTION. SNAILS.

712   **Kipling, Rudyard.** *How the Whale Got His Throat.* **Illus. by Pauline Baynes. Peter Bedrick, 1987. ISBN 0-87226-135-2**

Before the fish-eating whale devours him—the last small fish in the sea, the 'Stute Fish—he convinces the whale to eat instead a nice but nubbly man, a shipwrecked mariner in suspenders who puts an end to the whale's voracious eating habits. Robert McCloskey's *Burt Dow, Deep-Water Man* also ends up in a whale's belly. Continue underwater exploration with Bill Peet's *Cyrus the Unsinkable Sea Serpent*, Bernard Waber's *I Was All Thumbs*, and Susan Russo's *The Ice Cream Ocean and Other Delectable Poems of the Sea.* POURQUOI TALES. WHALES.

713   **Korschunow, Irina.** *The Foundling Fox.* **Illus. by Reinard Michl. Harper & Row, 1984. ISBN 0-06-023244-7**

A kindhearted vixen rescues a starving kit whose mother has been shot, protects him from a hunter's hound and fierce badger, and brings him home to raise with her own three fox children. Simple language, short chapters, and small masterful paintings mark a compelling drama of animal adoption, loyalty, and love. Set the mood with Tejima's *Fox's Dream.* FOXES. MOTHERS.

714   **Krauss, Ruth.** *Is This You?* **Illus. by Crockett Johnson. Scholastic, 1988. ISBN 0–590–41196–9**

How to write, illustrate, and put together a 10-page book about yourself. A good starting point for young authors along with Henry Drescher's *Simon's Book*. AUTHORS. BOOKS. CREATIVE WRITING. ILLUSTRATION OF BOOKS. WRITING.

715   **Kroll, Steven.** *Amanda and Giggling Ghost.* **Illus. by Dick Gackenbach. Holiday House, 1980. ISBN 0–8234–0408–0**

A little girl is blamed for a ghost's thefts throughout town one wild night. Witch Maggie is the culprit when the town's sweets are missing in Kroll's *The Candy Witch*. GHOSTS. HONESTY. STEALING.

716   **Kroll, Steven.** *Friday the 13th.* **Illus. by Dick Gackenbach. Holiday House, 1981. ISBN 0–8234–0392–0**

About the misfortunes of Harold who spills, breaks, and falls and, finally, changes for the better during his little league baseball game. Other boys having a bad day include the main characters in Patricia Reilly Giff's *Today Was a Terrible Day* and Judith Viorst's *Alexander and the Terrible, Horrible, No Good, Very Bad Day*. BASEBALL. LUCK.

717   **Kroll, Steven.** *Happy Mother's Day.* **Illus. by Marylin Hafner. Holiday House, 1985. ISBN 0–8234–0504–4**

A sequential surprise of finished chores and presents awaits Mom when she comes home to her six children and Dad, all of whom give proof that a valuable present doesn't need to be store bought. Students can decide what similar types of chores they can give for Mother's Day. FAMILY LIFE. GIFTS. MOTHER'S DAY.

718   **Kroll, Steven.** *Oh, What a Thanksgiving!* **Illus. by S. D. Schindler. Scholastic, 1988. ISBN 0–590–40613–2**

With his active imagination, modern day David has no trouble conjuring up a picture of life in Plymouth Colony and the first Thanksgiving. Large, clear illustrations juxtapose life now with scenes back then as David comes to realize that Thanksgiving is a time for family no matter what the year. Also read Eileen Spinelli's *Thanksgiving at the Tappletons'* and top off the feast with Jack Prelutsky's dozen rhymes in *It's Thanksgiving*. FAMILY LIFE. PILGRIMS. THANKSGIVING.

719   **Kroll, Steven.** *The Tyrannosaurus Game.* **Illus. by Tomie dePaola. Holiday House, 1976. ISBN 0–8234–0275–4**

One at a time, a group of schoolchildren spin a long yarn about a Tyrannosaurus who crashes through the window. Your students can conjure up their own story in sequence. Try this after reading, retelling, and making up an all-class variant of Remy Charlip's *Fortunately*. DINOSAURS. STORYTELLING.

720   **Lauber, Patricia.** *Clarence and the Burglar.* **Illus. by Paul Galdone. Coward, 1973.**

A playful, TV-loving beagle becomes a hero when he unwittingly thwarts a robbery by untying the burglar's shoes. Highlight animal heroism with Steven Kellogg's *Pinkerton, Behave* and Tomi Ungerer's *Crictor*. DOGS. ROBBERS AND OUTLAWS.

721   **Levine, Ellen.** *I Hate English.* **Illus. by Peter Bjorkman. Scholastic, 1989.**

Now living in New York where her family has moved from Hong Kong, Mei Mei resists speaking English until a new teacher shows her how she will benefit from her new language. Undidactic and believable, here is a story for not just the bilingual students who will identify with Mei Mei's anxiety but the English-speaking ones who have never had to know two languages at once. CHINESE AMERICANS. ENGLISH LANGUAGE.

722   **Levitin, Sonia.** *Nobody Stole the Pie.* **Illus. by Fernando Krahn. Harcourt, 1980.**

After the residents of Little Digby bake their annual tremendous lollyberry pie for all to share, each self-righteous person can't resist tasting it ahead of time, thinking "a little bit, a little bit, a little bit won't hurt." A lighthearted lesson on collective responsibility that goes along splendidly with the lemon pudding chapter in Ann Cameron's *The Stories Julian Tells* and John Vernon Lord's *The Giant Jam Sandwich.* CHANTABLE REFRAIN. FOOD. PIE.

723   **Lewis, Thomas P.** *Hill of Fire.* **Illus. by Joan Sandin. Harper & Row, 1971. ISBN 0-06-023804-6**

How an ordinary Mexican farmer discovered a volcano growing in his cornfield in this fictionalized version of the birth of Paricutin in 1943. Helen Garrett's *Angelo the Naughty One* gives a less explosive view of Mexican life. For a science unit on volcanoes, also read Lonzo Anderson's *The Ponies of Mykillenji* and Seymour Simon's dramatic *Volcanoes.* MEXICO. VOLCANOES.

724   **Lexau, Joan.** *I'll Tell on You.* **Illus. by Gail Owens. Dutton, 1982. ISBN 0-525-32542-5**

After his dog bites the baseball team coach's little girl, Mark is afraid to admit responsibility. A good discussion starter about the ethics of owning up, even when the stakes are high. Another child struggles with her conscience and a lie in Masako Matsuno's *A Pair of Red Clogs.* BASEBALL. DOGS. HONESTY.

725   **Lindgren, Astrid.** *The Tomten.* **Illus. by Harald Wiberg. Coward, 1961. ISBN 0-698-20147-7**

Poetic Swedish winter story about the silent, nocturnal, elflike creature in the barn. Maintain the mysterious mood with Tejima's *Fox's Dream.* ANIMALS, MYTHICAL. ELVES. FARM LIFE. SNOW. WINTER.

726   **Lionni, Leo.** *Alexander and the Wind-Up Mouse.* **Illus. by the author. Pantheon, 1970. ISBN 0-394-90914-3**

A mouse looks for a special purple pebble so the magic lizard will turn his toy mouse friend real. Read William Steig's *Sylvester and the Magic Pebble* and hand out pebbles for each child to keep and write about. Look in novelty toy stores for a classroom windup mouse. MICE. ROCKS. TRANSFORMATIONS. WISHES.

727   **Lionni, Leo.** *Frederick.* **Illus. by the author. Pantheon, 1967. ISBN 0-394-91040-0**

A mouse poet's imagery sustains his friends through a long harsh winter. An alternative interpretation of the old "Grasshopper and the Ant" fable from Aesop, this one can be used to kick off a poetry unit. Another mouse poet can be found in Lilian Moore's endearing *I'll Meet You at the Cucumbers.* MICE. POETS. WINTER.

728   **Lionni, Leo.** *Frederick's Fables: A Leo Lionni Treasury of Favorite Stories.* **Illus. by the author. Pantheon, 1985. ISBN 0-394-97710-6**

[13 stories, 132p.] Thirteen of Lionni's elegant animal fables, collected in one huge volume. ANIMALS. FABLES. MICE. SHORT STORIES.

729   **Lobel, Arnold.** *A Treeful of Pigs.* **Illus. by Anita Lobel. Greenwillow, 1979. ISBN 0-688-84177-5**

A lazy farmer is tricked by his clever wife into doing his chores. Another knowing wife proves her point in William Weisner's folktale *Happy-Go-Lucky*. FARM LIFE. LAZINESS. PIGS.

730   **Lord, John Vernon, and Janet Burroway.** *The Giant Jam Sandwich.* **Illus. by John Vernon Lord. Houghton Mifflin, 1975. ISBN 0-395-16033-2**

Poem-story about a wasp-filled town and the sandwich made to trap them. You'll also love Russell Hoban's *Bread and Jam for Frances*, Margaret Mahy's *Jam: a True Story*, and Nadine Bernard Westcott's *Peanut Butter and Jelly*. Finish up with some fruit and vegetable riddles from Charles Keller's *Alexander the Grape*. FOOD. INSECTS. STORIES IN RHYME.

731   **Low, Alice.** *The Witch Who Was Afraid of Witches.* **Illus. by Karen Gundersheimer. Pantheon, 1978.**

On Halloween night the youngest witch in the family finds her own special powers for broomstick flying and magic spells. Make up new rhyming spells for the abilities you desire. HALLOWEEN. WITCHES.

732   **Luttrell, Ida.** *One Day at School.* **Illus. by Jared D. Lee. Harcourt, 1984.**

On one of those days when everything goes wrong, Arnold B. Lipton, third-grader, takes over for his teacher and instructs his librarian, math, music, and other teachers in how to chew gum, run in the halls, read comic books, and other such useful lessons. Your students will undoubtedly come up with a few more suggestions. See also Mary Lystad's *Jennifer Takes Over P.S. 94*. SCHOOLS. TEACHERS.

733   **Lystad, Mary.** *Jennifer Takes Over P.S. 94.* **Illus. by Ray Cruz. Putnam, 1972.**

Jennifer imagines how she'd run her school if she were in charge. Your students will have plenty of their own ideas to write down and illustrate, especially if you also read Ida Luttrell's *One Day at School*. IMAGINATION. SCHOOLS.

734   **McCloskey, Robert.** *Make Way for Ducklings.* **Illus. by the author. Viking, 1941. ISBN 0-670-45149-5**

Two concerned mallard parents look for a suitable Boston site in which to raise their family. A must-read for anyone planning to visit Boston, where the ducks are memorialized in a Public Garden sculpture, and the swan boats still glide on the pond. CALDECOTT MEDAL. CITIES AND TOWNS. DUCKS. POLICE.

735   **McKissack, Patricia C.** *Flossie & the Fox.* **Illus. by Rachel Isadora. Dial, 1986. ISBN 0-8037-0251-5**

On her way to deliver a basket of eggs, a little girl encounters and outwits a fox when he tries to convince her of his true identity. Children can try the same line of reasoning to persuade the group that they are other animals, much like boy Herman does with the bears in *Not This Bear* by Bernice Myers, and Elsie Fay does in Edward Marshall's *Troll Country*. In the same mood, also read Molly Bang's *Wiley and the Hairy Man* and Mercer Mayer's *Liza Lou and the Yeller Belly Swamp*. AFRICAN AMERICANS. EGGS. FOXES.

736   **McNaughton, Colin.** *Anton B. Stanton and the Pirats.* **Illus. by the author. Benn, 1979.**

A swashbuckling miniature boy fights evil pirate rodents—pirats—walks the plank, and lives to help rescue the Water Rat Princess. Continue the pirate battles with Matt Faulkner's *The Amazing Voyage of Jackie Grace* or Bill Peet's *Cyrus the Unsinkable Sea Serpent,* and compare with the pint-sized adventures of Issun Boshi in the Japanese folktale *Little One Inch* by Barbara Brenner. PIRATES. RATS. SIZE.

737   **McPhail, David.** *The Magical Drawings of Mooney B. Finch.* **Illus. by the author. Doubleday, 1978.**

Much to the delight of some greedy bystanders, a young boy's prodigious artistic talent enables his creations to come to life as he finishes them. Read with Jon Agee's *The Incredible Painting of Felix Clousseau,* Molly Bang's *Tye May and the Magic Brush,* and Susan Jeschke's *Angela and Bear.* In addition to handing out magic crayons for a follow-up illustration, you may wish to provide pencil stubs to combine the activity with writing, using Diane Stanley's *The Magic Pencil* for inspiration. ARTISTS. DRAGONS. DRAWING. MAGIC.

738   **Madden, Don.** *The Wartville Wizard.* **Illus. by the author. Macmillan, 1986. ISBN 0-02-762100-6**

An old man who gains the "power over trash" sends back all the town's litter to stick to the slobs who threw it. The antilitter message will appeal to all civic-minded readers who are tired of mess in the United States and want to start an antilitter campaign with children. Good companion stories are Bill Peet's *The Wump World* and Dr. Seuss's *The Lorax.* POLLUTION. WIZARDS.

739   **Mahy, Margaret.** *The Boy Who Was Followed Home.* **Illus. by Steven Kellogg. Dial, 1986. ISBN 0-8037-0286-8**

Robert needs an eccentric witch's help to rid him of the 27 adoring hippos camped on his lawn. Related titles include Marilyn Sadler's *Alistair's Elephants* and David Cleveland's *The April Rabbits.* HIPPOPOTAMUS. WITCHES.

740   **Mahy, Margaret.** *Jam: A True Story.* **Illus. by Helen Craig. Little, Brown, 1986. ISBN 0-316-54396-9**

When Mrs. Castle goes back to work, Mr. Castle becomes an efficient househusband, taking care of the house and three children, and when the plums ripen, making pots and pots of jam. Bring in a jar and a loaf of bread, or better yet, try the plum jam recipe on the endpapers with your chefs. For a more far-reaching use of jam, don't miss John Vernon Lord's *The Giant Jam Sandwich* and Nadine Bernard Westcott's *Peanut Butter and Jelly.* Find more too-much-of-a-good-thing in Mary Rayner's *Mrs. Pig's Bulk Buy.* COOKERY. FAMILY LIFE. FOOD.

741   **Major, Beverly.** *Playing Sardines.* **Illus. by Andrew Glass. Scholastic, 1988. ISBN 0-590-41153-5**

Better than hide-and-seek is a summer nighttime game of sardines. "It" hides, and as each child finds her, he must hide there too, till everyone is crunched together like a can of sardines. After reading, take a few minutes to discuss favorite games and then play one. GAMES. SEASONS. SUMMER.

742   **Marshall, Edward.** *Space Case.* **Illus. by James Marshall. Dial, 1980. ISBN 0-8037-8007-9**

On Halloween, Buddy befriends a space creature who repays the favor the next day by posing as his school space project robot. Children can invent their own space creatures. Follow up with the sequel, *Merry Christmas, Space Case* and turn up new aliens in Daniel Pinkwater's *Guys from Space*, Marilyn Sadler's *Alistair in Space*, and Arthur Yorinks's *Company's Coming*. By the way, there is no Edward Marshall—it's really James Marshall in disguise. No fooling. EXTRATERRESTRIAL LIFE. HALLOWEEN. SCIENCE FICTION.

743   Marshall, James. *The Cut-Ups*. Illus. by the author. Viking, 1984. ISBN 0-670-25195-X

Two boys who usually get away with murder meet their match when Mary Frances lets them fly her homemade rocket ship right into ex-school principal Lamar J. Spurgle's prize zinnia bed. Wild, crazy, and a perfect back-to-school book. In the waggish sequel, *The Cut-Ups Cut Loose* (1987), Spud and Joe head back to school where they lock horns with Spurgle. Compare horror stories with Arthur in Marc Brown's *Arthur's Teacher Trouble* and Grandpa in James Stevenson's *That Dreadful Day*. BEHAVIOR. FRIENDSHIP. PICTURE BOOKS FOR ALL AGES. PRINCIPALS. SCHOOLS.

744   Marshall, James. *Merry Christmas, Space Case*. Illus. by the author. Dial, 1986. ISBN 0-8037-0216-7

Buddy McGee's outer space friend returns in time to show up the rotten Goober twins. Read after Edward Marshall's *Space Case*. BULLIES. CHRISTMAS. EXTRATERRESTRIAL LIFE. SCIENCE FICTION.

745   Marshall, James. *Wings: A Tale of Two Chickens*. Illus. by the author. Viking, 1986. ISBN 0-670-80961-6

Winnie, a dumb, book-disdaining chicken flies off with a fox in his balloon only to be rescued by quick-thinking Harriet who understands the value of reading. An object lesson for those too chicken to pick up a book and read. For more fox versus chicken mayhem, try Denys Cazet's *Lucky Me*. BOOKS AND READING. CHICKENS. FOXES. PICTURE BOOKS FOR ALL AGES.

746   Martin, Bill, Jr., and John Archambault. *Listen to the Rain*. Illus. by James Endicott. Henry Holt, 1988. ISBN 0-8050-0682-6

Brief as an autumn thundershower is this mood poem of the sounds of rain, from whisper to roar. The spare text and wispy illustrations should put you in the mood to lead the "rain" activity—as described in the Creative Dramatics chapter—with your students as they sit in a circle. Mary Stolz's *Storm in the Night* and Jack Prelutsky's poems in *Rainy Rainy Saturday* will fit the mood. RAIN AND RAINFALL. WEATHER.

747   Matsuno, Masako. *A Pair of Red Clogs*. Illus. by Kazue Mizamura. World, 1960.

Grandmother recalls how as a girl she broke her beautiful new clogs and was afraid to admit it to her mother. Start a discussion on honesty and how to own up to a lie. For a unit on old Japan, also read folktales such as Momoko Ishii's *The Tongue-Cut Sparrow*, Patricia Montgomery Newton's *The Five Sparrows*, and Taro Yashima's *Crow Boy*. Ina R. Friedman's *How My Parents Learned to Eat* brings you more up to date. HONESTY. JAPAN. SHOES.

748   Mayer, Mercer. *Liza Lou and the Yeller Belly Swamp*. Illus. by the author. Parents, 1976. ISBN 0-02-765220-3

While doing errands for her mamma, a fearless girl outsmarts the creatures she encounters, including a good-for-nothing swamp haunt, a wicked swamp witch, a slithery gobby gook, and a sly swamp devil. Pair with Molly Garrett Bang's folktale *Wiley and the Hairy Man*, Patricia C. McKissack's *Flossie & the Fox*, and Don Arthur Torgersen's *The Girl Who Tricked the Troll*. AFRICAN AMERICANS. MONSTERS.

749   **Mayer, Mercer. *Mrs. Beggs and the Wizard*. Illus. by the author. Four Winds, 1973.**

A reclusive wizard wreaks havoc in Mrs. Beggs's boardinghouse until she digs up an incantation of her own. Children can continue this open-ended tale, predicting what the scaly-tailed boarder might have up his sleeve the next time. MAGIC. WIZARDS.

750   **Merriam, Eve. *The Birthday Door*. Illus. by Peter J. Thornton. Morrow, 1986. ISBN 0-688-06194-X**

On Helen's birthday, she and her kitten Clio must decipher rhyming messages and go on a treasure hunt that leads them to her birthday present. Aside from guessing the location of each new clue in the story, your sleuths would love to try their own classroom treasure hunt, or perhaps even make up their own clues, like those in Eric Carle's *The Secret Birthday Message*. BIRTHDAYS.

751   **Modell, Frank. *One Zillion Valentines*. Illus. by the author. Greenwillow, 1981. ISBN 0-688-00569-1**

Marvin and Milton make valentines for everyone in the neighborhood and more to spare. Other heart-filled titles include Marjorie Weinman Sharmat's *The Best Valentine in the World*, Lillian Hoban's *Arthur's Great Big Valentine*, Eve Bunting's *The Valentine Bears*, Nancy L. Carlson's *Louanne Pig in the Mysterious Valentine*, and James Stevenson's *Happy Valentine's Day, Emma*. Inaugurate a class assembly line for production of valentines to distribute to every child in your school. One last treasure: Jack Prelutsky's easy-to-read poems in *It's Valentine's Day*. VALENTINE'S DAY.

752   **Modell, Frank. *Tooley! Tooley!* Illus. by the author. Greenwillow, 1979.**

Planning on earning reward money to use at the movies, Marvin and Milton look for a lost dog and find mutts galore in their search, though none of them is the right one. First in a series about two fast friends, including *Goodbye Old Year, Hello New Year* and the preceding *One Zillion Valentines*. DOGS. LOST.

753   **Moore, Clement C. *The Night before Christmas*. Illus. by Tomie dePaola. Holiday House, 1980. ISBN 0-8234-0414-5**

Saint Nick and his reindeer prance again, thanks to dePaola's jaunty watercolors, but also look for other versions, such as Anita Lobel's (Knopf, 1984) with its Victorian paintings and James Marshall's cavorting menagerie (Scholastic, 1985). CHRISTMAS—POETRY. NARRATIVE POETRY. PICTURE BOOKS FOR ALL AGES. SANTA CLAUS. STORIES IN RHYME.

754   **Myers, Bernice. *Sidney Rella and the Glass Sneaker*. Illus. by the author. Macmillan, 1985. ISBN 0-02-767790-7**

In a wonderful tongue-in-cheek send-up of *Cinderella*, poor Sidney does all the dirty work at home until his fairy godfather helps him become a football star. Other fairy tale parodies include A. Vesey's *The Princess and the Frog*, Jane Yolen's *Sleeping Ugly*, and Raymond Briggs's *Jim and the Beanstalk*. For another modern-day counterpart, read Charlotte Pomerantz's *The Downtown Fairy Godmother*. FAIR-IES. FAIRY TALES—SATIRE. FOOTBALL. PARODIES. SPORTS.

755 **Myller, Rolf.** *A Very Noisy Day.* **Illus. by the author. Atheneum, 1981.**

An almost typical sound-filled day in one dog's life as he cavorts outside and even captures a burglar. Full of noises children will love to make as you read. DOGS. ROBBERS AND OUTLAWS. SOUND EFFECTS.

756 **Nerlove, Miriam.** *I Made a Mistake.* **Illus. by the author. Atheneum, 1985. ISBN 0-689-50327-X**

"I went to the bathroom to brush my hair, I made a mistake . . . and brushed a bear." Rhyming nonsense couplets, based on an old jump rope rhyme, will make everyone giggle and try to predict each new mistake. Write and illustrate new ones for your own class book, and then try them all out with a jump rope in an all-class jumpathon or act them out in narrative pairs pantomime. CREATIVE DRAMA. CREATIVE WRITING. JUMP ROPE RHYMES. STORIES IN RHYME.

757 **Ness, Evaline.** *Sam, Bangs and Moonshine.* **Illus. by the author. Henry Holt, 1966. ISBN 0-8050-0314-2**

When Samantha tells gullible Thomas a lie that endangers both his life and her cat's, she finally learns the hard way the difference between real and moonshine. In *The Adventures of Obadiah* by Brinton Turkle, a story-spinning Quaker boy is not believed the one time he tells the truth. Tie these together with Aesop's fable, "The Boy Who Cried Wolf." CALDECOTT MEDAL. CATS. HONESTY. SEASHORE. STORY-TELLING.

758 **Neumeier, Marty, and Byron Glaser.** *Action Alphabet.* **Illus. by the authors. Greenwillow, 1985. ISBN 0-688-05704-7**

Each large black letter is incorporated into a black-and-white graphic word picture including an "I" on an ice skate, a jumping "J," and a twisted "T." Use with Suse MacDonald's *Alphabatics*; your viewers can guess all the words pictured. Older children can design new word-letters. ALPHABET BOOKS. PICTURE BOOKS FOR ALL AGES.

759 **Nikly, Michelle.** *The Emperor's Plum Tree.* **Illus. by the author. Greenwillow, 1982.**

Mourning the death of a tree that has spoiled his perfect garden, the emperor rejoices in its replacement until he realizes his selfishness has made a child unhappy and a nightingale homeless. This blends nicely with Hans Christian Andersen's *The Nightingale*, though that story is a more sophisticated one. A good way to introduce haiku, along with Kazue Mizamura's haiku collection, *Flower Moon Snow*; use with older grades when you want students to write their own. BIRDS. JAPAN. KINGS AND RULERS. POETS. TREES.

760 **Nixon, Joan Lowery.** *Gloria Chipmunk, Star!* **Illus. by Diane Dawson. Houghton Mifflin, 1980.**

[6 chapters, 1–2 sittings, 48p.] Eager for her big moment on stage, a chipmunk finds a way to take care of her baby brother and still be in the class play. For continued drama, see Miriam Cohen's *Starring First Grade* and Joanne Oppenheim's *Mrs. Peloki's Class Play*. ACTING. CHIPMUNKS. PLAYS. SCHOOLS.

761   **Noble, Trinka Hakes.** *The Day Jimmy's Boa Ate the Wash.* **Illus. by Steven Kellogg. Dial, 1980. ISBN 0-8037-1724-5**

A wild class trip to a farm sets off a chain of silly disasters when a student brings his boa constrictor to meet the other animals. Have children retell the story in the sequence it actually happened. More boa stories include C. Imbrior Kudrna's *To Bathe a Boa* and Tomi Ungerer's *Crictor.* You might also enjoy reading, singing, and acting out "I'm Being Eaten by a Boa Constrictor" from Shel Silverstein's *A Light in the Attic* and riddling with Diane L. Burns's *Snakes Alive!* CAUSE AND EFFECT. FARM LIFE. PETS. SLAPSTICK. SNAKES.

762   **Nolan, Dennis.** *Witch Bazooza.* **Illus. by the author. Prentice Hall, 1979.**

Preparing her house and yard for the Witches' Judging Society on Halloween night, Witch Bazooza has no choice but to use the magical carved vegetables created when her spells go wrong. Bring in odd-shaped gourds to paint or decorate with magic markers. CATS. HALLOWEEN. VEGETABLES. WITCHES.

763   **Oppenheim, Joanne.** *Mrs. Peloki's Class Play.* **Illus. by Joyce Audy dos Santos. Putnam, 1983. ISBN 0-396-08178-9**

The star of the second-grade production of *Cinderella,* narrator Stephanie describes the chaos of the final dress rehearsal and the successful performance, her newly erupted chicken pox notwithstanding. Other tales for thespians include Miriam Cohen's *Starring First Grade* and Joan Lowery Nixon's *Gloria Chipmunk, Star!* Read the Paul Galdone or Marcia Brown illustrated versions of the fairy tale to set the stage. ACTING. PLAYS. SCHOOLS. TEACHERS.

764   **Parish, Peggy.** *Amelia Bedelia.* **Illus. by Fritz Siebel. Harper & Row, 1963. ISBN 0-06-024641-3**

Looney maid takes everything literally. First of a series that children can read on their own, including *Play Ball, Amelia Bedelia* (1972), *Teach Us, Amelia Bedelia* (1977), *Amelia Bedelia and the Baby* (1981), *Amelia Bedelia Goes Camping* (1985), and *Amelia Bedelia's Family Album* (1988). Young authors of all ages can write new episodes using literal language. Don't forget the lemon meringue pie! ENGLISH LANGUAGE–IDIOMS.

765   **Paul, Anthony.** *The Tiger Who Lost His Stripes.* **Illus. by Michael Foreman. Harcourt, 1982.**

General MacTiger must convince the monkeys not to throw coconuts at the crocodiles who will then move out of the elephant's part of the river and build a house for python who will then give MacTiger back his stripes. A sequence story in the same vein as *One Fine Day* by Nonny Hogrogian. ANIMALS. SEQUENCE STORIES. TIGERS.

766   **Peet, Bill.** *Big Bad Bruce.* **Illus. by the author. Houghton Mifflin, 1982. ISBN 0-395-25150-8**

Bear bully who delights in tormenting smaller forest animals is tamed by Roxy, a no-nonsense witch who shrinks him to miniature size. Hold a Bill Peet festival to rile up the troops with this author's sensible yarns. BEARS. SIZE. WITCHES.

767   **Peet, Bill.** *Cyrus the Unsinkable Sea Serpent.* **Illus. by the author. Houghton Mifflin, 1975. ISBN 0-395-20272-8**

When a shark calls him a sissy, a peaceful sea monster sets out to wreck a ship, but ends up protecting it from ocean disasters, from sea squall to pirates. Sail on with Matt Faulkner's *The Amazing Voyage of Jackie Grace* and Colin McNaughton's *Anton B. Stanton and the Pirats*. MONSTERS. OCEAN. PIRATES. SHIPS.

768   Peet, Bill. *Encore for Eleanor.* Illus. by the author. Houghton Mifflin, 1981. ISBN 0-395-29860-1

Sent off to the zoo when she gets too old to perform, a retired circus elephant learns how to draw and becomes a star once more. Don Freeman's *Bearymore* also teaches himself new tricks. ARTISTS. DRAWING. ELEPHANTS. ZOOS.

769   Peet, Bill. *How Droofus the Dragon Lost His Head.* Illus. by the author. Houghton Mifflin, 1971. ISBN 0-395-15085-X

A harmless and helpful vegetarian dragon, sought by all the king's knights, is befriended by a farm family who find him worse for wear after a storm. Be sure to discuss the figure-of-speech title. Another stereotype-busting dragon awaits rescuing in Ruth Stiles Gannett's *My Father's Dragon*. DRAGONS. FRIENDSHIP. KNIGHTS AND KNIGHTHOOD.

770   Peet, Bill. *Hubert's Hair-Raising Adventure.* Illus. by the author. Houghton Mifflin, 1959. ISBN 0-395-15083-3

When lion Hubert's mane is burned off by accident, his animal friends seek a crocodile-tear cure that causes his locks to grow without stopping. A jaunty introduction to narrative poetry; try also *The Mean Old Mean Hyena* and *The Terrible Tiger*, both by Jack Prelutsky, and Dr. Seuss's *Thidwick, the Big-Hearted Moose*. ANIMALS. LIONS. NARRATIVE POETRY. STORIES IN RHYME.

771   Peet, Bill. *The Spooky Tail of Prewitt Peacock.* Illus. by the author. Houghton Mifflin, 1973. ISBN 0-395-15494-4

An outcast peacock redeems himself with his fellow fowl when his strange-faced tail feather formation frightens away a spry old tiger in the nick of time. Bring in peacock feathers to display, and talk about the burdens and rewards of being considered "different." Pete Seeger's *Abiyoyo* deals with the same theme from a human perspective. BIRDS. SELF-CONCEPT. TIGERS.

772   Peppé, Rodney. *The Mice Who Lived in a Shoe.* Illus. by the author. Lothrop, 1982. ISBN 0-688-00844-5

A many-member mouse family constructs a safe, snug, new house using a human shoe as their frame. On the last page is a photograph of the actual mouse-sized shoe house the author built as a model for the story. In *The Mice and the Clockwork Bus* (1986), they build another ingenious mouse-worthy contraption: an efficient bus that puts D. Rat's bicycle bus, the Rattletrap, out of business. Have your students bring in bags of odds and ends from home and then, using Peppé's own model photos at the back of each book for inspiration, construct your own mouse habitats, like a train, a car, or even a miniature spaceship. Read with Maryann Kovalski's sing-along *The Wheels on the Bus* to get in the mood for travel. CATS. HOUSES. MICE.

773   Peterson, Esther Allen. *Frederick's Alligator.* Illus. by Susanna Natti. Crown, 1979.

Though no one at school or home will believe he isn't exaggerating as usual, Frederick truly has found a baby alligator. Also see Brinton Turkle's *The Adventures of Obadiah* to meet up with a way-back-when tale-teller. ALLIGATORS. EXAGGERA-TION. HONESTY. SCHOOLS.

774   **Peterson, Esther Allen.** *Penelope Gets Wheels.* **Illus. by Susanna Natti. Crown, 1982.**

On the day of the big baseball game, a girl finds her new roller skates are the best wheels a kid can have. Compare Penelope's choice with what Rosa spends her birthday money on in Vera B. Williams's *Something Special for Me.* BIRTHDAYS. MONEY. TRANSPORTATION.

775   **Pittman, Helena Clare.** *Once When I Was Scared.* **Illus. by Ted Rand. Dutton, 1988. ISBN 0-525-44407-6**

In the drizzly autumn dusk, Daniel imagines himself a fox, bobcat, and eagle as he races next door—across two hills and through a dark wood—to get hot coals from the neighbors. Narrated by the grandson of Daniel, now a grandfather himself, there's a twist at the end to startle listeners. Contrast fear of the dark and the unknown then and now with Eve Bunting's *Ghost's Hour, Spook's Hour*, Alice Dalgliesh's *The Bears on Hemlock Mountain*, and Mary Stolz's *Storm in the Night*, another grandfather tale. AUTUMN. FEAR. FORESTS AND FORESTRY. GRANDFATHERS. IMAGINATION.

776   **Pomerantz, Charlotte.** *The Chalk Doll.* **Illus. by Frané Lessac. Lippincott, 1989. ISBN 0-397-32318-2**

Spending the day in bed with a cold is a good time for Rose to listen to her mother's stories of growing up poor in Jamaica where she had only a homemade rag doll, and three pennies constituted a fortune for a seven-year-old. Children who have no concept of being poor will see that having no money does not mean one can't be happy. This is another beautiful family story like Valerie Flournoy's *The Patchwork Quilt*, Ina R. Friedman's *How My Parents Learned to Eat*, or Cynthia Rylant's *When I Was Young in the Mountains*, all of which spark listeners with the need to uncover more of their own relatives' stories. DOLLS. FAMILY STORIES. MOTHERS AND DAUGH-TERS.

777   **Porte, Barbara Ann.** *Harry's Dog.* **Illus. by Yossi Abolafia. Greenwillow, 1984.**

When hiding his new dog, Girl, from his allergic father fails, Harry regales his sneezing dad with tall tales of how he found the dog, and lobbies to keep her. Allergy sufferers will sympathize with this and Marjorie N. Allen's *One, Two, Three —Ah-Choo!* ALLERGIES. DOGS. FATHERS AND SONS.

778   **Prelutsky, Jack.** *The Terrible Tiger.* **Illus. by Arnold Lobel. Macmillan, 1989. ISBN 0-689-71300-2**

He sings his terrible song in verse and swallows a baker, a grocer, and worse. While similar to Jack Kent's *The Fat Cat* and Paul Galdone's *The Greedy Old Fat Man*, this story boasts a wicked chorus for children to chant or sing like Prelutsky's *The Mean Old Mean Hyena.* CHANTABLE REFRAIN. STORIES IN RHYME. TIGERS.

779   **Quinn-Harkin, Janet.** *Peter Penny's Dance.* **Illus. by Anita Lobel. Dial, 1976. ISBN 0-8037-7184-3**

To win the hand of Lavinia, the ship captain's daughter, a sailor wagers he can dance around the world in five years or less. Use a map or globe to trace his toe-tapping geographical journey from England through France, Spain, Africa, China, India, and the United States. DANCING. SAILING.

780   **Raffi.** *Down by the Bay.* **Illus. by Nadine Bernard Westcott. Crown, 1987. ISBN 0-517-56644-3**

An illustrated version of the Canadian singer's wacky song about the animals' antics down by the bay where the watermelons grow. From a moose kissing a goose to llamas eating their pajamas, the silly, simply formatted rhymes beg to be sung over and over and will inspire children to write, illustrate, and sing dozens of new verses. See also Lynne Cherry's *Who's Sick Today?* with simple rhyming animal ailments, and Fritz Eichenberg's animal alphabet *Ape in a Cape* and counting rhyme book *Dancing in the Moon.* ANIMALS. CREATIVE WRITING. NONSENSE VERSES. SONGS. STORIES IN RHYME.

781   **Rayner, Mary.** *Garth Pig and the Ice Cream Lady.* **Illus. by the author. Atheneum, 1977. ISBN 0-689-30598-2**

Mrs. Wolf abducts Garth in her ice cream truck while his 9 piglet siblings rush to the rescue on their bicycle built for 10. For a human version, also read Audrey Wood's *Heckedy Peg.* BROTHERS AND SISTERS. FOOD. PIGS. WOLVES.

782   **Rayner, Mary.** *Mr. and Mrs. Pig's Evening Out.* **Illus. by the author. Atheneum, 1976. ISBN 0-689-30530-3**

Wicked Mrs. Wolf is the 10 piglets' new baby-sitter. For a point of view more sympathetic to the sitter, read Natalie Savage Carlson's *Marie Louise's Heyday* and Eileen Christelow's *Jerome the Babysitter.* BABY-SITTERS. BROTHERS AND SISTERS. PIGS. WOLVES.

783   **Rayner, Mary.** *Mrs. Pig's Bulk Buy.* **Illus. by the author. Atheneum, 1981. ISBN 0-689-30831-0**

The 10 piglets are cured of their ketchup overdoses when their mother feeds them nothing but. For kids who think they can never have too much of a good thing, pair with Margaret Mahy's *Jam: A True Story.* Finish up with a chapter a day of *Mrs. Pig Gets Cross and Other Stories* (1987), a collection of 7 more family tales of the 10 pigs and their parents. BROTHERS AND SISTERS. FOOD. PIGS.

784   **Rose, Anne.** *The Triumphs of Fuzzy Fogtop.* **Illus. by Tomie dePaola. Dial, 1979. ISBN 0-8037-8647-6**

Three comic stories, loosely based on Jewish folktales, of a foolish, forgetful man who loses his list of things to do, takes a train trip that goes nowhere, and meets an old friend who's changed. Try a medley of noodlehead tales including Tedd Arnold's *Ollie Forgot,* Joanna and Philip Cole's *Big Goof and Little Goof,* Paul Galdone's or Kathryn Hewitt's *The Three Sillies,* Galdone's *Hans in Luck,* and William Weisner's *Happy-Go-Lucky.* FOOLS. SLAPSTICK.

785   **Ross, Pat.** *M & M and the Santa Secrets.* **Illus. by Marylin Hafner. Viking, 1985. ISBN 0-317-62234-X**

A street corner Santa inadvertently helps best friends Mandy and Mimi surprise each other with special gifts. Use this and the preceding title to introduce other "M & M" books in the series for children to read themselves. CHRISTMAS. FRIENDSHIP. GIFTS. SANTA CLAUS.

786   **Ross, Tony.** *Super Dooper Jezebel.* **Illus. by the author. Farrar, 1988. ISBN 0-374-33660-1**

The most perfect girl ever gets hers, thanks to an escaped crocodile. A tongue-in-cheek reminder that being a normal, untidy, run-of-the-mill kid isn't so terrible. For a male version also read Myra Cohn Livingston's rhyming *Higgledy-Piggledy*. BEHAVIOR.

787   Sadler, Marilyn. *Alistair in Outer Space*. Illus. by Roger Bollen. Simon & Schuster, 1989. ISBN 0-671-68504-X

On his way to return his library books, unperturbable, brown-beanied Alistair is picked up by a Gootulan spaceship and whisked to an alien planet. Read when your students are receiving too many library overdue notices. A hoot, especially the surprise ending, which cries out for student-concocted sequels. Additional aliens lurk in James Marshall's *Space Case*, Daniel Pinkwater's *Guys from Space*, and Arthur Yorinks's *Company's Coming*. James Daugherty's *Andy and the Lion* is another on-the-way-to-the-library happening. BOOKS AND READING. SCIENCE FICTION. SPACE FLIGHT.

788   Sadler, Marilyn. *Alistair's Elephant*. Illus. by Roger Bollen. Prentice Hall, 1986. ISBN 0-13-022773-0

Future nerd Alistair finds it difficult to continue life as usual after an elephant follows him home from the zoo. Deadpan prose, rife with understatement, is made more hilarious by the large exaggerated illustrations. Continue the "following" theme with David Cleveland's *The April Rabbits* and Margaret Mahy's *The Boy Who Was Followed Home*, and look on the good side with Chris Riddell's *The Trouble with Elephants*. ELEPHANTS.

789   Sadler, Marilyn. *Alistair's Time Machine*. Illus. by Roger Bollen. Prentice Hall, 1986. ISBN 0-317-39621-8

Built for the science competition, his new time machine takes him to a French palace, pirate ship, Roman arena, and cave people campsite. Have students bring to life the scenes of his landings through narrative pantomime, and incorporate additional historical situations, that is, building the Great Wall or crossing the Delaware with Washington, or moon walking with the astronauts. SCIENCE FICTION. SPACE AND TIME.

790   Saunders, Susan. *Fish Fry*. Illus. by S. D. Schindler. Viking, 1982.

A young girl and her friend find fish and a live alligator at their turn-of-the-century Texas picnic. Contrast this with Carol Snyder's New York City story of the same era, *Ike and Mama and the Once-a-Year Suit*. COUNTRY LIFE. PICNICS. TEXAS.

791   Say, Allen. *The Bicycle Man*. Illus. by the author. Houghton Mifflin, 1982. ISBN 0-395-32254-5

A reminiscence from the author's childhood in postwar Japan of the time two American soldiers entertained the entire school at the end of its sports day festivities. If studying Japan, pair with other aspects of Japanese culture, old and modern, such as Ina R. Friedman's *How My Parents Learned to Eat* and Dianne Snyder's folktale *The Boy of the Three Year Nap* (both illustrated by Allen Say), Say's *Once under the Cherry Blossom Tree*, Masako Matsuno's *A Pair of Red Clogs*, and Taro Yashima's *Crow Boy*. AFRICAN AMERICANS. BICYCLES. JAPAN. SCHOOLS.

792   Schertle, Alice. *Bill and the Google-Eyed Goblins.* Illus. by Patricia Coombs. Lothrop, 1987. ISBN 0-688-06702-6

A dancing fool outsmarts a gaggle of gold-hoarding goblins on All Hallows' Eve. Read along with "The Old Man's Wen" from Molly Bang's *The Goblins Giggle and Other Stories.* DANCING. FAIRIES. HALLOWEEN. MONEY.

793   Schotter, Roni. *Captain Snap and the Children of Vinegar Lane.* Illus. by Marcia Sewall. Orchard, 1989. ISBN 0-531-08397-7

Little Sody and her gang of friends pester mean old Captain Snap until the day they find him ill in his shack and come to his aid with food and warm blankets. As an art project, bring in the same types of junk the Captain used to sculpt his toys and treasures, and create some small-scaled art pieces. FRIENDSHIP. SCULPTORS. SICK.

794   Schwartz, Amy. *Annabelle Swift, Kindergartner.* Illus. by the author. Orchard, 1988. ISBN 0-531-08337-3

Annabelle's affectionate know-it-all older sister Lucy gives her advice on all the "fancy stuff" she'll need to know when she starts school the next day. Read this one after the start of the school year, when everyone's just getting settled and can reminisce about how things went on that traumatic first day back, along with Rosemary Wells's *Timothy Goes to School.* Spur students in all grades to write their first day memoirs, and compare with Ramona's in Beverly Cleary's *Ramona the Pest.* PICTURE BOOKS FOR ALL AGES. SCHOOLS. SISTERS.

795   Schwartz, Amy. *Bea and Mr. Jones.* Illus. by the author. Bradbury, 1982. ISBN 0-02-781430-0

A kindergarten girl and her dad switch jobs so she can go into advertising and he can play the colored lollypop game. Good writing lead-in to the story starter, "What if *you* switched jobs with your mom or dad?" CREATIVE WRITING. FATHERS AND DAUGHTERS. PICTURE BOOKS FOR ALL AGES. SCHOOLS.

796   Schwartz, Amy. *Her Majesty, Aunt Essie.* Illus. by the author. Bradbury, 1984. ISBN 0-02-781450-5

Ruthie tries to prove that her aunt used to be a queen. You be Maisie, the skeptical friend, and let your students convince you, citing evidence of Essie's royalty. AUNTS. DOGS. KINGS AND RULERS.

797   Seeger, Pete, and Charles Seeger. *The Foolish Frog.* Illus. by Miloslav Jagr. Macmillan, 1973.

Story-song about a farmer's stupendous new tune and the wild party it inspires. If you don't sing, show the merry Weston Woods filmstrip version, sung and told by folksinger Pete Seeger, and invite your students to join in on each chorus. FOLK SONGS. FROGS. STORIES TO TELL. STORIES WITH SONGS.

798   Segal, Lore. *Tell Me a Mitzi.* Illus. by Harriet Pincus. Farrar, 1970. ISBN 0-374-37392-2

Martha's father makes up and tells to his daughter three family stories: the time Martha and baby brother Jacob tried to visit Grandma on their own, what happened when everyone in the house caught a terrible cold, and how Jacob called back a parade for the President. Continue with *Tell Me a Trudy* (1977), including three more family stories about copycatting, sharing, and robbers in the bathroom.

Encourage your students to ask their parents to tell them their own "Mitzi's" and "Trudy's." BROTHERS AND SISTERS. FAMILY LIFE. GRANDMOTHERS. STORYTELLING.

799   Selden, George. *Sparrow Socks*. Illus. by Peter Lippman. Harper & Row, 1965.

A Scottish sock factory caters to the birds when young Angus McPhee sets the family's sock machine to make wee pairs for their cold little feet. Read with your best brogue and have everyone move up close to see better. Other machine books include Eileen Christelow's *Mr. Murphy's Marvelous Invention* and William Pène du Bois's *Lazy Tommy Pumpkinhead*. BIRDS. CLOTHING AND DRESS. MACHINES. SCOTLAND.

800   Seuling, Barbara. *The Triplets*. Illus. by the author. Houghton Mifflin, 1980.

Three indistinguishable sisters who want to be recognized as individuals refuse to come out of their room until people stop mixing them up. Have each child make a list of what makes himself or herself unique. INDIVIDUALITY. SISTERS. TWINS.

801   Seuss, Dr. *Horton Hatches the Egg*. Illus. by the author. Random House, 1940. ISBN 0-394-90077-4

The accommodating 100 percent faithful elephant helps a lazy bird who takes a permanent vacation and leaves Horton responsible for sitting on her egg. Also read the sequel, *Horton Hears a Who!* (1954), where the sympathetic elephant valiantly tries to protect the tiny dust planet of Who-ville from the animals who doubt its existence. EGGS. ELEPHANTS. NARRATIVE POETRY. RESPONSIBILITY. STORIES IN RHYME.

802   Seuss, Dr. *How the Grinch Stole Christmas*. Illus. by the author. Random House, 1957. ISBN 0-394-90079-0

Classic rhyme of the evil Grinch who steals all the presents in Who-ville because of his heart, which is two sizes too small. Balance this tale of a Christmas meany with Eric Kimmel's *Hershel and the Hanukkah Goblins* about a brave man who outthinks a roomful of Hanukkah spoilsports. CHRISTMAS. GIFTS. NARRATIVE POETRY. STORIES IN RHYME.

803   Seuss, Dr. *If I Ran the Zoo*. Illus. by the author. Random House, 1950. ISBN 0-394-90081-2

Lots of looney animals in rhyme, which you can relate to Arnold Lobel's *The Ice Cream Cone Coot*, Bill Peet's *No Such Things*, Jack Prelutsky's *The Baby Uggs Are Hatching* and *The Snopp on the Sidewalk*, and Seuss's *McElligot's Pool* and *On Beyond Zebra*. ANIMALS, IMAGINARY–POETRY. CREATIVE WRITING. STORIES IN RHYME. ZOOS.

804   Seuss, Dr. *McElligot's Pool*. Illus. by the author. Random House, 1947. ISBN 0-394-90083-9

A boy imagines, in rhyme, all the wild fish he could catch there. Children will love making up their own unique species. Tie in the fish with the birds and then some by using Arnold Lobel's *The Ice Cream Cone Coot*, Bill Peet's *No Such Things*, Jack Prelutsky's *The Baby Uggs Are Hatching* and *The Snopp on the Sidewalk*, and Dr. Seuss's *If I Ran The Zoo* and *On Beyond Zebra*. ANIMALS, IMAGINARY–POETRY. CREATIVE WRITING. FISHES. STORIES IN RHYME.

805   Seuss, Dr. *On Beyond Zebra*. Illus. by the author. Random House, 1955. ISBN 0-394-90084-7

The crazy new alphabet letters will impel class poets to invent new alphabets and write rhymes about creatures to go along. More mythical beings cavort through Arnold Lobel's *The Ice Cream Cone Coot*, Bill Peet's *No Such Things*, and Dr. Seuss's *McElligot's Pool* and *If I Ran the Zoo*. ALPHABET BOOKS. ANIMALS, IMAGINARY—POETRY. CREATIVE WRITING. STORIES IN RHYME.

806 **Seuss, Dr.** *Thidwick, the Big-Hearted Moose.* **Illus. by the author. Random House, 1948. ISBN 0-394-90086-3**

While looking for nice tender moose moss to munch, Thidwick doesn't mind if a Bingle Bug rests in his horns, until it invites aboard scores of other freeloading animals from tree spider to Zinn-A-Zu Bird newlyweds. A tantalizing foil to Donald Carrick's *Harald and the Great Stag*. For more sheer rhyming madness, also do Edward Lear's similarly themed *The Quangle Wangle's Hat*. GENEROSITY. HUNTERS AND HUNTING. MOOSE. NARRATIVE POETRY. STORIES IN RHYME.

807 **Sharmat, Marjorie Weinman.** *The Best Valentine in the World.* **Illus. by Lilian Obligado. Holiday House, 1982. ISBN 0-8234-0440-4**

Ferdinand Fox makes a fancy one for his dear friend, Florette. Read the first week in February and then design your own gorgeous valentines. Also see Frank Modell's *One Zillion Valentines*, James Stevenson's *Happy Valentine's Day, Emma*, Lillian Hoban's *Arthur's Great Big Valentine*, Eve Bunting's *The Valentine Bears*, and Nancy L. Carlson's *Louanne Pig in the Mysterious Valentine*. Snappy poems abound in Jack Prelutsky's *It's Valentine's Day*. FOXES. FRIENDSHIP. VALENTINE'S DAY.

808 **Sharmat, Marjorie Weinman.** *Gila Monsters Meet You at the Airport.* **Illus. by Byron Barton. Macmillan, 1980. ISBN 0-02-782450-0**

An East Coast boy moves out West, expecting the worst. Ask children who have moved what they thought they'd find when they got there, and how their preconceived notions differed from reality. Larry L. King's *Because of Lozo Brown*, Elizabeth O'Donnell's *Maggie Doesn't Want to Move*, and Bernard Waber's octopus narrated *I Was All Thumbs* all deal with other aspects of the unexpected. MOVING, HOUSEHOLD. WEST.

809 **Sharmat, Marjorie Weinman.** *Gladys Told Me to Meet Her Here.* **Illus. by Edward Frascino. Harper & Row, 1970. ISBN 0-06-025550-1**

Irving looks for his best friend, and while imagining where she might be, muses on their great compatibility. Other accounts of true friendship include Bernard Waber's *Ira Says Goodbye* and Elizabeth Winthrop's *Lizzie & Harold*. FRIENDSHIP.

810 **Sharmat, Marjorie Weinman.** *Nate the Great.* **Illus. by Marc Simont. Coward, 1972. ISBN 0-698-30444-6**

The pancake-loving amateur boy detective solves his first mystery when friend Annie loses a picture she painted. Use as an introduction to the rest of this delightful hard-boiled series, which kids can handle on their own. DOGS. MYSTERY AND DETECTIVE STORIES.

811 **Silverstein, Shel.** *A Giraffe and a Half.* **Illus. by the author. Harper & Row, 1964. ISBN 0-06-025656-7**

Written in the cumulative style of "The House That Jack Built," this nonsense rhyme involves a boy's giraffe, a rose, a mouse, and other ridiculous interfering appendages. Ideal for recalling sequence and inspiring snickers. CUMULATIVE STO-RIES. GIRAFFES. SLAPSTICK.

812   **Silverstein, Shel.** *Who Wants a Cheap Rhinoceros?* **Illus. by the author. Macmillan, 1983. ISBN 0-02-782690-2**

What one will do for you when you get him, from eating bad report cards to letting you dress him up on Halloween. Think up and illustrate some more advantages. In the elephant department, see also Chris Riddell's *The Trouble with Elephants.* CREATIVE WRITING. RHINOCEROS.

813   **Skurzynski, Gloria.** *Martin by Myself.* **Illus. by Lynn Munsinger. Houghton Mifflin, 1979.**

Alone and lonely for 45 minutes on the first day his mother goes back to work, Martin makes a huge mess at home. Find out how your youngsters cope when both parents work. A good choice on the day after your class has given a substitute a hard time. DOGS. MOTHERS AND SONS.

814   **Small, David.** *Paper John.* **Illus. by the author. Farrar, 1987. ISBN 0-374-35738-2**

A gentle young man, who makes his living folding paper into origami-type knick-knacks and lives in a paper-folded house, rescues and gives shelter to a little gray devil who tries to do him wrong in return. Everyone will want to try a little bit of origami afterwards, so be prepared. In Anne Pellowski's *The Family Storytelling Handbook,* several terrific easy-to-learn paper and paper folding stories will wow your audience. DEVIL. ORIGAMI. WIND.

815   **Smith, Janice Lee.** *The Monster in the Third Dresser Drawer: And Other Stories about Adam Joshua.* **Illus. by Dick Gackenbach. Harper & Row, 1981. ISBN 0-06-025739-3**

[6 chapters, 86p.] A young boy reluctantly adjusts to large changes and other daily mishaps which include moving, a baby sister, and a new tooth. Let your students in on the sequel, *The Kid Next Door and Other Headaches* (1984), and consider reading aloud the third book in the series, which follows here. BABIES. BROTHERS AND SISTERS. FAMILY LIFE. MOVING, HOUSEHOLD.

816   **Smith, Janice Lee.** *The Show-and-Tell War: And Other Stories about Adam Joshua.* **Illus. by Dick Gackenbach. Harper & Row, 1988. ISBN 0-06-025815-2**

[5 chapters, 162p.] These five stories about Adam Joshua and his best friend Nelson are perfect for starting off the school year, dealing with the class bully, faking illness to stay home, and Halloween costumes. Librarians, be sure to check out "The Library Caper," where Adam Joshua can't help stealing his favorite book. HUMOR-OUS FICTION. SCHOOLS.

817   **Spier, Peter.** *Bored, Nothing to Do.* **Illus. by the author. Doubleday, 1978. ISBN 0-385-13177-1**

When they find an old propeller in the garage, two enterprising brothers scour the house for parts to the airplane they decide to build, using the motor of the family Volkswagen and other such useful household essentials. Understated text and detailed illustrations hilariously underscore modern children's low threshold of boredom. Also see Spier's *Oh, Were They Ever Happy,* about children who take it upon themselves to paint the house when Mom and Dad go out for the day, and James Stevenson's "Grandpa" yarn, *There's Nothing to Do!* AIRPLANES. BROTHERS.

818   **Spinelli, Eileen.** *Thanksgiving at the Tappletons'.* **Illus. by Maryann Cocca-Leffler. Harper & Row, 1984. ISBN 0-201-15892-2**

Just because there isn't any turkey and trimmings—due to a slapstick comedy of errors—doesn't mean the family gives up on their holiday dinner. While giving thanks, remember the pilgrims in Steven Kroll's *Oh, What a Thanksgiving!* and the rhymes in Jack Prelutsky's *It's Thanksgiving.* FAMILY LIFE. THANKSGIVING.

819   **Stadler, John.** *Animal Cafe.* **Illus. by the author. Macmillan, 1986. ISBN 0-689-71063-1**

Each night, as soon as proprietor Maxwell leaves his food shop, his mouser Casey and watchdog Sedgewick take over and open up the place as a restaurant for all the neighborhood animals. This could be considered the urban version of Bill Martin, Jr., and John Archambault's *Barn Dance.* Get a hold of Raffi's record "The Corner Grocery Store," about what happens when the groceries hold sway. Sing it with the group, and compose new verses as you go. CATS. DOGS. FOOD. RESTAURANTS.

820   **Steig, William.** *Brave Irene.* **Illus. by the author. Farrar, 1986. ISBN 0-374-30947-7**

One disaster follows another as a dressmaker's plucky daughter trudges through a snowstorm to deliver the duchess's ball gown on time. Once again, virtue is its own reward, as it was in the old folktales such as *Little Sister and the Month Brothers* by Beatrice Schenk de Regniers and *The Month Brother,* a variant by Samuel Marshak. CLOTHING AND DRESS. COURAGE. SNOW. WINTER.

821   **Steig, William.** *Sylvester and the Magic Pebble.* **Illus. by the author. Simon & Schuster, 1988. ISBN 0-13-881707-3**

Elated to find a red, shiny, round wishing pebble that lets him assume any form, a young donkey turns himself into a rock when a hungry lion frightens him. Either hand out or have children search for their own magic pebbles so they can write or tell about their wishes. Also read Steig's *Solomon, the Rusty Nail* and Leo Lionni's *Alexander and the Wind-Up Mouse.* CALDECOTT MEDAL. DONKEYS. ROCKS. TRANSFORMATIONS. WISHES.

822   **Stevenson, James.** *Could Be Worse.* **Illus. by the author. Greenwillow, 1977. ISBN 0-688-80075-0**

To impress his two grandchildren, Grandpa spins a wild yarn of night adventure through mountains, desert, ocean, and sky. First of a well-loved series about Louie and Mary Ann's indefatigable grandpa. In *We Can't Sleep* (1982), Grandpa describes how encounters with a shark, polar bear, dragon, and hurricane helped tire him out one sleepless night when he was a lad. Both are great to act out as group pantomimes. CREATIVE DRAMA. GRANDFATHERS. TALL TALES.

823   **Stevenson, James.** *Happy Valentine's Day, Emma!* **Illus. by the author. Greenwillow, 1987. ISBN 0-688-07358-1**

After receiving chocolate covered worms and stinky flowers from nasty witches Dolores and Lavinia, young witch Emma enlists the help of her animal friends to repay them in kind. One of a cartoon-style, dialogue-filled series, including *Emma, Fried Feathers for Thanksgiving* (1985) and *Yuck!* Celebrate Valentine's Day with a bouquet of books including Eve Bunting's *The Valentine Bears,* Nancy L. Carlson's *Louanne Pig in the Mysterious Valentine,* Lillian Hoban's *Arthur Great Big Valentine,* Frank Modell's *One Zillion Valentines,* and Marjorie Weinman Sharmat's *The Best*

Valentine in the World. And don't forget the poetry, as in Jack Prelutsky's *It's Valentine's Day.* ANIMALS. FRIENDSHIP. VALENTINE'S DAY. WITCHES.

824   **Stevenson, James. *That Terrible Halloween Night.* Illus. by the author. Greenwillow, 1980. ISBN 0-688-84281-X**

Grandpa describes the fright of his life when as a young boy he ventured into a haunted house. The sound effects should be ghastly. Have your students draw and describe what they think Grandpa found behind that door which changed him overnight from a young boy to an old man. FEAR. GRANDFATHERS. HALLOWEEN. HAUNTED HOUSES. SOUND EFFECTS.

825   **Stevenson, James. *There's Nothing to Do!* Illus. by the author. Greenwillow, 1986. ISBN 0-688-04699-1**

Grandpa tells Louie and Mary Ann about the time he and his baby brother, Wainey, were bored. The usual marvelous mixture of sound effects and narrative pantomime opportunities makes this one a must to whip out the next time your children complain they're bored. Top it off with Peter Spier's *Bored, Nothing to Do* and a carton of strawberry ice cream. BROTHERS AND SISTERS. CREATIVE DRAMA. GRANDFATHERS. SOUND EFFECTS.

826   **Stevenson, James. *What's Under My Bed?* Illus. by the author. Greenwillow, 1983. ISBN 0-688-02327-4**

When Mary Ann and Louie are afraid of night noises and can't sleep, Grandpa recalls a similar experience from his own childhood and how his fears were dispelled. Similar scary noises give a boy and his dog pause in *Ghost's Hour, Spook's Hour* by Eve Bunting and make Nick squirm in *My Mama Says There Aren't Any Zombies, Ghosts, Vampires, Creatures, Demons, Monsters, Fiends, Goblins or Things* by Judith Viorst. BEDTIME STORIES. FEAR. GRANDFATHERS. NOISE. SLEEP.

827   **Stevenson, James. *Worse Than Willy!* Illus. by the author. Greenwillow, 1984. ISBN 0-688-02597-8**

Louie and Mary Ann think their new baby brother's a bore until Grandpa regales them with the long ago tall tale hijinks of his baby brother, Wainey. Useful for defusing new-baby blues for jealous older siblings. BABIES. BROTHERS AND SISTERS. SIBLING RIVALRY.

828   **Stolz, Mary. *Storm in the Night.* Illus. by Pat Cummings. Harper & Row, 1988. ISBN 0-06-025913-2**

One wild rainy night with the electricity out, Thomas's grandfather tells the story of how he overcame his own boyhood fear of thunderstorms. Dark, bold, lightening-lit paintings and affectionate dialogue create an intimate scene your children may seek to duplicate by asking their own grandparents to reminisce. You may want to tape-record the resulting stories. For more storms and shivers, read Eve Bunting's *Ghost's Hour, Spook's Hour* and Helena Clare Pittman's *Once When I Was Scared,* another grandfather's recollection. AFRICAN AMERICANS. FEAR. GRANDFATHERS. RAIN AND RAINFALL. WEATHER.

829   **Swope, Sam. *The Araboolies of Liberty Street.* Illus. by Barry Root. Crown, 1989. ISBN 0-517-56960-4**

General Pinch's periodic threats of "I'll call in the army" keep the children on the block properly cowed and quiet until the multicolored, glow-in-the-dark Araboolie family moves next door along with their elephants, anteaters, one wild barumpuss, and other such pets. What a way to begin a discussion on accepting and celebrating the differences between people! Arthur Yorinks's *Company's Coming* ponders the same themes when aliens drop in by flying saucer to pay a quick visit. INDIVIDUALITY. PICTURE BOOKS FOR ALL AGES.

830 **Titus, Eve.** *Anatole.* **Illus. by Paul Galdone. McGraw-Hill, 1956.**

An industrious French mouse creates his own job as a secret taster at the local cheese factory, much to the delight of the company president who is thrilled to see business boom. Naturally, you'll want to have a cheese-tasting party. Other French animals you will find *très charmants* include Louise Fatio's *The Happy Lion* and Tomi Ungerer's *Crictor.* Another stalwart mouse who astonishes the humans is Don Freeman's *Norman the Doorman.* FOOD. FRANCE. MICE.

831 **Tobias, Tobi.** *Chasing the Goblins Away.* **Illus. by Victor Ambrus. Warne, 1977.**

Jimmy is terrified of night goblins until he gets up the nerve to fight them back. Elaine Willoughby's *Boris and the Monsters* and Elizabeth Winthrop's *Maggie and the Monster* are among the many books of bedtime creatures who keep us up all night. BEDTIME STORIES. FEAR. MONSTERS.

832 **Torgersen, Don Arthur.** *The Girl Who Tricked the Troll.* **Illus. by Tom Dunnington. Childrens Press, 1978.**

Angry when Karin eats his troll berries, a nasty troll settles in to ruin the family farm unless Karin can ask him a question he can't answer. Before reading the ending, have children come up with the questions they'd try. Read a medley of child tricked creature tales like Molly Garrett Bang's folktale *Wiley and the Hairy Man,* Edward Marshall's *Troll Country,* and Mercer Mayer's *Liza Lou and the Yeller Belly Swamp.* For the truth about trolls, read *D'Aulaire's Trolls.* FARM LIFE. QUESTIONS. TROLLS.

833 **Tresselt, Alvin.** *Hide and Seek Fog.* **Illus. by Roger Duvoisin. Lothrop, 1965. ISBN 0-688-51169-4**

Sailors and lobstermen are beached for three days when the worst fog in 20 years rolls over a seaside town. This will compliment a weather or seashore unit along with Robert McCloskey's *Time of Wonder* and *Burt Dow, Deep-Water Man.* SEASHORE. WEATHER.

834 **Turkle, Brinton.** *The Adventures of Obadiah.* **Illus. by the author. Viking, 1972. ISBN 0-670-10614-3**

His family has a hard time believing the truth-avoiding Quaker lad's seeming tall tale of riding a ram, dancing with sailors, and watching fire-eaters at the yearly sheepshearing. Take advantage of the early eighteenth-century Nantucket setting to explore life way back when. On the theme of exaggerating and not being believed, also read Esther Allen Peterson's *Frederick's Alligator.* FAMILY LIFE. HISTORICAL FICTION. HONESTY. STORYTELLING.

835 **Van Allsburg, Chris.** *The Polar Express.* **Illus. by the author. Houghton Mifflin, 1985. ISBN 0-395-38949-6**

On Christmas eve, a young boy rides the Polar Express train to the North Pole, where he is chosen by Santa Claus to receive the first gift—a sleigh bell that only believers can hear. Contrast this introspective fantasy of a dream fulfilled with the realism of *The Year of the Perfect Christmas Tree* by Gloria Houston. CALDECOTT MEDAL. CHRISTMAS. GIFTS. PICTURE BOOKS FOR ALL AGES. SANTA CLAUS.

836   **Vaughn, Marcia K.** *Wombat Stew.* **Illus. by Pamela Lofts. Silver Burdett, 1986. ISBN 0-382-09211-2**

After a clever dingo catches a wombat, he stirs up an unflavorful brew with additional ingredients as suggested by echidna, platypus, ostrich, and others intent on rescuing the hapless wombat. A singable refrain makes this a dream for reading or telling, though you'll want to first provide background on Australian animals. ANIMALS. AUSTRALIA. STORIES TO TELL. STORIES WITH SONGS.

837   **Vesey, A.** *The Princess and the Frog.* **Illus. by the author. Little, Brown, 1985. ISBN 0-316-90036-2**

After reading the original "Frog Prince" from either a collection of Grimm's fairy tales or Paul Galdone's version, bring on the satire with this Edwardian-styled recounting of the demanding frog who didn't turn into a prince, even when kissed. Use with other pairs of fairy tales and parodies, such as Bernice Myers's *Sidney Rella and the Glass Sneaker*, Raymond Briggs's *Jim and the Beanstalk*, and Jane Yolen's *Sleeping Ugly.* FAIRY TALES—SATIRE. FROGS. KINGS AND RULERS. PARODIES. PRINCES AND PRINCESSES.

838   **Viorst, Judith.** *Alexander and the Terrible, Horrible, No Good, Very Bad Day.* **Illus. by Ray Cruz. Atheneum, 1972. ISBN 0-689-30072-7**

Some days are just like that, as Alexander discovers when he wakes up with gum in his hair, the first of many indignities. "I think I'll move to Australia," he threatens. Now write about your own lousy days and compare with Patricia Reilly Giff's *Today Was a Terrible Day* and Steven Kroll's *Friday the 13th.* BEHAVIOR. EMOTIONS. FAMILY LIFE. PICTURE BOOKS FOR ALL AGES.

839   **Viorst, Judith.** *Alexander Who Used to Be Rich Last Sunday.* **Illus. by Ray Cruz. Atheneum, 1978. ISBN 0-689-30602-4**

A money-loving boy squanders his only dollar on gum, bets, snake rentals, bad language fines, and a one-eyed bear, and ends up with what he already had—bus tokens. Read when you're teaching about money. After everyone retells the story in sequence, do the subtraction using the same coins Alexander had. Then read the poem "Smart" from Shel Silverstein's *Where the Sidewalk Ends.* FAMILY LIFE. MONEY.

840   **Viorst, Judith.** *My Mama Says There Aren't Any Zombies, Ghosts, Vampires, Creatures, Demons, Monsters, Fiends, Goblins or Things.* **Illus. by Kay Chorao. Atheneum, 1973. ISBN 0-689-30102-2**

But mamas aren't always right, worrier Nick obsesses as he gives examples and tries to sleep in spite of the unsettling noises. Listeners can chime in on the spooky sound effects. Try this with Eve Bunting's *Ghost's Hour, Spook's Hour* and James Stevenson's more reassuring *What's under My Bed?* BEDTIME STORIES. FEAR. MONSTERS. MOTHERS AND SONS.

841   **Waber, Bernard.** *Ira Says Goodbye.* **Illus. by the author. Houghton Mifflin, 1988. ISBN 0-395-48315-8**

In this sequel to *Ira Sleeps Over*, Ira is horrified to learn that his best friend, Reggie, is moving away in two weeks. A new perspective on friendship from the one who's left behind expands the moving theme already sensitively represented by Larry King's *Because of Lozo Brown*, Elizabeth O'Donnell's *Maggie Doesn't Want to Move*, and Marjorie Weinman Sharmat's *Gila Monsters Meet You at the Airport*. On making and having friends, read Sharmat's *Gladys Told Me to Meet Her Here* and Elizabeth Winthrop's *Lizzie & Harold*. FRIENDSHIP. MOVING.

842 Waber, Bernard. *Ira Sleeps Over*. Illus. by the author. Houghton Mifflin, 1973. ISBN 0-395-13893-0

When Ira is invited to spend the night with best friend Reggie, he debates whether or not to take his teddy bear along. A classic for public library "pajama party" story times. Also read the chapter "A Night Away from Home" in Johanna Hurwitz's *Russell and Elisa* (Morrow, 1989). Follow up on Ira and Reggie's friendship with the sequel, *Ira Says Goodbye*. BEDTIME STORIES. FRIENDSHIP. NIGHT. TEDDY BEARS.

843 Wallace, Ian. *Chin Chiang and the Dragon Dance*. Illus. by the author. Atheneum, 1984. ISBN 0-689-50299-0

Afraid that his clumsy dancing will anger the Great Dragon, shame his grandfather, and bring bad fortune to his community, Chin Chiang runs off before the Chinese New Year's parade begins. His reconciliation will enrich your own New Year's festivities. If a Chinese store is accessible, buy each child a small red "luck money" envelope into which you can insert a penny. Relate this dragon to one of old in Jay Williams's *Everyone Knows What a Dragon Looks Like*. DANCING. DRAGONS. GRANDFATHERS. HOLIDAYS.

844 Ward, Lynd. *The Biggest Bear*. Illus. by the author. Houghton Mifflin, 1952. ISBN 0-395-14806-5

Johnny brings home to the farm a baby bear who grows and wreaks havoc in the neighbor's cornfields and smokehouses. Also read Alice Dalgliesh's *The Bears on Hemlock Mountain*. BEARS. CALDECOTT MEDAL. FARM LIFE. RESPONSIBILITY.

845 Waterton, Betty. *Petranella*. Illus. by Ann Blades. Vanguard, 1981. ISBN 0-8149-0844-6

On her way to the new family homestead in Wisconsin, a pioneer girl loses the flower seeds her grandmother gave her before the family sailed to North America. Steven Kellogg's *Johnny Appleseed* and Laura Ingalls Wilder's *Little House in the Big Woods* give additional portraits of life back then. FLOWERS. FRONTIER AND PIONEER LIFE. IMMIGRATION AND EMIGRATION.

846 Waterton, Betty. *A Salmon for Simon*. Illus. by Ann Blades. Salem House, 1987. ISBN 0-88894-533-7

A West Coast Canadian boy takes it upon himself to save a salmon when it is accidentally dropped into his clam hole by an eagle. Pair this with Jan Andrews's astonishing story of an Inuit girl who gathers mussels from under the frozen sea in *Very Last First Time*. BIRDS. CANADA. FISHES.

847 Watson, Clyde. *How Brown Mouse Kept Christmas*. Illus. by Wendy Watson. Farrar, 1980. ISBN 0-374-33494-3

For the first time, an attic mouse explores downstairs in the people part of the house on Christmas Eve. A curious bear finds out more about the holiday as well in Phyllis Reynolds Naylor's *Old Sadie and the Christmas Bear*. CHRISTMAS. MICE.

848   Weller, Frances Ward. *Riptide*. Illus. by Robert J. Blake. Philomel, 1990. ISBN 0-399-21675-8

Though the sign says, "No Dogs on Nauset Beach," Zack's golden dog Rip is a born beach patrol dog who finally proves his worth to the scolding lifeguards when he saves a young swimmer's life. Based on the life of a beloved pet, this poetic account will surely inspire your students to recall other remarkable dog tales. Help them along with a tribute to the noble beast, incorporating such memorable fictional characters as Jan Brett's *First Dog*, Beverly Cleary's *Risby*, Dick Gackenbach's *Beauty, Brave and Beautiful*, Steven Kellogg's *Pinkerton, Behave*, Bill Peet's *The Whingdingdilly*, and Susan Seligson and Howie Schneider's *Amos: The Story of an Old Dog and His Couch*. Don't forget Margaret Davidson's *Seven True Dog Stories* and Lee Bennett Hopkins's poetry collection *A Dog's Life*. DOGS. SEASHORE.

849   Willard, Nancy. *Simple Pictures Are Best*. Illus. by Tomie dePaola. Harcourt, 1978. ISBN 0-15-682625-9

When the shoemaker and his wife prepare to have a portrait taken by a photographer in front of their house, they can't resist draping themselves with all of their most treasured possessions. Don't forget to chant the title refrain. While *their* picture may have been spoiled, why not have children bring in and pose with all of the objects they can't do without—those things that reflect their interests and personalities—and then take a snapshot of each child. CHANTABLE REFRAIN. INDIVIDUALITY. PHOTOGRAPHY.

850   Williams, Barbara. *Donna Jean's Disaster*. Illus. by Margot Apple. Albert Whitman, 1986. ISBN 0-8075-1682-1

Her self-confidence eroded when Uncle Oscar is not in the front row as promised, Donna Jean forgets the words to her poem at Friday's Parent's Program. This would be a good lead-in to an informal poetry session for which each child chooses and learns his or her own poem. Take additional poetic license with Betsy Byars's *Beans on the Roof* and Lilian Moore's *I'll Meet You at the Cucumbers*. FEAR. SCHOOLS. SELF-CONCEPT.

851   Williams, Vera B. *A Chair for My Mother*. Illus. by the author. Greenwillow, 1982. ISBN 0-688-00915-8

After the disastrous fire that destroyed all their belongings and their apartment, a girl and her waitress mother and grandmother save change in a large glass jar until they have enough to buy a new chair for their new place. Vibrant illustrations dramatize a serious subject, handled in a reassuring way. First in a trilogy that continues with *Something Special for Me* (1983), where Rosa is given the contents of the household coin jar to spend on her own perfect birthday present, and *Music, Music for Everyone* (1984), where Rosa earns coins for the family money jar by playing her new accordian at a neighborhood party. APARTMENT HOUSES. CHAIRS. FAMILY LIFE. FIRE. MONEY.

852   Williams, Vera B. *Cherries and Cherry Pits*. Illus. by the author. Greenwillow, 1986. ISBN 0-688-05146-4

Young Bidemmi tells and illustrates four stories about people and cherries. Best read in June when you can sit with your children "eating cherries and spitting out the pits, eating cherries and spitting out the pits." The vibrant watercolor and magic marker pictures will prompt children to create their own draw-and-tell cherry stories, using their own cherry pits for inspiration. Then read Allen Say's Japanese folktale *Once under the Cherry Blossom Tree*. For another bout of unusual story-telling, see Moira Kalman's *Hey Willy, See the Pyramids*. CREATIVE WRITING. FOOD. FRUIT. WRITING.

853   Withers, Carl. *Tale of a Black Cat*. Illus. by Alan E. Cober. Holt, 1966.

A draw-as-you-tell story from American folklore. Hand out paper and black cray-ons so your students can follow along as you draw the story on the board. Follow up with the Paul O. Zelinsky variant, *The Maid and the Mouse and the Odd-Shaped House*. Keep drawing with *The Wild Ducks and the Goose* (1968), also from American folklore, about a foolish old man who sets out to shoot a duck but makes a goose of himself instead. Before presenting the story, induct your children into the Royal Order of Siam. Have them bow their heads and repeat after you—*owa tagoo Siam* until they "get it" . . . Oh, what a goose I am. CATS. DRAWING. ILLUSTRATION OF BOOKS. STORIES TO TELL.

854   Wood, Audrey. *Heckedy Peg*. Illus. by Don Wood. Harcourt, 1987. ISBN 0-15-233678-8

A devoted mother who comes home to find her seven children gone follows a blackbird to the home of an old witch who has turned them into food. A dramatic spellbinder, told in folktale style and based on a sixteenth-century day-of-the-week food-matching game, this is reminiscent in many ways of Jacob Grimm's *The Wolf and the Seven Little Kids* and Ed Young's *Lon Po Po*. For a lighter pig's point of view, try also Mary Rayner's *Garth Pig and the Ice Cream Lady*. DAYS OF THE WEEK. FOOD. WITCHES.

855   Wood, Audrey. *King Bidgood's in the Bathtub*. Illus. by Don Wood. Harcourt, 1985. ISBN 0-15-242730-9

The lusty, bearded, barrel-chested king spends the day in the tub, battling, eating, fishing, and dancing. Students can chant the page's lament and then act out the story, glub, glub, glub. For a real treat, the all-sung Random House filmstrip and video of this book are unsurpassed. Other bathing stories include Charlotte Pomer-antz's *Piggy in the Puddle*, Brock Cole's *No More Baths*, and Helen Garrett's *Angelo, the Naughty One*. BATHS. CHANTABLE REFRAIN. KINGS AND RULERS. PICTURE BOOKS FOR ALL AGES.

856   Wright, Jill. *The Old Woman and the Jar of Uums*. Illus. by Glen Rounds. Putnam, 1990. ISBN 0-399-21736-3

The funny-looking green glass jar that says, "Pick me up," causes the little old woman and rotten egg-throwing young Jackie McFee to get so "ummy" that they must visit the scary old Willy Nilly Man to lift the spell. Told in backwoods dialect, the colloquial language is sheer fun to read aloud, and your listeners will think about that there hainted jar ever time they jest starts to say "uuumm." Other magic objects can be found in your backyard, in the country, and at the beach as in Carol Chapman's *Barney Bippie's Magic Dandelions*, William Steig's *Sylvester and the Magic Pebble*, and Brinton Turkle's *Do Not Open*, respectively. MAGIC.

857   Yolen, Jane. *Owl Moon*. Illus. by John Schoenherr. Philomel, 1987. ISBN 0-399-21457-7

A young girl describes a snowy winter night's owling expedition into the woods with her father. Quiet and introspective, this Caldecott winner would work well with units on winter, birds, and families. Tejima's *Owl Lake* and *Fox's Dream* give two more breathtaking views of nature at night. BIRDS. CALDECOTT MEDAL. FATHERS AND DAUGHTERS. OWLS. WINTER.

858   **Zakhoder, Boris.** *How a Piglet Crashed the Christmas Party.* **Trans. from the Russian by Marguerita Rudolph. Illus. by Kurt Werth. Lothrop, 1971.**

Convincingly disguising himself as a boy with clothes and glasses, Oinky still makes a real pig of himself at the school Christmas party. Father Wolf has a similar idea in Michel Gay's *The Christmas Wolf*. Before the holidays is as good a time as any to review good manners. BEHAVIOR. CHRISTMAS. DOMESTIC ANIMALS. ETIQUETTE. PIGS.

859   **Zelinsky, Paul O.** *The Lion and the Stoat.* **Illus. by the author. Greenwillow, 1984. ISBN 0-688-02563-3**

Two painters vie to see who is the best artist in an animal-filled story of competition, based in part on Pliny's *Natural Histories*. Use in art class to introduce styles of illustration and, along with Alan Baker's *Benjamin's Portrait* and Cynthia Rylant's *All I See*, the role of the artist in children's books and life. ARTISTS. PAINTING.

860   **Zelinsky, Paul O.** *The Maid and the Mouse and the Odd-Shaped House.* **Illus. by the author. Dodd, Mead, 1986. ISBN 0-396-07938-5**

Another drawing story, this one's in rhyme, based on a story written in a teacher's notebook in 1897, and a variant of Carl Withers's *Tale of a Black Cat*, to which it can be compared. CATS. DRAWING. HOUSES. MICE. STORIES IN RHYME.

861   **Zolotow, Charlotte.** *The Quarreling Book.* **Illus. by Arnold Lobel. Harper & Row, 1963. ISBN 0-06-026976-6**

On a rainy gray morning, Mr. James forgets to kiss his wife good-bye, setting off a chain of bad feelings in the family until Eddie the dog reverses the ill-tempered tide. Byron Barton's *Buzz, Buzz, Buzz* and Jane Goodsell's *Toby's Toe* use the same format. Aside from recalling and acting out the sequence, you can use the pattern of nice deeds to set things right on grumpy days in your classroom. EMOTIONS. CAUSE AND EFFECT. CREATIVE DRAMA. FAMILY LIFE. SEQUENCE STORIES.

FICTION FOR GRADES 2–3

862   **Agee, John.** *The Incredible Painting of Felix Clousseau.* **Illus. by the author. Farrar, 1988. ISBN 0-374-33633-4**

At the Royal Palace's Grand Contest of Art in Paris, the judges are underwhelmed at an unknown artist's painting of a duck until it quacks and walks off the canvas. Clousseau's lifelike works cause chaos when they come to life, much like David McPhail's *The Magical Drawings of Mooney B. Finch* and Chris Van Allsburg's *Jumanji*. When teaching appreciation of illustration, have students paint their come-to-life masterpieces. If you buy or borrow a large picture frame or canvas stretcher, children can act out live tableau paintings that come alive. Other related titles include Henrik Drescher's *Simon's Book* and Paul Zelinsky's *The Lion and the Stoat.* ARTISTS. CREATIVE DRAMA. PAINTING.

863   **Andersen, Hans Christian.** *The Emperor's New Clothes: A Fairy Tale.* **Illus. by Dorothee Duntze. Retold by Anthea Bell. North-South Books, 1986. ISBN 1-55858-036-0**

Not until a little boy points out the obvious will anyone admit to not being able to see the emperor's posh new outfit. Discussion point: Have you ever agreed to do something you didn't want to do because you were afraid of what others might think of you? CLOTHING AND DRESS. HONESTY. KINGS AND RULERS. PICTURE BOOKS FOR ALL AGES.

864   **Andersen, Hans Christian.** *Thumbelina.* **Illus. by Susan Jeffers. Retold by Amy Ehrlich. Dial, 1979. ISBN 0-8037-8814-2**

Jeffers's dazzling watercolors draw the viewer into the classic Andersen tale of a tiny girl lost in the woods who almost is trapped into marriage with an insensitive mole. If she hadn't found a tiny prince she may have settled for the diminutive adventurers in Barbara Brenner's Japanese folktale *Little One Inch* or Colin McNaughton's *Anton B. Stanton and the Pirats*. Children can imagine what they would do if they were tiny, writing about and illustrating their excursions, or devising an updated survival guide for tiny travelers in an oversized world. CREATIVE WRITING. SIZE.

865   **Anderson, Lonzo.** *The Ponies of Mykillengi.* **Illus. by Adrienne Adams. Scribner, 1966.**

Stranded in a blizzard after an earthquake and an erupting volcano cut them off from their farm, an Icelandic brother and sister witness their pony giving birth.

Contrast with city and country blizzards of the past in Marietta Moskin's *The Day of the Blizzard* and Trinka Hakes Noble's *Apple Tree Christmas*. Use with Thomas P. Lewis's *Hill of Fire* about the Paricutin volcano in Mexico and with Seymour Simon's spectacular *Volcanoes* for a nonfiction view. BROTHERS AND SISTERS. HORSES. STORMS. VOLCANOES. WINTER.

866   **Andrews, F. Emerson.** *Upside-Down Town.* **Illus. by Louis Slobodkin. Little, Brown, 1958.**

[10 chapters, 64p.] On their way to visit their grandfather, the train makes an emergency stop and Rickie and Ann spend an unusual day in a town where everything is done backwards, from eating meals to playing baseball. Have children write or tell about other possible convoluted activities in town, such as taking a bath, reading books, getting dressed, or playing soccer. Take a subtrip to the land of Woosey in Dick Gackenbach's *King Wacky*. BROTHERS AND SISTERS. CREATIVE WRITING. HUMOROUS FICTION. OPPOSITES.

867   **Andrews, Jan.** *Very Last First Time.* **Illus. by Ian Wallace. Atheneum, 1986. ISBN 0-689-50388-1**

Today is the first day for Eva, a northern Canadian Inuit girl, to walk alone on the sea bottom under the ice to collect mussels. A breathtakingly different angle for units on winter, Eskimos, and Canada; students can also relate their own "first time" experiences. This works well with Jan Rogers's Eskimo winter story *Runaway Mittens* and Betty Waterton's *A Salmon for Simon*. CANADA. ESKIMOS. SEASONS. WINTER.

868   **Annett, Cora.** *How the Witch Got Alf.* **Illus. by Steven Kellogg. Franklin Watts, 1975.**

Jealous of the preferential treatment he thinks the cat, dog, and canary receive, the donkey craves affection from the old man and old woman and runs away onto the roof when he doesn't get enough. Mate this one with Brock Cole's *Nothing but a Pig*. DONKEYS. JEALOUSY. RUNAWAYS.

869   **Bang, Molly.** *Dawn.* **Illus. by the author. Morrow, 1983. ISBN 0-688-02404-1**

A somber first-person description, told to Dawn by her father, of the wounded goose he nursed to health and the beautiful dark-eyed woman who then appeared at his shipyard and offered to weave and sew sails. Freely adapted from the Japanese story "The Crane Wife," this haunting tale is set in eighteenth-century New England. Also see Bang's *The Paper Crane* for a similar theme and Sumiko Yagawa's *The Crane Wife* for the original. BIRDS. GEESE.

870   **Barrett, Judi.** *Animals Should Definitely Not Wear Clothing.*   **Illus. by Ron Barrett. Atheneum, 1970. ISBN 0-689-20592-9**

There are lots of reasons given. The hilarious writing and illustrating incentive will make a sidesplitting showcase when your children bring in stuffed animals, dress them, and write new reasons. ANIMALS. CLOTHING AND DRESS. CREATIVE WRITING.

871   **Barrett, Judi.** *Cloudy with a Chance of Meatballs.* **Illus. by Ron Barrett. Atheneum, 1978. ISBN 0-689-30647-4**

The town of ChewandSwallow undergoes a crisis when their normal edible weather turns nasty. Children can forecast the day's diet using weather terminology. Read after a weather lesson for a bizarre literary twist, along with *C.L.O.U.D.S.*

by Pat Cummings and *Bartholomew and the Oobleck* by Dr. Seuss. CREATIVE WRITING. FOOD. WEATHER.

872   **Baylor, Byrd.** *The Best Town in the World.* **Illus. by Ronald Himler. Scribner, 1983. ISBN 0-684-18035-9**

According to the narrator's father who grew up there, way back in the Texas hills, everything in his town—cooks, blackberries, dogs, summers, water, and candy—was perfect. Warm nostalgic watercolors evoke a bygone era. Have your listeners interview parents or grandparents to find out what their "perfect" towns were like. CITIES AND TOWNS. GRANDPARENTS.

873   **Baylor, Byrd.** *Everybody Needs a Rock.* **Illus. by Peter Parnall. Scribner, 1974. ISBN 0-684-13899-9**

Ten rules for finding a perfect one. A logical extension: Everyone must find his or her own rock, then write one or more new rules. Naturally, if you're studying rocks in science, this will fit right in, along with Joanna Cole's *The Magic School Bus Inside the Earth*, though you don't have to be able to identify a rock to like one. CREATIVE WRITING. ROCKS.

874   **Bennett, Anna Elizabeth.** *Little Witch.* **Illus. by Helen Stone. Lippincott, 1953. ISBN 0-397-30261-4**

[12 chapters, 128p.] Nine-year-old Minx, child of the vengeful witch Madam Snickasnee, rebels and sneaks off to school to be with normal children. Margaret Embry's *The Blue-Nosed Witch* also mingles with the human set, though she enjoys being a witch. Stretch the mood with poems from John E. Brewton's *In the Witch's Garden*, Lilian Moore's *See My Lovely Poison Ivy*, and Daisy Wallace's *Witch Poems*. MAGIC. SCHOOLS. WITCHES.

875   **Bess, Clayton.** *The Truth about the Moon.* **Illus. by Rosekrans Hoffman. Houghton Mifflin, 1983. ISBN 0-395-34551-0**

[1-2 sittings, 48p.] Sumu, a young, curious African boy, asks his sister, his parents, and the village chief to tell him. Their folklorelike responses will contrast with your astronomy unit and stimulate your students to invent their own explanations of the ways of the heavenly bodies. Also read Elphinstone Dayrell's African folktale *Why the Sun and the Moon Live in the Sky*, Gerald McDermott's *Anansi the Spider*, and James Thurber's *Many Moons*. AFRICA. MOON. STORYTELLING.

876   **Brooks, Walter Rollin.** *Jimmy Takes Vanishing Lessons.* **Illus. by Don Bolognese. Knopf, 1965.**

[1-2 sittings, unp.] To make his aunt's old deserted house rentable again, Jimmy makes a deal with the ghost who haunts it. A brave tinker makes a more dangerous bargain in Sibyl Hancock's Spanish folktale *Esteban and the Ghost*. *Ghost Poems* by Daisy Wallace should add the final chill. AUNTS. GHOSTS. HAUNTED HOUSES.

877   **Bulla, Clyde Robert.** *The Sword in the Tree.* **Illus. by Paul Galdone. Crowell, 1956. ISBN 0-690-79908-X**

[14 chapters, 114p.] In the days of King Arthur, a young boy's Uncle Lionel proves himself a wicked knight. Explore the flavor of the period with Donald Carrick's *Harald and the Giant Knight* and *Harald and the Great Stag*, and for sophisticated listeners, Selina Hasting's *Sir Gawain and the Loathly Lady* and Margaret Hodges's

Saint George and the Dragon. ENGLAND. HISTORICAL FICTION. KNIGHTS AND KNIGHT-HOOD. MIDDLE AGES.

878   **Burchardt, Nellie. *Project Cat.* Illus. by Fermin Rocker. Franklin Watts, 1966.**

[7 chapters, 66p.] Forbidden by the rules of her housing project to give shelter to a pregnant stray cat she has befriended, Betsy and her friends take on the mayor and the city council with their petition to repeal the ban. Use their determined example to discuss the functions of local government and explore how even children can make a difference. If there are injustices they would like to see addressed by local, state, or even federal government, students can write letters to public officials or the newspaper. AFRICAN AMERICANS. APARTMENT HOUSES. CATS.

879   **Byars, Betsy. *Beans on the Roof.* Illus. by Melodye Rosales. Delacorte, 1988. ISBN 0-440-50055-9**

[9 short chapters, 63p.] While Anna, Jenny, Mrs. Bean, and Mr. Bean each make up a poem when on their apartment building roof, son George has writer's block. An unpretentious demonstration of family love, and a great way to begin a poetry unit, especially paired with Lilian Moore's *I'll Meet You at the Cucumbers*, about a mouse poet, and Barbara Williams's *Donna Jean's Disaster*. Students can write their own roof, playground, or other "special place" poems to recite for the group. CREATIVE WRITING. FAMILY LIFE. POETS.

880   **Calhoun, Mary. *The Night the Monster Came.* Illus. by Leslie Morrill. Morrow, 1982.**

[9 chapters, 62p.] Left alone in the house and hearing loud noises outside, Andy fears Bigfoot is responsible for the huge animal-like footprints in the snow. *The Bears on Hemlock Mountain* by Alice Dalgliesh and *Once When I Was Scared* by Helena Clare Pittman are two other accounts of boys who deal with their fears and overcome them even in the face of danger. BEARS. COURAGE. MONSTERS. SNOW.

881   **Cameron, Ann. *The Stories Julian Tells.* Illus. by Ann Strugnell. Pantheon, 1981. ISBN 0-394-94301-5**

[6 chapters, 71p.] Lemon pudding, catalog cats, a loose tooth, and a best friend are the basis for wonderful family anecdotes of two young brothers and their parents. First of a series that children will want to continue on their own, including *More Stories Julian Tells* (1986), *Julian's Glorious Summer* (1987), and *Julian, Secret Agent* (1988). AFRICAN AMERICANS. BROTHERS. FAMILY LIFE.

882   **Carrick, Donald. *Harald and the Giant Knight.* Illus. by the author. Clarion, 1982. ISBN 0-89919-060-X**

When the much admired Baron's knights camp on his parents' farm, trampling the fields and destroying the trees and fences with their sharp swords, Harald comes up with a plan for constructing a huge woven basket to scare them off. Clyde Robert Bulla's *The Sword in the Tree* and Bill Peet's *Cowardly Clyde* introduce other knights, as do folktales *Sir Gawain and the Loathly Lady* by Selina Hastings and *Saint George and the Dragon* by Margaret Hodges. Other outwitted armies are sent packing in Mary Blount Christian's *April Fool* and Tomie dePaola's *The Mysterious Giant of Barletta.* ENGLAND. KNIGHTS AND KNIGHTHOOD. MIDDLE AGES.

883   **Carrick, Donald. *Harald and the Great Stag.* Illus. by the author. Clarion, 1988. ISBN 0-89919-514-8**

In the sequel to *Harald and the Giant Knight*, the Baron and his hunters plan a hunt to bring down the Great Stag of the forest. Young Harald spreads the deer's droppings through the forest to throw the dogs off the scent, only to find himself hunted as well. Other hunting abuses are countered in Roald Dahl's *The Fantastic Mr. Fox* and *The Magic Finger*, Bill Peet's *The Gnats of Knotty Pine*, and Dr. Seuss's *Thidwick, the Big-Hearted Moose*. Also pair with Susan Cooper's haunting Welsh folktale *The Silver Cow*. DEER. ENGLAND. FORESTS AND FORESTRY. HUNTERS AND HUNTING. MIDDLE AGES.

884 **Catling, Patrick Skene. *The Chocolate Touch*. Illus. by Margot Apple. Morrow, 1979. ISBN 0-688-32187-9**

[12 chapters, 126p.] A modern-day Midas story of a greedy boy whose passion for candy leads to a magical affliction where everything that touches his lips turns to chocolate. Go to the source and read Kathryn Hewitt's *King Midas and the Golden Touch*. CANDY. MAGIC. SCHOOLS.

885 **Chapman, Carol. *The Tale of Meshka the Kvetch*. Illus. by Arnold Lobel. Dutton, 1980. ISBN 0-525-40745-6**

The village complainer comes down with Kvetch's Itch, a malady where everything she complains about comes true, until she learns to praise the good in her life. Compare cures with those in Marilyn Hirsch's *Could Anything Be Worse?*, Arthur Yorinks's *It Happened in Pinsk*, and Margot Zemach's *It Could Always Be Worse*. SELF-CONCEPT.

886 **Charlip, Remy. *Harlequin and the Gift of Many Colors*. Illus. by the author. Parents, 1973.**

A touching, lyrical story of the first harlequin, too poor to buy a costume for the carnival, and his friends who tried to help. Take some time to talk about the value of friendship as opposed to wealth or possessions. CLOTHING AND DRESS. COSTUMES. FRIENDSHIP. ITALY.

887 **Cleary, Beverly. *Beezus and Ramona*. Illus. by Louis Darling. Morrow, 1955. ISBN 0-688-31076-1**

[6 long chapters, 159p.] Beezus must learn to cope with the world's brattiest little sister, everyone's favorite incorrigible, who even ruins her birthday cake twice. Follow up with Judy Blume's *Tales of a Fourth Grade Nothing* for a male counterpart to Ramona, and encourage your writers to pen chapters about their own siblings or themselves. FAMILY LIFE. HUMOROUS STORIES. SISTERS.

888 **Cleary, Beverly. *Henry Huggins*. Illus. by Louis Darling. Morrow, 1950. ISBN 0-688-31385-X**

[6 long chapters, 155p.] When third-grader Henry finds a stray mutt outside the drugstore, getting him home is just the first problem. The first of one of the most beloved series in children's book history, and as fresh and funny for kids today as it was in the 1950s when some of us were growing up. DOGS. HUMOROUS STORIES. SCHOOLS.

889 **Cleary, Beverly. *Ramona Quimby, Age 8*. Illus. by Alan Tiegreen. Morrow, 1981. ISBN 0-688-00478-4**

[9 chapters, 190p.] Former pest hits third grade. Not to be missed! If you're not already doing it, introduce the concept of DEAR—Drop Everything And Read—as described in Chapter 2, into your classroom. FAMILY LIFE. SCHOOLS.

890 **Cleary, Beverly. *Ramona the Pest*. Illus. by Louis Darling. Morrow, 1968. ISBN 0-688-31721-9**

[8 long chapters, 192p.] Kindergarten is Ramona's newest challenge. For another remarkable "first day" story that will bring students' early school memories to the fore, read *Annabelle Swift, Kindergartner* by Amy Schwartz. HUMOROUS STORIES. SCHOOLS.

891 **Cleary, Beverly. *Ribsy*. Illus. by Louis Darling. Morrow, 1964. ISBN 0-688-31662-X**

[7 long chapters, 192p.] Getting lost in a parking lot is the first step in Henry Huggins's dog's one-month sojourn from home. To introduce the difference between the two types of fiction, contrast this piece of realistic fiction with one of fantasy, such as Barbara Dillon's *What's Happened to Harry?*, where a boy is turned into a poodle by a body-stealing witch. DOGS. LOST.

892 **Cohen, Barbara. *The Carp in the Bathtub*. Illus. by Joan Halpern. Lothrop, 1972. ISBN 0-688-51627-0**

[1 sitting, 48p.] Grandmother recalls how, as children, she and her brother Harry once tried to save the live Passover fish from becoming gefilte fish by hiding it. Children can ask their parents and grandparents if they recall any memorable Easter or Passover holidays when they were young, and share their responses with the class. As another example of oral folklore, you may wish to tape-record their stories or have children write them down. BROTHERS AND SISTERS. FISHES. HOLIDAYS. JEWS. NEW YORK CITY.

893 **Cohen, Barbara. *Molly's Pilgrim*. Illus. by Michael Deraney. Lothrop, 1983. ISBN 0-688-02104-2**

A Jewish immigrant girl from Russia finally finds acceptance in her third-grade class at Thanksgiving time when, for a class project, her mother makes a clothespin pilgrim doll that looks Russian. Both the book and the Academy Award-winning film should spark a dialogue on overcoming prejudice and understanding those we may consider "different." For a first-hand look at Plymouth pilgrim life, read Kate Waters's photo-essay *Sara Morton's Day: A Day in the Life of a Pilgrim Girl*. DOLLS. IMMIGRATION AND EMIGRATION. PILGRIMS. SCHOOLS. THANKSGIVING.

894 **Cohen, Caron Lee. *Renata, Whizbrain and the Ghost*. Illus. by Blanche Simms. Atheneum, 1987.**

When Renata—the mayor, sheriff, and patent agent of Amarillo, Texas—grants Whizbrain Wallerbee an Ice Box Railroad Car Patent, the two of them must next think of a way to wrest a sunken treasure from Fearless Bones Kelly, a waterlogging Red River pirate ghost. Another Texas tall tale that fits the mood is *If You Say So, Claude* (Warne, 1980) by Joan Lowery Nixon. BURIED TREASURE. GHOSTS. PIRATES.

895 **Cole, Brock. *The King at the Door*. Illus. by the author. Doubleday, 1979.**

Trusting little Baggit believes the beggar at the inn is really the king in disguise, in spite of his innkeeper master's cynicism. As the innkeeper is a W. C. Fields look-alike, try using the comic's singular intonation when reading those bits of dialogue aloud. Talk over everyone's image of kingly appearance and bearing, and then humanize royalty a bit with stories like Dick Gackenbach's *King Wacky,* Dr. Seuss's *Bartholomew and the Oobleck,* and Audrey Wood's *King Bidgood's in the Bathtub*, plus folktales *King Midas and the Golden Touch* by Kathryn Hewitt and *Mufaro's Beautiful Daughters* by John Steptoe. KINGS AND RULERS.

896 **Cole, Joanna.** *Doctor Change.* **Illus. by Donald Carrick. Morrow, 1986. ISBN 0-688-06136-2**

Trapped in the employ of the nefarious doctor, young Tom finds the man's book of spells and learns to transform himself into any object, which makes possible his escape. Have students compose the transforming spells that Tom might have learned from the book. Mercer Mayer's *A Special Trick* and Brinton Turkle's *Do Not Open* also incorporate such magic. CREATIVE WRITING. MAGICIANS. TRANSFORMATIONS.

897 **Coletta, Irene, and Hallie Coletta.** *From A to Z: The Collected Letters of Irene and Hallie Coletta.* **Illus. by the authors. Prentice Hall, 1979.**

Twenty-six marvelous alphabet rebus poems surrounded with small, blue-tinged sketches of same-letter objects to guess. Have your children compose and illustrate their own rebus pages. ALPHABET BOOKS. CREATIVE WRITING. RIDDLES. STORIES IN RHYME.

898 **Conford, Ellen.** *Jenny Archer, Author.* **Illus. by Diane Palmisciano. Little, Brown, 1989. ISBN 0-316-15255-2**

[12 short chapters, 61p.] Assigned to write the story of her life, Jenny misunderstands the purpose and beefs it up with fascinating fictional details, which her teacher interprets as lies. Read before your students write their autobiographies (auto = self; bio = life; graphy = writing). IMAGINATION. WRITING.

899 **Conford, Ellen.** *A Job for Jenny Archer.* **Illus. by Diane Palmisciano. Little, Brown, 1988. ISBN 0-316-15262-5**

[15 short chapters, 3–4 sittings, 76p.] With only 27 cents to her name, Jenny tries dog training, baby-sitting, and selling real estate—all of which backfire—to earn money for her mother's birthday present. First in an easy chapter book series, including *A Case for Jenny Archer* (1988). Compare her business acumen with another cashless entrepreneur in Jean Van Leeuwen's *Benjy in Business.* MONEY.

900 **Coombs, Patricia.** *The Magician and McTree.* **Illus. by the author. Lothrop, 1984. ISBN 0-688-02111-5**

Thanks to the old, old magician's potion which goes awry, faithful cat McTree acquires human speech and is held captive at the castle to amuse the royalty there. A writing idea: What would happen if your favorite pet could speak? CATS. CREATIVE WRITING. KINGS AND RULERS. MAGICIANS.

901 **Coombs, Patricia.** *Molly Mullett.* **Illus. by the author. Lothrop, 1975.**

In spite of her father who considers her a mere girl, unflappable Molly defeats a ferocious ogre and is knighted by the king. A good-natured bit of modern feminist cheerleading in fairy tale format, this can stand alongside such tales as Tomie dePaola's *Fin M'Coul, the Giant of Knockmany Hill,* with Fin's clever wife Oonagh; Josepha Sherman's *Vassilisa the Wise;* and Dorothy Van Woerkom's *Alexandra the Rock-Eater.* COURAGE. KINGS AND RULERS. MOTHERS AND DAUGHTERS. OGRES.

902   Coren, Alan. *Arthur the Kid*. Illus. by John Astrop. Little, Brown, 1978. ISBN 0-316-15734-1

[4–5 sittings, 73p.] A level-headed ten-year-old boy shapes up an Old West gang of incompetent would-be bank-robbing outlaws. One of a tongue-in-cheek series, including *Buffalo Arthur* (1978), *The Lone Arthur* (1977), and *Railroad Arthur* (1978). Another wild West romp is Richard Kennedy's *Contests at Cowlick*, while a modern-day girl foils a bank robbery in Pat Ross's *Gloria and the Super Soaper*. ROBBERS AND OUTLAWS. WEST.

903   Cummings, Pat. *C.L.O.U.D.S.* Illus. by the author. Lothrop, 1986. ISBN 0-688-04683-5

Designing the skies over New York City seems like a bottom-of-the-barrel job to Chuku until he finds a little girl in Central Park who appreciates his work. Use as part of a cloud-weather unit along with Judi Barrett's *Cloudy with a Chance of Meatballs* and Tomie dePaola's *The Cloud Book,* and then have your junior forecasters design their own skies for their neighborhoods and make lists of the newly invented colors they'd need. Another in-the-sky creator is Artist Foreman in William Pène du Bois's *Lion*. CLOUDS. NEW YORK CITY. SKY. WEATHER.

904   Dahl, Roald. *The Fantastic Mr. Fox*. Illus. by Donald Chaffin. Knopf, 1970. ISBN 0-394-90497-4

[18 short chapters, 62p.] How a fearless fox outfoxes the three vengeful hunters who shot off his tail and plotted his demise. To complete a better-rounded portrait of foxes, also read Irina Korschunow's *The Foundling Fox*, Patricia C. McKissack's *Flossie and the Fox,* and Alice Mills Leighner's nonfiction *Reynard: The Story of a Fox Returned to the Wild*. FOXES. HUNTERS AND HUNTING.

905   Dahl, Roald. *The Magic Finger*. Illus. by William Pène du Bois. Harper & Row, 1966. ISBN 0-06-021382-5

[2 sittings, 141p.] An antihunting tale of a girl with a diabolical digit who turns her bird-shooting neighbors into ducks. Read in tandem with the above *The Fantastic Mr. Fox* and other like-minded stories such as Donald Carrick's *Harald and the Great Stag* and Bill Peet's *The Gnats of Knotty Pine*. DUCKS. HUNTERS AND HUNTING.

906   Day, Alexandra. *Frank and Ernest*. Illus. by the author. Scholastic, 1988. ISBN 0-590-41557-3

Two friends, a bear and an elephant, fill in at the diner for two days and learn all the special food lingo. The extensive list of flamboyant diner slang and its English-language counterparts will prove a challenge to patrons who will find a whole new vocabulary to fool with, and perhaps come up with more. For some old English wordplay, see the folktales *Arabella and Mr. Crack* by Dick Gackenbach and *Master of all Masters* by Marcia Sewall. BEARS. ELEPHANTS. ENGLISH LANGUAGE. FOOD. VOCABULARY.

907   dePaola, Tomie. *The Art Lesson*. Illus. by the author. Putnam, 1989. ISBN 0-399-21688-X

Convinced even before he started kindergarten that he would be an artist when he grew up, Tommy practiced drawing every chance he could get and waited stoically for the day, in first grade, when the art teacher would visit his class for a real art lesson. For all who have treasured their crayon boxes or been discouraged by an uncomprehending teacher, Tommy will inspire us to keep on drawing (or writing or creating), as this is an autobiographical success story. Introduce your listeners to dePaola's other works first and be sure to save time for sketching. A good mate with this one is Cynthia Rylant's *All I See*. ARTISTS. AUTOBIOGRAPHY. DRAWING. INDIVIDUALITY. PICTURE BOOKS FOR ALL AGES.

908   dePaola, Tomie. *Big Anthony and the Magic Ring*. Illus. by the author. Harcourt, 1979. ISBN 0-15-207124-5

In an original sequel to dePaola's retelling of the Italian folktale *Strega Nona*, the good witch's bumbling assistant finds a way to become so handsome, the besotted village girls won't leave him alone. Another funny companion story, *Strega Nona's Magic Lessons* (1982), has the ever-incompetent Big Anthony disguised as Antonia so that Strega Nona will instruct him in her witch's secrets. The ever-vital message to be yourself is also stressed in *The Whingdingdilly* by Bill Peet and *It Happened in Pinsk* by Arthur Yorinks. LOVE. MAGIC. SELF-CONCEPT. WITCHES.

909   dePaola, Tomie. *Merry Christmas, Strega Nona*. Illus. by the author. Harcourt, 1986. ISBN 0-15-253183-1

Covering up his real plans by acting like his usual bumbling, forgetful self, Big Anthony plans a surprise feast for Strega Nona for *Natale*. Aside from reading the other "Strega Nona" books in the series, this might be a good time to teach your linguists a few key phrases in Italian. CHRISTMAS. ITALY. WITCHES.

910   Dillon, Barbara. *What's Happened to Harry?* Illus. by Chris Conover. Morrow, 1982.

[6 chapters, 125p.] Witch Hepzibah the Hateful turns a young trick-or-treater into a poodle on Halloween night and inhabits his skin to impersonate him and cause witchy havoc in town. Act out the confrontation scenes between Harry and Hepzibah, Hepzibah at school and at home, and Harry as the poodle trying desperately to communicate with his parents. DOGS. HALLOWEEN. WITCHES.

911   Du Bois, William Pène. *Lazy Tommy Pumpkinhead*. Illus. by the author. Harper & Row, 1966.

Machines wake him, bathe him, brush his teeth, dress him, and feed him, until the day the power fails. Act out the machinery as a group. For other malfunctioning machines, try out Eileen Christelow's *Mr. Murphy's Marvelous Invention* and the retooled one in George Selden's *Sparrow Socks*. Rube Goldberg's outrageous inventions in *The Best of Rube Goldberg* will make everyone wild, and Lee Bennett Hopkins's *Click, Rumble, Roar: Poems about Machines* fits right in here. LAZINESS. MACHINES.

912   Du Bois, William Pène. *Lion*. Illus. by the author. Penguin, 1983. ISBN 0-14-050417-6

Artist Foreman, working in the Animal Factory to create a new creature he calls "Lion," draws it multicolored with feathers, fur, and scales until he asks his fellow artists for advice. Originally published in 1956. Foreman is a kindred spirit to Chuku in Pat Cummings's *C.L.O.U.D.S.* Other animal creation stories include Rudyard Kipling's *The Elephant's Child* and *The Beginning of the Armadillos*. ANIMALS—CREATION. ARTISTS. LIONS.

913   Embry, Margaret. *The Blue-Nosed Witch*. Illus. by Carl Rose. Bantam, 1984. ISBN 0-553-15435-4

[3 short chapters, 47p.] An always tardy witch child with an unusual lighted proboscis sets her alarm for Halloween and awakens early enough for an evening of trick-ortreating with human children. Originally published in 1956. Anna Elizabeth Bennett's *Little Witch* also encounters regular children when she goes to school against her mother's wishes, while Harry has nothing but trouble from Hepzibah the Hateful in Barbara Dillon's *What's Happened to Harry?* HALLOWEEN. NOSES. WITCHES.

914   **Estes, Eleanor.** *The Hundred Dresses.* **Illus. by Louis Slobodkin. Harcourt, 1944. ISBN 0-15-237374-8**

[7 chapters, 80p.] Because she claims to have 100 dresses in her closet, best friends Peggy and Maddie tease poor, motherless Wanda Petronski in school each day until Wanda moves away and it's almost too late to make amends. This is a thoughtul discussion starter on the meaning of prejudice and the cruelty we can thoughtlessly inflict on each other. Also read Barbara Cohen's *Molly's Pilgrim* and Taro Yashima's Japanese school story of another talented outcast, *Crow Boy.* CLOTHING AND DRESS. PREJUDICE. SCHOOLS.

915   **Etra, Jonathan, and Stephanie Spinner.** *Aliens for Breakfast.* **Illus. by Steve Björkman. Random House, 1988. ISBN 0-394-92093-7**

Richard Bickerstaff is convinced by Aric, the little pink alien he finds in his cereal bowl, to stand up to Dorp, the dazzling, smiling new kid at school who, as a planet-conquering Drane, will divide every four days unless Richard can figure out what food will cause him to self-destruct. A witty introduction to the "human child helps good alien creature save the world from bad alien creature" science fiction genre, along with Daniel Pinkwater's *Fat Men from Space.* EXTRATERRESTRIAL LIFE. SCIENCE FICTION.

916   **Feagles, Anita.** *Casey the Utterly Impossible Horse.* **Illus. by Dagmar Wilson. Shoe String Press, 1989. ISBN 0-208-02239-2**

[9 chapters, 80p.] Mike's moody but endearing talking horse companion insists on his own striped pajamas for a start. Next read Barbara Rinkoff's *The Remarkable Ramsey*, about a talking dog. HORSES.

917   **Fife, Dale.** *Who's in Charge of Lincoln?* **Illus. by Paul Galdone. Coward, 1965.**

[7 chapters, 61p.] Third-grader Lincoln Farnum, named after the sixteenth president and well known for his vivid imagination, ends up in Washington, D.C., with a satchel of money when no one believes his latest wild story, which happens to be true. Now is the time for a vicarious trip to our nation's capital through books and encyclopedias. AFRICAN AMERICANS. IMAGINATION. TRAINS. WASHINGTON, D.C.

918   **Fleischman, Sid.** *The Ghost on Saturday Night.* **Illus. by Eric Von Schmidt. Little, Brown, 1974. ISBN 0-316-28583-8**

[9 short chapters, 57p.] The scoundrel who claims to be able to raise the ghost of Crookneck John has a shady motive, but young narrator Opie and his Aunt Etta save the day, with the help of a tule fog. Ghosts raise mayhem in James Flora's *Grandpa's Ghost Stories*, Sibyl Hancock's Spanish folktale *Esteban and the Ghost*, and Lee Bennett Hopkins's *A-Haunting We Will Go: Ghostly Stories and Poems.* AUNTS. GHOSTS. ROBBERS AND OUTLAWS.

919   **Flora, James.** *Grandpa's Ghost Stories.* **Illus. by the author. Atheneum, 1978. ISBN 0-689-50112-9**

[1–2 sittings, unp.] While the thunder crashes outside, Grandpa tells his frightened grandson funny spine-tickling tales of a hungry skeleton, a warty witch, and a ghastly ghost. Students can write their own Grandpa adventures, while ghoulish types will also get a charge out of George Mendoza's *Gwot!*, plus Sibyl Hancock's *Esteban and the Ghost*, and Lee Bennett Hopkins's collection *A-Haunting We Will Go: Ghostly Stories and Poems.* CREATIVE WRITING. GHOST STORIES. GRANDFATHERS. WITCHES.

920   **Flora, James.** *Grandpa's Witched-Up Christmas.* **Illus. by the author. Atheneum, 1982. ISBN 0-689-50232-X**

[1–2 sittings, unp.] In the sequel to *Grandpa's Ghost Stories*, Grandpa recalls how, when he was a boy, a nasty witch turned him into a porker on Christmas Eve. Cat Chester and dog Harold's holiday encounter also gives them pause in *The Fright before Christmas* by James Howe. CHRISTMAS. GRANDFATHERS. PIGS. SANTA CLAUS. WITCHES.

921   **Flora, James.** *The Great Green Turkey Creek Monster.* **Illus. by the author. Atheneum, 1976. ISBN 0-689-50060-2**

Growing madly by the minute, the almost unstoppable Great Green Hooligan Vine escapes and overtakes the town until young Argie Bargle plays his trombone. This wild story would make a riotous detailed mural for your walls especially if you've been studying plants and how they grow. MONSTERS. PLANTS. TALL TALES.

922   **Flora, James.** *The Joking Man.* **Illus. by the author. Harcourt, 1968.**

Wild and crazy stunts are pulled when the mysterious Joking Man comes to town, as narrated by the two jovial boys from *My Friend Charlie*. Before you reveal the ending, have your students draw quick sketches of how they envision this character. TRICKS.

923   **Flora, James.** *Little Hatchy Hen.* **Illus. by the author. Harcourt, 1969.**

Grandpa's talented hen that can hatch anything, including a box of spaghetti into 200 feet of fire hose, is kidnapped by Big Bruno, the world's champion chicken thief. Dream up new pairs of objects the hen could hatch, and draw them side by side as "before" and "after" examples. CHICKENS. ROBBERS AND OUTLAWS.

924   **Flora, James.** *My Friend Charlie.* **Illus. by the author. Harcourt, 1964.**

[12 short chapters, 2–3 sittings, unp.] The young narrator gives reasons for being friends with Charlie who borrows dreams, makes a horse laugh, talks to fish, eats peanuts with his foot, and more. A good chapter for writing skills: "Things *not* to do." Children can also write their own reasons for liking their best friends. The two pals return in *The Joking Man.* CREATIVE WRITING. FRIENDSHIP.

925   **Flournoy, Valerie.** *The Patchwork Quilt.* **Illus. by Jerry Pinkney. Dial, 1985. ISBN 0-8037-0098-9**

A quilt can tell your life story, Tanya learns from her grandmother, as its creation brings the whole family closer together. A classroom quilt, with squares narrating the year's activities and designed by students on construction paper or write-on fabric, would be a logical conclusion to the story. FAMILY LIFE. FAMILY STORIES. GRANDMOTHERS. QUILTS.

926   Gauch, Patricia Lee. *This Time, Tempe Wick?* Illus. by Margot Tomes. Coward, 1974. ISBN 0-698-20300-3

This fictionalized account is based on the true story of the Jockey Hollow, New Jersey, colonial heroine who hid her horse in her bedroom to save it from mutinous Pennsylvania soldiers in the winter of 1781. Books on other Revolutionary War females who counter all stereotypes include Drollene P. Brown's *Sybil Rides for Independence,* Judith Berry Griffin's *Phoebe and the General,* and Ann McGovern's *Secret Soldier.* HISTORICAL FICTION. HORSES. U.S.—HISTORY—REVOLUTION—FICTION. WAR.

927   Graeber, Charlotte. *Mustard.* Illus. by Donna Diamond. Macmillan, 1982. ISBN 0-02-736690-1

[7 chapters, 42p.] Alex's beloved old cat, after a confrontation with a dog, has a heart attack and dies. Sad, but beautifully handled. Move from realistic fiction to fantasy with *Catwings* by Ursula K. Le Guin. CATS. DEATH.

928   Green, Melinda. *Rachel's Recital.* Illus. by the author. Little, Brown, 1979.

[1-2 sittings, 41p.] Rachel, a Lower East Side New York City girl who hates to practice, must fake it when she neglects to learn her piano piece in time for the recital. The turn-of-the-century city setting adds charm to a still-universal theme. Play the recording of a familiar piano piece and have students play an imaginary keyboard—the classical alternative to "air guitar." BROTHERS AND SISTERS. MUSIC.

929   Haas, Dorothy F. *Tink in a Tangle.* Illus. by Margot Apple. Albert Whitman, 1984. ISBN 0-8075-7952-1

[15 chapters, 132p.] Eight-year-old Tink is convinced that her red hair is what gets her into trouble every time she thinks up another good idea. Turn out the lights and have your storytellers make up Tink-like "spookies." Continue the mischief with Joanna Hurwitz's *Class Clown* or Natalie Honeycutt's *The All New Jonah Twist.* HAIR. IMAGINATION. SCHOOLS. STORYTELLING.

930   Hale, Lucretia. *The Lady Who Put Salt in Her Coffee.* Illus. by Amy Schwartz. Harcourt, 1989. ISBN 0-15-243475-5

It takes the lady from Philadelphia's simple sensible solution to remedy Mrs. Peterkin's bad-tasting coffee, after the chemist and herb woman have a try at removing the salt. This excerpt from the famed Victorian *Peterkin Papers,* first published in 1867, has lost none of its zest and understated humor. For another problem-solver among fools, read either Paul Galdone or Kathryn Hewitt's version of the English folktale *The Three Sillies.* Another inept problem-solver is Wallace Tripp's *My Uncle Podger.* FOOLS.

931   Hall, Donald. *Ox-Cart Man.* Illus. by Barbara Cooney. Viking, 1979. ISBN 0-670-53328-9

The cycle of seasons, crops, and chores on a nineteenth-century farm leads a farmer to market with his wares in a compelling and spare description of life back then. Also don't miss Tony Johnston's *Yonder* and Barbara Cooney's *Island Boy.* CALDECOTT MEDAL. COUNTRY LIFE. FAMILY LIFE. FARM LIFE. SEASONS.

932   Hall, Malcolm. *Headlines.* Illus. by Wallace Tripp. Coward, 1973.

An animal newspaper begins printing baffling headlines such as "SaDeeRoBanks." Print out each headline in giant print on the typewriter or computer so your students can decode them as you read the story, and then think up new ones. If they write stories to go along with their headlines, you can print up a class newspaper. ANIMALS. CREATIVE WRITING.

933   **Hirsch, Marilyn.** *Potato Pancakes All Around: A Hanukkah Tale.* **Illus. by the author. Jewish Publication Society, 1982. ISBN 0-8276-0217-0**

A "Stone Soup" variant for Hanukkah. The recipe's included, so get out your frying pan as a peddler shows two competing Grandmas how to make potato pancakes from a simple crust of bread. See also Marcia Brown's French folktale *Stone Soup*, Ann McGovern's easy-to-read *Stone Soup*, and Harve Zemach's Swedish folktale *Nail Soup*. COOKERY. FOOD. GRANDMOTHERS. HANUKKAH. PEDDLERS AND PEDDLING.

934   **Honeycutt, Natalie.** *The All New Jonah Twist.* **Bradbury, 1986. ISBN 0-02-744840-1**

[11 chapters, 110p.] Jonah vows that third grade will find him the best, most responsible eight-year-old ever, in spite of his new enemy, the pint-sized Granville Jones, who claims he can glow in the dark. Readers will enjoy the sequel *The Best Laid Plans of Jonah Twist* (1988) where the two boys have become best friends. On par with Dorothy Haas's *Tink in a Tangle*, Joanna Hurwitz's *Class Clown*, and Suzy Kline's "Herbie Jones" series. FRIENDSHIP. SCHOOLS.

935   **Howe, James.** *The Fright before Christmas.* **Illus. by Leslie Morrill. Morrow, 1988. ISBN 0-688-07665-3**

Dog narrator Harold and cat Chester try to convince terrified puppy Howie that the appearance of Santa Claus should be no cause for terror. A witty first picture book for the characters of the "Bunnicula" series, the best of which are more suitable for grades four and up, though younger listeners may have enjoyed the cartoon version on television. *Scared Silly*, Howe's Halloween picture book, is also irresistible. CATS. CHRISTMAS. DOGS. FEAR. SANTA CLAUS.

936   **Hurwitz, Johanna.** *Class Clown.* **Illus. by Sheila Hamanaka. Morrow, 1987. ISBN 0-688-06723-9**

[8 chapters, 98p.] Obstreperous third-grader Lucas fakes an eye exam, brings in a whole huge plastic bag of leaves to school instead of just one, and gets his head stuck in a chair during a school assembly. Teachers will recognize this student, and children will warmly identify with his good intentions gone wrong. Other less-than-perfect kids abound in Dorothy Haas's *Tink in a Tangle*, Lynn Hall's *In Trouble Again, Zelda Hammersmith*, Natalie Honeycutt's *The All New Jonah Twist*, and Suzy Kline's "Herbie Jones" books. BEHAVIOR. SCHOOLS.

937   **Hurwitz, Johanna.** *Much Ado about Aldo.* **Illus. by John Wallner. Morrow, 1978. ISBN 0-688-32160-7**

[11 chapters, 95p.] Upset when the classroom crickets face being eaten by the classroom chameleons, third-grader Aldo becomes a vegetarian. Research, plan out, and prepare a vegetarian meal together. Also see the sequel, *Aldo Applesauce* (1979), where now fourth-grader Aldo Sossi moves to the New Jersey suburbs midyear and gains a new nickname. FOOD. INSECTS. SCHOOLS.

938   **Johnson, Elizabeth.** *Stuck with Luck.* **Illus. by Trina Schart Hyman. Little, Brown, 1967.**

[7 chapters, 88p.] Magruder McGillicuddy O'Toole, a leprechaun on vacation in the United States, can't go home again until he gets his Lilt back. Also read Joan

Lowery Nixon's *The Gift* about an American boy who seeks a leprechaun while visiting relatives in Ireland. LEPRECHAUNS.

939 **Johnston, Tony. *Yonder*. Illus. by Lloyd Bloom. Dial, 1988. ISBN 0-8037-0278-7**

Mesmerizing, glowing oil paintings and rhythmic, gentle prose verses mark the passing of three generations of a nineteenth-century farm family through all seasons and the growth of a plum tree. Don't be surprised if you feel compelled to plant a tree or grow tiny seedlings with your children after reading this one. On the same generational wavelength are Barbara Cooney's *Island Boy* and *Miss Rumphius* and Donald Hall's *Ox-Cart Man*. CHANTABLE REFRAIN. COUNTRY LIFE. FAMILY LIFE. FARM LIFE. SEASONS.

940 **Julian, Nancy R. *The Peculiar Miss Pickett*. Illus. by Donald E. Cooke. Winston, 1951.**

[8 chapters, 73p.] Each time Carol and Bobby's white haired, little old lady baby-sitter takes off her big black-rimmed glasses, magic happens. Bring in a pair of specs and have your students write about what might happen to themselves if they had special eye powers. BABY-SITTERS. BROTHERS AND SISTERS. MAGIC.

941 **Kalman, Maira. *Hey Willy, See the Pyramids*. Illus. by the author. Viking, 1988. ISBN 0-670-82163-2**

In bed at night, Alexander's older sister Lulu tells him stories about cross-eyed dogs, tiny people, green-faced cousin Ervin, and Max the dog who wanted to live in Paris and be a poet. Without a doubt, one very bizarre book that draws you back to gape over the odd-faced illustrations and wonder what the dreamlike vignettes mean. The class can come up with tomorrow night's stories and pictures. Kindred spirits include Vera B. Williams's *Cherries and Cherry Pits* and Henrik Drescher's *Simon's Book*. BEDTIME STORIES. BROTHERS AND SISTERS. CREATIVE WRITING. PICTURE BOOKS FOR ALL AGES. STORYTELLING.

942 **Keats, Ezra Jack. *Apt. 3*. Illus. by the author. Macmillan, 1971. ISBN 0-02-749510-8**

Tracking down the lonely harmonica music in their apartment building, Sam and Ben listen to many sounds before they locate a blind man's room. Bring in a harmonica and have everyone make the various sound effects heard behind each door. APARTMENT HOUSES. BLIND. CITIES AND TOWNS. SOUND EFFECTS.

943 **Kimmel, Eric A. *Charlie Drives the Stage*. Illus. by Glen Rounds. Holiday House, 1989. ISBN 0-8234-0738-1**

What with avalanches in the pass, armed road agents on the road, Indians on the warpath, and the river rising fast, there's only one driver with a ghost of a chance of getting Senator McCorkle to his five o'clock train: Charlie Drummond. The madcap adventure, filled with split second escapes, rolls you through the western landscape, and not until the final page do you learn that the fearless Charlie is really Charlene. Read this alongside Alan Coren's *Arthur the Kid*, Richard Kennedy's *The Contests at Cowlick*, and Joan Lowery Nixon's *Beats Me, Claude*; then throw in some facts with Russell Freedman's *Children of the Wild West*. TRANSPORTATION. WEST.

944 **Kimmel, Eric A. *Hershel and the Hanukkah Goblins*. Illus. by Trina Schart Hyman. Holiday House, 1989. ISBN 0-8234-0769-1**

Arriving tired and hungry at the next village on the first night of Hanukkah, Hershel promises the villagers that he will rid their synagogue of Hanukkah-hating goblins by spending the next eight nights there, lighting the menorah candles. Bring in dreidels and teach all to play for peanuts. FAIRIES. HANUKKAH. JEWS. PICTURE BOOKS FOR ALL AGES.

945   **Kipling, Rudyard.** *The Beginning of the Armadillos.* **Illus. by Lorinda Bryan Cauley. Harcourt, 1985. ISBN 0-15-206380-3**

The story, O Best Beloved, of how a Stickley-Prickley Hedgehog and a Slow-and-Solid Tortoise who lived on the banks of the turbid Amazon joined forces to befuddle their natural enemy, the Painted Jaguar, and thus evolved as armadillos. Use with other Kipling "Just So Stories," such as *The Elephant's Child* and with William Pène du Bois's *Lion.* ANIMALS–CREATION. RIVERS.

946   **Kipling, Rudyard.** *The Elephant's Child.* **Illus. by Lorinda Bryan Cauley. Harcourt, 1983. ISBN 0-15-225385-8**

[1 sitting, 48p.] Undeterred by the hard spankings his family gives him, the bulgy boot-nosed Elephant's Child sets off through these promiscuous parts to the banks of the great grey-green greasy Limpopo River where he learns what the crocodile eats for dinner. This one's a charming complete version of Kipling's most famous "Just So" story, though you might also enjoy Tim Raglin's slightly abridged, illustrated version (Knopf, 1986), which was released as a video from Random House, narrated by Jack Nicholson. CROCODILES. CURIOSITY. ELEPHANTS. POURQUOI TALES. SNAKES.

947   **Kipling, Rudyard.** *How the Camel Got His Hump.* **Illus. by Quentin Blake. Bedrick, 1985. ISBN 0-87226-029-1**

Back when the world was so new and all, the horse, dog, and ox were so put out when the disdainful camel refused to do his share of work that they complained to the magical Djinn of All Deserts who set things right. After hearing a batch of such pourquoi tales, children can write new ones. ANIMALS. CAMELS. MAGIC. POURQUOI TALES.

948   **Kipling, Rudyard.** *Just So Stories.* **Illus. by Victor Ambrus. Rand, 1982.**

[5 short stories, 64p.] Vivid illustrations dazzle the pages of five of the best "Just So Stories," if you want them all together. ANIMALS. POURQUOI TALES. SHORT STORIES.

949   **Kline, Suzy.** *What's the Matter with Herbie Jones?* **Illus. by Richard Williams. Putnam, 1987. ISBN 0-14-032324-4**

[10 chapters, 111p.] Much to the relief of best friend Ray, third-grader Herbie's crush on bossy classmate Annabelle doesn't last long after he spends the whole day with her. Second in the winning "Herbie Jones" series, though your listeners may also coerce you into reading the sequel *Herbie Jones and the Class Gift* (1987), where the two boys are horrified when they accidentally drop their teacher's gift box and shatter the ceramic owl inside. Children can read *Herbie Jones* (1985) and *Herbie Jones and the Monster Ball* (1988) on their own. FRIENDSHIP. HUMOROUS FICTION. SCHOOLS.

950   **Le Guin, Ursula K.** *Catwings.* **Illus. by S. D. Schindler. Orchard, 1988. ISBN 0-531-08359-4**

[4 chapters, 1–2 sittings, 40p.] About to marry Mr. Tom Jones and afraid for her children in their current deprived urban environment, Mrs. Jane Tabby encourages her four inexplicably winged kittens to fly off in search of a better life. A small-sized treasure that can be read in one long or two short sittings, along with the sequel *Catwings Return* (1989), where cats James and Harriet fly back to the city and find, hiding alone in a soon-to-be demolished building, a scared and starving black winged kitten. Continuing the motif of unexpected wings, also read Betsy Byars's *The Winged Colt of Casa Mia* and Leo Lionni's *Tico and the Golden Wings*. Other endearing cat books include Mary Calhoun's *Cross-Country Cat* and Mary Stolz's *Cat Walk*. CATS. FLIGHT. WINGS.

951   Levy, Elizabeth. *Frankenstein Moved in on the Fourth Floor.* **Illus. by Mordicai Gerstein. Harper & Row, 1979. ISBN 0-06-023811-9**

[4 chapters, 57p.] Suspicious of the strange noises coming from Mr. Frank's apartment, Sam and Robert investigate their scary new neighbor. On their own, children will thrill to the summer camp sequel *Dracula Is a Pain in the Neck* (1983). APARTMENT HOUSES. BROTHERS. NEIGHBORS.

952   Lionni, Leo. *Tico and the Golden Wings.* **Illus. by the author. Knopf, 1987. ISBN 0-394-83078-4**

When a wingless bird is granted his wish, his friends reject him for looking different until he gives away each golden feather to someone in need. The message introduced—that we are all unique regardless of our common looks—can ignite a welcome spark of self-analysis. Bill Peet's *The Spooky Tail of Prewett Peacock* introduces another bird with feather problems. BIRDS. GENEROSITY. WINGS.

953   Livingston, Myra Cohn. *Higgledy-Piggledy: Verses & Pictures.* **Illus. by Peter Sis. Macmillan, 1986. ISBN 0-689-50407-1**

Higgledy-Piggledy is utterly perfect. / Two dozen plus verses recount him as so; / the narrator hates him. Your listeners will likewise. / The child that each teacher'd give eyeteeth to know! Try also his female counterpart *Super Dooper Jezebel* by Tony Ross. BEHAVIOR–POETRY. STORIES IN RHYME.

954   Lobel, Arnold. *The Ice Cream Cone Coot and Other Rare Birds.* **Illus. by the author. Parents, 1971.**

Humorous, rhyming, illustrated ditties about unique feathered flyers. Children love to create their own. Try switching animals, such as Marshmallowed Malamutes or Sandpaper Siamese. See also Bill Peet's *No Such Things*, Jack Prelutsky's *The Baby Uggs Are Hatching* and *The Snoop on the Sidewalk*, Dr. Seuss's *McElligot's Pool*, and Robert Tallon's *Zoophabets* for more invented creatures. ANIMALS, IMAGINARY–POETRY. BIRDS. CREATIVE WRITING. STORIES IN RHYME.

955   McCloskey, Robert. *Burt Dow, Deep-Water Man.* **Illus. by the author. Viking, 1963. ISBN 0-670-19748-3**

[2–3 sittings, 64p.] A crusty old Maine fisherman catches and is then swallowed by a whale, boat and all. In the whale's belly, Burt creates a Jackson Pollock-like painting. Try your hands at spatter painting, and read Rudyard Kipling's *How the Whale Got His Throat*. BIRDS. BOATS AND BOATING. FISHES. MAINE. WHALES.

956   McCloskey, Robert. *Lentil.* **Illus. by the author. Viking, 1940. ISBN 0-670-42357-2**

When contentious old Sneep tries to spoil the homecoming celebration for Colonel Carter, the town's most illustrious citizen, young Lentil saves the day with his harmonica. Bring in lemons for your students to suck and a harmonica to play "She'll Be Comin' Round the Mountain." FRUIT. MUSIC. STORIES WITH SONGS.

957   **McCloskey, Robert.** *Time of Wonder.* **Illus. by the author. Viking, 1957. ISBN 0-670-71512-3**

A low-key poetic description of a family's summer on a Maine island, ending in a hurricane. Ask your students to describe or write about their special places. CALDECOTT MEDAL. ISLANDS. MAINE. STORMS. SUMMER.

958   **McKissack, Patricia C.** *Mirandy and Brother Wind.* **Illus. by Jerry Pinkney. Knopf, 1988. ISBN 0-394-98765-9**

Determined to catch the wind and win the junior cakewalk contest with him as her partner, Mirandy even visits a conjure woman for a special spell. Find out from parents and grandparents the dances that were popular when they were growing up and how to do them. Pair this Caldecott Honor book with the same year's Caldecott Award, Stephen Gammell's *Song and Dance Man* for the dancing angle and with Caroline Feller Bauer's *Windy Day Stories and Poems* for another breath of air. AFRICAN AMERICANS. DANCING. WIND.

959   **McMillan, Bruce, and Brett McMillan.** *Puniddles.* **Photos by Bruce McMillan. Houghton Mifflin, 1982. ISBN 0-395-32076-3**

Each page features a pair of black-and-white photos that, when put together, constitute a word or phrase. Some are obvious (bear + feet = bare feet), others are less so (Collie +flower = cauliflower), and students will delight in guessing each one and composing new combinations. RIDDLES. WORD GAMES.

960   **Massie, Diane Redfield.** *Chameleon Was a Spy.* **Illus. by the author. Crowell, 1979. ISBN 0-690-03910-7**

Eager for supersecret spy work, Chameleon comes to the rescue when a pickle company's magic formula disappears in this slapstick melodrama which should be followed by pickles for all. Sequels for your readers to puzzle out include *Chameleon the Spy and the Terrible Toaster Trap* (1982) and *Chameleon the Spy and the Case of the Vanishing Jewels* (1984). CHAMELEONS. FOOD. MYSTERY AND DETECTIVE STORIES. REPTILES.

961   **Mayer, Mercer.** *A Special Trick.* **Illus. by the author. Dial, 1976. ISBN 0-8037-8103-2**

Ellroy tries out a magician's monster-filled book of magic spells and calls up six-eyed galaplops and other horrors before he has a chance to practice his skill. Have each student compose one page of a new classroom magic book with one spell, describe how it works, and include a drawing. Follow up with Joanna Cole's *Doctor Change*, Eloise Jarvis McGraw's *Joel and the Great Merlini*, and Barbara Rinkoff's *The Dragon's Handbook*, if you can find it. MAGIC. MAGICIANS. MONSTERS.

962   **Mendoza, George.** *Gwot! Horribly Funny Hairticklers.* **Illus. by Steven Kellogg. Harper & Row, 1967.**

[3 short stories, 42p.] A collection of short tales, along with the companion volume *The Crack in the Wall and Other Terribly Weird Tales* (1968), based in part on folktales that will appeal to those who love feeling squeamish. Fans of James Flora's *Grandpa's Ghost Stories* and Maria Leach's *The Thing at the Foot of the Bed* will feel right at home here. SHORT STORIES. STORIES TO TELL. SUSPENSE.

963   **Mendoza, George.** *A Wart Snake in a Fig Tree.* **Illus. by Etienne Delessert. Dial, 1968.**

A creature-minded parody of "The Twelve Days of Christmas" for those of us who have been naughty, not nice. Sing along and then have everyone come up with new versions. Also hum Carol Green's *The Thirteen Days of Halloween,* and refer back to Jan Brett's striking edition of the original song. CHRISTMAS. PARODIES. SONGS.

964   **Milne, A. A. *Winnie-the-Pooh.* Illus. by Ernest H. Shepard. Dutton, 1988. ISBN 0-525-44443-2**

[10 chapters, 161p.] The story in which we meet Pooh Bear and the other animals in the Hundred Acre Wood. Originally published in 1926. Also read the sequel *The House at Pooh Corner* (1928), as well as an assortment of your favorite poems from *Now We Are Six* and *When We Were Very Young.* Bring in a jar of honey for a midmorning nibble, and hum some Pooh hums, tiddly pom. ANIMALS. BEARS. FANTASY. TEDDY BEARS. TOYS.

965   **Molarsky, Osmond. *Take It or Leave It.* Illus. by Trina Schart Hyman. Walck, 1971.**

[2–3 sittings, 63p.] Master-swapper Chester trades baseball cards, yo-yo, skate-scooter, boomerang, monobike, toy submarine, kangaroo bucking ball, and finally a young puppy which, in order to give it a good home, he swaps for his yo-yo back again. Why not hold a paperback book swap, where children ask permission to bring in paperbacks they no longer want and trade them for new treasures. BARTERING. DOGS.

966   **Monjo, F. N. *The Drinking Gourd.* Illus. by Fred Brenner. Harper & Row, 1969. ISBN 0-06-024330-9**

Tommy and his father help a family of slaves escape to Canada on the Underground Railroad. For another first-rate explanation of a difficult topic, see Ann McGovern's biography *Runaway Slave: The Story of Harriet Tubman* and Jeanette Winter's *Follow the Drinking Gourd.* AFRICAN AMERICANS. COURAGE. HISTORICAL FICTION. SLAVERY. U.S.–HISTORY–1783–1865–FICTION.

967   **Moore, Lilian. *I'll Meet You at the Cucumbers.* Illus. by Sharon Wooding. Atheneum, 1988. ISBN 0-689-31243-1**

[2–3 sittings, 63p.] Country mouse poet Adam works up the nerve to visit the feared city where he meets his pen friend Amanda and discovers some mouse-oriented poetry at the public library. Use with Betsy Byars's *Beans on the Roof* as an introduction to writing poetry, with Sandy Clifford's mice in *The Roquefort Gang,* or as a follow-up to Lorinda Bryan Cauley's *The Town Mouse and the Country Mouse* or Leo Lionni's *Frederick.* For more mouse-sized poems, read a sampling from Valerie Worth's "Small Poems" books. FRIENDSHIP. MICE. POETS.

968   **Moore, Lilian. *The Snake That Went to School.* Illus. by Richard Williams. Scholastic, 1987. ISBN 0-590-40761-9**

[10 chapters, 99p.] Hank's pet hognose snake, Puffy, disappears from its cage when he takes it to school. See also Eth Clifford's *Harvey's Horrible Snake Disaster.* BROTHERS. SCHOOLS. SNAKES.

969   **Murphy, Jim. *The Call of the Wolves.* Illus. by Mark Alan Weatherby. Scholastic, 1989. ISBN 0-590-41097-0**

A two-year-old wolf hunting caribou is wounded and separated from the rest of his pack when he attempts to flee a plane of illegal hunters. After all the stories and folktales about the rapacious, heartless wolf, it is fitting to set the record straight with this realistic portrayal. Make a chart of misconceptions versus facts, bolstered with some class research. HUNTERS AND HUNTING. WOLVES.

970 **Myller, Rolf.** *How Big Is a Foot?* **Illus. by the author. Atheneum, 1969.**

When the King commissions a bed three feet wide and six feet long for his Queen, the lack of a standard foot measurement results in a bed that is way too small. Assign your math class the task of measuring everything in sight—first with their feet, then with a ruler or yardstick—including the length of the whole school. KINGS AND RULERS. MEASUREMENT.

971 **Nixon, Joan Lowery.** *Beats Me, Claude.* **Illus. by Tracey Campbell Pearson. Viking, 1986. ISBN 0-670-80781-8**

Each time Shirley bakes husband Claude an apple pie, she leaves out a vital ingredient which causes mayhem with a bank robber, three army deserters, and a nice orphan boy who needs a home. Second in a series of old-time down-home Texas frontier adventures, the first being the wittily deadpan *If You Say So, Claude* (Warne, 1980) where Claude and his calamity prone wife travel the state in their covered wagon looking for the perfect spot to settle. Bring in an apple pie for dessert and follow up with Sonia Levitin's *Nobody Stole the Pie*; then further gauge your senses of humor with *Wild Pill Hickock and Other Old West Riddles* by David A. Adler. FOOD. FRONTIER AND PIONEER LIFE. PIE. TALL TALES. TEXAS.

972 **Nixon, Joan Lowery.** *If You Were a Writer.* **Illus. by Bruce Degen. Four Winds, 1988. ISBN 0-02-768210-2**

Melia's mother, a writer, gives her writing tips on finding words that make pictures and show what is happening in a story, looking for and nurturing interesting story ideas, and developing characters with problems to solve. Use as a springboard for writing original stories and critiquing books, along with Henrik Drescher's *Simon's Book*. AUTHORS. BOOKS. CREATIVE WRITING. MOTHERS AND DAUGHTERS. WRITING.

973 **Noble, Trinka Hakes.** *Apple Tree Christmas.* **Illus. by the author. Dial, 1984. ISBN 0-8037-0103-9**

After the blizzard of 1881 hits their family farm, Katrina is heartsick when their treasured apple tree, where she sat and drew all summer, is felled by ice. Contrast farm life with the New York City perspective in Marietta Moskin's *The Day of the Blizzard* about the famed 1888 storm, and an Icelandic one in Lonzo Anderson's *Ponies of Mykillengi*. CHRISTMAS. DRAWING. FARM LIFE. SNOW. TREES.

974 **Noble, Trinka Hakes.** *Meanwhile Back at the Ranch.* **Illus. by Tony Ross. Dutton, 1987. ISBN 0-8037-0354-6**

While bored Rancher Hicks drives 84 miles to the town of Sleepy Gulch to see what's happening, his wife Elna wins a new refrigerator, wins the lottery, strikes oil, becomes a movie star, and meets the president. Listeners will love to chant the "meanwhile . . ." refrains that introduce each slapstick page. FARM LIFE. SLAPSTICK. TALL TALES.

975 **Peet, Bill.** *Chester the Worldly Pig.* **Illus. by the author. Houghton Mifflin, 1965.**

Running away to join the circus is just the first in a series of calamities for a fame-seeking, nose-balancing pig. Have a globe handy for the surprise ending, and swing right into a social studies lesson on the seven continents. CIRCUS. GEOGRAPHY. PIGS.

976   Peet, Bill. *Cowardly Clyde*. Illus. by the author. Houghton Mifflin, 1979. ISBN 0-395-27802-3

A fearless knight's fainthearted horse proves his mettle when he tangles with an ogre. Compare ogres with the one in *Molly Mullett* by Patricia Coombs. COURAGE. HORSES. KNIGHTS AND KNIGHTHOOD. MONSTERS. OGRES.

977   Peet, Bill. *Gnats of Knotty Pine*. Illus. by the author. Houghton Mifflin, 1975. ISBN 0-395-21405-X

On the first day of hunting season, gnats band together by the billions to foil hunters from shooting their fellow forest creatures. An antihunting tract that should invoke strong reactions, along with Donald Carrick's *Harald and the Great Stag* and Roald Dahl's *Fantastic Mr. Fox* and *The Magic Finger*. ANIMALS. HUNTERS AND HUNTING. INSECTS.

978   Peet, Bill. *No Such Things*. Illus. by the author. Houghton Mifflin, 1983. ISBN 0-395-33888-3

Simple rhymes about outrageous creatures such as Glubzunks, Juggarums, and Grabnabbits. Similar in scope to Arnold Lobel's *The Ice Cream Cone Coot* and Dr. Seuss's *McElligot's Pool* and *If I Ran the Zoo*; children can invent new animals and rhymes to go along and compile a second edition. ANIMALS, IMAGINARY–POETRY. CREATIVE WRITING. STORIES IN RHYME.

979   Peet, Bill. *The Whingdingdilly*. Illus. by the author. Houghton Mifflin, 1977. ISBN 0-395-24729-2

Impatient with his unglamorous country life, dog Scamp accepts and then regrets a witch's spell that turns him into a freak one-of-a-kind creature, part elephant, camel, zebra, rhinoceros, and reindeer. Comparable in intent to Bernard Waber's *"You Look Ridiculous," Said the Rhinoceros to the Hippopotamus*. DOGS. SELF-CONCEPT. WITCHES.

980   Peet, Bill. *The Wump World*. Illus. by the author. Houghton Mifflin, 1974. ISBN 0-395-19841-0

The usually peaceful Wump planet is invaded by the Pollutians from the planet Pollutus. Ties in well to any ecology lesson, along with Don Madden's *The Wartville Wizard* and Dr. Seuss's *The Lorax*. ANIMALS, IMAGINARY. ECOLOGY. POLLUTION.

981   Pomerantz, Charlotte. *The Downtown Fairy Godmother*. Illus. by Susanna Natti. Addison-Wesley, 1978.

[2–3 sittings, 44p.] Pining for a beautiful stuffed black cat in a store window, Olivia makes a wish and acquires her own grade C fairy godmother, pink curlers and all. For equal time, also read Bernice Myers's parody *Sidney Rella and the Glass Sneaker*, where Sidney meets up with his fairy godfather. FAIRIES. MAGIC. NEW YORK CITY. WISHES.

982   Porter, David Lord. *Help! Let Me Out*. Illus. by David Macaulay. Houghton Mifflin, 1982.

When Hugo learns to throw his voice, it leaves him speechless, preferring to go off on its own until it gets homesick and tries to find him again. Dig up some Sunday newspaper comics, white out the dialogue, and have everyone "throw" their own dialogue into the balloons. VOICE.

983   **Prelutsky, Jack. *The Mean Old Mean Hyena.* Illus. by Arnold Lobel. Greenwillow, 1978. ISBN 0-688-84163-5**

A wickedly funny poem-story, reminiscent of Joel Chandler Harris's Uncle Remus "The Tar Baby" story, of a nasty, practical joke-playing hyena who does not learn his lesson. If you can, make up a tune for the refrain so all can sing it with you. ANIMALS. CHANTABLE REFRAIN. NARRATIVE POETRY. STORIES IN RHYME.

984   **Rinkoff, Barbara. *The Dragon's Handbook.* Illus. by Kelly Oechsli. Nelson, 1966.**

[6 chapters, 88p.] Before returning Culhane's book of magic formulas, Brian convinces the dragon to sign a pact to teach him one spell that works. If you can find a copy of this green-paged gem, it makes a good match with Mercer Mayer's *A Special Trick.* Students can compose additional formulas for a classroom handbook of spells. DRAGONS. MAGIC. SCHOOLS.

985   **Rinkoff, Barbara. *The Remarkable Ramsey.* Illus. by Leonard Shortall. Morrow, 1965. ISBN 0-8446-6195-3**

[7 chapters, 77p.] Charlie meets a talking dog who cures him of being shy. This was also released as a 1976 Scholastic paperback, retitled *Remarkable Ramsey the Talking Dog.* Pair with Anita Feagles's verbal *Casey, the Utterly Impossible Horse.* DOGS. SELF-CONCEPT.

986   **Robinson, Nancy K. *Just Plain Cat.* Four Winds, 1983. ISBN 0-02-777350-7**

[19 short chapters, 119p.] Chris survives the traumas of third grade, from getting a screamer for a teacher to having trouble with his new cat. More third-grade trials envelop Beverly Cleary's *Henry Huggins*, Dorothy Haas's *Tink in a Tangle*, Natalie Honeycutt's *The All New Jonah Twist*, Johanna Hurwitz's *Much Ado about Aldo* and *Class Clown*, and Suzy Kline's "Herbie Jones" books. CATS. SCHOOLS.

987   **Ross, Pat. *Gloria and the Super Soaper.* Illus. by Susan Paradis. Little, Brown, 1982.**

[10 chapters, 60p.] A gun-loving girl supplies an important clue when she and her father witness a bank robbery committed with a gun made out of soap. While you're on the subject of banks and money, take a look at David M. Schwartz's *How Much Is a Million?*, and talk about ways to earn your share using Ellen Conford's *A Job for Jenny Archer* and Jean Van Leeuwen's *Benjy in Business* for practical and impractical ideas. ROBBERS AND OUTLAWS. TOYS.

988   **Rylant, Cynthia. *All I See.* Illus. by Peter Catalanotto. Orchard, 1988. ISBN 0-531-08377-2**

Each summer day, young Charlie watches from the bushes to see what artist Gregory is painting on his lakeside easel. Using the story as a thought provoking lead-in to a lesson on painting and imagination, have students paint the pictures that are in their minds' eyes. For other art-related titles, see Alan Baker's *Benjamin's Portrait*, Tomie dePaola's autobiographical *The Art Lesson*, and Paul O. Zelinsky's *The Lion and the Stoat.* ARTISTS. IMAGINATION. PAINTING.

989   **Rylant, Cynthia. *When I Was Young in the Mountains.* Illus. by Diane Goode. Dutton, 1982. ISBN 0-525-42525-X**

The author affectionately reminisces about her youth in Appalachia. Good for all ages, especially as the starting point for discussing or writing about childhood memories. For another glimpse of "life in the old days," students can interview parents or grandparents about their childhoods. Contrast with Dayal Kaur Khalsa's urban narrator in *Tales of a Gambling Grandma*. COUNTRY LIFE. CREATIVE WRITING. GRANDPARENTS. MOUNTAINS. PICTURE BOOKS FOR ALL AGES.

990   **Sachs, Marilyn.** *Matt's Mitt and Fleet-Footed Florence.* **Illus. by Hilary Knight and Charles Robinson. Dutton, 1989. ISBN 0-525-44450-5**

During World Series week, read these two books rereleased as one, about a great father-daughter baseball-playing combination. In the first story, the greatest catcher of all time owes his skill to his treasured blue baseball mitt. In the sequel, Matt's daughter, Florence, named after the famous nurse, astounds everyone by surpassing even her father and becoming the greatest baseball star who ever lived. Your astronomy lessons on stars will twinkle with this, plus Barbara Juster Esbensen's *The Star Maiden* and Paul Goble's *Her Seven Brothers*, both American Indian star myths. BASEBALL. STARS.

991   **Schertle, Alice.** *The April Fool.* **Illus. by Emily Arnold McCully. Lothrop, 1981.**

A "fool" leads the king to his first pair of comfortably fitting shoes. Meet a town of "fools" in Mary Blount Christian's *April Fool* and read both on the appropriate holiday. FOOLS. KINGS AND RULERS. SHOES.

992   **Schwartz, Amy.** *Yossel Zissel & the Wisdom of Chelm.* **Illus. by the author. Jewish Publication Society, 1986. ISBN 0-8276-0258-8**

How the wisdom of Chelm, Jewish town of fools, travels through the world today. Yossel Zissel, town butcher, trades his heavy gold inheritance for lightweight feathers which he tosses into the wind so he won't have to carry them home. A good tale to tell, along with traditional "Chelm" stories in Isaac Bashevis Singer's folklore collections, including *When Shlemiel Went to Warsaw* and *Zlateh the Goat*. Also consider reading with other noodlehead tales like Paul Galdone's or Kathryn Hewitt's *The Three Sillies* and Jacob Grimm's *Hans in Luck*. FOOLS.

993   **Scieszka, Jon.** *The True Story of the 3 Little Pigs.* **Illus. by Lane Smith. Viking Kestrel, 1989. ISBN 0-670-82759-2**

You may think you know what happened to those three house-constructing pig brothers, but, as narrated and explained by Alexander T. Wolf ("You can call me Al"), the truth is that the wolf was framed when the pigs died accidentally, brought on by Al's sneezing cold and the simple request to borrow a cup of sugar. Telling other well-known tales from the villains' points of view might lend a whole new perspective to the motives of bad guys like Rumpelstiltskin, the troll from *The Three Billy Goats Gruff*, the giant in *Jack and the Beanstalk*, and the witch in *Hansel and Gretel*. FAIRY TALES—SATIRE. PICTURE BOOKS FOR ALL AGES. PIGS. WOLVES.

994   **Seuss, Dr.** *Bartholomew and the Oobleck.* **Illus. by the author. Random House, 1949. ISBN 0-394-90075-8**

Thanks to the whim of selfish King Derwin, his royal magicians concoct a new type of sticky weather that confounds the kingdom of Didd and challenges the ingenuity of the king's young page in this sequel to *The 500 Hats of Bartholomew Cubbins*. Read on a rainy or snowy day and count your blessings, or append to a weather unit along with *Cloudy with a Chance of Meatballs* by Judi Barrett. KINGS AND RULERS. MAGIC. MAGICIANS. RESPONSIBILITY. WEATHER.

995   **Seuss, Dr.** *The 500 Hats of Bartholomew Cubbins.* **Illus. by the author. Vanguard, 1938. ISBN 0-8149-0388-6**

An innocent young country lad can't remove his multiplying hats fast enough to suit King Derwin who orders him beheaded for not showing proper respect to his majesty. Design and model your own outrageous hats. HATS. KINGS AND RULERS.

996   **Seuss, Dr.** *The King's Stilts.* **Illus. by the author. Random House, 1939. ISBN 0-394-90082-0**

Eric, a page boy, returns the king's beloved stilts in time to save the kingdom from the terrible Nizzards and the threatening ocean in an otherworld variant of Norma B. Green's *The Hole in the Dike.* BIRDS. KINGS AND RULERS. OCEAN.

997   **Seuss, Dr.** *The Lorax.* **Illus. by the author. Random House, 1971. ISBN 0-394-92337-5**

An epic poem of the old Once-ler and how he and his cut down all the Truffula trees and polluted the land, this is a nonsense story with a grim message that offers a ray of hope as we watch our own ozone layer thin. Read with Don Madden's *The Wartville Wizard* and Bill Peet's *The Wump World.* ECOLOGY. NARRATIVE POETRY. POLLUTION. STORIES IN RHYME. TREES.

998   **Sharmat, Marjorie Weinman.** *Chasing after Annie.* **Illus. by Marc Simont. Harper & Row, 1981. ISBN 0-06-025562-5**

[2 sittings, 63p.] Eager to get Annie Alpert to like him, braggart Richie Carr searches for her lost dog Fritz and comes up with a look-alike. Told from both characters' points of view via Richie's journal and Annie's diary entries during the month of May, the two-pronged story details their changes in attitudes about each other. Use as an incentive to keep classroom journals for a month or more, but also discuss how people seem to change the better you get to know them. CREATIVE WRITING. DOGS. LOST.

999   **Shulevitz, Uri.** *The Treasure.* **Illus. by the author. Farrar, 1979. ISBN 0-374-37740-5**

A magnificent, spare tale of a poor man who, after a journey to seek it, finds his treasure at home. Discuss what treasures we might find at home that are worth more than jewels. PICTURE BOOKS FOR ALL AGES. STORIES TO TELL.

1000   **Siebert, Diane.** *Mojave.* **Illus. by Wendell Minor. Crowell, 1988. ISBN 0-690-04569-7**

One long, gracious, descriptive rhyming poem, told from the desert's point of view, with sweeping full-page paintings of the life that inhabits the desert and the forces of nature within. Tuck this into your landforms lesson, and read with Byrd Baylor's narrative story poem *Amigo* about a desert boy and a prairie dog. DESERTS– POETRY. PICTURE BOOKS FOR ALL AGES.

1001   **Silverstein, Shel.** *The Giving Tree.* **Illus. by the author. Harper & Row, 1964. ISBN 0-06-025666-4**

Little by little, a generous tree gives up everything to the boy she loves until she is left with nothing but a stump. An unusual discussion starter on the meaning of friendship and sacrifice. LOVE. TREES.

1002   **Slote, Alfred.** *My Robot Buddy.* **Illus. by Joel Schick. Lippincott, 1975. ISBN 0-397-31641-0**

[5 chapters, 92p.] Jack Jameson must save his new human-looking robot companion, Danny One, from nefarious robot-nappers. First in the exciting series about Jack and Danny, including *C.O.L.A.R.* (1981), *Omega Station* (1983), and *Trouble on Janus* (1985), which good readers will be eager to attack on their own. FRIENDSHIP. SCIENCE FICTION.

1003   **Smith, Robert Kimmell.** *Chocolate Fever.* **Illus. by Gioia Fiammenghi. Putnam, 1989. ISBN 0-399-61224-6**

[12 chapters, 93p.] Henry Green's chocolate fetish goes too far and his body erupts in chocolate pox. Fun with Patrick Skene Catling's *The Chocolate Touch*. CANDY. RUNAWAYS. SICK.

1004   **Snyder, Carol.** *Ike and Mama and the Once-a-Year Suit.* **Illus. by Charles Robinson. Coward, 1978.**

[5 chapters, 47p.] Mama takes nine neighborhood boys downtown to bargain for new suits in New York City of 1918 in the first "Ike and Mama" book series. Compare settings with Susan Saunders's country outing, *Fish Fry*. CITIES AND TOWNS. CLOTHING AND DRESS. HISTORICAL FICTION. MOTHERS AND SONS. NEW YORK CITY.

1005   **Stanley, Diane.** *The Good-Luck Pencil.* **Illus. by Bruce Degen. Four Winds, 1986. ISBN 0-02-786800-1**

Convinced that her life is boring, Mary Ann writes whoppers about her family and talents for a school assignment that backfires when her pencil stub renders her glamorous daydreams real. Hand out pencil stubs and magic crayons so your students can record their fondest secret lives. Pair the imaginations of writers and illustrators by also reading David McPhail's *The Magical Drawings of Mooney B. Finch*. Other wishes come true in *Barney Bipple's Magic Dandelions* by Carol Chapman. CREATIVE WRITING. MAGIC. WRITING.

1006   **Steig, William.** *The Amazing Bone.* **Illus. by the author. Farrar, 1976. ISBN 0-374-30248-0**

Pearl the Pig's loyal talking bone saves her from a hungry fox. Cut bones out of oak tag for each listener, and have them write down the text of what their conversations together might be. BONES. FOXES. PIGS.

1007   **Steig, William.** *Dr. DeSoto.* **Illus. by the author. Farrar, 1982. ISBN 0-374-31803-4**

A kind-hearted mouse dentist and his wife relieve the toothache of an untrustworthy fox who plans on eating them for a snack. A Caldecott Honor book and a classic example of a picture book that is perfect in every way. Give a copy to your dentist. FOXES. MICE. TEETH.

1008   **Steig, William.** *Solomon the Rusty Nail.* **Illus. by the author. Farrar, 1985. ISBN 0-374-37131-8**

What is to become of a rabbit, who can turn into a nail at will, when he is captured and held prisoner by a vindictive and hungry cat? Similar in theme to Steig's *Sylvester and the Magic Pebble*, but with charms all its own. CATS. MAGIC. RABBITS. TRANSFORMATIONS.

1009   **Steig, William.** *Spinky Sulks.* **Illus. by the author. Farrar, 1988. ISBN 0-374-38321-9**

Furious at his whole family, Spinky retreats to the outside hammock and stubbornly refuses to acknowledge their existence for two long days. Work everyone into a bad-tempered frenzy with Jane Goodsell's *Toby's Toe* and William Cole's poetry collection *I'm Mad at You*, and then have a class discussion on how to deal with anger in a more realistic way. EMOTIONS. FAMILY LIFE.

1010 **Steptoe, John.** *Stevie.* **Illus. by the author. Harper & Row, 1969. ISBN 0-06-025764-4**

Robert recounts how he resented looking after his new foster brother until he moved out, leaving good memories too. Talk over how you can feel two ways at once about someone. With Steptoe's Roualt-styled, stained glass, colored illustrations and honest narration, the striking output of the then-18-year-old author/ illustrator caused a stir when the book came out. Introduce your group to other examples of the late Steptoe's brilliance, including *Jumping Mouse* and *Mufaro's Beautiful Daughters*, which show his remarkable growth as an artist. AFRICAN AMERICANS. BROTHERS.

1011 **Stevenson, James.** *That Dreadful Day.* **Illus. by the author. Greenwillow, 1985. ISBN 0-688-04035-7**

Just when you were convinced Miss Viola Swamp was the meanest teacher ever, along came the green-faced ogre, Mr. Smeal, Grandpa's first and worst teacher. This first day of school story, filled with dismal cheerleading and terrorized pupils, should convince you to get out your dunce cap and assuage the fears of your nervous new class who will be relieved to see you smile before Thanksgiving. GRANDFATHERS. PICTURE BOOKS FOR ALL AGES. SCHOOLS. TEACHERS.

1012 **Swallow, Pam.** *Melvil and Dewey in the Chips.* **Illus. by Judith Brown. Shoe Tree, 1986. ISBN 0-936915-03-X**

[6 chapters, 47p.] Longing for adventure and excitement, school library gerbil Dewey convinces his fearful cage mate Melvil to join him when he breaks out to explore the school and try the library's computer. Every library needs a copy of this one, and introducing the wonders of the Dewey Decimal System is so much more fun with these two rodents. Get a hold of the sequel—*Melvil and Dewey in the Fast Lane* (1989)—for fans to follow. DOGS. FANTASY. GERBILS. HUMOROUS STORIES. LIBRARIES.

1013 **Talbott, Hudson.** *We're Back!* **Illus. by the author. Crown, 1987. ISBN 0-517-56599-4**

Taken from their primitive planet onto a spaceship by alien Vorb and given Brain Gain ultramegavitamins to make them smart, seven dinosaurs voyage to New York's Museum of Natural History, arriving in time for the Macy's Thanksgiving Day Parade and a chase through the city. Throw in some dinosaur poetry via William Cole, Lee Bennett Hopkins, or Jack Prelutsky to get in the mood, and have everyone dream up ideas for the sequel. DINOSAURS. MUSEUMS. NEW YORK CITY. PICTURE BOOKS FOR ALL AGES.

1014 **Talon, Robert.** *Zoophabets.* **Illus. by the author. Scholastic, 1979.**

An arresting alliteration of invented creatures from Alpok to Zurk, detailing where they live and what they eat. An off-the-wall variant of Jane Bayer's *A My Name Is Alice*, a relative of Arnold Lobel's *The Ice Cream Cone Coot,* and a friend to Alvin Schwartz's *Kickle Snifters and Other Fearsome Critters*. Compile your own dictionary of additional alliterative beasts, using black paper and pastels for illustrations and the dictionary for interesting new words. ALPHABET BOOKS. ANIMALS, IMAGINARY. CREATIVE WRITING.

1015 **Thurber, James.** *Many Moons.* **Illus. by Louis Slobodkin. Harcourt, 1973. ISBN 0-15-656980-9**

[2–3 sittings, unp.] Princess Lenore, ill from a surfeit of raspberry tarts, wants to have the moon so she can be well again. Reprinted from the 1943 edition. Compare Lenore's explanation of how the moon reappears each month to the scientific one. Additional fictional details turn up in Clayton Bess's *The Truth about the Moon* and in the African folktales *Why the Sun and the Moon Live in the Sky* by Elphinstone Dayrell and *Anansi the Spider* by Gerald McDermott. CALDECOTT MEDAL. KINGS AND RULERS. MOON. PRINCES AND PRINCESSES. SICK.

1016   **Turkle, Brinton.** *Do Not Open.* **Illus. by the author. Dutton, 1981. ISBN 0-525-28785-X**

Treasure hunting with her cat on the beach after a big storm, Miss Moody finds a mysterious bottle and, against her better judgment, listens to the voice within that pleads with her to pull the stopper. Wonderfully scary with an ending motif common in folklore; similar to Molly Bang's *Wiley and the Hairy Man* and Mercer Mayer's *Liza Lou and the Yeller Belly Swamp*. Introduce the original cooperative genie in Andrew Lang's *Aladdin and the Wonderful Lamp*. CATS. CLOCKS. MAGIC. MONSTERS. SEASHORE.

1017   **Udry, Janice May.** *Angie.* **Illus. by Hilary Knight. Harper & Row, 1971.**

[11 chapters, 64p.] Daily incidents in the school and home life of Angie Brinker, an amiable girl who keeps a goose for a pet, eats the same breakfast every day, and befriends the school principal. If you work in a school, ask your principal to read aloud a pertinent chapter or two. PRINCIPALS. SCHOOLS. TEACHERS.

1018   **Ungerer, Tomi.** *The Beast of Monsieur Racine.* **Illus. by the author. Farrar, 1971. ISBN 0-374-30640-0**

Never guessing its true identity, a solitary retired French tax collector befriends the shaggy-maned, droopy, lumpy, gentle, unidentifiable creature who has been eating his prize pears. Share a few pears with your own beastly audience, and see if they can guess the beast's big secret. FRANCE. FRIENDSHIP. MONSTERS. SCIENTISTS.

1019   **Van Allsburg, Chris.** *The Garden of Abdul Gasazi.* **Illus. by the author. Houghton Mifflin, 1979. ISBN 0-395-27804-X**

Did the ominous magician really turn Fritz, the dog Alan is minding for the day, into a duck? Children should discuss their conclusions, citing supporting evidence. One Van Allsburg title won't do the trick—read them all. Art teachers may wish to give some guidance in drawing in pencil for the many who admire the artist's compelling technique. DOGS. DUCKS. MAGICIANS.

1020   **Van Allsburg, Chris.** *Jumanji.* **Illus. by the author. Houghton Mifflin, 1981. ISBN 0-395-30448-2**

Judy and Pete find a jungle board game that comes to life as they play. Have students write the sequel, act out the game after they've written new moves, and/or design their own board games. For another game that works, see Florence Parry Heide's odd *The Shrinking of Treehorn*. Related come-to-life titles include Jon Agee's *The Incredible Painting of Felix Clousseau*, Henrik Drescher's *Simon's Book*, and David McPhail's *The Magical Drawings of Mooney B. Finch*. BROTHERS AND SISTERS. CALDECOTT MEDAL. GAMES.

1021   **Van Leeuwen, Jean.** *Benjy in Business.* **Illus. by Margot Apple. Dial, 1983. ISBN 0-8037-0873-4**

[11 chapters, 152p.] With a Clyde Johnson baseball mitt as his goal, an undauntable Benjy sets out to earn $22.95 by baby-sitting for his fast-moving baby sister, selling lemonade, washing cars, and weeding. Second in a series that includes *Benjy and the Power of Zingies* (Dial, 1982) and *Benjy the Football Hero* (Dial, 1985). See how another broke kid comes up with the dough in *A Job for Jenny Arthur* by Ellen Conford. BABY-SITTERS. BROTHERS AND SISTERS. FAMILY LIFE. MONEY.

1022   **Waber, Bernard. *Dear Hildegarde*. Illus. by the author. Houghton Mifflin, 1980.**

An advice-dispensing owl writes a "Dear Abby"-ish column for disgruntled letter-writing animals. Your class can write and answer problem letters from the point of view of other animals or from specific animal book characters with problems, like Wilbur the pig or mouse Dr. DeSoto. CREATIVE WRITING. LETTER WRITING. OWLS.

1023   **Waber, Bernard. *I Was All Thumbs*. Illus. by the author. Houghton Mifflin, 1975. ISBN 0-395-21404-1**

Having lived his whole life in Captain Pierre's laboratory tank, Legs the Octopus describes his predicament as he must learn to adapt and make new friends after being released into the sea. Not only splendid to use with aquatic-minded science units, along with Susan Russo's collection of sea poems, *The Ice Cream Ocean*, but also a unique comment on not following the crowd and how to fit in to a new environment. A useful allegory for the first week of school, along with Marjorie Weinman Sharmat's classic on preconceived notions, *A Gila Monster Meets You at the Airport*. FISHES. FRIENDSHIP. MOVING, HOUSEHOLD. OCEAN.

1024   **Ward, Lynd. *The Silver Pony*. Illus. by the author. Houghton Mifflin, 1973. ISBN 0-395-14753-0**

A farm boy rides his wild winged horse around the world, visiting and helping children in the city, arctic, flooded town, and lighthouse, in eight wordless chapters of majestic gray-toned illustrations. Show the whole story and elicit reactions on plot and possible dialogue. Then, ask for volunteers to narrate the story, verbally dramatizing one chapter at a time. Working in small groups, students can attempt written versions of various chapters and perhaps invent new adventures. Also consider Betsy Byars's *The Winged Colt of Casa Mia* as a companion read aloud. CREATIVE WRITING. HORSES. IMAGINATION. STORIES WITHOUT WORDS. STORYTELLING.

1025   **Warner, Gertrude Chandler. *The Boxcar Children*. Illus. by Kate L. Deal. Albert Whitman, 1950. ISBN 0-8075-0851-9**

[13 chapters, 154p.] An abandoned train boxcar is home to four orphaned, self-sufficient children who run away from the grandfather they've never met. Easy to read alone, but there's something wonderfully compelling about this story that hits a wish-fulfilling nerve in children. BROTHERS AND SISTERS. GRANDFATHERS. RUN-AWAYS.

1026   **Weil, Lisl. *Owl and Other Scrambles*. Illus. by the author. Dutton, 1980. ISBN 0-525-36527-3**

Figure out each alphabetical word picture made from the letters in the word. Give these as spelling words, and then your students can design new ones using other nouns. ALPHABET BOOKS. WORD GAMES.

1027 **White, E. B.** *Charlotte's Web.* **Illus. by Garth Williams. Harper & Row, 1952. ISBN 0-06-026386-5**

[12 chapters, 184p.] Spider saves pig. The classic, perfect for all ages. For grades three and up, extend the theme with Shirley Climo's *Someone Saw a Spider: Spider Facts and Folktales.* FARM LIFE. PIGS. SPIDERS.

1028 **Wilder, Laura Ingalls.** *Little House in the Big Woods.* **Illus. by Garth Williams. Harper & Row, 1953. ISBN 0-06-026431-4**

[13 chapters, 238p.] First in an autobiographical series about a pioneer family in 1870s Wisconsin, detailing their customs, day-to-day and season-to-season activities, family stories, and songs. Have children collect, write down, and tell their own family stories from parents and grandparents. AUTOBIOGRAPHY. FAMILY LIFE. FRONTIER AND PIONEER LIFE. HISTORICAL FICTION. U.S.–HISTORY–1865–1898–FICTION.

1029 **Williams, Jay.** *Everyone Knows What a Dragon Looks Like.* **Illus. by Mercer Mayer. Four Winds, 1976. ISBN 0-02-793090-4**

The Great Cloud Dragon, disguised as a small, fat, bald old man, saves the city of Wu from war and ruin, thanks to young Han the gate sweeper, the only one who believes him. Other books with which to celebrate Chinese New Year include Leonard Everett Fisher's bold *The Great Wall of China* and Ian Wallace's *Chin Chiang and the Dragon Dance.* CHINA. DRAGONS.

1030 **Williams, Jay.** *One Big Wish.* **Illus. by John O'Brien. Macmillan, 1980.**

Farmer Fred Butterspoon's million dollar wish, granted by an old woman he helps, causes nothing but trouble. Before reading his final wish aloud, ask your listeners what it might be. For more impetuous wish making, read Margot Zemach's English folktale *The Three Wishes.* FARM LIFE. MONEY. WISHES.

1031 **Wisniewski, David.** *The Warrior and the Wise Man.* **Illus. by the author. Lothrop, 1989. ISBN 0-688-07890-7**

Sent by their father the emperor to bring back the five eternal elements: Earth, Water, Fire, Wind, and Cloud, twin brothers Tozaemon and Toemon differ in their approaches to defeating the demons who guard each prize. Dramatically illustrated with cut paper, this folktale-like story demonstrates the advantage of wisdom and ideas over brute force. The Japanese folktale *The Stonecutter* by Gerald McDermott is an apt follow-up. BROTHERS. JAPAN. TWINS.

1032 **Yashima, Taro.** *Crow Boy.* **Illus. by the author. Viking, 1955. ISBN 0-670-24931-9**

Chibi, an outcast boy in his Japanese village school, proves his value to his unkind classmates, as narrated by one of them. Insightful and a fine stimulus for a class discussion on how they'd treat people who are different. One the same topic, read Barbara Cohen's *Molly's Pilgrim* and Eleanor Estes's *The Hundred Dresses.* INDIVIDUALITY. JAPAN. SCHOOLS. SELF-CONCEPT.

1033 **Yolen, Jane.** *Sleeping Ugly.* **Illus. by Diane Stanley. Coward, 1981. ISBN 0-698-30721-6**

An alternative version of the 100-year nap, whereby a nasty, bad-tempered but beautiful princess meets up with Plain Jane and a fairy who grants three wishes. When reading fairy tales, like the Jacob Grimm *Sleeping Beauty* illustrated by Trina Schart Hyman, contrast them with parodies such as Raymond Briggs's *Jim and the Beanstalk*, Bernice Myers's *Sidney Rella and the Glass Sneaker*, and A. Vesey's *The*

Princess and the Frog. FAIRIES. FAIRY TALES—SATIRE. PARODIES. PRINCES AND PRINCESSES. WISHES.

1034   **Yorinks, Arthur.** *Company's Coming.* **Illus. by the author. Crown, 1988. ISBN 0-517-56751-2**

The little aliens who landed in Shirley and Moe's backyard and whom Shirley invited for dinner at six o'clock seem nonplussed when they return and find the house surrounded by tanks and the military. The punch line will knock you out. If you can stand the suspense, have your children draw pictures of what they think is in the alien's gift box. Also take off with Edward Marshall's *Space Case*, Daniel Pinkwater's *Guys from Space*, and Marilyn Sadler's *Alistair in Outer Space*. EXTRA-TERRESTRIAL LIFE. PICTURE BOOKS FOR ALL AGES. SCIENCE FICTION.

1035   **Yorinks, Arthur.** *It Happened in Pinsk.* **Illus. by the author. Farrar, 1983. ISBN 0-374-33651-2**

Envious of everyone else's good fortune, shoe salesman Irv Irving learns to appreciate his own when he wakes up one morning to find his head missing, compelling him to wear a stuffed pillowcase in its place. Tales of others who learn to value what they already have include Carol Chapman's *The Tale of Meshka the Kvetch* and Margot Zemach's *It Could Always Be Worse*. SELF-CONCEPT.

1036   **Yorinks, Arthur.** *Oh, Brother.* **Illus. by Richard Egielski. Farrar, 1989. ISBN 0-374-35599-1**

After causing a sorry accident at sea that leaves them alone in the world, querulous English twins Milton and Morris drift from orphanage to circus to tailor shop, where they learn a trade that takes them back to England for a surprise reunion with their parents and the Queen. After trading tales of sibling rivalry, regale your charges with Barbara Park's modern tale of brotherly loathing, *Operation: Dump the Chump*. BROTHERS. SIBLING RIVALRY.

1037   **Zemach, Harve.** *The Judge: An Untrue Tale.* **Illus. by Margot Zemach. Farrar, 1969. ISBN 0-374-33960-0**

A pompous and derisive judge won't believe his prisoners' increasingly horrific descriptions of an approaching monster, thus sealing his own doom. In rhyme and great to act out. CREATIVE DRAMA. MONSTERS. STORIES IN RHYME.

Illustration from FAT MEN FROM SPACE, written and illustrated by Daniel Manus Pinkwater. Dodd, Mead & Company, 1977. Reprinted by permission.

FICTION FOR GRADES 3–4

1038   **Aiken, Joan.** *The Moon's Revenge.* **Illus. by Alan Lee. Knopf, 1988. ISBN 0-394-99380-2**

[1 long sitting, unp.] Intent on becoming the best fiddler in the country, Seppy, the seventh son of a seventh son, makes a deal with the moon that leaves him barefoot for seven years and exposes his family to an unnamed danger. This magnificent and engrossing literary fairy tale about the power of love makes a fascinating complement to Hans Christian Andersen's *The Wild Swans.* FANTASY. MOON. MUSIC. SHOES. WISHES.

1039   **Andersen, Hans Christian.** *The Nightingale.* **Illus. by Beni Montresor. Crown, 1985. ISBN 0-517-55211-6**

[1 sitting, unp.] Montresor's huge jewel-toned illustrations grace this adaption of Andersen's famous tale about a Chinese emperor's fascination with first a real and then a mechanical bird. On the same wavelength is Michelle Nikly's *The Emperor's Plum Tree.* BIRDS. KINGS AND RULERS.

1040   **Andersen, Hans Christian.** *The Wild Swans.* **Illus. by Susan Jeffers. Retold by Amy Ehrlich. Dial, 1987. ISBN 0-8037-0451-8**

[1 sitting, 40p.] Flamboyantly romantic is this spellbinding literary fairy tale of Elise who must remain mute while she knits tunics from stinging nettles to set free her enchanted brothers. Elise had a hard row to hoe, almost being executed as a witch and all. Start up an ethics debate as to whether students would have emulated her noble behavior. In a similar mood is Joan Aiken's *The Moon's Revenge.* BIRDS. KINGS AND RULERS.

1041   **Anderson, Margaret.** *The Brain on Quartz Mountain.* **Illus. by Charles Robinson. Knopf, 1982. ISBN 0-394-85385-7**

[10 chapters, 114p.] David helps an eccentric professor educate a growing chicken brain with the help of *The Guinness Book of World Records.* Prolong the Guinness theme with Mary Francis Shura's *Chester.* BASEBALL. CHICKENS. SCIENTISTS.

1042   **Atwater, Richard, and Florence Atwater.** *Mr. Popper's Penguins.* **Illus. by Robert Lawson. Little, Brown, 1938. ISBN 0-316-05842-4**

[20 chapters, 139p.] Much to his son and daughter's delight, a placid housepainter receives his first of 12 live penguins as a gift from South Pole explorer Admiral

Drake. Another intelligent bird companion is parrot Madison in Dick King-Smith's *Harry's Mad*. BIRDS. HUMOROUS FICTION.

1043   **Bacon, Peggy. *The Magic Touch*. Illus. by the author. Little, Brown, 1968.**

[6 chapters, 112p.] In a seaside cottage, the four Lurie children try out a recipe book of magic spells and are transformed into cats, dogs, rabbits, and birds. Have children write about their own projected experiences as each animal. ANIMALS. COOKERY. CREATIVE WRITING. MAGIC. TRANSFORMATIONS.

1044   **Baum, Arline, and Joseph Baum. *Opt: An Illusionary Tale*. Illus. by the authors. Viking, 1987. ISBN 0-670-80870-9**

[1 sitting, 32p.] The story—preparing for the prince's birthday party—is slight, but each brightly illustrated page includes at least one familiar but no less ingenious optical illusion for viewers to puzzle. Make sure your listeners sit close. Explanations for each illusion are included in the back, along with ideas for making your own. Read as a splendid accompaniment to a science lesson on the eye, or just because you're in the mood for puzzlement. OPTICAL ILLUSIONS. TRICKS.

1045   **Birch, David. *The King's Chessboard*. Illus. by Devis Grebu. Dial, 1988. ISBN 0-8037-0367-8**

[1 sitting, unp.] When the King of Deccan commands a wise man to choose a reward, the wise man asks for one grain of rice to be doubled each day for 64 days, the number of squares on a chessboard. See also Helena Clare Pittman's folktale *A Grain of Rice* for a similar story. Set up the math question for your students midway through reading, and be sure to bring in a jar of rice for them to estimate and then count out. KINGS AND RULERS. MATHEMATICS.

1046   **Blume, Judy. *Tales of a Fourth Grade Nothing*. Illus. by Roy Doty. Dutton, 1972. ISBN 0-525-40720-0**

[10 chapters, 120p.] Peter must learn to cope with his incorrigible two-and-a-half-year-old little brother, Fudgie, the male equivalent to Beverly Cleary's Ramona in *Beezus and Ramona*. BROTHERS. FAMILY LIFE. HUMOROUS FICTION.

1047   **Byars, Betsy. *The Midnight Fox*. Illus. by Ann Grifalconi. Viking, 1968. ISBN 0-670-47473-8**

[19 chapters, 159p.] Tom, a nine-year-old city boy, reluctantly spends what turns out to be a memorable summer on his aunt and uncle's farm, tracking and saving a black fox and her kit. *Reynard: The Story of a Fox Returned to the Wild* by Alice Mills Leighner is a photo-filled nonfiction book that will make Tom's experience all the more compelling for urban children who only know foxes from fairy tales. FARM LIFE. FOXES.

1048   **Byars, Betsy. *The Winged Colt of Casa Mia*. Illus. by Richard Cuffari. Viking, 1973. ISBN 0-670-77318-2**

[15 chapters, 128p.] The narrator—a former movie stuntman—and his bookish nephew attempt to train a newborn horse that can fly. Also show Lynd Ward's wordless epic *The Silver Pony*. ANIMALS, MYTHICAL. FLIGHT. HORSES. UNCLES. WINGS.

1049 **Carey, Valerie Scho.** *The Devil & Mother Crump.* **Illus. by Arnold Lobel. Harper, 1987. ISBN 0-06-020982-8**

[1–2 sittings, 39p.] The devil himself is curious to meet the stingy old baker woman reported to be even meaner than he is, so he pays her a visit. This one's a literary variant of the folktale *Jack-O'-Lantern* by Edna Barth and *Mean Jake and the Devils* by William H. Hooks, to which you can compare it. DEVIL.

1050 **Cleary, Beverly.** *The Mouse and the Motorcycle.* **Illus. by Louis Darling. Morrow, 1965. ISBN 0-688-31698-0**

[13 chapters, 158p.] When his parents check into the Old Mountain View Inn, Keith meets a remarkable mouse named Ralph who delights in riding Keith's red toy motorcycle. Your students will want to read the 1970 sequel, *Runaway Ralph*. FANTASY. MICE.

1051 **Cleary, Beverly.** *Ralph S. Mouse.* **Illus. by Paul O. Zelinsky. Morrow, 1982. ISBN 0-688-01455-0**

[9 chapters, 160p.] In this third book in the "Mouse and the Motorcycle" trilogy, Ralph the mouse moves to the school of his human friend Keith, where he hides in anger after his precious red motorcycle is broken. If you have access to mice, you might want to duplicate the maze running experiment described here. FANTASY. MICE. SCHOOLS.

1052 **Clifford, Eth.** *Harvey's Horrible Snake Disaster.* **Houghton Mifflin, 1984. ISBN 0-395-35378-5**

[12 chapters, 108p.] Harvey's lying cousin Nora starts off her annual two-month visit by stealing Slider, a hognose snake belonging to the visiting herpetologist at Harvey's school. First in a series, followed by *Harvey's Marvelous Monkey Mystery* (1987). Snake fans will also enjoy Lilian Moore's *The Snake That Went to School*. COUSINS. HUMOROUS STORIES. SCHOOLS. SNAKES.

1053 **Clifford, Sandy.** *The Roquefort Gang.* **Illus. by the author. Houghton Mifflin, 1981.**

[5 chapters, 79p.] To baby-sitter mouse Nicole's horror, her mouse twin charges disappear into the dreaded wild berry lot. Compare these poetry-spouting mice and cats to the lyrical mice in *I'll Meet You at the Cucumbers* by Lilian Moore, and have children compose new mouse verse. CATS. CREATIVE WRITING. LOST. MICE. POETS.

1054 **Clymer, Eleanor.** *My Brother Stevie.* **Dell, 1989. ISBN 0-440-40125-9**

[6 chapters, 76p.] With her mother gone and her grandmother raising them in her project apartment, twelve-year-old Annie feels helpless to control her eight-year-old brother's misbehavior until she confides in Miss Stover, Stevie's teacher. John Steptoe's *Stevie*, which can be read in one short sitting, is about the pesky foster brother the narrator never appreciates until he's gone. BEHAVIOR. BROTHERS AND SISTERS. CITIES AND TOWNS. TEACHERS.

1055 **Cooney, Barbara.** *Island Boy.* **Illus. by the author. Viking, 1988. ISBN 0-670-81749-X**

[1 sitting, unp.] The life of Matthias, youngest of 12, who grew up on Tibbetts Island in nineteenth-century Maine, went to sea, and returned home to live out his days on the island where his heart lay. An affecting social studies lesson on life back then, along with Cooney's own *Miss Rumphius*, Donald Hall's *Ox-Cart Man*, and Tony Johnston's *Yonder*, and a catalyst for children to interview their grandparents and write their life histories. While in picture-book format, the slow pace and matter-of-fact narrative will be best appreciated by an older audience. FAMILY LIFE. HISTORICAL FICTION. ISLANDS.

1056   Corbett, Scott. *The Lemonade Trick*. Illus. by Paul Galdone. Little, Brown, 1960. ISBN 0-316-15694-9

[11 chapters, 103p.] First in the "trick" series about Kirby Maxwell's old magic chemistry set, given to him by old Mrs. Graymalkin, that always produces unexpected and amusing results—in this case, causing Kirby to do only good deeds all day long. Have each child submit one card to a good-deed jar; each person can then pull out a card and perform that good deed for someone in the school. BEHAVIOR. MAGIC. SCIENCE—EXPERIMENTS.

1057   Corbett, Scott. *The Limerick Trick*. Illus. by Paul Galdone. Little, Brown, 1964.

[9 chapters, 103p.] Using his magic chemistry set to try to win the bicycle prize for the school poetry contest causes Kirby to speak in rhyme all the time. Call a poetry break in the day, where your students are only permitted to speak aloud in rhyme. *The Turnabout Trick* (1964), where cat and dog switch roles, is another clever one in the series. MAGIC. POETS. SCIENCE—EXPERIMENTS.

1058   Dahl, Roald. *Charlie and the Chocolate Factory*. Illus. by Joseph Schindelman. Knopf, 1964. ISBN 0-394-91011-7

[30 chapters, 162p.] Only the five children who find the gold ticket in their candy bars —including our deserving hero, Charlie Bucket—will win a trip through Mr. Wonka's fabulous factory. Compare the book with the movie, and talk about how movies rarely ever capture all the good parts in a book. CANDY. FANTASY.

1059   Dahl, Roald. *James and the Giant Peach*. Illus. by Nancy Ekholm Burkert. Knopf, 1962. ISBN 0-394-91282-9

[39 short chapters, 119p.] Escaping from his odious Aunts Spiker and Sponge, orphan James and his new giant insect friends travel over the ocean in the stone of an enormous peach. Filled with several clever narrative poems including a sickeningly luscious one about favorite foods that will make everyone gag. FANTASY. FRUIT. INSECTS. ORPHANS.

1060   DeJong, Meindert. *Hurry Home, Candy*. Illus. by Maurice Sendak. Harper & Row, 1953. ISBN 0-06-021486-4

[19 chapters, 244p.] A nameless stray dog finds human companionship and finally the love of a kind man in his travels in and out of people's lives. Give the cats equal time with Mary Stolz's *Cat Walk*. DOGS. LOST.

1061   Delton, Judy. *Angel in Charge*. Illus. by Leslie Morrill. Houghton Mifflin, 1985. ISBN 0-395-37488-X

[9 chapters, 152p.] While their mother takes a much deserved vacation, Angel and her little brother Rags must cope with unexpected crises, starting when their sitter breaks her leg and the children are left with no one to take care of them. Another good read aloud, *Backyard Angel* (1983), is the first in the series which continues with *Angel's Mother's Boyfriend* (1986), *Angel's Mother's Wedding* (1987), and *Angel's Mother's Baby* (1989). In the great Cleary tradition, these chapter books about Angel, Rags, and their mother have a unique resonance that Hurwitz, Blume, and later Lowry readers will appreciate. Other children who cope on their own include those in Eleanor Clymer's *My Brother Stevie*, Dale Fife's *Who's in Charge of Lincoln*, and Gertrude Chandler Warner's *The Boxcar Children*. BABY-SITTERS. BROTHERS AND SISTERS. FAMILY LIFE. RESPONSIBILITY.

1062   Dillon, Barbara. *Mrs. Tooey & the Terrible Toxic Tar*. Lippincott, 1988. ISBN 0-397-32276-3

[7 chapters, 88p.] Craig and Margo's strange new sitter, a witch with a soft spot for mortals, enlists their help in thwarting her sister, Velma the Vindictive, who plans to destroy the town of Summerton. Meet Dillon's other incorrigible witch character, Hepzibah the Hateful, in the Halloween romp *What's Happened to Harry?* BABY-SITTERS. BROTHERS AND SISTERS. MAGIC. WITCHES.

1063   Edwards, Julie. *The Last of the Really Great Whangdoodles*. Harper & Row, 1974. ISBN 0-06-021805-3

[23 chapters, 209p.] Professor Savant instructs three children in their search via their imaginations for this elusive animal in the kingdom of Whangdoodleland, where they first encounter a Whiffle Bird, the Splintercat, and a mob of Swamp Gaboons. Vivid descriptions of each unusual character should enable children to draw portraits of them as they are introduced in the story and also make their own scrappy caps to wear each time you read a chapter. Also see Edward Ormondroyd's *David and the Phoenix* for a get-together with better-known mythical beasts. ANIMALS, MYTHICAL. BROTHERS AND SISTERS. FANTASY.

1064   Farley, Walter. *The Black Stallion*. Illus. by Keith Ward. Random House, 1977. ISBN 0-394-90601-2

[18 chapters, 187p.] Sailing home from India on the tramp steamer Drake, Alec and a wild horse are the only survivors after a storm at sea deposits them on an island. Follow the voyage on the globe as you read. First of a classic series, originally published in 1941. ADVENTURE AND ADVENTURERS. HORSES. ISLANDS. SURVIVAL.

1065   Fleischman, Paul. *Finzel the Farsighted*. Illus. by Marcia Sewall. Dutton, 1983. ISBN 0-525-44057-7

[1 sitting, 48p.] Being nearsighted proves an ultimate blessing to Finzel, a wise fortune-teller who can see deep into the past and future of both simpleton and rogue. Speaking of noodleheads, don't forget Amy Schwartz's *Yossel Zissel & the Wisdom of Chelm*. BROTHERS.

1066   Fleischman, Sid. *McBroom Tells the Truth*. Illus. by Walter H. Lorraine. Little, Brown, 1981. ISBN 0-316-28550-1

[1–2 sittings, 48p.] Tall tale of a farmer's 11 children and their fabulous one-acre farm. A reprint of the 1966 edition. Get students exaggerating by having them write their own fabrications, with Alvin Schwartz's *Whoppers* providing extra stimulus. Look for other "McBroom" books in the series, rereleased by Little, Brown and illustrated by Walter Lorraine. CREATIVE WRITING. EXAGGERATION. FARM LIFE. TALL TALES.

1067   Gardiner, John Reynolds. *Stone Fox*. Illus. by Marcia Sewall. Crowell, 1980. ISBN 0-690-03984-0

[2 sittings, 10 chapters, 81p.] With no money left in the strongbox, $500 in taxes due on their Wyoming farm, and a grandfather who's given up on life, ten-year-old Willy enters the National Dog Sled Races in hopes of winning the cash prize. Watch out for the powerful ending which might well bring you to tears. Afterward, start everyone thinking by asking if they would have entered the race, knowing how it all turned out. DOGS. FARM LIFE. GRANDFATHERS. INDIANS OF NORTH AMERICA. RESPONSIBILITY.

1068   Gwynne, Fred. *A Chocolate Moose for Dinner.* Illus. by the author. Simon & Schuster, 1988. ISBN 0-671-66685-1

[1 sitting, unp.] Picture book of figures of speech, taken literally, as narrated by a young boy who misunderstands them. Several will be over your children's heads, so explain the funny parts as needed. The group can compile an additional list and illustrate their own. Upper-grade teachers take note: This one's for you, too, as is *The King Who Rained* (1970), both of which were created by the man who played Herman Munster in the old TV comedy "The Munsters" and Muldoon in "Car 54, Where Are You?" CREATIVE WRITING. ENGLISH LANGUAGE–IDIOMS.

1069   Hall, Lynn. *In Trouble Again, Zelda Hammersmith?* Harcourt, 1987. ISBN 0-15-299964-7

[5 chapters, 138p.] Wittily narrated by the irrepressible Zelda who kidnaps a dog in order to steal a kiss from the boy she likes, fakes a car accident to camouflage an "F" in arithmetic, and buys a half-dead $17 horse for her mother's birthday. More chaos awaits in the trailer park where she and her mother live in *Zelda Strikes Again* (1988). HUMOROUS FICTION. MOTHERS AND DAUGHTERS.

1070   Harding, Lee. *The Fallen Spaceman.* Illus. by John Schoenherr and Ian Schoenherr. Bantam, 1982. ISBN 0-553-15694-2

[9 chapters, 86p.] Two boys discover the enormous spacesuit that holds Tyro, an alien trapped on Earth after his spaceship leaves him behind by mistake. Pair with Daniel Pinkwater's *Fat Men from Space* to go along with your astronomy unit and compare types of aliens—believable and slapstick. EXTRATERRESTRIAL LIFE. SCIENCE FICTION. SPACE FLIGHT.

1071   Heide, Florence Parry. *The Shrinking of Treehorn.* Illus. by Edward Gorey. Holiday House, 1971. ISBN 0-8234-0189-8

[1 sitting, unp.] No one, including parents or teacher, seems to notice or mind that Treehorn is getting smaller, thanks to a strange new board game under his bed. For another unusual game with disturbing properties, read Chris Van Allsburg's *Jumanji*; next, have students design new ones. GAMES. SIZE.

1072   Henry, Marguerite. *Misty of Chincoteague.* Illus. by Wesley Dennis. Rand, 1947. ISBN 0-02-689090-9

[18 chapters, 173p.] A classic Virginia horse story involving Paul and Maureen, a brother and sister who help to capture and tame a wild mare and her colt. Pair this realistic fiction with Betsy Byars's realistic fantasy *The Winged Colt of Casa Mia.* BROTHERS AND SISTERS. GRANDPARENTS. HORSES.

1073   Hildick, E. W. *The Case of the Condemned Cat.* Illus. by Lisl Weil. Macmillan, 1975.

[14 chapters, 106p.] With their new client accused of murder and under a possible death sentence, the McGurk Organization sets out to prove that Whiskers the cat did not kill Mrs. Overshaw's pet dove. One of the tongue-in-cheek series about a neighborhood group of kid detectives; just one should be enough to get your students hooked. CATS. MYSTERY AND DETECTIVE STORIES.

1074   Hooks, William H. *Mean Jake and the Devils*. Illus. by Dirk Zimmer. Dial, 1981. ISBN 0-8037-5564-3

[3 chapters, 61p.] Three Halloween-time tales, taken from North Carolina folklore, about the meanest man in the world who gave the devil some unpleasant memories. A variant of Edna Barth's *Jack-O-Lantern*, to which you can compare it. DEVIL. HALLOWEEN.

1075   Hughes, Ted. *The Iron Giant: A Story in Five Nights*. Illus. by Robert Nadler. Harper & Row, 1988. ISBN 0-06-022639-0

[5 chapters, 56p.] The metal-devouring giant settles contentedly in a junkyard until a space-bat-angel-dragon monster threatens Earth's existence. Read the five chapters over the course of one thrilling week. FANTASY. GIANTS. MONSTERS.

1076   Hunter, Mollie. *A Furl of Fairy Wind*. Illus. by Stephen Gammell. Harper & Row, 1977. ISBN 0-06-022674-9

[4 short stories, 58p.] Gentle, lyrical tales by a gifted Scottish writer, of people who encounter Brownies and other fairies. Meet a nontraditional fairy in Lynne Reid Banks's enthralling *The Fairy Rebel*. Shirley Climo's folktales, *Piskies, Spriggans, and Other Magical Beings*, fit in here as well. FAIRIES. FANTASY. SHORT STORIES.

1077   Hutchins, Hazel. *The Three and Many Wishes of Jason Reid*. Illus. by Julie Tennent. Viking, 1988. ISBN 0-317-69255-0

[10 chapters, 87p.] Granted wishes by Quicksilver, Elster of the third order, eleven-year-old Jason finds a loophole in the rules that allows his third wish to be for three more. Your students can compile their own list of wishes, both regular and important. Contrast with Bill Brittain's *All the Money in the World*, Elizabeth Johnson's *Stuck with Luck*, and Betsy Sterman's *Too Much Magic*. BASEBALL. FANTASY. MAGIC. WISHES.

1078   Ipcar, Dahlov. *I Love My Anteater with an A*. Illus. by the author. Knopf, 1964.

[1 sitting, unp.] This animal alliteration picture book, a vocabulary-building variant of Jane Bayer's *A My Name Is Alice*, makes a great dictionary, geography, and writing activity. ALPHABET BOOKS. ANIMALS. CREATIVE WRITING. PICTURE BOOKS FOR ALL AGES. VOCABULARY.

1079   Kaye, M. M. *The Ordinary Princess*. Doubleday, 1984. ISBN 0-671-60383-3

[4 chapters, 112p.] Bestowed at her christening the gift of "ordinary-ness" by her fairy godmother, Princess Amy grows up to eschew her palace life-style, runs away, and becomes a kitchen maid in a neighboring kingdom. An affectionate send-up of fairy tale customs, told with humor and a touch of wonder. Other marvelous folktale fictions include Pamela Stearns's *Into the Painted Bear Lair*, Elizabeth Winthrop's *The Castle in the Attic*, and Vivian Vande Velde's *A Hidden Magic*. FANTASY.

1080   Kennedy, Richard. *Come Again in the Spring*. Illus. by Marcia Sewall. Harper & Row, 1976.

[1 sitting, 47p.] Unwilling to leave the wild birds he's fed all his life, old Hark refuses to go with Death who has come to take him away, but agrees to a wager. Have your listeners write down or tell their earliest childhood memories to share with the group. BIRDS. CREATIVE WRITING. DEATH.

1081   **Kennedy, Richard.** *The Leprechaun's Story.* **Illus. by Marcia Sewall. Dutton, 1979. ISBN 0-525-33472-6**

[1 sitting, unp.] A leprechaun tricks a gullible tradesman out of his pot of gold by telling him a real sob story. Compare with "Patrick O'Donnell and the Leprechaun" in Virginia Haviland's *Favorite Fairy Tales Told in Ireland* and Linda Shute's variant *Clever Tom and the Leprechaun.* IRELAND. LEPRECHAUNS. PICTURE BOOKS FOR ALL AGES.

1082   **Kennedy, Richard.** *The Lost Kingdom of Karnica.* **Illus. by Uri Shulevitz. Scribner, 1979.**

[1 sitting, unp.] A greedy king is willing to destroy his entire kingdom to dig up the giant precious stone that a wise man claims is the heart of the kingdom. Explore the interesting parallels to our destruction of the ozone layer or our lack of conservation-consciousness leading to the deforestation of the Amazon. In the name of progress gone wrong, read also Bill Peet's *The Wump World* and Dr. Seuss's *The Lorax.* GREED. KINGS AND RULERS.

1083   **Kennedy, Richard.** *The Rise and Fall of Ben Gizzard.* **Illus. by Marcia Sewall. Little, Brown, 1978.**

[1 sitting, 41p.] The corrupt sheriff of the silver mining town of Depression Gulch finally gets his due when an old Indian's prophecy comes true. Talk about story structure, as this one has a dramatic climax, and the makeup of villains versus heroes. BIRDS. WEST.

1084   **Khalsa, Dayal Kaur.** *Tales of a Gambling Grandma.* **Illus. by the author. Clarkson N. Potter, 1986. ISBN 0-517-56137-9**

[1 sitting, 32p.] An affectionate, clear remembrance of the narrator's hard boiled grandma who taught her to play cards and gave her friendly advice on the Laws of Life. In picture-book format, but best used with older students who can ask and then write about their own grandmas' early memories. Use with Cynthia Rylant's *When I Was Young in the Mountains.* CREATIVE WRITING. GRANDMOTHERS.

1085   **King-Smith, Dick.** *Martin's Mice.* **Illus. by Jez Alborough. Crown, 1989. ISBN 0-517-57113-7**

[17 chapters, 128p.] Unlike his more conformist siblings, farm kitten Martin has no interest in catching mice to eat; he wants one as a pet, and finds his wish granted in pregnant mouse Drusilla whom he installs in an old bathtub at the top of the hayloft. Other books about those who don't care to fit their stereotypes include Roald Dahl's *The BFG*, King-Smith's *Harry's Mad*, and Janwillem Van de Wetering's *Hugh Pine.* CATS. FANTASY. FARM LIFE. MICE.

1086   **Laroche, Michel.** *The Snow Rose.* **Illus. by Sandra Laroche. Holiday House, 1986. ISBN 0-8234-0594-X**

A handsome Christmas-season picture book of Roland the troubadour who, seeking to win the hand of the vain Princess Ermina, successfully undergoes one contest for each season, only to realize who his true love really is. Intriguingly illustrated with detailed watercolors of the French chateau Chenonceaux and the Loire Valley countryside, contrasted with black silhouettes of all human participants. LOVE. PRINCES AND PRINCESSES. SEASONS.

1087   **Levy, Elizabeth.** *Lizzie Lies a Lot.* **Illus. by John Wallner. Delacorte, 1976. ISBN 0-440-04920-2**

[12 chapters, 102p.] The dreadful lies that Lizzie tells to her friends, parents, and grandmother finally catch up with her. Irma faces a similar problem in *The Bad Times of Irma Baumline* by Carol Ryrie Brink. Talk over why we lie and what we can do about it.   FAMILY PROBLEMS. GRANDMOTHERS. HONESTY.

1088   **Lewis, C. S.** *The Lion, the Witch and the Wardrobe.* **Illus. by Pauline Baynes. Macmillan, 1950. ISBN 0-02-758120-9**

[17 chapters, 154p.] The classic fantasy of four children who discover the enchanted winter-locked land of Narnia through the back wall of a large wooden clothes wardrobe in their uncle's old house. The first book in a series of seven, you may wish to also read *The Magician's Nephew* to find out how Narnia originated.   ANIMALS, MYTHICAL. FANTASY. LIONS. WINTER. WITCHES.

1089   **Lindgren, Astrid.** *The Ghost of Skinny Jack.* **Illus. by Ilon Wikland. Viking, 1988. ISBN 0-670-81913-1**

[1 sitting, unp.] The narrator recalls the time her grandmother told her and her brother a terrifying story of a wild young man who became an undead ghost. A deceptively young-looking picture book that will scare the socks off your horror fans. Not for the faint of heart, this is on par with some of the creepier stories in Molly Bang's folktale collection *The Goblins Giggle*.   BROTHERS AND SISTERS. GHOST STORIES. GRANDMOTHERS. STORYTELLING. SUSPENSE.

1090   **Lindgren, Astrid.** *Pippi Longstocking.* **Illus. by Louis S. Glanzman. Viking, 1950. ISBN 0-670-55745-5**

[11 chapters, 160p.] Zany eccentricities of a free-spirited, nine-year-old, red-haired Swedish girl who lives in Villa Villekulla with her pet monkey. First of a series, this one's been made into several bad movies; compare them with the original.   HUMOROUS FICTION. MONKEYS.

1091   **Lofting, Hugh.** *The Story of Doctor Dolittle.* **Illus. by the author. Delacorte, 1988. ISBN 0-385-29662-2**

[21 chapters, 156p.] The good doctor of Puddleby-on-the-Marsh, with his good friends Polynesia the parrot, Dab-Dab the duck, Jip the dog, Chee-Chee the monkey, and a homesick crocodile, sets sail for Africa to cure the monkeys there of a dreaded disease. With a slightly altered text that omits the original less-than-acceptable racist overtones, and including the author's original illustrations, this new edition of the 1920 classic is a rediscovered treasure. Children can break into groups to develop original language dictionaries for each species mentioned in the book, as Dr. Dolittle speaks each animal's dialect, but he never clues us in on their vocabularies. Ketu is much amused when he learns to understand animal speech in Verna Aardema's African folktale *What's So Funny, Ketu?*   AFRICA. ANIMALS. FANTASY.

1092   **MacDonald, Betty.** *Mrs. Piggle-Wiggle.* **Illus. by Hilary Knight. Lippincott, 1957. ISBN 0-397-31712-3**

[8 chapters, 119p.] A combination doctor, herbalist, witch doctor, child psychiatrist, and magician, she cures all those children of bad habits and manners that drive adults crazy. Read a chapter a day and perhaps your students will become angels too. Choose your favorite stories from sequels *Mrs, Piggle-Wiggle's Magic* (1949) and *Hello, Mrs. Piggle-Wiggle* (1957). BEHAVIOR. ETIQUETTE.

1093   **McGraw, Eloise Jarvis.** *Joel and the Great Merlini.* **Illus. by Jim Arnosky. Pantheon, 1979. ISBN 0-394-94193-4**

[11 chapters, 59p.] Joel is able to perform stupendous magic tricks, thanks to the help of an overzealous wizard. Follow up by demonstrating a few elementary magic tricks for children to master from Ray Broekel and Laurence B. White, Jr.'s *Now You See It*, and then read Robert Kraske's *Magicians Do Amazing Things*, where he reveals the secrets of six famous magic tricks by the Masters. FANTASY. MAGIC. WIZARDS.

1094   **MacLachlan, Patricia.** *Sarah, Plain and Tall.* **Harper & Row, 1985. ISBN 0-06-024102-0**

[9 chapters, 58p.] Anna and Caleb's father sends to Maine for a mail-order bride who comes for a month to see if she will like living on the prairie. Told in a spare, poetic style by Anna, and based on a true event in the author's family history, use this with Russell Freedman's *Children of the Wild West* and Laura Ingalls Wilder's "Little House" books, and ask children to burrow into their family stories for a window to the past. BROTHERS AND SISTERS. FAMILY LIFE. FRONTIER AND PIONEER LIFE. HISTORICAL FICTION. NEWBERY MEDAL.

1095   **Manes, Stephen.** *Be a Perfect Person in Just Three Days.* **Illus. by Tom Huffman. Clarion, 1982. ISBN 0-89919-064-2**

[6 chapters, 76p.] Milo Crinkley finds a strange library book by Dr. K. Pinkerton Silverfish, which gives step-by-step instructions, starting with the assignment to wear broccoli as a necklace for an entire day. Begin the school year with this one to show students they don't need to be perfect for you to like them. Ask them to think up and write down other crackpot directions for becoming faultless. BEHAVIOR. HUMOROUS FICTION.

1096   **Miles, Betty.** *The Secret Life of the Underwear Champ.* **Illus. by Dan Jones. Knopf, 1981. ISBN 0-394-84563-3**

[13 chapters, 117p.] Making TV commercials is not all fun for Larry, especially when they interfere with Little League practice and require him to model underwear. Now's the time to analyze the commercials your students are watching on television and perhaps to write and videotape some original book advertisements. BASEBALL. CLOTHING AND DRESS. HUMOROUS FICTION. TELEVISION.

1097   **Moeri, Louise.** *Star Mother's Youngest Child.* **Illus. by Trina Schart Hyman. Houghton Mifflin, 1980. ISBN 0-395-29929-2**

[1 sitting, unp.] A forgotten old woman who longs for a real Christmas plays reluctant host to the homely star child who ventures to Earth on Christmas Day in search of a holiday celebration. The small format, with most pictures too small to show, is a small drawback, though the story shines with the true meaning of love and generosity. CHRISTMAS. FANTASY. STARS.

1098   **Moskin, Marietta.** *The Day of the Blizzard.* **Illus. by Stephen Gammell. Coward, 1978.**

[6 chapters, 79p.] Her mother sick with fever and her train conductor father still away at work, Katie ventures out on an important errand during the Great Blizzard of

1888 in New York City. Contrast with rural blizzards in Lonzo Anderson's Icelandic *The Ponies of Mykillengi* and Trinka Hakes Noble's country *Apple Tree Christmas*. HISTORICAL FICTION. NEW YORK CITY. SNOW. STORMS. WEATHER.

1099 **Nixon, Joan Lowery.** *The Gift.* **Illus. by Andrew Glass. Macmillan, 1983. ISBN 0-02-768160-2**

[7 chapters, 86p.] Staying in Ireland for six weeks with his storytelling Great Granddad and other relatives gives Brian the chance to look for a real leprechaun. Read in early March, and then send your students to search out and share all the Irish folktales in the library, along with other leprechaun blather including Bill Brittain's *All the Money in the World* and Elizabeth Johnson's *Stuck with Luck*. GRANDFATHERS. IRELAND. LEPRECHAUNS. STORYTELLING.

1100 **Ormondroyd, Edward.** *David and the Phoenix.* **Illus. by Joan Raysor. Follett, 1957.**

[10 chapters, 171p.] Climbing the mountain behind his new house, David meets the mythical bird who flies him all around the world to encounter creatures from Griffen to Faun, as part of his practical education. Compile an illustrated mythical creatures encyclopedia of these and other well-known animals. Julie Edwards's *The Last of the Really Great Whangdoodles* fits this mood. ANIMALS, MYTHICAL. BIRDS. FANTASY. SCIENTISTS.

1101 **Park, Barbara.** *Operation: Dump the Chump.* **Knopf, 1982. ISBN 0-394-95179-4**

[11 chapters, 113p.] Oscar thinks up an eight-step foolproof plan to get rid of his pesty younger brother, Robert, by giving him away to the neighbors for the summer, but the whole thing backfires. Use this truly hilarious book and the true anecdotes in Eric H. Arnold and Jeffrey Loeb's *I'm Telling! Kids Talk about Brothers and Sisters* to recount and laugh over your class's sibling horror stories. BROTHERS. HUMOROUS FICTION. SIBLING RIVALRY.

1102 **Phelan, Terry Wolfe.** *The Week Mom Unplugged the TVs.* **Illus. by Joel Schick. Four Winds, 1979.**

[6 chapters, 37p.] Steve finds there's more to life than cartoon reruns. Here's a good kickoff for no TV week, or a means to get students thinking about alternatives to the idiot box. FAMILY LIFE. PLAY. TELEVISION.

1103 **Pinkwater, Daniel.** *Fat Men from Space.* **Illus. by the author. Dodd, Mead, 1977. ISBN 0-396-07461-8**

[2–3 sittings, 57p.] Aliens plan to invade Earth, rob it of all its junk food, and make Earthlings their slaves, and William, the boy with a radio-receiving filling in his mouth, is their first captive. Beef up your nutrition unit in a healthful way with the Fat Men acting as your negative role models. EXTRATERRESTRIAL LIFE. HUMOROUS FICTION. SCIENCE FICTION. TEETH.

1104 **Pinkwater, Daniel.** *The Hoboken Chicken Emergency.* **Illus. by the author. Prentice Hall, 1977. ISBN 0-13-392514-5**

[14 chapters, 83p.] When Arthur's friendly, new, 6-foot, 266-pound pet chicken, Henrietta, escapes, the New Jersey town is terrified. A very funny Thanksgiving saga, this is the New Jersey equivalent of Seymour Reit's dragon tale *Benvenuto*. CHICKENS. FANTASY. HUMOROUS FICTION. LOST. THANKSGIVING.

1105 **Pinkwater, Daniel.** *The Magic Moscow.* **Illus. by the author. Four Winds, 1980. ISBN 0-02-774630-5**

[6 chapters, 57p.] Excitable Hoboken ice cream parlor owner Steve Nickelson buys Edward, an Alaskan malamute that is supposedly the grandson of a TV wonder dog. Though this book and *Fat Men from Space* have little in common except the setting, the sequel to both is *Slaves of Spiegel*, where the Fat Men come back and kidnap Steve, a junk food cooking maestro. DOGS. HUMOROUS FICTION.

1106 **Reit, Seymour.** *Benvenuto.* **Illus. by Will Winslow. Addison-Wesley, 1974.**

[14 chapters, 126p.] Paolo finds a baby dragon at summer camp and takes it home to his New York City apartment until it gets away. True to New York form, no one blinks an eye at a dragon wandering the streets. On the other side of the Holland Tunnel, you can follow up with Daniel Pinkwater's *The Hoboken Chicken Emergency.* DRAGONS. FANTASY. NEW YORK CITY.

1107 **Richler, Mordecai.** *Jacob Two-Two Meets the Hooded Fang.* **Illus. by Fritz Wegner. Knopf, 1975.**

[15 chapters, 87p.] Charged with insulting behavior to a big person, six-year-old Jacob, who says everything twice, everything twice, is sent to Slimer's Isle dungeon, where he thwarts the rotten kid-hating villain who runs the prison. Act out the trial scene where Jacob is found guilty. BROTHERS AND SISTERS. FANTASY.

1108 **Riley, James Whitcomb.** *The Gobble-Uns'll Git You Ef You Don't Watch Out.* **Illus. by Joel Schick. Lippincott, 1975. ISBN 0-397-31621-6**

[1 sitting, unp.] The original "Little Orphan Annie" warns her charges of the dangers of being bad in this ghoul-filled nineteenth-century poem. Hone your down-home Indiana dialect, and invite your listeners to join in on the title refrain. More behavior problems cavort through X. J. Kennedy's poetry collection *Brats.* BEHAVIOR. HUMOROUS POETRY. STORIES IN RHYME.

1109 **Rockwell, Thomas.** *How to Eat Fried Worms.* **Illus. by Emily Arnold McCully. Franklin Watts, 1973. ISBN 0-531-02631-0**

[41 short chapters, 116p.] A bet to eat a worm a day for 15 days with a $50 payoff is accepted by Billy, who claims he can eat anything. Hilarious, but not before lunch. Bring in gummy worms as a treat, unless you'd like to sample the real thing. Another wormy story is Patricia Reilly Giff's *The Winter Worm Business.* FOOD. HUMOROUS FICTION. WORMS.

1110 **Sachar, Louis.** *Sideways Stories from Wayside School.* **Illus. by Dennis Hockerman. Avon, 1985. ISBN 0-380-69871-4**

[30 short chapters, 134p.] Thirty wacky chapters about the children of the top floor classroom in a school that is 30 stories high. Write your own "Wayside School" inspired book with each student writing chapters about him or herself. Fifth- and sixth-grade people also, don't miss this one or the sequel below. CREATIVE WRITING. HUMOROUS FICTION. SCHOOLS. TEACHERS.

1111 **Sachar, Louis.** *Wayside School Is Falling Down.* **Illus. by Joel Schick. Lothrop, 1989. ISBN 0-688-07868-0**

[30 short chapters, 179p.] More strange goings-on with the kids at the top of Wayside, including new student Mark Miller whose real name is Benjamin Mushmutt, Jason the compulsive pencil-chewer, and un-silly Allison who ends up in the nonexistent Miss Zarves's class on the nonexistent nineteenth floor. Adults include teacher Mrs. Jewls; ballroom dancing instructor, the wonderful Miss Waloosh; and a surprise evil appearance, in potato salad form, of former teacher Miss Gorf, who was turned into an apple in the first book. Why can't more books be this much fun? CREATIVE WRITING. HUMOROUS FICTION. SCHOOLS. TEACHERS.

1112 **Shura, Mary Francis.** *Chester.* **Illus. by Susan Swan. Dodd, Mead, 1985. ISBN 0-396-07800-1**

[7 chapters, 92p.] Narrator Jamie's friendly new neighbor has the most freckles, siblings, and unusual pets on the whole block. Poll your class to see what unique talents they possess to compile your own "Guinness Book" of class records and investigate the original Guinness, as does Margaret J. Anderson's *The Brain on Quartz Mountain.* FRIENDSHIP. PETS.

1113 **Slobodkin, Louis.** *The Spaceship under the Apple Tree.* **Illus. by the author. Collier, 1952.**

[10 chapters, 116p.] Earth boy Eddie befriends and helps cover up for Marty, a science explorer from the planet Martinea, after his Astral Rocket Dish malfunctions and he crash-lands in Eddie's family's apple orchard. Lee Harding's *The Fallen Spaceman* is a variation on the theme, as is Daniel Pinkwater's looney *Fat Men from Space.* EXTRATERRESTRIAL LIFE. SCIENCE FICTION.

1114 **Slote, Alfred.** *My Trip to Alpha I.* **Illus. by Harold Berson. Lippincott, 1978. ISBN 0-397-31810-3**

[11 chapters, 96p.] In the sophisticated future Jack visits his aunt on another planet via VOYA-CODE body travel, and while there uncovers a sinister plot to defraud her. Children can anticipate what futuristic developments they expect in the near and far future. SCIENCE FICTION. SPACE FLIGHT.

1115 **Smith, Robert Kimmell.** *The War with Grandpa.* **Illus. by Richard Lauter. Delacorte, 1984. ISBN 0-385-29314-3**

[37 short chapters, 140p.] Torn between love and resentment, Peter recounts his escalating battles to reclaim his bedroom from his grandfather. Written by Peter for a fifth-grade English assignment. What a good idea! FAMILY LIFE. GRANDFATHERS.

1116 **Sobol, Donald J.** *Encyclopedia Brown, Boy Detective.* **Illus. by Leonard Shortall. Nelson, 1963. ISBN 0-525-67200-1**

[10 chapters, 83p.] America's "Sherlock Holmes in sneakers" solves his first 10 mysteries. Try any in the extensive series; all are guaranteed to test your powers of deductive reasoning, and the solutions are in the back of the book. After your detectives hear the first few stories, have them attempt to solve the other mysteries —noting clues and discussing them—before you read the solutions aloud. For science-based mysteries in a similar vein, try Seymour Simon's "Einstein Anderson" series. MYSTERY AND DETECTIVE STORIES.

1117 **Stanley, Diane.** *Fortune.* **Illus. by the author. Morrow, 1989. ISBN 0-688-07211-9**

[1–2 sittings, 32p.] Searching for a way to earn his fortune, farmer's son Omar finds it in the form of a tame tiger that leads him first to a princess, and then back to his betrothed, the good-natured Sunny. The notion that the fulfillment of our fondest dreams can be found at home or within ourselves is also explored in Uri Shulevitz's tantalizing *The Treasure*. LITERARY FAIRY TALES. PRINCES AND PRINCESSES. TIGERS. TRANSFORMATIONS.

1118   **Steig, William.** *Caleb and Kate.* **Illus. by the author. Farrar, 1977. ISBN 0-374-31016-5**

[1 sitting, unp.] Unbeknownst to his wife, with whom he has just had a terrible quarrel, a carpenter is turned into a dog by a mischief-making witch, rendering him unrecognizable to his beloved spouse. Steig's sophisticated picture books of unusual transformations and anguished separations are often best appreciated by older children. See also *The Amazing Bone, Dr. DeSoto,* and *Solomon the Rusty Nail.* DOGS. ROBBERS AND OUTLAWS. WITCHES.

1119   **Sterman, Betsy, and Samuel Sterman.** *Too Much Magic.* **Illus. by Judy Glasser. Lippincott, 1987. ISBN 0-317-57066-8**

[11 chapters, 154p.] When everything younger brother Jeff wishes for comes to him, from a hot dog to a motorbike, he shares his marvelous secret find—a shiny metal "wishing cube"—with his older brother, narrator Bill. Also don't miss Hazel Hutchins's *The Three and Many Wishes of Jason Reid* and Willo Davis Roberts's *The Magic Book.* BROTHERS. MAGIC. SCIENCE FICTION. WISHES.

1120   **Stolz, Mary.** *The Bully of Barkham Street.* **Illus. by Leonard Shortall. Harper & Row, 1963. ISBN 0-06-025821-7**

[8 chapters, 194p.] The psychology behind bully Martin Hastings—overweight, always in trouble, yet a decent kid inside—allows us to understand his boorish ways and empathize with his problems. Your students may want to read *A Dog on Barkham Street* (1960) for the same story, but from the bully's victim's point of view. BULLIES. DOGS.

1121   **Stolz, Mary.** *Cat Walk.* **Illus. by Eric Blegvad. Harper & Row, 1983. ISBN 0-06-025975-2**

[16 chapters, 120p.] A six-toed barn cat who yearns for a human-given name and a real home ends up with both. Move from a believable fantasy about cats to a realistic depiction of a stray dog with Meindert DeJong's *Hurry Home, Candy.* ANIMALS. CATS. FANTASY.

1122   **Storr, Catherine.** *Clever Polly and the Stupid Wolf.* **Illus. by Marjorie-Ann Watts. Faber, 1979.**

[13 chapters, 95p.] Polly continues to outwit the fairy tale-influenced wolf who tries time after time to make her his supper. Students can write new Polly versus Wolf stories using folktales for inspiration. CREATIVE WRITING. FAIRY TALES–SATIRE. FANTASY. WOLVES.

1123   **Tripp, Wallace.** *My Uncle Podger.* **Illus. by the author. Little, Brown, 1975.**

[1 sitting, unp.] The narrator's self-important rabbit uncle attempts to hang a simple picture on the wall and upsets the whole household in the interim. Based on a passage from Jerome K. Jerome's satire of three pompous young English twits in *Three Men in a Boat.* Using judicious editing, narrate the action and have your students enact Uncle Podger's bumbling attempts. Next, each person can write an account of an eccentric or memorable relative. CREATIVE DRAMA. CREATIVE WRITING. HUMOROUS FICTION. UNCLES.

1124   Van Allsburg, Chris. *The Stranger*. Illus. by the author. Houghton Mifflin, 1986. ISBN 0-395-42331-7

[1 sitting, unp.] There is a connection between the silent stranger Farmer Bailey and his family take in for two weeks and the lateness of fall on the farm. Ask your students to be alert to clues in the story as to the stranger's identity. While you can certainly read this to younger children, they often miss the "Jack Frost"-like analogy until you talk it over. AUTUMN. FARM LIFE. PICTURE BOOKS FOR ALL AGES. SEASONS.

1125   Van Allsburg, Chris. *Two Bad Ants*. Illus. by the author. Houghton Mifflin, 1988. ISBN 0-395-48668-8

[One sitting, unp.] After a dangerous journey to gather crystals for the ant queen, two ants choose to stay behind, but find their new surroundings life threatening. Shown and described from an ant's perspective, so students will need to translate each danger into human terms, from the sugar cube crystals the ants gather to the coffee, toaster, garbage disposal, and electric socket which almost prove their undoing. Students can describe and illustrate other human/household perils from an insect's point of view, and then read them aloud for everyone else to identify. ANTS. CREATIVE WRITING. INSECTS.

1126   Van Allsburg, Chris. *The Wreck of the Zephyr*. Illus. by the author. Houghton Mifflin, 1983. ISBN 0-395-33075-0

[1 sitting, unp.] The narrator meets an old sailor who tells him an improbable tale about an airborne sailboat and how it came to be wrecked nearby. Read a medley of Van Allsburg's unusual and haunting tales, including *Jumanji*, *The Polar Express*, and *The Mysteries of Harris Burdick*, as well as those above. BOATS AND BOATING. SAILING. STORYTELLING.

1127   Van de Wetering, Janwillem. *Hugh Pine*. Illus. by Lynn Munsinger. Houghton Mifflin, 1980. ISBN 0-395-29459-2

[11 chapters, 83p.] A one-of-a-kind intelligent Maine porcupine who has taught himself to walk and talk must save his fellow porcupines from the cars that are killing them in increasing numbers. Go from rural to urban with Jean Van Leeuwen's crafty mice in *The Great Cheese Conspiracy* (Dell, 1976) and *The Great Christmas Kidnapping Caper*. FANTASY. MAINE. PORCUPINES.

1128   Van Leeuwen, Jean. *The Great Christmas Kidnapping Caper*. Illus. by Steven Kellogg. Dial, 1975. ISBN 0-8037-5415-9

[14 chapters, 133p.] After the Macy's department store Santa disappears, three daring street-smart New York City mice, now living in the toy department's dollhouse, come to the rescue. Sequel to *The Great Cheese Conspiracy* (Dell, 1976) where they plot a cheese store heist and encounter a ferocious cat and to *The Great Rescue Operation*, all of which can be read independently, this might be your students' first exposure to hard-boiled, present-tense narration. FANTASY. MICE. MYSTERY AND DETECTIVE STORIES. SANTA CLAUS.

1129   Wagner, Jane. *J. T.* Illus. by Gordon Parks. Dell, 1972. ISBN 0-440-44275-3

[3 sittings, 124p.] A lonely city boy, escaping the violence and toughness of the streets for a short while, adopts a mangy stray cat and nurses it back to health.

Illustrated with stills from the original television movie. (Have tissues handy.) AFRICAN AMERICANS. CATS. CITIES AND TOWNS.

1130   **Wetterer, Margaret. *The Giant's Apprentice*. Illus. by Elise Primavera. Atheneum, 1982.**

[1–2 sittings, unp.] Apprenticed to his storytelling blacksmith uncle, nine-year-old Liam McGowen is kidnapped by a giant on Halloween night and held for seven years before his uncle finds him. This dramatic tale is good to read on St. Patrick's Day as well, along with a dash of other Irish yarns like Virginia Haviland's *Favorite Fairy Tales Told in Ireland* and Tomie dePaola's *Fin M'Coul, the Giant of Knockmany Hill*. FANTASY. GIANTS. HALLOWEEN. IRELAND. UNCLES.

1131   **White, E. B. *Stuart Little*. Illus. by Garth Williams. Harper & Row, 1945. ISBN 0-06-026396-2**

[15 chapters, 131p.] In spite of his diminutive size, a mouse born to a human family thrives in New York City until his beloved bird friend, Margalo, leaves home and he is compelled to follow. Compare the ways Stuart copes in a giant-sized world with the quandary in which Ripple finds herself in *Moth-Kin Magic* by Kathy Kennedy Tapp. BIRDS. FANTASY. MICE. NEW YORK CITY. SIZE.

1132   **Wilder, Laura Ingalls. *Farmer Boy*. Illus. by Garth Williams. Harper & Row, 1953. ISBN 0-06-026421-7**

[29 chapters, 372p.] About the ninth year in the New York farm childhood of Laura Ingalls Wilder's husband, Almonzo, this gives an engrossing, detailed picture of farm life and schools in the 1870s. Traveling to the midwest, other slices of life back then are Susan Kirby's *Ike and Porker* and Patricia MacLachlan's *Sarah, Plain and Tall*. Russell Freedman's photo-filled *Children of the Wild West* includes a fascinating chapter on school back then that duplicates Almonzo's experiences in his one-room schoolhouse, rowdies and all. FARM LIFE. HISTORICAL FICTION. U.S.–HISTORY–1865–1898–FICTION.

1133   **Wilson, Gahan. *Harry the Fat Bear Spy*. Illus. by the author. Scribner, 1973.**

[14 chapters, 109p.] Agent Three Five Zero small case b, otherwise known as Harry, is instructed to infiltrate Bearmania's National Macaroon Factory to discover who is causing their famous confections to come out green. Bake up a batch, with or without green food coloring, for sharing. BEARS. FOOD. HUMOROUS FICTION. MYSTERY AND DETECTIVE STORIES. SPIES.

1134   **Winter, Jeanette. *Follow the Drinking Gourd*. Illus. by the author. Knopf, 1989. ISBN 0-394-99694-1**

[One sitting, unp.] Incorporating the title song that instructed slaves on how to escape on the Underground Railroad, this is a breathtakingly suspenseful tale of five slaves who cross into Canada and freedom. Music is appended. An unusual tie-in would be Paul Goble's *Her Seven Brothers*, of how the North Star and the Big Dipper came to be. Studies for Black History Month will also be enhanced by this and Stacy Chbosky's perceptive *Who Owns the Sun* and Ann McGovern's *Runaway Slave: The Story of Harriet Tubman*. AFRICAN AMERICANS. HISTORICAL FICTION. SLAVERY. STORIES WITH SONGS. U.S.–HISTORY–1783–1865.

1135 **Wolkoff, Judie.** *Wally.* **Bradbury, 1977.**

[19 chapters, 199p.] Contrary to explicit instructions from his mother, Michael agrees to reptile-sit his friend's pet chuckwalla for two weeks, during which he and his younger brother successfully hide the large fellow in the closet—until it escapes. For more slapstick and hidden reptiles, see also *Harvey's Horrible Snake Disaster* by Eth Clifford. BROTHERS AND SISTERS. HUMOROUS FICTION. MOVING, HOUSEHOLD. PETS. REPTILES.

1136 **Zhitkov, Boris.** *How I Hunted the Little Fellows.* **Illus. by Paul O. Zelinsky. Putnam, 1979. ISBN 0-396-07692-0**

[1 sitting, unp.] Based on the author's own experiences, the nineteenth-century Russian boy's imagination gets the better of him when he pries apart his grandmother's model steamship, convinced there are tiny people hidden inside. Note the good dramatic scenes for narrative pantomime, encompassing the character's emotional development. Students can then tell or write the worst things *they* ever did and what happened to them. Since Zhitkov ended the story before it was fully resolved, ask your frustrated and anguished listeners what they think happened to him. GRANDMOTHERS. HISTORICAL FICTION. IMAGINATION. SHIPS.

Illustration from THE WHIPPING BOY by Sid Fleischman. Illustration © 1986 by
Peter Sis. By permission of Greenwillow Books, William Morrow & Co.

FICTION FOR GRADES 4–5

1137   **Adler, David A.** *Eaton Stanley & the Mind Control Experiment.*   **Illus. by Joan Drescher. Dutton, 1985. ISBN 0-525-44117-4**

[15 chapters, 88p.] The scientific attempts of Brian's brainy new friend and classmate to influence the actions of their sixth-grade teacher seem to work. Eaton's idea of making history birthday cards is a clever kickoff for a reference unit. Read when the yearly science fair is looming. SCHOOLS. SCIENCE–EXPERIMENTS. TEACHERS.

1138   **Ainsworth, Ruth.** *The Phantom Carousel and Other Ghostly Tales.* **Illus. by Shirley Hughes. Follett, 1977.**

[11 chapters, 176p.] More puzzling and thought-provoking than scary, here are 11 intriguing short stories of children who meet up with spirits of the past. The title story is a real knockout. Compare these literary ghost tales with folklore like *A Book of Ghosts and Goblins* by Ruth Manning-Sanders or *Ghosts and Goblins* by Whilhelmina Harper. GHOST STORIES. MAGIC. SHORT STORIES.

1139   **Babbitt, Natalie.** *The Search for Delicious.* **Illus. by the author. Farrar, 1985. ISBN 0-374-46536-3**

[13 short chapters, 159p.] With the kingdom in violent disagreement over which food best fits the new dictionary's definition of "delicious," Gaylen, the prime minister's 12-year-old adopted son, is sent to poll every subject. Write your own classroom dictionary of food choices and organize a school poll or census just for the experience. DICTIONARIES. FANTASY. FOOD. KINGS AND RULERS. VOCABULARY.

1140   **Baldwin, Ann Norris.** *A Little Time.* **Viking, 1978.**

[11 chapters, 119p.] Matt, Ginny's Down's syndrome-afflicted little brother, causes her to swing between emotions of resentment and love when her new friend is repelled by him. Sheila Garrigue's *Between Friends* deals with the same basic conflict of embarrassment and loyalty. FAMILY PROBLEMS. HANDICAPS.

1141   **Banks, Lynne Reid.** *The Fairy Rebel.* **Illus. by William Geldart. Doubleday, 1988. ISBN 0-385-24483-5**

[8 chapters, 125p.] Jan, a former famous actress made lame by a stage accident, befriends a tiny nonconformist fairy, Tiki, who uses forbidden magic to help her fulfill her wish for a baby girl. Talk over what makes Tiki different from the other

fairies and whether or not being different from your peers is a bad thing. FAIRIES.
FANTASY.

1142 **Beatty, Jerome.** *Matthew Looney's Invasion of the Earth.* **Illus. by Gahan Wilson. Harper
& Row, 1965. ISBN 0-201-09273-5**

[15 chapters, 157p.] An adventure-prone Moon boy joins an earthbound expedition
searching for intelligent life in one of a series about the Looney family that will
spice up your space studies curriculum. Recommend as read alones the "Maria
Looney" books about Matthew's younger sister. EARTH. MOON. SCIENCE FICTION.
SPACE FLIGHT.

1143 **Bellairs, John.** *The House with a Clock in Its Walls.* **Illus. by Edward Gorey. Dial, 1973.
ISBN 0-8037-3823-4**

[11 chapters, 179p.] After orphaned Lewis moves into magician Uncle Jonathan's
mansion, they investigate the constant and insidious ticking within the walls
caused by evil wizard Isaac Izard. If the class insists, follow up with the 1975 sequel,
The Figure in the Shadows. For science or for fun, bring in an old nonfunctioning
alarm clock and take it apart with your group. CLOCKS. FANTASY. SUSPENSE. UN-
CLES.

1144 **Birdseye, Tom.** *I'm Going to Be Famous.* **Holiday House, 1986. ISBN 0-8234-0630-X**

[26 chapters, 160p.] Eating 17 bananas in under 2 minutes is all it will take for fifth-
grader Arlo to break into the Guinness Book of World Records. Logical follow-ups
include a wild unit on reference skills; a banana eating, watermelon seed spitting
contest; and a class record-breaking stint of your students' choosing. For another
Guinness striver, read Janet Taylor Lisle's *The Dancing Cats of Applesap* or Phyllis
Reynolds Naylor's *The Bodies in the Besseldorf Hotel.* HUMOROUS FICTION.

1145 **Blume, Judy.** *Superfudge.* **Dutton, 1980. ISBN 0-525-40522-4**

[12 chapters, 166p.] A new baby named Tootsie adds to the mayhem when the
Hatcher family moves from New York City to Princeton, New Jersey, in this
hilarious sequel to *Tales of a Fourth Grade Nothing.* BROTHERS AND SISTERS. FAMILY
LIFE. HUMOROUS FICTION.

1146 **Bond, Michael.** *A Bear Called Paddington.* **Illus. by Peggy Fortnum. Houghton Mifflin,
1960. ISBN 0-395-06636-0**

[8 chapters, 128p.] First in a long series about that well-meaning but trouble-causing
English bear from darkest Peru. Filled with Briticisms, which you can compare to
U.S. lingo, and straight-faced slapstick. Many of his antics make marvelous narra-
tive pantomimes, such as his first bath experience. BEARS. CREATIVE DRAMA. ENG-
LAND. HUMOROUS FICTION.

1147 **Bond, Michael.** *Paddington's Storybook.* **Illus. by Peggy Fortnum. Houghton Mifflin,
1984. ISBN 0-395-36667-4**

[10 chapters, 160p.] A sampling of 10 of the most memorable Paddington Bear stories
culled from 8 of the books in the series published over the last 30 years. Uncap the
orange marmalade and unwrap the biscuits for your Elevenses. BEARS. ENGLAND.
FANTASY. HUMOROUS FICTION.

1148 **Brady, Esther Wood.** *Toliver's Secret.* **Illus. by Richard Cuffari. Crown, 1976.**

[13 chapters, 166p.] Disguised as a boy, timid Toliver must cross through Redcoat territory to deliver to General Washington a message that has been hidden in a loaf of bread. Another female heroine, one who actually saved the General's life, is Phoebe Fraunces in Judith Berry Griffin's true account, *Phoebe and the General.* COURAGE. HISTORICAL FICTION. U.S.–HISTORY–REVOLUTION–FICTION.

1149 **Brenner, Barbara.** *A Year in the Life of Rosie Bernard.* **Illus. by Joan Sandin. Harper & Row, 1971.**

[14 chapters, 179p.] Ten-year-old Rosie, daughter of a traveling actor, spends 1932 with her cousins and grandparents in Brooklyn, living through "hard times" with her usual aplomb. For a rural view of life then, read Robert Burch's *Ida Early Comes Over the Mountain.* FAMILY LIFE. HISTORICAL FICTION. U.S.–HISTORY–20TH CENTURY –FICTION.

1150 **Brink, Carol Ryrie.** *The Bad Times of Irma Baumline.* **Illus. by Trina Schart Hyman. Macmillan, 1972. ISBN 0-02-714220-5**

[15 chapters, 134p.] When Irma tells a classmate that she owns the largest doll in the world, her lie backfires, leading to more deception and even to stealing. Lizzie is also trapped by a lie even she cannot overcome in *Lizzie Lies a Lot* by Elizabeth Levy. DOLLS. HONESTY.

1151 **Brink, Carol Ryrie.** *Caddie Woodlawn.* **Illus. by Kate Seredy. Macmillan, 1973. ISBN 0-02-713670-1**

[24 chapters, 270p.] Published originally in 1935 and based on true stories of the author's grandmother who, in 1864, was a 12-year-old tomboy in a Wisconsin frontier family. Look into descriptions of U.S. life in other regions from the same approximate time period, such as California in Sid Fleischman's Gold Rush tale *By the Great Horn Spoon,* the Maine wilderness in Elizabeth George Speare's *The Sign of the Beaver,* and New York state in Laura Ingalls Wilder's *Farmer Boy.* FRONTIER AND PIONEER LIFE. HISTORICAL FICTION. INDIANS OF NORTH AMERICA . NEWBERY MEDAL. U.S.–HISTORY–1783–1865–FICTION.

1152 **Brittain, Bill.** *All the Money in the World.* **Illus. by Charles Robinson. Harper & Row, 1979. ISBN 0-06-020676-4**

[12 chapters, 150p.] After Quentin helps leprechaun Flan out of a well, he is granted three wishes that make him alarmingly, uselessly rich. Ask your class to decide what their wishes would have been and how they might have backfired. In the leprechaun lexicon, also read Joan Lowery Nixon's *The Gift.* For more wishes and cash read Hazel Hutchins's *The Three and Many Wishes of Jason Reid,* Sonia Levitin's *Jason and the Money Tree,* and Marianna Mayer's expanded folktale *Aladdin and the Enchanted Lamp.* AFRICAN AMERICANS. LEPRECHAUNS. MAGIC. MONEY. WISHES.

1153 **Burch, Robert.** *Ida Early Comes Over the Mountain.* **Viking, 1980. ISBN 0-670-39169-7**

[18 chapters, 145p.] Ida, a young, six-foot-tall, overall-clad housekeeper, cares for the four motherless Sutton children in rural Georgia during the Depression. An exuberant character, she is an excellent subject for a portrait, both drawn and described in prose, by your listeners. Discussion point: Would you be embarrassed or proud of Ida as your baby-sitter? BROTHERS AND SISTERS. COUNTRY LIFE. FAMILY LIFE. HISTORICAL FICTION. U.S.–HISTORY–20TH CENTURY–FICTION.

1154   Butterworth, Oliver. *The Enormous Egg*. Illus. by Louis Darling. Little, Brown, 1956. ISBN 0-316-11904-0

[17 chapters, 188p.] An ordinary chicken hatches a Freedom, New Hampshire, dinosaur egg, giving farmboy Nate his own pet triceratops until the media gets in on the act. In *Weird Henry Berg* by Sarah Sargeant, another odd egg hatches, this one belonging to a large dragon. DINOSAURS. EGGS. FARM LIFE. HUMOROUS FICTION. SCIENTISTS.

1155   Byars, Betsy. *The 18th Emergency*. Illus. by Robert Grossman. Viking, 1973. ISBN 0-670-29055-6

[10 chapters, 124p.] Prepared for every unlikely catastrophe except this one, a weakling known as "Mouse" awaits a beating from Marv Hammerman, the school's biggest bully. An examination of bullying behavior and ways to confront it would make for a useful class discussion, with examples culled from life and books including *The Revenge of the Incredible Dr. Rancid and His Youthful Assistant, Jeffrey* by Ellen Conford, *The Monster's Ring* by Bruce Coville, *Veronica Ganz* by Marilyn Sachs, and *The Bully of Barkham Street* by Mary Stolz. BULLIES. HUMOROUS FICTION. SCHOOLS.

1156   Byars, Betsy. *The Not-Just-Anybody Family*. Illus. by Jacqueline Rogers. Delacorte, 1986. ISBN 0-385-29443-3

[34 short chapters, 149p.] With their mother away working the rodeo, Vern and Maggie must figure out a plan of action when Pop, their grandfather, is arrested for disturbing the peace and Junior, their younger brother, lands in the hospital with two broken legs. First in the outstanding Blossom family quartet, which also includes *The Blossoms Meet the Vulture Lady* (1986), *The Blossoms and the Green Phantom* (1987), and *A Blossom Promise* (1987). Note how Byars shifts the characters' points of view in each short chapter and juggles four distinct but interrelated story lines simultaneously in this masterwork. BROTHERS AND SISTERS. DOGS. FAMILY PROBLEMS. GRANDFATHERS.

1157   Chase, Mary. *Loretta Mason Potts*. Illus. by Harold Berson. Peter Smith, 1958. ISBN 0-8446-6428-6

[15 chapters, 221p.] After Colin's mysterious, rotten older sister comes home for the first time in 10 years, he sets out to find the fantastic secret of the hill that holds such a powerful influence over her. From the worst-behaved child in the world move to the best: canned-kid *Konrad* by Christine Nöstlinger. BEHAVIOR. BROTHERS AND SISTERS. FANTASY. SIZE.

1158   Chbosky, Stacey. *Who Owns the Sun?* Illus. by the author. Landmark Editions, 1988. ISBN 0-933849-14-1

[1 sitting, 26p.] Learning from his revered father that no one can own the sun, stars, rain, wind, birds, or flowers, the young narrator is stunned to realize they are both "owned" as slaves. Winner of the 1987 National Written & Illustrated By . . . Awards Contest, the 15-year-old author packs an unexpected emotional wallop that should spark much debate during Black History Month along with Jeanette Winter's Underground Railroad tale *Follow the Drinking Gourd*. AFRICAN AMERICANS. FATHERS AND SONS. SLAVERY.

1159   Cohen, Barbara. *Thank You, Jackie Robinson*. Illus. by Richard Cuffari. Lothrop, 1988. ISBN 0-688-07909-1

[6 sittings, 125p.] Sam Greene, a 10-year-old New Jersey baseball nut, becomes best friends with Davy, a 60-year-old black cook who shares his passion for the old time Brooklyn Dodgers. Get the class involved in baseball research as you read, and follow the World Series. Check out the World Almanac for statistics. Since most children no longer know about Jackie Robinson, an investigation of his life and record-breaking career would be a good idea. Indulge their passion with William Jaspersohn's fascinating photo essay *The Ballpark: One Day Behind the Scenes at a Major League Game*. AFRICAN AMERICANS. BASEBALL. FRIENDSHIP.

1160   Collodi, Carlo. *The Adventures of Pinocchio*. Illus. by Roberto Innocenti. Knopf, 1988. ISBN 0-394-82110-6

[36 chapters, 142p.] Originally published in 1882, this brilliant Italian serial is a "Perils of Pauline" for backsliding children and puppets. New listeners will worship an adventure where the hero is imprisoned, hung, cheated, made to be a watchdog, almost fried as a fish, turned into a donkey, and swallowed by a shark *before* he can accept that work, study, truthfulness, and kindness are the way to go. If you've only seen the Disney version, you're in for a delicious surprise. ADVENTURE AND ADVENTURERS. BEHAVIOR. FANTASY. FATHERS AND SONS.

1161   Conford, Ellen. *Me and the Terrible Two*. Illus. by Charles Carrol. Little, Brown, 1974. ISBN 0-316-15303-6

[11 chapters, 117p.] When Dorrie's best friend moves away to Australia, she is saddled with obnoxious identical twin boys as new neighbors. Hearing about Dorrie's class project—the four-page newspaper with headlines, articles, and even classified ads from children's books—your readers should be fired up to do the same, using Newsroom on your Apple Computer for the layout. Claudia Mills's *After Fifth Grade, the World!* also incorporates a class newspaper and has a mean teacher to boot. FRIENDSHIP. SCHOOLS. TWINS.

1162   Conford, Ellen. *Revenge of the Incredible Dr. Rancid and His Youthful Assistant, Jeffrey*. Little, Brown, 1980. ISBN 0-316-15288-9

[9 chapters, 119p.] Thanks to his secret notebook, the skinniest boy in the sixth grade becomes a bully-liquidating hero in his own imagination every time Dewey Belasco won't leave him alone. Use in September when you're just starting the year's journal writing. Louise Fitzhugh's *Harriet the Spy* also deals with her frustrations by recording every thought and observation in a secret notebook. BULLIES. SCHOOLS. SELF-CONCEPT. WRITING.

1163   Corbett, Scott. *The Donkey Planet*. Illus. by Troy Howell. Dutton, 1979. ISBN 0-525-28825-2

[16 chapters, 89p.] Two Earth scientists are transformed into a boy and a donkey when they are sent, by speed of thought, to the planet Vanaris on a dangerous mission to trade aluminum bars for guundar, a heavy metal. Children can describe other aspects of life on the planet, giving thought to food, housing, customs, and other amenities not already detailed by the author. Compare the setting with the planet Shine in Jill Paton Walsh's *The Green Book*. DONKEYS. SCIENCE FICTION. SPACE FLIGHT. TRANSFORMATIONS.

1164   Corbett, Scott. *The Red Room Riddle*. Illus. by Geff Gerlach. Little, Brown, 1972. ISBN 0-316-15719-8

[12 chapters, 104p.] While seeking out a haunted house one memorable but terrifying Halloween night in the 1920s, Bruce and Bill meet Jamie Bly, a boy who claims to live with ghosts. With each side citing supporting evidence, debate whether the boys' experience was real or an illusion. GHOST STORIES. HALLOWEEN.

1165   Coville, Bruce. *The Monster's Ring*. Illus. by Katherine Coville. Pantheon, 1982. ISBN 0-394-95320-7

[13 chapters, 87p.] Russell obtains and uses a magic ring that turns him into a monster and scares the meanness out of bully Eddy Tacker. Students can act out his horrifying transformations in narrative pantomime. Another bully is thwarted by magic in *The Magic Book* by Willo Davis Roberts. Scare up some supporting monster data with Lee Bennett Hopkins's poetry collection *Creatures*, Ruth Manning-Sanders's folktales *A Book of Monsters* (Dutton, 1975), and Joseph Rosenbloom's *Monster Madness: Riddles, Jokes, Fun*. BULLIES. HALLOWEEN. MONSTERS. SCHOOLS.

1166   Dahl, Roald. *The BFG*. Illus. by Quentin Blake. Farrar, 1982. ISBN 0-374-30469-6

[24 chapters, 221p.] Befriended by the big friendly giant who has kidnapped her, young orphan Sophie enlists his help in preventing nine repulsive, human-guzzling giants from eating innocent children. The BFG is a language mangler of the highest order, making each of his speeches an event to be savored. Your linguists should make up new gobblefunk to translate and write original definitions to go along. ENGLISH LANGUAGE. FANTASY. GIANTS. ORPHANS.

1167   Dahl, Roald. *The Witches*. Illus. by Quentin Blake. Farrar, 1983. ISBN 0-374-38458-4

[22 chapters, 202p.] According to the young male narrator's Norwegian grandmamma, real witches wear gloves to hide their curvy claws, use wigs to hide their bald scalps, have pink, curvy nose holes for smelling out the stench of clean children, and have blue spit. Satisfyingly chilling, eccentric, outrageous, and *not to be missed*! Since the book ends ambiguously, ask the crew to write their own endings, or at least a postscript describing what might have become of the boy turned mouse. FANTASY. GRANDMOTHERS. MICE. TRANSFORMATIONS. WITCHES.

1168   DeJong, Meindert. *The Wheel on the School*. Illus. by Maurice Sendak. Harper & Row, 1954. ISBN 0-06-021586-0

[15 chapters, 298p.] Lina, her five friends, and their teacher make a plan to lure the storks back to their Dutch fishing village of Shora. So everyone has a clear image of the beauty and wonder of storks, also read Margaret Wise Brown's Caldecott Medal picture book published the same year, *Wheel on the Chimney*. BIRDS. NETHERLANDS. NEWBERY MEDAL. SCHOOLS.

1169   Drury, Roger W. *The Champion of Merrimack County*. Illus. by Fritz Wegner. Little, Brown, 1976. ISBN 0-316-19349-6

[25 chapters, 199p.] Mouse bicyclist O'Crispin hurts his tail and his bicycle when he shows off while riding around Mr. Berryfield's antique bathtub. Introduce other vehicle-owning mice, such as Ralph in Beverly Cleary's *The Mouse and the Motorcycle* and sequels and E. B. White's *Stuart Little* who skippers a boat in Central Park. BICYCLES. HUMOROUS FICTION. MICE.

1170   **Drury, Roger W.** *The Finches' Fabulous Furnace.* **Illus. by Eric Blegvad. Little, Brown, 1971. ISBN 0-316-19348-8**

[20 chapters, 149p.] There's a volcano in their cellar, and it's growing! Use with William Pène du Bois's *The Twenty-One Balloons,* a wildly fictitious account of Krakatoa's eruption, Patricia Lauber's *Volcano: The Eruption and Healing of Mount St. Helens,* and Seymour Simon's *Volcanoes* for a science unit with zip. VOLCANOES.

1171   **Fitzgerald, John D.** *The Great Brain.* **Illus. by Mercer Mayer. Dial, 1967. ISBN 0-8037-3076-4**

[8 chapters, 175p.] Uproarious autobiographical tales of growing up Catholic in Mormon turn-of-the-century Utah by the brother of a money-hungry, conniving young genius. First in a series of seven "Great Brain" books. AUTOBIOGRAPHY. BROTHERS. FAMILY LIFE. HISTORICAL FICTION. U.S.–HISTORY–20TH CENTURY–FICTION.

1172   **Fleischman, Sid.** *The Whipping Boy.* **Illus. by Peter Sís. Greenwillow, 1986. ISBN 0-688-06216-4**

[20 chapters, 90p.] When Prince Brat runs away, his maltreated whipping boy, Jimmy-of-the-streets, is obliged to go along right into the hands of highwaymen Cutwater and Hold-Your-Nose Billy, who hold them for ransom. Contrast the prince with the untypical princess in *A Hidden Magic* by Vivian Vande Velde. ADVENTURE AND ADVENTURERS. PRINCES AND PRINCESSES. ROBBERS AND OUTLAWS.

1173   **Fleming, Susan.** *Trapped on the Golden Flyer.* **Illus. by Alex Stein. Westminster, 1978.**

[16 chapters, 123p.] On his way to stay with his California aunt and uncle after his mother's death, Paul and 200 other passengers spend days on the train when it becomes marooned in a Sierra Nevada blizzard. *True Escape and Survival Stories* by Gurney Williams allows your listeners to feel even less safe and sound as they talk over how to react in an emergency. SNOW. STORMS. SURVIVAL. TRAINS. WINTER.

1174   **Garfield, James B.** *Follow My Leader.* **Illus. by Robert Greiner. Viking, 1957. ISBN 0-670-32332-2**

[17 chapters, 191p.] After being blinded by a firecracker, 11-year-old Jimmy slowly adjusts to his handicap with the help of a German shepherd guide dog. *Child of the Silent Night* by Edith Fisher Hunter is the biography of blind, deaf-mute Laura Bridgman who, in the nineteenth century, became the first child so handicapped to be successfully educated. BLIND. DOGS. HANDICAPS.

1175   **Garrigue, Sheila.** *Between Friends.* **Bradbury, 1978. ISBN 0-02-736620-0**

[17 chapters, 160p.] Jill's loyalty is tested by her new friendship with Dede, a retarded girl with Down's syndrome. Also see Ann Norris Baldwin's *A Little Time.* BROTHERS AND SISTERS. FRIENDSHIP. HANDICAPS. MOVING, HOUSEHOLD.

1176   **George, Jean Craighead.** *My Side of the Mountain.* **Illus. by the author. Dutton, 1967. ISBN 0-525-35530-8**

[22 chapters, 166p.] Sam learns to survive by his wits when he camps out alone in his self-built Catskill mountain tree house and lives off the land for 12 months. In *The Sign of the Beaver* by Elizabeth Speare, 12-year-old Matt also stays alone in his family's cabin for several months in the Maine wilderness. Contrast the survival skills of modern-day Sam and eighteenth-century Matt. MOUNTAINS. SURVIVAL.

1177 Giff, Patricia Reilly. *The Winter Worm Business.* Illus. by Leslie Morrill. Delacorte, 1981. ISBN 0-385-29154-X

[15 chapters, 132p.] Leroy's most unfavorite whiz kid, cousin Mitchell, moves to town and horns in on his friendship with Tracy Matson, with whom he digs worms to sell for fishing bait. Speaking of worms, why not continue the theme with Thomas Rockwell's delectable *How to Eat Fried Worms.* COUSINS. FRIENDSHIP. WINTER. WORMS.

1178 Gilson, Jamie. *Dial Leroi Rupert, D.J.* Illus. by John Wallner. Lothrop, 1979. ISBN 0-688-41888-0

[9 chapters, 126p.] Three boys who need to earn $30 fast, before their parents find out how they broke Dr. Scharff's window and flowerpot, turn to a popular radio D.J. for help. Set up a radio talk show interview where each character, as played by your students, can discuss his or her part in the story. HUMOROUS FICTION. MONEY.

1179 Gilson, Jamie. *Harvey the Beer Can King.* Illus. by John Wallner. Lothrop, 1978.

[12 chapters, 127p.] Hoping to win the town's Superkid Contest with his beer can collection, Harvey suffers a setback when his father orders him to get rid of the cans by Sunday. Organize your own class Superkid Contest. CONTESTS. HUMOROUS FICTION.

1180 Gipson, Fred. *Old Yeller.* Illus. by Carl Burger. Harper & Row, 1956. ISBN 0-06-011546-7

[16 chapters, 158p.] A classic 1860s Texas tale narrated by Travis, who looks back to his fourteenth year when the mangy, big, yellow, ugly stray dog came to stay. After weeping over the ending, go for a more cheerful slant with a bit of a mongrel fantasy like James Howe's *Bunnicula* or George Selden's *Harry Cat's Pet Puppy.* DOGS. FRONTIER AND PIONEER LIFE. WEST.

1181 Gormley, Beatrice. *Fifth-Grade Magic.* Illus. by Emily Arnold McCully. Dutton, 1982. ISBN 0-525-44007-0

[13 chapters, 131p.] When her rival gets the lead in the fifth-grade play, Gretchen turns to her bumbling young fairy godmother, Agent Errora, who tries to rectify the situation with her magic Enchantulator. For children who have never seen a melodrama, dig up a good one from *Plays* magazine and have a class reading. FAIRIES. FANTASY. PLAYS. SCHOOLS.

1182 Gormley, Beatrice. *Mail-Order Wings.* Illus. by Emily Arnold McCully. Dutton, 1981. ISBN 0-525-34450-0

[12 chapters, 164p.] From a Chilling Tales comic, Andrea buys wings that, once assembled properly, really work. After reading this, a flying contest will be in order, not to mention a bit of bird research. Diane Wolkstein's lovely Chinese folktale *The Magic Wings* gives us another young girl whose dream is fulfilled. BIRDS. FANTASY. FLIGHT. WINGS.

1183 Greene, Bette. *Philip Hall Likes Me. I Reckon, Maybe.* Illus. by Charles Lilly. Dial, 1974. ISBN 0-8037-6096-5

[7 chapters, 135p.] Beth Lambert's first crush on the number-one student in class may be the reason she is number two in her rural Arkansas class. AFRICAN AMERICANS. FARM LIFE. FRIENDSHIP. MYSTERY AND DETECTIVE STORIES.

1184 Greenwald, Sheila. *The Atrocious Two*. Illus. by the author. Dell, 1989. ISBN 0-440-40141-0

[18 chapters, 153p.] An obnoxious brother and sister from New York City become reformed when they are sent to spend the summer in Connecticut with tough Aunt Tessie and find themselves embroiled in a mystery. Explore the dynamics of sibling relationships with *I'm Telling! Kids Talk about Brothers and Sisters*, edited by Eric H. Arnold and Jeffrey Loeb, and poll your class for true-life tales of mischief. AUNTS. BEHAVIOR. BROTHERS AND SISTERS. MYSTERY AND DETECTIVE STORIES.

1185 Haynes, Betsy. *The Ghost of the Gravestone Hearth*. Nelson, 1977.

[20 chapters, 128p.] Charlie meets up with the ghost of a real pirate who died at age 16 in 1712 and now needs help in locating a buried chest of gold. Judy Donnelly's *True-Life Treasure Hunts* should help establish the mood, as will Alvin Schwartz's *Gold and Silver, Silver and Gold: Tales of Hidden Treasure*. BROTHERS AND SISTERS. BURIED TREASURE. GHOSTS. PIRATES. SEASHORE.

1186 Herman, Charlotte. *Our Snowman Had Olive Eyes*. Dutton, 1977. ISBN 0-525-36490-0

[10 chapters, 103p.] The year Sheila's 79-year-old grandmother moves in, they share a bedroom and special closeness. Pete establishes a more combative relationship when his grandfather takes over his room in *The War with Grandpa* by Robert Kimmell Smith. GRANDMOTHERS.

1187 Hicks, Clifford B. *Alvin's Swap Shop*. Illus. by Bill Sokol. Holt, 1976.

[18 chapters, 143p.] The day after magnificent-brained Alvin Fernald swaps an ant for more valuable items, he opens a junk-filled Swap Shop and solves another mystery. Make available the rest of the adventure-prone "Alvin Fernald" books, as well as E. W. Hildick's plentiful and equally entertaining "McGurk" series, such as *The Case of the Condemned Cat* or *McGurk Gets Good and Mad*. BARTERING. MYSTERY AND DETECTIVE STORIES.

1188 Hicks, Clifford B. *Peter Potts*. Avon, 1989. ISBN 0-380-43273-0

[7 chapters, 105p.] About an accident-prone boy and his grand schemes, one per chapter, for pulling a loose tooth, winning the state Spelldown, and throwing a big wedding for sister Betts. Read the April Fools' Day chapter *after* April Fools' Day, if you know what's good for you! HUMOROUS FICTION. SCHOOLS.

1189 Hildick, E. W. *McGurk Gets Good and Mad*. Illus. by Lisl Weil. Macmillan, 1982.

[12 chapters, 136p.] Who is trying to sabotage the McGurk Organization's first annual Open House? Another delightful mystery in this ongoing series about neighborhood kids who can solve anything. MYSTERY AND DETECTIVE STORIES.

1190 Holland, Barbara. *Prisoners at the Kitchen Table*. Houghton Mifflin, 1979. ISBN 0-395-28969-6

[11 chapters, 121p.] Polly Conover and Josh Blake are kidnapped and held captive in a remote farmhouse by a man and woman who first pretend to be Polly's relatives. Also responsible for ensuring their own safety and escape are the boy from Richard Kennedy's *Inside My Feet*, when a giant kidnaps both his parents, and orphaned Emily of Barbara Brooks Wallace's *Peppermints in the Parlor*, who is kept as a scullery slave by the evil Mrs. Meeching. ADVENTURE AND ADVENTURERS. KIDNAPPING.

1191   Holman, Felice. *The Blackmail Machine.* Illus. by Victoria de Larrea. Macmillan, 1968.

[20 chapters, 182p.] Adding a propeller to a treehouse enables it to fly, giving four children a powerful chance to have the town authorities and other apathetic grown-ups pay attention to their demands. Set up a panel where your children's rights advocates can give voice to their own concerns. FLIGHT. SELF-CONCEPT.

1192   Howard, Ellen. *A Circle of Giving.* Atheneum, 1984. ISBN 0-689-31027-7

[18 chapters, 99p.] Two sisters in 1920 Los Angeles find their ordinary neighborhood anything but mundane after they befriend Francie, the cerebral palsied daughter of the glamorous Mrs. Hanisian. As this gives an unsentimental look at children's reactions to a handicapped child, build on the theme by researching handicaps and diseases, including such sobering books as Janet Kamien's *What If You Couldn't* (Macmillan, 1979) and Mary Beth Sullivan's *Feeling Free* (Harper & Row, 1979). FRIENDSHIP. HANDICAPS. MOVING, HOUSEHOLD. SISTERS.

1193   Howe, Deborah, and James Howe. *Bunnicula: A Rabbit-Tale of Mystery.* Illus. by Alan Daniel. Atheneum, 1979. ISBN 0-380-51094-4

[9 chapters, 98p.] Is the Monroe family's new pet really a vampire bunny? A wild tale of exorcism gone amok, as related by Harold, the family dog. First in a series of pun-filled adventures of hare-raising horrors, including *Howliday Inn* (1982), *The Celery Stalks at Midnight* (1983), and *Nighty-Nightmare* (1987). Also priceless are the seasonal picture books *Scared Silly* and *The Fright before Christmas.* CATS. DOGS. MYSTERY AND DETECTIVE STORIES. RABBITS.

1194   Howe, James. *Nighty-Nightmare.* Illus. by Leslie Morrill. Atheneum, 1987. ISBN 0-689-31207-5

[9 chapters, 122p.] Fourth in the pun-laden "Bunnicula" series. When dog narrator Harold, cat Chester, and dim dachshund Howie are lost in the midnight woods on evil spirit-filled St. George's Day, Chester tells a ghost story of how Bunnicula, the vampire rabbit, came to be. CAMPING. CATS. DOGS. HUMOROUS FICTION. MYSTERY AND DETECTIVE STORIES.

1195   James, Mary. *Shoebag.* Scholastic, 1990. ISBN 0-590-43029-7

[22 chapters, 135p.] In a black comedic twist on Franz Kafka's grim adult classic *Metamorphosis*, a contented young cockroach awakens one morning to find he has been transformed into a little boy, and is taken in by the apartment's human occupants, the Biddle family. Discussions on topics from school outcasts to the banality of television should abound after each off-beat chapter. To see life from an insect's perspective, read *James and the Giant Peach* by Roald Dahl; *Joyful Noise,* insect poems by Paul Fleischman; and *Two Bad Ants* by Chris Van Allsburg. FANTASY. INSECTS.

1196   Jones, Rebecca C. *Germy Blew It.* Dutton, 1987. ISBN 0-525-44294-4

[22 chapters, 105p.] Pretending to be sick, but actually on a one-day strike from school to protest the cancellation of all field trips, Jeremy is horrified to find he's missed his big chance to be on TV and plots another opportunity with a bubble gum blowing contest. If video equipment is accessible, set it up and produce a class news show where everyone takes an active part. CONTESTS. TELEVISION.

1197   Jones, Terry. *The Saga of Erik the Viking.* Illus. by Michael Foreman. Penguin, 1986. ISBN 0-14-031713-9

[27 chapters, 144p.] A brave Viking warrior and his heroic crew set sail on the *Golden Dragon* to seek the land where the sun goes at night. While studying the factual history of the Vikings, read a chapter a day of this handsome and spellbinding collection of offbeat literary fairy tales. ADVENTURE AND ADVENTURERS. FANTASY.

1198   Keller, Beverly. *The Genuine, Ingenious Thrift Shop Genie, Clarissa Mae Bean and Me.* Illus. by Raymond Davidson. Coward, 1977.

[4 chapters, 62p.] In spite of her own misgivings, Marcie is best friends with the weirdest girl in school in this offbeat comedy that champions the nonconformist. At the end of each chapter, ask listeners what they think of Clarissa and if they would be friends with her. BALLET. DANCING. FRIENDSHIP. HUMOROUS FICTION.

1199   King-Smith, Dick. *Harry's Mad.* Illus. by Jill Bennett. Crown, 1987. ISBN 0-517-56254-5

[15 chapters, 123p.] The last thing Harry expects when he inherits his American Great-Uncle George's most cherished possession is a talking parrot named Madison who can play the piano, use the telephone, and do the London Sunday *Times* crossword puzzle. Compare this jolly fantasy with one of a darker nature, such as Beatrice Gormley's *Mail-Order Wings*, where Andrea's new bird wings work too well. BIRDS. HUMOROUS FICTION. PARROTS. PETS.

1200   Kirby, Susan. *Ike and Porker.* Houghton Mifflin, 1983.

[16 chapters, 145p.] Though his father is convinced that 11 is too young for helping to drive the family's pigs to the far-off Chicago stockyards, Isaac is determined to make 1837 the year he leaves the frontier for the big city. In the barnyard vein, consider also Larry Callen's realistic *Pinch* and fantasies such as Dick King-Smith's *Babe the Gallant Pig* or *Pigs Might Fly*, Emily Rodda's *The Pig's Are Flying*, and Mary Stolz's *Quentin Corn*. FRONTIER AND PIONEER LIFE. HISTORICAL FICTION. PICS. U.S.– HISTORY–1783–1865–FICTION.

1201   Konigsburg, E. L. *From the Mixed-Up Files of Mrs. Basil E. Frankweiler.* Illus. by the author. Atheneum, 1967. ISBN 0-689-20586-4

[10 chapters, 162p.] Claudia and her nine-year-old brother Jamie run away to the Metropolitan Museum of Art in New York City, where they spend an art-filled week and solve a mystery. Show off a small part of that museum's vast holdings with Dan Fox's songbook *Go In and Out the Window* and Kenneth Koch and Kate Farrell's poetry anthology *Talking to the Sun*, both crammed with breathtaking reproductions of paintings, sculptures, and other art. MUSEUMS. MYSTERY AND DETECTIVE STORIES. NEW YORK CITY. NEWBERY MEDAL. RUNAWAYS.

1202   Krensky, Stephen. *The Dragon Circle.* Illus. by A. Delaney. Atheneum, 1977.

[12 chapters, 116p.] The unexpected appearance of five dragons in a small western Massachusetts village causes the Wynd family's usual magic spells to go awry. Having seen so many illustrations and cartoon dragons, children can now draw and describe how they think modern-day dragons should look and act. BROTHERS AND SISTERS. DRAGONS. FANTASY. MAGIC.

1203   Levitin, Sonia. *Jason and the Money Tree.* Illus. by Pat Grant Porter. Harcourt, 1974.

[11 chapters, 121p.] Jason plants the soiled, crumpled $10 bill his grandfather left him in his will and grows a bill-bearing plant in his backyard. Worthwhile follow-ups include Bill Brittain's *All the Money in the World*, Susan Beth Pfeffer's *Kid Power*, and Ron Roy's *Million Dollar Jeans*. FANTASY. MONEY.

1204　**Lewis, C. S. *The Magician's Nephew*. Illus. by Pauline Baynes. Macmillan, 1988. ISBN 0-02-758340-6**

[15 chapters, 167p.] How Aslan, the noble lion, created the land of Narnia, and about Digory and Polly, the English children who find themselves there due to two magic rings. Sixth of the seven "Chronicles of Narnia" that began with *The Lion, the Witch and the Wardrobe*, this actually takes place first. Fans can illustrate and describe each character. FANTASY. MAGICIANS. WITCHES.

1205　**Lisle, Janet Taylor. *The Dancing Cats of Applesap*. Illus. by Joelle Shefts. Bradbury, 1984. ISBN 0-02-759140-9**

[20 chapters, 169p.] The metamorphosis of Melba from introverted Milquetoast to crusader is spurred when Jiggs's Drug Store is set to close, leaving its 100 alley cats homeless. As Melba strives to get the cats recognized in the Guinness Book of World Records, so do Arlo in Tom Birdseye's *I'm Going to Be Famous* and Bernie in Phyllis Reynolds Naylor's *The Bodies in the Besseldorf Hotel*. CATS. SELF-CONCEPT.

1206　**Little, Jean. *Home from Far*. Illus. by Jerry Lazare. Little, Brown, 1965. ISBN 0-316-52792-0**

[19 chapters, 145p.] Six months after her twin brother Michael died in an auto accident, Jenny must adjust to the new foster brother and sister that her parents take in. BROTHERS AND SISTERS. DEATH. FAMILY PROBLEMS.

1207　**Lobel, Arnold. *Fables*. Illus. by the author. Harper & Row, 1980. ISBN 0-06-023974-3**

[20 fables, 42p.] While these 20 original animal fables may be read to younger children as well, many of the sophisticated morals will go over their heads. Integrated with reading and acting out of other traditional fables and, for older students, updated ones by James Thurber, these wise, insightful jewels will stir students into writing their own. (Teachers: Try reading the priceless "The Bad Kangaroo" at a faculty meeting.) ANIMALS. CALDECOTT MEDAL. CREATIVE DRAMA. CREATIVE WRITING. FABLES.

1208　**McCloskey, Robert. *Homer Price*. Illus. by the author. Viking, 1943. ISBN 0-670-37729-5**

[6 chapters, 149p.] A levelheaded, sensible Ohio boy contends with a pet skunk, robbers, and an overloaded doughnut machine. Act out the doughnut machine with each child responsible for a different mechanism to make it work, sound effects and all. The Weston Woods video of "The Doughnuts" is worth showing. Fans can follow up with *Centerburg Tales* (1951). CREATIVE DRAMA. HUMOROUS FICTION.

1209　**McMullin, Kate. *The Great Ideas of Lila Fenwick*. Illus. by Diane de Groat. Dial, 1986. ISBN 0-8037-0317-1**

[5 chapters, 118p.] Fifth grade is the year that klutzy Lila's great ideas all seem to work out for the best, from Halloween costumes to the perfect farewell present for her teacher. Also, what a bonus to meet Mr. Sherman, a teacher who loves books and reads aloud to his students! Contrast this school experience with Heidi's in *After Fifth Grade, the World!* by Claudia Mills. SCHOOLS. TEACHERS.

1210 McMurtry, Stan. *The Bunjee Venture*. Illus. by the author. Scholastic, 1986. ISBN 0-590-40396-6

[14 chapters, 128p.] After Mr. Winsborrow and his flimsy homemade time machine disappear from the family garage, his two plucky children construct a sturdier model and travel back to prehistoric times where they find not only him but Bunjee, an astonishingly odd elephantlike creature. Continue the time travel theme with Gery Greer and Bob Ruddick's *Max and Me and the Time Machine* and Jay Williams and Raymond Abrashkin's *Danny Dunn, Time Traveler*. ANIMALS, IMAGINARY. BROTHERS AND SISTERS. FANTASY. HUMOROUS FICTION. SPACE AND TIME.

1211 Manes, Stephen. *Chicken Trek: The Third Strange Thing That Happened to Oscar J. Noodleman*. Illus. by Ron Barrett. Dutton, 1987. ISBN 0-525-44312-6

[20 chapters, 110p.] Resigned to spending a rotten summer in Secaucus, New Jersey, working for his second cousin—mad inventor Dr. Peter Prechtwinkle—Oscar is thrilled to travel cross-country via Picklemobile instead, eating numerous greasy "Chicken in the Bag" dinners to win the $99,999.99 contest prize. Third in the "Oscar Noodleman" series; in *The Oscar J. Noodleman Television Network* (1984), also wild to read aloud, bully Billy Norval gets more than he bargained for when Oscar plots revenge using a one-of-a-kind video camera, flavored Jell-O, and a dead octopus. For more goofy humor about odd relatives, see Daniel Pinkwater's *Yobgorgle*. CHICKENS. FANTASY. HUMOROUS FICTION.

1212 Masterman-Smith, Virginia. *The Treasure Trap*. Illus. by Roseanne Litzinger. Four Winds, 1979.

[14 chapters, 200p.] Billy Beak and his feisty new neighbor Angel dig up her new yard in search for millionaire miser Old Man Waterman's cash that disappeared from the property when he died, seven years before. Read about other ways of acquiring money, including wishing for it, as in Bill Brittain's *All the Money in the World*; growing it, as in Sonia Levitin's *Jason and the Money Tree*; and even earning it, as in Susan Beth Pfeffer's *Kid Power*. BURIED TREASURE. FRIENDSHIP. MYSTERY AND DETECTIVE STORIES.

1213 Miles, Miska. *Annie and the Old One*. Illus. by Peter Parnall. Little, Brown, 1972. ISBN 0-316-57117-2

[1 sitting, unp.] An Indian girl who fears her grandmother's inevitable death seeks to prevent it by undoing the weaving on her grandmother's loom. While the old man in Richard Kennedy's *Come Again in the Spring* manages to outsmart Death, Annie's wise grandmother helps her to accept the inevitable. DEATH. GRANDMOTHERS. INDIANS OF NORTH AMERICA.

1214 Mills, Claudia. *After Fifth Grade, the World!* Macmillan, 1989. ISBN 0-02-767041-4

[12 chapters, 125p.] Heidi (aka H. P. Ahlenslager to herself) goes on the offensive when her sarcastic and rigid fifth-grade teacher, Mrs. Richardson, requires all students to write with cartridge pens. Heidi's final battle, where she organizes a class newspaper, may spur your writers into doing the same, as will Ellen Conford's *Me and the Terrible Two*. Make two lists with your class of bad and good things about school, and work together to overcome the bad and celebrate the good. FRIENDSHIP. SCHOOLS. TEACHERS.

1215   **Mooser, Stephen.** *Orphan Jeb at the Massacree.* **Illus. by Joyce Audy dos Santos. Knopf, 1984.**

[15 chapters, 87p.] February 16, 1860, Jeb's twelfth birthday, marks the start of his escapade encompassing a dead man, buried gold, a cure-peddling medicine man in a hot air balloon, and several western outlaws. In the same Wild West mood are Gary Greer and Bob Ruddick's *Max and Me and the Wild West* and Sid Fleischman's *By the Great Horn Spoon.* For the truth about the times, see Russell Freedman's *Children of the Wild West* and Ellen Levine's *If You Travelled West in a Covered Wagon.* BURIED TREASURE. HISTORICAL FICTION. ROBBERS AND OUTLAWS. U.S.-HISTORY-1783-1865-FICTION. WEST.

1216   **Naylor, Phyllis Reynolds.** *The Bodies in the Besseldorf Hotel.* **Atheneum, 1986. ISBN 0-689-31304-7**

[21 chapters, 132p.] Seemingly dead bodies appear and then disappear without warning in this comedy-mystery about a family who manage a 30-room, small-town hotel. Since 11-year-old Bernie, who unravels the intrigue, yearns to set a new skateboard record for the Guinness Book of World Records, this would be a fine time to introduce this fascinating reference and trivia tool, along with Tom Birdseye's *I'm Going to Be Famous* and Janet Taylor Lisle's *The Dancing Cats of Applesap.* HUMOROUS FICTION. MYSTERY AND DETECTIVE STORIES.

1217   **Naylor, Phyllis Reynolds.** *Witch's Sister.* **Illus. by Gail Owens. Macmillan, 1980. ISBN 0-689-70471-2**

[8 chapters, 150p.] Lynn and her best friend Mouse join forces against Mrs. Tuggle, whom they suspect of being a witch. First in a chilling quartet, followed by *Witch Water* (1977), *The Witch Herself* (1978), and *The Witch's Eye* (Delacorte, 1990). While reading, ask children to debate if Mrs. Tuggle is a witch or not, citing evidence to prove their points of view. SISTERS. WITCHES.

1218   **Nesbit, E.** *Melisande.* **Illus. by P. J. Lynch. Harcourt, 1989. ISBN 0-15-253164-5**

[1-2 sittings, unp.] Owing to bad fairy Malevola's spiteful christening gift, sweet Princess Melisande is as bald as an egg until she grows up and makes her own wish to have hair a yard long that grows twice as long each time it is cut. Written almost a century ago, this sensible fairy tale send-up has lost none of its good-natured punch, while the stunning full-page paintings endow it with additional personality. Lead off with the traditional tale of flowing locks, *Rapunzel,* incorporate the first few chapters of Lewis Carroll's *Alice in Wonderland,* and wind up with Jacob Grimm's *The Sleeping Beauty* to complete a discussion of the literary references incorporated in the story. Math teachers and students should also have fun devising word problems about rates of hair growth. HAIR. LITERARY FAIRY TALES. PRINCES AND PRINCESSES. SIZE.

1219   **Nostlinger, Christine.** *Konrad.* **Illus. by Carol Nicklaus. Franklin Watts, 1977.**

[11 chapters, 135p.] A factory-produced canned kid is delivered by mistake to Mrs. Bartolotti, an eccentric weaver who has no experience with children, especially perfect ones. Working in pairs, develop and act out new situations where your children try to teach Konrad to act like them. BEHAVIOR. FANTASY. HUMOROUS FICTION. MOTHERS AND SONS.

1220   **Park, Barbara.** *Don't Make Me Smile.* **Knopf, 1981. ISBN 0-394-84978-7**

[13 chapters, 114p.] Furious when he learns of his parents' impending divorce, Charlie Hickle lashes out at both of them and even runs away to the park to live in a tree. A serious subject is treated with much humor and empathy and from a child's point of view.   DIVORCE. FAMILY PROBLEMS.

1221   **Park, Barbara.** *The Kid in the Red Jacket.* **Knopf, 1987. ISBN 0-394-98189-8**

[10 chapters, 113p.] Intent on fitting in with the boys in his class, Howard, the new kid in town, is aghast when first-grader, chatterbox Molly Vera Thompson, his new neighbor, pesters him to be her friend. Park deals with the common problems of moving to a new place, which most children know all too well, and breaks new ground with her subplot of how Howard ignores his conscience to impress his new friends. Have students discuss and write about their own "moving" experiences, after you've tweaked their memories with Marjorie Weinman Sharmat's picture book *Gila Monsters Meet You at the Airport.*   FAMILY LIFE. HUMOROUS FICTION. MOVING, HOUSEHOLD.

1222   **Park, Barbara.** *Skinnybones.* **Knopf, 1982. ISBN 0-394-82596-9**

[12 chapters, 112p.] A wild sense of humor saves Alex Frankovitch, Little League's worst player. I defy anyone to read this aloud without laughing uproariously. Ask each child to submit his own Kittyfritters Contest entry blank; give prizes for the most interesting ones.   BASEBALL. CATS. HUMOROUS FICTION.

1223   **Peck, Robert Newton.** *Soup and Me.* **Illus. by Charles Lilly. Knopf, 1975. ISBN 0-394-93157-2**

[7 chapters, 115p.] Growing up in rural Vermont, Rob and his best friend Soup lose their clothes skinny-dipping in Putt's Pond in the first of many close calls with the infamously ornery Janice Riker. Look for other titles in the autobiographical "Soup" series.   FRIENDSHIP. HUMOROUS FICTION. SCHOOLS.

1224   **Pfeffer, Susan Beth.** *Kid Power.* **Illus. by Leigh Grant. Franklin Watts, 1977. ISBN 0-531-00123-7**

[11 chapters, 121p.] Janice starts a burgeoning odd-jobs business, advertising "No Job Too Big or Too Small," to earn money for her new bike. Find out more about earning big bucks in *If You Made a Million* by David M. Schwartz.   FAMILY LIFE. MONEY.

1225   **Pinkwater, Daniel.** *Lizard Music.* **Putnam, 1976. ISBN 0-396-07357-3**

[18 chapters, 157p.] Home alone with both parents and sister away on vacation, Victor starts seeing lizards everywhere, on television and off. Organize a "House of Memory" display where your students bring in their most treasured items from their younger days.   FANTASY. LIZARDS. REPTILES. SCIENCE FICTION.

1226   **Pinkwater, Daniel.** *The Slaves of Spiegel: A Magic Moscow Story.* **Four Winds, 1982.**

[26 very short chapters, 88p.] Fat men from the planet Spiegel hold an intergalactic junk food cook-off for which they abduct Magic Moscow owner Steve Nickelson and his helper Norman Bleistift from Hoboken, New Jersey, in a bizarre sequel to both *The Magic Moscow* and *Fat Men from Space.* Have your junk food experts concoct their own contest entries.   EXTRATERRESTRIAL LIFE. FOOD. HUMOROUS FICTION. SCIENCE FICTION.

1227 Pinkwater, Daniel. *Yobgorgle: Mystery Monster of Lake Ontario*. **Houghton Mifflin, 1979.**

[23 chapters, 156p.] Eugene and his junk food-addicted Uncle Mel join in the search for the newest unidentified creature since Nessie. Equally looney is Stephen Manes's *Chicken Trek*. BOATS AND BOATING. FOOD. HUMOROUS FICTION. UNCLES.

1228 Pollack, Pamela, ed. *The Random House Book of Humor for Children*. **Illus. by Paul O. Zelinsky. Random House, 1988. ISBN 0-394-98049-2**

[36 chapters, 310p.] A large treasury of laugh-out-loud chapters, excerpts, and short stories, ranging from ever-popular chunks of Judy Blume, Beverly Cleary, and Roald Dahl to lesser-known bits from Shirley Jackson, Garrison Keillor, and Sam Levenson. Also see Joanna Cole's treasury *The Laugh Book*. Declare Humorous Fiction Week, where each child brings in his or her favorite funny chapter or passage to read aloud in class. Compile these selections into a new collection for all to guffaw over. HUMOROUS FICTION. SHORT STORIES.

1229 Roberts, Willo Davis. *The Magic Book*. **Atheneum, 1986. ISBN 0-689-31120-6**

[19 chapters, 150p.] At the library's used-book sale, Alex finds a book of magic spells and potions published in 1802 that has his own name inscribed in it. As in Bruce Coville's *The Monster's Ring*, Alex undertakes to dispatch a dreaded bully with a spell. BOOKS. BULLIES. MAGIC.

1230 Robinson, Barbara. *The Best Christmas Pageant Ever*. **Illus. by Judith Gwyn Brown. Harper & Row, 1972. ISBN 0-06-025044-5**

[7 chapters, 80p.] The worst kids in the history of the world, known to all in town as the horrible Herdmans, steal all the main parts in the church Christmas play. As you progress, your listeners can trace the changes in attitude of both the Herdman kids and themselves. BEHAVIOR. BROTHERS AND SISTERS. CHRISTMAS. HUMOROUS FICTION. PLAYS.

1231 Rodda, Emily. *The Pigs Are Flying*. **Illus. by Noela Young. Greenwillow, 1988. ISBN 0-688-08130-4**

[11 chapters, 137p.] Transported on a unicorn's back, Rachel finds herself an outsider in a strange land during a grunter, a storm during which pigs rise and float in the air. An original "Oz"-like fantasy that would pair well with Larry Callen's *Pinch* and Susan Kirby's *Ike and Porker*, both realistic, and fantasies Mary Stolz's *Quentin Corn* and Dick King-Smith's *Pigs Might Fly*. Compile a new volume of rewritten pig nursery rhymes. Arnold Lobel's *Pigericks* should help you make a start. FANTASY. PIGS. WEATHER.

1232 Rounds, Glen. *Mr. Yowder and the Train Robbers*. **Illus. by the author. Holiday House, 1981. ISBN 0-8234-0394-7**

[1 sitting, unp.] Taking a fishing holiday out in the boondocks, the unperturbable sign painter foils dangerous outlaws with the help of cooperative rattlesnakes. Act out the scene with the outlaws, using improvised dialogue. In *Mr. Yowder and the Lion Roar Capsules* (1976), he is given a broken-down lion in payment for his work. The dry, understated humor tells like a laid-back tall tale. HUMOROUS FICTION. ROBBERS AND OUTLAWS. SNAKES. TALL TALES.

1233   Roy, Ron. *Million Dollar Jeans*. Illus. by Joyce Audy dos Santos. Dutton, 1983. ISBN 0-525-44047-X

[20 chapters, 88p.] Tommy and Twig race from a rummage sale to the Salvation Army to the city dump in search of Tommy's paint-stained blue jeans with a million dollar winning lottery ticket in the back pocket. Share the wealth with Bill Brittain's *All the Money in the World* or Sonia Levitin's *Jason and the Money Tree*. Ask your students to plan what they'd do with a million bucks, and give them a few ideas with David M. Schwartz's *If You Made a Million*.   CLOTHING AND DRESS. MONEY.

1234   Roy, Ron. *Nightmare Island*. Illus. by Robert MacLean. Dutton, 1981. ISBN 0-525-35905-2

[11 chapters, 69p.] Two brothers out camping on a tiny Maine island are trapped by the resulting fire when they unwittingly throw a burning stick into the oil-slicked ocean. Research different types of fires and ways to escape them.   BROTHERS. CAMPING. FIRE. ISLANDS. SURVIVAL.

1235   Ruckman, Ivy. *Night of the Twisters*. Crowell, 1984. ISBN 0-690-04409-7

[12 chapters, 153p.] Dan's hour-by-hour recounting lets us experience the horror of the tornadoes that leveled most of Grand Island, Nebraska, on June 3, 1980, when he was alone with his best friend Arthur and baby brother Ryan. Other disaster survival stories include Walter R. Brown and Norman D. Anderson's *Rescue! True Stories of Winners of the Young American Medal for Bravery*, Susan Fleming's *Trapped on the Golden Flyer*, Gurney Williams's *True Escape and Survival Stories*, and William Steig's *Abel's Island*.   SURVIVAL. TORNADOES. WEATHER.

1236   Sachs, Marilyn. *Veronica Ganz*. Illus. by Louis Glanzman. Scholastic, 1987. ISBN 0-590-40405-9

[11 chapters, 156p.] A girl bully meets her match in Peter Wedermeyer, the shrimpy new boy in her class who isn't afraid of her. A reprint of the 1968 edition. Compare this to the plight of the runty kid terrified by the prospect of bodily harm when a bully stalks him in *The 18th Emergency* by Betsy Byars.   BULLIES. FRIENDSHIP. SELF-CONCEPT.

1237   Selden, George. *The Cricket in Times Square*. Illus. by Garth Williams. Farrar, 1960. ISBN 0-374-31650-3

[15 chapters, 151p.] An unusually musical cricket from Connecticut is befriended by Harry Cat, Tucker Mouse, and young Mario Bellini in the 42nd Street subway station in New York City where Mario's parents run a newsstand. Play a bit of classical music on the record player to introduce each chapter. Raising a puppy in a New York subway station drainpipe is not an easy task for Harry Cat and Tucker Mouse in the sequel *Harry Cat's Pet Puppy* (1974). Present another trio of animals trying to get by in the Big Apple: Fats the Fuse, Raymond the Rat, and Marv the Magnificent in Jean Van Leeuwen's *The Great Christmas Kidnapping Caper* and *The Great Rescue Operation*.   CATS. DOGS. INSECTS. MICE. NEW YORK CITY.

1238   Shura, Mary Francis. *Mister Wolf and Me*. Illus. by Konrad Hack. Putnam, 1979. ISBN 0-396-07666-1

[10 chapters, 126p.] If Miles cannot prove that his pet German shepherd is not responsible for killing a hostile farmer's sheep, the dog will be destroyed. Encourage students to give both sides equal weight in discussing the moral issues involved.   DOGS.

1239   Simon, Seymour. *Einstein Anderson, Science Sleuth.* Illus. by Fred Winkowski. Penguin, 1986. ISBN 0-14-032098-9

[10 chapters, 73p.] First of an "Encyclopedia Brown"-like series of science-based mysteries your students will delight in solving, using knowledge of motion, friction, astronomy, buoyancy, and other such principles. Key specific chapters into your science lessons. MYSTERY AND DETECTIVE STORIES. SCIENCE–EXPERIMENTS.

1240   Sleator, William. *Among the Dolls.* Illus. by Trina Schart Hyman. Dutton, 1975. ISBN 0-525-25563-X

[9 chapters, 70p.] Dolls imprison Vicky in her own antique dollhouse to retaliate for her abuse of them. Equally alarming is the life-sized doll who takes over Hollis's life in *Is There Life on a Plastic Planet?* by Mildred Ames. DOLLS. FANTASY. SIZE. SUSPENSE.

1241   Slote, Alfred. *Hang Tough, Paul Mather.* Lippincott, 1973. ISBN 0-397-31451-5

[17 chapters, 156p.] Being unable to play baseball is an overwhelming side effect of having leukemia for a Little League pitcher. No one writes better children's baseball novels; booktalk Slote's other titles for your student fans. BASEBALL. SICK.

1242   Sperry, Armstrong. *Call It Courage.* Illus. by the author. Macmillan, 1940. ISBN 0-02-786030-2

[5 chapters, 95p.] Mafatu, a Polynesian chief's son who must overcome his fear of the sea to become accepted, sets out in his canoe alone on the ocean except for his tamed albatross, Kiri. True tales of courage include Walter R. Brown and Norman D. Anderson's *Rescue! True Stories of Winners of the Young American Medal for Bravery* and Gurney Williams's *True Escape and Survival Stories.* ADVENTURE AND ADVENTURERS. COURAGE. NEWBERY MEDAL. OCEAN. SURVIVAL.

1243   Stearns, Pamela. *Into the Painted Bear Lair.* Illus. by Ann Strugnell. Houghton Mifflin, 1976.

[9 chapters, 153p.] After Gregory inexplicably finds himself in a hungry bear's sitting room, he enlists the help of a female knight, Sir Rosemary, to get him home again. Other entertaining folklore-based tales include M. M. Kaye's *The Ordinary Princess,* Vivian Vande Velde's *A Hidden Magic,* and Elizabeth Winthrop's *The Castle in the Attic.* BEARS. FAIRY TALES–SATIRE. FANTASY. KNIGHTS AND KNIGHTHOOD.

1244   Stolz, Mary. *Zekmet, the Stone Carver.* Illus. by Deborah Nourse Lattimore. Harcourt, 1988. ISBN 0-15-299961-2

[1 sitting, unp.] A fictional account of how a pharaoh's vanity, a vizier's desperation, and a stone carver's talent inspired the building of the sphinx. Be forewarned that this unusually handsome picture book, easily read in one sitting, bordered in Egyptian hieroglyphics, will stimulate an early precurricular interest in Egyptian culture, writing, and art. Preface your reading with an overview of ancient Egypt, as children will most likely have very little background. Irene and Laurence Swinburn's *Behind the Sealed Door: The Discovery of the Tomb and Treasures of Tutankhamen* is bewitching, if you can find it. Also uncover Shirley Climo's ancient folktale *The Egyptian Cinderella* and Gerald McDermott's *The Voyage of Osiris.* ARTISTS. EGYPT, ANCIENT. HISTORICAL FICTION. SCULPTORS.

1245 Stonely, Jack. *Scruffy.* **Knopf, 1988. ISBN 0-394-82039-8**

[19 chapters, 156p.] An abandoned puppy survives to become the most famous dog in England as recorded in the English press by the author/reporter who found her at the pound. Mary Stolz's *Cat Walk* provides equal time for both lost felines and fantasy. DOGS. LOST. SURVIVAL.

1246 Sutton, Jane. *Me and the Weirdos.* **Illus. by Sandy Kossin. Houghton Mifflin, 1981.**

[10 chapters, 117p.] Cindy Krinkle decides to "unweird" her eccentric family and learns to accept their zany ways in the process. Everyone's family is weird; ask your bunch to record their interesting examples. FAMILY LIFE. HUMOROUS FICTION.

1247 Tapp, Kathy Kennedy. *Moth-Kin Magic.* **Illus. by Michele Chessare. Atheneum, 1983. ISBN 0-689-50288-5**

[11 chapters, 122p.] On the day of the gathering—a once-a-year celebration of her colony's legends, stories, and magic—young Ripple, her mother, and her Uncle Kane are captured and imprisoned by giants. This sparkling survival tale of a band of insect-sized people unwittingly caught by human children will change your perception of the classroom terrarium forever. Listeners can write their own adventures from the perspective of the tiny humanlike winged creatures. Their escape is chronicled in the equally innovative sequel, *Flight of the Moth-Kin* (McElderry, 1987). FANTASY. SIZE. SURVIVAL.

1248 Taylor, Mildred D. *The Gold Cadillac.* **Illus. by Michael Hays. Dial, 1987. ISBN 0-8037-0343-0**

[1 sitting, 43p.] When Lois's father plans to drive his glamorous new 1950 Cadillac from their home in Ohio down to racially segregated Mississippi, the whole family goes along to stave off possible trouble. Based on the author's recollection of her own family's car and the prejudice she encountered as an African American child growing up after World War II, this is an eye-opening presentation of a subject that deserves discussion. AFRICAN AMERICANS. AUTOMOBILES. PREJUDICE.

1249 Titus, Eve. *Basil of Baker Street.* **Illus. by Paul Galdone. McGraw-Hill, 1958. ISBN 0-07-064907-3**

[15 chapters, 96p.] The mouse detective who lives in Sherlock Holmes's basement and patterns himself after the great detective solves the toughest case of his career in this first book in the series. Also acknowledge the talents of America's "Sherlock Holmes in Sneakers," Idaville's own *Encyclopedia Brown, Boy Detective* as told by Donald J. Sobol. MICE. MYSTERY AND DETECTIVE STORIES.

1250 Van Allsburg, Chris. *The Mysteries of Harris Burdick.* **Illus. by the author. Houghton Mifflin, 1984. ISBN 0-395-35393-9**

[1 sitting, unp.] A collection of 14 intriguing and compelling pencil illustrations, each accompanied by a story title and picture caption. According to the author's introduction, they were left at a publisher's office by Mr. Burdick, who never returned with the completed stories. Students in grades two and up will be eager to write and discuss their own versions of the stories behind the illustrations. CREATIVE WRITING. IMAGINATION.

1251 Vande Velde, Vivian. *A Hidden Magic.* **Illus. by Trina Schart Hyman. Crown, 1985. ISBN 0-517-55534-4**

[16 chapters, 117p.] Jennifer, a plain, good-natured princess from a small unassuming kingdom, braves the magic of two witches, a dragon, and a giant to lift the sleeping spell cast over a handsome but vain prince. Vande Velde pokes gentle fun at stock fairy tale characters, to whom you can compare this cast. For more giddy parody, see Pamela Stearns's *Into the Painted Bear Lair* and M. M. Kaye's *The Ordinary Princess*. FAIRY TALES–SATIRE. MAGIC. PRINCES AND PRINCESSES. WITCHES.

1252   **Van Leeuwen, Jean.** *The Great Rescue Operation.* **Illus. by Margot Apple. Dial, 1982. ISBN 0-8037-3139-6**

[15 chapters, 167p.] Accidentally kidnapped from Macy's toy department when the fancy doll carriage he is snoozing in is sold, Fats the Fuse is tracked down by his two remaining mouse pals in the comic sequel to *The Great Cheese Conspiracy* (Dell, 1976) and *The Great Christmas Kidnapping Caper*. HUMOROUS FICTION. MICE. NEW YORK CITY.

1253   **White, E. B.** *The Trumpet of the Swan.* **Illus. by Edward Frascino. Harper & Row, 1970. ISBN 0-06-026398-9**

[21 chapters, 210p.] Louis, an intelligent trumpeter swan born without a voice, finds a unique way to make himself heard after his father robs a trumpet from a music store window. Use Jay Featherly's nonfiction *Ko-Oh: The Call of the Trumpeter Swan* (Carolrhoda, 1986) for background, as well as Hans Christian Andersen's *The Ugly Duckling*, to make sure all have heard that classic tale. For a bird with the opposite in linguistic and vocal acuity, introduce Madison the parrot from *Harry's Mad* by Dick King-Smith. BIRDS. FANTASY. HANDICAPS.

1254   **Williams, Jay.** *The Magic Grandfather.* **Illus. by Gail Owens. Four Winds, 1979. ISBN 0-02-793100-5**

[11 chapters, 149p.] Sam is the only one in his family who doesn't mind grandpa being a "bum" and is astonished to discover he is a sorcerer as well. The narrator's grandmother in Roald Dahl's *The Witches* has her own knowledge of magic. Compare these extraordinary grandparents with tin-can collecting salt-of-the-earth Pop of *The Not-Just-Anybody Family* by Betsy Byars. Encourage children to find out more and write about their own grandparents. FANTASY. GRANDFATHERS. MAGIC.

1255   **Williams, Jay, and Raymond Abrashkin.** *Danny Dunn and the Homework Machine.* **Illus. by Ezra Jack Keats. McGraw-Hill, 1958.**

[17 chapters, 141p.] Although written long before the advent of the home computer, this tale, one of a habit-forming science adventure series starring science-loving Danny and his two sidekicks, Joe and Irene, is one your homework-haters will relish. Also fun is David A. Adler's *Eaton Stanley & the Mind Control Experiment*, where two boys try to get around their teacher by thought. SCHOOLS. SCIENCE–EXPERIMENTS.

1256   **Williams, Jay, and Raymond Abrashkin.** *Danny Dunn, Time Traveler.* **Illus. by Owen Kampen. McGraw-Hill, 1963.**

[14 chapters, 136p.] When he accidentally breaks Professor Bullfinch's time machine, Danny and his cohorts are stranded in 1763 where they meet and exchange scientific data with Ben Franklin. Some research into the life and times of the great scientist would not be amiss, from the historical fantasy *Ben and Me* by Robert

Lawson to biographies including Ingri and Edgar Parin D'Aulaire's *Benjamin Franklin* and Jean Fritz's *What's the Big Idea, Ben Franklin?* Continue time exploration with Gery Greer and Bob Ruddick's *Max and Me and the Time Machine* and Stan McMurtry's *The Bunjee Venture.* HISTORICAL FICTION. SCIENCE FICTION. SPACE AND TIME.

Illustration from THE PIGS ARE FLYING by Emily Rodda, illustrated by Noela Young. Illustrations copyright © 1986 by Noela Young. Published in the United States by Greenwillow Books, William Morrow & Co., 1988. First published by Angus & Robertson Publishers in Australia and the United Kingdom, 1986, as PIGS MIGHT FLY. Reproduced by permission of Collins / Angus & Robertson Publishers.

Illustration from INSIDE MY FEET: THE STORY OF A GIANT by Richard Kennedy, illustrated by Ronald Himler. Illustrations copyright © 1979 by Ronald Himler. Harper & Row, Publishers, 1979. Reprinted by permission of HarperCollins Publishers.

FICTION FOR GRADES 5–6

1257 **Alcock, Vivien.** *The Monster Garden.* **Delacorte, 1988. ISBN 0-440-50053-2**

[20 chapters, 134p.] After lonely Frankie Stein finagles from her older brother a bit of grayish living tissue he's stolen from their father's lab, she incubates it in a petri dish and raises a fast-growing, nonhuman creature she names Monnie. As you read each description of the growing monster, your listeners can draw what they think he looks like in each stage of development. FANTASY. MONSTERS. SCIENCE FICTION.

1258 **Alexander, Lloyd.** *The Book of Three.* **Henry Holt, 1964. ISBN 0-8050-0874-8**

[20 chapters, 217p.] Taran, an enchanter's assistant pigkeeper, dreams of glory and adventure. First of five in the riveting "Prydain Chronicles" fantasy, based on Welsh mythology. ADVENTURE AND ADVENTURERS. FANTASY.

1259 **Alexander, Lloyd.** *The Cat Who Wished to Be a Man.* **Dutton, 1977. ISBN 0-525-27545-2**

[19 chapters, 107p.] Granted the power of human speech by his enchanter master, cat Lionel now talks his way into becoming human, with hilarious results. *Quentin Corn*, Mary Stolz's farm pig, also turns human; compare their acclimations. CATS. FANTASY. MAGIC. TRANSFORMATIONS.

1260 **Alexander, Lloyd.** *The First Two Lives of Lucas-Kasha.* **Dutton, 1978. ISBN 0-525-29748-0**

[23 chapters, 213p.] A lazy, young, ne'er-do-well with a horror of working becomes king of an unknown land, thanks to his encounter with a marketplace conjurer. Based on a theme from Persian folklore, with strong, outspoken characters students can draw, describe, and judge. ADVENTURE AND ADVENTURERS. FANTASY.

1261 **Alexander, Lloyd.** *The Town Cats and Other Tales.* **Illus. by Laslo Kubinyi. Dutton, 1977. ISBN 0-525-41430-4**

[8 chapters, 126p.] These eight folktale-like short stories about shrewd felines can mark the start of a cat celebration. Charles Keller's riddles in *It's Raining Cats and Dogs*, Nancy Larrick's stunning poetry collection *Cats Are Cats*, and Marjorie Zaum's *Catlore: Tales from Around the World* should start the ball rolling. CATS. SHORT STORIES.

1262 **Alexander, Lloyd.** *The Wizard in the Tree.* **Illus. by Laslo Kubinyi. Dutton, 1974. ISBN 0-525-43128-4**

[16 chapters, 138p.] After Mallory, servant girl at the local inn, discovers and helps free an ill-tempered old enchanter long trapped inside an oak tree, she feels obliged to help him regain his once-considerable powers. Other powerful enchanters include an evil one in Bill Brittain's *Dr. Dredd's Wagon of Wonders* and a kindly one in Tom McGowen's *The Magician's Apprentice.* FANTASY. WIZARDS.

1263   **Ames, Mildred.** *Is There Life on a Plastic Planet?* **Dutton, 1975. ISBN 0-525-32594-8**

[15 chapters, 134p.] Overweight, insecure Hollis, beguiled by the empathetic owner of The Shop of Living Dolls, agrees to switch places with her double—a life-sized doll who ultimately refuses to recognize Hollis's status and tries to keep Hollis from returning to her own house. Another tale of a child who escapes her troubled life with the help of dolls is *The Bears' House* by Marilyn Sachs. DOLLS. FANTASY. SCIENCE FICTION. SELF-CONCEPT.

1264   **Armstrong, William.** *Sounder.* **Illus. by James Barkley. Harper & Row, 1969. ISBN 0-06-020144-4**

[8 chapters, 116p.] A poor southern black sharecropper is jailed for stealing a ham, leaving behind his family and their wounded hound. Discussion points: Is stealing ever justified? Are laws always just? AFRICAN AMERICANS. DOGS. NEWBERY MEDAL.

1265   **Arthur, Robert.** *The Secret of Terror Castle.* **Illus. by Harry Kane. Random House, 1964.**

[19 chapters, 179p.] After setting up their agency in Jupiter Jones's uncle's junkyard and winning the use of a gold Rolls Royce for one month, three teenage detectives are hired by Alfred Hitchcock to investigate a haunted mansion. First in the genuinely scary "Three Investigators" series, which can prove an addiction for suspense lovers. MYSTERY AND DETECTIVE STORIES. SUSPENSE.

1266   **Avi.** *Bright Shadow.* **Bradbury, 1985. ISBN 0-02-707750-0**

[12 chapters, 167p.] Before he dies, the wizard Pindel passes along the kingdom's last five wishes to twelve-year-old Morwenna, a chambermaid's assistant at the fortress palace of ruthless King Ruthvin. A thoughtful and rich depiction of the opposite consequences power can bring: corruption and greed versus moral responsibility. *The First Two Lives of Lukas-Kasha* by Lloyd Alexander is a stimulating companion for discussion. FANTASY. WISHES.

1267   **Avi.** *The Fighting Ground.* **Lippincott, 1984. ISBN 0-397-32074-4**

[69 very short chapters, 152p.] A 24-hour accounting of 12-year-old Jonathan who, on April 3, 1778, bored with his New Jersey farm work, runs off to fight the British and is captured by Hessians, where he learns firsthand of the terrors of war. For easier access, the German spoken by the Hessians is translated at the back of the book. See also James Lincoln Collier's *My Brother Sam Is Dead.* HISTORICAL FICTION. U.S.–HISTORY–REVOLUTION–FICTION.

1268   **Avi.** *Night Journeys.* **Pantheon, 1979.**

[6 chapters, 143p.] Peter York, the orphaned ward of a Quaker justice of the peace, assists two young indentured servants in their escape from New Jersey into Pennsylvania in 1767. When studying colonial times, Ann McGovern's *If You Lived in Colonial Times* gives a flavor of the period. Avi's book paints a dark picture of a type of slavery most children know nothing about and weaves in Peter's ethical dilemma of disobeying an unjust law. HISTORICAL FICTION. RUNAWAYS. U.S.–HISTORY –COLONIAL PERIOD–FICTION.

1269   **Avi.** *Shadrach's Crossing.* **Pantheon, 1983. ISBN 0-394-95816-0**

[22 chapters, 178p.] Liquor smugglers have terrorized Lucker's Island where 12-year-old Shad lives, and he skirts danger, intent on bringing the crooks to justice. A thrilling Depression-era story; compile character studies of each possible suspect. BROTHERS. COURAGE. ISLANDS.

1270   **Babbitt, Natalie.** *The Devil's Storybook.* **Illus. by the author. Farrar, 1974. ISBN 0-374-31770-4**

[10 chapters, 101p.] Match these 10 entertaining short stories about the ever-scheming, often-bested Devil with the title story in Alfred Slote's *The Devil Rides with Me and Other Fantastic Stories* and a sprinkling of folktales, such as Jacob Grimm's *The Bearskinner*, Charles Scribner's *The Devil's Bridge*, and Harve Zemach's *Duffy and the Devil.* DEVIL. SHORT STORIES.

1271   **Babbitt, Natalie.** *Tuck Everlasting.* **Illus. by the author. Farrar, 1975.**

[26 chapters, 123p.] Ten-year-old Winnie Foster longs for adventure until she meets the Tuck family and learns the secret of the spring that gave them everlasting life. While it might be desirable to put off death for a time as old Hark does in Richard Kennedy's *Come Again in the Spring*, ask students if they would drink from the spring themselves and why. The Norse gods almost lose their source of nonstop youth in Marianna Mayer's *Iduna and the Magic Apples.* All of these are interesting to consider when social studies turn to Ponce de Leon's search for the elusive Fountain of Youth. ADVENTURE AND ADVENTURERS. MURDER.

1272   **Banks, Lynne Reid.** *The Indian in the Cupboard.* **Illus. by Brock Cole. Doubleday, 1985. ISBN 0-385-17051-3**

[16 chapters, 181p.] Omri does not value the miniature plastic toy Indian his friend Patrick gives him as a birthday present until it comes to life as Little Bear. First in a thrilling trilogy, Bank's characters are remarkable for their depth, even the ones who are only thumb-sized. Explore the world from a tiny perspective with the added outlook of *The Borrowers* by Mary Norton. ENGLAND. FANTASY. INDIANS OF NORTH AMERICA. SIZE. TOYS.

1273   **Bauer, Marion Dane.** *On My Honor.* **Clarion, 1986. ISBN 0-89919-439-7**

[12 chapters, 90p.] A Newbery honor book that will start a serious discussion of friendship and accountability for one's own actions. After his best friend Tony drowns while they are swimming in the forbidden Vermillion River, Joel is panicked by guilt, fear, and grief into denying any knowledge or responsibility for his friend's death. DEATH. FRIENDSHIP. OBEDIENCE. RESPONSIBILITY. RIVERS.

1274   **Beatty, Patricia.** *That's One Ornery Orphan.* **Morrow, 1980.**

[13 chapters, 216p.] In 1889, after her grandfather dies, headstrong 13-year-old Hallie May looks for a way out of the Texas orphanage where she's been sent. Around the same time period, orphan Emily also perseveres through adversity in *Peppermints in the Parlor* by Barbara Brooks Wallace. HISTORICAL FICTION. ORPHANS. TEXAS. U.S.–HISTORY–1865–1898–FICTION. WEST.

1275   Bellairs, John. *The Treasure of Alpheus Winterborn.* **Illus. by Judith Gwyn Brown. Harcourt, 1978.**

[17 chapters, 180p.] While working in the town library, 13-year-old Anthony finds the first clue to a treasure hidden decades ago by the town's wealthy practical joker. Your class may enjoy setting up a similar mystery treasure hunt with clues for another class to figure out. BURIED TREASURE. LIBRARIES. MYSTERY AND DETECTIVE STORIES.

1276   Brittain, Bill. *Devil's Donkey.* **Illus. by Andrew Glass. Harper & Row, 1981. ISBN 0-06-020683-7**

[8 chapters, 120p.] Headstrong Dan'l Pitt angers Old Magda the witch and the devil himself after he cuts a branch off the forbidden Coven Tree. The scene from where Dan'l arrives back at the store from gathering firewood to where old Magda casts her first spell, turning him into a donkey, makes a fine bit of Readers Theater or creative drama. DEVIL. FANTASY. MAGIC. WITCHES.

1277   Brittain, Bill. *Dr. Dredd's Wagon of Wonders.* **Illus. by Andrew Glass. Harper & Row, 1987. ISBN 0-06-020714-0**

[10 chapters, 179p.] Narrator Stew Meat relates his third spooky tale of the New England town of Coven Tree when drought turns everyone desperate enough to strike a deal with the odious and evil Dr. Dredd who promises them rain in exchange. Also read Gloria Skurzynski's *What Happened in Hamelin* to see how a similar bargain was struck with the Pied Piper. FANTASY. MAGIC. SUPERNATURAL. WEATHER.

1278   Brittain, Bill. *The Wish Giver: Three Tales of Coven Tree.* **Illus. by Andrew Glass. Harper & Row, 1983. ISBN 0-06-020687-X**

[5 chapters, 181p.] At the Coven Tree church social, three children each spend fifty cents for wish cards that make their wishes come true—literally. Write new literal wishes and chapters to go along with them. For another wish that backfires, read also Brittain's *All the Money in the World.* CREATIVE WRITING. FANTASY. MAGIC. WISHES.

1279   Burnford, Sheila. *The Incredible Journey.* **Illus. by Carl Burger. Little, Brown, 1961. ISBN 0-316-11714-5**

[11 chapters, 145p.] A Labrador retriever, a bull terrier, and a Siamese cat brave the Canadian wilds on their 250-mile trip to find their human family. Other loyal pets include *Sounder* by William Armstrong, *Old Yeller* by Fred Gipson, and Michael Morpurgo's *War Horse*, an otherwise realistic World War I tale narrated by the horse. In a less serious vein, see Mary Calhoun's picture book *Cross-Country Cat* and introduce some animal fantasy with *Harry Cat's Pet Puppy* by George Selden and *Cat Walk* by Mary Stolz. CANADA. CATS. DOGS. SURVIVAL.

1280   Byars, Betsy. *Cracker Jackson.* **Viking, 1985. ISBN 0-670-80546-7**

[24 chapters, 146p.] When he suspects Alma, his former baby-sitter, is being beaten up by her husband, Jackson tries to help her and her baby Nicole. Few authors could tackle as sensitive a topic with such empathy, savoir faire, and humor. This is one no one will forget. FAMILY PROBLEMS. FRIENDSHIP.

1281 Byars, Betsy. *The Pinballs.* **Harper & Row, 1977. ISBN 0-06-020918-6**

[26 chapters, 136p.] Three unwanted, neglected children—Harvey, whose alcoholic father ran over and broke both Harvey's legs; Thomas J., who was taken in as a baby by octogenarian twin sisters until they broke their hips; and tough Carlie, whose stepfather beat her—are placed with foster parents Mr. and Mrs. Mason. As always, Byars is a master at fleshing out engrossing, unique characters to whom we become attached. Listeners will empathize with the three troubled children who, in banding together, begin to heal their emotional wounds. FAMILY PROBLEMS. FRIENDSHIP.

1282 Byars, Betsy. *The Summer of the Swans.* **Illus. by Ted CoConis. Viking, 1970. ISBN 0-670-68190-3**

[23 short chapters, 142p.] When Sara's retarded brother disappears, her daylong search for him helps her begin to understand herself better. Along with Ann Baldwin's *A Little Time*, Sheila Garrigue's *Between Friends*, and Marlene Fanta Shyer's *Welcome Home, Jellybean*, Byars's award-winning story enables children to gain a large measure of sensitivity toward the retarded. BROTHERS AND SISTERS. HANDICAPS. LOST. SELF-CONCEPT.

1283 Byars, Betsy. *The Two-Thousand Pound Goldfish.* **Harper & Row, 1982. ISBN 0-06-020890-2**

[16 chapters, 152p.] Warren yearns for his mother, a radical underground fugitive wanted by the FBI, and invents horror movie scenarios as his own escape from life's rougher moments. The hard-hitting intensity mixed with wild humor should stir a class discussion on the difference between legitimate protest and extremism, as well as the responsibilities a parent has to her children. BROTHERS AND SISTERS. FAMILY LIFE. GRANDMOTHERS. IMAGINATION. MOTHERS.

1284 Callen, Larry. *The Deadly Mandrake.* **Illus. by Larry Johnson. Little, Brown, 1978.**

[27 chapters, 163p.] Evil erupts in the small country town of Four Corners when Sorrow Nix's father dies after arranging to have his secret Mandrake root buried nearby. Travel back to America's past to examine other rural customs and beliefs through folklore collections including Richard Chase's *Grandfather Tales* and Virginia Haviland's *North American Legends*. COUNTRY LIFE. SUSPENSE.

1285 Callen, Larry. *Pinch.* **Illus. by Marvin Friedman. Little, Brown, 1976. ISBN 0-316-12495-8**

[24 chapters, 179p.] In this first of a trilogy, small town boy Pinch Grimball trains his new pig in hopes of winning a bird hunting contest. Hog the following to share with your class: Dick King-Smith's sheepherding *Babe the Gallant Pig* and *Pig's Might Fly*, Susan Kirby's *Ike and Porker*, Emily Rodda's *The Pigs Are Flying*, and Mary Stolz's *Quentin Corn*. COUNTRY LIFE. HUMOROUS FICTION. PIGS.

1286 Callen, Larry. *Sorrow's Song.* **Illus. by Marvin Friedman. Little, Brown, 1979.**

[31 short chapters, 150p.] Pinch's mute friend Sorrow tries to shield a wounded whooping crane from the Zoo Man and others who seek it. Third in the "Pinch" trilogy, with the eloquently silent Sorrow Nix. If you want to focus on the handicap, also read Paul Fleischman's gripping *The Half-a-Moon Inn* and the biography of deaf-mute Laura Bridgman, *Child of the Silent Night* by Edith Fisher Hunter. BIRDS. COUNTRY LIFE. HANDICAPS.

1287   **Cassedy, Sylvia.** *Behind the Attic Wall.* **Crowell, 1983. ISBN 0-690-04337-6**

[37 chapters, 315p.] After being kicked out of numerous boarding schools, sullen friendless Maggie is sent to live with her two forbidding aunts in a mansion where the very walls seem to have voices and the dolls are alive. After these benevolent dolls, introduce a few malevolent ones, such as those in Mildred Ames's *Is There Life on a Plastic Planet?* or William Sleator's *Among the Dolls*. BEHAVIOR. DOLLS. FANTASY. GHOSTS. ORPHANS.

1288   **Collier, James Lincoln, and Christopher Collier.** *My Brother Sam Is Dead.* **Four Winds, 1974. ISBN 0-02-722980-7**

[15 chapters, 216p.] In 1775, Tim's 16-year-old brother leaves Yale to join the Rebel troops, much to his Tory father's fury. A graphic and tragic account of how war affects one family, as is Avi's *The Fighting Ground*. BROTHERS. HISTORICAL FICTION. U.S.–HISTORY–REVOLUTION–FICTION.

1289   **Conford, Ellen.** *And This Is Laura.* **Little, Brown, 1977. ISBN 0-316-15300-1**

[13 chapters, 179p.] Laura considers herself the unexceptional one in her talented family until she discovers her gift of predicting the future. Pair this with Roald Dahl's *Matilda*, whose parents disregard her even though she's a five-year-old genius with her own extraordinary powers. EXTRASENSORY PERCEPTION. FAMILY LIFE. INDIVIDUALITY.

1290   **Conford, Ellen.** *Lenny Kandell, Smart Aleck.* **Illus. by Walter Gaffney-Kessell. Little, Brown, 1983. ISBN 0-316-15313-3**

[12 chapters, 120p.] In 1946, Lenny is determined to become a great stand-up comic, in spite of setbacks like ruining his aunt's fur scarf, not memorizing "Hiawatha," and being threatened by bully Mousie Blatner. Play tapes of old-time comedian Jack Benny to set the mood. BULLIES. HUMOROUS FICTION. SCHOOLS.

1291   **Dahl, Roald.** *Danny, the Champion of the World.* **Illus. by Jill Bennett. Knopf, 1975. ISBN 0-394-93103-3**

[22 chapters, 198p.] In his ninth year, narrator Danny and his marvelous father go pheasant poaching in Hazell's Wood to spite the sneering, smug Mr. Victor Hazell. In the first chapter, note the germination of the idea for the author's book *The BFG*. BIRDS. FATHERS AND SONS.

1292   **Dahl, Roald.** *Matilda.* **Illus. by Quentin Blake. Viking, 1988. ISBN 0-670-82439-9**

[21 chapters, 240p.] The extraordinarily brilliant five-year-old daughter of horrid, low-life parents matches wits with the treacherously evil headmistress, Miss Trunchbull. Warning: Watching intrepid schoolchildren best stupid, malicious adults may disturb grown-ups, but kids will cheer. Preview first to see in which category you fit. EXTRASENSORY PERCEPTION. HUMOROUS FICTION. SCHOOLS. TEACHERS.

1293   **Dahl, Roald.** *The Wonderful Story of Henry Sugar and Six More.* **Bantam, 1979. ISBN 0-553-15445-1**

[7 short stories, 215p.] Seven mystifying tales, some purportedly autobiographical. Follow up or precede with his revealing autobiography *Boy: Tales of Childhood*. SHORT STORIES.

1294   Du Bois, William Pène. *The Giant.* **Illus. by the author. Dell, 1987. ISBN 0-440-42994-3**

[11 chapters, 124p.] While touring Europe to complete work on "A Bear's Guide to the World's Pleasure Spots," the author meets El Muchacho, the biggest boy on Earth. Go from large to small with Mary Norton's classic of the tiny family that lives under the grandfather clock, *The Borrowers.* FANTASY. GIANTS. SIZE.

1295   Du Bois, William Pène. *The Twenty-One Balloons.* **Illus. by the author. Viking, 1947. ISBN 0-670-73441-1**

[10 chapters, 180p.] Professor Sherman provides a detailed account of his fantastic balloon voyage to the island of Krakatoa and the secret diamond-rich colony of citizens he discovers there before the volcanic eruption of 1883. Also let off steam with Roger W. Drury's *The Finches' Fabulous Furnace* and Seymour Simon's nonfiction *Volcanoes.* ADVENTURE AND ADVENTURERS. BALLOONS. FANTASY. NEWBERY MEDAL. VOLCANOES.

1296   Fife, Dale. *North of Danger.* **Illus. by Haakon Saether. Dutton, 1978. ISBN 0-525-36035-2**

[16 chapters, 72p.] In 1940, 12-year-old Arne must brave snow and hardships to warn his underground leader father of the impending Nazi occupation of their Norwegian town of Spitsbergen in a thrilling survival story based on a true incident. See how other children survived World War II in England with Noel Streatfeild's *When the Siren's Wailed*, in Denmark in Lois Lowry's *Number the Stars*, in the United States with Yoshiko Uchida's *Journey Home*, and in Poland with Eva-Lis Wuorio's *Code: Polonaise.* ADVENTURE AND ADVENTURERS. HISTORICAL FICTION. SKIING. SURVIVAL. WORLD WAR, 1939–1945.

1297   Fisk, Nicholas. *Grinny: A Novel of Science Fiction.* **Nelson, 1974.**

[28 short chapters, 124p.] Tim's diary entries from January to April detail his growing suspicion that Great-Aunt Emma might really be an evil alien from space. Your diarists can record their normal and not-so-normal observations in their own journals, especially if you also read Louise Fitzhugh's *Harriet the Spy.* BROTHERS AND SISTERS. EXTRATERRESTRIAL LIFE. SCIENCE FICTION. SUSPENSE.

1298   Fitzhugh, Louise. *Harriet the Spy.* **Illus. by the author. Harper & Row, 1964. ISBN 0-06-021911-4**

[16 chapters, 298p.] A young Manhattan snooper's secret notebook, in which she obsessively records all her observations about the people around her including nursemaid Ole Golly, is filched by her curious and indignant classmates. Look into some basic spy techniques with books on codes and ciphers in the 652 section of the library. Perhaps if Harriet had written her notebook in code, things would have gone easier for her. FRIENDSHIP. SCHOOLS. WRITING.

1299   Fleischman, Paul. *The Half-a-Moon Inn.* **Illus. by Kathy Jacobi. Harper & Row, 1980. ISBN 0-06-021918-1**

[9 chapters, 88p.] While searching for his mother after a blizzard, mute Aaron takes shelter at an eerie inn where he is held captive by the ominous old proprietress, Miss Grackle. In a similar mood, Oliver from *The Ghost in the Noonday Sun*, written by Fleischman's father Sid, is expected to find riches for an unscrupulous pirate. Turning to folklore, the Russian witch *Baba Yaga*, as retold by Ernest Small, has a similar sinister feel. HANDICAPS. KIDNAPPING. ROBBERS AND OUTLAWS. SUSPENSE.

1300   **Fleischman, Sid.** *By the Great Horn Spoon.* **Illus. by Eric Von Schmidt. Little, Brown, 1963. ISBN 0-316-28577-3**

[17 chapters, 193p.] Stowaways on a ship from Boston, young Jack Flagg and his faultless butler, Praiseworthy, plan to hunt for gold in the 1849 California gold rush. Moving forward almost a century, reveal how Norwegian children helped hide their country's gold from the Nazis during World War II in Marie McSwigan's *Snow Treasure*, based on an actual incident. CALIFORNIA. HISTORICAL FICTION. U.S.– HISTORY–1783–1865–FICTION. WEST.

1301   **Fleischman, Sid.** *The Ghost in the Noonday Sun.* **Illus. by Peter Sis. Greenwillow, 1989. ISBN 0-688-08410-9**

[16 chapters, 173p.] Because he was born on the stroke of midnight with the supposed power to see ghosts, Oliver is kidnapped by pirates intent on using him to help them find the late Gentlemen Jack's buried treasure. Find out where some real treasures were dug up from Judy Donnelly's *True-Life Treasure Hunts.* ADVENTURE AND ADVENTURERS. BURIED TREASURE. KIDNAPPING. PIRATES. SHIPS.

1302   **Fleischman, Sid.** *Jingo Django.* **Illus. by Eric Von Schmidt. Little, Brown, 1988. ISBN 0-316-28554-4**

[24 chapters, 172p.] After escaping from his chimney sweep master, General Dirty Face Jim Scurlock, Jingo Hawks meets up with gypsies while searching for his scoundrel father. Though the setting and plot are quite different, longing for an absent parent is also Warren's dilemma in the contemporary novel *The Two-Thousand-Pound Goldfish* by Betsy Byars. ADVENTURE AND ADVENTURERS. RUN-AWAYS.

1303   **Gardiner, John Reynolds.** *Top Secret.* **Illus. by Marc Simont. Little, Brown, 1985. ISBN 0-316-30368-2**

[12 chapters, 110p.] Spurred on by his grandpop who encourages him to use his brain and think crazy, Allen defies his rigid science teacher and continues to pursue his science project of human photosynthesis until he turns into a green plantlike boy. Dean Hughes's *Nutty Knows All* and Jim Murphy's *Weird and Wacky Inventions* would fit in fine here. As teachers, let's emulate grandpop and see what new ideas our budding scientists will generate. If plants are part of your science curriculum, don't resist this one. GRANDFATHERS. PLANTS. SCHOOLS. SCIENCE–EXPERIMENTS. TEACHERS.

1304   **George, Jean Craighead.** *Julie of the Wolves.* **Illus. by John Schoenherr. Harper & Row, 1972. ISBN 0-06-021944-0**

[approx. 12 sittings, 170p.] Torn between her Eskimo traditions and modern life, Miyax runs away and lives with the wolves on the Alaskan tundra. For children raised on wicked wolves à la "Little Red Riding Hood," the portrait of loyal, affectionate, and nurturing animals painted here should come as a shock. Assign some wolf research to compare the legends with reality. ADVENTURE AND ADVEN-TURERS. ESKIMOS. NEWBERY MEDAL. SURVIVAL. WOLVES.

1305   **Grahame, Kenneth.** *The Wind in the Willows.* **Illus. by Ernest H. Shepard. Scribner, 1983. ISBN 0-684-17957-1**

[12 chapters, 255p.] The classic British river tale of Ratty, Mole, Badger, and Toad of Toad Hall, originally published in 1908, is a challenging read, but one of a tradition of brilliant British animal fantasies, the most recent of which is Brian Jacques's *Redwall*. ANIMALS. FANTASY. RIVERS.

1306   **Greer, Gery, and Bob Ruddick.** *Max and Me and the Time Machine.* **Harcourt, 1983. ISBN 0-15-253134-3**

[22 chapters, 114p.] With the aid of Professor Flybender's fantastic time machine, two boys find themselves in the midst of knights and mayhem in thirteenth-century England. Try out other time travel books, going back to the dinosaur era with Stan McMurtry's *The Bunjee Venture* and U.S. colonial days with Jay Williams and Raymond Abrashkin's *Danny Dunn, Time Traveler*. ENGLAND. HISTORICAL FICTION. HUMOROUS FICTION. MIDDLE AGES. SPACE AND TIME.

1307   **Greer, Gery, and Bob Ruddick.** *Max and Me and the Wild West.* **Harcourt, 1988. ISBN 0-15-253136-X**

[22 chapters, 138p.] If your students are studying western expansion (and even if they're not), a perfect complement to Russell Freedman's nonfiction *Children of the Wild West* and *Cowboys of the Wild West* (Clarion, 1985) is this slapstick old-time adventure of Max and narrator Steve as they take another journey with their garage sale time machine and find themselves transformed into a traveling actor and a newspaper man. Outlaws, a flimflam man, and dime novels add to the 1882 boomtown atmosphere of Silver Gulch. Also see Sid Fleischman's *By the Great Horn Spoon* and Stephen Mooser's *Orphan Jeb at the Massacree*. Round it off with David A. Adler's *Wild Pill Hickock and Other Old West Riddles*. HISTORICAL FICTION. HUMOROUS FICTION. ROBBERS AND OUTLAWS. SPACE AND TIME. WEST.

1308   **Hayes, William.** *Project: Genius.* **Atheneum, 1962.**

[22 chapters, 135p.] Pete's first attempts to win first prize for Franklin school's most original outside project contest backfires and even breaks windows until he proves the earth is round. His enthusiasm can be a source of inspiration for your own science curriculum. A wide variety of entertaining science-based fiction makes for satisfying read alouds, among them John Reynolds Gardiner's *Top Secret*, Dean Hughes's *Nutty Knows All*, and Seymour Simon's "Einstein Anderson." With the exception of Irene in the "Danny Dunn" series by Jay Williams and Raymond Abrashkin, female scientists as main characters are conspicuously scarce. One exception is Frankie in *The Monster Garden* by Vivian Alcock, which begins to give equal time for curious science-minded girls. SCHOOLS. SCIENCE–EXPERIMENTS.

1309   **Heath, W. L.** *Max the Great.* **Illus. by Dorothy Koda. Crane, 1977.**

[19 chapters, 88p.] An organ-grinder's monkey takes over a hound dog's popularity in the small town of Greenwillow, Alabama. Move from realism to the realistic fantasy of *Castaways on Chimp Island* by Sandy Landsman. DOGS. MONKEYS.

1310   **Heide, Florence Parry.** *Banana Twist.* **Holiday House, 1978. ISBN 0-8234-0334-3**

[9 chapters, 111p.] While in the process of writing his application to the permissive Fairlee boarding school, Jonah D. Krock, TV and fast-food freak, meets up with Goober Grube, the world's creepiest neighbor. Bring in bananas as a snack, of course, but also consider having students fill in their own Fairlee school applications. Written as short scripts, Jonah's many encounters in the elevator of his apartment building would make a grand bit of Readers Theater. FRIENDSHIP. HUMOROUS FICTION. WRITING.

1311   Holland, Isabella. *Alan and the Animal Kingdom*. Lippincott, 1977.

[7 chapters, 190p.] Fearful that the authorities will take away his six precious pets, Alan keeps the death of his only relative a secret from the child authorities and stays alone in the relative's New York City apartment. Orphaned Emily keeps her kitten secret in a different type of survival story in *Peppermints in the Parlor* by Barbara Brooks Wallace. Also try pairing this with another New York story, *The Cricket in Times Square* by George Selden, where the animals must look out for themselves, even with boy Mario's help. NEW YORK CITY. ORPHANS. PETS.

1312   Hughes, Dean. *Nutty Knows All*. Atheneum, 1988. ISBN 0-689-31410-8

[15 chapters, 150p.] With only one week left to think up a spectacular science fair project to impress his skeptical friends and classmates, Nutty Nutsell goes along with friend and genius William Bilks in a one-of-a-kind experiment with photons that makes his head glow in the dark. Fifth in the naturally funny "Nutty" series, which your Alvin Fernald and McGurk fans will especially enjoy. Another partner in scientific wackiness is John Reynolds Gardiner's *Top Secret*. Have your mad scientists write new short stories about their own experiments run amok. CREATIVE WRITING. PRINCES AND PRINCESSES. SCHOOLS. SCIENCE–EXPERIMENTS.

1313   Hunter, Mollie. *Wicked One: A Story of Suspense*. Harper & Row, 1977. ISBN 0-06-022648-X

[11 chapters, 136p.] This Scottish tale of the Grollican, a mischievous otherworld creature who plagues a quick-tempered forester and his family, will go along wickedly well with Shirley Climo's *Piskies, Spriggans, and Other Magical Beings: Tales from the Droll-Teller* and Virginia Haviland's *Favorite Fairy Tales Told in Scotland*. MAGIC. SCOTLAND.

1314   Hurmence, Belinda. *A Girl Called Boy*. Clarion, 1982. ISBN 0-395-31022-9

[18 chapters, 168p.] Blanche Overtha Yancy, rebellious modern girl who cares nothing for her family's past history, finds herself a slave in 1850s North Carolina after she rubs a carved soapstone conjure bird. Read this as part of a packet including Stacey Chbosky's *Who Owns the Sun*, Jeanette Winter's bold picture book *Follow the Drinking Gourd*, Ellen Levine's factual *If You Traveled on the Underground Railroad*, and Ann McGovern's *Runaway Slave: The Story of Harriet Tubman*, all of which give valuable background on the slave experience in America. In addition, complete the study and discussion with a sampling of "Uncle Remus" tales retold by Julius Lester or Van Dyke Parks. AFRICAN AMERICANS. HISTORICAL FICTION. SLAVERY. SPACE AND TIME. U.S.–HISTORY–1783–1865–FICTION.

1315   Jacques, Brian. *Redwall*. Philomel, 1987. ISBN 0-399-21424-0

[58 chapters, 351p.] During the summer of the Late Rose, the peaceful abbey mouse of Mossflower Wood is laid siege by Cluny the Scourge, a savage bilge rat known for his whiplike tail and his menacing band of rats, 500 strong. This a masterpiece to remember. Compile an illustrated biographical dictionary that includes a description of each character, a forest cookbook, and an outline, battle by battle, of both sides' military strategy. ANIMALS. FANTASY. MICE. RATS.

1316   Juster, Norton. *The Phantom Tollbooth*. Illus. by Jules Feiffer. Knopf, 1988. ISBN 0-394-82037-1

[20 chapters, 256p.] The ultimate fantasy—reprinted from the 1961 edition—as indifferent Milo journeys, via toy car, to Dictionopolis and Digitopolis with Tock, a ticking watchdog. Here is a feast of word and number play around which you could build your entire language arts curriculum. Boost everyone's word power with Paul Levitt's vocabulary stories from *The Weighty Word Book*, Eve Merriam's *Chortles: New and Selected Wordplay Poems*, and Marvin Terban's wordplay explanations and riddles, including *In a Pickle and Other Funny Idioms*. DOGS. ENGLISH LANGUAGE. FANTASY. VOCABULARY.

1317   **Kehret, Peg. *Deadly Stranger*. Dodd, Mead, 1987. ISBN 0-399-21701-0**

[14 chapters, 174p.] When Katie's new friend Angie is abducted and held in a remote barn by a deranged young man, Katie, as the only witness, becomes the man's next target. The plot device of shifting between two main characters' point of view is an effective one for maintaining the tension in a story. Betsy Byars does the same thing in her "Blossoms" quartet, starting with *The Not-Just-Anybody Family*, which creates a different type of suspense. KIDNAPPING. SUSPENSE.

1318   **Kennedy, Richard. *Inside My Feet*. Illus. by Ronald Himler. Harper & Row, 1979. ISBN 0-06-023119-X**

[2–3 sittings, 71p.] A horrifying tale about a boy who saves himself and his parents from a pair of enchanted boots and the murderous giant who controls them. The crazed giant's question "What became of the child I was?" is an interesting one to pose to listeners. ADVENTURE AND ADVENTURERS. FANTASY. GIANTS. RATS. SUSPENSE.

1319   **King-Smith, Dick. *Babe, the Gallant Pig*. Illus. by Mary Rayner. Crown, 1985. ISBN 0-517-55556-5**

[12 chapters, 118p.] An intelligent and determined young pig learns the ropes of sheepherding from his adopted mother, a collie. Sheep figure in Mary Francis Shura's realistic *Mister Wolf and Me*, when Miles risks having his German shepherd put down for possibly killing several of a farmer's flock. DOMESTIC ANIMALS. FARM LIFE. PIGS.

1320   **King-Smith, Dick. *Pigs Might Fly*. Illus. by Mary Rayner. Viking, 1982. ISBN 0-670-55506-1**

[21 chapters, 158p.] Daggie Dogfoot, the runt of the litter, proves himself to the rest of the barnyard by learning to swim and saving the day when the farm is flooded. Move from fantasy to realism with the bird-hunting pig in Larry Callen's *Pinch*. ENGLAND. FANTASY. FARM LIFE. PIGS.

1321   **Korman, Gordon. *This Can't Be Happening at Macdonald Hall*. Illus. by Affie Mohammed. Scholastic, 1978. ISBN 0-590-40534-9**

[14 chapters, 123p.] Headmaster Sturgeon, alias The Fish, tries to split up the infamous roommate team of Boots and Bruno. First of an overwhelmingly funny series about an all-boys' boarding school across the road from an all-girls' school; you'll also want to booktalk *Beware the Fish* (1980), *Go Jump in the Pool* (1979), *The War with Mr. Wizzle* (1982), and *The Zucchini Warriors* (1988). For added inspiration, this book was written as an English assignment when the author was 13! FRIENDSHIP. HUMOROUS FICTION. SCHOOLS.

1322 Kotzwinkle, William. *Trouble in Bugland: A Collection of Inspector Mantis Mysteries.* Illus. by Joe Servello. Godine, 1983. ISBN 0-87923-472-5

[5 chapters, 152p.] For Sherlock Holmes fans and the most discerning of mystery lovers, this collection of cases, populated entirely by insect characters, is ingenious, challenging, and worth savoring. Look in the 595 section of the library for factual evidence to back up the story, along with Paul Fleischman's insect duet poems, *Joyful Noise.* INSECTS. MYSTERY AND DETECTIVE STORIES.

1323 Landsman, Sandy. *Castaways on Chimp Island.* Atheneum, 1986. ISBN 0-689-31214-8

[18 chapters, 203p.] Sick of daily language labs where he learns American sign language, aspiring actor Danny pretends to forget everything he's learned, which backfires and results in his being sent with three other chimps to a jungle island. Hold on to your hats: Narrator Danny is a chimp, too! This beguiling survival adventure is a natural extension of Francine Patterson's *Koko's Kitten* and *Koko's Story.* CHIMPANZEES. SURVIVAL.

1324 Lawson, Robert. *Ben and Me.* Illus. by the author. Little, Brown, 1939. ISBN 0-316-51732-1

[15 chapters, 114p.] "A New and Astonishing *Life* of *Benjamin Franklin* as written by his Good Mouse *Amos,*" in which said mouse takes credit for many inventions and Ben's success in Paris during the American Revolution. Use this to start research on the man, the times, and the inventions, with the able assistance of Ingri and Edgar Parin D'Aulaire's *Benjamin Franklin* and Jean Fritz's *What's the Big Idea, Ben Franklin?* Danny and his companions also meet up with the great inventor in *Danny Dunn, Time Traveler* by Jay Williams and Raymond Abrashkin. FRANCE. HISTORICAL FICTION. INVENTIONS. MICE. U.S.–HISTORY–REVOLUTION–FICTION.

1325 L'Engle, Madeleine. *A Wrinkle in Time.* Farrar, 1962. ISBN 0-374-38613-7

[12 chapters, 211p.] Meg travels with her little brother Charles Wallace and friend Calvin through time and space to rescue her scientist father from the sinister planet of Camazotz. For science rediscovered, follow up with Tom McGowen's *The Magician's Apprentice* set in the distant ruined future; for pure magic versus more evil, thrill to L. J. Smith's *The Night of the Solstice.* BROTHERS AND SISTERS. NEWBERY MEDAL. SCIENCE FICTION. SPACE AND TIME.

1326 Levitt, Paul M., Douglas A. Burger, and Elissa S. Guralnick. *The Weighty Word Book.* Illus. by Janet Stevens. Bookmaker's Guild, 1989. ISBN 0-917665-13-9

[26 short stories, 99p.] Twenty-six difficult words—from abasement to zealot—are each presented in unforgettable story form, each ending with a word pun that makes it impossible not to recall the meaning. Each story and accompanying illustration is delightfully entertaining as well, and you will be stirred to writing new pun-full anecdotes of vocabulary words with your class. Read one a day, and by the end of the month your future SAT takers will be scintillating, winsome, and of course raucous. *Not to be missed!* Fans of Norton Juster's *The Phantom Tollbooth* will find this stimulating. CREATIVE WRITING. SHORT STORIES. VOCABULARY. WORD GAMES.

1327 Lowry, Lois. *All about Sam.* Illus. by Diane de Groat. Houghton Mifflin, 1988. ISBN 0-395-48662-9

[13 chapters, 135p.] An introduction to Anastasia Krupnik's little brother, from birth to four, taking him through diaper changing, the terrible two's, and preschool highs and lows. An ecstatic and endearing trip down memory lane for students who will relive their own "childhoods" and perhaps write about them. Don't neglect to have the rest of the "Anastasia" series at hand, as she is a character all will value knowing. BABIES. FAMILY LIFE. HUMOROUS FICTION.

1328   **Lowry, Lois. *Number the Stars*. Houghton Mifflin, 1989. ISBN 0-395-51060-0**

[18 chapters, 137p.] In Nazi-occupied Copenhagen of 1943, 10-year-old Annemarie becomes a small part of the Danish Resistance when her family helps her best friend, Ellen Rosen, escape with her family to Sweden. Based on actual events, Lowry's story helps introduce the Holocaust to children who are just starting to develop a sense of history. Other books of heroic wartime children include Dale Fife's *North of Danger*, Noel Streatfeild's *When the Sirens Wailed*, Yoshiko Uchida's *Journey Home*, Hilma Wolitzer's *Introducing Shirley Braverman*, and Eva-Lis Wuorio's *Code: Polonaise*. Chana Byers Abels's photo essay, *The Children We Remember*, is a good way to introduce a topic that is difficult for children to comprehend. *Clara's Story*, Clara Isaacman's autobiography of hiding from the Nazis in Belgium, is also unforgettable. FRIENDSHIP. HISTORICAL FICTION. JEWS. NEWBERY MEDAL. WORLD WAR, 1939–1945–FICTION.

1329   **McGowen, Tom. *The Magician's Apprentice*. Illus. by the author. Dutton, 1987. ISBN 0-525-67189-7**

[17 chapters, 119p.] Intending to rob the house of Armindor the Magician, young pickpocket Tigg is startled to discover the old man has singled him out to become his apprentice. While this begins as standard otherworld fantasy, readers will slowly become aware that it actually takes place 3,000 years in Earth's primitive future, long after the Fire from the Sky ended our current Age of Magic. As scissors, compass, kaleidoscope, and magnet are physically described for us to discern during the final chapter, have your students each bring to class a common object, hidden in a bag, and write a description for others to identify. Life after cataclysm is also dealt with in Jill Paton Walsh's *The Green Book*. FANTASY. MAGIC. MAGICIANS.

1330   **McSwigan, Marie. *Snow Treasure*. Illus. by Andre LaBlanc. Dutton, 1967. ISBN 0-525-39556-3**

[30 chapters, 179p.] Based on a true event where children smuggled gold bars on their sleds, a small Norwegian village saved millions of dollars worth of gold bullion from the clutches of the Nazis during World War II. Originally published in 1942. Another dangerous mission is carried out by Norwegian boy Arne when he must ski north to find his father before the Nazis do in *North of Danger* by Dale Fife and by Danish Annemarie who helps her Jewish friend's family escape to Sweden in Lois Lowry's *Number the Stars*. COURAGE. HISTORICAL FICTION. NORWAY. WORLD WAR, 1939–1945–FICTION.

1331   **Merrill, Jean. *The Pushcart War*. Illus. by Ronni Solbert. Addison-Wesley, 1964. ISBN 0-201-09313-8**

[36 chapters, 223p.] Pushcart peddlers fight back against the giant trucks in crowded New York City after Morris the florist's cart is deliberately crushed by Mack's mammoth moving truck. Over 25 years after publication, this tale is more current than ever. NEW YORK CITY. TRANSPORTATION. TRUCKS.

1332   **Morey, Walt. *Gentle Ben*. Illus. by John Schoenherr. Dutton, 1965. ISBN 0-525-30429-0**

[15 chapters, 191p.] Mark struggles to keep his beloved "pet," a wild Alaskan brown bear, in the northern Alaskan town of Orca City. Pair this with another Alaskan adventure, *Julie of the Wolves* by Jean Craighead George. ALASKA. BEARS.

1333   **Morey, Walt. *Sandy and the Rock Star*. Dutton, 1979. ISBN 0-525-38785-4**

[12 chapters, 171p.] Paul, a 15-year-old singing idol, runs away to an island owned by a big game hunter, where he tries to save a trained cougar from sure death. Hunting, specifically poaching, is given a far different slant in Roald Dahl's *Danny, the Champion of the World*. ADVENTURE AND ADVENTURERS. CATS. HUNTERS AND HUNTING. ISLANDS.

1334   **Morpurgo, Michael. *War Horse*. ABC Clio, 1989. ISBN 1-85089-943-6**

[21 chapters, 148p.] A harrowing and engrossing personal account of World War I, as narrated by Joey, the horse who survived it. Be sure to set aside time for discussion and study of the Great War. William Cole's *The Poetry of Horses* is a lovely collection to read from as a preface to each chapter. HISTORICAL FICTION. HORSES. WORLD WAR, 1914-1918-FICTION.

1335   **Newman, Robert. *The Case of the Baker Street Irregular*. Macmillan, 1984. ISBN 0-689-70766-5**

[16 chapters, 216p.] After being taken to London by his guardian, who is then kidnapped, orphan Anthony must seek aid from the world's greatest detective, Mr. Sherlock Holmes. Undoubtedly, after meeting the human detective, your sleuths will appreciate his insect counterpart, Inspector Mantis, in *Trouble in Bugland* by William Kotzwinkle, not to mention the mouse who lives in Holmes's basement, *Basil of Baker Street* by Eve Titus. ENGLAND. MYSTERY AND DETECTIVE STORIES.

1336   **Norton, Mary. *The Borrowers*. Illus. by Beth Krush and Joe Krush. Harcourt, 1953. ISBN 0-15-209987-5**

[20 chapters, 180p.] First in a classic series about the tiny family that lives under the old grandfather clock and makes a living borrowing from "human beans." Other interesting accounts of small folk include Lynne Reid Banks's *Indian in the Cupboard*, William Sleator's *Among the Dolls*, Kathy Kennedy Tapp's *Moth-Kin Magic*, and Elizabeth Winthrop's *The Castle in the Attic*. An interesting comparison is William Pène du Bois's *The Giant*, as his problems of surviving in a human-sized world are quite different. ADVENTURE AND ADVENTURERS. FANTASY. SIZE.

1337   **O'Brien, Robert C. *Mrs. Frisby and the Rats of NIMH*. Illus. by Zena Bernstein. Atheneum, 1971. ISBN 0-689-20651-8**

[28 chapters, 233p.] Brilliant laboratory rats plot their escape from the National Institutes of Mental Health. Lead your readers to the excellent sequel *Racso and the Rats of NIMH* written by O'Brien's daughter, Jane Leslie Conly. Read a contrasting treatment of animal laboratories in Ron Roy's realistic *The Chimpanzee Kid*. FANTASY. MICE. NEWBERY MEDAL. RATS.

1338   **O'Dell, Scott. *The Black Pearl*. Illus. by Milton Johnson. Houghton Mifflin, 1967. ISBN 0-395-06961-0**

[18 chapters, 96p.] Ramon recalls his life-and-death struggle when he sought the elusive Pearl of Heaven from the undersea clutches of Manta Diablo. Another splendid "Robinson Crusoe"-like survival story is *Island of the Blue Dolphins*, also by Scott O'Dell. ADVENTURE AND ADVENTURERS. FISHES. OCEAN.

1339   **O'Dell, Scott.** *Island of the Blue Dolphins.* **Houghton Mifflin, 1960. ISBN 0-395-06962-9**

[29 chapters, 181p.] An early 1800s survival story is narrated by Karana, an Indian girl who spent 18 years alone on an island off the California coast when her tribe relocated and she was inadvertently left behind. As spoiled modern folk, discuss what we might feel we could not do without on a desert island and what books we'd bring if we had a choice. See how Sam coped alone on his New York mountain in Jean Craighead George's *My Side of the Mountain*. Gurney Williams relates seven sagas of people who made it in *True Escape and Survival Stories*. ADVENTURE AND ADVENTURERS. HISTORICAL FICTION. INDIANS OF NORTH AMERICA . NEWBERY MEDAL. SURVIVAL.

1340   **Paterson, Katherine.** *Bridge to Terabithia.* **Illus. by Donna Diamond. Crowell, 1977. ISBN 0-690-01359-0**

[13 chapters, 128p.] When Leslie moves to Lark Creek, Jess loses his chance to be the fastest runner in school but gains an invaluable friend in a story of friendship and devastating loss. *On My Honor* by Marion Dane Bauer is another recounting of the death of a friend. DEATH. FRIENDSHIP. NEWBERY MEDAL. TEACHERS.

1341   **Paton Walsh, Jill.** *The Green Book.* **Illus. by Lloyd Bloom. Farrar, 1982. ISBN 0-374-32778-5**

[5 sittings, 74p.] Four years after leaving a doomed planet Earth in one of the last spaceships, a group of families settle on a small planet they name Shine and struggle to master the new unfamiliar environment. One loss everyone feels is the lack of books and stories. What books and personal items would your students choose to take along? Writing possibilities include filling in descriptions of what other natural phenomena the children might find on Shine, from food to animals, and how to use them in daily life. Another view of life after Earth's disaster is Tom McGowen's *The Magician's Apprentice*. BOOKS AND READING. CREATIVE WRITING. FAMILY LIFE. SCIENCE FICTION.

1342   **Pearce, Philippa.** *Tom's Midnight Garden.* **Illus. by Susan Einzig. Lippincott, 1984. ISBN 0-397-30475-7**

[27 chapters, 229p.] Each night during Tom's visit to his relatives, when the grandfather clock strikes 13, he goes back in time where he befriends a girl named Hattie. Julia L. Sauer's *Fog Magic* and David Wiseman's *Jeremy Visick* also use the device of a child moving back and forth to one time and place. Children can interview grandparents to find out what was strikingly different way back then and then write their own time travel stories, making themselves the main characters. ENGLAND. SPACE AND TIME.

1343   **Peck, Robert Newton.** *Mr. Little.* **Doubleday, 1979.**

[13 chapters, 87p.] Small-town boys Findley and his best friend Drag play a series of practical jokes on their new teacher before they realize what a special person he is. Move to fantasy to meet another unique teacher and a terror of a headmistress in Roald Dahl's *Matilda*. HUMOROUS FICTION. SCHOOLS. TEACHERS.

1344 **Pfeffer, Susan Beth.** *What Do You Do When Your Mouth Won't Open?* **Illus. by Lorna Tomei. Delacorte, 1981. ISBN 0-440-09471-2**

[11 chapters, 114p.] Reesa sets out to cure her public-speaking phobia when she wins an essay contest that requires her to read her composition to a large audience. On the humorous front, Alex enters an essay contest for Kittyfritters in the hilarious *Skinnybones* by Barbara Park. FEAR. SCHOOLS. SELF-CONCEPT.

1345 **Roberts, Willo Davis.** *The Girl with the Silver Eyes.* **Atheneum, 1980. ISBN 0-689-30786-1**

[14 chapters, 181p.] Although her telekenetic powers have always made her seem different, Katie discovers the identities of three more children her age who have her same abilities. Mind powers also dominate the two children who are having the same nightmare in William Sleator's *Into the Dream.* EXTRASENSORY PERCEPTION. FANTASY. SCIENCE FICTION.

1346 **Roberts, Willo Davis.** *The View from the Cherry Tree.* **Atheneum, 1975. ISBN 0-689-30483-8**

[16 chapters, 181p.] Everyone called it a tragic accident, but what Rob witnessed was old lady Calloway's murder, and no one will believe him. Fast paced and suspenseful, though sharp-eared listeners may be able to deduce the killer before the end. Make a chart of the suspects to help sort the clues. MURDER. MYSTERY AND DETECTIVE STORIES. SUSPENSE.

1347 **Robertson, Keith.** *Henry Reed's Baby-Sitting Service.* **Illus. by Robert McCloskey. Viking, 1966. ISBN 0-670-36825-3**

[16 chapters, 204p.] In the second of the witty "Henry Reed" series, Henry keeps his usual diary describing how he and his friend Midge earned money and trouble with their new summer jobs in small town Grover's Corner, New Jersey. It's easy come, easy go when Quentin asks for too much cash from a leprechaun in Bill Brittain's *All the Money in the World.* BABY-SITTERS. MONEY.

1348 **Roy, Ron.** *The Chimpanzee Kid.* **Clarion, 1985. ISBN 0-89919-364-1**

[19 chapters, 151p.] After his parents divorce and his dog is put to sleep, animal rights activist, school loner, and misfit Harold takes it upon himself to rescue a chimp from the nearby Laboratory for Primate Studies. This makes an unusual contrast to Robert C. O'Brien's mouse fantasy, *Mrs. Frisby and the Rats of NIMH,* where intelligent lab rats escape on their own, and to Sandy Landsman's tale of signing chimps in *Castaways on Chimp Island.* CHIMPANZEES. DIVORCE. FAMILY PROBLEMS. FRIENDSHIP.

1349 **Rylant, Cynthia.** *Children of Christmas: Stories for the Seasons.* **Illus. by S. D. Schindler. Orchard, 1987. ISBN 0-531-08306-3**

[6 chapters, 38p.] Six descriptive slice-of-life character situation studies, told in a blunt but emotionally moving present tense, about a Christmas tree man, a diner cat, a grieving grandfather, a solitary New York City girl, and a bag lady. Rylant cuts through the cynical commercialization of the season with an alternative vision to the usual sugarplums. CHRISTMAS. SHORT STORIES.

1350 **Sachs, Marilyn.** *The Bears' House.* **Dutton, 1987. ISBN 0-525-44286-3**

[6 chapters, 67p.] With the family on welfare, her father gone, and her mother depressed and unable to care for the five children, thumb-sucking outcast Fran

Ellen retreats into a fantasy life at school, where she joins the three toy bears and Goldilocks in the Bears' House, a dollhouse belonging to her teacher. Originally published in 1971. Continue with the sequel *Fran Ellen's House* (1987), where the family comes back together after being sent out to foster homes and Fran Ellen and her sisters restore the dollhouse together. DOLLS. FAMILY PROBLEMS. SCHOOLS. TEACHERS.

1351 **Salway, Lance.** *A Nasty Piece of Work and Other Ghost Stories.* **Illus. by Jeremy Ford. Clarion, 1985. ISBN 0-899-19-360-9**

[7 short stories, 128p.] Provocative original short stories about such unsettling subjects as a vengeful little sister and her obedient ghost, an eternally jealous twin, and a fly-infested bedroom will set your listeners' teeth on edge on a gloomy day. Light a candle, turn out the lights, and scare their socks off. Also intriguing is Ruth Ainsworth's *The Phantom Carousel and Other Ghostly Tales.* GHOST STORIES. SHORT STORIES.

1352 **Sargeant, Sarah.** *Weird Henry Berg.* **Dell, 1981. ISBN 0-440-49346-3**

[11 chapters, 113p.] Henry's antique egg, originally discovered by his great-grandfather almost a century before, hatches, yielding a baby dragon he names Vincent. Dragons interfere with a family's magic powers in Stephen Krensky's *The Dragon Circle.* Throw in some classic folklore such as Gail E. Haley's *Jack and the Fire Dragon*, Margaret Hodges's retelling of Spenser's *Saint George and the Dragon*, and Ruth Manning-Sanders's collection *A Book of Dragons.* A final good egg is Oliver Butterworth's *The Enormous Egg*, about a triceratops that is hatched by a chicken. DRAGONS. EGGS. FANTASY. LIZARDS.

1353 **Sauer, Julia L.** *Fog Magic.* **Illus. by Lynd Ward. Penguin, 1986. ISBN 0-14-032163-2**

[10 chapters, 107p.] Greta, who loves the fog, finds she can go through it back in time to the Blue Cove village of her ancestors. David Wiseman's *Jeremy Visick* also goes back 100 years to find out what happened to a boy trapped in a mining accident. FANTASY. HISTORICAL FICTION. SPACE AND TIME. U.S.–HISTORY–COLONIAL PERIOD– FICTION.

1354 **Service, Pamela F.** *Stinker from Space.* **Scribner, 1988. ISBN 0-684-18910-0**

[13 chapters, 96p.] After crashing to Earth in his desperate bid to escape an enemy Zarnk cruiser, Tsynq Yr takes on a new life form—that of a skunk—and seeks help from two science-minded Earth children with his plan to get back home. Correlate this with space studies, especially if a space shuttle launch is coming up. After you finish the book, children can write about how Karen and Jonathan might have rationalized their behavior to their parents and to government authorities. EXTRA-TERRESTRIAL LIFE. SCIENCE FICTION. SKUNKS.

1355 **Service, Robert W.** *The Cremation of Sam McGee.* **Illus. by Ted Harrison. Greenwillow, 1987. ISBN 0-688-06903-7**

[1 sitting, unp.] Famed early twentieth-century versifier's grisly Yukon gold rush classic about the Tennessee man who, on his deathbed, extracts from his friend, the narrator, a hard promise to keep. Be sure to practice this a few times before reading to your students, and talk over why building a fire is a tricky business in the frozen North. U.S. gold rush days are chronicled in Sid Fleischman's *By the Great Horn Spoon.* CANADA–POETRY. NARRATIVE POETRY. SNOW–POETRY. WINTER–POETRY.

1356   **Shyer, Marlene Fanta.** *My Brother, the Thief.* **Scribner, 1980. ISBN 0-684-16434-5**

[20 chapters, 137p.] Twelve-year-old Carolyn suspects her 15-year-old half-brother and his shady friend Flim-Flam of stealing team jackets from the town swim club. Talk about ethics and whether it's right to turn in or tell on a friend or relative if you know they've done something wrong. BROTHERS AND SISTERS. FAMILY PROBLEMS. STEALING.

1357   **Shyer, Marlene Fanta.** *Welcome Home, Jellybean.* **Macmillan, 1978. ISBN 0-689-71213-8**

[20 chapters, 152p.] When his 13-year-old retarded sister Geraldine comes home to live after having been institutionalized most of her life, Ned is unprepared for the drastic changes her presence makes in his family's routine. Shyer pulls no punches in her description of life with a retarded adolescent, and her description of a family in turmoil will win empathy for all characters involved. Ann Norris Baldwin's *A Little Time* and Sheila Garrigue's *Between Friends* deal with different aspects of the same handicap. BROTHERS AND SISTERS. FAMILY LIFE. HANDICAPS.

1358   **Skurzynski, Gloria.** *What Happened in Hamelin.* **Four Winds, 1979.**

[21 chapters, 173p.] How, after ridding the town of rats, the Pied Piper led the children away as payment for his deed, as told by Geist, the baker's apprentice who stayed behind. Most people do not realize the famed story is based on a true event that took place in Germany in 1284, and Skurzynski's harrowing account is unforgettable. See also Sara and Stephen Corrin's folktale *The Pied Piper of Hamelin,* and update the struggle between good and evil with Bill Brittain's fearful *Dr. Dredd's Wagon of Wonders.* "Willie Saxophone" from Alfred Slote's *The Devil Rides with Me* is also a good tie-in. GERMANY. HISTORICAL FICTION. MIDDLE AGES. ORPHANS. RATS.

1359   **Sleator, William.** *Into the Dream.* **Illus. by Ruth Sanderson. Dutton, 1979. ISBN 0-525-32583-2**

[10 chapters, 137p.] Paul discovers that Francine, a girl from his class, is having the same terrifying dream as he, night after night. Willo Davis Roberts's *The Girl with the Silver Eyes* has trouble adapting to her mind-reading gift, while Nicholas Fisk's *Grinny* is another novel of invading aliens. DREAMS. EXTRASENSORY PERCEPTION. SCIENCE FICTION.

1360   **Slote, Alfred.** *The Devil Rides with Me and Other Fantastic Stories.* **Methuen, 1980.**

[6 short stories, 83p.] Short stories about the Devil, dividing worms, a reverse Pied Piper in Hamelin, an extraordinary frog, a realistic painter, and a hero robot. Read "Thanks, Mr. Divido" along with Thomas Rockwell's *How to Eat Fried Worms* and "Willie Saxophone" with Gloria Skurzynski's *What Happened in Hamelin.* FANTASY. SHORT STORIES. SUPERNATURAL.

1361   **Smith, Alison.** *Help! There's a Cat Washing in Here.* **Illus. by Amy Rowen. Dutton, 1981. ISBN 0-525-31630-2**

[18 chapters, 152p.] Henry Walker attempts to take care of the housework and his younger brother and sister for two wild weeks while his mother prepares her portfolio for a new job illustrating children's books. Talk over the scope of chores children do at home and what it might be if they ran their households for a while. BABY-SITTERS. BROTHERS AND SISTERS. FAMILY LIFE. HUMOROUS FICTION. MOTHERS.

1362 Smith, L. J. *The Night of the Solstice.* Macmillan, 1987. ISBN 0-02-785840-5

[21 chapters, 230p.] Being lured to the old house on the hill by a beautiful talking fox is the first step of a perilous rescue mission that involves young Claudia and her three siblings in saving the human world from the sinister plans of the Wildworld Sorcerer, Cadel Forge. An exhilarating, credible, and original high fantasy that will leave you gasping. For more magic, read Madeleine L'Engle's *A Wrinkle in Time*, or try the distant future with Tom McGowen's *The Magician's Apprentice*. BROTHERS AND SISTERS. FANTASY. MAGIC.

1363 Speare, Elizabeth George. *The Sign of the Beaver.* Houghton Mifflin, 1983. ISBN 0-395-33890-5

[25 chapters, 135p.] Alone in his family's newly built cabin in the Maine wilderness of 1768 while his father fetches the rest of the family, 13-year-old Matt learns about survival from Attean, an aloof Indian boy. Compare life alone for Matt with that of an orphaned New York boy determined to keep his plight a secret in Isabelle Holland's *Alan and the Animal Kingdom*. FRIENDSHIP. FRONTIER AND PIONEER LIFE. HISTORICAL FICTION. INDIANS OF NORTH AMERICA. U.S.–HISTORY–COLONIAL PERIOD –FICTION.

1364 Steig, William. *Abel's Island.* Illus. by the author. Farrar, 1976. ISBN 0-374-40016-4

[20 chapters, 119p.] After attempting to retrieve his beloved wife Amanda's scarf, a chivalrous gentleman mouse is stranded on an island apart from her and must learn to fend for himself. Also read Steig's perfect picture book *Dr. DeSoto*, about a mouse couple in the dental profession who deal with large, sometimes ravenous, patients. ISLANDS. MICE. SURVIVAL.

1365 Stolz, Mary. *Quentin Corn.* Illus. by Pamela Johnson. Godine, 1985. ISBN 0-87923-553-5

[14 chapters, 122p.] To escape becoming a barrow and a barbecue, an intelligent pig runs away from the farm, disguises himself as a boy, and starts a new life as a small town handyman's helper. Another animal-turns-human tale, Lloyd Alexander's *The Cat Who Wished to Be a Man*, will make a nifty comparison novel when exploring the difficulties of becoming human. Additional tantalizing pig stories include Larry Callen's *Pinch*, Dick King-Smith's *Babe the Gallant Pig* and *Pigs Might Fly*, and Susan Kirby's *Ike and Porker*. FANTASY. PIGS. TRANSFORMATIONS.

1366 Streatfeild, Noel. *When the Sirens Wailed.* Illus. by Judith Gwyn Brown. Random House, 1976.

[18 chapters, 176p.] The three Clark children are evacuated from London to the countryside during World War II. Other gripping accounts of surviving the war include Dale Fife's *North of Danger*, Lois Lowry's *Number the Stars*, Yoshiko Uchida's *Journey Home*, Hilma Wolitzer's *Introducing Shirley Braverman*, and Eva-Lis Wuorio's *Code: Polonaise*. BROTHERS AND SISTERS. ENGLAND. HISTORICAL FICTION. WORLD WAR, 1939–1945–FICTION.

1367 Tannen, Mary. *The Wizard Children of Finn.* Knopf, 1981.

[18 chapters, 214p.] Fiona, a red-haired, headstrong 11-year-old, and her little brother Bran are transported to ancient Ireland 2,000 years back with an enchanted boy. Loosely based on the Irish legend "The Boyhood of Finn," about Finn M'Cool; children will want to read the splendid 1982 sequel, *The Lost Legend of Finn*.

Afterward, read Tomie dePaola's clever folktale *Finn M'Coul, the Giant of Knockmany Hill.* BROTHERS AND SISTERS. FANTASY. IRELAND. SPACE AND TIME.

1368   **Thayer, Ernest Lawrence.** *Casey at the Bat: A Ballad of the Republic, Sung in the Year 1888.* **Illus. by Wallace Tripp. Coward, 1978. ISBN 0-698-20486-7**

[1 sitting, unp.] A picture-book version of the classic narrative poem; read during the tumult of World Series week, and compare with Paul Frame's illustrated version (Prentice Hall, 1964). Frame's illustrations are reminiscent of old photos, while Tripp's multicolored sketches show Casey as a pompous, uniformed bear alongside his animal teammates. BASEBALL–POETRY. NARRATIVE POETRY. STORIES IN RHYME.

1369   **Thomas, Jane Resh.** *The Princess in the Pigpen.* **Clarion, 1989. ISBN 0-395-51587-4**

[16 chapters, 130p.] Sick with the fever, Elizabeth, daughter to the Duke of Umberland, is aghast to find herself not in her family's fine London house but on an Iowa farm almost 500 years in the future where modern life is beyond her comprehension. Students can delve into the life and times of Queen Elizabeth I, the main character's namesake, and those of other historical folk mentioned, such as William Shakespeare, Sir Walter Raleigh, and the Earl of Essex. Make a time line of inventions and discoveries from 1600 to the present to see the developments in science and social customs since then. ENGLAND. FARM LIFE. HISTORICAL FICTION. SPACE AND TIME.

1370   **Uchida, Yoshiko.** *Journey Home.* **Illus. by Charles Robinson. Atheneum, 1978. ISBN 0-689-50126-9**

[18 chapters, 131p.] Problems of getting their lives back together in California beset 12-year-old Yuki and her Japanese American family after leaving Topaz, a World War II concentration camp in Utah. This is the sequel to the hard-to-find *Journey to Topaz* (Scribner, 1971), which describes their internment. Contrast with Hilma Wolitzer's *Introducing Shirley Braverman* about 1944 Brooklyn, a different sort of home front story. FAMILY LIFE. HISTORICAL FICTION. PREJUDICE. WORLD WAR, 1939–1945–FICTION.

1371   **Ullman, James Ramsay.** *Banner in the Sky.* **Lippincott, 1988. ISBN 0-06-447048-2**

[19 chapters, 252p.] In 1865, 16-year-old Rudi yearns to conquer the Citadel, a great Swiss mountain overlooking his village where his father, a guide, died 15 years before. A reprint of the 1954 edition. Mafatu proves his courage by going out on the ocean alone in William Sperry's *Call It Courage.* ADVENTURE AND ADVENTURERS. COURAGE. HISTORICAL FICTION. MOUNTAINS. SURVIVAL.

1372   **Wallace, Barbara Brooks.** *Peppermints in the Parlor.* **Atheneum, 1980. ISBN 0-689-30790-X**

[18 chapters, 198p.] Orphaned little rich girl Emily Luccock becomes a servant when she arrives at her aunt's San Francisco mansion and finds it transformed into an old people's home, under the iron rule of the wicked Mrs. Meeching. California is also the setting for Sid Fleischman's gold rush adventure, *By the Great Horn Spoon.* ADVENTURE AND ADVENTURERS. AUNTS. ORPHANS.

1373   **Wallace, Bill.** *Beauty.* **Holiday House, 1988. ISBN 0-8234-0715-2**

[22 chapters, 177p.] With Luke's mama laid off from her job and no other way to make ends meet, they move from Denver to her father's farm in Oklahoma where

Luke confronts his feelings about his parents' separation, gets to know his crusty old Grampa, and learns to ride his mother's old horse. From realistic fiction, move to historical fantasy with Michael Morpurgo's World War I drama *War Horse*. FAMILY PROBLEMS. FARM LIFE. GRANDFATHERS. HORSES.

1374   **Winthrop, Elizabeth.** *The Castle in the Attic.* **Holiday House, 1985. ISBN 0-8234-0579-6**

[17 chapters, 179p.] Planning after 10 years as beloved housekeeper to go back to England, Mrs. Philips entrusts her family heirloom, a toy castle, to her disconsolate 10-year-old charge William, who finds a living knight within. This medieval quest fantasy will go along well with Lynne Reid Bank's more modern *The Indian in the Cupboard* and Pamela Stearn's lighthearted *Into the Painted Bear Lair*. FANTASY. KNIGHTS AND KNIGHTHOOD. SIZE.

1375   **Wiseman, David.** *Jeremy Visick.* **Houghton Mifflin, 1981. ISBN 0-395-30449-0**

[23 chapters, 170p.] Stumbling upon an old carved tombstone in a nearby graveyard, Matthew is driven to find the remains of a 12-year-old boy lost in a mining accident in his town in Cornwall, England, over 100 years before. If you have access to an old graveyard, a class trip to read the headstones and research local history might be in order. ENGLAND. HISTORICAL FICTION. SPACE AND TIME.

1376   **Wolitzer, Hilma.** *Introducing Shirley Braverman.* **Farrar, 1975. ISBN 0-374-33646-6**

[22 chapters, 153p.] Growing up in Brooklyn during the last year of World War II when she was 12, Shirley's experiences make that distant era comprehensible to today's children who have never known war times. Also read *Journey Home*, Yoshiko Uchida's account of a Japanese American family after internment in a U.S. concentration camp during the war. FAMILY LIFE. HISTORICAL FICTION. NEW YORK CITY. WORLD WAR, 1939-1945-FICTION.

1377   **Wuorio, Eva-Lis.** *Code: Polonaise.* **Holt, 1971.**

[23 chapters, 198p.] During the Nazi occupation of Poland, a group of brave, home-less children in Warsaw start an underground newspaper. Play a recording of Chopin's "Polonaise Militaire," the tune they use as a unifying call to resistance. Other essential World War II books include Dale Fife's *North of Danger*, Lois Lowry's *Number the Stars*, Noel Streatfeild's *When the Sirens Wailed*, Yoshiko Uchida's *Journey Home*, and Hilma Wolitzer's *Introducing Shirley Braverman*. COUR-AGE. HISTORICAL FICTION. SURVIVAL. WORLD WAR, 1939-1945-FICTION.

1378   **York, Carol Beach.** *I Will Make You Disappear.* **Nelson, 1974. ISBN 0-525-66410-6**

[14 chapters, 111p.] After moving into a cheerless summer house, the four Astin children discover a witch's room hidden under a trapdoor in the backyard shed. Your conjurers can make up new spells that do marvelous deeds, though, as in Willo Davis Roberts's *The Magic Book* or Jay Williams's *The Magic Grandfather*, sometimes spells backfire or work differently than you expect. BROTHERS AND SISTERS. SUSPENSE. WITCHES.

Illustration from ONCE UNDER THE CHERRY BLOSSOM TREE: AN OLD JAPA-
NESE TALE, retold and illustrated by Allen Say. Copyright © Harper & Row,
Publishers, 1974. Reprinted by permission of HarperCollins Publishers.

FOLK & FAIRY TALES, MYTHS AND LEGENDS: SINGLE STORIES

1379   Aardema, Verna. *Bimwili and the Zimwi*. Illus. by Susan Meddaugh. Dial, 1985. ISBN 0-8037-0213-2

[Gr. K–2] When the youngest sister runs back to the seashore to retrieve the shell she left behind, an ugly creature kidnaps her, hides her inside his drum, and makes her sing at each village he visits. Bring in a seashell so everyone can hear the sea's whisper. Also read Joanna Galdone's Slavic *The Little Girl and the Big Bear* and draw the parallels. FOLKLORE—AFRICA. MUSIC—FOLKLORE. SONGS—FOLKLORE.

1380   Aardema, Verna. *Bringing the Rain to Kapiti Plain*. Illus. by Beatriz Vidal. Dial, 1981. ISBN 0-8037-0809-2

[Gr. Pre–2] An African cumulative tale in rhyming "This Is the House That Jack Built" style, which explains how Ki-Pat shot an arrow into the clouds to end the drought. Children can join in on each refrain and continue the fun with Arnold Lobel's *The Rose in My Garden*, Rose Robart's *The Cake That Mack Ate*, Janet Stevens's *The House That Jack Built*, and Colin West's *The King of Kennelwick Castle*. CUMULATIVE STORIES. STORIES IN RHYME.

1381   Aardema, Verna. *Princess Gorilla and a New Kind of Water*. Illus. by Victoria Chess. Dial, 1988. ISBN 0-8037-0412-7

[Gr. Pre–2] When Princess Gorilla's father decrees he will marry her off to whoever can drink a barrel of vinegar, an elephant, hippopotamus, hog, and leopard all try and fail. A chantable refrain and evocative animal sound effects round out the merriment of this West African pourquoi tale, which complements Ruby Dee's Liberian tale, *Two Ways to Count to Ten*. Before reading, give each student a wee taste of vinegar; afterwards act out the story. CREATIVE DRAMA–FOLKLORE. FOLK-LORE–AFRICA. GORILLAS–FOLKLORE.

1382   Aardema, Verna. *Rabbit Makes a Monkey Out of Lion*. Illus. by Jerry Pinkney. Dial, 1989. ISBN 0-8037-0298-1

[Gr. Pre–3] Unable to keep his paws out of Lion's personal bee hive high in the calabash tree, Rabbit and his friends Bush-rat and Turtle outsmart the outraged big cat time and time again. Filled with Aardema's trademark storytelling sound effects and a few satisfying refrains to bellow, this story will lead you to Julius Lester's or Van Dyke Parks's "Uncle Remus" tales where Brer Rabbit takes on Brers Fox and

Bear in similar fashion. ANIMALS−FOLKLORE. FOLKLORE−AFRICA. LIONS−FOLKLORE. RABBITS−FOLKLORE. TRICKSTER TALES.

1383   **Aardema, Verna. *The Riddle of the Drum.* Illus. by Tony Chen. Four Winds, 1979.**

[Gr. 1−4] Cumulative Mexican folktale of a princess' suitor who must prove himself worthy by guessing what kind of animal skin covers the King's drum. Listeners will love repeating the name-filled refrain. Compare this with its Russian variant, Arthur Ransome's *The Fool of the World and the Flying Ship,* and extend the drum theme with Maggie Duff's drum-wielding blackbird from India in *Rum Pum Pum.* CHANTABLE REFRAIN. CUMULATIVE STORIES. FOLKLORE−MEXICO.

1384   **Aardema, Verna. *What's So Funny, Ketu?* Illus. by Marc Brown. Dial, 1982. ISBN 0-8037-9364-2**

[Gr. 1−4] Mirthful African story of a man who helps a snake and is rewarded with the magic gift of understanding animal speech. In the revised edition of Hugh Lofting's classic *The Story of Dr. Dolittle,* the kindly vet, who speaks a wide variety of animal dialects, travels to Africa to help cure a colony of sick monkeys. FOLK-LORE−AFRICA. SNAKES−FOLKLORE.

1385   **Aardema, Verna. *Who's in Rabbit's House?* Illus. by Leo Dillon and Diane Dillon. Dial, 1977. ISBN 0-8037-9550-5**

[Gr. 2−4] Masai story of how Rabbit and his friends got The Long One out of the house. Perfect to act out as Readers Theater, especially since the illustrations present the story as a play and the characters as costumed actors. ANIMALS−FOLKLORE. CREATIVE DRAMA−FOLKLORE. FOLKLORE−AFRICA. PLAYS.

1386   **Aardema, Verna. *Why Mosquitoes Buzz in People's Ears.* Illus. by Leo Dillon and Diane Dillon. Dial, 1975. ISBN 0-8037-6089-2**

[Gr. Pre−2] Cumulative African pourquoi tale of the chain of events that began when mosquito told a lie to iguana. Fun for recalling sequence and acting out, along with cause-and-effect tales such as Paul Galdone's folktale *The Old Woman and Her Pig,* Helen Lester's *It Wasn't My Fault,* and Jack Tworkov's *The Camel Who Took a Walk.* ANIMALS−FOLKLORE. CALDECOTT MEDAL. CUMULATIVE STORIES. FOLKLORE−AFRICA. POURQUOI TALES.

1387   **Aesop. *The Miller, His Son and Their Donkey: A Fable from Aesop.* Illus. by Eugen Sopko. North-South, 1988. ISBN 1-55858-067-0**

[Gr. K−2] Who should ride and who should walk? The farmer and his son learn the hard way that you never can please everyone, though sometimes, as in Antony Maitland's *Idle Jack,* things can work out for the best. DONKEYS−FOLKLORE. FABLES.

1388   **Aesop. *The Tortoise and the Hare: An Aesop Fable.* Illus. by Janet Stevens. Adapted by Janet Stevens. Holiday House, 1984. ISBN 0-8234-0510-9**

[Gr. Pre−2] The classic story, jazzed up a bit with running shorts and sneakers in the cheerful pictures, though the outcome remains the same. See also Brian Wild-smith's version, *The Hare and the Tortoise.* Mwenye Hadithi's *Tricky Tortoise* features another fast-thinking turtle. FABLES. RABBITS−FOLKLORE. TURTLES−FOLKLORE.

1389   **Alexander, Ellen. *Llama and the Great Flood: A Folktale from Peru.* Illus. by the author. Crowell, 1989. ISBN 0-690-04727-4**

[Gr. 2–4] A Peruvian llama's dream of a five-day flood helps him save his owner's family who climb to the top of a mountain with a sampling of every type of animal before the rains begin. One of the world's many flood myths, of which Noah's Ark is the best known. ANIMALS–FOLKLORE. FOLKLORE–PERU. RAIN AND RAINFALL–FOLKLORE. STORMS–FOLKLORE.

1390   **Aliki.** *The Twelve Months.* **Illus. by the author. Greenwillow, 1978.**

[Gr. 1–3] Greek folktale of a poor, humble widow and a jealous, rich one who each get what they deserve. Compare with variants Beatrice Schenk de Regniers's *Little Sister and the Month Brothers* and Samuel Marshak's *The Month Brothers.* FOLKLORE –GREECE. MONTHS–FOLKLORE.

1391   **Anderson, Lonzo.** *Arion and the Dolphins.* **Illus. by Adrienne Adams. Scribner, 1978.**

[Gr. K–3] Based on an ancient Greek legend where a lute-playing boy is thrown overboard into the sea, then rescued, and brought ashore by dolphins who appreciated his music. Miraculous modern-day *Nine True Dolphin Stories* by Margaret Davidson give this folktale credence. DOLPHINS–FOLKLORE. FOLKLORE–GREECE. MUSIC–FOLKLORE.

1392   **Arnold, Caroline.** *The Terrible Hodag.* **Illus. by Lambert Davis. Harcourt, 1989. ISBN 0-15284750-2**

[Gr. 1–5] In the far north woods, Lumberjack Ole Swenson and his compatriots enlist the aid of the feared Hodag, a 40-foot creature with the head of an ox, feet of a bear, back of a dinosaur, and tail of an alligator, to deal with their greedy boss man. A U.S. legend worthy of the tall-tale heroes like Paul Bunyan and his blue ox, Babe, and a contrast in temperament to Sasquatch and the Jersey Devil stories. ANIMALS, MYTHICAL–FOLKLORE. FOLKLORE–U.S.

1393   **Aruego, Jose, and Ariane Dewey.** *A Crocodile's Tale.* **Illus. by the authors. Scholastic, 1974. ISBN 0-590-09899-3**

[Gr. Pre–1] Philippine folk story of an ungrateful crocodile who decides to eat Juan after the boy has freed him from a trap. Act this one out with improvised dialogue and compare escapes with Paul Galdone's Indian fable *The Monkey and the Crocodile.* CREATIVE DRAMA–FOLKLORE. CROCODILES–FOLKLORE. FOLKLORE–PHILIPPINES.

1394   **Asbjørnsen, P. C.** *The Runaway Pancake.* **Illus. by Svend Otto S. Larousse, 1980.**

[Gr. Pre–1] Funny Norwegian cumulative tale to act out and to compare with variants such as Lorinda Bryan Cauley's *The Pancake Boy*, Paul Galdone's *The Gingerbread Boy*, and Ruth Sawyer's *Journey Cake, Ho!* CREATIVE DRAMA–FOLKLORE. CUMULATIVE STORIES. FOLKLORE–NORWAY.

1395   **Asbjørnsen, P. C.** *The Squire's Bride.* **Illus. by Marcia Sewall. Atheneum, 1975.**

[Gr. 1–4] The Squire wants to marry the farmer's pretty young daughter, but she, not the least bit interested, sends a horse in her stead. Clarify the humor by having pairs of children act out each scene. FOLKLORE–NORWAY. HORSES–FOLKLORE.

1396   **Asbjørnsen, P. C.** *The Three Billy Goats Gruff.* **Illus. by Marcia Brown. Harcourt, 1957.**

[Gr. Pre–2] The classic Norwegian tale of a nasty troll who gets his just deserts. Perfect to dramatize using improvised dialogue, but first discuss ways to pantomime the ending so children do not try to make the violence real. Compare with the version illustrated by Paul Galdone. Other troll-trickers include Edward Marshall's

Troll Country, Ingri and Edgar Parin D'Aulaire's *D'Aulaire's Trolls*, Tomie dePaola's *The Cat on the Dovrefell*, and Don Arthur Torgersen's *The Girl Who Tricked the Troll*. CREATIVE DRAMA—FOLKLORE. FOLKLORE—NORWAY. TROLLS—FOLKLORE.

1397 **Baker, Olaf. *Where the Buffaloes Begin*. Illus. by Stephen Gammell. Penguin, 1985. ISBN 0-14-050560-1**

[Gr. 3–6] American Indian story of Little Wolf who finds the fabled buffalo lake and saves his people from a marauding tribe. Buffalo play other roles in Paul Goble's Great Plains legends such as *Buffalo Woman* and *Her Seven Brothers*. Also read Russell Freedman's engrossing nonfiction *Buffalo Hunt* for an absorbing portrait of the Native American past. BUFFALOES—FOLKLORE. FOLKLORE—INDIANS OF NORTH AMERICA.

1398 **Bang, Molly. *Tye May and the Magic Brush*. Illus. by the author. Greenwillow, 1981.**

[Gr. K–3] A poor iron-willed Chinese girl's paintings come to life, much to the envy of the greedy emperor. Contrast with David McPhail's picture book, *The Magical Drawings of Mooney B. Finch*. ARTISTS—FOLKLORE. FOLKLORE—CHINA. PAINTING—FOLKLORE.

1399 **Bang, Molly. *Wiley and the Hairy Man*. Illus. by the author. Macmillan, 1976. ISBN 0-02-708370-5**

[Gr. K–3] Black American folktale about a boy who must fool the swamp-dwelling Hairy Man three times to be rid of him. Do not miss Mercer Mayer's *Liza Lou and the Yeller Belly Swamp*, Patricia McKissack's *Flossie and the Fox*, or Brinton Turkle's *Do Not Open* for comparisons. FOLKLORE, AFRICAN AMERICAN.

1400 **Barth, Edna. *Jack-O'-Lantern*. Illus. by Paul Galdone. Clarion, 1982. ISBN 0-89919-123-1**

[Gr. 3–6] American Halloween fare of how ornery Jack outwitted the Devil. For other fictionalized versions see Valerie Scho Carey's *The Devil & Mother Crump* and William H. Hooks's *Mean Jake and the Devils*. DEVIL—FOLKLORE. HALLOWEEN—FOLKLORE.

1401 **Basile, Giambattista. *Petrosinella: A Neopolitan Rapunzel*. Illus. by Diane Stanley. Warne, 1981.**

[Gr. 4–6] Compare this oversized, elegant Italian variant to the two Grimm renditions of *Rapunzel* illustrated by Trina Schart Hyman and the other by Bernadette Watts (Crowell, 1975). For another Italian princess overcome by witchery see Inna Rayevsky's *The Talking Tree*. CREATIVE DRAMA—FOLKLORE. DEVIL—FOLKLORE. FOLKLORE—ITALY. OGRES.

1402 **Belpré, Pura. *Oté*. Illus. by Paul Galdone. Pantheon, 1969.**

[Gr. 1–4] Puerto Rican tale of a nearsighted greedy devil who eats up a poor family's food, and the littlest boy who foils him. Good play material for either improvised drama or Readers Theater. CREATIVE DRAMA—FOLKLORE. DEVIL—FOLKLORE. FOLKLORE—PUERTO RICO.

1403 **Bennett, Jill. *Teeny Tiny*. Illus. by Tomie dePaola. Putnam, 1986. ISBN 0-399-21293-0**

[Gr. Pre–2] "Give me my bone!" the voice demands of the teeny tiny woman in her teeny tiny bed. The second time around, have everyone tell it with you. Paul Galdone's *The Teeny-Tiny Woman* is a good version too, and both are nonthreateningly scary, like Linda Williams's *The Little Old Lady Who Was Not Afraid of*

Anything. BONES—FOLKLORE. FEAR—FOLKLORE. FOLKLORE—ENGLAND. STORIES TO TELL.

1404 Blia, Xiong. *Nine-in-One, Grr! Grr! A Folktale from the Hmong People of Laos.* Illus. by Nancy Hom. Adapted by Cathy Spagnoli. Children's Book Press, 1989. ISBN 0-89239-048-4

[Gr. K–3] The Eu bird takes it upon herself to subvert tiger's song of how many cubs she will bear in a year, thus reducing the possible number of tigers on the earth today. Written up as a Readers Theater script, this would make a charming three-person skit. In *The Spooky Tail of Prewett Peacock* by Bill Peet, meet another tiger waylaid by a feathered fellow. BIRDS—FOLKLORE. CHANTABLE REFRAIN. FOLKLORE—LAOS. TIGERS.

1405 Bowden, Joan Chase. *The Bean Boy.* Illus. by Sal Murdocca. Macmillan, 1979.

[Gr. Pre–1] An amusing sequence story similar in intent to Paul Galdone's *What's in Fox's Sack?* and Jennifer Westwood's *Going to Squintum's.* All three are satisfying for telling and acting out with improvised dialogue. CHANTABLE REFRAIN. CREATIVE DRAMA—FOLKLORE. SEQUENCE STORIES.

1406 Bowden, Joan Chase. *Why the Tides Ebb and Flow.* Illus. by Marc Brown. Houghton Mifflin, 1979. ISBN 0-395-28378-7

[Gr. 1–6] When stubborn Old Woman takes the rock from the bottom of the sea, water begins to pour down through the bottomless hole uncovered there until Sky Spirit intervenes. An original explanation to use with your science lesson on oceans and tides. OCEAN. POURQUOI TALES.

1407 Brenner, Barbara. *Little One Inch.* Illus. by Fred Brenner. Coward, 1977.

[Gr. K–4] The Japanese Tom Thumb, named Issun Boshi, meets up with demons in the great outside world. For another miniature adventurer read Hans Christian Andersen's *Thumbelina* and Colin McNaughton's *Anton B. Stanton and the Pirats.* Go from vigilant to indolent with Dianne Snyder's *The Boy of the Three-Year Nap* and finish up with Linda Shute's rousing *Momotaro, the Peach Boy.* FOLKLORE—JAPAN. SIZE—FOLKLORE.

1408 Brett, Jan. *Goldilocks and the Three Bears.* Illus. by the author. Putnam, 1987. ISBN 0-396-08925-9

[Gr. Pre–1] Richly detailed, with bear-filled borders and ornaments. See also those versions by Lorinda Bryan Cauley, Armand Eisen, Paul Galdone, James Marshall, and Janet Stevens, as well as Brinton Turkle's wordless *Deep in the Forest* and Jane Yolen's poetic tie-in, *The Three Bears Rhyme Book.* BEARS—FOLKLORE. OBEDIENCE—FOLKLORE.

1409 Brett, Jan. *The Mitten.* Illus. by the author. Putnam, 1989. ISBN 0-399-21920-X

[Gr. Pre–2] When Nicki drops his newly knitted white mitten in the snow, the animals put it to good use, burrowing inside it and stretching it to keep warm. Alvin Tresselt retold a similar version of the same title, though Brett's illustrations are more lush. On the same topic, don't forget Lorinda Bryan Cauley's *The Three Little Kittens* or Jean Rogers's *Runaway Mittens.* ANIMALS—FOLKLORE. FOLKLORE—UKRAINE. MITTENS—FOLKLORE. WINTER—FOLKLORE.

1410 Brown, Marcia. *Cinderella: Or, The Little Glass Slipper*. Illus. by the author. Scribner, 1954. ISBN 0-684-12676-1

[Gr. 1–4] Illustrated in French baroque style; compare this award-winner with many versions including Shirley Climo's *The Egyptian Cinderella*, the Grimm version illustrated by Nonny Hogrogian, Paul Galdone's and Barbara Karlin's retellings, William H. Hook's *Moss Gown* from the Southern U.S., Charlotte Huck's *Princess Furball*, Dang Manh Kha's *In the Land of Small Dragon* from Vietnam, Ai-Ling Louie's *Yeh-Shen* from China, and Flora Annie Steel's *Tattercoats*. CALDECOTT MEDAL. FOLKLORE–FRANCE. PRINCES AND PRINCESSES–FOLKLORE.

1411 Brown, Marcia. *Dick Whittington and His Cat*. Illus. by the author. Scribner, 1988. ISBN 0-684-18998-4

[Gr. 1–4] Classic English story of the poor boy whose cat brought him riches and fame, ultimately as Lord Mayor of London. Compare the cat and circumstances with those in Lorinda Bryan Cauley's *Puss in Boots*. CATS–FOLKLORE. FOLKLORE–ENGLAND.

1412 Brown, Marcia. *Stone Soup*. Illus. by the author. Scribner, 1947. ISBN 0-684-92296-7

[Gr. 1–4] In a French village, some hungry soldiers teach the stingy villagers a cooking lesson. Use with Marilyn Hirsch's Hanukkah story *Potato Pancakes All Around*, Ann McGovern's simple version of *Stone Soup*, Harve Zemach's *Nail Soup*, and try out the recipes for lunch. A large cast of characters makes this suitable for acting out using improvised dialogue. FOLKLORE–FRANCE. FOOD–FOLKLORE. SOLDIERS–FOLKLORE. SOUP–FOLKLORE.

1413 Carrick, Carol. *Aladdin and the Wonderful Lamp*. Illus. by Donald Carrick. Scholastic, 1989. ISBN 0-590-41679-0

[Gr. 2–4] An elegantly illustrated retelling of the Arabian Nights tale, simpler in text than Andrew Lang's version or Marianne Mayer's expanded text, *Aladdin and the Enchanted Lamp*. FOLKLORE–ARABIA. GENIES–FOLKLORE. PRINCES AND PRINCESSES–FOLKLORE. WISHES–FOLKLORE.

1414 Cauley, Lorinda Bryan. *The Cock, the Mouse and the Little Red Hen*. Illus. by the author. Putnam, 1982. ISBN 0-399-20740-6

[Gr. Pre–2] An industrious hen saves the three title characters from a hungry fox. Lots of sound effects and a simple plot make this fun to act out. Continue Cauley's saga with Paul Galdone's *The Little Red Hen*, where the hen bakes bread without the help of her lazy companions. CHICKENS–FOLKLORE. CREATIVE DRAMA–FOLKLORE. FOXES–FOLKLORE.

1415 Cauley, Lorinda Bryan. *Goldilocks and the Three Bears*. Illus. by the author. Putnam, 1981. ISBN 0-399-20794-5

[Gr. Pre–2] Marvelous illustrations give new vitality to this old chestnut. Compare with other versions including those by Jan Brett, Armand Eisen, Paul Galdone, James Marshall, and Janet Stevens, along with Brinton Turkle's wordless *Deep in the Forest* and Jane Yolen's related *The Three Bears Rhyme Book*. BEARS–FOLKLORE. OBEDIENCE–FOLKLORE.

1416 Cauley, Lorinda Bryan. *The Goose and the Golden Coins*. Illus. by the author. Harcourt, 1981.

[Gr. K–1] Italian folktale about two poor sisters who buy an extraordinary gold-coin-laying goose. See how other gold-dispensing animals fare in Leslie L. Brooke's *The Golden Goose Book* and Jacob Grimm's *The Table, the Donkey and the Stick*. GEESE-FOLKLORE. MONEY.

1417 **Cauley, Lorinda Bryan. *Jack and the Beanstalk*. Illus. by the author. Putnam, 1983. ISBN 0-399-20901-8**

[Gr. 1–3] The original English "Fe Fi Fo Fum." Along with Susan Pearson's retelling, draw in all the other related tales, such as Raymond Briggs's modern day spoof *Jim and the Beanstalk*, Paul Galdone's English poetry rendition from 1807, *The History of Mother Twaddle and the Marvelous Achievements of Her Son, Jack*, and the U.S. Appalachian kin, Gail E. Haley's *Jack and the Bean Tree*, and James Still's *Jack and the Wonder Beans*. FOLKLORE-ENGLAND. GIANTS-FOLKLORE.

1418 **Cauley, Lorinda Bryan. *The Pancake Boy: An Old Norwegian Folk Tale*. Illus. by the author. Putnam, 1988. ISBN 0-399-21505-0**

[Gr. 1–3] Goody Poody's seven children race after the sweet-milk pancake that jumps out of the pan and gives them, Manny Panny, Henny Penny, Cocky Locky, Ducky Lucky, and Goosey Poosey, the slip. P. C. Asbjørnsen's *The Runaway Pancake* is another Norwegian version. Unlike Scott Cook's or Paul Galdone's *The Gingerbread Boy* or Ruth Crawford's *Journey Cake, Ho!* it's Piggy Wiggy who gets the last bite here. The added pancake recipe is one you can make in class and acting this out will give everyone an appetite. ANIMALS-FOLKLORE. CHANTABLE REFRAIN. FOLKLORE-NORWAY. FOOD-FOLKLORE.

1419 **Cauley, Lorinda Bryan. *Puss in Boots*. Illus. by the author. Harcourt, 1988. ISBN 0-15-264227-7**

[Gr. K–4] Thanks to the ingenuity and cunning of his fine-booted cat, a poor young man takes over the estates of an ogre and, as the marquis of Carabas, marries the king's lovely daughter. Contrast his fortunes with those of a poor English boy in Marcia Brown's *Dick Whittington and His Cat*. CATS-FOLKLORE. FOLKLORE-FRANCE.

1420 **Cauley, Lorinda Bryan. *The Three Little Pigs*. Illus. by the author. Putnam, 1980.**

[Gr. Pre–2] You will be surprised by the number of children who have never heard the whole story. Humorously and colorfully illustrated; see also versions illustrated by Erik Blegvad (Atheneum, 1980), Paul Galdone, James Marshall, and Margot Zemach. Break your group into pairs, with half portraying the savviest pigs, and the other half wolves who try every verbal angle to convince the pigs to open the door; then switch roles and try again. Try some down-home dialogue with William H. Hooks's American variant, *The Three Little Pigs and the Fox*, and hear the wolf's side of the story in Jon Scieszka's *The True Story of the 3 Little Pigs*. CREATIVE DRAMA-FOLKLORE. PIGS-FOLKLORE. WOLVES-FOLKLORE.

1421 **Cauley, Lorinda Bryan. *The Town Mouse and the Country Mouse*. Illus. by the author. Putnam, 1984. ISBN 0-399-21123-3**

[Gr. Pre–2] Mouse cousins visit each other to find they much prefer their own habitats. Based on an Aesop fable, this Victorian update can precede Lilian Moore's mouse poet story, *I'll Meet You at the Cucumbers*. Set up a friendly debate between town and country "mice" and let each side defend their way of life and, with supporting details, attempt to convince the others that their home is best. FABLES. MICE – FOLKLORE.

1422   Cheng, Hou-Tien. *The Six Chinese Brothers: An Ancient Tale.* **Illus. by the author. Holt, 1979.**

[Gr. Pre–2] Black-and-red scissors cuttings depict the saga of the identical brothers who cannot be executed. Compare with Claire Hutchet Bishop's *The Five Chinese Brothers* and Gerald McDermott's African tale, *Anansi the Spider,* which also boasts six unusual sons and a father in trouble. FOLKLORE – CHINA.

1423   Christian, Mary Blount. *April Fool.* **Illus. by Diane Dawson. Macmillan, 1986. ISBN 0-689-71075-5**

[Gr. 1–3] Foolish behavior by the townsfolk of Gotham convinces King John to build his hunting lodge elsewhere. Read this and Alice Schertle's *The April Fool* on the first of that month. Also, see Donald Carrick's *Harald and the Giant Knight,* Mirra Ginsburg's Russian *The Night It Rained Pancakes,* and Tomie dePaola's *The Mysterious Giant of Barletta* for more clever tricks. FOLKLORE – ENGLAND. FOOLS – FOLKLORE. KINGS AND RULERS – FOLKLORE.

1424   Climo, Shirley. *The Egyptian Cinderella.* **Illus. by Ruth Heller. Crowell, 1989. ISBN 0-690-04822-X**

[Gr. 2–6] One of the world's oldest Cinderella stories, first recorded in the first century B.C., this is loosely based on the true existence of Rhodopis, a Greek slave girl whose rose-red gold slipper is dropped into the bored Pharaoh's lap by a falcon. What a way to demonstrate the staying power of folklore! Among the 500 variants of the Cinderella story, choose from Marcia Brown's or Paul Galdone's French versions, Nonny Hogrogian's Grimm retelling, William H. Hooks's U.S. relative, *Moss Gown,* Charlotte Huck's *Princess Furball,* Dang Manh Kha's Vietnamese *In the Land of Small Dragon,* Ai-Ling Louie's *Yeh-Shen,* and Flora Annie Steel's English *Tattercoats.* Ancient Egypt units will be enriched with this and Gerald McDermott's *The Voyage of Osiris,* Mary Stolz's *Zekmet the Stone Carver,* and Irene and Laurence Swinbern's King Tut account, *Behind the Sealed Door.* FOLKLORE – EGYPT. KINGS AND RULERS – FOLKLORE.

1425   Climo, Shirley. *King of the Birds.* **Illus. by Ruth Heller. Harper, 1988. ISBN 0-690-04621-9**

[Gr. K–3] How wren won that honor and the right to keep all quarreling birds in line. This is a good lead-in to a bird unit in science, as so many species are identified and handsomely depicted in the course of the ancient tale. Read with Joanna Troughton's South American Indian tale *How the Birds Changed Their Feathers.* BIRDS – FOLKLORE. POURQUOI TALES.

1426   Cole, Joanna. *Bony-Legs.* **Illus. by Dirk Zimmer. Four Winds, 1983. ISBN 0-02-722970-X**

[Gr. K–2] Simplified but nicely chilling Baba Yaga story of how kind Sasha escapes her stew-pot fate with the aid of the witch's gate, dog, and cat, who give her a magic mirror and comb. Also read Ernest Small's *Baba Yaga* and Maida Silverman's *Anna and the Seven Swans.* FOLKLORE – RUSSIA. WITCHES – FOLKLORE.

1427   Conger, Leslie. *Tops and Bottoms.* **Illus. by Imero Gobbato. Four Winds, 1970.**

[Gr. Pre–3] How a devil is outsmarted by a quick-thinking farmer who promises him corn bottoms and carrot tops. If you are in a gardening mode, try Lois Ehlert's

Growing Vegetable Soup and Bruce McMillan's *Growing Colors*. DEVIL−FOLKLORE. FARM LIFE−FOLKLORE.

1428   Conover, Chris. *Mother Goose and the Sly Fox*. Illus. by the author. Farrar, 1989. ISBN 0-374-35072-8

[Gr. Pre−1] As in Jacob Grimm's *The Wolf and the Seven Little Kids*, once the mother is out of the house, leaving her seven children behind, the hungry fox disguises his paws and his voice to gain entrance and throw six of the seven goslings in his sack. Another fox who is deceived by the contents of his sack and meets an unhappy end can be found in both Paul Galdone's *What's in Fox's Sack* and Jennifer Westwood's *Going to Squintum's*. FOXES−FOLKLORE. GEESE−FOLKLORE.

1429   Cook, Scott. *The Gingerbread Boy*. Illus. by the author. Knopf, 1987. ISBN 0-394-88698-4

[Gr. Pre−1] The original dough boy runs away from the little old woman who made him, and a slew of other chasers, until the Fox comes along. Other versions include P. C. Asbjørnsen's *The Runaway Pancake*, Lorinda Bryan Cauley's *The Pancake Boy*, Paul Galdone's *The Gingerbread Boy*, and Ruth Sawyer's American variant, *Journey Cake, Ho!* CHANTABLE REFRAIN. CREATIVE DRAMA−FOLKLORE. FOXES−FOLKLORE. SEQUENCE STORIES.

1430   Cooper, Susan. *The Silver Cow: A Welsh Tale*. Illus. by Warwick Hutton. Atheneum, 1983. ISBN 0-689-50236-2

[Gr. 2−5] Until it is too late, Huw's small-hearted father will not believe the gentle cow in their field is magic, sent out of the lake by the Tylwyth Teg to acknowledge Huw's harp-playing. Zuzo Otsuka's *Suho and the White Horse* is another touching story of a boy who loses his animal friend but gains a fiddle in return. COWS− FOLKLORE. FAIRIES−FOLKLORE. FOLKLORE−WALES.

1431   Corrin, Sara, and Stephen Corrin. *The Pied Piper of Hamelin*. Illus. by Errol Le Cain. Harcourt, 1989. ISBN 0-15-261596-2

[Gr. 2−6] Dark, brooding, Breughel-style paintings haunt this legend that stems from a true incident in Germany in 1284. With grades five and six, read this along with Gloria Skurzynski's riveting fiction tale, *It Happened in Hamelin*. FOLKLORE- GERMANY. MIDDLE AGES−FOLKLORE. RATS−FOLKLORE.

1432   Dasent, George Webbe. *The Cat on the Dovrefell: A Christmas Tale*. Illus. by Tomie dePaola. Putnam, 1979. ISBN 0-399-20685-X

[Gr. Pre−2] A Norwegian Christmas yarn about Halvor who, with the help of a large white bear, scares away marauding trolls. See how these trolls measure up to the one from *The Three Billy Goats Gruff* as illustrated by Marcia Brown or Paul Galdone. Also try *D'Aulaire's Trolls* by Ingri and Edgar Parin D'Aulaire. BEARS− FOLKLORE. CHRISTMAS−FOLKLORE. FOLKLORE−NORWAY. TROLLS−FOLKLORE.

1433   Dasent, George Webbe. *East o' the Sun & West o' the Moon: An Old Norse Tale*. Illus. by Gillian Barlow. Philomel, 1988. ISBN 0-399-21570-0

[Gr. 2−6] So that her family might gain riches, the youngest daughter of a poor peasant family goes off to live with a White Bear who throws off his beast shape each night to become a man. Barlow's golden-toned, bordered paintings are almost primitive in style, a striking contrast to the somber-colored ones in Kathleen and Michael Hague's *East of the Sun and West of the Moon*. Stack this tale up against the

French variant, *Beauty and the Beast* as retold by either Rosemary Harris or Marianna Mayer, and also take time for the American "Whitebear Whittington" from Richard Chase's *Grandfather Tales* and Elizabeth Isele's Russian tale *The Frog Princess*. BEARS—FOLKLORE. FOLKLORE—NORWAY. TRANSFORMATIONS—FOLKLORE. TROLLS—FOLKLORE.

1434 **D'Aulaire, Ingri, and Edgar Parin D'Aulaire. *D'Aulaire's Trolls.* Illus. by the authors. Doubleday, 1972.**

[2 sittings, Gr. K–3] The truth about Norwegian trolls and their relatives, from hulder-maidens to gnomes. Read an assortment of troll stories, old and new, from Marcia Brown or Paul Galdone's *The Three Billy Goats Gruff* and Tomie dePaola's *The Cat on the Dovrefell*, to Edward Marshall's *Troll Country* and Don Arthur Torgersen's *The Girl Who Tricked the Troll*. FOLKLORE—NORWAY. TROLLS—FOLKLORE.

1435 **Dayrell, Elphinstone. *Why the Sun and Moon Live in the Sky.* Illus. by Blair Lent. Houghton Mifflin, 1990. ISBN 0-395-53963-3**

[Gr. Pre–2] The African folktale explanation of sky phenomena will relate to your astronomy lesson. Children can compose their own interpretations, especially after hearing Bess Clayton's *The Truth about the Moon* and Gerald McDermott's *Anansi the Spider*. FOLKLORE—AFRICA. MOON—FOLKLORE. SUN—FOLKLORE. WATER—FOLKLORE.

1436 **Dee, Ruby. *Two Ways to Count to Ten: A Liberian Folktale.* Illus. by Susan Meddaugh. Henry Holt, 1988. ISBN 0-8050-0407-6**

[Gr. K–3] Chanting "I will be king. I can do this thing!" Elephant, Bush Ox, Chimpanzee, and Lion all try and fail to throw a spear that must remain in the air until the count of ten in order to win the title of future king. Read this as you begin to teach or review the "two-times" table. Another African tale of fast-thinking contestants is Verna Aardema's *Princess Gorilla and a New Kind of Water*. ANIMALS—FOLKLORE. FOLKLORE—AFRICA. MATHEMATICS—FOLKLORE.

1437 **DeFelice, Cynthia C. *The Dancing Skeleton.* Illus. by Robert Andrew Parker. Macmillan, 1989. ISBN 0-02-726452-1**

[Gr. 2–4] Though mean and ornery Aaron Kelly is dead and buried, he feels just fine, so he comes home to sit in his rocking chair until he turns into nothing but a skeleton. After this humorous chiller, scare younger listeners with Sibyl Hancock's *Esteban and the Ghost* and the older ones with Astrid Lindgren's *The Ghost of Skinny Jack*. BONES—FOLKLORE. FOLKLORE—U.S. GHOST STORIES.

1438 **dePaola, Tomie. *The Comic Adventures of Old Mother Hubbard and Her Dog.* Illus. by the author. Harcourt, 1981. ISBN 0-15-219541-6**

[Gr. Pre–1] A rendition of the famous early nineteenth-century nursery rhyme by Sarah Catherine Martin. At the end of each verse, let students supply the rhyming word. Read again and act it out, with the children playing the dog, and make up some new verses to add to the folk process. See also versions illustrated by Evaline Ness (Holt, 1972), Paul Galdone, and the Swedish version by Lennart Hellsing (Coward, 1976). CREATIVE DRAMA—FOLKLORE. DOGS—FOLKLORE. NURSERY RHYMES. STORIES IN RHYME.

1439 dePaola, Tomie. *Fin M'Coul, the Giant of Knockmany Hill.* Illus. by the author. Holiday, 1981. ISBN 0-8234-0384-X

[Gr. 1–4] The famed Irish giant and his clever wife, Oonah, put an end to giant Cucullin's powers that lay in his brass finger. A welcome diversion from leprechauns for St. Patrick's or any day, though you may feel inspired to do a giant medley, including such well-known big guys as the ones from *Jack and the Beanstalk*, dePaola's *The Mysterious Giant of Barletta* and Jacob Grimm's *The Valiant Little Tailor*. FOLKLORE–IRELAND. GIANTS–FOLKLORE.

1440 dePaola, Tomie. *The Legend of the Bluebonnet: An Old Tale of Texas.* Illus. by the author. Putnam, 1983.

[Gr. 1–4] Sacrificing to the fire her beloved buckskins warrior doll, the only link to her now-dead parents, She-Who-Is-Alone appeases the great spirits who send rain and flowers to the drought-starved Comanche. Additional American Indian flower origin tales include dePaola's *The Legend of the Indian Paintbrush* and Barbara Juster Esbensen's *The Star Maiden*. As both of dePaola's works relate the legends behind the Texas and Wyoming state flowers, children could research the stories behind and draw other state flowers as well. FLOWERS–FOLKLORE. FOLKLORE–INDIANS OF NORTH AMERICA. TEXAS–FOLKLORE.

1441 dePaola, Tomie. *The Legend of the Indian Paintbrush.* Illus. by the author. Putnam, 1987. ISBN 0-399-21534-4

[Gr. 1–3] After Little Gopher's dream-vision tells him that he will paint his People's pictures for them to see and remember forever, the Plains Indian boy searches to capture the colors of the sunset. Take the opportunity to paint flowers and sunsets with watercolors or plan a joint lesson with your art teacher. This complements *The Legend of the Bluebonnet*, as both are about state flowers; this title is about Wyoming's. Another flower origin tale is Barbara Juster Esbensen's *The Star Maiden*, of how water lilies came to be. FLOWERS–FOLKLORE. FOLKLORE–INDIANS OF NORTH AMERICA. PAINTING–FOLKLORE.

1442 dePaola, Tomie. *The Mysterious Giant of Barletta: An Italian Folktale.* Illus. by the author. Harcourt, 1988. ISBN 0-15-256349-0

[Gr. 1–4] How the town's giant statue came to life and dissuaded an outside army from invading his peaceful village. Halve an onion, as the giant did, and see how it affects your listeners. Compare his tactics to those used by the boy who stopped the Baron's knights in Donald Carrick's *Harald and the Giant Knight* and the English townsmen who dissuaded King John's visit in Mary Blount Christian's *April Fool*. FOLKLORE–ITALY. GIANTS–FOLKLORE.

1443 dePaola, Tomie. *The Prince of the Dolomites: An Old Italian Tale.* Illus. by the author. Harcourt, 1980. ISBN 0-15-674432-5

[Gr. 2–4] Zio Narratore, the local storyteller, tells the village children how a prince's love for a moon princess caused the once-dark Italian Dolomite mountains to turn into the gleaming pink, white, and blue Alps of today. Add this dash of romance to your moon or mountain studies. FOLKLORE–ITALY. MOON–FOLKLORE. MOUNTAINS–FOLKLORE.

1444 dePaola, Tomie. *Strega Nona.* Illus. by the author. Prentice Hall, 1975.

[Gr. K–4] Italian tale of lotsa pasta, a helpful witch, and Big Anthony, who does not listen. Do not miss the Weston Woods film, video, or filmstrip version. Bring in an assortment of dried pastas to show, or better yet, to cook and eat, after working up your appetite by singing Tom Glazer's *On Top of Spaghetti*. For younger grades also read Paul Galdone's overflowing *The Magic Porridge Pot*. While *Strega Nona* is a folktale, the delightful sequels *Big Anthony and the Magic Ring*; *Merry Christmas, Strega Nona*; and *Strega Nona's Magic Lessons* are original fictions also written by dePaola. FOLKLORE–ITALY. FOOD–FOLKLORE. MAGIC–FOLKLORE.

1445   **De Regniers, Beatrice Schenk.** *Little Sister and the Month Brothers.* **Illus. by Margot Tomes. Clarion, 1976. ISBN 0-8164-3147-7**

[Gr. K–3] A Slavic story about a hardworking, good-hearted young girl, and the downfall of her malicious stepmother and stepsister who send her out in the snows of January to find violets and strawberries. Use with Aliki's Greek variant *The Twelve Months* and Samuel Marshak's *The Month Brothers* to whirl through each month of the year. Also use Sara Coleridge's 1834 nursery rhyme *January Brings the Snow: A Book of Months* and Maurice Sendak's comforting *Chicken Soup with Rice*. FOLKLORE, SLAVIC. MONTHS–FOLKLORE. WINTER–FOLKLORE.

1446   **Domanska, Janina.** *King Krakus and the Dragon.* **Illus. by the author. Greenwillow, 1979.**

[Gr. K–2] The ravenous dragon goes on a rampage in the Polish town of Krakow until an orphan shoemaker's apprentice creates an antidote. Take your dragon-slayers with you and tell them *I'm Going on a Dragon Hunt*, with help from the author, Maurice Jones. DRAGONS–FOLKLORE. FOLKLORE–POLAND. KINGS AND RULERS–FOLKLORE.

1447   **Domanska, Janina.** *Little Red Hen.* **Illus. by the author. Macmillan, 1973.**

[Gr. Pre–1] No one wants to help her with the bread-making until it is time to eat it. Paul Galdone's version is nice too; then read Lorinda Bryan Cauley's *The Cock, the Mouse and the Little Red Hen* for more chicken travails. CHANTABLE REFRAIN. CHICKENS–FOLKLORE. COOKERY–FOLKLORE. COOPERATION–FOLKLORE.

1448   **Domanska, Janina.** *The Turnip.* **Illus. by the author. Macmillan, 1969.**

[Gr. Pre–1] Everyone tries to pull up the turnip in this Russian tale, perfect for group narrative pantomime. Compare with Pierr Morgan's *The Turnip* (Philomel, 1990), Alexei Tolstoi's *The Great Big Enormous Turnip*, and if you are in a planting mood, Ruth Krauss's *The Carrot Seed* and Bruce McMillan's *Growing Colors*. CREATIVE DRAMA–FOLKLORE. VEGETABLES–FOLKLORE.

1449   **Duff, Maggie.** *Rum Pum Pum.* **Illus. by Jose Aruego and Ariane Dewey. Macmillan, 1978.**

[Gr. Pre–2] All the while beating on his walnut-shell kettledrum, General Blackbird wages war on the king who has stolen his wife in this cumulative Indian tale with a lively chant for children to repeat. Practice rolling your "r's" and bring in walnuts for eating, cracking, or making mini-drums. An interesting variant is Jeanne M. Lee's Vietnamese *Toad Is the Uncle of Heaven*. Other stories with similar motifs include Verna Aardema's Mexican *The Riddle of the Drum* and Arthur Ransome's Russian *The Fool of the World and the Flying Ship*. BIRDS–FOLKLORE. CHANTABLE REFRAIN. CUMULATIVE STORIES. FOLKLORE–INDIA. KINGS AND RULERS–FOLKLORE.

1450 Eisen, Armand. *Goldilocks and the Three Bears*. Illus. by Lynn Bywaters Ferris. Knopf, 1987.

[Gr. Pre–1] Another glowing version. Compare this with renditions by Jan Brett, Lorinda Bryan Cauley, Paul Galdone, James Marshall, and Janet Stevens, along with Brinton Turkle's wordless turnaround *Deep in the Forest* and Jane Yolen's *The Three Bears Rhyme Book*. BEARS–FOLKLORE. OBEDIENCE–FOLKLORE.

1451 Esbensen, Barbara Juster. *The Star Maiden: An Ojibway Tale*. Illus. by Helen K. Davie. Little, Brown, 1988. ISBN 0-316-24951-3

[Gr. 2–5] Tired of wandering across the sky, a glowing star longs to live among people as a flower, which is how water lilies came to be. Also read Tomie dePaola's *The Legend of the Bluebonnet* and *The Legend of the Indian Paintbrush* for more flower origins, and Paul Goble's *Her Seven Brothers* and Marilyn Sachs's *Fleet-Footed Florence* for more star myths, old and new. FLOWERS–FOLKLORE. FOLKLORE–INDIANS OF NORTH AMERICA. STARS–FOLKLORE.

1452 Fisher, Leonard Everett. *Theseus and the Minotaur*. Illus. by the author. Holiday House, 1988. ISBN 0-8234-0703-9

[Gr. 4–6] The son of King Aegus volunteers to go to Crete and free Athens from the yearly burden of sacrificing 14 youths to the labyrinth-bound Minotaur. To give your students an idea of how the labyrinth was set up, give them copies of a complex maze puzzle to meander through with a pencil. This book and Penelope Proddow's *Demeter and Persephone* are exceptionally handsome introductions to the heroics and tragedy of Greek myths. FOLKLORE–GREECE. MONSTERS–FOLKLORE. MYTHOLOGY.

1453 Forest, Heather. *The Woman Who Flummoxed the Fairies: An Old Tale from Scotland*. Illus. by Susan Gaber. Harcourt, 1990.

[Gr. 1–4] Determined to have a taste of the fine cakes made by the bakerwoman, the King of the Fairies sends his fairie folk to spirit the bakerwoman away to his underworld kingdom. Ellin Greene also retold this lighthearted tale in her collection of recipe-filled, food-focused folktales, *Clever Cooks*. Serve a wee bit of cake after this one. FAIRIES–FOLKLORE. FOLKLORE–SCOTLAND. FOOD–FOLKLORE.

1454 Gackenbach, Dick. *Arabella and Mr. Crack*. Illus. by the author. Macmillan, 1982.

[Gr. K–3] A short English tale of a new housekeeper who must adapt to her master's eccentric vocabulary; compare this with Marcia Sewall's version, *Master of All Masters*. Brainstorm with your group to come up with new noodlehead vocabulary for common classroom objects and then write stories incorporating these words. For restaurant jargon of renamed food you will hunger for Alexandra Day's *Frank and Ernest*, while Alvin Schwartz comes up with plenty of odd words from American folklore in *Chin Music*. FOLKLORE–ENGLAND. VOCABULARY–FOLKLORE.

1455 Galdone, Joanna. *The Little Girl and the Big Bear*. Illus. by Paul Galdone. Houghton Mifflin, 1980. ISBN 0-395-29029-5

[Gr. Pre–2] After losing her way in the forest and being captured as a bear's servant, Little Girl devises a plan for her escape back to her grandparents. Little Red Riding Hood should have been this cunning. Pair this with Jacob Grimm's *Little Red Riding Hood*, Whilhelmina Harper's *The Gunniwolf*, and Ed Young's *Lon Po Po*. BEARS–FOLKLORE. FOLKLORE, SLAVIC.

1456 Galdone, Joanna. *The Tailypo: A Ghost Story.* Illus. by Paul Galdone. Clarion, 1984. ISBN 0-395-30084-3

[Gr. 2-4] A scruffy old man is terrified when the varmint whose tail he has chopped off and eaten returns to get him. This one tells so well, though it is scarier than *Teeny Tiny* by Jill Bennett, *The Teeny-Tiny Woman* by Paul Galdone, or "The Hairy Toe" in George Mendoza's *Gwot!* FOLKLORE–U.S. GHOST STORIES. STORIES TO TELL.

1457 Galdone, Paul. *The Amazing Pig.* Illus. by the author. Clarion, 1981. ISBN 0-395-29101-1

[Gr. 2-4] A Hungarian tale-teller outwits the king by telling him something to which the king cannot reply, "I believe you." Afterward, students can hone their own exaggerating skills by thinking up other stories that might have stumped the king. One of the best-known children's book illustrators of folklore, Galdone's retellings are authentic and his drawings bright, cheery, and unpretentious. He makes the old standards seem fresh and immediate, and fills a great gap for children raised on only television versions. When reading folktales, children should be introduced to Galdone's body of work, listed here and also under Grimm, Jacob, later in this chapter. EXAGGERATION. FOLKLORE–HUNGARY. KINGS AND RULERS–FOLKLORE. PIGS –FOLKLORE.

1458 Galdone, Paul. *Cinderella.* Illus. by the author. McGraw-Hill, 1978. ISBN 0-07-022684-9

[Gr. 1-4] The classic French fairy tale. Use this with the numerous variants such as Marcia Brown's French and Jacob Grimm's German *Cinderella*, Barbara Karlin's humorous-minded version, Shirley Climo's *The Egyptian Cinderella*, William H. Hooks's U.S. *Moss Gown*, Charlotte Huck's *Princess Furball*, Dang Manh Kha's Vietnamese *In the Land of Small Dragon* Ai-Ling Louie's Chinese *Yeh-Shen*, and Flora Annie Steel's English *Tattercoats*. FOLKLORE–FRANCE. PRINCES AND PRINCESSES–FOLKLORE.

1459 Galdone, Paul. *The Gingerbread Boy.* Illus. by the author. Clarion, 1979. ISBN 0-395-28799-5

[Gr. Pre-1] The talking cookie escapes only to meet his end in the jaws of a fox. Chant the refrain together and act it out. Also see P. C. Asbjørnsen's *The Runaway Pancake*, Scott Cook's version, Lorinda Bryan Cauley's *The Pancake Boy*, and Ruth Sawyer's American variant *Johnny Cake, Ho!* If you are not up to a class baking session, at least bring in gingerbread boy cookies to eat after you read the story. CHANTABLE REFRAIN. CREATIVE DRAMA-FOLKLORE. FOXES-FOLKLORE. SEQUENCE STORIES.

1460 Galdone, Paul. *The Greedy Old Fat Man: An American Folktale.* Illus. by the author. Clarion, 1983. ISBN 0-89919-188-6

[Gr. Pre-2] After scarfing down 100 biscuits and a barrel of milk, the greedy Old Fat Man consumes a little boy, girl, dog, cat, fox, and some little rabbits before he's stymied by a squirrel. Substitute a bear for the man and you will have "Sody Saleratus" from Richard Chase's *Grandfather Tales*. Other ravenous, related stories include Jack Kent's *The Fat Cat* and Jack Prelutsky's rhyming *The Terrible Tiger*. Act these out and chant all the "Gingerbread Man"-like refrains. CHANTABLE REFRAIN. CREATIVE DRAMA-FOLKLORE. CUMULATIVE STORIES. FOLKLORE–U.S.

1461 Galdone, Paul. *Henny Penny.* Illus. by the author. Clarion, 1979. ISBN 0-395-28800-2

[Gr. Pre–1] "The sky is falling!" cries the simple hen when struck on the head by a falling acorn. Act this one out and then read Rafe Martin's *Foolish Rabbit's Big Mistake*. CHANTABLE REFRAIN. CHICKENS–FOLKLORE. FOXES–FOLKLORE. SEQUENCE STORIES.

1462   Galdone, Paul. *The History of Mother Twaddle and the Marvelous Achievements of Her Son, Jack*. Illus. by the author. Clarion, 1979. ISBN 0-395-28801-0

[Gr. K–3] Adapted from the verse version of *Jack in the Beanstalk* published in England in 1807, this good-humored edition features one bean and an easily overcome giant. Be sure to bring in the other versions, including Lorinda Bryan Cauley's traditional retelling, Raymond Briggs's modern parody *Jim and the Beanstalk*, and two down-home American ones: Gail E. Haley's *Jack and the Bean Tree* and James Still's *Jack and the Wonder Beans*. FOLKLORE–ENGLAND. GIANTS–FOLKLORE. STORIES IN RHYME.

1463   Galdone, Paul. *King of the Cats*. Illus. by the author. Houghton Mifflin, 1980. ISBN 0-395-29030-9

[Gr. 2–4] A grave digger witnesses a cat's midnight funeral and learns a bit of shocking information about his own tom cat in the process. Listeners will be eager to supply meowing sound effects. CATS–FOLKLORE. FOLKLORE–ENGLAND.

1464   Galdone, Paul. *The Little Red Hen*. Illus. by the author. Clarion, 1979. ISBN 0-395-28803-7

[Gr. Pre–1] A lazy cat, dog, and mouse refuse to help out with the cake-making chores. Children can chime in on the "Not I" refrain. There is also a bread-baking version by Janina Domanska. Follow up with Lorinda Bryan Cauley's *The Cock, the Mouse and the Little Red Hen*, where the hen protagonist fixes a fox. CHANTABLE REFRAIN. CHICKENS–FOLKLORE. COOKERY–FOLKLORE. FOOD–FOLKLORE.

1465   Galdone, Paul. *The Magic Porridge Pot*. Illus. by the author. Clarion, 1979. ISBN 0-395-28805-3

[Gr. Pre–2] The porridge overflows through the whole village and won't stop. Fun to use with Tomie dePaola's *Strega Nona*. COOKERY–FOLKLORE. FOOD–FOLKLORE. MAGIC–FOLKLORE.

1466   Galdone, Paul. *The Monkey and the Crocodile: A Jataka Tale from India*. Illus. by the author. Clarion, 1979. ISBN 0-395-28806-1

[Gr. Pre–2] Fable of a hungry crocodile and the cunning monkey he plans to eat. See how a human boy handles a similar dilemma in Jose Aruego's Philippine *A Crocodile's Tale*. CROCODILES–FOLKLORE. FOLKLORE–INDIA. MONKEYS–FOLKLORE.

1467   Galdone, Paul. *The Monster and the Tailor*. Illus. by the author. Clarion, 1982. ISBN 0-89919-116-9

[Gr. 2–4] While stitching the Grand Duke's trousers in the graveyard at midnight, the tailor must fend off a horrific monster. Children should take the part of the terrified tailor repeating "I see that but I'll sew this" each awful time. CLOTHING AND DRESS–FOLKLORE. MONSTERS–FOLKLORE. TAILORS–FOLKLORE.

1468   Galdone, Paul. *Old Mother Hubbard and Her Dog*. Illus. by the author. McGraw-Hill, 1960.

[Gr. Pre–1] This presents the complete text of the well-known nursery rhyme of a dame's dotty dog. Compare with versions illustrated by Tomie dePaola and Evaline

Ness (Holt, 1972), and the Swedish one by Lennart Hellsing (Coward, 1976), and try acting out the nursery rhyme in narrative pantomime. CHANTABLE REFRAIN. CREATIVE DRAMA—FOLKLORE. DOGS—FOLKLORE. NURSERY RHYMES. STORIES IN RHYME.

1469 **Galdone, Paul.** *The Old Woman and Her Pig.* **Illus. by the author. McGraw-Hill, 1960.**

[Gr. Pre–1] A cumulative English folktale of the dog, stick, fire, water, ox, butcher, rat, and cat needed to nudge a stubborn pig over a stile so the old woman can get home that night. There are plenty of parts for acting out in narrative pantomime and the "I won't" refrain will let children feel wonderfully stubborn for a bit. Also see Priscilla Lamont's *The Troublesome Pig* and Nonny Hogrogian's *One Fine Day* for more sequential trouble. CHANTABLE REFRAIN. CREATIVE DRAMA-FOLKLORE. CUMULATIVE STORIES. FOLKLORE–ENGLAND.

1470 **Galdone, Paul.** *Puss in Boots.* **Illus. by the author. Clarion, 1979. ISBN 0-395-28808-8**

[Gr. K–4] After the miller dies, his youngest son ends up with the princess by entrusting his good fortune to his quick-witted cat. Also see Lorinda Bryan Cauley's version and contrast it with the more realistic *Dick Whittington and His Cat* by Marcia Brown. CATS—FOLKLORE. FOLKLORE—FRANCE.

1471 **Galdone, Paul.** *The Teeny-Tiny Woman: A Ghost Story.* **Illus. by the author. Clarion, 1984.**

[Gr. Pre–2] "Take it!" she cries to the voice who pursues her, seeking its teeny-tiny bone. In *Teeny Tiny,* Jill Bennett also retells this coy, disquieting tale that children learn to tell instantly. Also titillating is Linda Williams's *The Little Old Lady Who Was Not Afraid of Anything.* Joanna Galdone's *The Tailypo* is an American variant, but it is too terrifying for younger than second grade. BONES—FOLKLORE. FEAR—FOLKLORE. FOLKLORE—ENGLAND. STORIES TO TELL.

1472 **Galdone, Paul.** *The Three Bears.* **Illus. by the author. Clarion, 1979. ISBN 0-395-28811-8**

[Gr. Pre–1] Goldilocks strikes again. Also check out retellings by Jan Brett, Lorinda Bryan Cauley, Armand Eisen, James Marshall, and Janet Stevens. Tie them together with Brinton Turkle's wordless switch *Deep in the Forest* and Jane Yolen's *The Three Bears Rhyme Book.* BEARS—FOLKLORE. OBEDIENCE—FOLKLORE.

1473 **Galdone, Paul.** *The Three Billy Goats Gruff.* **Illus. by the author. Clarion, 1979. ISBN 0-395-28812-6**

[Gr. Pre–1] "Who's that tripping over my bridge?" Compare the gruesome troll in this version of the P. C. Asbjørnsen story with the one in Marcia Brown's book, and in Tomie dePaola's *The Cat on the Dovrefell,* and then have a look at some more modern trolls, as in James Marshall's *Troll Country* and Don Arthur Torgersen's *The Girl Who Tricked the Troll.* FOLKLORE—NORWAY. GOATS—FOLKLORE. TROLLS—FOLKLORE.

1474 **Galdone, Paul.** *The Three Little Pigs.* **Illus. by the author. Clarion, 1979. ISBN 0-395-28813-4**

[Gr. Pre–1] The whole sordid tale from the huffing and puffing to the final cooking pot. See also known versions by Erik Blegvad (Atheneum, 1980), Lorinda Bryan Cauley, James Marshall, and Margot Zemach, and the southern U.S. variant *The Three Little Pigs and the Fox* by William H. Hooks. Jon Scieszka's *The True Story of the 3 Little Pigs* gives the wolf's account of the whole affair. CREATIVE DRAMA—FOLKLORE. PIGS—FOLKLORE. WOLVES—FOLKLORE.

1475 Galdone, Paul. *The Three Sillies.* Illus. by the author. Clarion, 1981. ISBN 0-395-30172-6

[Gr. 1–4] English noodlehead tale of a suitor who sets out to find three people who are sillier than his sweetheart and her parents. Compare with Kathryn Hewitt's pig-based version and read other "nitwit" tales such as Tedd Arnold's *Ollie Forgot*, Jacob Grimm's *Hans in Luck*, and Anne Rose's *The Triumphs of Fuzzy Fogtop*. FOLKLORE—ENGLAND. FOOLS—FOLKLORE.

1476 Galdone, Paul. *What's in Fox's Sack?* Illus. by the author. Clarion, 1982. ISBN 0-89919-062-6

[Gr. Pre–2] A greedy fox parlays his fortune from bee to boy. A good tale to act out; check Anne Rockwell's *The Old Woman and Her Pig and Ten Other Stories* and Jennifer Westwood's *Going to Squintum's* for other versions. CREATIVE DRAMA—FOLKLORE. FOLKLORE—ENGLAND. FOXES—FOLKLORE.

1477 Ginsburg, Mirra. *The Chinese Mirror.* Illus. by Margot Zemach. Harcourt, 1988. ISBN 0-15-200420-3

[Gr. 1–4] A Korean man brings home a magical treasure from his travels in China—a small hand mirror—which distresses his wife, mother, father, and son no end when each sees a different unfamiliar face. Have a mirror on hand so your listeners can describe and draw what *they* see. Relate this to Demi's *Reflective Fables* from China. A science lesson on mirrors would fit in nicely here, as would a mirror pantomime activity and Jack Kent's story *Jim Jimmy James*. Magic mirrors turn up in Mirra Ginsburg's *The Fisherman's Son* and Jacob Grimm's *Snow White and the Seven Dwarfs*. FOLKLORE—KOREA.

1478 Ginsburg, Mirra. *The Fisherman's Son.* Illus. by Tony Chen. Greenwillow, 1979.

[Gr. 2–5] A story whereby a young Russian boy saves a fish, a deer, a fox, and a stork from death, and is later assisted by said animals in winning the hand of the maiden he loves. Examine that maiden's magic mirror in the context of those in Ginsburg's *The Chinese Mirror* and Jacob Grimm's *Snow White and the Seven Dwarfs*. ANIMALS—FOLKLORE. FOLKLORE—RUSSIA.

1479 Ginsburg, Mirra. *The Magic Stove.* Illus. by Linda Heller. Coward, 1983. ISBN 0-698-20566-9

[Gr. K–3] An unscrupulous Russian king steals a poor couple's little stove that makes pies on command, but their faithful rooster gets it back and makes the king suffer for it. Thieves make off with magic food-producing objects in Jacob Grimm's *The Table, the Donkey and the Stick* and Freya Littledale's *Peter and the North Wind*, while General Blackbird in Maggie Duff's *Rum Pum Pum* also gets even with a thoughtless king. FOLKLORE—RUSSIA. KINGS AND RULERS—FOLKLORE. ROOSTERS—FOLKLORE.

1480 Ginsburg, Mirra. *The Night It Rained Pancakes.* Illus. by Douglas Florian. Greenwillow, 1980.

[Gr. Pre–2] A humorous Russian tale of two peasant brothers who find a way to keep the pot of gold they dug up. Other so-called fools who get the last laugh can be found in Mary Blount Christian's *The April Fool*. BROTHERS—FOLKLORE. FOLKLORE—RUSSIA. FOOLS—FOLKLORE.

1481   Goble, Paul. *Buffalo Woman.* Illus. by the author. Bradbury, 1984. ISBN 0-02-737720-2

[Gr. 2–6] In spite of his tribe's disapproval, a young man bravely follows his beloved wife and child to her Buffalo Nation people to whom he demonstrates his love and courage, and becomes one of them. Contrast his choice with that of a girl who becomes a star to escape marriage to the Buffalo people in Goble's *Her Seven Brothers*. Olaf Baker's *Where the Buffaloes Begin* and Russell Freedman's stunning nonfiction text *Buffalo Hunt* are also memorable. BUFFALOES–FOLKLORE. FOLKLORE–INDIANS OF NORTH AMERICA. LOVE–FOLKLORE.

1482   Goble, Paul. *Her Seven Brothers.* Illus. by the author. Bradbury, 1988. ISBN 0-02-737960-4

[Gr. 3–6] A Cheyenne legend of the girl who sews clothes for her adopted brothers, and, to escape the Buffalo People, becomes part of the Big Dipper in the northern sky. Unusual complements to your astronomy unit would be this and Marilyn Sachs's baseball star story, *Fleet Footed Florence*, along with Seymour Simon's *Stars* for the facts. For still another view of the buffalo read Olaf Baker's *Where the Buffaloes Begin* and Goble's *Buffalo Woman* who, as one of the Buffalo Nation, turns human for a while to marry a mortal. BROTHERS AND SISTERS–FOLKLORE. BUFFALOES –FOLKLORE. FOLKLORE–INDIANS OF NORTH AMERICA. STARS–FOLKLORE.

1483   Goble, Paul. *Iktomi and the Boulder: A Plains Indian Story.* Illus. by the author. Orchard, 1988. ISBN 0-531-05760-7

[Gr. K–3] When the clever but lazy trickster is trapped by an angry bounding boulder, he enlists the animals to help lift it off his legs. The straightforward and humorous storyteller's narrative explains why there are now rocks scattered all over the Great Plains, and why bats have flattened faces, rendering this useful for both geology and mammal studies. FOLKLORE–INDIANS OF NORTH AMERICA. POUR-QUOI TALES. ROCKS–FOLKLORE. TRICKSTER TALES.

1484   Grant, Joan. *The Monster That Grew Small: An Egyptian Folktale.* Illus. by Jill Karla Schwarz. Lothrop, 1987. ISBN 0-688-06808-1

[Gr. 1–4] Miobi, an Egyptian boy, is terrified of all things until a Hare he has rescued bestows upon him a dagger and shows him the road to courage. Originally published in England in 1943, this tale of fears overcome by confronting the monster "What Might Happen" should provoke much discussion, especially for those who loved Dick Gackenbach's *Harry and the Terrible Whatzit* in their "youths." COUR-AGE–FOLKLORE. FEAR–FOLKLORE. FOLKLORE–EGYPT. MONSTERS–FOLKLORE.

1485   Grifalconi, Ann. *The Village of Round and Square Houses.* Illus. by the author. Little, Brown, 1986. ISBN 0-316-32862-6

[Gr. K–4] A storytelling grandmother in the West African village of Tos describes the eruption of Old Naka long ago and explains how it led to the villagers living in two types of houses: the men in square ones and the women in round ones. Aside from imparting a taste of rural African customs, the story portrays a terrifying volcanic eruption, which you may want to compare with those in Lonzo Anderson's *The Ponies of Mykillengi*, set in Iceland; Thomas P. Lewis's *Hill of Fire* from Mexico; and Seymour Simon's dramatic color-photo-filled *Volcano.* FOLKLORE–AFRICA. GRAND-MOTHERS–FOLKLORE. STORYTELLING.

1486   Grimm, Jacob. *The Bearskinner.* Illus. by Felix Hoffman. Atheneum, 1978.

[Gr. 2–4] A young soldier's deal with the Devil includes wearing a bearskin as a cloak and not bathing for seven years. From Wanda Gag's *Tales from Grimm*, see how three young soldiers get the best of the bargain in "The Dragon and His Grandmother," while an old soldier has his day in Michael McCurdy's *The Devils Who Learned to Be Good*. DEVIL–FOLKLORE. FOLKLORE–GERMANY. SOLDIERS–FOLK-LORE.

1487   Grimm, Jacob. *The Bremen Town Musicians*. Trans. by Anthea Bell. Illus. by Josef Palecek. Retold by Anthea Bell. Picture Book Studios, 1988. ISBN 0-88708-071-5

[Gr. Pre–3] To avoid being killed by their owners, four old animals—a donkey, a dog, a cat, and a rooster—band together and head through the woods for Bremen, when they come upon a house inhabited by robbers. Conduct the animal choir in your room so all can hear firsthand the dreadful noise that frightened the robbers away. Another version of the same story is retold by Ilse Plume (Doubleday, 1980). A rooster manages the same single-handedly in Arnold Lobel's *How the Rooster Saved the Day*. ANIMALS–FOLKLORE. FOLKLORE–GERMANY. ROBBERS AND OUTLAWS–FOLKLORE.

1488   Grimm, Jacob. *Cinderella*. Illus. by Nonny Hogrogian. Retold by Nonny Hogrogian. Greenwillow, 1981.

[Gr. 1–4] In this German retelling, Cinderella is aided by white doves and a hazel tree. Compare with Marcia Brown or Paul Galdone's French versions, Barbara Karlin's rendition, as well as Asian variants *In the Land of Small Dragon* by Dang Manh Kha and *Yeh-Shen* by Ai-Ling Louie, Shirley Climo's *The Egyptian Cinderella*, William H. Hooks's *Moss Gown*, Charlotte Huck's *Princess Furball*, and Flora Annie Steel's English *Tattercoats*. FOLKLORE–GERMANY. PRINCES AND PRINCESSES–FOLK-LORE.

1489   Grimm, Jacob. *The Devil with the Three Golden Hairs*. Illus. by Nonny Hogrogian. Retold by Nonny Hogrogian. Knopf, 1983. ISBN 0-394-95560-9

[Gr. 2–4] The king is determined to kill the poor boy who is destined to marry the princess, and when that fails, to assign him an impossible task. Also read the Russian variants *The Three Wonderful Beggars* by Sally Scott and *Vasily and the Dragon* by Simon Stern. DEVIL–FOLKLORE. FOLKLORE–GERMANY.

1490   Grimm, Jacob. *The Donkey Prince*. Illus. by Barbara Cooney. Adapted by M. Jean Craig. Doubleday, 1977.

[Gr. 2–4] Cheating the wizard who promised them a child, the greedy king and vain queen are rewarded with a donkey child who will never look normal until someone can forget its shape and love it as a human being is loved. Discuss ways the donkey's dilemma of always being unfairly judged for his looks and not his personality applies to your children's experiences. Also see Grimm's *The Frog Prince*, Elizabeth Isele's *The Frog Princess*, and Jane Langton's Latvian *The Hedgehog Boy*. DONKEYS–FOLKLORE. FOLKLORE–GERMANY. PRINCES AND PRINCESSES–FOLK-LORE. WIZARDS–FOLKLORE.

1491   Grimm, Jacob. *The Elves and the Shoemaker*. Illus. by Paul Galdone. Retold by Paul Galdone. Clarion, 1984. ISBN 0-89919-226-2

[Gr. Pre–2] With only enough leather to make one pair of shoes, a poor but honest shoemaker goes to bed and two naked elves step in to help out. An able candidate for improvised drama. Adrienne Adams did another fine version titled *The Shoe-maker and the Elves* (Scribner, 1961). ELVES—FOLKLORE. FOLKLORE—GERMANY. SHOES—FOLKLORE.

1492   **Grimm, Jacob.** *The Fisherman and His Wife.* **Trans. by Randall Jarrell. Illus. by Margot Zemach. Retold by Randall Jarrell. Farrar, 1980. ISBN 0-374-32340-2**

[Gr. 2–4] Not satisfied with the wish granted by a magic fish, a covetous woman demands and gets more, until she asks to be made God. Compare Zemach's riotous illustrations with the glowing paintings in Elizabeth Shub's version, illustrated by Monika Laimgruber (Greenwillow, 1978). FISHES—FOLKLORE. FOLKLORE—GERMANY. HUSBANDS AND WIVES—FOLKLORE. WISHES—FOLKLORE.

1493   **Grimm, Jacob.** *The Frog Prince.* **Illus. by Paul Galdone. McGraw-Hill, 1974.**

[Gr. K–3] After the frog retrieves the princess' golden ball from the bottom of the well, he visits the palace to make her keep her promise to be his friend. For more royalty in animal's skins also read Jacob Grimm's *The Donkey Prince*, *The Frog Prince*, and *The Glass Mountain*, Elizabeth Isele's Russian *The Frog Princess*, and Jane Lanton's Latvian tale *The Hedgehog Boy*. A. Vesey's *The Princess and the Frog* is an amusing parody of the whole situation. FOLKLORE—GERMANY. FROGS—FOLKLORE. PRINCES AND PRINCESSES—FOLKLORE. TRANSFORMATIONS—FOLKLORE.

1494   **Grimm, Jacob.** *The Glass Mountain.* **Illus. by Nonny Hogrogian. Retold by Nonny Hogrogian. Knopf, 1985. ISBN 0-394-86724-6**

[Gr. 2–6] A king's daughter, who has been put under a spell and turned into a raven due to her mother's hasty spoken wish, enlists the aid of a young man in the forest to set her free. Unique marbelized paper borders around each page may set you out on a messy but interesting paper-making project with spectacular results. Squeeze dabs of oil paint into small containers, mix with a bit of paint thinner, and pour colors into a large pan of water. Quickly dip or insert blank sheets of paper into the water and remove, letting them dry on newspaper. You can swirl the colors a bit to mix them in the water. Other enchanted bird tales include Hans Christian Andersen's *The Wild Swans* and Grimm's *Jorinda and Joringel*. BIRDS—FOLKLORE. FOLKLORE—GERMANY.

1495   **Grimm, Jacob.** *Hans in Luck.* **Illus. by Paul Galdone. Parents, 1979.**

[Gr. K–3] Hans takes his wages for seven years' work and makes trade after trade, ending up with nothing. Similar in theme to Amy Schwartz's original folktale, *Yossel Zissel and the Wisdom of Chelm* and William Wiesner's *Happy-Go-Lucky*, and partner-in-silliness with Tedd Arnold's *Ollie Forgot*, Paul Galdone or Kathryn Hewitt's *The Three Sillies*, and Anne Rose's *The Triumphs of Fuzzy Fogtop*. FOLKLORE—GERMANY. FOOLS—FOLKLORE.

1496   **Grimm, Jacob.** *Hansel and Gretel.* **Illus. by Paul Galdone. McGraw-Hill, 1982. ISBN 0-07-022727-6**

[Gr. 2–4] Two children find their way to a witch's gingerbread house after being abandoned in the woods by their parents. More proof that wicked witches do not prevail can be found in the version retold by Charles Scribner, Jr., and illustrated by Adrienne Adams (Scribner, 1975). Increase the witchery with Grimm's *Jorinda and Joringel*, and, for a real scare, read Barbara Walker's Turkish variant *Teeny Tiny and the Witch Woman.* BROTHERS AND SISTERS—FOLKLORE. FOLKLORE—GERMANY. WITCHES—FOLKLORE.

1497 **Grimm, Jacob.** *Hansel and Gretel.* **Illus. by Paul O. Zelinsky. Retold by Rika Lesser. Putnam, 1989. ISBN 0-399-21725-8**

[Gr. 2–4] Zelinsky's haunting medieval-style paintings, comparable to those in his *Rumpelstiltskin* for which he won a silver Caldecott medal, make this book unforgettable. Compare moods, texts, and illustrations of Evaline Ness's *Tom Tit Tot* and Harve Zemach's *Duffy and the Devil,* and of course the original Grimm tales retold by Jacqueline Ayer (Harcourt, 1967), Paul Galdone, and Edith Tarcov (Four Winds, 1973). BROTHERS AND SISTERS—FOLKLORE. FOLKLORE—GERMANY. WITCHES—FOLKLORE.

1498 **Grimm, Jacob.** *Jorinda and Joringel.* **Trans. by Elizabeth Shub. Illus. by Adrienne Adams. Scribner, 1968.**

[Gr. 2–4] A witch who turns maidens into caged birds puts her spell on two young sweethearts. In Audrey Wood's literary folktale *Heckedy Peg,* based on an old children's rhyme, the witch turns seven children into food to which their mother must match them correctly if they are to be freed. BIRDS—FOLKLORE. FOLKLORE—GERMANY. TRANSFORMATIONS—FOLKLORE. WITCHES—FOLKLORE.

1499 **Grimm, Jacob.** *Little Brother and Little Sister.* **Illus. by Barbara Cooney. Retold by Barbara Cooney. Doubleday, 1982.**

[Gr. 2–5] After fleeing their abusive stepmother, Little Brother is transformed into a faun in this romantic fairy tale that melds well with Grimm's *Hansel and Gretel, Jorinda and Joringel,* and *Snow White.* BROTHERS AND SISTERS—FOLKLORE. FOLKLORE—GERMANY. KINGS AND RULERS—FOLKLORE. WITCHES—FOLKLORE.

1500 **Grimm, Jacob.** *Little Red Cap.* **Trans. by Elizabeth D. Crawford. Illus. by Lisbeth Zwerger. Morrow, 1983.**

[Gr. Pre–2] A delicately illustrated version of the universally known tale. Compare with Grimm's *Little Red Riding Hood,* illustrated by Paul Galdone (McGraw-Hill, 1974) or Trina Schart Hyman; the mirthful revision *Red Riding Hood* by James Marshall; Wilhelmina Harper's *The Gunniwolf;* and Ed Young's Chinese variant *Lon Po Po.* FOLKLORE—GERMANY. GRANDMOTHERS—FOLKLORE. OBEDIENCE—FOLKLORE. WOLVES—FOLKLORE.

1501 **Grimm, Jacob.** *Little Red Riding Hood.* **Illus. by Trina Schart Hyman. Retold by Trina Schart Hyman. Holiday House, 1983.**

[Gr. Pre–2] Many children have never heard the traditional version of the wolf in Granny's clothing. Compare with other Grimm retellings: Lisbeth Zwerger's illustrated *Little Red Cap* above, the one illustrated by Paul Galdone (McGraw-Hill, 1974), James Marshall's outrageous *Red Riding Hood,* and Ed Young's Chinese version *Lon Po Po;* then finish off with Wilhelmina Harper's *The Gunniwolf.* FOLKLORE—GERMANY. GRANDMOTHERS—FOLKLORE. OBEDIENCE—FOLKLORE. WOLVES—FOLKLORE.

1502 **Grimm, Jacob.** *Mother Holly.* **Illus. by Bernadette Watts. Retold by Bernadette Watts. Crowell, 1972. ISBN 0-690-56363-9**

[Gr. Pre–2] Sent by her mother to fetch the spindle from the well, the good sister finds herself with old Mother Holly, who makes the snow come and rewards her for working hard. Like Beatrice Schenk de Regniers's *Little Sister and the Month Brothers* and Samuel Marshak's *The Month Brothers*, the bad sister gets what she deserves in the end. FOLKLORE–GERMANY. SISTERS–FOLKLORE. WINTER–FOLKLORE.

1503   **Grimm, Jacob. *Rapunzel*. Illus. by Trina Schart Hyman. Retold by Barbara Rogasky. Holiday House, 1982. ISBN 0-8234-0454-4**

[Gr. 2–4] A handsomely illustrated retelling of the story of a young maid locked in a tower with only her opulent tresses for company. See also the edition illustrated by Bernadette Watts (Crowell, 1975) and the Italian variant, *Petrosinella*, retold by Giambattista Basile. FOLKLORE–GERMANY. WITCHES–FOLKLORE.

1504   **Grimm, Jacob. *Rumpelstiltskin*. Illus. by Paul O. Zelinsky. Retold by Paul O. Zelinsky. Dutton, 1986. ISBN 0-525-44265-0**

[Gr. 1–4] As a reward for spinning straw into gold, the little man demands the miller's daughter's first-born child if she cannot guess his name. Magnificent medieval-style paintings brought Zelinsky's radiant retelling a well-deserved Caldecott honor award. Note the diverse styles of illustration in this and each of the following excellent versions: Jacqueline Ayer's book (Harcourt, 1967); Edith Tarcov's retelling, illustrated by Edward Gorey (Four Winds, 1973); and Paul Galdone's (Clarion, 1985). Compare with variants like Evaline Ness's *Tom Tit Tot* and Harve Zemach's *Duffy and the Devil*, both of which hail from England. Read Tarcov's simpler version as a lead in to Elizabeth Vreeken's *The Boy Who Would Not Say His Name*. FOLKLORE–GERMANY. KINGS AND RULERS–FOLKLORE. NAMES–FOLKLORE.

1505   **Grimm, Jacob. *The Sleeping Beauty*. Illus. by Trina Schart Hyman. Retold by Trina Schart Hyman. Little, Brown, 1983. ISBN 0-316-38702-9**

[Gr. 2–5] The prophecy of a wicked fairy comes true when Briar Rose pricks her finger and falls into a 100-year sleep. Both this and Jane Yolen's version (Random House, 1986) incorporate romantically lyrical retellings and illustrations. Compare the style of these with Errol Le Cain's illustrated Grimm variant *Thorn Rose*. Act out as a tableau the scene where the court, frozen in its tracks, comes to life. Jane Yolen also wrote *Sleeping Ugly*, an alternative version for children who need to reassess their standards of beauty. FOLKLORE–GERMANY. PRINCES AND PRINCESSES–FOLKLORE. SLEEP–FOLKLORE.

1506   **Grimm, Jacob. *Snow White*. Trans. by Paul Heins. Illus. by Trina Schart Hyman. Little, Brown, 1979. ISBN 0-316-35450-3**

[Gr. 2–5] A gloomy forest and seven dwarfs await the lovely young girl who has aroused her stepmother's murderous jealousy. Compare illustrations with Randall Jarrell's translation of *Snow-White and the Seven Dwarfs*, illustrated by Nancy Ekholm Burkert (Farrar, 1972), as both are uncommonly exquisite editions of the romantic standard. FOLKLORE–GERMANY. PRINCES AND PRINCESSES–FOLKLORE.

1507   **Grimm, Jacob. *The Table, the Donkey and the Stick*. Illus. by Paul Galdone. McGraw-Hill, 1976. ISBN 0-07-022701-2**

[Gr. 1–4] Thanks to a lying goat, three brothers are sent into the world to seek their fortunes where they earn three magic rewards. Follow up with Warwick Hutton's similar-themed *The Nose Tree*, Freya Littledale's Norse *Peter and the North Wind*, Gerald McDermott's Irish *Tim O'Toole and the Wee Folk*, James Riordan's Russian variant *The Three Magic Gifts*, and Harve Zemach's *Too Much Nose*. DONKEYS–FOLKLORE. FOLKLORE–GERMANY. GOATS–FOLKLORE.

1508 **Grimm, Jacob.** *Thorn Rose: or, The Sleeping Beauty.* **Illus. by Errol Le Cain. Puffin, 1978. ISBN 0-14-050222-X**

[Gr. 1–4] Another gloriously illustrated edition of the tale of a princess' 100-year snooze. See also both editions of Grimm's *The Sleeping Beauty*, cited previously. FOLKLORE–GERMANY. PRINCES AND PRINCESSES–FOLKLORE. SLEEP–FOLKLORE.

1509 **Grimm, Jacob.** *The Twelve Dancing Princesses.* **Illus. by Errol Le Cain. Puffin, 1981. ISBN 0-14-050322-6**

[Gr. 1–4] With the aid of a cloak that makes him invisible, a sharp-witted soldier solves the mystery of the princesses' nightly disappearances. In Warwick Hutton's *The Nose Tree*, three soldiers must trick a wily princess into returning their magic possessions, including another cloak of invisibility. DANCING–FOLKLORE. FOLKLORE–GERMANY. PRINCES AND PRINCESSES–FOLKLORE.

1510 **Grimm, Jacob.** *The Valiant Little Tailor.* **Illus. by Victor Ambrus. Oxford, 1980. ISBN 0-19-279727-1**

[Gr. 1–4] After the tailor kills seven flies with one blow, he takes on two giants. See Christine Price's *Sixty at a Blow* (Dutton, 1968) for a similar story from Turkey, and Dorothy Van Woerkom's *Alexandra the Rock-Eater* that hails from Russia. FOLKLORE–GERMANY. GIANTS–FOLKLORE. TAILORS–FOLKLORE.

1511 **Grimm, Jacob.** *The Water of Life.* **Illus. by Trina Schart Hyman. Retold by Barbara Rogasky. Holiday House, 1986. ISBN 0-8234-0552-4**

[Gr. 3–6] To cure their father, the king, three brothers—two proud and evil-hearted, the third pure and true—set out to find the only medicine that will work. As in the Chinese tale *The Enchanted Tapestry* by Robert D. San Souci, only the youngest son can manage the obstacles, though in Cheng Hou-Tien's *The Six Chinese Brothers*, the brothers work together to obtain the necessary magic pearl that will help their father. BROTHERS–FOLKLORE. FOLKLORE–GERMANY. KINGS AND RULERS–FOLKLORE. PRINCES AND PRINCESSES–FOLKLORE.

1512 **Grimm, Jacob.** *The Wolf and the Seven Little Kids.* **Illus. by Martin Ursell. Retold by Linda M. Jennings. Silver Burdett, 1986. ISBN 0-382-09306-2**

[Gr. Pre–1] Convinced that the wolf is their mother, given his soft voice and white paws, the kids open the door and let him in. The retelling and illustration style is similar to the version translated by Anne Rogers and illustrated by Svend Otto S. (Larousse, 1977); contrast situations with that of the seven geese in Chris Conover's *Mother Goose and the Sly Fox* and the seven children and the witch in Audrey Wood's *Heckedy Peg*. FOLKLORE–GERMANY. GOATS–FOLKLORE. WOLVES–FOLKLORE.

1513 **Hague, Kathleen, and Michael Hague.** *East of the Sun and West of the Moon.* **Illus. by Michael Hague. Harcourt, 1989. ISBN 0-15-224703-3**

[Gr. 3–5] A Norwegian girl must seek the man she loves after she ignores his instructions and discovers his identity as bear by day, man by night. The George Dasent/Gillian Barlow version *East o' the Sun & West o' the Moon* makes an interesting comparison, as the style of illustration is so different. Similar in theme to both the French *Beauty and the Beast* as retold by Rosemary Harris or Marianna Mayer and the Russian *The Frog Princess* by Elizabeth Isele; for an American

version read "Whitebear Whittington" from Richard Chase's *Grandfather Tales*.
BEARS–FOLKLORE. FOLKLORE–NORWAY. TRANSFORMATIONS–FOLKLORE.

1514   **Hague, Kathleen, and Michael Hague.** *The Man Who Kept House.* **Illus. by Michael Hague. Harcourt, 1981. ISBN 0-15-251698-0**

[Gr. K–4] A pragmatic Norwegian housewife swaps jobs with her disdainful farmer husband for one day. See also William Wiesner's version, *Turnabout*. FOLKLORE–NORWAY. HUSBANDS AND WIVES–FOLKLORE.

1515   **Haley, Gail E.** *Jack and the Bean Tree.* **Illus. by the author. Crown, 1986. ISBN 0-517-55717-7**

[Gr. 1–4] An Appalachian variant of the beanstalk story, told in dialect by an old woman storyteller, Poppy. Serve up a mess of variants, all well worth hearing, including Raymond Briggs's parody *Jim and the Beanstalk*, Lorinda Bryan Cauley's *Jack and the Beanstalk*, Paul Galdone's *The History of Mother Twaddle and the Marvelous Achievements of Her Son, Jack* in verse, and James Still's Kentucky-bred *Jack and the Wonder Beans*. FOLKLORE–U.S. GIANTS–FOLKLORE.

1516   **Haley, Gail E.** *Jack and the Fire Dragon.* **Illus. by the author. Crown, 1988. ISBN 0-517-56814-4**

[Gr. 2–5] An Appalachian Jack tale of how he defeated the giant Fire Dragoman and found a wife as well. Read and tell an assortment of Jack tales from both the United States and England, from Richard Chase's *Jack Tales* to Lorinda Bryan Cauley's *Jack and the Beanstalk* and Haley's *Jack and the Bean Tree*. BROTHERS–FOLKLORE. DRAGONS–FOLKLORE. FOLKLORE–U.S.

1517   **Haley, Gail E.** *A Story, a Story.* **Illus. by the author. Atheneum, 1970. ISBN 0-689-20511-2**

[Gr. K–3] An African tale of Anansi the Spider and how he spread the world's first stories. Also try Gerald McDermott's *Anansi the Spider* and the following exemplary collections: Peggy Appiah's *Tales of an Ashanti Father* (Deutsch, 1967), Joyce Cooper Arkhurst's *The Adventures of Spider*, and Harold Courlander's *The Hat-Shaking Dance*. CALDECOTT MEDAL. FOLKLORE–AFRICA. STORYTELLING.

1518   **Hancock, Sibyl.** *Esteban and the Ghost.* **Illus. by Dirk Zimmer. Dial, 1983. ISBN 0-8037-2443-8**

[Gr. 2–4] On All Hallow's Eve, a merry tinker sets off to drive a ghost out of a haunted castle, for which he will receive a thousand gold reals—if he lives to tell the tale. Read this after you have told the spooky chant "And Still She Sat," which you can find in Caroline Feller Bauer's gold mine *Handbook for Storytellers*. For another bag of old bones, see Cynthia C. DeFelice's *The Dancing Skeleton*. FOLKLORE–SPAIN. GHOST STORIES. HALLOWEEN–FOLKLORE.

1519   **Harper, Wilhelmina.** *The Gunniwolf.* **Illus. by William Wiesner. Dutton, 1978. ISBN 0-525-31139-4**

[Gr. Pre–1] Little Girl breaks her promise to her mother when she wanders into the jungle, meets up with the Gunniwolf, and sings him "that guten sweeten song again." Compare this variant with any of the Grimm versions of *Little Red Riding Hood*. Act out in pairs, with all the little girls on one side of the room and all the Gunniwolves on the other, and then switch roles. CHANTABLE REFRAIN. CREATIVE DRAMA–FOLKLORE. OBEDIENCE–FOLKLORE. STORIES WITH SONGS. WOLVES–FOLKLORE.

1520 **Harris, Rosemary.** *Beauty and the Beast.* **Illus. by Errol Le Cain. Doubleday, 1980.**

[Gr. 2–5] To save her father's life, the merchant's youngest daughter agrees to move to the palace of a monstrous beast. Compare with Marianna Mayer's retelling and identify similar motifs in the George Dasent/Gillian Barlow version of the Norwegian fairy tale *East o' the Sun & West o' the Moon* and Kathleen and Michael Hague's *East of the Sun and West of the Moon,* as well as Elizabeth Isele's Russian *The Frog Princess.* FOLKLORE–FRANCE. MONSTERS–FOLKLORE. TRANSFORMATIONS–FOLKLORE.

1521 **Hastings, Selina.** *Sir Gawain and the Loathly Lady.* **Illus. by Juan Wijngaard. Lothrop, 1985. ISBN 0-688-05823-X**

[Gr. 3–6] Destined to die at the hands of the Black Knight unless he can answer the question, "What is it that women most desire," King Arthur learns the answer from a monstrous hag who wants, in return, one of Arthur's knights for a husband. Before the answer is revealed by the Loathly Lady, poll your listeners for their responses to the riddle. Read in tandem with Margaret Hodges's *Saint George and the Dragon,* another gorgeous English tale with illuminated manuscript-style paintings. FOLKLORE–ENGLAND. KINGS AND RULERS–FOLKLORE. KNIGHTS AND KNIGHTHOOD–FOLKLORE.

1522 **Hewitt, Kathryn.** *King Midas and the Golden Touch.* **Illus. by the author. Harcourt, 1987. ISBN 0-15-242800-3**

[Gr. 1–4] This is a story in which the Greek King finds out the hard way that gold isn't everything. Hewitt's detailed golden watercolors are a treat. Also read Patrick Skene Catling's modern update, *The Chocolate Touch,* along with Nathaniel Hawthorne's *The Golden Touch* (McGraw-Hill, 1959). FOLKLORE–GREECE. GREED–FOLKLORE. KINGS AND RULERS–FOLKLORE. MYTHOLOGY.

1523 **Hewitt, Kathryn.** *The Three Sillies.* **Illus. by the author. Harcourt, 1986. ISBN 0-15-286855-0**

[Gr. 1–4] Classic English tale of a young girl—in this version, all characters are pigs—who, envisioning the disaster it could bring, cries over an ax in the cellar ceiling. Compare the illustrations with Paul Galdone's version, and read the Italian variant "Bastianello" from Virginia Haviland's *Favorite Fairy Tales Told in Italy* (Little, Brown, 1965). FOLKLORE–ENGLAND. FOOLS–FOLKLORE.

1524 **Hirsch, Marilyn.** *The Rabbi and the Twenty-Nine Witches.* **Illus. by the author. Holiday House, 1976.**

[Gr. K–2] Based on a Jewish tale from the Talmud, a crafty rabbi finds a way for the villagers to see the full moon and rid their town of the witches as well. On the same theme do not miss Eric A. Kimmel's *Hershel and the Hanukkah Goblins.* FOLKLORE, JEWISH. WITCHES–FOLKLORE.

1525 **Hodges, Margaret.** *The Little Humpbacked Horse.* **Illus. by Chris Conover. Farrar, 1987. ISBN 0-374-44495-1**

[Gr. 3–5] A Russian fool prospers with the aid of his wise and faithful horse companion. Ride another helpful beast with Sally Scott's Persian *The Magic Horse.* FOLKLORE–RUSSIA. FOOLS–FOLKLORE. HORSES–FOLKLORE.

1526 **Hodges, Margaret.** *Saint George and the Dragon: A Golden Legend.* **Illus. by Trina Schart Hyman. Little, Brown, 1984.**

[Gr. 3–6] Una recruits the Red Cross Knight to slay the mighty dragon that plagues her father's kingdom. Based on Edmund Spenser's sixteenth-century epic poem, "The Faerie Queen," this elegant retelling and the glorious illustrations will leave you breathless. Also read Selina Hastings's Arthurian tale *Sir Gawain and the Loathly Lady* and Jay Williams's China-based *Everyone Knows What a Dragon Looks Like.* CALDECOTT MEDAL. DRAGONS—FOLKLORE. FOLKLORE—ENGLAND. KNIGHTS AND KNIGHTHOOD—FOLKLORE.

1527 **Hodges, Margaret.** *The Wave.* **Illus. by Blair Lent. Houghton Mifflin, 1964. ISBN 0-395-06818-5**

[Gr. K–4] Burning his own rice fields is the only way a wealthy old Japanese grandfather can warn the villagers of an impending tidal wave. Discuss the meaning of sacrifice for the common good, and ask if anyone knows any true tales of people who have acted in a selfless manner toward their fellow humans. FOLKLORE—JAPAN. SEASHORE—FOLKLORE.

1528 **Hogrogian, Nonny.** *One Fine Day.* **Illus. by the author. Macmillan, 1971. ISBN 0-02-744000-1**

[Gr. Pre–2] Cumulative tale of a fox who must barter for milk to give to an old woman before she will sew his tail back on. Children can retell this in sequence and act it out. Similarly formatted is Paul Galdone's *The Old Woman and Her Pig.* CALDECOTT MEDAL. CREATIVE DRAMA—FOLKLORE. FOXES—FOLKLORE. SEQUENCE STORIES.

1529 **Hooks, William H.** *Moss Gown.* **Illus. by Donald Carrick. Clarion, 1987. ISBN 0-89919-460-5**

[Gr. 2–6] A Southern U.S. variant of an originally European story that is a close relative to *Cinderella.* To demonstrate the effect of salt, as Candace does when she tells her father, "I love you more than meat loves salt," first serve your class something without it, like homemade chicken soup or mashed potatoes. Of the many possible *Cinderella* tales, select from the following: Shirley Climo's *The Egyptian Cinderella,* those by Marcia Brown, Jacob Grimm, Paul Galdone, Nonny Hogrogian, and Barbara Karlin, plus Charlotte Huck's *Princess Furball,* Dang Manh Kha's Vietnamese *In the Land of Small Dragon,* Ai-Ling Louie's Chinese *Yeh-Shen,* and Flora Annie Steel's English *Tattercoats.* FATHERS AND DAUGHTERS—FOLKLORE. FOLKLORE—U.S.

1530 **Hooks, William H.** *The Three Little Pigs and the Fox.* **Illus. by S. D. Schindler. Macmillan, 1989. ISBN 0-02-744431-7**

[Gr. Pre–2] While her two brothers are captured and detained by that mean, tricky old drooly mouth fox, Hamlet is sharp enough to trap the fox in a butter churn and make the forest safe for piglets leaving home to seek their fortunes. This down-home Appalachian variant will whet your whistle for James Marshall's *The Three Little Pigs* and Jon Scieszka's outrageous turnaround *The True Story of the 3 Little Pigs* as told by A. Wolf. FOLKLORE—U.S. FOXES—FOLKLORE. PIGS—FOLKLORE.

1531 **Huck, Charlotte.** *Princess Furball.* **Illus. by Anita Lobel. Greenwillow, 1989. ISBN 0-688-07838-9**

[Gr. 1–4] Before she will marry the Ogre to whom her father has betrothed her, the Princess insists on three fancy gowns and a coat made of a thousand different kinds of fur. This European Cinderella variant will make a handsome match with Shirley Climo's *The Egyptian Cinderella*, Nonny Hogrogian's *Cinderella*, Dang Manh Kha's *In the Land of Small Dragon*, Ai-Ling Louie's *Yeh-Shen*, Flora Annie Steel's *Tattercoats*, and William Hooks's *Moss Gown*. FOLKLORE–ENGLAND. PRINCES AND PRINCESSES–FOLKLORE.

1532 **Hurlimann, Ruth.** *The Proud White Cat.* **Trans. by Anthea Bell. Illus. by the author. Morrow, 1977.**

[Gr. Pre–2] In this German sequence story, Tom Cat asks Mrs. Vixen the fox for advice about the worthiest lady for him to marry. In a more somber format is Gerald McDermott's similar *The Stonecutter* from Japan. CATS–FOLKLORE. FOLKLORE–GERMANY. SEQUENCE STORIES.

1533 **Hutton, Warwick.** *The Nose Tree.* **Illus. by the author. Atheneum, 1980.**

[Gr. 2–5] Apples from a nose-growing tree enable three German soldiers to retrieve their magical possessions from a scheming princess. See also Harve Zemach's earthy version, *Too Much Nose*, plus Paul Galdone's *The Table, the Donkey and the Stick*, Freya Littledale's *Peter and the North Wind*, Gerald McDermott's *Tim O'Toole and the Wee Folk*, and James Riordan's *The Three Magic Gifts*. FOLKLORE–GERMANY. NOSES–FOLKLORE. SOLDIERS–FOLKLORE.

1534 **Isele, Elizabeth.** *The Frog Princess.* **Illus. by Michael Hague. Crowell, 1984.**

[Gr. 2–5] In this Russian folktale—which incorporates elements of both Jacob Grimm's *The Frog Prince* and the Norwegian *East of the Sun and West of the Moon*, in retellings by George Webbe Dasent or Kathleen and Michael Hague—Ivan, the czar's youngest son, must marry a frog who is really Princess Vasilisa the Wise under a spell. Another resourceful and quick-witted heroine is the take-charge *Vasilisa the Wise* by Josepha Sherman, though she appears to be unrelated to the princess in Isele's tale. FOLKLORE–RUSSIA. FROGS–FOLKLORE. PRINCES AND PRINCESSES–FOLKLORE.

1535 **Ishii, Momoko.** *The Tongue-Cut Sparrow.* **Trans. by Katherine Paterson. Illus. by Suekichi Akaba. Lodestar, 1987. ISBN 0-525-67199-4**

[Gr. Pre–3] An old man's wife snips out the tongue of his beloved sparrow, whom the old man then seeks in the mountain. Have students chant the refrain and join in on the onomatopoeic sound effects. A tale of goodness rewarded and selfishness punished, compare this to Patricia Montgomery Newton's Japanese variant *The Five Sparrows*. BIRDS–FOLKLORE. CHANTABLE REFRAIN. FOLKLORE–JAPAN.

1536 **Johnston, Tony.** *The Badger and the Magic Fan: A Japanese Folktale.* **Illus. by Tomie dePaola. Putnam, 1990. ISBN 0-399-21945-5**

[Gr. Pre–2] Transforming himself into a little girl, Badger outsmarts the tengu goblin children, steals their fan, and with it, causes the nose of a beautiful girl to grow long, long, long, *long*. Meet up with other spirited creatures from Japanese folklore in *The Funny Little Woman* by Arlene Mosel and *Momotaro, the Peach Boy* by Linda Shute. BADGERS–FOLKLORE. FOLKLORE–JAPAN. MAGIC–FOLKLORE.

1537 Karlin, Barbara. *Cinderella.* Illus. by James Marshall. Little, Brown, 1989. ISBN 0-316-54654-2

[Gr. Pre–2] The traditional story, but with Marshall's own goofy kitty-infested illustrations. More sedate versions are by Marcia Brown, Jacob Grimm, Paul Galdone, and Nonny Hogrogian, while Bernice Myers lampoons the tale in *Sidney Rella and the Glass Sneaker.* FOLKLORE–FRANCE. PRINCES AND PRINCESSES–FOLKLORE.

1538 Keats, Ezra Jack. *John Henry: An American Legend.* Illus. by the author. Knopf, 1987. ISBN 0-394-99052-8

[Gr. 1–4] How the steel-driving man beat the steam drill and died with his hammer in his hand. Tuck this into a lesson on machines, railroads, or Westward expansion. For older students also read Steve Sanfield's *A Natural Man.* FOLKLORE, AFRICAN AMERICAN. FOLKLORE–U.S. TALL TALES.

1539 Kent, Jack. *The Fat Cat.* Illus. by the author. Scholastic, 1972. ISBN 0-590-02174-5

[Gr. Pre–2] Here is a long-standing favorite cumulative Danish tale of a greedy cat who eats everyone in his path. Perfect for acting out, along with Paul Galdone's similar U.S. folktale *The Greedy Old Fat Man,* Virginia Haviland's "The Cat and the Parrot" from *Favorite Fairy Tales Told in India* (Little, Brown, 1973), Robert Leydenfrost's *The Snake That Sneezed,* and Jack Prelutsky's *The Terrible Tiger.* CATS–FOLKLORE. CREATIVE DRAMA–FOLKLORE. CUMULATIVE STORIES.

1540 Kha, Dang Manh. *In the Land of Small Dragon: A Vietnamese Folktale.* Illus. by Tony Chen. Viking, 1979.

[Gr. 3–5] A poetic, magnificent *Cinderella* variant. Contrast with other retellings such as Marcia Brown's French *Cinderella,* Shirley Climo's *The Egyptian Cinderella,* those by Jacob Grimm, William H. Hooks's American *Moss Gown,* Charlotte Huck's *Princess Furball,* Ai-Ling Louie's Chinese *Yen-Shen,* and Flora Annie Steel's English *Tattercoats.* FOLKLORE–VIETNAM.

1541 Kimmel, Eric A. *Anansi and the Moss-Covered Rock.* Illus. by Janet Stevens. Holiday House, 1990. ISBN 0-8234-0798-5

[Gr. Pre–2] Anansi takes great advantage of the discovery that every time another animal says, "Isn't this a strange moss-covered rock," he falls down senseless for an hour, leaving the cunning spider free to steal that animal's food supply. Rabbit pulls the same sort of pranks in *Rabbit Makes a Monkey Out of Lion,* another African trickster tale, by Verna Aardema. For more about Anansi, see Peggy Appiah's *Tales of an Ashanti Father* (Deutsch, 1967), Joyce Cooper Arkhurst's *Adventures of Spider,* Harold Courlander's *The Cow-Tail Switch,* Gail E. Haley's *A Story, a Story,* and Gerald McDermott's *Anansi the Spider.* ANIMALS–FOLKLORE. FOLKLORE–AFRICA. SPIDERS–FOLKLORE. STORIES TO TELL. TRICKSTER TALES.

1542 Kismaric, Carole. *The Rumor of Pavel and Paali: A Ukrainian Folktale.* Illus. by Charles Mikolaycak. Harper & Row, 1988. ISBN 0-06-023277-3

[Gr. 3–6] Twin brothers, one happy and generous, the other sour and stingy, make a wager of all their worldly goods on whether the first three authorities they meet believe in doing good or evil as the better way to live. Of course, goodness prevails, but not until the kind brother loses his possessions and even his eyes to the nasty one. Poll your students as to their opinions on this ever-timely issue of ethics. In the same vein, peace triumphs over violence in David Wisniewski's *The Warrior and the Wise Man*. BROTHERS—FOLKLORE. FOLKLORE—UKRAINE.

1543 **Lamont, Priscilla.** *The Troublesome Pig: A Nursery Tale.* **Illus. by the author. Crown, 1985. ISBN 0-517-55546-8**

[Gr. Pre–2] The stubborn pig won't jump over the stile to go home with the old woman until she summons help. Chant the refrain together, then act this one out. Compare the text and illustrations with Paul Galdone's classic *The Old Woman and Her Pig*. ANIMALS-FOLKLORE. CHANTABLE REFRAIN. CUMULATIVE STORIES. FOLK-LORE-ENGLAND. PIGS-FOLKLORE.

1544 **Lang, Andrew.** *Aladdin and the Wonderful Lamp.* **Illus. by Errol Le Cain. Viking, 1981.**

[Gr. 2–5] Lured into an underground treasure trove by a magic lamp-seeking magician who poses as his uncle, Aladdin gains inadvertent control of the lamp, giving him never-ending wealth through genie-power. With large, meticulous illustrations modeled after Persian miniatures, this telling is more elemental than Marianna Mayer's gussied up *Aladdin and the Enchanted Lamp*. Contrast the old-time genie with the bullying one in Brinton Turkle's New England-based *Do Not Open*. Continue with the breathtaking *Ali Baba and the Forty Thieves* by Walter McVitty. FOLKLORE—ARABIA. GENIES—FOLKLORE. PRINCES AND PRINCESSES—FOLK-LORE. WISHES—FOLKLORE.

1545 **Langton, Jane.** *The Hedgehog Boy: A Latvian Folktale.* **Illus. by Ilse Plume. Harper & Row, 1985. ISBN 0-06-023696-5**

[Gr. K–3] Prickly coated boy, the enchanted only child of an old farming couple, marries the King's youngest daughter. Pair this with Jacob Grimm's *The Donkey Prince* and *The Frog Prince*, and Elizabeth Isele's *The Frog Princess*. FOLKLORE—LATVIA. PRINCES AND PRINCESSES—FOLKLORE. TRANSFORMATIONS—FOLKLORE.

1546 **Lee, Jeanne M.** *Toad Is the Uncle of Heaven.* **Illus. by the author. Henry Holt, 1985. ISBN 0-8050-1146-3**

[Gr. Pre–2] How Toad visited the King of Heaven and brought rain to Vietnam. This makes a good companion piece to the Indian folktale *Rum Pum Pum* by Maggie Duff. FOLKLORE—VIETNAM. TOADS—FOLKLORE.

1547 **Littedale, Freya.** *Peter and the North Wind.* **Illus. by Troy Howell. Scholastic, 1988. ISBN 0-590-40756-2**

[Gr. Pre–3] A retelling of the Norse tale "The Lad Who Went to the North Wind," this variant of Jacob Grimm's *The Table, the Donkey and the Stick* pits young Peter and a magic cloth, goat, and stick against a greedy innkeeper. Also see Warwick Hutton's German *The Nose Tree*, Gerald McDermott's *Tim O'Toole and the Wee Folk*, James Riordan's Russian *The Three Magic Gifts,* and Harve Zemach's Italian *Too Much Nose*. FOLKLORE—NORWAY.

1548 **Louie, Ai-Ling.** *Yeh-Shen: A Cinderella Story from China.* **Illus. by Ed Young. Philomel, 1982. ISBN 0-399-20900-X**

[Gr. 3–5] A magic fish is the girl's confidant in this tale that predates by 1,000 years the earliest-known European version of *Cinderella*, as retold by Marcia Brown. Compare with traditional versions by Jacob Grimm and Paul Galdone, Shirley Climo's *The Egyptian Cinderella*, William H. Hooks's American *Moss Gown*, Charlotte Huck's *Princess Furball*, Dang Manh Kha's Vietnamese *In the Land of Small*

Dragon, and Flora Annie Steel's English *Tattercoats.* FISHES—FOLKLORE. FOLKLORE—CHINA.

1549   McCurdy, Michael. *The Devils Who Learned to Be Good.* Illus. by the author. Little, Brown, 1987. ISBN 0-316-55527-4

[Gr. K–3] An old soldier's generosity to two beggars nets him a magic deck of cards and an old sack that he uses to outwit and then tame the rowdy devils in the czar's palace. In Wanda Gag's *Tales from Grimm,* three young soldiers outsmart the devil in "The Dragon and His Grandmother." DEVIL—FOLKLORE. FOLKLORE—RUSSIA. SOLDIERS—FOLKLORE.

1550   McDermott, Gerald. *Anansi the Spider: A Tale from the Ashanti.* Illus. by the author. Henry Holt, 1972. ISBN 0-8050-0310-X

[Gr. Pre–3] West African story from Ghana about Anansi's six talented sons and of how the moon came to be. Other explanations are found in Elphinstone Dayrell's *Why the Sun and Moon Live in the Sky* and Bess Clayton's *The Truth about the Moon.* For more Anansi see Gail E. Haley's ideal *A Story, a Story,* along with these other collections: Peggy Appiah's *Tales of an Ashanti Father* (Deutsch, 1967), Joyce Cooper Arkhurst's *The Adventures of Spider,* and Harold Courlander's *The Hat-Shaking Dance.* For a bit of cross-cultural comparison see Cheng Hou-Tien's *The Six Chinese Brothers.* FOLKLORE—AFRICA. MOON—FOLKLORE. SPIDERS—FOLKLORE.

1551   McDermott, Gerald. *Daniel O'Rourke: An Irish Tale.* Illus. by the author. Puffin, 1988. ISBN 0-317-69623-8

[Gr. 1–4] After dining on green cheese and goose livers at a grand party, Daniel heads home past the pooka's tower and is taken on a wild ride out to sea, up to the moon, and into the water. This would be a good time to talk about some of the wild and woolly dreams your children have had and to make stories out of them. FOLKLORE—IRELAND. MOON—FOLKLORE.

1552   McDermott, Gerald. *The Stonecutter: A Japanese Folk Tale.* Illus. by the author. Puffin, 1978. ISBN 0-14-050289-0

[Gr. K–4] A humbling cyclical tale where the dissatisfied lowly stonecutter, filled with envy for that which is more powerful than he, is transformed by the mountain spirit into a prince, the sun, a cloud, and finally, the mountain with another lowly stonecutter chipping away at his feet. Ruth Hurlimann's *The Proud White Cat* covers some of the same ground. The eternal elements are tamed by peace instead of war in David Wisniewski's *The Warrior and the Wise Man.* On a lighter note read and act out Arnold Lobel's *Ming Lo Moves the Mountain.* FOLKLORE—JAPAN. JEALOUSY—FOLKLORE. MOUNTAINS—FOLKLORE.

1553   McDermott, Gerald. *Tim O'Toole and the Wee Folk: An Irish Tale.* Illus. by the author. Viking, 1990. ISBN 0-670-80393-6

[Gr. 1–4] Sent by his wife to find work, penniless Tim chances upon a troop of wee folk who give him a little grey goose that lays golden eggs, a food-producing tablecloth, and a hat filled with club-bearing little men. Tim first squanders and then recovers his gifts, as do the fellows in Jacob Grimm's *The Table, the Donkey and the Stick,* Warwick Hutton's *The Nose Tree,* Freya Littledale's *Peter and the North Wind,* James Riordan's *The Three Magic Gifts,* and Harve Zemach's *Too Much Nose.* FAIRIES—FOLKLORE. FOLKLORE—IRELAND.

1554 **McDermott, Gerald.** *The Voyage of Osiris: A Myth of Ancient Egypt.* **Illus. by the author. Dutton, 1977.**

[Gr. 2–6] Dazzling illustrations uplift this account of how Osiris became Lord of the Underworld after being killed by his evil brother, animal-headed Set. Add Shirley Climo's *The Egyptian Cinderella,* Mary Stolz's Sphinx story *Zekmet, the Stone Carver,* and Irene and Laurence Swinburn's smashing *Behind the Sealed Door: The Discovery of the Tomb and Treasures of Tutankhamun,* all a boon to ancient Egypt studies. FOLKLORE–EGYPT. MYTHOLOGY.

1555 **McGovern, Ann.** *Stone Soup.* **Illus. by Winslow Pinney Pels. Scholastic, 1986. ISBN 0-590-40526-8**

[Gr. Pre–2] An easy-to-read version with the repeated refrain "Soup from a stone, fancy that," which the little old lady says to the hungry young man. Variants include Marcia Brown's French *Stone Soup,* Marilyn Hirsch's Hanukkah tale *Potato Pancakes All Around,* and Harve Zemach's Swedish *Nail Soup.* COOKERY–FOLKLORE. FOOD–FOLKLORE. SOUP–FOLKLORE.

1556 **McGovern, Ann.** *Too Much Noise.* **Illus. by Simms Taback. Houghton Mifflin, 1967. ISBN 0-395-18110-0**

[Gr. Pre–2] Similar to Marilyn Hirsch's *Could Anything Be Worse?* (Holiday House, 1974) and Margot Zemach's *It Could Always Be Worse,* this story about a man who couldn't sleep until he acquired and then let go a houseful of animals is the easiest of the three to read or tell. Almost every line can be accompanied by sound effects and the large animal cast makes acting it out a pleasure. ANIMALS–FOLKLORE. CREATIVE DRAMA–FOLKLORE. CUMULATIVE STORIES. NOISE–FOLKLORE. SOUND EFFECTS.

1557 **McVitty, Walter.** *Ali Baba and the Forty Thieves.* **Illus. by Margaret Early. Abrams, 1989.**

[Gr. 3–6] "Open sesame," are the magic words a poor woodcutter overhears that lead him into a den of robbers' riches in this most famous Arabian Nights tale. With outstanding Persian miniaturelike illustrations gleaming gold, this makes an outstanding companion to Andrew Lang's *Aladdin and the Wonderful Lamp* or Marianna Mayer's longer telling, *Aladdin and the Enchanted Lamp.* FOLKLORE–ARABIA. ROBBERS AND OUTLAWS–FOLKLORE.

1558 **Mahy, Margaret.** *The Seven Chinese Brothers.* **Illus. by Jean Tseng and Mou-sien Tseng. Scholastic, 1990. ISBN 0-590-42055-0**

[Gr. K–4] Like Claire Bishop's *The Five Chinese Brothers* and Cheng Hou-Tien's *The Six Chinese Brothers,* these seven siblings each have one amazing power that saves them from being killed by the Celestial Emperor. Introduce this Han tale, about how the brothers mend a hole in the Great Wall and then escape death, by reading Leonard Everett Fisher's *The Great Wall of China.* BROTHERS–FOLKLORE. FOLKLORE–CHINA.

1559 **Maitland, Antony.** *Idle Jack.* **Illus. by the author. Farrar, 1979. ISBN 0-374-33628-8**

[Gr. K–3] Lazy English noodlehead tries to earn an honest living and the comical results cure a rich man's daughter. The nonsensical way he takes advice will remind you of Aesop's *The Miller, His Son and His Donkey.* DAYS OF THE WEEK–FOLKLORE. FOLKLORE–ENGLAND. FOOLS–FOLKLORE.

1560   **Marshak, Samuel.** *The Month Brothers: A Slavic Tale.* **Trans. by Thomas P. Whitney. Illus. by Diane Stanley. Morrow, 1983. ISBN 0-688-01510-7**

[Gr. K–3] Czechoslovakian story about a girl sent by her stepmother into a winter blizzard to pick snowdrops. Compare with variants: Aliki's *The Twelve Months*, Beatrice Schenk de Regniers's *Little Sister and the Month Brothers*, and Jacob Grimm's *Mother Holly*. Marshak produced the play in postwar Russia; you might do the same with your own student actors. CREATIVE DRAMA–FOLKLORE. FOLKLORE –CZECHOSLOVAKIA. MONTHS–FOLKLORE. WINTER–FOLKLORE.

1561   **Marshall, James.** *Goldilocks and the Three Bears.* **Illus. by the author. Dial, 1988. ISBN 0-8037-0542-5**

[Gr. Pre–1] An irreverent romp through scalding porridge, unsuitable chairs, and a comfy bed. Other more traditional versions include those by Jan Brett, Lorinda Bryan Cauley, Armand Eisen, Paul Galdone, and Janet Stevens. Don't forget Brinton Turkle's wordless parody *Deep in the Forest* and Jane Yolen's *The Three Bears Rhyme Book* for poems written by and about Baby Bear. BEARS–FOLKLORE. OBEDIENCE–FOLKLORE.

1562   **Marshall, James.** *Red Riding Hood.* **Illus. by the author. Dial, 1987. ISBN 0-8037-0344-9**

[Gr. Pre–2] Put off reading this almost-slapstick rendition, where Granny is furious at having her reading interrupted by the wolf, until children have heard some of the more traditional Jacob Grimm retellings such as *Little Red Cap* or *Little Red Riding Hood*. An American variant, Wilhelmina Harper's *The Gunniwolf* is an addictive act-it-out story as well. FOLKLORE–GERMANY. GRANDMOTHERS–FOLKLORE. WOLVES–FOLKLORE.

1563   **Marshall, James.** *The Three Little Pigs.* **Illus. by the author. Dial, 1989. ISBN 0-8037-0591-3**

[Gr. Pre–1] While sticking closely to the story, Marshall injects hilarious touches into his dialogue and illustrations. See also versions by Erik Blegvad (Atheneum, 1980), Lorinda Bryan Cauley, Paul Galdone, and Margot Zemach. Cap it off with William Hook's Appalachian *The Three Little Pigs and the Fox*, and Jon Scieszka's hilarious *The True Story of the 3 Little Pigs* as explained by the wolf. CREATIVE DRAMA– FOLKLORE. PIGS–FOLKLORE. WOLVES–FOLKLORE.

1564   **Martin, Rafe.** *Foolish Rabbit's Big Mistake.* **Illus. by Ed Young. Putnam, 1985. ISBN 0-399-21178-0**

[Gr. Pre–2] Like Chicken Little or Paul Galdone's *Henny Penny*, a rabbit, thinking the earth is breaking up when he hears a loud noise, panics and runs off to warn the other animals. Based on a Jataka tale, this boasts staggeringly vivid illustrations that are spectacular from a distance. Hand out apple chunks while all contemplate the story's message: To investigate that which scares you before you panic. Then, contrast rabbits by reading Charlotte Zolotow's *Mr. Rabbit and the Lovely Present* or try Steven Kellogg's tongue-in-cheek *Chicken Little*, a wild reinterpretation of the old story. ANIMALS–FOLKLORE. FOOD–FOLKLORE. FRUIT–FOLKLORE. LIONS–FOLK-LORE.

1565   **Mayer, Marianna.** *Aladdin and the Enchanted Lamp.* **Illus. by Gerald McDermott. Macmillan, 1985. ISBN 0-02-765360-9**

[8 chapters, 80p., Gr. 4–6] An elaborately expanded version of the Arabian Nights tale about a boy, his genie, and a thwarted sorcerer who seeks vengeance. For a less detailed retelling see also Andrew Lang's *Aladdin and the Wonderful Lamp*. Compare these with what happens to Quentin's wished-for wealth in Bill Brittain's modern-day leprechaun fantasy *All the Money in the World*. Walter McVitty's retelling of *Ali Baba and the Forty Thieves* is another gorgeous Arabian Nights story. FOLKLORE–ARABIA. GENIES–FOLKLORE. PRINCES AND PRINCESSES–FOLKLORE. WISHES –FOLKLORE.

1566   **Mayer, Marianna. *Beauty and the Beast*. Illus. by Mercer Mayer. Four Winds, 1978. ISBN 0-02-765270-X**

[Gr. 2–5] Compare the lyric text and the voluptuous illustrations with the mannered tapestry style of the Rosemary Harris version, with pictures by Errol Le Cain. Other suitors in animal disguise who depend on their beloveds' steadfast devotion can be found in the George Dasent/Gillian Barlow version of the Norwegian fairy tale *East o' the Sun & West o' the Moon*, Kathleen and Michael Hague's *East of the Sun and West of the Moon*, and Elizabeth Isele's Russian *The Frog Princess*. FOLKLORE–FRANCE. MONSTERS–FOLKLORE. TRANSFORMATIONS–FOLKLORE.

1567   **Mayer, Marianna. *Iduna and the Magic Apples*. Illus. by Laszlo Gal. Macmillan, 1988. ISBN 0-02-765120-7**

[Gr. 4–6] Based on the tenth-century Norse poem about Iduna, the beloved mistress of a garden where she grows the apples that keep Odin and the other gods forever young, this details the trouble that befalls her when the evil giant Thiassi intervenes. Discuss the concept of living forever and expand on its pitfalls by reading Natalie Babbitt's *Tuck Everlasting*. FOLKLORE–NORWAY. FOOD–FOLKLORE. FRUIT–FOLKLORE. GIANTS–FOLKLORE. MYTHOLOGY.

1568   **Miller, Moira. *The Moon Dragon*. Illus. by Ian Deuchar. Dial, 1989. ISBN 0-8037-0566-2**

[Gr. 1–4] Trapped by his own braggadocio when the Emperor commands him to build a kite to fly to the moon, Ling Po learns a lesson in humility. In Diane Wolkstein's Chinese folktale *The Magic Wings*, the goose girl sets all the women to yearning for the means to fly. FLIGHT–FOLKLORE. FOLKLORE–CHINA.

1569   **Morgan, Pierr. *The Turnip: An Old Russian Folktale*. Illus. by the author. Philomel, 1990. ISBN 0-399-22229-4**

[Gr. Pre–1] Dedoushka plants the turnip seed and enlists the help of wife Baboushka, granddaughter Mashenka, dog Geouchka, cat Keska, and an unnamed field mouse before he can pull up the huge vegetable. The sequence is infectious for chanting, and can be compared with Janina Domanska's *The Turnip* and Alexei Tolstoi's *The Great Big Enormous Turnip* before you act it out. Bring in a fresh turnip to slice up so everyone can have a nibble. CREATIVE DRAMA. FOLKLORE–RUSSIA. SEQUENCE STORIES. STORIES TO TELL. VEGETABLES–FOLKLORE.

1570   **Morris, Winifred. *The Magic Leaf*. Illus. by Ju-Hong Chen. Atheneum, 1987. ISBN 0-689-31358-6**

[Gr. 2–4] Although Lee Foo thought of himself as a very smart fellow, he will remind you of every other fool who graces the pages of international noodlehead, numskull, and nitwit tales, from the elders of Chelm and Anne Rose's *The Triumphs of Fuzzy Fogtop* to *The Three Sillies* by Paul Galdone or Kathryn Hewitt. Your students can plan what they would do if they found a leaf that could render them invisible. FOLKLORE—CHINA. FOOLS—FOLKLORE.

1571   **Mosel, Arlene.** *The Funny Little Woman.* **Illus. by Blair Lent. Dutton, 1972. ISBN 0-525-30265-4**

[Gr. Pre–3] Japanese ogres, the wicked oni, kidnap the Funny Little Woman to become their cook after she loses her rice dumpling underground. Look for the superb Weston Woods filmstrip by the same title. Linda Shute's *Momotaro, the Peach Boy* also takes on oni and wins, while both Helena Clare Pittman's *A Grain of Rice* and David Birch's *The King's Chessboard* deal with a quantity of rice that is doubled. CALDECOTT MEDAL. FOLKLORE—JAPAN.

1572   **Mosel, Arlene.** *Tikki Tikki Tembo.* **Illus. by Blair Lent. Henry Holt, 1968. ISBN 0-8050-0662-1**

[Gr. Pre–3] Chinese tale of a long-named boy who falls into a well. Your children will not be able to resist chanting that great long name every time you do. BROTHERS—FOLKLORE. CHANTABLE REFRAIN. FOLKLORE—CHINA. NAMES—FOLKLORE. OBEDIENCE—FOLKLORE.

1573   **Ness, Evaline.** *Mr. Miacca: An English Folktale.* **Illus. by the author. Holt, 1967.**

[Gr. Pre–2] Bad Tommy Grimes is captured by wicked Mr. Miacca, who plans to boil the boy and eat him for supper. Tommy is as clever as the monkey in Paul Galdone's *The Monkey and the Crocodile.* FOLKLORE—ENGLAND. OBEDIENCE—FOLKLORE.

1574   **Ness, Evaline.** *Tom Tit Tot.* **Illus. by the author. Scribner, 1965.**

[Gr. 2–4] An English variant of *Rumpelstiltskin,* told in catchy dialect. Compare with the Jacob Grimm versions retold by Jacqueline Ayer (Harcourt, 1967), Paul Galdone, Edith Tarcov (Four Winds, 1973), and Paul O. Zelinsky, and Harve Zemach's Yorkshire *Duffy and the Devil.* FOLKLORE—ENGLAND. NAMES—FOLKLORE.

1575   **Newton, Patricia Montgomery.** *The Five Sparrows: A Japanese Folktale.* **Illus. by the author. Atheneum, 1982.**

[Gr. 1–4] After nursing a wounded sparrow, an old woman is rewarded for her kindness with a never-ending supply of rice, while her greedy neighbor deserves and receives only flies. For another Japanese variant read Momoko Ishii's *The Tongue-Cut Sparrow.* BIRDS—FOLKLORE. FOLKLORE—JAPAN.

1576   **Otsuka, Zuzo.** *Suho and the White Horse: A Legend of Mongolia.* **Illus. by Suekichi Akaba. Viking, 1981.**

[Gr. 2–4] A poor peasant boy of the steppes finds a newborn foal that he raises, races, and loses tragically in a tale of how the first horse-head fiddle came to be. Also about music and loss is Susan Cooper's sensitive Welsh folktale *The Silver Cow.* FOLKLORE—MONGOLIA. HORSES—FOLKLORE. MUSIC—FOLKLORE.

1577   **Pearson, Susan.** *Jack and the Beanstalk.* **Illus. by James Warhola. Simon & Schuster, 1989. ISBN 0-671-67196-0**

[Gr. K–4] Bright, large-scale illustrations take us high into the clouds with brash Jack who absconds with the giant's gold, hen, and harp. Compare this with Lorinda Bryan Cauley's version, as well as with all the variants: Raymond Briggs's update *Jim and the Beanstalk,* Paul Galdone's *The History of Mother Twaddle and the*

Marvelous Achievements of Her Son, Jack, Gail E. Haley's *Jack and the Bean Tree*, and James Still's *Jack and the Wonder Beans*. FOLKLORE—ENGLAND. GIANTS—FOLKLORE.

1578 **Pevear, Richard.** *Mr. Cat-and-a-Half.* **Illus. by Robert Rayevsky. Macmillan, 1986.**

[Gr. 1–3] An entertaining Ukrainian folktale about Mistress Fox's sleek new husband, an opportunistic cat who unwittingly scares the daylights out of the boar, bear, rabbit, and wolf who invite him for supper. For another cat who comes to dinner and causes consternation, read "The Cat and the Parrot" from Virginia Haviland's *Favorite Fairy Tales Told in India* (Little, Brown, 1973). Greed interrupts Big Daizo and Little Suki's food supply in Yoshiko Uchida's Japanese *Two Foolish Cats*. CATS—FOLKLORE. FOLKLORE—RUSSIA. FOXES—FOLKLORE.

1579 **Pevear, Richard.** *Our King Has Horns!* **Illus. by Robert Rayevsky. Macmillan, 1987. ISBN 0-02-773920-1**

[Gr. 2–5] Finding it overwhelming to keep such a burdening secret, the King's barber tells the reeds about the king's unusual head adornments. This is the Russian companion to Hans Christian Andersen's familiar *The Emperor's New Clothes* and, of course, the old King Midas tale, of which Peggy Thomson's *The King Has Horse's Ears* is a droll, baroque-style retelling. FOLKLORE—RUSSIA. KINGS AND RULERS—FOLKLORE.

1580 **Pittman, Helena Clare.** *A Grain of Rice.* **Illus. by the author. Hastings House, 1986. ISBN 0-8038-2728-8**

[Gr. 2–4] When the Emperor of China will not allow Pong Lo to marry princess Chang Wu, even after the farmer's son has cured her of her malaise, the young peasant asks instead for one grain of rice to be doubled daily for 100 days. Your students will clamor to attack the math problem within and perhaps count out some rice grains to calculate volume. David Brich's *The King's Chessboard* encompasses the same burgeoning rice bags. FOLKLORE—CHINA. KINGS AND RULERS—FOLKLORE. PRINCES AND PRINCESSES—FOLKLORE.

1581 **Proddow, Penelope.** *Demeter and Persephone.* **Illus. by Barbara Cooney. Doubleday, 1972.**

[Gr. 5–6] Homeric hymn of the goddess' daughter who is stolen away by Hades, Lord of the Underworld. Read this during cold weather as an explanation of winter, and afterward, share a pomegranate with your listeners. Another dramatic Greek myth in striking picture book format is Leonard Everett Fisher's *Theseus and the Minotaur*. FOLKLORE—GREECE. MYTHOLOGY. SEASONS—FOLKLORE. WINTER—FOLKLORE.

1582 **Quigley, Lillian F.** *The Blind Men and the Elephant.* **Illus. by Janice Holland. Scribner, 1959.**

[Gr. K–5] Indian fable of six blind men who each determine what the great beast is like, with significant differences in their conclusions. For an involving follow-up that takes a bit of advance plannning, choose three or four unique animals, for example, giraffe, lion, and kangaroo. For each animal, write a clear, basic description for each of the following parts: head, body, legs, and tail, including size, shape, color, and markings for each part. Divide your class into groups of four to eight, and hand out each description to one or two children who will then draw that body part using the clues you have offered. As each group finishes, they cut out the body parts, assemble the animal, determine what animal they have just drawn, and then share descriptions and results with the rest of the class. BLIND—FOLKLORE. ELEPHANTS—FOLKLORE. FABLES. FOLKLORE—INDIA.

1583   **Ransome, Arthur.** *The Fool of the World and His Flying Ship.* **Illus. by Uri Shulevitz. Farrar, 1968. ISBN 0-374-32442-5**

[Gr. 2–4] Russian Fool wins the Czar's daughter, thanks to the singular talents of his traveling companions. Also try Verna Aardema's Mexican variant, *The Riddle of the Drum.* CALDECOTT MEDAL. FOLKLORE—RUSSIA. FOOLS—FOLKLORE. SHIPS—FOLKLORE.

1584   **Rayevsky, Inna.** *The Talking Tree.* **Illus. by Robert Rayevsky. Putnam, 1990. ISBN 0-399-21631-6**

[Gr. 2–5] Collector of the rarest treasures in the world, an acquisitive king seeks the talking tree described by a stranger, and finds within a princess under a witch's enchantment. Other Italian folktales involving unusual transformations and witchcraft include Giambattista Basile's *Petrosinella*, Tomie dePaola's *The Mysterious Giant of Barletta*, and Harve Zemach's *Too Much Nose.* FOLKLORE—ITALY. KINGS AND RULERS—FOLKLORE. PRINCES AND PRINCESSES—FOLKLORE. WITCHES—FOLKLORE.

1585   **Reuter, Bjarne.** *The Princess and the Sun, Moon and Stars.* **Illus. by Svend Otto S. Viking, 1987.**

[Gr. 1–4] Thanks to a humble but clever soldier, who lies about the size of her nose but gives her his heart, the beautiful princess is rejected by the three princes who offer her the moon, the stars, and the sun. This Chinese folktale is an amusing companion to Warwick Hutton's *The Nose Tree*, where the princess truly does grow a long nose. FOLKLORE—CHINA. PRINCES AND PRINCESSES—FOLKLORE. SOLDIERS—FOLKLORE.

1586   **Riordan, James.** *The Three Magic Gifts.* **Illus. by Errol Le Cain. Oxford University Press, 1980. ISBN 0-19-520194-9**

[Gr. 1–4] A poor Russian man loses his magic cloth and goat to his rich brother. A familiar theme in folklore, compare this with Jacob Grimm's *The Table, the Donkey and the Stick*, Warwick Hutton's *The Nose Tree*, Freya Littledale's *Peter and the North Wind*, Gerald McDermott's *Tim O'Toole and the Wee Folk*, and Harve Zemach's *Too Much Nose.* BROTHERS—FOLKLORE. FOLKLORE—RUSSIA.

1587   **Roth, Susan L.** *Kanahena: A Cherokee Story.* **Illus. by the author. St. Martin's, 1988. ISBN 0-312-01722-7**

[Gr. Pre–2] While stirring the *kanahena* or cornmeal mush, an old woman tells a little girl the story of how Terrapin tricked Bad Wolf and had his own shell broken in return. Illustrated with a collage of natural materials such as leaves, grasses, and cotton, this is an Indian variant of the Brer Rabbit brier patch story to which you can compare it, using the retelling in Van Dyke Parks's collection *Jump Again!* Rudyard Kipling used the same theme in his *The Beginning of the Armadillos.* FOLKLORE—INDIANS OF NORTH AMERICA. POURQUOI TALES. TRICKSTER TALES.

1588   **Sanfield, Steve.** *A Natural Man: The True Story of John Henry.* **Illus. by Peter J. Thornton. Godine, 1986. ISBN 0-87923-630-2**

[48p., Gr. 4–6] An intense prose version of the folk song about the great steel-driving man who took on the new steam drill. Words and music to the ballad are appended.

See also Ezra Jack Keats's *John Henry*. FOLKLORE, AFRICAN AMERICAN. FOLKLORE—
U.S. MACHINES—FOLKLORE. TALL TALES.

1589 **San Souci, Robert. *The Enchanted Tapestry: A Chinese Folktale*. Illus. by Laszlo Gal. Dial, 1987. ISBN 0-8037-0304-X**

[Gr. 1–4] After completing the magnificent tapestry into which she has woven her dreams and all she holds dear, Li Ju's mother is stricken ill when the masterpiece blows away to the fairies of Sun Mountain, leaving it up to her three sons to retrieve it. Compare this to Jacob Grimm's *The Water of Life*, where the youngest son prevails. For better-behaved brothers who work together read Cheng Hou-Tien's *The Six Chinese Brothers*. BROTHERS—FOLKLORE. FAIRIES—FOLKLORE. FOLKLORE—CHINA.

1590 **San Souci, Robert. *The Talking Eggs*. Illus. by Jerry Pinkney. Dial, 1989. ISBN 0-8037-0620-0**

[Gr. 1–4] Sweet and kind and sharp as 40 crickets, Blanche is rewarded for her kindness to an old woman, while mean sister Rose, who doesn't know beans from birds' eggs, is punished for her nasty ways. In the same vein as Beatrice Schenk de Regniers's *Little Sister and the Month Brothers*, Jacob Grimm's *Mother Holly*, and Samuel Marshak's *The Month Brothers*, the story in this large, stunningly illustrated Caldecott honor book most likely originally migrated from Europe to Louisiana by French émigrés way back when. EGGS—FOLKLORE. FOLKLORE, AFRICAN AMERICAN. FOLKLORE—U.S. SISTERS—FOLKLORE.

1591 **Sawyer, Ruth. *Journey Cake, Ho!* Illus. by Robert McCloskey. Puffin, 1978. ISBN 0-14-050275-0**

[Gr. Pre–2] Johnny's pancake gets away from him. This American version of a familiar theme includes two refrains for your listeners to sing or chant. Compare with P. C. Asbjørnsen's *The Runaway Pancake*, Lorinda Bryan Cauley's *The Pancake Boy*, and Scott Cook and/or Paul Galdone's *The Gingerbread Boy*. ANIMALS—FOLK-LORE. CHANTABLE REFRAIN. FOLKLORE—U.S.

1592 **Say, Allen. *Once Under the Cherry Blossom Tree: An Old Japanese Tale*. Illus. by the author. Harper, 1974.**

[Gr. 1–4] When he accidentally swallows a cherry pit, a miserly village landlord grows a large cherry tree atop his head. Discuss the difference between old tales and new fiction, using Vera B. Williams's *Cherries and Cherry Pits* as an example of modern storytelling. FOLKLORE—JAPAN. FRUIT—FOLKLORE. TREES—FOLKLORE.

1593 **Schwartz, Alvin, comp. *Kickle Snifters and Other Fearsome Critters Collected from American Folklore*. Illus. by Glen Rounds. Lippincott, 1976. ISBN 0-39732161-9**

[63p., Gr. 2–5] If squonks, goofus birds, and wunks are unfamiliar species, the descriptions and portraits of these and other peculiar animals will inspire students to make up an illustrated booklet of their own beasts. See also Robert Talon's *Zoophabets* and Jack Prelutsky's poetic collections: *The Baby Uggs Are Hatching* and *The Snopp on the Sidewalk*. ANIMALS, MYTHICAL—FOLKLORE. FOLKLORE—U.S.

1594 **Scott, Sally. *The Magic Horse*. Illus. by the author. Greenwillow, 1986. ISBN 0-688-05897-3**

[Gr. 1–4] An adaptation of Richard Burton's *Arabian Nights* story "The Ebony Horse," about a Persian wizard who tries to use his carved, wooden flying horse to thwart a prince in love. Note the similarities to Margaret Hodges's *The Little Humpbacked Horse* from Russia. FOLKLORE—PERSIA. PRINCES AND PRINCESSES—FOLKLORE.

1595 Scott, Sally. *The Three Wonderful Beggars.* Illus. by the author. Greenwillow, 1988. ISBN 0-688-06656-9

[Gr. 1–4] In this story Mark the Rich, a hard-hearted merchant, tries to circumvent the prophecy that young Vassili will take all his riches. As usual, good triumphs, so Vassili marries Mark's daughter, and Mark takes over for the ferryman in a lush Russian tale with jewel-toned illustrations. Compare stories and art styles with Simon Stern's *Vasily and the Dragon* and with the Jacob Grimm variant, *The Devil with the Three Golden Hairs.* DRAGONS—FOLKLORE. FOLKLORE—RUSSIA.

1596 Scribner, Charles. *The Devil's Bridge.* Illus. by Evaline Ness. Scribner, 1978.

[Gr. 2–4] After a French village's bridge is destroyed in a storm, a sinister stranger appears and offers to rebuild it—for a price. Pacts with Old Scratch are also made in Jacob Grimm's *The Bearskinner* and Krystyna Turska's *The Magician of Cracow.* DEVIL—FOLKLORE. FOLKLORE—FRANCE.

1597 Sewall, Marcia. *Master of All Masters: An English Folktale.* Illus. by the author. Little, Brown, 1972.

[Gr. K–3] A young servant girl must learn silly new names for ordinary household objects. Compare with the Dick Gackenbach rendition, *Arabella and Mr. Crack,* and make up your own words for everyday school articles such as chalk, pencils, and desks. For a restauranteur's tour of diner slang, do not miss Alexandra Day's *Frank and Ernest.* FOLKLORE—ENGLAND. VOCABULARY—FOLKLORE.

1598 Sherman, Josepha. *Vassilisa the Wise: A Tale of Medieval Russia.* Illus. by Daniel San Souci. Harcourt, 1988. ISBN 0-15-293240-2

[Gr. 2–5] Based on a twelfth-century Russian folk ballad, this is the story of a resourceful young woman who disguises herself as a Tartar ambassador so she may outwit Prince Vladimir and save her boasting husband from the Prince's dungeon. Another Russian protagonist of the same name but otherwise apparently unrelated is *The Frog Princess* by Elizabeth Isele. FOLKLORE—RUSSIA. PRINCES AND PRINCESSES—FOLKLORE.

1599 Shute, Linda. *Clever Tom and the Leprechaun.* Illus. by the author. Lothrop, 1988. ISBN 0-688-07488-X

[Gr. Pre–3] Tom ties a red garter around the boliarin bush to mark the place where a leprechaun claims his gold is buried, runs off for a spade, and returns to find a garter on every bush in sight. Similar to "Patrick O'Donnell and the Leprechaun" from Virginia Haviland's *Favorite Fairy Tales Told in Ireland* (Little, Brown, 1961); both make good tales to tell. For more fairy tricks also read Lorna Balian's *Leprechauns Never Lie,* Richard Kennedy's *The Leprechaun's Story,* and Gerald McDermott's *Tim O'Toole and the Wee Folk.* FOLKLORE-IRELAND. LEPRECHAUNS-FOLKLORE. STORIES TO TELL.

1600 Shute, Linda. *Momotaro the Peach Boy: A Traditional Japanese Tale.* Illus. by the author. Lothrop, 1986. ISBN 0-688-05863-9

[Gr. 1–4] Said to be the most popular folktale of Japan, this quest of a brave young man and his monkey, dog, and pheasant companions who roust a castleful of ugly oni dates to the eighth century A.D. Barbara Brenner's *Little One Inch* also thwarts oni and wicked demons, as does Arlene Mosel's *The Funny Little Woman*. FOLKLORE —JAPAN. MONSTERS—FOLKLORE.

1601   **Silverman, Maida.** *Anna and the Seven Swans.* **Illus. by David Small. Morrow, 1984. ISBN 0-688-02756-3**

[Gr. K–3] When the Russian witch Baba Yaga has her swans steal little Ivan away, his sister Anna runs to rescue him, but stops along the way to help a needy stove, apple tree, and river of milk. Rewritten into script form, this would work fine as Readers Theater. Other Baba Yaga tales include Joanna Cole's *Bony-Legs* and Ernest Small's *Baba Yaga*. BIRDS—FOLKLORE. CREATIVE DRAMA—FOLKLORE. FOLKLORE—RUSSIA. WITCHES—FOLKLORE.

1602   **Small, Ernest.** *Baba Yaga.* **Illus. by Blair Lent. Houghton Mifflin, 1966. ISBN 0-395-16975-5**

[Gr. 1–4] The iron-toothed Russian witch who lives in a hut that walks on chicken legs catches a bad Russian child for her stew-pot. Other Baba Yaga stories include Joanna Cole's *Bony-Legs* and Maida Silverman's *Anna and the Seven Swans*. FOLKLORE—RUSSIA. WITCHES—FOLKLORE.

1603   **Snyder, Dianne.** *The Boy of the Three Year Nap.* **Illus. by Allen Say. Houghton Mifflin, 1988. ISBN 0-395-44090-4**

[Gr. 2–5] While the lazy Japanese boy Taro tricks a rich merchant into arranging a marriage with the rich man's daughter, Taro's mother has her own agenda when she convinces the merchant to fix up her house and give her son his first real job. Try some other folktales of idle folk, including Mirra Ginsburg's *The Lazies* and Diane Woklstein's *Lazy Stories*. Also showcase Allen Say's other Japan-based stories and folktales including *The Bicycle Man* and *Once Under the Cherry Blossom Tree*, and Ina R. Friedman's *How My Parents Learned to Eat*. FOLKLORE—JAPAN. LAZINESS.

1604   **Spray, Carole.** *The Mare's Egg: A New World Folk Tale.* **Illus. by Kim La Fave. Camden House, 1981.**

[Gr. 2–5] A gullible Canadian rube settler spends ten dollars for a pumpkin that he thinks will hatch into a colt. This gives a taste of backwoods living to children studying the day-to-day life of the pioneers. Similar in theme to *The Gollywhopper Egg* by Anne Rockwell. FOLKLORE—CANADA. FOOLS—FOLKLORE. FRONTIER AND PIONEER LIFE. HORSES—FOLKLORE.

1605   **Stamm, Claus.** *Three Strong Women: A Tall Tale.* **Illus. by Jean Tseng and Mou-sien Tseng. Viking, 1990. ISBN 0-670-83323-1**

[Gr. 2–4] On his way to wrestle before the Emperor, Forever-Mountain meets up with a young girl, her mother, and grandmother, all of whom are stronger than he could ever be, who make him over into a truly strong man. Compare his power with that of the tricksters in Tomie dePaola's Irish *Fin M'Coul, the Giant of Knockmany Hill*, Jacob Grimm's *The Valiant Little Tailor*, and Dorothy Van Woerkom's *Alexandra the Rock-Eater*. FOLKLORE—JAPAN. WOMEN—FOLKLORE.

1606   **Steel, Flora Annie.** *Tattercoats: An Old English Tale.* **Illus. by Diane Goode. Bradbury, 1976.**

[Gr. 2–5] Dressed in rags and shunned by her grandfather and his servants, Tattercoats has but one friend, the lame gooseherd, whose haunting pipe-playing entrances the king's son and causes him to fall in love with her. Out of the hundreds of the world's *Cinderella* stories, present some of the following: Shirley Climo's *The Egyptian Cinderella*, Marcia Brown's or Paul Galdone's French *Cinderella*, Nonny Hogrogian's Grimm retelling, William H. Hooks's U.S. *Moss Gown*, Charlotte Huck's *Princess Furball*, Dang Manh Kha's Vietnamese *In the Land of Small Dragon*, Ai-Ling Louie's Chinese *Yeh-Shen*, and John Steptoe's African *Mufaro's Beautiful Daughters*. FOLKLORE–ENGLAND. PRINCES AND PRINCESSES–FOLKLORE.

1607   Steptoe, John. *Mufaro's Beautiful Daughters: An African Tale.* Illus. by the author. Lothrop, 1987. ISBN 0-688-04045-4

[Gr. 1–4] One good daughter and one bad daughter set off to appear before the king who plans to choose his queen. The sumptuous, stately paintings will astonish your listeners. As this Caldecott Honor book incorporates elements of *Cinderella*, compare it with some of the variants listed under Flora Annie Steel's *Tattercoats*. FOLKLORE–AFRICA. KINGS AND RULERS–FOLKLORE. SISTERS–FOLKLORE. SNAKES–FOLKLORE.

1608   Steptoe, John. *The Story of Jumping Mouse: A Native American Legend.* Illus. by the author. Lothrop, 1984. ISBN 0-688-01902-1

[Gr. Pre–4] Inspired by stories of the far-off land, an unselfish, compassionate young mouse sets off on a perilous journey, aided by Magic Frog, to fulfill his dream. On this journey the mouse is transformed into an eagle. Huge, dignified, often larger-than-life gray-and-white pencil illustrations are breathtaking to behold. When learning about birds, this tale of how the eagle came to be works well with other feathered folktales such as Shirley Climo's *King of the Birds*, Joanna Troughton's *How the Birds Changed Their Feathers*, and Sumiko Yagawa's *The Crane Wife*. Leo Lionni's *Tico and the Golden Wings* is also about a bird rewarded for his generosity. BIRDS–FOLKLORE. FOLKLORE–INDIANS OF NORTH AMERICA. MICE–FOLKLORE. POURQUOI TALES.

1609   Stern, Simon. *The Hobyas: An Old Story.* Illus. by the author. Prentice Hall, 1977.

[Gr. Pre–1] Such a gleeful adaptation of Joseph Jacob's English tale about the little dog who scares the creatures away from his owner's turnip house makes a fine puppet show or a play using repetitive dialogue. Speaking of turnips, bring in a few and read either Janina Domanska's *The Turnip* or Alexei Tolstoi's *The Great Big Enormous Turnip*. CHANTABLE REFRAIN. CREATIVE DRAMA–FOLKLORE. DOGS–FOLKLORE. FOLKLORE–ENGLAND.

1610   Stern, Simon. *Vasily and the Dragon: An Epic Russian Fairy Tale.* Illus. by the author. Pelham Books, 1982.

[Gr. 3–6] Because of Marko the Rich's miserly nature, two beggars—really St. Nicholas and the Lord God in disguise—offer the prophecy that a young man will possess all of Marko's wealth in fewer than 16 years. Compare with Nonny Hogrogian's Grimm variant, *The Devil with the Three Golden Hairs* and Sally Scott's *The Three Wonderful Beggars*. DRAGONS–FOLKLORE. FOLKLORE–RUSSIA.

1611   Stevens, Janet. *Goldilocks and the Three Bears.* Illus. by the author. Holiday House, 1986. ISBN 0-8234-0608-3

[Gr. Pre–1] Yet another excellent version. See also those illustrated by Jan Brett, Lorinda Bryan Cauley, Armand Eisen, Paul Galdone, and James Marshall. Don't forget to tie this story in with Brinton Turkles's wordless *Deep in the Forest* and Jane Yolen's *The Three Bears Rhyme Book.* BEARS—FOLKLORE. OBEDIENCE—FOLKLORE.

1612   **Still, James.** *Jack and the Wonder Beans.* **Illus. by Margot Tomes. Putnam, 1977.**

[Gr. 2–4] This Kentucky-bred *Jack and the Beanstalk* comes replete with irresistible Appalachian dialect. Hand out beans to plant, and link with Raymond Briggs's parody, *Jim and the Beanstalk,* Lorinda Bryan Cauley's *Jack and the Beanstalk,* and Gail E. Haley's *Jack and the Bean Tree,* another mountain version. FOLKLORE—U.S. GIANTS—FOLKLORE.

1613   **Thomson, Peggy.** *The King Has Horse's Ears.* **Illus. by David Small. Simon & Schuster, 1988. ISBN 0-671-64953-1**

[Gr. 2–5] Sworn to secrecy by the King, the court barber lets out his burdensome knowledge by whispering it to the water's edge, from whence a telltale reed grows. Set in a French baroque milieu, this retelling of the King Midas myth has far-ranging relatives, including Hans Christian Andersen's *The Emperor's New Clothes* and Richard Pevear's Russian variant *Our King Has Horns.* KINGS AND RULERS—FOLKLORE.

1614   **Tolstoi, Alexei.** *The Great Big Enormous Turnip.* **Illus. by Helen Oxenbury. Heinemann, 1968.**

[Gr. Pre–1] Everyone must work together to pull up the turnip. Compare with *The Turnip* by Janina Domanska or Pierr Morgan (Philomel, 1990), and have your students act it out. For a gardening unit use with Ruth Kraus's *The Carrot Seed* and Bruce McMillan's *Growing Colors.* CREATIVE DRAMA—FOLKLORE. FOLKLORE—RUSSIA. VEGETABLES—FOLKLORE.

1615   **Tresselt, Alvin.** *The Mitten: An Old Ukrainian Folktale.* **Illus. by Yaroslava. Lothrop, 1964. ISBN 0-688-51053-1**

[Gr. Pre–2] One by one, the forest animals crowd into a boy's lost mitten in order to keep warm. Similar in theme to Mirra Ginsburg's *Mushroom in the Rain,* also act this one out with improvised dialogue, using a large sheet as the expanding mitten. More mitten tales include Lorinda Bryan Cauley's *The Three Little Kittens* and Jean Rogers's *Runaway Mittens.* ANIMALS—FOLKLORE. FOLKLORE—UKRAINE. MITTENS—FOLKLORE. WINTER—FOLKLORE.

1616   **Troughton, Joanna.** *How the Birds Changed Their Feathers: A South American Indian Folk Tale.* **Illus. by the author. Peter J. Bedrick Books, 1986. ISBN 0-87226-080-1**

[Gr. Pre–3] When he puts on a bright-colored stone necklace, a bird-hunting boy is transformed into the fearsome and dangerous Rainbow Snake until a brave white-feathered cormorant kills it and, with the rest of the white birds, carries away the skin. Follow up this tale of how the birds became so colorful with Shirley Climo's *King of the Birds* that explains how they chose a leader. BIRDS—FOLKLORE. FOLKLORE —INDIANS OF SOUTH AMERICA. POURQUOI TALES.

1617   **Troughton, Joanna.** *Mouse-Deer's Market.* **Illus. by the author. Peter J. Bedrick Books, 1984. ISBN 0-911745-63-7**

[Gr. Pre–2] When none of the animals take notice of Mouse-deer's cries from the hole in which she has fallen, she tricks them into coming in by claiming to be selling marvelous goods there and then climbs out using the animals as her stepping-stones. Compare with Betsy and Giulio Maestro's similar-themed *A Wise Monkey Tale*. ANIMALS—FOLKLORE. FOLKLORE—BORNEO.

1618   **Troughton, Joanna.** *Tortoise's Dream.* **Illus. by the author. Peter J. Bedrick Books, 1986. ISBN 0-87226-039-9**

[Gr. Pre–2] Though Grandmother Koko tells each animal how to find the marvelous multifruited Omumbo-rombonga tree, they don't mind her instructions and so don't find it until it's Tortoise's turn to look. Chant Grandmother Koko's refrain each time. After, have children draw and name a tree filled with all of their favorite fruits or foods. ANIMALS—FOLKLORE. DREAMS—FOLKLORE. FOLKLORE—AFRICA. SEQUENCE STORIES. TREES—FOLKLORE.

1619   **Turska, Krystyna.** *The Magician of Cracow.* **Illus. by the author. Greenwillow, 1975.**

[Gr. 2–5] Eager to be the first man on the moon, a Polish magician makes a pact with the Devil who, in exchange, must do anything requested of him. *Daniel O'Rourke* also finds himself on the moon in Gerald McDermott's Irish folktale, while a whole French village agrees to the Devil's deal in *The Devil's Bridge* by Charles Scribner. DEVIL—FOLKLORE. FOLKLORE—POLAND. MAGICIANS—FOLKLORE.

1620   **Uchida, Yoshiko.** *The Two Foolish Cats.* **Illus. by Margot Zemach. McElderry, 1987. ISBN 0-689-50397-0**

[Gr. Pre–2] Big Daizo and Little Suki can't decide who should get the biggest rice cake until wise Mr. Monkey mediates and takes the problem right out of their paws. Here is a personal commonsense solution for food-related "his piece is bigger" woes: One child divides it in half, the other chooses the first piece. Richard Pevear's *Mr. Cat-and-a-Half* gets all of the food when the other forest animals become convinced he is a danger to them. CATS—FOLKLORE. FOLKLORE—JAPAN. GREED—FOLKLORE.

1621   **Van Woerkom, Dorothy.** *Alexandra the Rock-Eater.* **Illus. by Rosekrans Hoffman. Knopf, 1978. ISBN 0-394-83536-0**

[Gr. 1–4] In this witty Russian tale, two dragons are outwitted by pragmatic and cunning Alexandra, mother of 100 children. Compare with Jacob Grimm's *The Valiant Little Tailor* for similar exploits, but with a male protagonist. DRAGONS—FOLKLORE. FOLKLORE—RUSSIA.

1622   **Vernon, Adele.** *The Riddle.* **Illus. by Robert Rayevsky and Vladimir Radunsky. Dodd, 1987.**

[Gr. 3–6] Lost in the forest, the king comes upon a poor charcoal maker who explains how, on the meager wage of ten cents a day, he manages to make enough to live on, pay back a debt, save for his old age, and still have something left to throw out the window. Be sure to explain what a dowry is before you read this Catalan tale. A young Chinese peasant makes an equally propitious agreement with the emperor in Helena Clare Pittman's *A Grain of Rice*. FOLKLORE—SPAIN. KINGS AND RULERS—FOLKLORE. RIDDLES—FOLKLORE.

1623   **Walker, Barbara.** *Teeny-Tiny and the Witch Woman.* **Illus. by Michael Foreman. Pantheon, 1975.**

[Gr. 2–4] How the smallest of three brothers saves them all from a knife-sharpening witch in a frightening Turkish variant of Jacob Grimm's *Hansel and Gretel*. If you can't find the book, order the chilling filmstrip from Random House. BROTHERS—FOLKLORE. FOLKLORE—TURKEY. WITCHES—FOLKLORE.

1624 **Westwood, Jennifer.** *Going to Squintum's: A Foxy Folktale.* **Illus. by Fiona French. Dial, 1985. ISBN 0-8037-0015-6**

[Gr. Pre–2] Fox leaves his bag at houses along the way and increases his fortune each time when the woman of each house gets curious and peeks inside. Compare the use of language with Paul Galdone's *What's in Fox's Sack.* Both are dandy for retelling and acting out. CREATIVE DRAMA—FOLKLORE. FOLKLORE—ENGLAND. FOXES—FOLKLORE. SEQUENCE STORIES.

1625 **Wiesner, William.** *Happy-Go-Lucky.* **Illus. by the author. Seabury, 1970.**

[Gr. 1–4] A Norwegian farmer wins when he bets that his understanding wife will not be angry after he relates to her his misfortunes in selling their cow. Jacob Grimm's *Hans in Luck* is another poor trader who ends up with nothing. Jack fares better with his trade in Lorinda Bryan Cauley or Susan Pearson's versions of *Jack and the Beanstalk.* FARM LIFE—FOLKLORE. FOLKLORE—NORWAY. HUSBANDS AND WIVES—FOLKLORE.

1626 **Wiesner, William.** *Turnabout.* **Illus. by the author. Seabury, 1972.**

[Gr. K–4] A Norwegian farmer, scornful of his wife's housekeeping chores, offers to exchange jobs for the day. See also Kathleen and Michael Hague's *The Man Who Kept House.* FARM LIFE—FOLKLORE. FOLKLORE—NORWAY. HUSBANDS AND WIVES—FOLKLORE.

1627 **Wildsmith, Brian.** *The Hare and the Tortoise.* **Illus. by the author. Franklin Watts, 1966.**

[Gr. Pre–3] Slow and steady wins every time in this adaptation of seventeenth-century French author La Fontaine's retelling of an Aesop fable. You will also snicker over Janet Stevens's more modern rendition, *The Tortoise and the Hare.* Another quick-witted tortoise, one who manages to outsmart an elephant, is *Tricky Tortoise* by Mwenye Hadithi. FABLES. RABBITS—FOLKLORE. TURTLES—FOLKLORE.

1628 **Wildsmith, Brian.** *The Lion and the Rat.* **Illus. by the author. Oxford, 1987. ISBN 0-19-279607-0**

[Gr. Pre–3] Mouse repays lion in kind after the lion frees him. A fable by French storyteller La Fontaine based on the ancient Aesop fable; act this one out in pairs. For an updated variant see Bill Peet's *The Ant and the Elephant.* CREATIVE DRAMA—FOLKLORE. FABLES. LIONS—FOLKLORE. RATS—FOLKLORE.

1629 **Wolkstein, Diane.** *The Banza: A Haitian Story.* **Illus. by Marc Brown. Dial, 1981. ISBN 0-8037-0428-3**

[Gr. Pre–2] About Teegra, a little tiger who gives his treasured banjo to his goat friend, Cabree, for protection. The story of a bond between tiger and goat who are supposed to be enemies should start your children thinking about what it means to be a friend. FOLKLORE—HAITI. FRIENDSHIP—FOLKLORE. GOATS—FOLKLORE. STORIES WITH SONGS. TIGERS—FOLKLORE.

1630 **Wolkstein, Diane.** *The Magic Wings: A Tale from China.* **Illus. by Robert Andrew Parker. Dutton, 1983. ISBN 0-525-44062-3**

[Gr. Pre–4] When the goose girl takes it into her head that she might grow wings to greet spring, the grocer's and judge's daughters, the princess, queen, and then every female in town also wet their shoulders, flap their arms, and wait. Ling Po builds his own wings—a kite to fly to the moon—in Moira Miller's *The Moon Dragon*. For older children, read with Beatrice Gormley's modern fiction *Mail-Order Wings*. FLIGHT—FOLKLORE. FOLKLORE—CHINA. SPRING—FOLKLORE. STORIES TO TELL. WINGS—FOLKLORE.

1631   **Wolkstein, Diane.** *White Wave: A Chinese Tale.* **Illus. by Ed Young. Crowell, 1979. ISBN 0-690-03893-3**

[Gr. 2–6] The moon goddess assists a poor farmer when he brings home a live moon snail to care for. Similar in many ways to Molly Bang's *Dawn* and Sumiko Yagawa's *The Crane Wife*, this offers a touching explanation of the significance of stories. FARM LIFE—FOLKLORE. FOLKLORE—CHINA. SNAILS—FOLKLORE.

1632   **Yagawa, Sumiko.** *The Crane Wife.* **Illus. by Suekichi Akaba. Morrow, 1981. ISBN 0-688-00496-2**

[Gr. 2–5] After healing a wounded crane, a Japanese peasant meets and marries a beautiful and mysterious woman who weaves exquisite cloth. Compare with *Dawn*, Molly Bang's updated telling set in New England; *The Paper Crane*, also by Bang; and Diane Wolkstein's *White Wave*. BIRDS—FOLKLORE. FOLKLORE—JAPAN.

1633   **Young, Ed.** *Lon Po Po: A Red-Riding Hood Story from China.* **Illus. by the author. Philomel, 1989. ISBN 0-399-21619-7**

[Gr. K–2] Disguised as their grandmother, an old wolf plans to eat the three sisters staying home alone, but he is undone by his greed for gingko nuts and the sisters' cleverness. Compare this haunting variant with the Grimm versions of *Little Red Riding Hood* and with Audrey Wood's *Heckedy Peg*. CALDECOTT MEDAL. FOLKLORE—CHINA. SISTERS—FOLKLORE. WOLVES—FOLKLORE.

1634   **Young, Ed.** *The Terrible Nung Gwama: A Chinese Folktale.* **Illus. by the author. Collins-World, 1978.**

[Gr. 1–4] A poor young woman finds a way to avoid becoming supper for a repulsive monster who delights most in eating people. Retell this one in sequence and then act it out. FOLKLORE—CHINA. MONSTERS—FOLKLORE.

1635   **Zemach, Harve.** *Duffy and the Devil.* **Illus. by Margot Zemach. Farrar, 1986. ISBN 0-374-41897-7**

[Gr. 2–5] Squire Lovel's new wife makes a deal with the squinty-eyed devil to do all her knitting and spinning in an uproarious Cornish variant of Jacob Grimm's *Rumpelstiltskin*. Do not miss the wonderful Miller-Brody filmstrip narrated with throaty perfection by Tammy Grimes. See also Evaline Ness's *Tom Tit Tot* for another rendition, and of course the original Grimm tales retold by Jacqueline Ayer (Harcourt, 1967), Paul Galdone, Edith Tarcov (Four Winds, 1973), and especially Paul O. Zelinsky. CALDECOTT MEDAL. DEVIL—FOLKLORE. FOLKLORE—ENGLAND. NAMES—FOLKLORE.

1636   **Zemach, Harve.** *Nail Soup: A Swedish Folk Tale.* **Illus. by Margot Zemach. Follett, 1964.**

[Gr. 1–4] A tramp cajoles food out of a stingy old woman when he claims to be able to make soup with a mere nail. Also see both Marcia Brown's and Ann McGovern's *Stone Soup* and Marilyn Hirsch's Hanukkah story *Potato Pancakes All Around*. COOKERY—FOLKLORE. FOLKLORE—SWEDEN. FOOD—FOLKLORE. SOUP—FOLKLORE.

1637   **Zemach, Harve.** *Too Much Nose: An Italian Tale.* **Illus. by Margot Zemach. Holt, 1967.**

[Gr. 2–5] Italian folktale of a greedy queen who gets what she deserves after she steals a magic coin purse, hat, and horn from three gullible brothers. See also Jacob Grimm's *The Table, the Donkey and the Stick* and Warwick Hutton's German version, *The Nose Tree*, as well as Freya Littledale's *Peter and the North Wind*, Gerald McDermott's *Tim O'Toole and the Wee Folk*, and James Riordan's *The Three Magic Gifts*. BROTHERS–FOLKLORE. FOLKLORE–ITALY. NOSES–FOLKLORE.

1638   **Zemach, Margot.** *It Could Always Be Worse.* **Illus. by the author. Farrar, 1990. ISBN 0-374-33650-4**

[Gr. 1–4] A poor, unfortunate man needs the rabbi's advice when he can no longer stand his overcrowded one-room hut. The large cast offers great possibilities for acting the story out with improvised dialogue. See also Marilyn Hirsch's version *Could Anything Be Worse?* (Holiday House, 1974), and the sound effects-filled *Too Much Noise* by Ann McGovern. Equally sensible are Carol Chapman's *The Tale of Meshka the Kvetch*, Arnold Lobel's *Ming Lo Moves the Mountain*, and Arthur Yorinks's *It Happened in Pinsk*. CREATIVE DRAMA–FOLKLORE. FOLKLORE, JEWISH.

1639   **Zemach, Margot.** *The Three Little Pigs: An Old Story.* **Illus. by the author. Farrar, 1988. ISBN 0-374-37527-5**

[Gr. Pre–2] Another competently, affectionately illustrated version to use with the best of all the others, including those by Erik Blegvad (Atheneum, 1980), Lorinda Bryan Cauley, Paul Galdone, and James Marshall, and William H. Hooks's country variant, *The Three Little Pigs and the Fox*. The wolf gives his own account of the sordid events in Jon Scieszka's *The True Story of the 3 Little Pigs*. CREATIVE DRAMA–FOLKLORE. PIGS–FOLKLORE. WOLVES–FOLKLORE.

1640   **Zemach, Margot.** *The Three Wishes: An Old Story.* **Illus. by the author. Farrar, 1986. ISBN 0-374-37529-1**

[Gr. 1–4] Granted wishes by the imp they free from under a fallen tree, the poor woodcutting husband and wife squander them in one impetuous, peevish, sausage-filled moment. This story offers a fine example of why we need to think before we speak. Also read Paul Galdone's version of the same title (McGraw-Hill, 1961) and Jay Williams's *One Big Wish*. Everyone can write down what he or she would wish for, wisely of course. WISHES–FOLKLORE.

Illustration from WHOPPERS: TALL TALES AND OTHER LIES COLLECTED
FROM AMERICAN FOLKLORE by Alvin Schwartz, illustrated by Glen Rounds.
Illustrations copyright © 1975 by Glen Rounds. J. B. Lippincott Company, 1975.
Reprinted by permission of HarperCollins Publishers.

FOLK & FAIRY TALES, MYTHS
AND LEGENDS: COLLECTIONS

1641   **Aesop.** *The Aesop for Children.* **Illus. by Milo Winter. Macmillan, 1984. ISBN 0-02-689022-4**

[126 fables, 96p., Gr. K–3] A hefty, handsome facsimile of a popular 1919 edition. The wise animal lessons from the fifth-century B. C. Greek slave have not dulled with age. Retell the stories in this book and in the others that follow, act them out, write and illustrate new ones, compare different versions of the same tale, update them to modern day, and incorporate the lessons learned into everyday school life. For an oriental point of view that older listeners can correlate with Aesop, also read Demi's intriguing delicate collections, *A Chinese Zoo* and *Demi's Reflective Fables*, plus Arnold Lobel's own *Fables*. ANIMALS—FOLKLORE. FABLES.

1642   **Aesop.** *Aesop's Fables.* **Illus. by Michael Hague. Selected by Michael Hague. Henry Holt, 1985. ISBN 0-8050-0210-3**

[13 fables, 28p., Gr. 2–4] Mostly well-known fables, each accompanied by a full-color page, ''old-timey'' English-style painting. ANIMALS—FOLKLORE. CREATIVE DRAMA—FOLKLORE. FABLES.

1643   **Aesop.** *Aesop's Fables.* **Illus. by Heidi Holder. Viking, 1981. ISBN 0-670-10643-7**

[9 fables, 25p., Gr. 3–6] Striking, gentle, brown-toned watercolors embellish an assortment of tales. ANIMALS—FOLKLORE. CREATIVE DRAMA—FOLKLORE. FABLES.

1644   **Aesop.** *Aesop's Fables.* **Illus. by A. J. McClaskey. Retold by Ann McGovern. Scholastic, 1963. ISBN 0-590-40569-1**

[67 fables, 80p., Gr. 2–6] A workmanlike collection that children will readily understand. ANIMALS—FOLKLORE. CREATIVE DRAMA—FOLKLORE. FABLES.

1645   **Aesop.** *Aesop's Fables.* **Illus. by Alice Provensen and Martin Provensen. Selected by Louis Untermeyer. Golden Press, 1965.**

[40 fables, 92p., Gr. K–3] In this large, indispensable, amusingly illustrated classic anthology, most stories are ideal for acting out in pairs or small groups for Readers Theater. Compare the prose fables with the rhymed versions by folksinger Tom Paxton in his *Aesop's Fables*. ANIMALS—FOLKLORE. CREATIVE DRAMA—FOLKLORE. FABLES.

1646   Aesop. *Aesop's Fables.* Illus. by Robert Rayevsky. Retold by Tom Paxton. Morrow, 1988. ISBN 0-688-07361-1

[10 fables, unp. Gr. 3–6] Ten known and not-so-known tales, set into verse by an American folksinger. Compare these with the traditional versions including those retold by Eric Carle in *Twelve Tales from Aesop*, Paul Galdone's *Three Aesop Fox Fables*, the collections illustrated by Michael Hague and Heidi Holder, and Louis Untermeyer's large collection illustrated by Alice and Martin Provensen. ANIMALS –FOLKLORE. FABLES. STORIES IN RHYME.

1647   Aesop. *The Fables of Aesop.* Illus. by David Levine. Retold by Joseph Jacobs. Schocken, 1966. ISBN 0-8052-3068-8

[82 fables, 115p., Gr. 2–6] An extensive collection by the noted eighteenth-century English folklorist. ANIMALS–FOLKLORE. CREATIVE DRAMA–FOLKLORE. FABLES.

1648   Aesop. *Once in a Wood: Ten Tales from Aesop.* Illus. by Eve Rice. Adapted by Eve Rice. Greenwillow, 1979.

[10 fables, 64p., Gr. Pre–2] Familiar fables in a clear, easy-to-read format, with rhyming morals. Ideal for acting out in pairs or small groups. ANIMALS–FOLKLORE. CREATIVE DRAMA–FOLKLORE. FABLES.

1649   Aesop. *Seven Fables from Aesop.* Illus. by R. W. Alley. Retold by R. W. Alley. Putnam, 1986. ISBN 0-396-08820-1

[7 fables, 32p., Gr. 1–4] Clearly told and appealingly illustrated in pen and ink and watercolors, these will work out well for Readers Theater. ANIMALS–FOLKLORE. CREATIVE DRAMA–FOLKLORE. FABLES.

1650   Aesop. *Three Aesop Fox Fables.* Illus. by Paul Galdone. Retold by Paul Galdone. Houghton Mifflin, 1979. ISBN 0-395-28810-X

[3 fables, unp., Gr. K–2] Fox has dealings with grapes, a stork, and a cheese-carrying crow. CREATIVE DRAMA–FOLKLORE. FABLES. FOXES–FOLKLORE.

1651   Aesop. *Twelve Tales from Aesop.* Illus. by Eric Carle. Retold by Eric Carle. Philomel, 1980.

[12 fables, 30p., Gr. K–3] Old favorites retold, one per double-page spread, with bright full-page illustrations. Short and sweet for reenacting. ANIMALS–FOLKLORE. CREATIVE DRAMA–FOLKLORE. FABLES.

1652   Afanasev, Alexander, ed. *Russian Folk Tales.* Trans. by Robert Chandler. Illus. by Ivan I. Bilibin. Shambhala, 1980. ISBN 0-87773-195-0

[7 tales, 78p., Gr. 3–6] Classic stories collected by an eighteenth-century Russian folklorist and illustrated by a well-known artist of that era. For short tales of Russian sillies see the collections by Mirra Ginsburg and don't miss Virginia Haviland's *Favorite Fairy Tales Told in Russia* (Little, Brown, 1961). FOLKLORE-RUSSIA.

1653   Appiah, Peggy. *Tales of an Ashanti Father.* Illus. by Mora Dickson. Beacon Press, 1989. ISBN 0-8070-8312-7

[22 tales, 157p., Gr. 3–6] African trickster stories from Ghana about the spiderman, Kwaku Ananse, and other animals. Also read Joyce Cooper Arkhurst's *The Adventures of Spider*, Harold Courlander's *The Hat-Shaking Dance*, Julius Lester's *How Many Spots Does a Leopard Have?*, and Adjai Robinson's *Singing Tales of Africa*.

Contrast these African trickster tales with Julius Lester's *More Tales of Uncle Remus* and *The Tales of Uncle Remus*, plus Van Dyke Park and Malcolm Jones's *Jump!* and *Jump Again!* ANIMALS—FOLKLORE. FOLKLORE—AFRICA. SPIDERS—FOLKLORE. TRICK-STER TALES.

1654   **Arkhurst, Joyce Cooper.** *The Adventures of Spider: West African Folktales.* **Illus. by Jerry Pinkney. Little, Brown, 1964.**

[6 tales, 58p., Gr 1–4] Good-natured trickster tales from Liberia and Ghana. Do read aloud the mood-setting introduction. See also Peggy Appiah's *Tales of an Ashanti Father*, Harold Courlander's *The Hat-Shaking Dance*, Julius Lester's *How Many Spots Does a Leopard Have?* and Adjai Robinson's *Singing Tales of Africa.* ANIMALS—FOLKLORE. FOLKLORE—AFRICA. SPIDERS—FOLKLORE. TRICKSTER TALES.

1655   **Bang, Molly.** *The Goblins Giggle and Other Stories.* **Illus. by the author. Peter Smith, 1988. ISBN 0-8446-6360-3**

[5 tales, 57p., Gr. 3–6] With varying degrees of suspense, these chillers from Japan, Ireland, Germany, France, and China go well with Wilhelmina Harper's *Ghosts and Goblins.* "The Old Man's Wen" is just dandy for retelling. SUPERNATURAL—FOLK-LORE. SUSPENSE—FOLKLORE.

1656   **Benson, Sally.** *Stories of the Gods and Heroes.* **Illus. by Steele Savage. Dial, 1940. ISBN 0-8037-8291-8**

[28 tales, 256p., Gr. 4–6] Over 20 mostly familiar Greek and Roman myths, using Roman names. Rewritten and simplified from Thomas Bulfinch's famous *The Age of Fable.* Other useful volumes include *D'Aulaire's Book of Greek Myths* and Miriam Cox's *The Magic and the Sword*, Mary Pope Osborne's *Favorite Greek Myths*, and Margaret Evans Price's *Myths and Enchantment Tales.* MYTHOLOGY.

1657   **Biro, Val.** *Hungarian Folk-Tales.* **Illus. by the author. Oxford University Press, 1987. ISBN 0-19-274126-8**

[21 tales, 192p., Gr. 3–6] Competent stories, including trickster tales and old friends like "The Mayor's Egg," which we know from Ann Rockwell's *The Gollywhopper Egg* and Carole Spray's *The Mare's Egg*, and "The Hedgehog," a variant of *The Hedgehog Boy* as told by Jane Langton. FOLKLORE—HUNGARY.

1658   **Brooke, L. Leslie.** *The Golden Goose Book.* **Illus. by the author. Warne, 1905.**

[4 tales, unp., Gr. Pre–3] The title tale and three other well-known stories: "The Three Bears," "The Three Little Pigs," and "Tom Thumb," as interpreted by the classic illustrator, are still fresh and fun. ANIMALS—FOLKLORE.

1659   **Bruchac, Joseph.** *Iroquois Stories: Heroes and Heroines, Monsters and Magic.* **Illus. by Daniel Burgevin. Crossing Press, 1985. ISBN 0-89594-167-8**

[32 tales, 198p., Gr. 3–6] An essential and engrossing collection of tales with an inviting, large-print format, and an easy rhythm and familiarity to each retelling. This is a requisite for units on Native Americans and a rich source for storytellers. FOLKLORE—INDIANS OF NORTH AMERICA.

1660   **Carlson, Natalie Savage.** *King of the Cats and Other Tales.* **Illus. by David Frampton. Doubleday, 1980.**

[9 tales, 72p., Gr. 3–6] Folktales about such legendary creatures as a lutin, a Korrigan, and a Loup Garou, all from the Brittany province of France can cross the Channel to accompany Shirley Climo's Cornwall creatures in *Piskies, Spriggans, and Other Magical Beings.* ANIMALS, MYTHICAL−FOLKLORE. FOLKLORE−FRANCE.

1661   **Chase, Richard.** *Grandfather Tales.* **Illus. by Berkeley Williams, Jr. Houghton Mifflin, 1948. ISBN 0-395-06692-1**

[25 tales, 240p., Gr. K−6] These sensational American-English folktales, collected by the author in North Carolina, Virginia, and Kentucky, and containing recognizable variants of many well-known stories, comprise a storyteller's feast. FOLKLORE−U.S. STORYTELLING.

1662   **Chase, Richard.** *Jack Tales.* **Illus. by Berkeley Williams, Jr. Houghton Mifflin, 1943. ISBN 0-395-06694-8**

[18 tales, 202p., Gr. 4−6] More Southern Appalachian folktales, collected in North Carolina and Virginia and retold by the author. These tales are about clever Jack, alternately lazy and hardworking, as he seeks his fortune from kings, farmers, and giants. Some other long-lost relatives of the English folktales about Jack are Gail E. Haley's *Jack and the Bean Tree* and *Jack and the Fire Dragon*, and James Still's *Jack and the Wonder Beans.* FOLKLORE−U.S. STORYTELLING.

1663   **Climo, Shirley.** *Piskies, Spriggans, and Other Magical Beings: Tales from the Droll-Teller.* **Illus. by Joyce Audy dos Santos. Crowell, 1981. ISBN 0-690-04064-4**

[17 tales, 122p., Gr. 3−6] All about supernatural types from Cornwall, England, such as knackers, small people, changelings, giants, sea people, witches, and devils. Compare Climo's version of the Rumpelstiltskin-like "Duffy and the Devil" with the one by Harve Zemach. FAIRIES−FOLKLORE. FOLKLORE−ENGLAND. SUPERNATURAL−FOLKLORE.

1664   **Climo, Shirley.** *Someone Saw a Spider: Spider Facts and Folktales.* **Illus. by Dirk Zimmer. Crowell, 1985. ISBN 0-690-04436-4**

[9 tales, 133p., Gr. 3−6] This illuminating compendium of spider stories, superstitions, cures, and lesser-known facts will aid in dispelling spider phobias and instill admiration for all arachnids. Use E. B. White's *Charlotte's Web* as a starting point; then give your class the opportunity to do a little reference work for more spider-wise details. SPIDERS−FOLKLORE.

1665   **Coatsworth, Emerson, and David Coatsworth, comps.** *The Adventures of Nanabush: Ojibway Indian Stories.* **Illus. by Francis Kagige. Atheneum, 1980.**

[16 tales, 85p., Gr. 2−5] How the great magician, Nanabush, created and improved the world, as originally told to the compilers by Sam Snake, Chief Elija Yellowhead, and other elders of the Canadian tribe in the 1930s. Compare these with other creation myths and trickster tales such as Ronald Melzack's *Raven, Creator of the World* (Little, Brown, 1970) and Gail Robinson's *Raven the Trickster.* FOLKLORE−CANADA. FOLKLORE−INDIANS OF NORTH AMERICA. TRICKSTER TALES.

1666   **Cole, Joanna.** *Best Loved Folktales of the World.* **Illus. by Jill Karla Schwarz. Doubleday, 1983. ISBN 0-385-18949-4**

[200 tales, 792p., Gr. 2−6] A resource book of tales both familiar and lesser-known, broken down by continents. The cramped layout makes this more appropriate for teachers to read aloud than for children to tackle alone. FOLKLORE−ANTHOLOGIES.

1667 **Corrin, Sara, and Stephen Corrin.** *The Faber Book of Favourite Fairy Tales.* **Illus. by Juan Wijngaard. Faber, 1988. ISBN 0-571-14854-9**

[26 tales, 244p., Gr. 1–5] The Corrins have tracked down the first published version of each of these well-known tales, including samples from such folklorists as Grimm, Perrault, Jacobs, and Andersen, and translated them anew. FOLKLORE–ANTHOLOGIES.

1668 **Courlander, Harold.** *The Hat-Shaking Dance: And Other Tales from the Gold Coast.* **Illus. by Enrico Arno. Harcourt, 1957.**

[21 tales, 143p., Gr. 2–6] About Anansi the Spider and other animals as told by the Ashanti people of Ghana. Also see Peggy Appiah's *Tales of an Ashanti Father,* Joyce Cooper Arkhurst's *The Adventures of Spider,* Julius Lester's *How Many Spots Does a Leopard Have?* and the collections of African American Brer Rabbit stories by Julius Lester and/or Van Dyke Parks. ANIMALS–FOLKLORE. FOLKLORE–AFRICA. SPIDERS–FOLKLORE. TRICKSTER TALES.

1669 **Courlander, Harold.** *The Piece of Fire and Other Haitian Tales.* **Illus. by Beth Krush and Joe Krush. Harcourt, 1942.**

[26 tales, 128p., Gr. 3–6] Within are many whimsical tales of Bouki, a trickster and fool. These will go well with other "fools" collections such as Isaac Bashevis Singer's Jewish "Chelm" tales, *When Shlemiel Went to Warsaw* and *Zlateh the Goat;* Barbara Walker's Nasreddin Hoca stories from Turkey, *Watermelon, Walnuts, and the Wisdom of Allah* (Parents, 1967); or any of the African "Anansi the Spider" stories retold by Joyce Cooper Arkhurst in *The Adventures of Spider* and Peggy Appiah in *Tales of an Ashanti Father.* For more splendid Haitian tales see Diane Wolkstein's *The Magic Orange Tree.* FOLKLORE–HAITI. FOOLS–FOLKLORE. TRICKSTER TALES.

1670 **Courlander, Harold, and George Herzog.** *The Cow-Tail Switch and Other West African Stories.* **Illus. by Madye Lee Chastain. Henry Holt, 1988. ISBN 0-8050-0288-X**

[17 tales, 143p., Gr. 2–6] Collected by Courlander and Herzog, these are superb for reading and telling. Also see Courlander's *The Hat-Shaking Dance,* Julius Lester's *How Many Spots Does a Leopard Have?* and Adjai Robinson's *Singing Tales of Africa.* ANIMALS–FOLKLORE. FOLKLORE–AFRICA. SPIDERS–FOLKLORE. TRICKSTER TALES.

1671 **Cox, Miriam.** *The Magic and the Sword: The Greek Myths Retold.* **Illus. by Harold Price. Harper & Row, 1962.**

[51 tales, 224p., Gr. 4–6] Familiar myths including those of the Trojan War and the travels of Odysseus. Includes pronunciation guide, index, and glossary. Sally Benson's *Stories of the Gods and Heroes,* D'Aulaire's *Book of Greek Myths,* Mary Pope Osborne's *Favorite Greek Myths,* and Margaret Evans Price's *Myths and Enchantment Tales* are also worthy of note. FOLKLORE–GREECE. MYTHOLOGY.

1672 **Credle, Ellis.** *Tall Tales from the High Hills and Other Stories.* **Illus. by Richard Bennett. Nelson, 1957.**

[20 tales, 156p., Gr. 4–6] Droll whoppers collected by Credle from Hank Huggins, a yarn spinner who lived in the Blue Ridge Mountains. More American stories collected in the neighborhood can be found in Richard Chase's *Grandfather Tales.* FOLKLORE–U.S. TALL TALES.

1673   Crouch, Marcus. *The Whole World Storybook.* **Illus. by William Stobbs. Oxford University Press, 1987. ISBN 0-19-278103-0**

[25 tales, 168p., Gr. 3–6] An unusual array of international folktales including several little-known relatives of such well-known tales as "The Brave Little Tailor," "Puss in Boots," "Molly Whuppie," "The Twelve Dancing Princesses," and "East of the Sun and West of the Moon" from Greece, Hungary, Finland, Portugal, and Scotland, respectively. FOLKLORE–ANTHOLOGIES.

1674   D'Aulaire, Ingri, and Edgar Parin D'Aulaire. *D'Aulaire's Book of Greek Myths.* **Illus. by the authors. Doubleday, 1980. ISBN 0-385-07108-6**

[46 tales, 192p., Gr. 4–6] An oversized dramatic compilation of stories about the gods and goddesses. There is an index, but no guide to pronunciation. Sally Benson's *Stories of the Gods and Heroes*, Miriam Cox's *The Magic and the Sword*, Mary Pope Osborne's *Favorite Greek Myths*, and Margaret Evans Price's *Myths and Enchantment Tales* are just as stirring. FOLKLORE–GREECE. MYTHOLOGY.

1675   Demi. *A Chinese Zoo: Fables and Proverbs.* **Illus. by the author. Harcourt, 1987. ISBN 0-15-217510-5**

[13 tales, unp., Gr. 2–6] An outstanding visual feast of Chinese fables, each one written beside a double-page fan-shaped illustration. Both tales and morals are certain to churn up much thought and discussion, whether used in conjunction with Aesop or alone. Also read Demi's Chinese nursery rhymes *Dragon Kites and Dragonflies*, plus Ed Young's Chinese riddle-poems *High on a Hill*. For more Chinese folktales see M. A. Jagendorf and Virginia Weng's *The Magic Boat*, Carol Kendall and Yao-wen Li's *Sweet and Sour*, and Catherine Edwards Sadler's *Treasure Mountain*. FABLES. FOLKLORE–CHINA.

1676   Demi. *Demi's Reflective Fables.* **Illus. by the author. Putnam, 1988. ISBN 0-448-09281-6**

[13 tales, unp., Gr. 2–6] In a format like *A Chinese Zoo*, preceding this entry, the front jacket flap incorporates a large mirror that can be used to reflect each illustration while the reader contemplates each story's meaning. Present these with a dash of Aesop and ask students how each tale applies to their own lives. FABLES. FOLKLORE–CHINA.

1677   Finger, Charles. *Tales from Silver Lands.* **Illus. by Paul Honore. Doubleday, 1924. ISBN 0-385-07513-8**

[19 tales, 207p., Gr. 3–6] Collected by Finger from the Indians of South America. FOLKLORE–SOUTH AMERICA. NEWBERY MEDAL.

1678   Garner, Alan. *A Bag of Moonshine.* **Illus. by Patrick James Lynch. Delacorte, 1986. ISBN 0-385-29517-0**

[22 tales, 144p., Gr. 2–5] Compact, rowdy tales, eager to be told, from England and Wales. Another fine collection from Great Britain is Shirley Climo's *Piskies, Spriggans, and Other Magical Beings*. FOLKLORE–ENGLAND. FOLKLORE–WALES.

1679   Gates, Doris. *Lord of the Sky: Zeus.* **Illus. by Robert Handville. Penguin, 1982. ISBN 0-14-031532-2**

[16 tales, 126p., Gr. 5–6] Greek myths about the father of the gods and his influence over mortals and immortals alike. Gates's *The Warrior Goddess: Athena* (Viking,

1972), about Pallas Athena and the mortals she assists, uses the same format. FOLKLORE—GREECE. MYTHOLOGY.

1680   **Ginsburg, Mirra.** *The Lazies.* **Illus. by Marian Parry. Macmillan, 1973.**

[15 tales, 70p., Gr. 2–4] Short yarns of Russian fools and do-nothings. Compare with the idlers in Diane Wolkstein's *Lazy Stories.* FOLKLORE—RUSSIA. FOOLS—FOLKLORE.

1681   **Ginsburg, Mirra.** *Three Rolls and One Doughnut: Fables from Russia.* **Illus. by Anita Lobel. Dial, 1970.**

[28 tales, 52p., Gr. 1–5] An interesting mix of animals and noodlehead stories to contrast with Aesop. ANIMALS—FOLKLORE. FABLES. FOLKLORE—RUSSIA.

1682   **Ginsburg, Mirra.** *The Twelve Clever Brothers and Other Fools.* **Illus. by Charles Mikolaycak. Lippincott, 1979. ISBN 0-397-31862-6**

[14 tales, 89p., Gr. 2–5] Brief vignettes of Russian noodleheads who try to be smart but fail hilariously. Maria Leach's *Noodles, Nitwits and Numskulls* proves that Russia has no corner on the fools market. FOLKLORE—RUSSIA. FOOLS—FOLKLORE.

1683   **Greene, Ellin.** *Clever Cooks: A Concoction of Stories, Charms, Recipes and Riddles.* **Illus. by Trina Schart Hyman. Lothrop, 1973.**

[12 tales, 154p., Gr. 2–5] Food-related folktales starring quick-witted chefs, both male and female. Get out your aprons. FOOD-FOLKLORE. WOMEN-FOLKLORE.

1684   **Grimm, Jacob.** *The Brothers Grimm Popular Folk Tales.* **Trans. by Brian Alderson. Illus. by Michael Foreman. Doubleday, 1978.**

[31 tales, 192p., Gr. 2–5] An appealing collection of mostly familiar stories. FOLKLORE—GERMANY.

1685   **Grimm, Jacob.** *Fairy Tales of the Brothers Grimm.* **Illus. by Kay Nielsen. Viking, 1979.**

[12 tales, 121p., Gr. 2–5] A beautiful fascimile edition of familiar choices, originally published in 1925. Compare these illustrations with those in *Grimm's Fairy Tales: 20 Stories*, as illustrated by another classic children's illustrator, Arthur Rackham. FOLKLORE—GERMANY.

1686   **Grimm, Jacob.** *Grimm's Fairy Tales: 20 Stories.* **Illus. by Arthur Rackham. Viking, 1973.**

[20 tales, 127p., Gr. 3–6] Facsimile of the beautiful early twentieth-century edition. FOLKLORE—GERMANY.

1687   **Grimm, Jacob.** *The Juniper Tree: And Other Tales from Grimm.* **Illus. by Maurice Sendak. Trans. by Lore Segal and Randall Jarrell. Farrar, 1973. ISBN 0-374-18057-1**

[27 tales, 332p., Gr. 3–6] A small, handsome two-volume set including many of the Grimms' lesser-known and more melancholy sagas. FOLKLORE—GERMANY.

1688   **Grimm, Jacob.** *Tales from Grimm.* **Trans. by Wanda Gag. Illus. by Wanda Gag. Coward, 1981. ISBN 0-698-20533-2**

[16 tales, 237p., Gr. 1–4] Along with *More Tales from Grimm* (1947), these are two classic collections no library should be without. Originally published in 1936. FOLKLORE—GERMANY.

1689   **Grimm, Jacob.** *The Twelve Dancing Princesses and Other Tales from Grimm.* **Illus. by Lydia Postma. Edited by Naomi Lewis. Dial, 1986. ISBN 0-8037-0237-X**

[14 tales, 99p., Gr. 3–6] A large, appealing volume of mostly lesser-known tales. FOLKLORE–GERMANY.

1690   **Harper, Wilhelmina.** *Ghosts and Goblins: Stories for Halloween.* **Illus. by William Wiesner. Dutton, 1965. ISBN 0-525-30516-5**

[34 tales, 250p., Gr. 2–5] An anthology of short, traditional chillers, good for telling along with Maria Leach's *The Thing at the Foot of the Bed*, Ruth Manning Sanders's "A Book of. . ." series, and Alvin Schwartz's *Scary Stories to Tell in the Dark* and *More Scary Stories to Tell in the Dark*. GHOST STORIES. HALLOWEEN–FOLKLORE. SUPERNATURAL–FOLKLORE. WITCHES–FOLKLORE.

1691   **Harris, Christie.** *Mouse Woman and the Mischief-Makers.* **Illus. by Douglas Tait. Atheneum, 1977.**

[7 tales, 114p., Gr. 4–6] Entertaining Northwest Coastal Indian stories of the tiny supernatural narnauk grandmother who comes to the aid of young people in trouble. Other wonderful books in the series include *Mouse Woman and the Muddleheads* (1979) and *Mouse Woman and the Vanished Princesses* (1976). FOLKLORE–INDIANS OF NORTH AMERICA. PRINCES AND PRINCESSES–FOLKLORE. SUPERNATURAL –FOLKLORE.

1692   **Harris, Christie.** *The Trouble with Adventurers.* **Illus. by Douglas Tait. Atheneum, 1982.**

[6 tales, 160p., Gr. 4–6] To go along with the "Mouse Woman" stories, preceding, are a variety of fascinating Northwest Coast Indian legends of the Eagle, Raven, Bear, and Wolf clans. More can be found in Harris's *Once Upon a Totem* (1966) and *The Trouble with Princesses* (1980). FOLKLORE–INDIANS OF NORTH AMERICA.

1693   **Haviland, Virginia, ed.** *The Fairy Tale Treasury.* **Illus. by Raymond Briggs. Dell, 1986. ISBN 0-440-42556-5**

[32 tales, 192p., Gr. Pre–3] A huge format and delightful illustrations accompany some of our favorite old friends. A "must have." FOLKLORE–ANTHOLOGIES.

1694   **Haviland, Virginia, ed.** *Favorite Fairy Tales Told around the World.* **Illus. by S. D. Schindler. Little, Brown, 1985. ISBN 0-316-35044-3**

[35 tales, 327p., Gr. 1–4] Two or three tales culled from each country of her 16 original volumes of fairy tales give a global view of some superb stories. The distinguished folklorist, former Head of Children's Book Selection at the Library of Congress, originally retold a selection of five to eight tales in each of these splendid national collections, all published by Little, Brown: *Favorite Fairy Tales Told in Czechoslovakia* (1966), *Denmark* (1971), *England* (1959), *France* (1959), *Greece* (1970), *India* (1973), *Ireland* (1961), *Italy* (1965), *Japan* (1967), *Norway* (1961), *Russia* (1961), *Scotland* (1963), *Spain* (1963), and *Sweden* (1966). FOLKLORE–ANTHOLOGIES.

1695   **Haviland, Virginia, ed.** *North American Legends.* **Illus. by Ann Strugnell. Putnam, 1979. ISBN 0-399-20810-0**

[29 tales, 214p., Gr. 4–6] Traditional American folk and tall tales of Indians, Eskimos, European immigrants, and African Americans. FOLKLORE, AFRICAN AMERICAN. FOLKLORE–ANTHOLOGIES. FOLKLORE–INDIANS OF NORTH AMERICA. FOLKLORE–U.S.

1696   **Hayes, Sarah.** *Robin Hood.* **Illus. by Patrick Benson. Henry Holt, 1989. ISBN 0-8050-1206-0**

[13 chapters, 76p., Gr. 4–6] A most enthralling and romantic retelling of the Robin Hood legends, neither too violent nor too difficult to fathom, and spanning Robin's first encounter with the maniacal Sir Guy of Gisborne, his exploits with his green-clad fellows of Sherwood as they bedevil Sir Guy and the Sheriff, and his tragic, untimely passing. Stay in the medieval mood with Selina Hastings's *Sir Gawain and the Loathly Lady* and Margaret Hodges's *Saint George and the Dragon*. FOLKLORE–ENGLAND.

1697   **Hoke, Helen.** *Witches, Witches, Witches.* **Illus. by W. R. Lohse. Franklin Watts, 1958.**

[27 tales, 230p., Gr. 2–5] Satisfyingly spooky tales for October 31. Also don't forget Wilhelmina Harper's *Ghosts and Goblins*, Lee Bennett Hopkins's *Witching Time* (Albert Whitman, 1977), and Ruth Manning Sanders's *A Book of Witches*. WITCHES–FOLKLORE.

1698   **Hopkins, Lee Bennett.** *Witching Time: Mischievous Stories and Poems.* **Illus. by Vera Rosenberry. Albert Whitman, 1977.**

[9 tales, 128p., Gr. 2–4] This title, along with its two companion volumes *A-Haunting We Will Go* (1977) and *Monsters, Ghoulies and Creepy Creatures* (1977), is a collection of folktales, poems, and contemporary spine-tinglers for the young reader. Of varying degrees of scariness are Wilhelmina Harper's *Ghosts and Goblins*, Maria Leach's *The Thing at the Foot of the Bed*, George Mendoza's *The Crack in the Wall* and *Gwot!*, Ruth Manning-Sanders's *A Book of Witches*, and Alvin Schwartz's *Scary Stories to Tell in the Dark* and *More Scary Stories to Tell in the Dark*. For more poetry see John E. Brewton's *In the Witches' Garden*, Lilian Moore's *See My Lovely Poison Ivy*, and Jack Prelutsky's *It's Halloween* and *Nightmares*. WITCHES–FOLKLORE. WITCHES–POETRY.

1699   **Jagendorf, M. A., and Virginia Weng.** *The Magic Boat: And Other Chinese Folk Stories.* **Illus. by Wan-go Weng. Vanguard, 1980.**

[33 tales, 236p., Gr. 2–6] An imposing collection representing the many ethnic groups in China. See also Demi's *A Chinese Zoo: Fables and Proverbs* and *Demi's Reflective Fables*, Carol Kendall and Yo-Wen Li's *Sweet and Sour*, and Catherine Edwards Sadler's *Treasure Mountain*. FOLKLORE–CHINA.

1700   **Jaquith, Priscilla.** *Bo Rabbit Smart for True: Folktales from the Gullah.* **Illus. by Ed Young. Philomel, 1981. ISBN 0-399-61179-7**

[4 tales, 56p., Gr. K–4] Brief and amusing African-based animal tales from the Sea Islands of Georgia and South Carolina, these can be compared with the Brer Rabbit stories in Julius Lester's *The Tales of Uncle Remus* and Van Dyke Parks and Malcolm Jones's *Jump! The Adventures of Brer Rabbit*. FOLKLORE, AFRICAN AMERICAN. FOLKLORE–U.S.

1701   **Kendall, Carol, and Yao-wen Li.** *Sweet and Sour: Tales from China.* **Illus. by Shirley Felts. Houghton Mifflin, 1979. ISBN 0-395-28958-0**

[24 tales, 112p., Gr. 3–6] Stories from ancient China from the third century B.C. to the early twentieth century. See also Demi's *A Chinese Zoo: Fables and Proverbs* and *Demi's Reflective Fables*, M. A. Jagendorf and Virginia Weng's *The Magic Boat and Other Folk Stories*, and Catherine Edwards Sadler's *Treasure Mountain*. FOLKLORE–CHINA.

1702 **Lang, Andrew.** *Blue Fairy Book.* **Illus. by Antony Maitland. Edited by Brian Alderson. Penguin, 1988. ISBN 0-14-035090-X**

[32 tales, 373p., Gr. 2–6] One from the marvelous series of "color" collections of international folktales originally compiled by folklorist Andrew Lang in the late nineteenth century and recently reissued as follows: *Green Fairy Book* (1978), *Pink Fairy Book* (1982), *Red Fairy Book* (1976), and *Yellow Fairy Book* (1980). Each includes interesting appendixes of source notes and the text of Lang's original introductions. According to *Books in Print,* the other seven colors—Brown, Crimson, Grey, Lilac, Olive, Orange, and Violet—are available from publishers Peter Smith and Dover Press. FOLKLORE–ANTHOLOGIES.

1703 **Leach, Maria.** *The Rainbow Book of American Folk Tales and Legends.* **Illus. by Marc Simont. World, 1958.**

[74 tales, 318p., Gr. 3–6] Oversized format includes tall tales, state lore, bad men, scary stories, local legends, and then some. Use this as part of a class study on the states. FOLKLORE–ANTHOLOGIES. FOLKLORE–U.S.

1704 **Leach, Maria.** *The Thing at the Foot of the Bed and Other Scary Tales.* **Illus. by Kurt Werth. Putnam, 1987. ISBN 0-399-21496-8**

[35 tales, 126p., Gr. 2–6] Short, easy-to-learn, ghostly folktales. Get out a candle, turn off the lights, and practice your screams with the additional assistance of Leach's similar *Whistle in the Graveyard: Folktales to Chill Your Bones* (Viking, 1974), and Alvin Schwartz's *Scary Stories to Tell in the Dark* and *More Scary Stories to Tell in the Dark.* GHOST STORIES. SUPERNATURAL–FOLKLORE. SUSPENSE–FOLKLORE.

1705 **Lester, Julius.** *How Many Spots Does a Leopard Have? And Other Tales.* **Illus. by David Shannon. Scholastic, 1989. ISBN 0-590-41973-0**

[12 tales, 72p., Gr. 1–5] Told in a colloquial, often hip, style are ten African and two Jewish folktales, accompanied by large, compelling paintings. Also fascinating are Peggy Appiah's *Tales of an Ashanti Father,* Joyce Cooper Arkhurst's *The Adventures of Spider,* Harold Courlander's *The Hat-Shaking Dance and Other Tales from the Gold Coast,* and the collections of African American Brer Rabbit stories by Julius Lester and/or Van Dyke Parks. ANIMALS–FOLKLORE. FOLKLORE–AFRICA.

1706 **Lester, Julius.** *The Knee-High Man and Other Tales.* **Illus. by Ralph Pinto. Dial, 1972. ISBN 0-8037-4593-1**

[6 tales, 32p., Gr. K–4] Boisterous African American folktales of animals and humans including pourquoi stories perfect for telling. ANIMALS–FOLKLORE. FOLKLORE, AFRICAN AMERICAN. POURQUOI TALES.

1707 **Lester, Julius.** *The Tales of Uncle Remus: The Adventures of Brer Rabbit.* **Illus. by Jerry Pinkney. Dial, 1987. ISBN 0-8037-0272-8**

[48 tales, 151p., Gr. 2–5] Liberated from Joel Chandler Harris's use of heavy dialect, these retellings of famous African American trickster tales of animal mischief and its often violent consequences are made even more amusing through the use of modern day slang. Along with the second volume, *More Tales of Uncle Remus* (1988), compare the use of language with Van Dyke Park and Malcolm Jones's *Jump! The Adventures of Brer Rabbit* and Park's *Jump Again! More Adventures of Brer Rabbit,* as well as to African trickster tales such as Peggy Appiah's *Tales of an Ashanti Father,* Joyce Cooper Arkhurst's *The Adventures of Spider,* and Harold

Courlander's *The Hat-Shaking Dance and Other Tales from the Gold Coast*. ANIMALS—FOLKLORE. FOLKLORE, AFRICAN AMERICAN. FOLKLORE—U.S. RABBITS—FOLKLORE. TRICKSTER TALES.

1708   **Lurie, Alison.** *Clever Gretchen and Other Forgotten Folktales.* **Illus. by Margot Tomes. Crowell, 1980. ISBN 0-690-03944-1**

[15 tales, 113p., Gr. 4–6] Resourceful European heroines prove that it is not always the prince who is brave and stout-hearted. Also grab Rosemary Minard's *Womenfolk and Fairy Tales* and James Riordan's *Woman in the Moon and Other Tales of Forgotten Heroines*. WOMEN—FOLKLORE.

1709   **McCormick, Dell J.** *Paul Bunyan Swings His Axe.* **Illus. by the author. Caxton, 1936. ISBN 0-87004-093-6**

[17 tales, 111p., Gr. 3–6] Straight-faced tall tales of the famous U.S. logger and his blue ox, Babe. Other classics include Roberta Feuerlicht's *The Legends of Paul Bunyan* (Collier, 1966) and Glen Rounds's *Ol' Paul, the Mighty Logger*. FOLKLORE—U.S. TALL TALES.

1710   **Manning-Sanders, Ruth.** *A Book of Witches.* **Illus. by Robin Jacques. Dutton, 1965.**

[12 tales, 127p., Gr. 2–6] This is just one book in a terrific series of folktale collections, now out of print, but to be found in many library collections. As a source for reading and telling also keep an eagle eye out for: *A Book of Charms and Changelings* (1971), *A Book of Devils and Demons* (1970), *A Book of Dragons* (1964), *A Book of Dwarfs* (1963), *A Book of Enchantments and Curses* (1976), *A Book of Ghosts and Goblins* (1968), *A Book of Giants* (1962), *A Book of Kings and Queens* (1977), *A Book of Magic Animals* (1974), *A Book of Mermaids* (1967), *A Book of Monsters* (1975), *A Book of Ogres and Trolls* (1972), *A Book of Princes and Princesses* (1969), *A Book of Sorcerers and Spells* (1973), *A Book of Spooks and Spectres* (1979), and *A Book of Wizards* (1966). WITCHES—FOLKLORE.

1711   **Martin, Eva.** *Tales of the Far North.* **Illus. by Laszlo Gal. Dial, 1987. ISBN 0-8037-0319-8**

[12 tales, 123p., Gr. 4–6] Among these French and English Canadian folktales are several variants of well-known European tales. These are to Canada what Richard Chase's *Grandfather Tales* and Virginia Haviland's *North American Legends* are to the United States. FOLKLORE—CANADA.

1712   **Minard, Rosemary.** *Womenfolk and Fairy Tales.* **Illus. by Suzanne Klein. Houghton Mifflin, 1975. ISBN 0-395-20276-0**

[18 tales, 163p., Gr. 3–6] From the Chinese Red Riding Hoods to Kate Crackernuts, these female protagonists save the day. Also savor Alison Lurie's *Clever Gretchen and Other Forgotten Folktales* and James Riordan's *The Woman in the Moon & Other Tales of Forgotten Heroines*. WOMEN—FOLKLORE.

1713   **Osborne, Mary Pope.** *Favorite Greek Myths.* **Illus. by Troy Howell. Scholastic, 1989. ISBN 0-590-41338-4**

[12 tales, 81p., Gr. 5–6] An elegant compilation of stories about famous pairs. See also *D'Aulaire's Book of Greek Myths*, Sally Benson's *Stories of the Gods and Heroes*, Miriam Cox's *The Magic and the Sword*, and Margaret Evans Price's *Myths and Enchantment Tales*. FOLKLORE—GREECE. MYTHOLOGY.

1714   **Parks, Van Dyke, and Malcolm Jones.** *Jump! The Adventures of Brer Rabbit.* **Illus. by Barry Moser. Harcourt, 1986. ISBN 0-15-241350-2**

[5 tales, 40p., Gr. 2–5] Southern black folktales with African roots, originally written by Joel Chandler Harris in the late 1800s in heavy dialect, these were for years a source of contention for blacks and whites. Retold here in an easygoing manner, illustrated with personable watercolor portraits, these stories of Brers Fox, Rabbit, Wolf, and Bear are now accessible and entertaining for all, although some will object to the humorous acceptance of violence between the animals. Compare these tales and the five in Parks and Jones's *Jump Again! More Adventures of Brer Rabbit* (1987) to Julius Lester's contemporary-minded versions in *The Tales of Uncle Remus* and *More Tales of Uncle Remus* to demonstrate how the same stories can be retold in different styles. ANIMALS–FOLKLORE. FOLKLORE, AFRICAN AMERICAN. FOLKLORE–U.S. RABBITS–FOLKLORE. TRICKSTER TALES.

1715   **Perl, Lila.** *Don't Sing before Breakfast, Don't Sleep in the Moonlight: Everyday Superstitions and How They Began.* **Illus. by Erika Weihs. Clarion, 1988. ISBN 0-89919-504-0**

[5 chapters, 90p., Gr. 4–6] A conversational explanation, this dispels common superstitions, many of which are ingrained in our daily routines. Also see Jane Sarnoff's *Take Warning! A Book of Superstitions* and Alvin Schwartz's *Cross Your Fingers, Spit in your Hat.* Compile a list of class superstitions; then have children look each up in the books and read aloud how it began. SUPERSTITIONS–FOLKLORE.

1716   **Price, Margaret Evans.** *Myths and Enchantment Tales.* **Illus. by Evelyn Urbanowich. Rand, 1960.**

[26 tales, 192p., Gr. 4–6] Assorted familiar Greek myths using mostly Roman names. Though no pronunciation guide is included, these tales are accessible and skillfully told nevertheless. *D'Aulaire's Book of Greek Myths,* Sally Benson's *Stories of the Gods and Heroes,* Miriam Cox's *The Magic and the Sword,* and Mary Pope Osborne's *Favorite Greek Myths* are also well worth a browse. MYTHOLOGY.

1717   **Riordan, James.** *The Woman in the Moon: And Other Tales of Forgotten Heroines.* **Illus. by Angela Barrett. Dial, 1985. ISBN 0-8037-0196-9**

[13 tales, 86p., Gr. 4–6] Expertly and amusingly told, these are mostly little-known stories of feisty females. Two additional similarly themed collections are Alison Lurie's *Clever Gretchen and Other Forgotten Folktales* and Rosemary Minard's *Womenfolk and Fairy Tales.* WOMEN–FOLKLORE.

1718   **Robinson, Adjai.** *Singing Tales of Africa.* **Illus. by Christine Price. Scribner, 1974.**

[7 tales, 80p., Gr. 1–4] The musical refrains for each of these captivating stories are included for you to learn and use with the tales. Similar in feel is Diane Wolkstein's *The Magic Orange Tree and Other Haitian Folktales.* FOLKLORE–AFRICA. STORIES WITH SONGS–FOLKLORE.

1719   **Robinson, Gail.** *Raven the Trickster: Legends of the North American Indians.* **Illus. by Joanna Troughton. Atheneum, 1982.**

[9 tales, 125p., Gr. 4–6] North American Indian legends about troublemaking heroes including Coyote, Raven, and Fox. Also see the companion volume, Gail Robinson and Douglas Hill's *Coyote the Trickster* (Crane Russak, 1976), and Ronald Melzack's *Raven, Creator of the World* (Little, Brown, 1970). ANIMALS–FOLKLORE. BIRDS–FOLKLORE. FOLKLORE–INDIANS OF NORTH AMERICA. TRICKSTER TALES.

1720   Rockwell, Anne. *Puss in Boots & Other Stories.* **Illus. by the author. Macmillan, 1988. ISBN 0-02-777781-2**

[12 tales, 88p., Gr. Pre–3] A collection of simply told well-known tales, illuminated with bright, childlike watercolors on almost every page, this accompanies two earlier collections: *The Three Bears & 15 Other Stories* (Crowell, 1975) and *The Old Woman and Her Pig and 10 Other Stories* (Crowell, 1979). ANIMALS–FOLKLORE.

1721   Rounds, Glen. *Ol' Paul, the Mighty Logger.* **Illus. by the author. Holiday House, 1976. ISBN 0-8234-0269-X**

[11 tales, 94p., Gr. 4–6] "Being a True Account of the Seemingly Incredible Exploits and Inventions of the Great Paul Bunyan," this was reissued on the fortieth anniversary of the original publication. Roberta Feuerlicht's *The Legends of Paul Bunyan* (Collier, 1966) and Dell J. McCormack's *Paul Bunyan Swings His Axe* are also well worth reading. EXAGGERATION. FOLKLORE–U.S. TALL TALES.

1722   Sadler, Catherine Edwards. *Treasure Mountain: Folktales from Southern China.* **Illus. by Cheng Mung Yun. Atheneum, 1982.**

[6 tales, 66p., Gr. 4–6] Tales of the minority Chuang, T'ung, and Yao tribes and the Han rulers. Other worthy collections include Demi's *A Chinese Zoo: Fables and Proverbs* and Demi's *Reflective Fables*, M. A. Jagendorf and Virginia Weng's *The Magic Boat and Other Chinese Folk Stories*, and Carol Kendall and Yao-wen Li's *Sweet and Sour: Tales from China*. FOLKLORE–CHINA.

1723   Sarnoff, Jane. *Take Warning! A Book of Superstitions.* **Illus. by Reynold Ruffins. Scribner, 1978.**

[159p., Gr. 4–6] An alphabetical encyclopedia of world superstitions. Students can compile their own lists. See also Lila Perl's *Don't Sing before Breakfast, Don't Sleep in the Moonlight: Everyday Superstitions and How They Began* and Alvin Schwartz's *Cross Your Fingers, Spit in Your Hat.* SUPERSTITIONS–FOLKLORE.

1724   Schwartz, Alvin, comp. *Cross Your Fingers, Spit in Your Hat: Superstitions and Other Beliefs.* **Illus. by Glen Rounds. Lippincott, 1990. ISBN 0-397-32436-7**

[161p., Gr. 3–6] Witches, numbers, weather, school, and money are some of the 21 subjects investigated. See also Lila Perl's *Don't Sing before Breakfast, Don't Sleep in the Moonlight: Everyday Superstitions and How They Began* and Jane Sarnoff's *Take Warning.* FOLKLORE–U.S. SUPERSTITIONS.

1725   Schwartz, Alvin. *Scary Stories to Tell in the Dark.* **Illus. by Stephen Gammell. Lippincott, 1981. ISBN 0-397-31927-4**

[29 tales, 111p., Gr. 4–6] Don't forget your flashlight and beware of the terrifying illustrations in this and its companion, *More Scary Stories to Tell in the Dark* (Lippincott, 1984). Other short chillers to tell include Wilhelmina Harper's *Ghosts and Goblins* and Maria Leach's *The Thing at the Foot of the Bed.* FOLKLORE–U.S. GHOST STORIES. SUSPENSE–FOLKLORE.

1726   Schwartz, Alvin. *Whoppers: Tall Tales and Other Lies.* **Illus. by Glen Rounds. Lippincott, 1975. ISBN 0-397-31575-9**

[6 chapters, 127p., Gr. 3–6] As fine a collection of ranting bunkum as any liar could assemble from American folklore. The concept of straight-faced exaggeration does not make sense to many children, particularly younger ones. Reading these, along with Sid Fleischman's "McBroom" books and assorted tall tales collections such as

Ellis Credle's *Tall Tales from the High Hills*, Dell J. McCormick's *Paul Bunyan Swings His Axe*, or Glen Rounds's *Ol' Paul, the Mighty Logger*, exposes readers to a whole new type of humor, even if you do need to explain some of the funny parts. The class can then write a series of lies about homework, chores, pets, and other familiar situations, with a final judging to pick the biggest gallyflopper. CREATIVE WRITING. EXAGGERATION. FOLKLORE—U.S. TALL TALES.

1727   **Schwartz, Betty Ann, and Leon Archibald.** *The Old-Fashioned Storybook.* **Illus. by Troy Howell. Simon & Schuster, 1985.**

[20 tales, 143p., Gr. 1–4] A handsome assortment of 20 mostly known tales illustrated with formal full-page paintings. FOLKLORE—ANTHOLOGIES.

1728   **Schwartz, Howard.** *Elijah's Violin and Other Jewish Fairy Tales.* **Illus. by Linda Heller. Harper & Row, 1983. ISBN 0-06-015108-0**

[36 tales, 302p., Gr. 4–6] An impressive compilation from Eastern Europe, Palestine, the Middle East, and even India, some dating from the fifth century. Isaac Bashevis Singer tells other Jewish tales in *When Shlemiel Went to Warsaw & Other Stories* and *Zlateh the Goat and Other Stories* (Harper & Row, 1966). FOLKLORE, JEWISH.

1729   **Shannon, George.** *Stories to Solve: Folktales from Around the World.* **Illus. by Peter Sis. Greenwillow, 1985. ISBN 0-688-04304-6**

[14 tales, 55p., Gr. 2–5] Very brief folktales, each with a problem or mystery for the listener to figure out using deductive reasoning and general ingenuity. Before reading each solution aloud, let the children either hammer out the possibilities together or write down their own answers. Also challenging are Louis Philip's *263 Bruin Busters*, Donald J. Sobol's "Encyclopedia Brown" series, Alvin Schwartz's *Unriddling*, and Ed Young's Chinese riddle puzzles *High on a Hill*. RIDDLES—FOLKLORE.

1730   **Singer, Isaac Bashevis.** *When Shlemiel Went to Warsaw & Other Stories.* **Illus. by Margot Zemach. Farrar, 1968. ISBN 0-374-38316-2**

[8 tales, 116p., Gr. 4–6] Both the foolish and the unfortunate prevail in these luscious, folklore-based Yiddish stories of fools and devils, just right for Hanukkah celebrations. See also the companion volume *Zlateh the Goat and Other Stories* (Harper & Row, 1966) and Howard Schwartz's *Elijah's Violin and Other Jewish Fairy Tales*. FOLKLORE, JEWISH. FOOLS—FOLKLORE.

1731   **Tashjian, Virginia.** *Once There Was and Was Not: Armenian Tales Retold.* **Illus. by Nonny Hogrogian. Little, Brown, 1966.**

[7 tales, 85p., Gr. 2–6] Stories of underdog peasants, some foolish and some wise. Also see Tashjian's *Three Apples Fell from Heaven* (1971). FOLKLORE—ARMENIA.

1732   **Uchida, Yoshiko.** *The Sea of Gold and Other Tales from Japan.* **Illus. by Marianne Yamaguchi. Gregg, 1988. ISBN 0-88739-056-0**

[12 tales, 136p., Gr. 2–6] Spellbinding stories of goodness and cleverness abound in this and in Uchida's *The Dancing Kettle and Other Japanese Folk Tales* (Harcourt, 1949) and *The Magic Listening Cap* (Harcourt, 1955). Also see Virginia Haviland's *Favorite Fairy Tales Told in Japan*, which includes variants of some of the same stories. FOLKLORE—JAPAN.

1733   **Vuong, Lynette Dyer.** *The Brocaded Slipper and Other Vietnamese Tales.* **Illus. by Vo-Dinh Mai. Harper & Row, 1982. ISBN 0-201-08088-5**

[5 tales, 111p., Gr. 3–6] Five tales reminiscent of Cinderella, Tom Thumb, Rip Van Winkle, and other familiar characters. Also read Dang Manh Kha's Cinderella story, *In the Land of Small Dragon.* FOLKLORE–VIETNAM.

1734   **Walker, Barbara K.** *A Treasury of Turkish Folktales for Children.* **Shoe String Press, 1988. ISBN 0-208-02206-6**

[34 tales, 155p., Gr. 2–6] More a resource collection for tellers than a book children will read alone, these Turkish Hoca stories and fairy tales boast unusual and whimsical beginning and ending lines, often starting with "Once there was and twice there wasn't." Additional excellent collections by Walker include Turkish tales of the bald-headed peasant boy, Keloglan, *Once There Was and Twice There Wasn't* (Follett, 1968), and *Watermelons, Walnuts, and the Wisdom of Allah and Other Tales of the Hoca* (Parents, 1967), about Nasreddin Hoca, the Turkish religious leader and consummate fool. Introduce an international medley of clever numskulls and tricksters such as Bouki in Harold Courlander's *The Piece of Fire and Other Haitian Tales*; the Jewish elders of Chelm in Isaac Bashevis Singer's *When Shlemiel Went to Warsaw* or *Zlateh the Goat* (Harper & Row, 1966); and African Anansi the Spider in collections such as Peggy Appiah's *Tales of an Ashanti Father*, Joyce Cooper Arkhurst's *The Adventures of Spider*, and Harold Courlander's *The Hat-Shaking Dance.* FOLKLORE–TURKEY. FOOLS–FOLKLORE.

1735   **Withers, Carl.** *I Saw a Rocket Walk a Mile: Nonsense Tales, Chants and Songs from Many Lands.* **Illus. by John E. Johnson. Holt, 1965.**

[69 tales and chants, 160p., Gr. K–6] Chock-full of short, tellable ditties from North America, Europe, Asia, and Africa. Combine these with Withers's *A World of Nonsense: Strange and Humorous Tales from Many Lands* (Holt, 1968) and Virginia A. Tashjian's *Juba This and Juba That* and *With a Deep Sea Smile*, and you will never run dry of stories that practically tell themselves. FOLKLORE–ANTHOLOGIES. NONSENSE. STORIES TO TELL.

1736   **Wolkstein, Diane.** *Lazy Stories.* **Illus. by James Marshall. Seabury, 1976.**

[3 tales, 39p., Gr. 1–4] Three funny stories from Japan, Mexico, and Laos. The stories include helpful notes for the storyteller. Keep your eyes open as well with Mirra Ginsburg's Russian *The Lazies.* FOLKLORE–JAPAN. FOLKLORE–LAOS. FOLKLORE–MEXICO.

1737   **Wolkstein, Diane.** *The Magic Orange Tree and Other Haitian Folktales.* **Illus. by Elsa Henriquez. Knopf, 1987. ISBN 0-8052-0650-7**

[27 tales, 212p., Gr. 2–6] Stories collected in Haiti by Wolkstein, who has appended excellent storytellers' notes and music for each tale. See also Harold Courlander's Haitian trickster/fool stories in *The Piece of Fire and Other Haitian Tales.* FOLKLORE–HAITI. SONGS–FOLKLORE. STORIES WITH SONGS–FOLKLORE.

1738   **Zaum, Marjorie.** *Catlore: Tales from Around the World.* **Illus. by the author. Atheneum, 1985. ISBN 0-689-31173-7**

[10 tales, 83p., Gr. 2–6] A well-researched assortment of little-known cat tales, plus folk sayings and rhymes, from the United States, Europe, Asia, and Africa. Extend the cat theme with Lloyd Alexander's folktale-like *The Town Cats and Other Tales* and *The Cat Who Wished to Be a Man*; Charles Keller's riddles, *It's Raining Cats and Dogs*; and assorted cat poems from Jean Chapman's *Cat Will Rhyme with Hat*, Lee Bennett Hopkins's *I Am the Cat*, Nancy Larrick's *Cats Are Cats*, and Myra Cohn Livingston's *Cat Poems*. CATS—FOLKLORE.

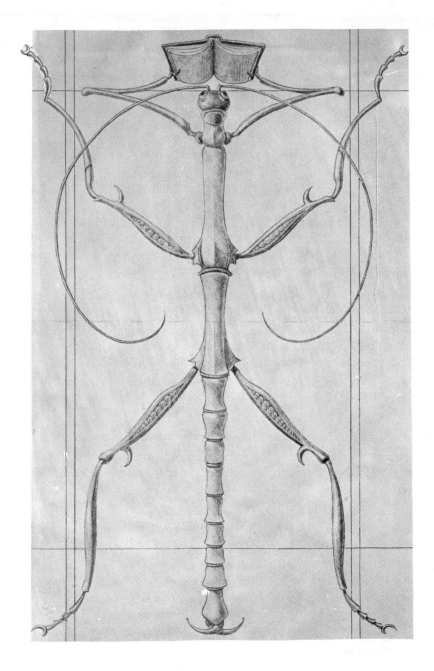

Illustration from JOYFUL NOISE: POEMS FOR TWO VOICES by Paul Fleischman, illustrated by Eric Beddows. Copyright © Harper & Row, Publishers, 1988. Reprinted by permission of HarperCollins Publishers.

POETRY, NONSENSE, AND
LANGUAGE-ORIENTED NONFICTION

1739 **Adler, David A., comp.** *The Carsick Zebra and Other Animal Riddles.* **Illus. by Tomie dePaola. Holiday House, 1983. ISBN 0-8234-0479-X**

[unp, Gr. K–3] "Which dogs make the best librarians? Hush puppies"—and other amusing ones, one per page. Other simple riddle books include Bennett Cerf's *Bennett Cerf's Book of Riddles* and *More Riddles.* ANIMALS–RIDDLES. RIDDLES.

1740 **Adler, David A.** *Remember Betsy Floss: And Other Colonial American Riddles.* **Illus. by John Wallner. Holiday House, 1987. ISBN 0-8234-0664-4**

[unp., Gr. 2–6] One riddle and illustration per page—60 in all—for you history buffs, much like Charles Keller's *The Star-Spangled Banana and Other Revolutionary Riddles.* RIDDLES. U.S.–HISTORY–RIDDLES.

1741 **Adler, David A.** *Wild Pill Hickok and Other Old West Riddles.* **Illus. by Glen Rounds. Holiday House, 1988. ISBN 0-8234-0718-7**

[unp., Gr. 2–5] Sixty mostly original riddles, one per page, about cowboys, outlaws, cows, and horses. Lead off with a few of these when you are reading Wild West fiction such as Alan Coren's *Arthur the Kid,* Gery Greer and Bob Ruddick's *Max and Me and the Wild West,* and Stephen Mooser's *Orphan Jeb at the Massacree.* FRONTIER AND PIONEER LIFE. RIDDLES. U.S.–HISTORY–RIDDLES. WEST.

1742 **Adoff, Arnold.** *Eats.* **Illus. by Susan Russo. Lothrop, 1979. ISBN 0688-51901-6**

[unp., Gr. 2–6] Free-form food poems for those who love to indulge. Read a few before lunch along with Rose H. Agree's *How to Eat a Poem and Other Morsels,* William Cole's *Poem Stew,* and Lee Bennett Hopkins's *Munching.* FOOD–POETRY. POETRY–SINGLE AUTHOR.

1743 **Agree, Rose H., comp.** *How to Eat a Poem and Other Morsels: Food Poems for Children.* **Illus. by Peggy Wilson. Pantheon, 1967.**

[87p., Gr. 2–6] A collection of poems divided into edible categories. See also Arnold Adoff's *Eats,* William Cole's *Poem Stew,* and Lee Bennett Hopkins's *Munching.* FOOD–POETRY.

1744 **Arbuthnot, May Hill, comp.** *Time for Poetry.* **Scott, Foresman, 1968. ISBN 0-673-05549-3**

[228p., Gr. Pre–6] A large anthology of poetry for all days and moods that includes valuable chapters with instructions for reading poetry to children and choral reading. Other essential collections include Joanna Cole's *A New Treasury of Children's Poetry*, Nancy Larrick's *Piping Down the Valleys Wild*, Jack Prelutsky's *The Random House Book of Poetry for Children*, and Louis Untermeyer's *The Golden Treasury of Poetry*. POETRY—ANTHOLOGIES.

1745   **Barrol, Grady. *The Little Book of Anagrams*. Illus. by Liz Victor. Harvey House, 1978.**

[unp., Gr. 3–6] By rearranging letters in a word or phrase, you can create new ones. Just enough examples to get you and your students started. WORD GAMES.

1746   **Bauer, Caroline Feller. *Windy Day: Stories and Poems*. Illus. by Dirk Zimmer. Lippincott, 1988.**

[74p., Gr. 1–4] A carefully chosen anthology, including some fine stories to tell, to go along with your weather studies or just feel good on a blustery day. Tie in some weather folklore with Hubert Davis's *A January Fog Will Freeze a Hog*. SHORT STORIES. STORIES TO TELL. WEATHER—POETRY. WIND.

1747   **Bennett, Jill, comp. *Tiny Tim: Verses for Children*. Illus. by Helen Oxenbury. Delacorte, 1982. ISBN 0-440-08910-7**

[unp., Gr. Pre–2] Twenty enchantingly illustrated humorous poems, one per page, for the younger set. Compare this version of the title poem with Nadine Bernard Westcott's picture book adaption, *The Lady with the Alligator Purse*. HUMOROUS POETRY. NONSENSE VERSES.

1748   **Bernstein, Joanne E., and Paul Cohen. *Creepy Crawly Critter Riddles*. Illus. by Rosekrans Hoffman. Albert Whitman, 1986. ISBN 0-8075-1345-8**

[unp., Gr. 2–5] Like wine, these get better with age. If your charges want more, read them Katy Hall and Lisa Eisenberg's *Buggy Riddles* and *Fishy Riddles* and Mary Ann Hoberman's *Bugs: Poems*. INSECTS—RIDDLES. JOKES. RIDDLES.

1749   **Bernstein, Joanne E., and Paul Cohen. *What Was the Wicked Witch's Real Name? And Other Character Riddles*. Illus. by Ann Iosa. Albert Whitman, 1986. ISBN 0-8075-8854-7**

[unp., Gr. 2–6] "Literacy Lunacy," one of the chapter headings, aptly describes this wide ranging riddle assemblage that draws inspiration from fairy tales, Mother Goose, super heroes, the Bible, the funnies, and assorted kid's books. BOOKS AND READING. RIDDLES.

1750   **Bodecker, N. M. *"It's Raining," Said John Twaining: Danish Nursery Rhymes*. Illus. by the author. Macmillan, 1977. ISBN 0-689-70437-2**

[unp., Gr. Pre–2] In picture book format are 15 rhymes to chant over and over again. Read these as well to broaden the horizons of Mother Goose fans: Brian Alderson's *Cakes and Custard*, Demi's Chinese *Dragon Kites and Dragonflies*, Arnold Lobel's *Gregory Griggs* and *Whiskers & Rhymes*, and Clyde Watson's original *Father Fox's Pennyrhymes*. NURSERY RHYMES.

1751   **Bodecker, N. M. *Let's Marry Said the Cherry and Other Nonsense Poems*. Illus. by the author. Atheneum, 1974.**

[79p., Gr. K–5] Silly, short, good-humored verse. For an extended poem similar to the title rhyme, don't miss Polly Cameron's *"I Can't," Said the Ant*. HUMOROUS POETRY. POETRY—SINGLE AUTHOR.

1752 Bodecker, N. M. *A Person from Britain Whose Head Was the Shape of a Mitten and Other Limericks*. Illus. by the author. Atheneum, 1980.

[60p., Gr. 3–6] Bodecker's whimsical line drawings add to the cheery good humor of more than 48 original limericks, one per page. Fourth-graders and older children will enjoy trying their hands at writing more. For other limerick books see also John E. Brewton's *They've Discovered a Head in the Box for the Bread*, Sara and John E. Brewton's *Laughable Limericks*, John Ciardi's *The Hopeful Trout and Other Limericks*, Edward Lear's *How Pleasant to Know Mr. Lear!*, Arnold Lobel's *The Book of Pigericks*, and Joseph Rosenbloom's *The Looniest Limerick Book in the World*. LIMERICKS. POETRY—SINGLE AUTHOR.

1753 Brandreth, Gyles, comp. *The Biggest Tongue Twister Book in the World*. Illus. by Alex Chin. Sterling, 1978. ISBN 0-8069-4594-X

[128p., Gr. 2–6] An alphabetical assortment, incorporating all 24 verses from the first tongue twister book in the United States, *Peter Piper's Practical Principles of Plain and Perfect Pronunciation*, and many more contemporary ones. Encourage your pupils to make up their own alliterative sentences. See also Joseph Rosenbloom's *Twist These on Your Tongue* and *World's Toughest Tongue Twisters* and Alvin Schwartz's *A Twister of Twists, a Tangler of Tongues*. ALLITERATION. CREATIVE WRITING. TONGUE TWISTERS.

1754 Brandreth, Gyles. *The Super Joke Book*. Illus. by Nick Berringer. Sterling, 1983. ISBN 0-8069-4673-3

[128p., Gr. 3–6] Pair up your class clowns and straight men so they can read aloud these comic routines à la Groucho and Chico Marx, especially if you happen to be reading Ellen Conford's *Lenny Kandell, Smart Aleck*, about a boy who dreams of becoming a comedian. Other joke books include *Syd Hoff's Joke Book*, Charles Keller's *School Daze* for beginners, and Joseph Rosenblooms's *The Gigantic Joke Book*. JOKES.

1755 Brett, Jan. *The Twelve Days of Christmas*. Illus. by the author. Dodd, Mead, 1986. ISBN 0-396-08821-X

[unp., Gr. Pre–6] Elegant watercolors with ornate borders make this old chestnut memorable. Sing it straight; then, if you're feeling wicked, turn to parodies like George Mendoza's *A Wart Snake in a Fig Tree* or Carol Greene's *The Thirteen Days of Halloween* and have students compose new lyrics. CHRISTMAS—SONGS. CREATIVE WRITING. FOLK SONGS. SONGS.

1756 Brewton, John E., and Lorraine A. Blackburn, comps. *They've Discovered a Head in the Box for the Bread: And Other Laughable Limericks*. Illus. by Fernando Krahn. Crowell, 1978. ISBN 0-690-01388-4

[129p., Gr. 3–6] Giggles abound in this book. Don't miss the final section: "Write the Last Line Yourself," as it's a good way to breed new poets. For more limericks see N. M. Bodecker's *A Person from Britain Whose Head Was the Shape of a Mitten*, Sara and John E. Brewton's original *Laughable Limericks* (Crowell, 1965), John Ciardi's *The Hopeful Trout and Other Limericks*, Edward Lear's *How Pleasant to Know Mr. Lear!*, Arnold Lobel's *The Book of Pigericks*, and Joseph Rosenbloom's *The Looniest Limerick Book in the World*. CREATIVE WRITING. HUMOROUS POETRY. LIMERICKS.

1757 **Brewton, John E., Lorraine A. Blackburn, and George M. Blackburn, III, comps.** *In the Witch's Kitchen: Poems for Halloween.* **Illus. by Harriet Barton. Crowell, 1980. ISBN 0-690-04062-8**

[88p., Gr. K–3] Pleasantly spooky rhymes about an assortment of spooks, ghosts, witches, and the like. Add to the rhyme-fest with Lilian Moore's *See My Lovely Poison Ivy* and Jack Prelutsky's *It's Halloween*. HALLOWEEN–POETRY. SUPERNATU-RAL–POETRY.

1758 **Brewton, Sara, and John E. Brewton, comps.** *Shrieks at Midnight: Macabre Poems, Eerie and Humorous.* **Illus. by Ellen Raskin. Crowell, 1969. ISBN 0-690-73518-9**

[177p., Gr. 4–6] From famous poets to unknown epitaph composers, a collection to intrigue lovers of horror. If you need more chills see Jack Prelutsky's *Nightmares: Poems to Trouble Your Sleep,* along with folktale collections such as Maria Leach's *The Thing at the Foot of the Bed* and Alvin Schwartz's *Scary Stories to Tell in the Dark* and *More Scary Stories to Tell in the Dark*. HALLOWEEN–POETRY. SUPERNATURAL–POETRY. SUSPENSE–POETRY.

1759 **Brewton, Sara, John E. Brewton, and G. Meredith Blackburn, III, comps.** *My Tang's Tungled and Other Ridiculous Situations.* **Illus. by Graham Booth. Crowell, 1973. ISBN 0-690-57223-9**

[111p., Gr. 2–6] Short, droll poems including some tongue twisters and limericks, all ripe for memorizing. William Cole also collects funny verse; see his *Oh, How Silly; Oh, Such Foolishness; Oh, That's Ridiculous;* and *Oh, What Nonsense*. HUMOROUS POETRY. LIMERICKS. NONSENSE VERSES. TONGUE TWISTERS.

1760 **Brown, Marc.** *Hand Rhymes.* **Illus. by the author. Dutton, 1985. ISBN 0-525-44201-4**

[32p., Gr. Pre–2] This soft colored-pencil paged collection, along with its companions—*Finger Rhymes* (1980), *Party Rhymes* (1988), and *Play Rhymes* (1987)—includes a dozen or so fingerplays and singing games with accompanying diagrams to show how to do each one and music appended for singing. Sources for additional classics include Tom Glazer's *Eye Winker, Tom Tinker, Chin Chopper: Fifty Musical Fingerplays,* and *Do Your Ears Hang Low? Fifty More Musical Fingerplays,* and Nancy and John Langstaff's *Jim Along, Josie*. FINGERPLAYS. GAMES. NURSERY RHYMES. SONGS.

1761 **Brown, Marc.** *Spooky Riddles.* **Illus. by the author. Random House, 1983. ISBN 0-394-96093-9**

[unp., Gr. K–3] The usual cast of nocturnal terrors populates this good-natured collection of easy-to-read, one-per-page, full-color illustrated riddles. Pair this with Halloween stories including Janet and Allan Ahlberg's *Funnybones,* Brown's own *Arthur's Halloween,* and Eileen Christelow's *Jerome and the Witchcraft Kids*. More laughs abound in the slightly more sophisticated *Count Draculations! Monster Riddles* by Charles Keller. HALLOWEEN–RIDDLES. MONSTERS–RIDDLES. RIDDLES. SUPERNATURAL–RIDDLES.

1762 **Brown, Marcia.** *Peter Piper's Alphabet.* **Illus. by the author. Scribner, 1959.**

[unp., Gr. 1–6] This is the original 1813 version of *Peter Piper's Practical Principals of Plain and Perfect Pronunciation* of which Peter is only one alliterative tongue twister out of 24. Not only will speech teachers have a hoot, but students can update the alphabet once they've mastered some of these. Additional compilations include

Gyles Brandreth's *The Biggest Tongue Twister Book in the World*, Foley Curtis's *The Little Book of Big Tongue Twisters*, Joseph Rosenbloom's *Twist These on Your Tongue* and *World's Toughest Tongue Twisters*, and Alvin Schwartz's *Busy Buzzing Bumblebees* and *A Twister of Twists, a Tangler of Tongues*. ALLITERATION. CREATIVE WRITING. TONGUE TWISTERS.

1763 **Burns, Diane L.** *Snakes Alive! Jokes about Snakes.* **Illus. by Joan Hanson. Lerner, 1988. ISBN 0-8225-0996-2**

[unp., Gr. 1–4] Tiny-format collection of over 50 never boa-ring snake riddles to add bite to reptile studies or warm up for fiction like Trinka Hakes Noble's *The Day Jimmy's Boa Ate the Wash* and Tomi Ungerer's *Crictor.* REPTILES–RIDDLES. RIDDLES. SNAKES–RIDDLES.

1764 **Calmenson, Stephanie, comp.** *Never Take a Pig to Lunch: And Other Funny Poems about Animals.* **Illus. by Hilary Knight. Doubleday, 1972.**

[32p., Gr. Pre–4] A slapstick collection that will complement William Cole's *I Went to the Animal Fair* and Jack Prelutsky's *Zoo Doings.* ANIMALS–POETRY. HUMOROUS POETRY.

1765 **Carlson, Bernice Wells, comp.** *Listen! And Help Tell the Story.* **Illus. by Burmah Burris. Abingdon, 1965. ISBN 0-687-22096-3**

[176p., Gr. Pre–2] Using sound effects and chanting refrains, children will join in on these enticing nursery rhymes, fingerplays, poems, ballads, and stories. Also don't miss Virginia A. Tashjian's collections *Juba This and Juba That* and *With a Deep Sea Smile.* CALL-AND-RESPONSE STORIES. CHANTABLE REFRAIN. FINGERPLAYS. SOUND EFFECTS. STORYTELLING.

1766 **Cerf, Bennett.** *Bennett Cerf's Book of Riddles.* **Illus. by Roy McKie. Beginner Books, 1966. ISBN 0-394-90015-4**

[64p., Gr. Pre–2] The most basic groaners for the youngest joke-lovers, along with the follow-up *More Riddles* (1961). Also try David A. Adler's *The Carsick Zebra*, Katy Hall and Lisa Eisenberg's *Buggy Riddles*, Giulio Maestro's *Razzle-Dazzle Riddles*, Joseph Rosenbloom's *The Funniest Riddle Book Ever*, and Alvin Schwartz's *Ten Copycats in a Boat.* RIDDLES.

1767 **Chapman, Jean, comp.** *Cat Will Rhyme with Hat: A Book of Poems.* **Illus. by Peter Parnall. Scribner, 1986. ISBN 0-684-18747-7**

[80p., Gr. 3–6] A pleasing pile of more than 60 cat poems. Even more can be had in Beatrice Schenk de Regniers's *This Big Cat and Other Cats I've Known*, Lee Bennett Hopkins's *I Am the Cat*, Nancy Larrick's *Cats Are Cats*, and Myra Cohn Livingston's *Cat Poems.* CATS–POETRY.

1768 **Churchill, E. Richard, comp.** *The Six-Million Dollar Cucumber: Riddles and Fun for Children.* **Illus. by Carol Nicklaus. Franklin Watts, 1976.**

[85p., Gr. Pre–6] Over 200 wonderfully dumb animal riddles guaranteed to make you chortle. Have each child pick a riddle to illustrate with the riddle on the top of the page, the answer upside down on the bottom, and the picture in the middle. Start your own dumb riddle collection. ANIMALS–RIDDLES. RIDDLES.

1769 **Ciardi, John.** *Doodle Soup.* **Illus. by Merle Nacht. Houghton Mifflin, 1985. ISBN 0-395-38395-1**

[57p., Gr. 1–4] Thirty-eight assorted witty rhymes about tigers and turtles and everything else. Introduce Ciardi's other works (following) at the same time. HUMOROUS POETRY. POETRY—SINGLE AUTHOR.

1770   Ciardi, John. *Fast and Slow: Poems for Advanced Children and Beginning Parents*. Illus. by Becky Gaver. Houghton Mifflin, 1975. ISBN 0-395-20282-5

[67p., Gr. 2–5] Whimsical verse for days you feel like being silly. HUMOROUS POETRY. POETRY—SINGLE AUTHOR.

1771   Ciardi, John. *The Hopeful Trout and Other Limericks*. Illus. by Susan Meddaugh. Houghton Mifflin, 1989. ISBN 0-395-43606-0

[52p., Gr. 3–6] Foibles of people and animals fill up 41 thoughtful limericks by the master wordsmith. Read a compendium of limericks with N. M. Bodecker's *A Person from Brittain Whose Head Was Shaped Like a Mitten*, John Brewton's *They've Discovered a Head in the Box for the Bread and Other Laughable Limericks*, John Ciardi's *The Hopeful Trout and Other Limericks*, Arnold Lobel's *The Book of Pigericks*, and Joseph Rosenbloom's *The Looniest Limerick Book in the World*. HUMOROUS POETRY. LIMERICKS. POETRY—SINGLE AUTHOR.

1772   Ciardi, John. *You Read to Me, I'll Read to You*. Illus. by Edward Gorey. Harper & Row, 1962. ISBN 0-397-30646-6

[64p., Gr. 1–3] A mix of easy-to-read poems (in blue print) and more challenging ones (in black print), 35 in all, to alternate reading aloud with your children. Try some choral reading. HUMOROUS POETRY. POETRY—SINGLE AUTHOR.

1773   Cole, Joanna, comp. *A New Treasury of Children's Poetry: Old Favorites and New Discoveries*. Illus. by Judith Gwyn Brown. Doubleday, 1984. ISBN 0-385-18539-1

[224p., Gr. Pre–6] Over 200 of Cole's personal favorites, attractively laid out one per page and sorted into nine general areas. Additional large anthologies include May Hill Arbuthnot's *Time for Poetry*, Nancy Larrick's *Piping Down the Valleys Wild*, Jack Prelutsky's *The Random House Book of Poetry*, and Louis Untermeyer's *The Golden Treasury of Poetry*. POETRY—ANTHOLOGIES.

1774   Cole, Joanna, and Stephanie Calmenson, comps. *Laugh Book: A New Treasury of Humor for Children*. Illus. by Marylin Hafner. Doubleday, 1986. ISBN 0-385-18559-6

[302p., Gr. 2–5] Combining jokes, riddles, tongue twisters, tricks, games, puzzles, excerpted chapters from fiction, poems, and funny autographs ensure the success of this book as a "dip-into" read-aloud. Also see Pamela Pollock's collection *The Random House Book of Humor for Children*. HUMOROUS FICTION. HUMOROUS POETRY.

1775   Cole, William, comp. *Beastly Boys and Ghastly Girls*. Illus. by Tomi Ungerer. Dell, 1977. ISBN 0-440-40467-3

[125p., Gr. 2–6] Over 60 nimble-witted poems of and for obnoxious kids. Also meet X. J. Kennedy's *Brats* and Myra Cohn Livingston's perfect child, *Higgledy-Piggledy*. James Whitcomb Riley's classic poem *The Gobble-uns'll Git You Ef You Don't Watch Out* warns of dire consequences for bad behavior. BEHAVIOR—POETRY. HUMOROUS POETRY.

1776   Cole, William, comp. *Dinosaurs and Beasts of Yore*. Illus. by Susanna Natti. Philomel, 1989.

[62p., Gr. 1–4] Droll poetry of the prehistoric. Also showcase Lee Bennett Hopkins's collection *Dinosaurs* and Jack Prelutsky's original *Tyrannosaurus Was a Beast*. DINO-SAURS–POETRY.

1777   **Cole, William, comp. *Good Dog Poems*. Illus. by Ruth Sanderson. Scribner, 1981.**

[142p., Gr. 4–6] An anthology of 88, often serious, poems for lovers of mutts, thoroughbreds, and pups in between. Also sample Lee Bennett Hopkins's *A Dog's Life*. DOGS–POETRY.

1778   **Cole, William, comp. *I Went to the Animal Fair*. Illus. by Colette Rosselli. World, 1958.**

[unp., Gr. Pre–K] Thirty-five animal poems for the very young. Stephanie Calmenson's assortment *Never Take a Pig to Lunch* and Jack Prelutsky's *Zoo Doings* are equally entertaining. ANIMALS–POETRY.

1779   **Cole, William, comp. *I'm Mad at You*. Illus. by George MacClain. Collins, 1978.**

[63p., Gr. 1–4] When your students are feeling cranky, read them some of these poems. Weave in William Steig's *Spinky Sulks*, Jane Goodsell's *Toby's Toe*, and Charlotte Zolotow's *The Quarreling Book* to round out the tooth-gnashing. EMO-TIONS–POETRY.

1780   **Cole, William, comp. *Oh, Such Foolishness*. Illus. by Tomie dePaola. Lippincott, 1978. ISBN 0-397-31807-3**

[96p., Gr. 2–6] This is a collection of nonsense poems, along with companion volumes (all published by Viking) *Oh, How Silly* (1970), *Oh, That's Ridiculous* (1972), and *Oh, What Nonsense* (1966), for times of general hilarity. You will also get a kick out of Sara Brewton's *My Tang's Tungled and Other Ridiculous Situations*. HUMOROUS POETRY. NONSENSE VERSES.

1781   **Cole, William, comp. *Poem Stew*. Illus. by Karen Weinhaus. Lippincott, 1981. ISBN 0-397-31963-0**

[84p., Gr. 2–5] For gourmets and fast food junkies alike, these poems will tickle your appetite. If you are still hungry try Arnold Adoff's *Eats*, Rose H. Agree's *How to Eat a Poem and Other Morsels*, and Lee Bennett Hopkins's *Munching*. FOOD–POETRY.

1782   **Cole, William, comp. *The Poetry of Horses*. Illus. by Ruth Sanderson. Scribner, 1979.**

[180p., Gr. 4–6] A sturdy compilation of over 100 narrative poems about riders and their equine companions. HORSES–POETRY.

1783   **Corrin, Sara, and Stephen Corrin, comps. *Once Upon a Rhyme: 101 Poems for Young Children*. Illus. by Jill Bennett. Faber, 1982. ISBN 0-571-11913-1**

[157p., Gr. K–3] A pleasant anthology grouped into ten general subjects. POETRY–ANTHOLOGIES.

1784   **Cox, James A. *Put Your Foot in Your Mouth and Other Silly Sayings*. Illus. by Sam Q. Weissman. Random House, 1980. ISBN 0-394-94503-4**

[22 short chapters, 69p., Gr. 2–6] This entertaining, thorough, and easily understood explanation of such expressions as "cut off your nose to spite your face" and "spill the beans" will expand learners' command of the language. Ann Nevins's *From the Horse's Mouth*, Arthur Steckler's *101 Words and How They Began*, and Marvin Terban's *In a Pickle and Other Funny Idioms* and *Mad As a Wet Hen! And Other Funny Idioms* give more of the same. ENGLISH LANGUAGE–IDIOMS.

1785 Cricket Magazine, editors of, comp. *Cricket's Jokes, Riddles & Other Stuff*. Compiled by Marcia Leonard. Designed by John Grandits. Random House, 1977. ISBN 0-394-93545-4

[unp., Gr. K–5] The usual funny assortment. If your students are not familiar with *Cricket* magazine, it is never too late to make the introduction. LIMERICKS. RIDDLES. TONGUE TWISTERS. WORD GAMES.

1786 Curtis, Foley. *The Little Book of Big Tongue Twisters*. Illus. by David Ross. Harvey House, 1977.

[unp., Gr. 1–4] A brief palm-sized alphabetical assortment. Continue with Marcia Brown's *Peter Piper's Alphabet* and Alvin Schwartz's easy-to-read *Busy Buzzing Bumblebees* and alphabetical *A Twister of Twists, a Tangler of Tongues*. ALLITERATION. TONGUE TWISTERS.

1787 Dahl, Roald. *Roald Dahl's Revolting Rhymes*. Illus. by Quentin Blake. Knopf, 1982.

[39p., Gr. 3–6] In a bitingly flip tone reminiscent of Ogden Nash's, Dahl has rewritten six fairy tales: *Cinderella, Snow White, Jack and the Beanstalk, Goldilocks, Little Red Riding Hood*, and *The Three Pigs*. Not intended or suitable for young children—and some grown-ups will take offense as well—these are razor-sharp send-ups with twisted endings that will leave you light-headed. Children can attempt their own rhyming or prose parodies of other grand old chestnuts. With fifth- and sixth-graders you may want to introduce them to some of humorist James Thurber's marvelous fables, though these were not written for children, and you would need to dig them up from the adult room at the library. CREATIVE WRITING. FAIRY TALES–POETRY. HUMOROUS POETRY. NARRATIVE POETRY. PARODIES.

1788 Delamar, Gloria T., comp. *Children's Counting-Out Rhymes, Fingerplays, Jump-Rope and Bounce-Ball Chants and Other Rhythms: A Comprehensive English-Language Reference*. McFarland, 1983. ISBN 0-89950-064-1

[206p., Gr. Pre–3] While this is supposed to be an adult reference source, the sheer wealth of nonsense makes it too good for the grown-ups to hide away. If the format was just a tad more exciting and there was a dust jacket this would be an instant hit for kids to read themselves as are the Duncan Emrich and Alvin Schwartz books. My favorite chapter is "Staircase Tales," a collection of cumulative stories and tricks. For additional fun see Bernice Wells Carlson's *Listen! And Help Tell the Story*, Nancy and John Langstaff's *Jim Along, Josie*, Virginia A. Tashjian's *Juba This and Juba That* and *With a Deep Sea Smile*, and Carl Withers's *A Rocket in My Pocket*. FINGERPLAYS. GAMES. JUMP ROPE RHYMES.

1789 Demi. *Dragon Kites and Dragonflies: A Collection of Chinese Nursery Rhymes*. Illus. by the author. Harcourt, 1986. ISBN 0-15-224199-X

[unp., Gr. Pre–3] Vivid glossy watercolors, inspired by paper kites, embroideries, and other Chinese arts, fill huge double-page spreads for each of 22 rhymes collected and adapted by Demi, who also compiled and illustrated the magnificent *Chinese Zoo: Fables and Proverbs*. Don't forget Ed Young's Chinese riddle book *High on a Hill*, as well as the grand slew of Mother Goose rhymes (see Mother Goose) and other nursery rhyme collections such as N. M. Bodecker's Danish *"It's Raining," Said John Twaining*, Arnold Lobel's *Gregory Griggs* and *Whiskers & Rhymes*, and Clyde Watson's *Father Fox's Pennyrhymes*. CHINA–FOLKLORE. CHINESE POETRY. NURSERY RHYMES.

1790 dePaola, Tomie. *Tomie dePaola's Book of Poems*. Illus. by the author. Putnam, 1988. ISBN 0-399-21540-9

[95p., Gr. Pre–4] A large, lavishly illustrated compilation dealing with weather, hiding places, games, Halloween, siblings, old age, animals, and seasons. See also Beatrice Schenk de Regniers's *Sing a Song of Popcorn: Every Child's Book of Poems* and Jack Prelutsky's equally good *Read-Aloud Rhymes for the Very Young*. POETRY–ANTHOLOGIES.

1791 De Regniers, Beatrice Schenk. *It Does Not Say Meow and Other Animal Riddle Rhymes*. Illus. by Paul Galdone. Houghton Mifflin, 1983. ISBN 0-89919-043-X

[unp., Gr. Pre–1] These simplest of rhyming riddles allow children to listen for clues and identify a cow, cat, bird, elephant, ant, mouse, frog, dog, and bee. Each child can draw a large picture of an animal, dictate a description to write below it, or define its characteristics aloud for the others to guess before displaying the visual answer. Continue the fun with Marilee Robin Burton's *Tails, Toes, Eyes, Ears, Nose*; Beau Gardner's *Guess What?*; Deborah Guarino's *Is Your Mama a Llama?*; and Tana Hoban's *Look Again* and *Take Another Look*. ANIMALS–RIDDLES. RIDDLES.

1792 De Regniers, Beatrice Schenk, ed. *Sing a Song of Popcorn: Every Child's Book of Poems*. Illus. by Trina Schart Hyman. Scholastic, 1988. ISBN 0-590-40645-0

[142p., Gr. Pre–4] A large, elegant compilation of over 100 read-aloud poems radiantly illustrated by nine Caldecott artists. Also lovely are *Tomie dePaola's Book of Poems* and Jack Prelutsky's *Read-Aloud Rhymes for the Very Young*. POETRY–ANTHOLOGIES.

1793 De Regniers, Beatrice Schenk. *This Big Cat and Other Cats I've Known*. Illus. by Alan Daniel. Crown, 1985. ISBN 0-517-55538-7

[unp., Gr. Pre–2] The priceless dedication to cats everywhere sets off an affectionate, easy-to-understand collection, with endearing black-wash watercolors. Cat lovers will also want to purr over John Chapman's *Cat Will Rhyme with Hat*, Lee Bennett Hopkins's *I Am the Cat*, Nancy Larrick's *Cats Are Cats*, and Myra Cohn Livingston's *Cat Poems*. CATS–POETRY. POETRY–SINGLE AUTHOR.

1794 Doty, Roy, comp. *Tinkerbell Is a Ding-a-Ling*. Illus. by the author. Doubleday, 1980.

[unp., Gr. 4–6] Illustrated in cartoon style, here are more than enough corny jokes and riddles to satisfy even the most dented sense of humor. *Gunga Your Din-Din Is Ready* (1976), *King Midas Has a Gilt Complex* (1978), *Pinocchio Was Nosy* (1977), *Puns, Gags, Quips and Riddles* (1974), and *Q's Are Weird O's* (1975) are prequels, in the same format. RIDDLES. WORD GAMES.

1795 Eliot, T. S. *Old Possum's Book of Practical Cats*. Illus. by Edward Gorey. Harcourt, 1982. ISBN 0-15-168656-4

[56p., Gr. 4–6] Rum Tum Tugger, Old Deuteronomy, and Skimbleshanks are some of the felines cavorting through the poems, originally published in 1939, that inspired the Broadway musical *Cats*. CATS–POETRY. POETRY–SINGLE AUTHOR.

1796 Emrich, Duncan, comp. *The Hodgepodge Book*. Illus. by Ib Ohlsson. Four Winds, 1972.

[367p., Gr. 2–6] This, plus companion volumes *The Nonsense Book* (1970) and *The Whim-Wham Book* (1975), is a browser's paradise, jam-filled with jokes, riddles, puzzles, conundrums, tongue twisters, and rhymes, all from American folklore. For

more, see also all titles by Alvin Schwartz and Carl Withers's *A Rocket in My Pocket*.
FOLKLORE—U.S. NONSENSE. RIDDLES. TONGUE TWISTERS. WORD GAMES.

1797   **Esbensen, Barbara Juster.** *Cold Stars and Fireflies: Poems of the Four Seasons.* **Illus. by Susan Bonners. Crowell, 1984. ISBN 0-690-04362-7**

[70p., Gr. 3–6] Haunting free-verse poems to read straight through for a memorable portrait of a year. Also see Lee Bennett Hopkins's collections *Moments: Poems about Seasons* and *The Sky Is Full of Song*. POETRY—SINGLE AUTHOR. SEASONS—POETRY.

1798   **Feelings, Muriel.** *Jambo Means Hello: Swahili Alphabet Book.* **Illus. by Tom Feelings. Dial, 1974. ISBN 0-8037-4346-7**

[1 sitting, unp., Gr. 2–5] Learn a smattering of Africa's most widespread language while soaking up the culture and customs of East Africa through the expressive brown-and-wash paintings of this and *Moja Means One: Swahili Counting Book* (1971). Make February, Black History Month, a memorable one by incorporating folklore and Swahili vocabulary into your daily routine. AFRICA. ALPHABET BOOKS. LANGUAGE.

1799   **Fleischman, Paul.** *Joyful Noise: Poems for Two Voices.* **Illus. by Eric Beddows. Harper & Row, 1988. ISBN 0-06-021852-5**

[44p., Gr. 5–6] These 14 spare two-columned poems of grasshoppers, honey bees, cicadas, fireflies, and other insects will bring pleasure even if you are not studying invertebrates. Some are whimsical, some are touching. These poems, meant to be read aloud from top to bottom by two readers—one on the left and one on the right —are like spoken songs, with some lines read in harmony, some solo, and others in unison. Pairs of students can select, practice, and perform selections for the class or go all out and stage a costumed reading for the school. Sophisticated classes will appreciate these poems along with William Kotzwinkle's *Trouble in Bugland*. To see more from an insect's perspective show Chris Van Allsburg's *Two Bad Ants*. INSECTS—POETRY. NEWBERY MEDAL.

1800   **Foster, John, ed.** *A First Poetry Book.* **Illus. by Chris Orr, Martin White, and Joseph Wright. Oxford University Press, 1980. ISBN 0-19-918113-6**

[128p., Gr. K–2] Almost 100 brief poems of everyday life for young children. POETRY —ANTHOLOGIES.

1801   **Fox, Dan, ed.** *Go In and Out the Window: An Illustrated Songbook for Young People.* **Commentary by Claude Marks. Illus. Henry Holt, 1987. ISBN 0-8050-0628-1**

[144p., Gr. Pre–6] Words and music to 61 well-known or traditional folk songs, each one accompanied by one or more exquisite full-color reproductions of paintings, prints, or other artworks from the Metropolitan Museum of Art's collection. See also the companion poetry/art anthology, Kenneth Koch and Kate Farrell's *Talking to the Sun*. ART. FOLK SONGS. PAINTINGS. SONGBOOKS.

1802   **Garson, Eugenia, comp.** *The Laura Ingalls Wilder Songbook.* **Illus. by Garth Williams. Harper & Row, 1968. ISBN 0-06-021933-5**

[160p., Gr. 2–5] Sixty-two of the songs and hymns mentioned in the texts of the eight "Little House" books are included, along with piano and guitar arrangements and notes relating each tune to the book in which it was sung. FOLK SONGS. SONGBOOKS.

1803 **Gerler, William R., comp.** *A Pack of Riddles.* **Illus. by Giulio Maestro. Dutton, 1975. ISBN 0-525-36530-3**

[unp., Gr. Pre–2] One illustrated easy-to-read riddle per page, with more than 72 riddles in all. Keep them laughing with *Bennett Cerf's Book of Riddles* and Giulio Maestro's *Riddle Romp.* RIDDLES.

1804 **Glazer, Tom, comp.** *Eye Winker, Tom Tinker, Chin Chopper: Fifty Musical Fingerplays.* **Illus. by Ronald Himler. Doubleday, 1978. ISBN 0-385-08200-2**

[91p., Gr. Pre–2] Nursery songs and other clever ditties to be performed with actions as described in the text and in the continuation, *Do Your Ears Hang Low? Fifty More Musical Fingerplays* (1980). Also see Marc Brown's slim collections including *Finger Rhymes* (Dutton, 1980), *Hand Rhymes, Party Rhymes* (1988), and *Play Rhymes* (1987) and Nancy and John Langstaff's *Jim Along Josie.* CREATIVE DRAMA. FINGERPLAYS. FOLK SONGS. SINGING GAMES. SONGBOOKS.

1805 **Glazer, Tom, comp.** *Tom Glazer's Treasury of Songs for Children.* **Illus. by John O'Brien. Doubleday, 1988. ISBN 0-385-23693-X**

[256p., Gr. Pre–6] Over 100 popular folk songs for all occasions, with music and guitar chords included. Originally published by Grossett & Dunlap in 1964 as *Tom Glazer's Treasury of Folk Songs.* Also see Jane Hart's *Singing Bee*, Timothy John's *The Great Song Book*, and Ruth Crawford Seeger's *American Folk Songs for Children.* FOLK SONGS. SONGBOOKS.

1806 **Gounaud, Karen Jo, comp.** *A Very Mice Joke Book.* **Illus. by Lynn Munsinger. Houghton Mifflin, 1981. ISBN 0-395-30445-8**

[47p., Gr. 1–5] Mouse puns and riddles, decked out with mouse-terful illustrations. Let your class mouster-up some new ones to go along with mouse novels such as Beverly Cleary's "Ralph" books or Lilian Moore's *I'll Meet You at the Cucumbers.* MICE–RIDDLES. RIDDLES.

1807 **Greenfield, Eloise.** *Honey, I Love.* **Illus. by Diane Dillon and Leo Dillon. Crowell, 1978. ISBN 0-690-01334-5**

[unp., Gr. 2–5] A young black girl's poems about her world and the people in it. AFRICAN AMERICANS–POETRY. POETRY–SINGLE AUTHOR.

1808 **Greenfield, Eloise.** *Under the Sunday Tree.* **Illus. by Amos Ferguson. Harper & Row, 1988. ISBN 0-06-022254-9**

[38p., Gr. 2–5] Twenty poems accompany a Bahamian primitive artist's bright vibrant paintings of day-to-day life there. Show each painting and have your students compose their own poetic descriptions. In Charlotte Pomerantz's *The Chalk Doll*, island life is recalled by Rose's mother who grew up in Jamaica. ISLANDS. POETRY–SINGLE AUTHOR.

1809 **Hall, Katy, and Lisa Eisenberg.** *Buggy Riddles.* **Illus. by Simms Taback. Dial, 1986. ISBN 0-8037-0139-X**

[48p., Gr. Pre–2] With one colorful illustration and easy-to-read riddle per page, this is a companion to *Fishy Riddles* (1983). Surely, your own mites can infest your classroom with their own flea-bitten groaners. Unearth some others in Joanne E. Bernstein and Paul Cohen's *Creepy Crawly Critter Riddles* and learn to appreciate their charms with Mary Ann Hoberman's *Bugs: Poems.* INSECTS–RIDDLES. RIDDLES.

1810 Hart, Jane, comp. *Singing Bee! A Collection of Favorite Children's Songs.* Illus. by Anita Lobel. Lothrop, 1982. ISBN 0-688-41975-5

[160p., Gr. K-2] One hundred and twenty-five mostly well-known tunes for young children accompanied by large, beautiful illustrations, many in color. Other grand folk song collections include *Tom Glazer's Treasury of Songs for Children,* Eugenia Garson's *The Laura Ingalls Wilder Songbook,* Timothy John's *The Great Song Book,* and Ruth Crawford Seeger's *American Folk Songs for Children.* FOLK SONGS. SONGBOOKS.

1811 Heller, Ruth. *A Cache of Jewels and Other Collective Nouns.* Illus. by the author. Putnam, 1987. ISBN 0-448-19211-X

[unp., Gr. Pre-3] Large, luscious illustrations introduce a rhyming host of collective nouns. Reading teachers rejoice and set your students to compiling an additional sampling of nouns and verbs. See also Heller's *Kites Sail High,* for older children, and use this along with Patricia Hooper's poems, *A Bundle of Beasts.* ANIMALS-POETRY. ENGLISH LANGUAGE-GRAMMAR.

1812 Heller, Ruth. *Kites Sail High: A Book about Verbs.* Illus. by the author. Putnam, 1988. ISBN 0-448-10480-6

[unp., Gr. 3-5] Like Heller's *A Cache of Jewels and Other Collective Nouns,* this is a visual rhyming feast that reviews all types of verbs, including linking, helping, irregular and regular, and their three moods: imperative, indicative, and subjunctive. ENGLISH LANGUAGE-GRAMMAR. STORIES IN RHYME.

1813 Hoban, Russell. *Egg Thoughts and Other Frances Songs.* Illus. by Lillian Hoban. Harper & Row, 1972. ISBN 0-06-022332-4

[32p., Gr. K-2] After reading aloud Hoban's "Frances" books about the homey adventures of a versifying young badger, try a few of her original poems. Perhaps your children will want to set them to music. BADGERS-POETRY. HUMOROUS POETRY. POETRY-SINGLE AUTHOR. SONGBOOKS.

1814 Hoberman, Mary Ann. *Bugs: Poems.* Illus. by Victoria Chess. Viking, 1976.

[unp., Gr. 1-4] An affectionate look at our crawly friends, the insects. Laugh a bit with Joanne E. Bernstein and Paul Cohen's *Creepy Crawly Critter Riddles* and Katy Hall and Lisa Eisenberg's *Buggy Riddles.* INSECTS-POETRY.

1815 Hoff, Syd. *Syd Hoff's Animal Jokes.* Illus. by the author. Lippincott, 1985. ISBN 0-694-00145-7

[unp., Gr. K-2] More than 36 easy-to-fathom, one-liner cartoons and riddles, one per intensely colorful page. Good training for future *New Yorker* magazine readers. ANIMALS-RIDDLES. JOKES. RIDDLES.

1816 Hoff, Syd. *Syd Hoff's Joke Book.* Illus. by the author. Putnam, 1972.

[63p., Gr. 2-4] Organize class comedy teams to practice and read aloud pages of these punchy two-person jokes. Also try Charles Keller's *School Daze* and the slightly more sophisticated *The Super Joke Book* by Gyles Brandreth and *The Gigantic Joke Book* by Joseph Rosenbloom. JOKES.

1817 Hooper, Patricia. *A Bundle of Beasts.* Illus. by Mark Steele. Houghton Mifflin, 1987. ISBN 0-395-44259-1

[60p., Gr. 2–5] Twenty-five startlingly funny and ingenious poems about collective nouns, from a smack of jelly fish to a murder of crows. As a warm-up use Ruth Heller's *A Cache of Jewels and Other Collective Nouns*. ANIMALS–POETRY. ENGLISH LANGUAGE–GRAMMAR.

1818   **Hopkins, Lee Bennett, comp.** *Best Friends.* **Illus. by James Watts. Harper & Row, 1986. ISBN 0-06-022561-0**

[48p., Gr. 1–4] Sunny watercolors joyously present 18 friendship poems about children wrestling, playing, fighting, and sleeping over with and moving away from their favorite companions. Also make friends with the gang in Jack Prelutsky's *Rolling Harvey Down the Hill*. FRIENDSHIP–POETRY.

1819   **Hopkins, Lee Bennett, comp.** *Click, Rumble, Roar: Poems about Machines.* **Photos by Anna Held Audette. Crowell, 1987. ISBN 0-690-04587-5**

[40p., Gr. 2–5] From a car wash and laundromat to a pocket calculator and computer here are 18 noisy, banging poems accompanied by full-page black-and-white photographs. In this age of computers we should all be able to identify with Eve Merriam's final poem, "Think Tank," which is so satisfying to read aloud as you drape yourself with computer paper. Clunk. MACHINES–POETRY.

1820   **Hopkins, Lee Bennett, comp.** *Creatures.* **Illus. by Stella Ormai. Harcourt, 1985. ISBN 0-15-220875-5**

[32p., Gr. 2–5] Eighteen lighthearted poems of bump-in-the-night nasties and day-time fairies. See also Sara and John E. Brewton's *Shrieks at Midnight*, John E. Brewton's *In the Witches Kitchen*, and Jack Prelutsky's malevolent *Nightmares*. MONSTERS–POETRY. SUPERNATURAL–POETRY. WITCHES–POETRY.

1821   **Hopkins, Lee Bennett, comp.** *Dinosaurs.* **Illus. by Murray Tinkelman. Harcourt, 1987. ISBN 0-15-223495-0**

[46p., Gr. K–6] A universally adored reptile such as this deserves its own collection, along with the full-page black-and-white cross-hatched drawings. Also don't miss William Cole's *Dinosaurs and Beasts of Yore* and Jack Prelutsky's original poems, *Tyrannosaurus Was a Beast*. DINOSAURS–POETRY.

1822   **Hopkins, Lee Bennett, comp.** *A Dog's Life.* **Illus. by Linda Rochester Richards. Harcourt, 1983.**

[40p., Gr. K–6] Black-and-white cross-hatched pups spill across the pages of affec-tionate, often sober poems, paeans to man's best friend. Give equal time to Hop-kins's companion volume *I Am the Cat* and also take a walk through William Cole's *Good Dog Poems*. DOGS–POETRY.

1823   **Hopkins, Lee Bennett, comp.** *I Am the Cat.* **Illus. by Linda Rochester Richards. Harcourt, 1981.**

[40p., Gr. K–6] A sensitive collection of cat-based poems, laced with elegant cross-hatched line drawings, and a companion to *A Dog's Life*. Also see John Chapman's *Cat Will Rhyme with Hat*, Beatrice Schenk de Regniers's *This Big Cat and Other Cats I've Known*, Lee Bennett Hopkins's *I Am the Cat*, Nancy Larrick's *Cats Are Cats*, and Myra Cohn Livingston's *Cat Poems*. CATS–POETRY.

1824   **Hopkins, Lee Bennett, comp.** *Moments: Poems about the Seasons.* **Illus. by Michael Hague. Harcourt, 1980.**

[64p., Gr. 1–5] Divided into autumn, winter, spring, and summer; 50 poems by well-known poets. Also see Barbara Juster Esbensen's memorable *Cold Stars and Fireflies* and Hopkins's *The Sky Is Full of Song*. SEASONS–POETRY.

1825   **Hopkins, Lee Bennett, comp.** *More Surprises.* **Illus. by Megan Lloyd. Harper & Row, 1987. ISBN 0-06-022604-8**

[64p., Gr. Pre–3] Short, snappy delicious poetic bites, in "I Can Read" format, with a bit of everything, including a couple of just-right poems about books and reading. Also read the first one, *Surprises* (1984). POETRY–ANTHOLOGIES.

1826   **Hopkins, Lee Bennett, comp.** *Munching: Poems about Eating.* **Illus. by Nelle Davis. Little, Brown, 1985. ISBN 0-316-37269-2**

[46p., Gr. K–3] A bright, cheery, easy-to-read assortment of before-lunch short verse. Use with Adoff's *Eats*, Rose H. Agree's *How to Eat a Poem and Other Morsels*, and William Cole's *Poem Stew*, and plan a poetry lunch or snack with your students. FOOD–POETRY.

1827   **Hopkins, Lee Bennett, comp.** *Side by Side: Poems to Read Together.* **Illus. by Hilary Knight. Simon & Schuster, 1988. ISBN 0-671-63579-4**

[80p., Gr. K–2] Over 50 poetry oldies but goodies and newer destined-to-be favorites, all lavishly decorated with cozy, good-natured watercolors. Continue the sharing with *Tomie dePaola's Book of Poems*, John Ciardi's *You Read to Me, I'll Read to You*, and Jack Prelutsky's *Read-Aloud Rhymes for the Very Young*. POETRY–ANTHOLOGIES.

1828   **Hopkins, Lee Bennett, comp.** *The Sky Is Full of Song.* **Illus. by Dirk Zimmer. Harper & Row, 1983.**

[46p, Gr. K–3] Decorated with dainty colored woodblock prints are 38 short poems that run through the cycle of seasons. Related rhymes include Sara Coleridge's *January Brings the Snow: A Book of Months*, Shirley Hughes's *Out and About*, and Maurice Sendak's *Chicken Soup with Rice*. SEASONS–POETRY.

1829   **Hopkins, Lee Bennett, and Misha Arenstein, comps.** *Thread One to a Star: A Book of Poems.* **Illus. with photos. Four Winds, 1976.**

[124p., Gr. 4–6] An intriguing eclectic poetic assortment of seasons, people, cities, and personal feelings, interspersed with fitting, stark, black-and-white photographs. POETRY–ANTHOLOGIES.

1830   **Hughes, Langston.** *Don't You Turn Back.* **Illus. by Ann Grifalconi. Selected by Lee Bennett Hopkins. Knopf, 1969.**

[79p., Gr. 3–6] Forty-five short treasures, one per page, expressing dreams and despair, by the famous African American poet. AFRICAN AMERICANS–POETRY. POETRY–SINGLE AUTHOR.

1831   **Hughes, Shirley.** *Out and About.* **Illus. by the author. Lothrop, 1988. ISBN 0-688-07691-2**

[unp., Gr. Pre–1] The year in rhyme from a young girl's perspective. Eighteen simple, jubilant poems move from spring through winter, along with Hughes's cozily detailed child-filled pictures. For more round-the-year poetry also read Sara Coleridge's *January Brings the Snow: A Book of Months*, Lee Bennett Hopkins's *The Sky Is Full of Song*, and Maurice Sendak's *Chicken Soup with Rice*. SEASONS–POETRY. WEATHER–POETRY.

1832   John, Timothy, ed. *The Great Song Book*. Illus. by Tomi Ungerer. Benn, 1978.

[112p., Gr. Pre–5] A charming illustrated collection of over 60 well-known folk songs. Keep humming with *Tom Glazer's Treasury of Songs for Children*, Eugenia Garson's *The Laura Ingalls Wilder Songbook*, Jane Hart's *Singing Bee*, and Ruth Crawford Seeger's *American Folk Songs for Children*. FOLK SONGS. SONGBOOKS.

1833   Jones, Evelyn, comp. *World's Wackiest Riddle Book*. Illus. by Dennis Kendrick. Sterling, 1987. ISBN 0-8069-4737-3

[128p., Gr. 2–6] Over 500 riddles with a subject index for easy access and in the same style, format, and fun as the Joseph Rosenbloom books. RIDDLES.

1834   Keller, Charles, comp. *Alexander the Grape: Fruit and Vegetable Jokes*. Illus. by Gregory Filling. Prentice Hall, 1982. ISBN 0-13-021410-8

[44p., Gr. 2–6] More than enough riddles about pickles, bananas, and even broccoli. Also try a bit of gastronomic poetry with Arnold Adoff's *Eats*, Rose H. Agree's *How to Eat a Poem and Other Morsels*, William Cole's *Poem Stew*, and Lee Bennett Hopkins's *Munching*. All of these fit in with both James Howe's *Bunnicula*, where the vampire bunny sucks the juices out of vegetables and Steven Manes's *Be a Perfect Person in Just Three Days*, where Milo must wear a head of broccoli as a necklace around his neck for an entire day. FOOD–RIDDLES. FRUIT–RIDDLES. RIDDLES. VEGETABLES–RIDDLES.

1835   Keller, Charles, comp. *Ballpoint Bananas and Other Jokes for Kids*. Illus. by David Barrios. Prentice Hall, 1973.

[96p., Gr. 2–6] Along with *More Ballpoint Bananas* (1977), this is filled with riddles, rhymes, Tom Swifties, perverted proverbs, and other ticklish situations. HUMOROUS POETRY. NONSENSE VERSES. RIDDLES.

1836   Keller, Charles, comp. *Count Draculations! Monsters Riddles*. Illus. by Edward Frascino. Prentice Hall, 1986. ISBN 0-13-183641-2

[unp., Gr. 2–6] "Why does a skeleton go to the library? . . . To bone up on a few things"—and many others of that ilk for Halloween and everyday. Also use Marc Brown's *Spooky Riddles* and Joseph Rosenbloom's *Monster Madness*. HALLOWEEN–RIDDLES. MONSTERS–RIDDLES. RIDDLES. SUPERNATURAL–RIDDLES.

1837   Keller, Charles, comp. *It's Raining Cats and Dogs: Cat and Dog Jokes*. Illus. by Charles Quackenbush. Pippin, 1988. ISBN 0-945912-01-3

[unp., Gr. 2–5] Dozens of jokes, full of purrs and paws, some new and some not. Sample these when reading cat or dog stories and poems along with Marjorie Zaum's folktales *Catlore*. CATS–RIDDLES. DOGS–RIDDLES. RIDDLES.

1838   Keller, Charles, comp. *Llama Beans*. Illus. by Dennis Nolan. Prentice Hall, 1979.

[44p., Gr. 1–4] More animals jokes, one per two-sided page, with wonderfully goofy illustrations. See also David A. Adler's *The Carsick Zebra and Other Animal Riddles*. ANIMALS–RIDDLES. RIDDLES.

1839   Keller, Charles, comp. *Norma Lee I Don't Knock on Doors*. Illus. by Paul Galdone. Prentice Hall, 1983. ISBN 0-13-623587-5

[unp., Gr. K–3] More knock-knock jokes than anyone should ever tell. Also open the door on Joseph Rosenbloom's *Dr. Knock-Knock's Official Knock-Knock Dictionary;*

The Funniest Knock-Knock Book Ever; and *Knock-Knock! Who's There?* JOKES. KNOCK-KNOCK JOKES.

1840   **Keller, Charles, comp.** *The Nutty Joke Book.* **Illus. by Jean-Claude Suares. Prentice Hall, 1978. ISBN 0-13-627737-3**

[unp., Gr. 2–5] Riddles about peanuts and other unsuspecting nuts. FOOD–RIDDLES. RIDDLES.

1841   **Keller, Charles, comp.** *Remember the à la Mode! Riddles and Puns.* **Illus. by Lee Lorenz. Prentice Hall, 1983. ISBN 0-13-773342-9**

[unp., Gr. 2–6] An all-purpose, all-funny grouping of "What did," "What do you call," "Why," and "What do you get when you cross?" riddles. Encourage your punsters to create and illustrate new ones. RIDDLES. WORD GAMES.

1842   **Keller, Charles, comp.** *School Daze.* **Illus. by Sam Q. Weissman. Prentice Hall, 1981. ISBN 0-13-793612-5**

[64p., Gr. 2–5] Snappy two-person short-dialogue jokes about spelling, math, report cards, and teachers. Have two children at a time act out the jokes for the class, Readers Theater style. While you are geared up, all the students will identify with universal school tales such as Harry Allard's *Miss Nelson Is Missing,* Ida Luttrell's *One Day at School,* James Marshall's *The Cut-Ups,* Amy Schwartz's *Annabelle Swift, Kingergartner,* and James Stevenson's *That Dreadful Day.* CREATIVE DRAMA. JOKES. SCHOOLS–RIDDLES.

1843   **Keller, Charles, comp.** *Swine Lake: Music & Dance Riddles.* **Illus. by Gregory Filling. Prentice Hall, 1985. ISBN 0-13-879743-9**

[48p., Gr. 3–6] Now even the music teacher can yuck it up in class with riddle warm-ups. Scott K. Peterson's *Face the Music! Jokes about Music* (Lerner, 1988) is also noteworthy. MUSIC–RIDDLES. RIDDLES.

1844   **Keller, Charles, and Richard Baker, comps.** *The Star-Spangled Banana and Other Revolutionary Riddles.* **Illus. by Tomie dePaola. Prentice Hall, 1974. ISBN 0-13-842989-8**

[unp., Gr. 2–6] Your students probably never realized colonial history was so funny. Lighten up those social studies lessons with this book and David A. Alder's *Remember Betsy Floss.* RIDDLES. U.S.–HISTORY–RIDDLES.

1845   **Kennedy, X. J.** *Brats.* **Illus. by James Watts. McElderry, 1986. ISBN 0-689-50392-X**

[42p., Gr. 3–6] Forty-two rotten kids give and get some just deserts in these short, vengeful, irreverent little poems. For more behavior problems see William Cole's *Beastly Boys and Ghastly Girls* and James Whitcomb Riley's *The Gobble-Uns'll Git You Ef You Don't Watch Out.* BEHAVIOR–POETRY. HUMOROUS POETRY.

1846   **Kennedy, X. J.** *Ghastlies, Goops & Pincushions: Nonsense Verse.* **Illus. by Ron Barrett. McElderry, 1989. ISBN 0-689-50477-2**

[57p., Gr. 3–6] Short takes of rhyming silliness about animals, relatives, and other odd creations. *One Winter Night in August and Other Nonsense Jingles* (1975) and *The Phantom Ice Cream Man: More Nonsense Verse* (1979) are companions. HUMOROUS POETRY. NONSENSE VERSES. POETRY–SINGLE AUTHOR.

1847   **Kennedy, X. J., comp.** *Knock at a Star: A Child's Introduction to Poetry.* **Illus. by Karen Weinhaus. Little, Brown, 1985. ISBN 0-316-48853-4**

[148p., Gr. 4–6] Brief, brilliant nuggets of poems that make you laugh, tell stories, send messages, share feelings, and start you wondering, with sensible advice on how to appreciate them and numerous suggestions for the reluctant teacher. PO-ETRY—ANTHOLOGIES.

1848 **Klein, Robin.** *Snakes and Ladders: Poems about the Ups and Downs of Life.* **Illus. by Ann James. Oxford University Press, 1987. ISBN 0-19-276062-9**

[77p., Gr. 3–6] School and other rhyming complaints from the witty Australian humorist. Keep laughing with Judith Viorst's *If I Were in Charge of the World and Other Worries.* HUMOROUS POETRY. POETRY—SINGLE AUTHOR.

1849 **Koch, Kenneth, and Kate Farrell, comps.** *Talking to the Sun: An Illustrated Anthology of Poems for Young People.* **Illus. Henry Holt, 1985. ISBN 0-8050-0144-1**

[112p., Gr. Pre–6] From the first poem, the African "Hymn to the Sun," illustrated with a full-color photograph of the Metropolitan's Tiffany stained-glass window, "Autumn Landscape," you and your art and verse fans will pore over each lavish page filled with poems and paintings, prints, sculptures, and other glorious art from the Metropolitan Museum of Art's own collection. See the equally magnificent companion volume of songs *Go In and Out the Window,* compiled by Dan Fox. ART. PAINTINGS. POETRY—ANTHOLOGIES.

1850 **Langstaff, Nancy, and John Langstaff, comps.** *Jim Along Josie: A Collection of Folk Songs.* **Illus. by Jan Pienkowski. Harcourt, 1970.**

[127p., Gr. Pre–2] Eighty-one songs we all should know, with two-thirds of the book devoted to singing games and action songs. Other time-honored collections for young children include Jane Hart's *Singing Bee;* Tom Glazer's *Eye Winker, Tom Tinker, Chin Chopper: Fifty Musical Fingerplays; Do Your Ears Hang Low? Fifty More Musical Fingerplays;* and *Tom Glazer's Treasury of Songs for Children;* Timothy John's *The Great Song Book;* and Ruth Crawford Seeger's *American Folk Songs for Children.* FINGERPLAYS. FOLK SONGS. SINGING GAMES. SONGBOOKS.

1851 **Larrick, Nancy, comp.** *Cats Are Cats.* **Illus. by Ed Young. Philomel, 1988. ISBN 0-399-21517-4**

[80p., Gr. 3–6] Large paper-bag-colored, double-page spreads pulsate with each of the 42 grand poems of alley cats and their more fortunate siblings. More on the same topic includes John Chapman's *Cat Will Rhyme with Hat,* Beatrice Schenk de Regniers's *This Big Cat and Other Cats I've Known,* Lee Bennett Hopkins's *I Am the Cat,* and Myra Cohn Livingston's *Cat Poems.* CATS—POETRY.

1852 **Larrick, Nancy, comp.** *Piping Down the Valleys Wild.* **Illus. by Ellen Raskin. Delacorte, 1985. ISBN 0-385-29429-8**

[247p., Gr. 2–6] A classic treasury with over 200 good poems. Another collection distilled from this one is Larrick's *Piper, Pipe That Song Again: Poems for Boys and Girls* (Random House, 1965). Keep these company with May Hill Arbuthnot's *Time for Poetry,* Joanna Cole's *A New Treasury of Children's Poetry,* Jack Prelutsky's *The Random House Book of Poetry,* and Louis Untermeyer's *The Golden Treasury of Poetry.* POETRY—ANTHOLOGIES.

1853 **Lear, Edward.** *How Pleasant to Know Mr. Lear!* **Illus. by the author. Selected by Myra Cohn Livingston. Holiday House, 1982. ISBN 0-8234-0462-5**

[123p., Gr. 4–6] An insightful glimpse into the poetry, life, and illustrations of the grand master of limericks. For additional limericks by Lear and others see also N. M. Bodecker's *A Person from Britain Whose Head Was the Shape of a Mitten*, John Brewton's *They've Discovered a Head in the Box for the Bread and Other Laughable Limericks*, John Ciardi's *The Hopeful Trout and Other Limericks*, Arnold Lobel's *The Book of Pigericks*, and Joseph Rosenbloom's *The Looniest Limerick Book in the World*. HUMOROUS POETRY. LIMERICKS. NONSENSE VERSES. POETRY–SINGLE AUTHOR.

1854   **Lee, Dennis.** *Alligator Pie.* **Illus. by Frank Newfield. Houghton Mifflin, 1974.**

[64p., Gr. Pre–4] The title poem is just one of the little gems you will find here, along with the other books by Dennis Lee that follow. Also look for Lee's Caedmon recording. HUMOROUS POETRY. NONSENSE VERSES. NURSERY RHYMES. POETRY–SINGLE AUTHOR.

1855   **Lee, Dennis.** *Jelly Belly: Original Nursery Rhymes.* **Illus. by Juan Wijngaard. Peter Bedrick, 1985. ISBN 0-87226-001-1**

[64p., Gr. Pre–3] This, as well as *Garbage Delight* (1977) and *Nicholas Knock and Other People* (1974), contains delightful galloping nonsense poems and nursery rhymes, mostly for primary grades, but with a few for the older kids as well. Lee is to Canada what Shel Silverstein and Jack Prelutsky are to the United States. HUMOROUS POETRY. NONSENSE VERSES. NURSERY RHYMES. POETRY–SINGLE AUTHOR.

1856   **Lewis, Richard, ed.** *Miracles: Poems by Children of the English-Speaking World.* **Publishing Center for Cultural Resources, 1966. ISBN 0-671-42797-0**

[215p., Gr. 1–6] Exquisite examples of children's creative endeavors. POETRY–ANTHOLOGIES.

1857   **Livingston, Myra Cohn, comp.** *Callooh! Callay! Holiday Poems for Young Readers.* **Illus. by Janet Stevens. Atheneum, 1980.**

[131p., Gr. 2–5] From New Year's Day to Christmas Eve, and all the major holidays in between; several poems for each, over 80 in all. Oversized, bold, dynamic acrylics dominate the double-page spreads of one poem per holiday in Livingston's picture book-style *Celebrations* (Holiday House, 1985). HOLIDAYS–POETRY.

1858   **Livingston, Myra Cohn, comp.** *Cat Poems.* **Illus. by Trina Schart Hyman. Holiday House, 1987. ISBN 0-8234-0631-8**

[32p., Gr. 2–5] A slim but pleasing assortment with large black-and-white pencil drawings for fans of felines. Similar in tone to Lee Bennett Hopkins's *I Am the Cat* and felicitous with John Chapman's *Cat Will Rhyme with Hat*, Beatrice Schenk de Regniers's *This Big Cat and Other Cats I've Known*, and Nancy Larrick's *Cats Are Cats*. When introducing students to the card catalog, gather together this and other assorted cat books to book talk. CATS–POETRY.

1859   **Livingston, Myra Cohn, comp.** *Christmas Poems.* **Illus. by Trina Schart Hyman. Holiday House, 1984. ISBN 0-8234-0508-7**

[32p., Gr. 3–6] A brief assortment of 18 selections, some jauntily secular, some serious. For the younger listeners also read Jack Prelutsky's jocular originals in *It's Christmas*. CHRISTMAS–POETRY.

1860   **Livingston, Myra Cohn, comp.** *A Song I Sang to You: A Selection of Poems.* **Illus. by Margot Tomes. Harcourt, 1984. ISBN 0-15-277105-0**

[84p., Gr. K–3] A small-sized collection of 60 spare, sometimes rhyming, child-eyed poems from five of Livingston's earlier books. POETRY–SINGLE AUTHOR.

1861   **Lobel, Arnold.** *The Book of Pigericks.* **Illus. by the author. Harper & Row, 1983. ISBN 0-06-023982-4**

[48p., Gr. 2–6] More than 36 pig limericks. Try composing your own about porkers or any other interesting beasts. For other limerick books see also N. M. Bodecker's *A Person from Britain Whose Head Was the Shape of a Mitten,* John Brewton's *They've Discovered a Head in the Box for the Bread and Other Laughable Limericks,* John Ciardi's *The Hopeful Trout and Other Limericks,* Edward Lear's *How Pleasant to Know Mr. Lear!* and Joseph Rosenbloom's *The Looniest Limerick Book in the World.* Organize a party of pig books with such titles as *The Three Little Pigs,* Charlotte Pomerantz's *The Piggy in the Puddle,* or Mary Rayner's *Mr. and Mrs. Pig's Evening Out,* to name a few. HUMOROUS POETRY. LIMERICKS. PIGS–POETRY. POETRY–SINGLE AUTHOR.

1862   **Lobel, Arnold.** *Whiskers & Rhymes.* **Illus. by the author. Greenwillow, 1985. ISBN 0-688-03835-2**

[48p., Gr. Pre–3] Captivatingly bouncy original nursery rhymes. Also don't miss Lobel's *Gregory Griggs and Other Nursery Rhyme People,* along with N. M. Bodecker's Danish nursery rhymes *"It's Raining," Said John Twaining,* Dennis Lee's *Jelly Belly,* and Clyde Watson's original *Father Fox's Pennyrhymes,* as well as a healthy assortment of Mother Goose. HUMOROUS POETRY. NURSERY RHYMES. POETRY–SINGLE AUTHOR.

1863   **Longfellow, Henry Wadsworth.** *Paul Revere's Ride.* **Illus. by Paul Galdone. Crowell, 1963.**

[unp., Gr. 4–6] The famous poetic account in handsome picture-book format proves an appropriate supplement to your colonial history lesson. Contrast the bombast of poetic hero-worship with the true story as told by Jean Fritz in *And Then What Happened, Paul Revere?* Laugh it up afterward with David A. Adler's *Remember Betsy Floss and Other Colonial American Riddles* and Charles Keller and Richard Baker's *The Star-Spangled Banana and Other Revolutionary Riddles.* NARRATIVE POETRY. STORIES IN RHYME. U.S.–HISTORY–REVOLUTION.

1864   **McCord, David.** *One at a Time.* **Illus. by Henry B. Kane. Little, Brown, 1986. ISBN 0-316-55516-9**

[494p., Gr. K–4] A thick, luscious, one-volume treasury consisting of the well-loved poet's seven books: *All Day Long, Away and Ago, Every Time I Climb a Tree, For Me to Say, The Star in the Pail, Far and Few,* and *Take Sky.* POETRY–SINGLE AUTHOR.

1865   **McMillan, Bruce.** *One Sun: A Book of Terse Verse.* **Photos by author. Holiday House, 1990. ISBN 0-8234-0810-8**

[1 sitting, unp., Gr. Pre–2] Two-word rhyming poems about a day at the shore are accompanied by clear, full-page, color photographs. Class poets can think of new monosyllabic couplets to illustrate. Beach lovers will also appreciate Ken Robbins's *Beach Days,* Susan Russo's *The Ice Cream Ocean and Other Delectable Poems of the Sea,* and James Stevenson's *Clams Can't Sing.* SEASHORE–POETRY.

1866   Maestro, Giulio. *Razzle-Dazzle Riddles.* **Illus. by the author. Clarion, 1985. ISBN 0-89919-382-X**

[unp., Gr. Pre–3] "Why did the bookworm have an upset stomach? . . . He couldn't digest all the facts." One riddle per page with gleeful illustrations. More fodder for the easy-reader set includes the companion book *Riddle Romp* (1983), David A. Adler's *The Carsick Zebra*, Marc Brown's *Spooky Riddles*, Bennett Cerf's *Bennett Cerf's Book of Riddles*, Katy Hall and Lisa Eisenberg's *Buggy Riddles*, Joseph Rosenbloom's *The Funniest Riddle Book Ever*, and Alvin Schwartz's *Ten Copycats in a Boat*. RIDDLES. WORD GAMES.

1867   Margolis, Richard J. *Secrets of a Small Brother.* **Illus. by Donald Carrick. Macmillan, 1984. ISBN 0-02-762280-0**

[unp., Gr. 1–4] Perceptive, unrhyming poem-thoughts of a younger brother about his older brother. Read this book straight through like a storybook. Children will be sparked to write about their own sibling trials and joys. BROTHERS—POETRY. POETRY —SINGLE AUTHOR. SIBLING RIVALRY—POETRY.

1868   Merriam, Eve. *Blackberry Ink.* **Illus. by Hans Wilhelm. Morrow, 1985. ISBN 0-688-04150-7**

[unp., Gr. Pre–2] Twenty-three light and silly verses for chanting and fooling. Read an assortment of Merriam's poetry, as well as her *Catch a Little Rhyme* (Atheneum, 1966). HUMOROUS POETRY. POETRY—SINGLE AUTHOR.

1869   Merriam, Eve. *Chortles: New and Selected Wordplay Poems.* **Illus. by Sheila Hamanaka. Morrow, 1989. ISBN 0-688-08152-5**

[53p., Gr. 3–6] Puns, noises, word juggling, and fooling invade each of these almost 50 poems. Roy Doty's riddle books, along with Norton Juster's novel *The Phantom Tollbooth*, Paul M. Levitt's vocabulary pun stories in *The Weighty Word Book*, and the language books by Marvin Terban all go a long way toward developing one's sense of the absurd. ENGLISH LANGUAGE. POETRY—SINGLE AUTHOR. VOCABULARY. WORD GAMES.

1870   Merriam, Eve. *A Poem for a Pickle: Funnybone Verses.* **Illus. by Sheila Hamanaka. Morrow, 1989.**

[unp., Gr. K–4] These 28 short, simple rhymes read like Mother Goose at times, though they are much more hip. Also see collections by John Ciardi, X. J. Kennedy, Dennis Lee, and Lois Simmie's *Auntie's Knitting a Baby*. HUMOROUS POETRY. POETRY—SINGLE AUTHOR.

1871   Merriam, Eve. *You Be Good & I'll Be Night: Jump-on-the-Bed Poems.* **Illus. by Karen Lee Schmidt. Morrow, 1988. ISBN 0-688-06743-3**

[unp., Gr. Pre–1] More than 24 simple, nonsense-filled rhymes, ideal for call and response and charmingly illustrated with pigs, mice, and other rhythm-loving animals. BEDTIME—POETRY. POETRY—SINGLE AUTHOR.

1872   Milne, A. A. *Now We Are Six.* **Illus. by Ernest H. Shepard. Dutton, 1988. ISBN 0-525-44446-7**

[102p., Gr. Pre–3] This classic, originally published in 1927, along with its companion, *When We Were Very Young* (1924), is a book of poems of Pooh and Christopher Robin and their friends. Read along with *The House at Pooh Corner* and *Winnie-the-Pooh*. HUMOROUS POETRY. POETRY—SINGLE AUTHOR.

1873   Mizamura, Kazue. *Flower Moon Snow: A Book of Haiku*. Illus. by the author. Crowell, 1977. ISBN 0-690-01291-8

[unp., Gr. 2–6] Thirty delicate nature haiku with accompanying brown and black-and-white woodblock prints. NATURE–POETRY. POETRY–SINGLE AUTHOR. SEASONS –POETRY.

1874   Moore, Lilian, comp. *Go with the Poem*. McGraw-Hill, 1979. ISBN 0-07-042880-8

[125p., Gr. 3–6] An unforgettable collection of fascinating introspective verse, mostly unrhyming, by more than 50 twentieth-century poets. POETRY–ANTHOLOGIES.

1875   Moore, Lilian, comp. *See My Lovely Poison Ivy: And Other Verses about Witches, Ghosts and Things*. Illus. by Diane Dawson. Atheneum, 1979.

[42p., Gr. K–3] A treat for Halloween, Friday the 13th, and other dark days. Not as frightening, but in the same vein as Jack Prelutsky's *Nightmares: Poems to Trouble Your Sleep*. HALLOWEEN–POETRY.

1876   Morley, Diana. *Marms in the Marmalade*. Illus. by Kathy Rogers. Carolrhoda, 1984. ISBN 0-87614-258-7

[24p., Gr. 1–4] A rhyming jam session for words within words and how they sometimes make sense and sometimes don't. Your class will surely come up with new examples, which they can illustrate. CREATIVE WRITING. ENGLISH LANGUAGE. STORIES IN RHYME. VOCABULARY.

1877   Morrison, Lillian, comp. *Best Wishes, Amen*. Illus. by Loretta Lustig. Crowell, 1974. ISBN 0-690-00579-2

[195p., Gr. 2–6] A useful handbook of time-honored rhymes and sayings to write in autograph books. Also look for the companion book, *Yours Till Niagara Falls* (1950). HUMOROUS POETRY.

1878   Mother Goose. *Cakes and Custard*. Illus. by Helen Oxenbury. Compiled by Brian Alderson. Morrow, 1975.

[156p., Gr. Pre–1] A large luscious collection of over 150 mostly English traditional children's nursery and playground rhymes. Issued in a slightly bigger format, with the illustrations reproduced larger and darker is Alderson's *The Helen Oxenbury Nursery Rhyme Book* (Morrow, 1987), which consists of 60 rhymes distilled from this book. There are many magnificent collections of nursery rhymes so it is hard to decide which ones to use. Select several collections at one time, comparing illustrations, dipping into each volume for a sampling of whimsy, reciting well-known versions in unison, and digging up lesser-known tales to learn and repeat again and again. One can never read too much Mother Goose. Additional nursery rhyme books, not necessarily Mother Goose rhymes, are scattered through this chapter and are equally marvelous, including N. M. Bodecker's Danish *"It's Raining," Said John Twaining*, Demi's Chinese *Dragon Kites and Dragon Flies*, Dennis Lee's original *Jelly Belly*, Arnold Lobel's original *Whiskers & Rhymes*, and Clyde Watson's *Father Fox's Pennyrhymes*. NURSERY RHYMES.

1879   Mother Goose. *The Glorious Mother Goose*. Illus. by Cooper Edens. Compiled by Cooper Edens. Atheneum, 1988. ISBN 0-689-31434-5

[88p., Gr. Pre–2] Over 40 of the best-known nursery rhymes, printed one per double page, each of which includes a black-and-white and a color illustration from well-known artists of the last quarter of the nineteenth century up to the first quarter of the twentieth century. NURSERY RHYMES.

1880   **Mother Goose.** *Granfa' Grig Had a Pig: And Other Rhymes without Reason from Mother Goose.* **Illus. by Wallace Tripp. Compiled by Wallace Tripp. Little, Brown, 1976. ISBN 0-316-85282-1**

[96p., Gr. Pre–4] A sparkling frolic through nursery rhymes both known and obscure. For additional poems and captivating illustrations see Wallace Tripp's companion volumes, *A Great Big Ugly Man Came Up and Tied His Horse to Me* and *Marguerite, Go Wash Your Feet* (Houghton Mifflin, 1985). NONSENSE VERSES. NURSERY RHYMES.

1881   **Mother Goose.** *Gray Goose and Gander: And Other Mother Goose Rhymes.* **Illus. by Anne Rockwell. Compiled by Anne Rockwell. Crowell, 1980. ISBN 0-690-04048-2**

[64p., Gr. Pre–1] Cheerful watercolors illuminate over 48 easy-to-read nursery rhymes. NURSERY RHYMES.

1882   **Mother Goose.** *Gregory Griggs: And Other Nursery Rhyme People.* **Illus. by Arnold Lobel. Compiled by Arnold Lobel. Macmillan, 1987. ISBN 0-688-07042-6**

[48p., Gr. Pre–2] Close to 36 lesser-known but not-to-be-missed gems of maids and men, with the usual marvelous full-page watercolors. Other obscure nursery rhymes can be found in Iona and Peter Opie's *Tail Feathers from Mother Goose.* NURSERY RHYMES.

1883   **Mother Goose.** *James Marshall's Mother Goose.* **Illus. by James Marshall. Compiled by James Marshall. Farrar, 1986. ISBN 0-374-43723-8**

[unp., Gr. Pre–2] Thirty-four tried-and-trues filled with Marshall's dizzy comic creatures. NURSERY RHYMES.

1884   **Mother Goose.** *Mother Goose: A Collection of Classic Nursery Rhymes.* **Illus. by Michael Hague. Compiled by Michael Hague. Henry Holt, 1984. ISBN 0-8050-0214-6**

[61p., Gr. Pre–1] In picture book format with one large elegant painting per rhyme. NURSERY RHYMES.

1885   **Mother Goose.** *The Mother Goose Treasury.* **Illus. by Raymond Briggs. Compiled by Raymond Briggs. Dell, 1986. ISBN 0-440-46408-0**

[220p., Gr. Pre–2] A huge classic collection of over 400 rhymes taken from Iona and Peter Opie's compilations. NURSERY RHYMES.

1886   **Mother Goose.** *Over the Moon: A Book of Nursery Rhymes.* **Illus. by Charlotte Voake. Compiled by Charlotte Voake. Clarkson N. Potter, 1985. ISBN 0-517-55873-4**

[121p., Gr. Pre–2] More than 100 attractively illustrated children's chants and rhymes. NURSERY RHYMES.

1887   **Mother Goose.** *The Random House Book of Mother Goose.* **Illus. by Arnold Lobel. Compiled by Arnold Lobel. Random House, 1986. ISBN 0-394-86799-8**

[176p., Gr. Pre–2] A visual feast with over 500 rhymes. NURSERY RHYMES.

1888   Mother Goose. *The Real Mother Goose.* Illus. Rand, 1916. ISBN 0-528-82322-1

[128p., Gr. Pre–1] A grand oversized classic collection of more than 200 nursery rhymes with the original illustrations. NURSERY RHYMES.

1889   Mother Goose. *Richard Scarry's Best Mother Goose Ever.* Illus. by Richard Scarry. Compiled by Richard Scarry. Western, 1970. ISBN 0-307-15578-1

[94p., Gr. Pre–1] Large, boisterous double-page spreads enfold each of 50 rhymes. NURSERY RHYMES.

1890   Mother Goose. *Songs from Mother Goose: With the Traditional Melody for Each.* Illus. by Robin Spowart. Compiled by Nancy Larrick. Harper & Row, 1989. ISBN 0-06-023713-9

[70p., Gr. Pre–2] Now you can sing as well as chant these 56 rhymes laid out in a large, pleasant lap book just right for sharing. NURSERY RHYMES. SONGBOOKS.

1891   Mother Goose. *Tail Feathers from Mother Goose: The Opie Rhyme Book.* Compiled by Iona Opie and Peter Opie. Illus. Little, Brown, 1988. ISBN 0-316-65081-1

[124p., Gr. Pre–3] An exquisite, useful, and eclectic compilation of over 60 mostly lesser-known rhymes and other ditties to be sung, recited, chanted, and whispered, illustrated enchantingly by 60 well-known mostly English artists. Arnold Lobel's *Gregory Griggs and Other Nursery Rhyme People* also contains the more obscure selections. NURSERY RHYMES.

1892   Mother Goose. *Tomie dePaola's Mother Goose.* Illus. by Tomie dePaola. Compiled by Tomie dePaola. Putnam, 1985. ISBN 0-399-21258-2

[127p., Gr. Pre–2] Almost 200 rhymes with dePaola's trademark of large, cheery paintings. NURSERY RHYMES.

1893   Nash, Ogden. *Custard and Company.* Illus. by Quentin Blake. Little, Brown, 1980.

[128p., Gr. 3–6] Seven dozen captivatingly funny word-played rhymes about animals and people, accompanied by Blake's whimsical scratches. HUMOROUS POETRY. NONSENSE VERSES. POETRY–SINGLE AUTHOR.

1894   Nelson, Esther L. *The Funny Song Book.* Illus. by Joyce Behr. Sterling, 1984. ISBN 0-8069-4682-2

[96p., Gr. Pre–6] One of an indispensable series filled with wild and crazy songs with over 60 selections per book. The series also includes *The Fun to Sing Song Book* (1986), *The Great Rounds Song Book* (1985), and *The Silly Song Book* (1981). Another splendid favorite is Marie Winn's *The Fireside Book of Fun and Game Songs.* FOLK SONGS. HUMOROUS SONGS. SONGBOOKS.

1895   Ness, Evaline, comp. *Amelia Mixed the Mustard and Other Poems.* Illus. by the author. Scribner, 1975.

[47p., Gr. 2–5] A collection of 20 celebratory poems about independent-minded females of all ages and types. WOMEN–POETRY.

1896   Nevins, Ann. *From the Horse's Mouth.* Illus. by Dan Nevins. Prentice Hall, 1977.

[119p., Gr. 3–6] An alphabetical listing of over 100 idiomatic expressions along with short descriptions of their meanings. James A. Cox gives more detail but fewer phrases in *Put Your Foot in Your Mouth* and Marvin Terban's *In a Pickle and Other Funny Idioms* and *Mad As a Wet Hen! and Other Funny Idioms* are also valuable. Using a combination of these texts, students can research the origins of popular sayings and report back, demonstrate, or act out skits on their findings for the rest of the class. ENGLISH LANGUAGE–IDIOMS. VOCABULARY.

1897 **O'Neill, Mary L.** *Hailstones and Halibut Bones: Adventures in Color.* **Illus. by John Wallner. Doubleday, 1989. ISBN 0-385-24484-3**

[59p., Gr. Pre–3] Originally published in 1961, this edition is newly illustrated, with one perceptive poem for each of 12 colors, delving into those objects, feelings, and surroundings that depend on that color. For younger children intersperse the poems with color-empathetic titles such as Lois Ehlert's *Color Zoo*, Arnold Lobel's *The Great Blueness*, or Charlotte Zolotow's *Mr. Rabbit and the Lovely Present.* COLOR –POETRY.

1898 **O'Neill, Mary L.** *What Is That Sound!* **Illus. by Lois Ehlert. Atheneum, 1966.**

[54p., Gr. 2–5] Poems about the noises in our lives. Make sound-effects tapes to accompany the poems of your choice. POETRY–SINGLE AUTHOR. SOUND EFFECTS–POETRY.

1899 **Peck, Robert Newton.** *Bee Tree and Other Stuff.* **Illus. by Laura Lydecker. Walker, 1975.**

[118p., Gr. 4–6] Poems and commentary of a Vermont farm childhood, by the author of the autobiographical "Soup" series. FARM LIFE–POETRY. POETRY–SINGLE AUTHOR.

1900 **Phillips, Louis.** *How Do You Get a Horse Out of the Bathtub? Profound Answers to Preposterous Questions.* **Illus. by James Stevenson. Viking, 1983. ISBN 0-670-38119-5**

[71p., Gr. 5–6] Hundreds of punny answers, once again proving the "Ask a silly question . . ." statement. You will often need to explain the punch line or give students enough time to figure it out. When the students begin to catch on, see if they can write their answers to some of the questions and try them on each other. CREATIVE WRITING. JOKES. WORD GAMES.

1901 **Phillips, Louis.** *The Upside Down Riddle Book.* **Illus. by Beau Gardner. Lothrop, 1982. ISBN 0-688-00931-X**

[unp., Gr. K–2] Turn the book upside down to see the answer to each poem-riddle in brightly colored graphics. RIDDLES.

1902 **Pomerantz, Charlotte.** *If I Had a Paka.* **Illus. by Nancy Tafuri. Greenwillow, 1981. ISBN 0-688-00837-2**

[unp., Gr. K–4] Twelve brightly illustrated chantable poems using words from 11 different languages. If you supply your students with a list of key words translated into French or Spanish they can compose their own chantable poems. LANGUAGE–POETRY. POETRY–SINGLE AUTHOR.

1903 **Pooley, Sarah, comp.** *A Day of Rhymes.* **Illus. by the author. Knopf, 1988. ISBN 0-394-99497-3**

[75p., Gr. Pre–1] From Mother Goose to modern, 61 fingerplays and nursery rhymes for early morning until bedtime. Cheery, detailed shiny illustrations give visual directions for acting out. See also Marc Brown's collections of similar rhymes. FINGERPLAYS. NURSERY RHYMES.

1904 **Prelutsky, Jack.** *The Baby Uggs Are Hatching.* **Illus. by James Stevenson. Greenwillow, 1982. ISBN 0-688-00922-0**

[32p., Gr. K–4] These invented creepy crawlers go right along with those in Prelutsky's *The Snopp on the Sidewalk*. Hatch up an original rhyming batch using Arnold Lobel's *The Ice Cream Cone Coot and Other Rare Birds* and Bill Peet's *No Such Things* for additional inspiration. If you relish a galloping rhyme, sprinkled with wit, mishap, and glee, don't miss the genius of Prelutsky. Poems of holidays, horrifiers, and undefinable creatures skulk through the pages of his numerous collections, waiting to be intoned, burbled, and sung by each unsuspecting browser. ANIMALS, IMAGINARY–POETRY. HUMOROUS POETRY. NONSENSE VERSES.

1905   Prelutsky, Jack. *It's Christmas.* Illus. by Marylin Hafner. Greenwillow, 1981. ISBN 0-688-00439-3

[47p., Gr. Pre–3] The holidays will not be complete without these read-alone format collections, each containing 12 poems from a child's point of view, including Prelutsky's *It's Halloween, It's Thanksgiving,* and *It's Valentine's Day.* Don't bother picking and choosing separate poems; read each book aloud from start to finish. CHRISTMAS–POETRY.

1906   Prelutsky, Jack. *It's Halloween.* Illus. by Marylin Hafner. Greenwillow, 1977. ISBN 0-688-80102-1

[56p., Gr. Pre–3] From carving out the pumpkin to bobbing for apples these 12 poems encompass typical trick-or-treat experiences. Search out additional seasonal poems in John E. Brewton's *In the Witch's Kitchen* and in Lilian Moore's *See My Lovely Poison Ivy.* HALLOWEEN–POETRY.

1907   Prelutsky, Jack. *It's Snowing! It's Snowing!* Illus. by Jeanne Titherington. Greenwillow, 1984. ISBN 0-688-01512-3

[47p., Gr. Pre–3] When the flakes start to fall, take out this child-centered group of 17 poems and then drift into picture books with Virginia Lee Burton's *Katy and the Big Snow,* Ezra Jack Keats's *The Snowy Day,* Florence Slobodkin's *Too Many Mittens,* Harriet Ziefert's *Snow Magic,* and Charlotte Zolotow's *Something Is Going to Happen.* SEASONS–POETRY. SNOW–POETRY. WINTER–POETRY.

1908   Prelutsky, Jack. *It's Thanksgiving.* Illus. by Marylin Hafner. Greenwillow, 1982. ISBN 0-688-00442-3

[47p., Gr. Pre–3] Read this lighthearted group of poems with Steven Kroll's story *Oh, What a Thanksgiving* and Eileen Spinelli's *Thanksgiving at the Tappletons'* for starters. THANKSGIVING–POETRY.

1909   Prelutsky, Jack. *It's Valentine's Day.* Illus. by Yossi Abolafia. Greenwillow, 1983. ISBN 0-688-02312-6

[47p., Gr. Pre–3] Fourteen child-narrated rhymers for all aspects of the holiday. Read along with a picture book or two such as Eve Bunting's *The Valentine Bears,* Nancy L. Carlson's *Louanne Pig in the Mysterious Valentine,* Lillian Hoban's *Arthur's Great Big Valentine,* Frank Modell's *One Zillion Valentines,* Marjorie Weinman Sharmat's *The Best Valentine in the World,* and James Stevenson's *Happy Valentine's Day, Emma!* VALENTINE'S DAY–POETRY.

1910   Prelutsky, Jack. *My Parents Think I'm Sleeping.* Illus. by Yossi Abolafia. Greenwillow, 1985. ISBN 0-688-04018-7

[47p., Gr. Pre–3] A bedtime book of poems for the wide-awake. Children can elaborate on their personal sleep-inducing remedies after reading several related stories such as Felicia Bond's *Poinsettia and the Firefighters*, Bernie and Mati Karlin's *Night Ride*, Tom Paxton's *Jennifer's Rabbit*, Marjorie Weinman Sharmat's *Go to Sleep, Nicholas Joe*, and Bernard Waber's *Ira Sleeps Over*. BEDTIME–POETRY. SLEEP–POETRY.

1911   Prelutsky, Jack. *The New Kid on the Block*. Illus. by James Stevenson. Greenwillow, 1984. ISBN 0-688-02271-5

[159p., Gr. K–5] More than 100 of the funniest poems ever and an indispensable addition to the shelves for all poetry lovers. This one, along with Shel Silverstein's *A Light in the Attic* and *Where the Sidewalk Ends* and Judith Viorst's *If I Were in Charge of the World*, is guaranteed to turn the most rabid poetry-loathers into fans. HUMOROUS POETRY. NONSENSE VERSES. POETRY–SINGLE AUTHOR.

1912   Prelutsky, Jack. *Nightmares: Poems to Trouble Your Sleep*. Illus. by Arnold Lobel. Greenwillow, 1976. ISBN 0-688-80053-X

[38p., Gr. 3–6] Chilling descriptions of 12 odious mythical beings from bogeyman to ghoul. Keep up the suspense with Sara and John E. Brewton's collection, *Shrieks at Midnight* and Lee Bennett Hopkins's more benign *Creatures*. HALLOWEEN–POETRY. POETRY–SINGLE AUTHOR. SUPERNATURAL–POETRY. SUSPENSE–POETRY.

1913   Prelutsky, Jack, comp. *Poems of A. Nonny Mouse*. Illus. by Henrik Drescher. Knopf, 1989. ISBN 0-394-98711-X

[unp., Gr. K–4] Remember all those poems by Anonymous? According to compiler Prelutsky, they were all actually composed by one A. Nonny Mouse, a charming and clever rodent whose name was misspelled many years back by a publisher who subsequently ignored her efforts to set the record straight. Many of her well-known ditties are included here, and you will doubtless find more in other collections of humorous poetry and nursery rhymes such as Wallace Tripp's *A Great Big Ugly Man Came Up and Tied His Horse to Me*. HUMOROUS POETRY. NONSENSE VERSES.

1914   Prelutsky, Jack. *The Queen of Eene*. Illus. by Victoria Chess. Greenwillow, 1978. ISBN 0-688-80144-7

[32p., Gr. 2–4] A poetry assortment describing 14 odd humans. Pair these with Prelutsky's *The Sheriff of Rottenshot* for introducing odd characters. Children can each pick one favorite character about whom they can write new stories. HUMOROUS POETRY. POETRY–SINGLE AUTHOR.

1915   Prelutsky, Jack. *Rainy Rainy Saturday*. Illus. by Marylin Hafner. Greenwillow, 1980. ISBN 0-688-80252-4

[47p., Gr. K–2] Fourteen more first-person poems in read-alone format of what kids do on a no-school, bad-weather day. Also read Bill Martin, Jr., and John Archambault's *Listen to the Rain* and Audrey Wood's rainy day cumulative story *The Napping House*. RAIN AND RAINFALL–POETRY. WEATHER–POETRY.

1916   Prelutsky, Jack, comp. *The Random House Book of Poetry for Children*. Illus. by Arnold Lobel. Random House, 1983. ISBN 0-394-85010-6

[248p., Gr. 1–5] Sample and mosey your way through this treasury of over 500 poems, divided into general sections such as nature, seasons, living things, cities, and children. As grand a group as the older standards: May Hill Arbuthnot's *Time for Poetry*, Nancy Larrick's *Piping Down the Valleys Wild*, and Louis Untermeyer's

The Golden Treasury of Poetry. More subdued but also nice is Joanna Cole's *A New Treasury of Children's Poetry.* POETRY—ANTHOLOGIES.

1917   **Prelutsky, Jack, ed.** *Read-Aloud Rhymes for the Very Young.* **Illus. by Marc Brown. Knopf, 1986. ISBN 0-394-97218-X**

[97p., Gr. Pre–3] The oversized format and cheery, huge colored-pencil illustrations make this assemblage of more than 200 short assorted poems sparkle. Pair with Beatrice Schenk de Regniers's *Sing a Song of Popcorn: Every Child's Book of Poems* and *Tomie dePaola's Book of Poems.* POETRY—ANTHOLOGIES.

1918   **Prelutsky, Jack.** *Ride a Purple Pelican.* **Illus. by Garth Williams. Greenwillow, 1986. ISBN 0-688-04031-4**

[64p., Gr. Pre–2] From Seattle to New York, the more than 24 chantable snippets of nursery rhymelike poems are filled with people and animals from all over the United States and Canada. The large format and simply glorious full-color paintings cry out for a large audience, along with the usual Mother Goose, Dennis Lee's *Jelly Belly,* and Clyde Watson's *Father Fox's Pennyrhymes.* NONSENSE VERSES. NURSERY RHYMES. POETRY—SINGLE AUTHOR.

1919   **Prelutsky, Jack.** *Rolling Harvey Down the Hill.* **Illus. by Victoria Chess. Greenwillow, 1980. ISBN 0-688-80258-3**

[31p., Gr. 2–4] Fifteen poems of friendship by a nameless narrator, who describes his gang of five—flaws and all—and the fun they have together. Read the whole book straight through. Also see *Best Friends,* collected by Lee Bennett Hopkins. FRIENDSHIP—POETRY. HUMOROUS POETRY.

1920   **Prelutsky, Jack.** *The Sheriff of Rottenshot.* **Illus. by Victoria Chess. Greenwillow, 1982. ISBN 0-688-00205-6**

[32p., Gr. 2–4] Goofy humans and animals amble through 16 rib-tweaking poems. Prelutsky's *The Baby Uggs Are Hatching, The Queen of Eene,* and *The Snopp on the Sidewalk* are companion pieces. HUMOROUS POETRY. POETRY—SINGLE AUTHOR.

1921   **Prelutsky, Jack.** *The Snopp on the Sidewalk and Other Poems.* **Illus. by Byron Barton. Greenwillow, 1977. ISBN 0-688-84084-1**

[unp., Gr. K–3] More weird invented animal poems to read along with Prelutsky's *The Baby Uggs Are Hatching, The Queen of Eene,* and *The Sheriff of Rottenshot.* ANIMALS, IMAGINARY—POETRY. POETRY—SINGLE AUTHOR.

1922   **Prelutsky, Jack.** *Tyrannosaurus Was a Beast.* **Illus. by Arnold Lobel. Greenwillow, 1988. ISBN 0-688-06442-6**

[31p., Gr. 1–6] Fourteen limber, literate poems about dinosaurs, each kind with its own spellbinding full-page watercolor illustration. Use the eye-catching table of contents to introduce each poem. Do not wait for the curriculum to require these; dinosaurs are beloved at every level. Read William Cole's *Dinosaurs and Beasts of Yore* and Lee Bennett Hopkins's *Dinosaurs* as well as stories such as Carol Carrick's *Patrick's Dinosaurs* and *What Happened to Patrick's Dinosaurs?,* Steven Kellogg's *Prehistoric Pinkerton,* and Hudson Talbott's *We're Back.* Throw some books of facts in, such as Patricia Lauber's exquisite *The News about Dinosaurs.* DINOSAURS—POETRY.

1923   **Prelutsky, Jack.** *What I Did Last Summer.* **Illus. by Yossi Abolafia. Greenwillow, 1984.**

[47p., Gr. K–3] In easy-to-read format, these 13 poems cover the end of June to the first day back at school from one young boy's point of view. Read the first week back, along with a few start-the-year stories such as James Howe's *The Day the Teacher Went Bananas*, James Marshall's *The Cut-Ups*, and Amy Schwartz's *Annabelle Swift, Kindergartner*. Older children can write summer vacation events in rhyme. SEASONS–POETRY. SUMMER–POETRY.

1924   **Prelutsky, Jack.** *Zoo Doings.* **Illus. by Paul O. Zelinsky. Greenwillow, 1983.**

[79p., Gr. K–4] Included are all the animal poems from Prelutsky's first three books: *A Gopher in the Garden*, *The Pack Rat's Day*, and *Toucans Two*. Two fine and funny collections of animal poems are Stephanie Calmenson's *Never Take a Pig to Lunch* and William Cole's *I Went to the Animal Fair*. ANIMALS–POETRY. POETRY–SINGLE AUTHOR.

1925   **Quackenbush, Robert, comp.** *The Holiday Songbook.* **Illus. by the author. Lothrop, 1977.**

[128p., Gr. Pre–5] One hundred songs, many old standards, for 27 holidays include a brief one-page commentary for each holiday, plus piano music and guitar chords. Myra Cohn Livingston has assembled two collections of holiday poems as well: *Callooh! Callay!* and *Celebrations* (Holiday House, 1985). HOLIDAYS–SONGS. SONGBOOKS.

1926   **Raffi.** *The Raffi Singable Songbook: A Collection of 51 Songs from Raffi's First Three Records for Young Children.* **Illus. by Joyce Yamomoto. Crown, 1987. ISBN 0-517-56638-9**

[106p., Gr. Pre–2] If you or your students have never heard or seen the mellow-voiced Canadian singer Raffi, rush out to your record store and buy his records and /or videos to add to your Hap Palmer/Ella Jenkins/Pete Seeger collection. The spiral-bound songbook, along with *The Second Raffi Songbook: 42 Songs from Raffi's Albums—Baby Beluga; Rise and Shine;* and *One Light, One Sun* (1986), includes words, simple music, and guitar chords. FOLK SONGS. SONGBOOKS.

1927   **Rosenbloom, Joseph.** *Daffy Definitions.* **Illus. by Joyce Behr. Sterling, 1983.**

[128p., Gr. 4–6] A dictionary of puns and wordplays, to which your jokers can add new words and meanings while expanding their regular vocabularies. For additional nonsense read riddle books such as Charles Keller's *Remember the à la Mode* and anything by Roy Doty. CREATIVE WRITING. DICTIONARIES. JOKES. WORD GAMES.

1928   **Rosenbloom, Joseph.** *The Funniest Dinosaur Book Ever.* **Illus. by Hans Wilhelm. Sterling, 1987. ISBN 0-8069-6625-4**

[unp., Gr. Pre–3] Easy to read and with good-natured watercolors, these riddles can be used to introduce dinosaur poetry, fiction, or fact, as in Jack Prelutsky's *Tyrannosaurus Was a Beast*, Carol Carrick's *What Happened to Patrick's Dinosaurs?*, and Patricia Lauber's *The News about Dinosaurs*, respectively. DINOSAURS–RIDDLES. RIDDLES.

1929   **Rosenbloom, Joseph.** *The Funniest Knock-Knock Book Ever!* **Illus. by Hans Wilhelm. Sterling, 1987. ISBN 0-8069-4759-4**

[unp., Gr. Pre–3] An easier collection to which you can add Charles Keller's *Norma Lee I Don't Knock on Doors* and Rosenbloom's *Dr. Knock-Knock's Official Knock-Knock Dictionary* (1976) and *Knock Knock! Who's There?* JOKES. KNOCK-KNOCK JOKES.

1930 Rosenbloom, Joseph. *The Funniest Riddle Book Ever!* Illus. by Hans Wilhelm. Sterling, 1985. ISBN 0-8069-4699-7

[unp., Gr. Pre–3] Simple riddles indeed. Also try David A. Adler's *The Carsick Zebra*, Marc Brown's *Spooky Riddles*, Bennett Cerf's *Bennett Cerf's Book of Riddles*, Giulio Maestro's *Razzle-Dazzle Riddles*, and Alvin Schwartz's *Ten Copycats in a Boat*. RIDDLES.

1931 Rosenbloom, Joseph, comp. *The Gigantic Joke Book*. Illus. by Joyce Behr. Sterling, 1981. ISBN 0-8069-4591-5

[256p., Gr. 3–6] Comedy routines for pairs. Also try Gyles Brandreth's *The Super Joke Book*, Syd Hoff's *Syd Hoff's Joke Book*, and Charles Keller's *School Daze*. JOKES.

1932 Rosenbloom, Joseph. *Giggles, Gags & Groaners*. Illus. by Sanford Hoffman. Sterling, 1987. ISBN 0-8069-6447-2

[128p., Gr. 3–6] Rosenbloom's manic collections of jokes, riddles, tongue twisters, rhymes, and other silliness should satisfy even the most demanding nonsense lovers. Pick and choose your favorites from this one plus *Biggest Riddle Book in the World* (1976), *How Do You Make an Elephant Laugh? And 699 Other Zany Riddles* (1979), *Laughs, Hoots & Giggles* (1984), and *The Zaniest Riddle Book in the World* (1984). JOKES. RIDDLES.

1933 Rosenbloom, Joseph. *Knock Knock! Who's There?* Illus. by Sanford Hoffman. Sterling, 1984.

[128p., Gr. 3–6] Still more knock-knock jokes from the man who brought you *Dr. Knock-Knock's Official Knock-Knock Dictionary* (1976) and *The Funniest Knock-Knock Book Ever*, to which you may add Charles Keller's *Norma Lee I Don't Knock on Doors*. JOKES. KNOCK-KNOCK JOKES.

1934 Rosenbloom, Joseph. *The Looniest Limerick Book in the World*. Illus. by Sanford Hoffman. Sterling, 1982.

[128p., Gr. 4–6] Lots of limericks. See also N. M. Bodecker's *A Person from Britain Whose Head Was the Shape of a Mitten*, John Brewton's *They've Discovered a Head in the Box for the Bread*, John Ciardi's *The Hopeful Trout and Other Limericks*, Edward Lear's *How Pleasant to Know Mr. Lear!*, and Arnold Lobel's *The Book of Pigericks*. HUMOROUS POETRY. LIMERICKS.

1935 Rosenbloom, Joseph, comp. *Monster Madness: Riddles, Jokes, Fun*. Illus. by Joyce Behr. Sterling, 1980. ISBN 0-8069-4635-0

[127p., Gr. 3–6] Incorporate this with fiction such as Bruce Coville's *The Monster's Ring*, folklore collections such as Ruth Manning-Sanders's *A Book of Monsters*, and poetry such as Lee Bennett Hopkins's *Creatures* or Jack Prelutsky's *Nightmares*. Also see Charles Keller's *Count Draculations! Monster Riddles* and Rosenbloom's *Spooky Riddles and Jokes*. MONSTERS–RIDDLES. RIDDLES.

1936 Rosenbloom, Joseph, comp. *Silly Verse (and Even Worse)*. Illus. by Joyce Behr. Sterling, 1979.

[128p., Gr. 3–6] Short anonymous limericks, couplets, and other doggerel. The chapter on "Modern Nursery Rhymes" might spawn new ones from your students. HUMOROUS POETRY. LIMERICKS. NONSENSE VERSES.

1937   **Rosenbloom, Joseph.** *Spooky Riddles and Jokes.* **Illus. by Sanford Hoffman. Sterling, 1987. ISBN 0-8069-6577-0**

[128p., Gr. 2–6] This book includes a "spooky bestsellers" list of invented titles and authors to use when making up catalog cards or teaching the parts of a book, including *Screams in the Dark* by I. C. Fingers and *The Haunted House* by Terry Fide. Charles Keller's *Count Draculations! Monster Riddles* and Rosenbloom's *Monster Madness: Riddles, Jokes, Fun* will add to the ghoulish merriment, along with horror tales from Maria Leach's *The Thing at the Foot of the Bed* and Alvin Schwartz's *Scary Stories to Tell in the Dark*. HALLOWEEN–RIDDLES. JOKES. RIDDLES. SUPERNATURAL–RIDDLES.

1938   **Rosenbloom, Joseph, comp.** *Twist These on Your Tongue.* **Illus. by Joyce Behr. Lodestar Books, 1978. ISBN 0-525-66612-5**

[91p., Gr. 3–6] A more challenging alphabetical collection. Other good ones include Rosenbloom's *The World's Toughest Tongue Twisters* (Sterling, 1986), Gyles Brandreth's *The Biggest Tongue Twister Book in the World*, Marcia Brown's *Peter Piper's Alphabet*, Foley Curtis's *The Little Book of Big Tongue Twisters*, and Alvin Schwartz's *A Twister of Twists, a Tangler of Tongues*. ALLITERATION. TONGUE TWISTERS.

1939   **Rosenbloom, Joseph.** *The World's Best Sports Riddles and Jokes.* **Illus. by Sanford Hoffman. Sterling, 1988. ISBN 0-8069-6736-6**

[128p., Gr. 2–6] Let the gym teacher know about this book and Rosenbloom's *Sports Riddles* (1982). RIDDLES. SPORTS–RIDDLES.

1940   **Russo, Susan, comp.** *The Ice Cream Ocean and Other Delectable Poems of the Sea.* **Illus. by the author. Lothrop, 1984.**

[39p., Gr. Pre–3] Bright jelly bean-colored illustrations splash across the pages of 20 appealing water-based poems. Read with Katy Hall and Lisa Eisenberg's *Fishy Riddles* (Dial, 1986) and sea-centered fiction such as Leo Lionni's *Swimmy*, Ken Robbins's *Beach Day*, or Bernard Waber's *I Was All Thumbs*. OCEAN–POETRY.

1941   **Rylant, Cynthia.** *Waiting to Waltz: A Childhood.* **Illus. by Stephen Gammell. Bradbury, 1984. ISBN 0-02-778000-7**

[45p., Gr. 5–6] Thirty-one poignant slice-of-life remembrances, told in free verse, of Rylant's youth in the small town of Beaver, West Virginia. Read this straight through instead of at random. Your students can recall significant events or people in their lives and write their own poetic impressions. BIOGRAPHY. CREATIVE WRITING. POETRY–SINGLE AUTHOR. FAMILY LIFE–POETRY.

1942   **Sandburg, Carl.** *Rainbows Are Made.* **Illus. by Fritz Eichenberg. Harcourt, 1982. ISBN 0-15-265480-1**

[82p., Gr. 5–6] An elegant offering of poetry by the legendary American writer accompanied with distinguished wood engravings. POETRY–SINGLE AUTHOR.

1943   **Saunders, Dennis, comp.** *Magic Lights and Streets of Shining Jet.* **Photos by Terry Williams. Greenwillow, 1974.**

[142p., Gr. 1–4] Categorized into sections of creatures, weather and seasons, colors, and sea and shore; each appealing one-page poem is accompanied with a color photograph on the facing page. POETRY–ANTHOLOGIES.

1944 Schwartz, Alvin. *Busy Buzzing Bumblebees and Other Tongue Twisters.* Illus. by Kathie Abrams. Harper & Row, 1982. ISBN 0-06-025269-3

[63p., Gr. Pre–2] Fun, garish, and easy to read and repeat, with one twister per page. For a slightly tougher challenge, see also Schwartz's *A Twister of Twists, a Tangler of Tongues* and Marcia Brown's *Peter Piper's Alphabet*. ALLITERATION. TONGUE TWISTERS.

1945 Schwartz, Alvin, comp. *The Cat's Elbow and Other Secret Languages.* Illus. by Margot Zemach. Farrar, 1982. ISBN 0-374-41054-2

[82p., Gr. 2–6] How to speak Pig Latin, Iggity, Ku, and other coded languages for those who like to sound mysterious. Untranslated stories, riddles, and rhymes are included as practice problems. Students can put their own writings in code and practice on each other. CODES AND CIPHERS. LANGUAGE. RIDDLES.

1946 Schwartz, Alvin, comp. *Chin Music: Tall Talk and Other Talk, Collected from American Folklore.* Illus. by John O'Brien. Lippincott, 1979. ISBN 0-397-31869-3

[127p., Gr. 3–6] Extend the vocabulary of your pupils by reading from this grand dictionary of colorful folk speech and have yourself a frolicsome time to dream up additional bits of "jawbilation." For more outrageous real vocabulary see Susan Kelz Sperling's *Murfles and Wink-a-Peeps: Funny Old Words for Kids*. ENGLISH LANGUAGE. FOLKLORE–U.S. TALL TALES. VOCABULARY.

1947 Schwartz, Alvin. *I Saw You in the Bathtub and Other Folk Rhymes.* Illus. by Syd Hoff. Harper & Row, 1989. ISBN 0-06-025298-7

[64p., Gr. K–3] More than 36 funny child rhymes and chants, many of which you will recall from your own childhood, in easy-to-read format. Also consult Jill Bennett's *Tiny Tim: Verses for Children* and your children for additional ones. Make a class book of your favorite rhymes. HUMOROUS POETRY. NONSENSE VERSES.

1948 Schwartz, Alvin, comp. *Ten Copycats in a Boat and Other Riddles.* Illus. by Marc Simont. Harper & Row, 1980. ISBN 0-06-025238-3

[63p., Gr. Pre–2] Easy riddles, some from American folklore, one per page, that go along with David A. Adler's *The Carsick Zebra*, Marc Brown's *Spooky Riddles*, Bennett Cerf's *Bennett Cerf's Book of Riddles*, Katy Hall and Lisa Eisenberg's *Buggy Riddles*, Giulio Maestro's *Razzle-Dazzle Riddles*, and Joseph Rosenbloom's *The Funniest Riddle Book Ever*. RIDDLES.

1949 Schwartz, Alvin, comp. *Tomfoolery: Trickery and Foolery with Words.* Illus. by Glen Rounds. Lippincott, 1973. ISBN 0-397-31466-3

[127p., Gr. 1–6] A chuckle-filled volume of poetry, tricks, riddles, jokes, and word games, collected from American folklore, all of which demand to be tried out on unsuspecting students and friends. Just as wonderful are *Flapdoodle: Pure Nonsense from American Folklore* (1980), *Unriddling: All Sorts of Riddles to Puzzle Your Guessery* (1983), and *Witcracks: Jokes and Jests from American Folklore* (1973), all by Schwartz. Also don't miss Duncan Emrich's three massive compendiums, *The Hodgepodge Book*, *The Nonsense Book*, and *The Whim-Wham Book* and Laurence B. White Jr.'s *The Trick Book*. FOLKLORE–U.S. HUMOROUS POETRY. RIDDLES. WORD GAMES.

1950 Schwartz, Alvin, comp. *A Twister of Twists, a Tangler of Tongues.* Illus. by Glen Rounds. Lippincott, 1972. ISBN 0-397-31387-X

[125p., Gr. 2–6] Tie your tongue in knots with "lemon liniment," repeated five times fast, and many more, arranged by subject, even including a section in other languages. See also Gyles Brandreth's *The Biggest Tongue Twister Book in the World*, Foley Curtis's *The Little Book of Big Tongue Twisters*, and Joseph Rosenbloom's *Twist These on Your Tongue*, and *World's Toughest Tongue Twisters* (Sterling, 1986). ALLITERATION. TONGUE TWISTERS.

1951   **Seeger, Ruth Crawford, comp.** *American Folk Songs for Children.* **Illus. by Barbara Cooney. Doubleday, 1980. ISBN 0-385-15788-6**

[190p., Gr. Pre–4] A basic classic collection that includes an excellent guide for parents and teachers on ways to use folk songs with children. Also see the companion volume *Animal Folk Songs for Children* (1950), Engenia Garson's *The Laura Ingalls Wilder Songbook*, Jane Hart's *Singing Bee*, Timothy John's *The Great Song Book*, Nancy and John Langstaff's *Jim Along Josie*, and *Tom Glazer's Treasury of Songs for Children.* ANIMALS–SONGS. FOLK SONGS. SONGBOOKS.

1952   **Silverstein, Shel.** *Where the Sidewalk Ends.* **Illus. by the author. Harper & Row, 1974. ISBN 0-06-025667-2**

[166 p., Gr. Pre–6] Along with *A Light in the Attic* (1981), these are two of the funniest poetry books ever, illustrated with Silverstein's own whimsical line drawings. Read along with Jack Prelutsky's *The New Kid on the Block*, a trio for every teacher's desk. HUMOROUS POETRY. NONSENSE VERSES. POETRY–SINGLE AUTHOR.

1953   **Simmie, Lois.** *Auntie's Knitting a Baby.* **Illus. by Anne Simmie. Orchard, 1988. ISBN 0-531-05762-3**

[70p., Gr. 2–5] With 11 "Auntie" poems running through as a motif, here is an array of 50 catchy rhymes on what it is like to be a child. Fans of N. M. Bodecker, John Ciardi, X. J. Kennedy, Dennis Lee, Jack Prelutsky, Shel Silverstein, and Judith Viorst will all feel right at home. HUMOROUS POETRY. POETRY–SINGLE AUTHOR.

1954   **Singer, Marilyn.** *Turtle in July.* **Illus. by Jerry Pinkney. Macmillan, 1989. ISBN 0-02-782881-6**

[unp., Gr. 1–4] All told from the animals' perspectives are 14 brief, fresh poems spanning the year and the natural world. After spanning the calendar with these, have each student select a new animal, research its habits and habitats, and write four poems—one per season—in that creature's voice. Barbara Esbensen's spare, insightful *Cold Stars and Fireflies: Poems of the Four Seasons* will be appreciated as well. ANIMALS–POETRY. MONTHS–POETRY. SEASONS–POETRY.

1955   **Smith, William Jay.** *Laughing Time: Nonsense Poems.* **Illus. by Fernando Krahn. Delacorte, 1980.**

[116p., Gr. K–3] More than 100 entertaining and silly poems filled with beasts and a nonsense ABC. Also search out similar humorous verse by X. J. Kennedy, Dennis Lee, and Jack Prelutsky. HUMOROUS POETRY. NONSENSE VERSES. POETRY–SINGLE AUTHOR.

1956   **Sperling, Susan Kelz.** *Murfles and Wink-a-Peeps: Funny Old Words for Kids.* **Illus. by Tom Bloom. Clarkson N. Potter, 1985. ISBN 0-517-55659-6**

[1–2 sittings, unp., Gr. 2–6] Over 60 "lost" words like glop, sloomy, and dimpse are presented, along with definitions and sentences showing how they were used in the old days. Alvin Schwartz's *Chin Music* is also full of slang and entertaining lingo from American folklore. ENGLISH LANGUAGE. VOCABULARY.

1957 **Starbird, Kaye.** *The Covered Bridge House and Other Poems.* **Illus. by Jim Arnosky. Four Winds, 1979. ISBN 0-02-786850-8**

[53p., Gr. 3–6] A marvelous assemblage of 35 poems by a gifted poet. POETRY– SINGLE AUTHOR.

1958 **Steckler, Arthur.** *101 More Words and How They Began.* **Illus. by James Flora. Doubleday, 1980.**

[48p., Gr. 3–6] Get out your globe to chart the far-flung origins of many of the words we take for granted about people, food, clothing, and animals. Marvin Terban supplies explanations of additional eponyms in *Guppies in Tuxedos* (Clarion, 1988). ENGLISH LANGUAGE. VOCABULARY.

1959 **Steig, William.** *CDB.* **Illus. by the author. Dutton, 1968.**

[unp., Gr. 2–6] Each line drawing is captioned by a letter, phrase, or sentence written codelike, in sound-out letters. While some are too difficult or sophisticated— especially those in the sequel *CDC* (1984)—others are perfect for children to figure out, such as the one with Aladdin and his "R-A-B-N-G-N-E." Class linguists and cartoonists are bound to think up more examples for all to guess. ALPHABET BOOKS. CREATIVE WRITING. WORD GAMES.

1960 **Swann, Brian.** *A Basket Full of White Eggs.* **Illus. by Ponder Goembel. Orchard, 1988. ISBN 0-531-05734-8**

[32p., Gr. K–3] Fourteen spare riddle-poems from around the globe, each with an entrancing double-page illustration that contains the answer. Also see Ed Young's *High on a Hill: A Book of Chinese Riddles.* RIDDLES.

1961 **Tashjian, Virginia.** *Juba This and Juba That: Story Hour Stretches for Large or Small Groups.* **Illus. by Victoria de Larrea. Little, Brown, 1969. ISBN 0-316-83230-8**

[116p., Gr. Pre–4] A spectacular, indispensable collection of chants, poems, stories to tell, fingerplays, riddles, songs, tongue twisters, and jokes, along with its equally superb follow-up volume, *With a Deep Sea Smile* (1974). Also don't miss Bernice Wells Carlson's *Listen! And Help Tell the Story* and Gloria T. Delamar's *Children's Counting-Out Rhymes.* FINGERPLAYS. NONSENSE. STORYTELLING.

1962 **Terban, Marvin.** *The Dove Dove: Funny Homograph Riddles.* **Illus. by Tom Huffman. Clarion, 1988. ISBN 0-89919-810-4**

[64p., Gr. 3–6] There is no more entertaining way to learn about grammar, parts of speech, idioms, and a general passion for the quirks of the English language than to tease your emerging linguists with Terban's collections of riddles and other world-plays. With these and the riddles in Terban's *Eight Ate: A Feast of Homonym Riddles* (1982) close at hand there is no reason for language lessons to be dull or uninspired. Also challenging are Eve Merriam's *Chortles: New and Selected Wordplay Poems* and, for older punsters, Norton Juster's fantasy *The Phantom Tollbooth.* ENGLISH LAN-GUAGE–HOMONYMS. RIDDLES.

1963 **Terban, Marvin.** *I Think I Thought and Other Tricky Verbs.* **Illus. by Giulio Maestro. Clarion, 1984. ISBN 0-89919-231-9**

[64p., Gr. 2–4] Along with *Your Foot's on My Feet! and Other Tricky Nouns* (1986), this is filled with examples that take the "dull" out of grammar. ENGLISH LANGUAGE–GRAMMAR.

1964   Terban, Marvin. *In a Pickle and Other Funny Idioms*. Illus. by Giulio Maestro. Ticknor & Fields, 1983. ISBN 0-89919-153-3

[64p., Gr. 3–6] Explore the origin and meaning of familiar terms in this book, along with *Mad As a Wet Hen! And Other Funny Idioms* (1987). *Guppies in Tuxedos: Funny Eponyms* (1988), explains common words that originated from the names of people or places. James A. Cox's *Put Your Foot in Your Mouth and Other Silly Sayings* and Fred Gwynne's *A Chocolate Moose for Dinner* and *The King Who Rained* (Dutton, 1970) are also fun. ENGLISH LANGUAGE–IDIOMS. VOCABULARY.

1965   Terban, Marvin. *Too Hot to Hoot: Funny Palindrome Riddles*. Illus. by Giulio Maestro. Clarion, 1985. ISBN 0-89919-319-6

[64p., Gr. 2–6] After reading these riddles children can make up new ones. RIDDLES.

1966   Thaler, Mike. *The Chocolate Marshmelephant Sundae*. Illus. by the author. Franklin Watts, 1978.

[96p., Gr. 3–6] Visual jokes, riddles, puns, and other wordplays, such as a drawing of your basic peanut butter and jellyfish sandwich. Draw a few on the chalkboard for children to guess, then have them try their hands at creating new ones. See also Thaler's *What's Up Duck: Cartoons, Riddles and Jokes* (1978), which includes some truly dumb duck and other animal riddles and word puns, filled with Groucho Marx-like ducks in the line drawings. "What weighs 200 pounds, barks, and is filled with prunes?—A Great Danish" is a favorite. JOKES. RIDDLES.

1967   Tripp, Wallace, comp. *A Great Big Ugly Man Came Up and Tied His Horse to Me: A Book of Nonsense Verse*. Illus. by the author. Little, Brown, 1974. ISBN 0-316-85280-5

[46p., Gr. K–3] Tripp's endearingly nutty illustrations demand closer scrutiny; when reading these goofy verses, have everyone squeeze up close. See also Tripp's *Granfa' Grig Had a Pig*, listed under Mother Goose in this chapter. The poems in Tripp's *Marguerite, Go Wash Your Feet* (Houghton Mifflin, 1985) are waggishly merry, though much of the nonsense is well over the heads of children and will require you to "explain" the funny parts. HUMOROUS POETRY. NONSENSE VERSES.

1968   Untermeyer, Louis, comp. *The Golden Treasury of Poetry*. Illus. by Joan Walsh Anglund. Golden Press, 1959.

[324p., Gr. 2–6] A huge anthology with something for every taste and occasion. Comparable collections include May Hill Arbuthnot's *Time for Poetry*, Joanna Cole's *A New Treasury of Children's Poetry*, Nancy Larrick's *Piping Down the Valleys Wild*, and Jack Prelutsky's *The Ramdom House Book of Poetry*. POETRY–ANTHOLOGIES.

1969   Viorst, Judith. *If I Were in Charge of the World and Other Worries: Poems for Children and Their Parents*. Illus. by Lynne Cherry. Atheneum, 1981. ISBN 0-689-30863-9

[56p., Gr. 2–5] Truly funny musings of wishes and worries, wicked thoughts, and facts of life. When reading aloud from 398.2, you will love the ironic poems and parodies in the chapter "Fairy Tales." For more laughs read Robin Klein's *Snakes and Ladders*. FAIRY TALES–POETRY. HUMOROUS POETRY. POETRY–SINGLE AUTHOR.

1970 **Wallace, Daisy, comp.** *Ghost Poems.* **Illus. by Tomie dePaola. Holiday House, 1979. ISBN 0-8234-0344-0**

[30p., Gr. K–4] This alluring collection works well with fiction such as Walter Rollin Brooks's *Jimmy Takes Vanishing Lessons*, James Flora's *Grandpa's Ghost Stories*, and Emily Herman's *Hubknuckles*. Wallace's *Monster Poems* (1976) and *Witch Poems* (1976) are two more attractively ghoulish assemblages with spooky/funny illustrations for Halloween and other eerie times. John E. Brewton's *In the Witches Kitchen*, Sara and John E. Brewton's *Shrieks at Midnight*, Lee Bennett Hopkins's *Creatures*, Lilian Moore's *See My Lovely Poison Ivy*, plus Jack Prelutsky's benign *It's Halloween* and malevolent *Nightmares* are all good companions here. GHOSTS–POETRY. HALLOWEEN–POETRY.

1971 **Walton, Rich, and Ann Walton.** *What's Your Name, Again? More Jokes about Names.* **Illus. by Joan Hanson. Lerner, 1988. ISBN 0-8225-0997-0**

[unp., Gr. 1–6] Small sized, but full of wit about first names such as, "Who has a wet face and an apple in his mouth? Bob!" Surely the children in your school have first names with infinite ridde-making possibilities. Get the real lowdown with *Last, First, Middle and Nick: All about Names* by Barbara Shook Hazen. CREATIVE WRITING. NAMES. RIDDLES.

1972 **Watson, Clyde.** *Father Fox's Pennyrhymes.* **Illus. by Wendy Watson. Crowell, 1971. ISBN 0-690-29214-7**

[56p., Gr. Pre–1] More than 24 lovely, jingling, nursery-rhymish ditties. Use these along with the regular Mother Goose assortment, plus N. M. Bodecker's *"It's Raining," Said John Twaining*, Demi's Chinese *Dragon Kites and Dragonflies*, anything by Dennis Lee, Arnold Lobel's *Gregory Griggs* and *Whiskers & Rhymes*, and Jack Prelutsky's *Ride a Purple Pelican*. NURSERY RHYMES. POETRY–SINGLE AUTHOR.

1973 **Weiss, Nicki.** *If You're Happy and You Know It: Eighteen Story Songs Set to Pictures.* **Illus. by the author. Greenwillow, 1987. ISBN 0-688-06444-2**

[40p., Gr. Pre–2] You will not find a more appealing, colorful, child-focused songbook than this one with its unsurprising favorites like "This Old Man," "Hush Little Baby," and "My Tall Silk Hat," all illustrated line by line. FOLK SONGS. SONGBOOKS.

1974 **Whipple, Laura, comp.** *Eric Carle's Animals, Animals.* **Illus. by Eric Carle. Philomel, 1989. ISBN 0-399-21744-4**

[92p., Gr. K–4] A giant, gaudy, and gorgeous poetry and picture celebration of animals that swim, creep, fly, and leap. The match between the peerless verse and the tissue paper collage illustrations is memorable; you will refer to this grand volume again and again. Additional breathtaking collections include *Tomie dePaola's Book of Poems*, Beatrice Schenk de Regniers's *Sing a Song of Popcorn*, and Jack Prelutsky's *The Random House Book of Poetry for Children*. ANIMALS–POETRY. POETRY–ANTHOLOGIES.

1975 **Wilner, Isabel, comp.** *The Poetry Troupe: An Anthology of Poems to Read Aloud.* **Illus. by the author. Scribner, 1977. ISBN 0-684-15198-7**

[223p., Gr. K–4] A comfortable, familiar, whimsy-filled collection. POETRY–ANTHOLOGIES.

1976 Winn, Marie, comp. *The Fireside Book of Fun and Game Songs.* Illus. by Whitney Darrow, Jr. Simon & Schuster, 1974. ISBN 0-671-65213-3

[222p., Gr. Pre–6] You do not need a campfire to sing raucously; let the songs in this grand collection inspire you. For more musical lunacy, do not miss Esther Nelson's series starting with *The Funny Songbook.* FOLK SONGS. HUMOROUS SONGS. SONGBOOKS.

1977 Withers, Carl, comp. *A Rocket in My Pocket: The Rhymes and Chants of Young Americans.* Illus. by Susanne Suba. Henry Holt, 1988. ISBN 0-8050-0821-7

[214p., Gr. K–4] Rhymes, riddles, and chants for bouncing balls, jumping rope, spelling, counting, autographing albums, and twisting tongues—all from American folklore. For more of the same look for the Duncan Emrich books and Gloria T. Delamar's *Children's Counting-Out Rhymes.* FOLKLORE–U.S. NONSENSE VERSES. RIDDLES.

1978 Withers, Carl, and Sula Benet, comps. *The American Riddle Book.* Illus. by Marc Simont. Abelard, 1954.

[157p., Gr. 2–6] Found within are more than 1,000 groaners collected in the United States, together with a chapter of foreign ones. For more traditional riddles see also the collections of Duncan Emrich and Alvin Schwartz. RIDDLES.

1979 Worth, Valerie. *Small Poems.* Illus. by Natalie Babbitt. Farrar, 1972. ISBN 0-374-37072-9

[41p., Gr. 2–6] The first of four books. The others are *More Small Poems* (1976), *Still More Small Poems* (1978), and *Small Poems Again* (1986). All contain brilliant, spare, perceptive jewels to pore over about zinnias, pies, safety pins, magnets, acorns, crabs, pumpkins, horses, slugs, cat baths, sweets, anteaters, tigers, asparagus, fleas, coat hangers, and libraries, to name just a few. One poem per page, with small elegant pen-and-ink illustrations, guarantees you and your listeners will never take familiar everyday objects for granted again. Bring in a box full of items for children to handle and observe, some to go along with the poems as your read them and some not; then have them write some new small poems to go with the objects. Farrar released all four books in one paperback edition called *All the Small Poems* (1989). CREATIVE WRITING. POETRY–SINGLE AUTHOR.

1980 Yolen, Jane, comp. *The Fireside Song Book of Birds and Beasts.* Illus. by Peter Parnall. Simon & Schuster, 1972.

[223p., Gr. Pre–6] Nearly 100 animal tunes of the air, the land, the sea, and then some. ANIMALS–SONGS. FOLK SONGS. SONGBOOKS.

1981 Yolen, Jane. *The Three Bears Rhyme Book.* Illus. by Jane Dyer. Harcourt, 1987. ISBN 0-15-286386-9

[32p., Gr. Pre–2] Assuming that Baby Bear and Goldilocks became friends, this delectably illustrated, charming collection of 15 poems about porridge, chairs, and other bear-based concerns takes the old fairy tale several steps further. Use these poems in tandem with the myriad versions of the folktale including the ones illustrated by Jan Brett, Lorinda Bryan Cauley, Armand Eisen, James Marshall, and Janet Stevens. Tie it all together with Brinton Turkle's wordless turnaround, *Deep in the Forest.* BEARS–POETRY. FAIRY TALES–POETRY. POETRY–SINGLE AUTHOR.

1982 Young, Ed, comp. *High on a Hill: A Book of Chinese Riddles*. Illus. by the author. Collins, 1980.

[unp., Gr. 2–4] Collected in China by Young's family, here are more than 24 riddle-poems about animals, written in both Chinese and English, with delicately shaded pencil drawings supplying proof of the answers. Also marvel over *Dragon Kites and Dragonflies*, Demi's Chinese nursery rhyme collection. FOLKLORE–CHINA. RIDDLES.

1983 Zimmerman, Andrea Griffing, comp. *The Riddle Zoo*. Illus. by Giulio Maestro. Dutton, 1981. ISBN 0-525-38299-2

[62p., Gr. K–2] Simple, one-per-page animal riddles. See also David A. Adler's *The Carsick Zebra and Other Animal Riddles* and Beatrice Schenk de Regniers's *It Does Not Say Meow and Other Animal Riddle Rhymes*. ANIMALS–RIDDLES. RIDDLES.

1984 Zolotow, Charlotte. *Everything Glistens and Everything Sings*. Illus. by Margot Tomes. Harcourt, 1987. ISBN 0-15-226488-4

[96p., Gr. K–4] Over 70 poems, some rhyming, some not, about the world, the sea, colors, friendship, animals, seasons, growing things, and bedtime. POETRY–SINGLE AUTHOR.

Illustration from HOW TO DIG A HOLE TO THE OTHER SIDE OF THE WORLD by Faith McNulty, illustrated by Marc Simont. Illustrations copyright © 1979 by Marc Simont. Harper & Row, Publishers, 1979. Reprinted by permission of HarperCollins Publishers.

NONFICTION AND BIOGRAPHY

1985   **Abels, Chana Byers.** *The Children We Remember.* **Illus. with photos. Greenwillow, 1986. ISBN 0-688-06372-1**

[1 sitting, unp., Gr. 4–6] In simple language, this 21-sentence description of what happened to Jewish children when the Nazis came to power is made painfully clear and understandable for modern children who will see themselves in every haunting photograph. Read this as an introduction to Clara Isaacson's autobiography *Clara's Story* and Lois Lowry's Newbery Award–winning book, *Number the Stars.* JEWS. WORLD WAR, 1939–1945.

1986   **Arnold, Caroline.** *Kangaroo.* **Photos by Richard Hewett. Morrow, 1987. ISBN 0-688-06481-7**

[1–2 sittings, 48p., Gr. 2–6] Marsupial lovers will warm to the large color photographs of Sport, an orphaned baby kangaroo who was raised by a human family. Interspersed is information about kangaroos in the wild. A companion volume, *Koala* (1987), introduces endearing and photogenic Frangipani. Alice Leighner's *Reynard: The Story of a Fox Returned to the Wild* and Betty Leslie-Melville's *Daisy Rothschild: The Giraffe That Lives with Me* are also about the rescue and care of wild creatures. KANGAROOS.

1987   **Arnold, Caroline.** *Trapped in Tar: Fossils from the Ice Age.* **Photos by Richard Hewett. Clarion, 1987. ISBN 0-89919-415-X**

[1–2 sittings, 57p., Gr. 4–6] Since 1906 scientists have been excavating fossils of prehistoric beasts and plants from the tar pits at Rancho La Brea in California. The large black-and-white photographs of some of the findings—ranging from teratorns with a wingspan of almost 14 feet to imperial mammoths 13 feet tall—and the descriptions of how these excavations are made will please dinosaur-obsessed youngsters, as will Patricia Lauber's *The News about Dinosaurs.* ANIMALS, PREHISTORIC.

1988   **Arnold, Eric H., and Jeffrey Loeb, eds.** *I'm Telling! Kids Talk about Brothers and Sisters.* **Illus. by G. Brian Karas. Little, Brown, 1987. ISBN 0-316-05185-3**

[17 chapters, 137p., Gr. 4–6] Arnold and Loeb interviewed and taped hundreds of siblings, ages 10 to 14, about sharing, annoying habits, fighting, chores, jealousy, tattling, and advice—all of which is transcribed here in terrifically funny, real-life monologues. Read excerpts as needed and expect your listeners to drive you wild with their own true horror tales, which they can then record on cassette or paper. Perhaps your students would like to compile their own mini-book about parents, relatives, or school. Read along with Barbara Park's *Operation: Dump the Chump*, which deals with acute sibling rivalry in a hilarious way. BROTHERS AND SISTERS.

1989 Back, Christine. *Bean and Plant.* **Photos by Barrie Watts. Silver Burdett, 1984. ISBN 0-382-09286-4**

[1 sitting, 25p., Gr. Pre–3] A deceptively simple color photo essay. This stage-by-stage depiction of a bean seed that grows into a plant will make you want to plant your own, observe, and draw each change. This science lesson could not be clearer. See Gene Zion's *The Plant Sitter* for day-to-day maintenance problems. PLANTS.

1990 Banish, Roslyn. *Let Me Tell You about My Baby.* **Illus. with photos. Harper & Row, 1988. ISBN 0-06-020383-8**

[1 sitting, 61p., Gr. Pre–1] A black-and-white photo essay narrated by a young boy about his new brother, from anticipating his arrival to learning to like him. Including tasteful birth and nursing scenes, this runs a believable gamut of emotions from anger and jealousy to love. New baby books abound in fiction such as Marc Brown's *Arthur's Baby*, Judith Caseley's *Silly Baby*, Alane Ferguson's *That New Pet!*, Kathryn Osebold Galbraith's *Waiting for Jennifer*, Ezra Jack Keats's *Peter's Chair*, and Astrid Lindgren's *I Want a Brother or Sister*. BABIES. BROTHERS.

1991 Bare, Colleen Stanley. *Guinea Pigs Don't Read Books.* **Photos by author. Putnam, 1985. ISBN 0-396-08538-5**

[unp., Gr. Pre–1] Large adorable color photographs and a simple text explain what guinea pigs do and do not do. Tie this in with Kate Duke's basic-concepts wordbook *Guinea Pigs Far and Near* and Tricia Springstubb's *The Magic Guinea Pig*. GUINEA PIGS. PETS.

1992 Bare, Colleen Stanley. *To Love a Dog.* **Photos by author. Putnam, 1987. ISBN 0-396-09057-5**

[1 sitting, 47p., Gr. Pre–2] Labeled color snapshot poses of more than 24 breeds of dogs, with instructions for their loving care are in easy language for any child to comprehend. Put youself in the dog's place with Dick Gackenbach's *Dog for a Day* and Rolf Myller's *A Very Busy Day* and see what it's like to train one with Steven Kellogg's *Pinkerton, Behave* and Amy Schwartz's *Oma and Bobo*. DOGS.

1993 Barton, Byron. *Building a House.* **Illus. by the author. Greenwillow, 1981. ISBN 0-688-84291-7**

[1 sitting, unp., Gr. Pre–1] Starting with a hill, the bulldozer digs, builders hammer, and before you know it, the house is done. This easiest of nonfiction titles, in picture book format, perks up Virginia Lee Burton's comeback saga of an older place, *The Little House*, and makes your builders rush to the block corner to erect their own creations. HOUSES.

1994 Bash, Barbara. *Desert Giant: The World of the Saguaro Cactus.* **Illus. by the author. Sierra Club, 1989. ISBN 0-316-08301-1**

[1 sitting, unp., Gr. 2–5] How the Sonoran desert cactus grows, and after 150 years flowers, bears fruit, and supports a host of dependents, including owls, woodpeckers, hawks, long-nosed bats, and the Tohono O'odham Indians who use the juicy fruit to make jams and sweets. Relate this to Diane Siebert's majestic desert poem *Mojave* and Lynne Cherry's plea for conservation, *The Great Kapok Tree: A Tale of the Amazon Rain Forest*. DESERTS. ECOLOGY. PLANTS.

1995   **Berger, Gilda.** *Whales.* **Illus. by Lisa Bonforte. Doubleday, 1987. ISBN 0-385-23421-X**

[40p., Gr. 2–4] Huge paintings and intriguing facts make an already popular subject even more appealing. Berger's *Sharks* (1987) is just as nice, though much gorier. WHALES.

1996   **Blumberg, Rhoda.** *The Incredible Journey of Lewis & Clark.* **Illus. Lothrop, 1987. ISBN 0-688-06512-0**

[16 chapters, 141p., Gr. 5–6] A most spectacular, detailed, and riveting illustrated account of the expedition sponsored by Thomas Jefferson in 1804. This is a gorgeous volume and one of the best examples of nonfiction. Jammed with details of medicine, animal and plant life, and anecdotes of the explorers not usually made available for children; history-haters will be seduced. EXPLORERS. U.S.-HISTORY-1783–1865. WEST.

1997   **Brandreth, Gyles.** *Brain-Teasers and Mind-Benders.* **Illus. by Ann Axworthy. Sterling, 1979.**

[128p., Gr. 3–6] More than 100 challenging math, perception, and word puzzles, including a description of the Möbius strip, which you should demonstrate. Find more stunts in E. Richard Churchill's *Devilish Bets to Trick Your Friends*, Vicki Cobb and Kathy Darling's *Bet You Can!* and *Bet You Can't!*, Louis Phillip's *263 Brain Busters*, and Laurence B. White, Jr., and Ray Broekel's *The Trick Book*. GAMES. MATHEMATICS. TRICKS. WORD GAMES.

1998   **Branley, Franklyn M.** *Tornado Alert.* **Illus. by Giulio Maestro. Crowell, 1988. ISBN 0-690-04688-X**

[32p., Gr. 1–4] What causes tornadoes, how they move, and what to do if you are near one. Like tidal waves, earthquakes, and volcanoes, this is a topic of perennial fascination, handled in a clear and unsensationalized fashion. TORNADOES. WEATHER.

1999   **Broekel, Ray, and Laurence B. White, Jr.** *Now You See It: Easy Magic for Beginners.* **Illus. by Bill Morrison. Little, Brown, 1979. ISBN 0-316-93595-6**

[57p., Gr. 2–5] All 35 tricks are easy to understand and perform. Continue the trickery with Bob Brown's *How to Fool Your Friends* and Sid Fleischman's *Mr. Mysterious's Secrets of Magic*. MAGIC.

2000   **Brown, Bob.** *How to Fool Your Friends.* **Illus. by Robert Pierce. Golden Press, 1978.**

[48p., Gr. 3–5] All 46 simple, clearly explained, and often astonishing magic tricks, many science-based, are entirely within the realm of children. Also see Ray Broekel and Laurence B. White, Jr.'s *Now You See It*, Vicki Cobb and Kathy Darling's *Bet You Can!* and *Bet You Can't!* and M. S. Lehane's easy-to-read *Science Tricks*. MAGIC. SCIENCE-EXPERIMENTS.

2001   **Brown, Drollene P.** *Sybil Rides for Independence.* **Illus. by Margot Apple. Albert Whitman, 1985. ISBN 0-8075-7684-0**

[1 sitting, 48p., Gr. 2–4] On April 26, 1777, with Danbury, Connecticut, set ablaze by the British, 16-year-old Sybil Ludington set out on horseback through the country-side to rouse the patriot regiment to arms. Contrast this to the other famous rides detailed in Jean Fritz's *And Then What Happened, Paul Revere?* In a male-domint ed historical period other heroic female patriots include those in Patricia Lee Gauch's *This Time, Tempe Wick?*, Ann McGovern's *Secret Soldier*, and Judith Berry Griffin's *Phoebe and the General*. BIOGRAPHY. U.S.–HISTORY–REVOLUTION.

2002   Brown, Marc, and Stephen Krensky. *Dinosaurs, Beware! A Safety Guide*. Illus. by the authors. Little, Brown, 1982. ISBN 0-316-11228-3

[1–2 sittings, 32p., Gr. Pre–3] Green-tinged dinosaurs exaggerate each safety feature listed, from playing with matches to giving first aid, but young humans will find the practical advice useful in all emergencies. Discuss each illustration before reading the caption to elicit the safety knowledge your children already know. DINOSAURS. SAFETY.

2003   Brown, Marc, and Stephen Krensky. *Perfect Pigs: An Introduction to Manners*. Illus. by the authors. Little, Brown, 1983. ISBN 0-316-11080-9

[1 sitting, 32p., Gr. Pre–3] A pig-filled picture book approach with all the do's and don'ts of exquisite etiquette. For a refresher course read Sesyle Joslin's *What Do You Do, Dear?* and *What Do You Say, Dear?* and backslide with a barnyard-mannered animal in Boris Zakhoder's *How a Piglet Crashed the Christmas Party*. ETIQUETTE.

2004   Brown, Walter R., and Norman D. Anderson. *Rescue! True Stories of Winners of the Young American Medal for Bravery*. Walker, 1983.

[12 chapters, 92p., Gr. 3–6] Established in 1952 by Congress, the medal is given annually to two young people who, in the face of danger, risked their own lives to help others. The 12 episodes described here, plus an appendix of 42 capsule descriptions of fire; snake bites; tornado; airplane and car crashes; and water rescues, are a testament to American youth. Investigate methods of safety and survival with your class heroes who will also thrill to Gurney Williams III's *True Escape and Survival Stories*. BIOGRAPHY. COURAGE. HEROES.

2005   Churchill, E. Richard. *Devilish Bets to Trick Your Friends*.   Illus. by Sanford Hoffman. Sterling, 1985. ISBN 0-8069-7968-2

[128p., Gr. 3–6] Originally published in 1982 as *I Bet I Can, I Bet You Can't*, this is a collection of more than 60 science stunts, reading tricks, and math puzzlers to go along with the likes of Gyles Brandreth's *Brain-Teasers and Mind-Benders*, Vicki Cobb and Kathy Darling's *Bet You Can!* and *Bet You Can't!*, Louis Phillip's *263 Brain Busters*, and Laurence B. White, Jr., and Ray Broekel's *The Surprise Book*. GAMES. MATHEMATICS. TRICKS. WORD GAMES.

2006   Cobb, Vicki, and Kathy Darling. *Bet You Can! Science Possibilities to Fool You*. Illus. by Stella Ormai. Avon, 1983. ISBN 0-380-82180-X

[6 chapters, 108p., Gr. 3–6] Science tricks of gravity, liquids, energy, math, and mechanics to try out on willing victims who will be dazzled and mystified by the results and the follow-up explanations, along with the companion volume, *Bet You Can't! Science Impossibilities to Fool You* (Lothrop, 1980). On the simpler side try out Bob Brown's *How to Fool Your Friends* and M. S. Lehane's *Science Tricks*. SCIENCE– EXPERIMENTS.

2007   Coerr, Eleanor. *Sadako & the Thousand Paper Cranes*. Illus. by Ronald Himler. Putnam, 1977. ISBN 0-399-20520-9

[2 sittings, 9 chapters, 64p., Gr. 3–6] As the fiftieth anniversary of the atomic bombing of Hiroshima and Nagasaki approaches, honor the memory of the courageous 12-year-old girl who died of leukemia in 1954 before she could finish folding her 1,000 good-luck paper cranes. Make paper cranes with your students if origami is one of your talents. BIOGRAPHY. JAPAN. ORIGAMI. SICK. WORLD WAR, 1939–1945.

2008   Cole, Joanna. *The Magic School Bus at the Waterworks*. Illus. by Bruce Degen. Scholastic, 1988. ISBN 0-590-40360-5

[1 sitting, 39p., Gr. 2–4] Ms. Frizzle, the most wildly dressed, innovative science teacher in the business, takes her class on a field trip through the clouds, into the reservoir, and out of the sink pipes in the girl's bathroom. Sprinkled throughout are charts of ten water facts collected by her jaded, know-it-all students. First in a series, this is a stellar example of fictionalized nonfiction for teaching science skills that students will not be able to resist. Plan your own class trips à la Frizzle. SCHOOLS. SCIENCE–EXPERIMENTS. TEACHERS. WATER.

2009   Cole, Joanna. *The Magic School Bus Inside the Earth*. Illus. by Bruce Degen. Scholastic, 1987. ISBN 0-590-40759-7

[1 sitting, 40p., Gr. 2–4] Rock collecting on their class trip, Ms. Frizzle's crew digs right through the Earth, identifying sedimentary, metamorphic, and igneous rocks all the way. At the end of their journey there is a section of dialogue called "A Word with the Author and the Artist"; have three children read this aloud, Readers Theater style. Another incredible excavation on the same topic is Faith McNulty's *How to Dig a Hole to the Other Side of the World*. EARTH. GEOLOGY. ROCKS. SCIENCE–EXPERIMENTS. TEACHERS.

2010   Cole, Joanna. *The Magic School Bus Inside the Human Body*. Illus. by Bruce Degen. Scholastic, 1989. ISBN 0-590-41426-7

[1 sitting, unp., Gr. 2–4] On their way to the science museum, Ms. Frizzle's class takes a detour inside Arnold's body where they pass through the stomach, into a blood vessel, inside the four chambers of the heart, past the brain, and out his nose. Take time to read all the science notes on each page and examine each illustration; then give the True-or-False Test at the back of the book to keep the discussion going. As a health bonus offer a sampling of Barbara Seuling's *You Can't Sneeze with Your Eyes Open & Other Freaky Facts about the Human Body* (Lodestar, 1986). BODY, HUMAN. SCHOOLS. TEACHERS.

2011   Cross, Helen Reeder. *The Real Tom Thumb*. Illus. by Stephen Gammell. Four Winds, 1980.

[6 chapters, 92p., Gr. 3–6] Brought to the world's attention when he was but four years old by P. T. Barnum the "Prince of Humbug," the 31-inch tall dwarf Tom Thumb, né Charles Stratton of Connecticut, charmed queens and commoners alike with his performances of singing, dancing, and poetry recitations. BIOGRAPHY. DWARFS. HANDICAPS.

2012   Dahl, Roald. *Boy: Tales of Childhood*. Illus. with photos. Farrar, 1984. ISBN 0-374-37374-4

[25 chapters, 160p., Gr. 5–6] The background of Dahl's obsession with the macabre and the horrific becomes strikingly clear in this compelling autobiography, an exploration of his most vivid childhood family and school memories. Read in tandem with his fiction classics such as *The BFG; Matilda;* or *The Witches.* AUTHORS. AUTOBIOGRAPHY. BIOGRAPHY.

2013   **D'Aulaire, Ingri, and Edgar Parin D'Aulaire.** *Benjamin Franklin.* **Illus. by the authors. Doubleday, 1987. ISBN 0-385-24103-8**

[2 sittings, unp., Gr. 2–6] Of all the Revolutionary War figures, none is more fascinating than Benjamin Franklin, as this detailed, anecdotal biography with its large proverb-filled color illustrations ably proves. Read along with Jean Fritz's *What's the Big Idea, Ben Franklin?* to examine what facts each biographer chose to include. For older students more conversant with colonial history toss in a bit of fancy with Robert Lawson's mouse-narrated *Ben and Me.* BIOGRAPHY. INVENTIONS. U.S.–HISTORY–REVOLUTION.

2014   **Davidson, Margaret.** *Nine True Dolphin Stories.* **Illus. by Roger Wilson. Hastings House, 1974.**

[10 chapters, 67p., Gr. 2–4] Short anecdotes about dolphins who have saved lives and showed concern for humans. Lonzo Anderson's Greek folktale *Arion and the Dolphins* gives some historical perspective. DOLPHINS.

2015   **Davidson, Margaret.** *Seven True Dog Stories.* **Illus. by Susanne Suba. Hastings House, 1986. ISBN 0-8038-6738-7**

[8 chapters, 85p., Gr. 2–4] Heroic canines abound in real accounts of bravery and loyalty in this reprint of a 1977 edition. Intersperse each account with poems from Lee Bennett Hopkins's *It's a Dog's Life.* James Garfield's *Follow My Leader* and Jack Stonely's *Scruffy* are two realistic fiction books that make dog lovers out of all listeners. DOGS.

2016   **Davis, Hubert, ed.** *A January Fog Will Freeze a Hog and Other Weather Folklore.* **Illus. by John Wallner. Crown, 1977.**

[1 sitting, unp., Gr. 2–6] Collected from American folklore, these 30 rhyming weather sayings have more than a grain of truth to them. Perfect for weather studies, as endnotes explain each rhyme in more scientific terms. Judi Barrett's *Cloudy with a Chance of Meatballs,* Pat Cummings's *C.L.O.U.D.S.,* and Dr. Seuss's *Bartholomew and the Oobleck* all prove interesting companions, as children could write their own folklore rhymes to go with the stories. WEATHER.

2017   **dePaola, Tomie.** *The Cloud Book.* **Illus. by the author. Holiday House, 1975. ISBN 0-8234-0531-1**

[1 sitting, 32p., Gr. 1–3] The simplest explanation possible of all types of clouds includes delicious long names like cumulonimbus and cirrostratus for children to roll on their tongues. Delve deeper into weather lore with Hubert Davis's *A January Fog Will Freeze a Hog and Other Weather Folklore.* WEATHER.

2018   **dePaola, Tomie.** *The Popcorn Book.* **Illus. by the author. Holiday House, 1978. ISBN 0-8234-0314-9**

[1 sitting, unp., Gr. 1–4] Twins work together to make popcorn: one pops it, the other reads aloud interesting facts about it from a book. Simultaneously informative and funny; while Frank Asch's *Popcorn* is a story for younger children, it still works well with this, along with a snack of the real thing. POPCORN.

2019   dePaola, Tomie. *The Quicksand Book*. Illus. by the author. Holiday House, 1977. ISBN 0-8234-0291-6

[1 sitting, unp., Gr. 1–4] Instead of rescuing Jungle Girl when she falls in quicksand, Jungle Boy uses the chance of a captive audience to lecture her on the facts behind quicksand and how not to sink. Topped off by directions for making a bucketful of quicksand, this is one topic that will keep your class afloat. Dig further into Earth's mysteries with Joanna Cole's *The Magic School Bus Inside the Earth*, Bruce Hiscock's *The Big Rock*, Faith McNulty's *How to Dig a Hole to the Other Side of the World*, and Lisa Westberg Peter's *The Sun, the Wind, and the Rain*. GEOLOGY.

2020   Donnelly, Judy. *True-Life Treasure Hunts*. Illus. by Charles Robinson. Random House, 1984.

[5 chapters, 68p., Gr. 3–5] Compelling stories of pirates, sunken treasure, the Sacred Well at Chichén Itzá in the Yucatan, and King Tut's Tomb in Egypt make history thrilling. A U.S. lost treasure map at the back of the book shows where sunken ships, lost mines, and other loot are reported to be hidden, while well-chosen black-and-white photographs whet one's appetitie for more. "Tut-wise," see also Irene and Laurence Swinburn's *Behind the Sealed Door*; the color photographs alone will make you gasp. ARCHAEOLOGY. BURIED TREASURE.

2021   Dorros, Arthur. *Ant Cities*. Illus. by the author. Crowell, 1987. ISBN 0-690-04570-0

[1 sitting, 32p., Gr. K–3] One in Crowell's splendid "Let's Read and Find Out" science series, this explains how ants build their nests and run their empires, with the queen in charge. Larger than life watercolors allow children to see ants as creatures worthy of their respect, to the point where they may wish to make the simple "ant farm" described on the final page. Don't forget Bill Peet's story *The Ant and the Elephant*. ANTS. INSECTS.

2022   Epstein, Sam, and Beryl Epstein. *Secret in a Sealed Bottle: Lazzaro Spallanzani's Work with Microbes*. Illus. by Jane Sterrett. Coward, 1979.

[10 chapters, 63p., Gr. 5–6] About the eighteenth-century Italian naturalist and how he disproved the theory of spontaneous generation through his brilliant experiments with what were then called animacules. Your group can duplicate some of his work if you have access to microscopes. BIOGRAPHY. SCIENTISTS.

2023   Fisher, Leonard Everett. *The Great Wall of China*. Illus. by the author. Macmillan, 1986. ISBN 0-02-735220-X

[1 sitting, 32p., Gr. 2–6] Winding over 3,750 miles, the Mongol-repelling wall begun over 2,000 years ago still inspires awe and Fisher's stirring text and gray-toned paintings make it accessible to children. Set the mood with one or more of the following: Cheng Hou-Tien's *The Six Chinese Brothers*; Demi's *A Chinese Zoo* and Demi's *Reflective Fables*; M. A. Jagendorf and Virginia Weng's *The Magic Boat and Other Chinese Folk Stories*; Carol Kendall's *Sweet and Sour*; Ai-Ling Louie's *Yeh-Shen*, a Chinese Cinderella story over 1,000 years old; Catherine Edwards Sadler's folktale collection *Treasure Mountain*; and finish up by guessing the Chinese riddles in Ed Young's *High on a Hill*. CHINA. MONUMENTS.

2024 Fleischman, Sid. *Mr. Mysterious's Secrets of Magic.* **Illus. by Eric Von Schmidt. Little, Brown, 1975.**

[21 chapters, 81p., Gr. 3–6] What makes this magic book so much fun is the patter that Fleischman scripted in with each trick so that one can perform each illusion with finesse. Simpler magic for beginners can be found in Ray Broekel and Laurence B. White Jr.'s *Now You See It*, while famous magicians strut their stuff in Robert Kraske's *Magicians Do Amazing Things* and Florence White's *Escape! The Life of Harry Houdini.* MAGIC.

2025 Freedman, Russell. *Buffalo Hunt.* **Illus. with photos. Holiday House, 1988. ISBN 0-8234-0702-0**

[Gr. 5–6] Accompanied by exquisite historical full-page paintings, an inspired text describes the Plains Indians' hunt and uses of buffalo until the white man's conquest of the 1880s. For social studies units ranging from Indians to endangered species this is nonfiction at its best. Plains Indian legends such as Olaf Baker's *Where the Buffaloes Begin* or Paul Goble's *Buffalo Woman* and *Her Seven Brothers* round out the picture. BUFFALO. INDIANS OF NORTH AMERICA. U.S.–HISTORY–1865–1898. WEST.

2026 Freedman, Russell. *Children of the Wild West.* **Illus. with photos. Clarion, 1983. ISBN 0-89919-143-6**

[7 chapters, 104p., Gr. 3–6] What it was like for settlers and Indian children living and going to school in the West. Dotted with captivating period photographs, the beguiling narrative takes the distance out of long ago. For a "you are there" approach consult Ellen Levine's *If You Traveled West in a Covered Wagon* (Scholastic, 1986), then segue into Carol Ryrie Brink's *Caddie Woodlawn* or Laura Ingalls Wilder's *Little House in the Big Woods*, both based on true stories. Spice it up with a bit of slapstick in Alan Coren's *Arthur the Kid*, Gery Greer and Bob Ruddick's *Max and Me and the Wild West*, and Stephen Mooser's *Orphan Jeb at the Massacree.* U.S.–HISTORY–1865–1898. WEST.

2027 Freedman, Russell. *Immigrant Kids.* **Illus. with photos. Dutton, 1980. ISBN 0-525-32538-7**

[72p., Gr. 4–6] Chronicling the massive wave of immigration to the United States from 1890 to the early 1900s, through arresting black-and-white period photographs and remembrances of those who were growing up then, Freedman gives us an insider's eye on life in the teeming New York tenements. As an important symbol of the immigrant experience, *The Story of the Statue of Liberty* by Betsy Maestro is an appropriate cross-reference. CITIES AND TOWNS. IMMIGRATION AND EMIGRATION. U.S.–HISTORY.

2028 Freedman, Russell. *Lincoln: A Photobiography.* **Illus. with photos. Clarion, 1987. ISBN 0-89919-380-3**

[7 chapters, 150p., Gr. 5–6] In spite of the many fascinating anecdotes and the lively narrative style, this eloquent, elegant biography is not easy to read aloud, as it is riddled with political issues of which elementary schoolchildren know little, but for classes studying the Civil War, it is a treasure. Historical photographs of Lincoln abound, along with reproductions of letters, posters, and drawings, all of which make this book, a beacon in its field, all the more outstanding. Zachary Kent's *The Story of Ford's Theater and the Death of Lincoln* (Childrens, 1987) gives a competent account of John Wilkes Booth's crime, while Ann McGovern's *If You Grew Up with Abraham Lincoln* (Scholastic, 1966) answers questions commonly asked about his childhood. BIOGRAPHY. LINCOLN, ABRAHAM. NEWBERY MEDAL. PRESIDENTS—U.S. U.S. —HISTORY—1783–1865.

2029 **Fritz, Jean.** *And Then What Happened, Paul Revere?* **Illus. by Margot Tomes. Coward, 1973. ISBN 0-698-20274-0**

[1 sitting, 45p., Gr. 3–6] Did you know that the famous silversmith forgot his spurs on the night of the big ride? Compare Henry Wadsworth Longfellow's classic poem of the event, *Paul Revere's Ride,* with the facts here. For a lesser-known ride by a young female patriot read Drollene P. Brown's *Sybil Rides for Independence.* This book is Fritz's first in a brilliant series of biographies of Revolutionary War heroes including *Where Was Patrick Henry on the 29th of May?* (1975), the inside story of the dramatic orator Thomas Jefferson described as being all tongue; *Why Don't You Get a Horse, Sam Adams?* (1974); and *Will You Sign Here, John Hancock?* (1976), the latter title about the fancy-signatured, richest man in New England who spent his life buying approval and huzzahs. BIOGRAPHY. U.S.–HISTORY–REVOLUTION.

2030 **Fritz, Jean.** *Can't You Make Them Behave, King George?* **Illus. by Tomie dePaola. Coward, 1982. ISBN 0-698-20315-1**

[1–2 sittings, 48p., Gr. 3–6] Children accustomed to resenting the English king behind the American Revolution will be startled to meet a young, meticulous, well-liked ruler who liked music, collected clocks and zoo animals, and fathered 15 children. BIOGRAPHY. KINGS AND RULERS. U.S. HISTORY–REVOLUTION.

2031 **Fritz, Jean.** *The Double Life of Pocahontas.* **Illus. by Ed Young. Putnam, 1983. ISBN 0-399-21016-4**

[6 chapters, 85p., Gr. 4–6] Known to schoolchildren as the Indian princess who saved John Smith, Pocahontas was a unique historical figure: a pawn of her father, tribe, and the English settlers who took advantage of her position. Both a biography and a recounting of life among the early Jamestown settlers, this book covers the events from 1607 to 1617, when she died in England at age 21. Marcia Sewall's *The Pilgrims of Plimoth* and Kate Waters's *Sarah Morton's Day: A Day in the Life of a Pilgrim Girl* cover roughly the same period in Massachusetts, though not from the Native American perspective. BIOGRAPHY. INDIANS OF NORTH AMERICA—BIOGRA-PHY. U.S.—HISTORY—COLONIAL PERIOD.

2032 **Fritz, Jean.** *Shh! We're Writing the Constitution.* **Illus. by Tomie dePaola. Putnam, 1987. ISBN 0-399-21403-8**

[2–3 sittings, 44p., Gr. 4–6] All the turmoil and tittle-tattle behind that great docu-ment is chronicled, as the delegates battled out the format and content during the sweltering Philadelphia summer of 1786. Also see Elizabeth Levy's excellent *If You Were There When They Signed the Constitution* (Scholastic, 1987) and Betsy and Giulio Maestro's simplified picture book *A More Perfect Union.* U.S.—CONSTITU-TIONAL HISTORY.

2033 **Fritz, Jean.** *What's the Big Idea, Ben Franklin?* **Illus. by Margot Tomes. Coward, 1976. ISBN 0-698-20543-X**

[1–2 sittings, 48p., Gr. 3–6] Not as grandly illustrated as Ingri and Edgar Parin d'Aulaire's *Benjamin Franklin,* but every bit as entertaining and astonishing in its details that reveal the marvels of the man. For the fictional "truth" about the power behind the legend read Robert Lawson's *Ben and Me*, where good mouse Amos takes all the credit. BIOGRAPHY. INVENTIONS. U.S.–HISTORY–REVOLUTION.

2034 **Fritz, Jean.** *Where Do You Think You're Going, Christopher Columbus?* **Illus. by Margot Tomes. Putnam, 1980. ISBN 0-399-20734-1**

[80p., Gr. 4–6] Egotistical and intractable as he was, Columbus was a magnificent sailor according to Fritz's personable and unvarnished account, which is riddled with wonderful facts about Queen Isabella, the islands Columbus discovered, and the many setbacks he encountered. BIOGRAPHY. EXPLORERS.

2035 **Fritz, Jean.** *Who's That Stepping on Plymouth Rock?* **Illus. by J. B. Handelsman. Coward, 1975. ISBN 0-698-20325-9**

[1 sitting, 30p., Gr. 3–6] Where the Mayflower Pilgrims—or First Comers, as they called themselves—may have first landed in 1620 and what has become of the rock since then. Travel back in time with Ann McGovern's *If You Sailed on the Mayflower* (Scholastic, 1969), Marcia Sewall's *The Pilgrims of Plimoth,* and Kate Water's photo essay, *Sarah Morton's Day: A Day in the Life of a Pilgrim Girl.* PILGRIMS. ROCKS. U.S.–HISTORY–COLONIAL PERIOD.

2036 **Garrison, Webb.** *Why Didn't I Think of That? From Alarm Clocks to Zippers.* **Illus. by Ray Abel. Prentice Hall, 1977.**

[120p., Gr. 4–6] Over 60 stories behind ingenious inventions and the tenacious men (and one woman) who made them work. Provide extra inspiration to your own inventors when they research the origin of other common objects or dream up a useful new discovery. From odd to outlandish see also Jim Murphy's *Weird & Wacky Inventions* and its sequel *Guess Again: More Weird & Wacky Inventions* (Bradbury, 1986) and Rube Goldberg's *The Best of Rube Goldberg.* INVENTIONS.

2037 **George, William T.** *Box Turtle at Long Pond.* **Illus. by Lindsay Barrett George. Greenwillow, 1989. ISBN 0-688-08185-1**

[1 sitting, unp., Gr. Pre–2] Spend an autumn day in the field with a box turtle as he eats worms, draws into his shell to avoid a raccoon's prying paws, and feasts on wild grapes. The magnificent color paintings give a turtle's-eye view of the world, as do the "Just for a Day" books by Joanne Ryder. Contrast with such picture book stories as Frank Asch's *Turtle Tale,* Lorna Balian's *The Aminal,* Mwenye Hadithi's *Tricky Tortoise,* and Barbara Williams's *Albert's Toothache.* ANIMALS. POND LIFE. TURTLES.

2038 **Gerrard, Roy.** *Sir Francis Drake: His Daring Deeds.* **Illus. by the author. Farrar, 1988. ISBN 0-374-36962-3**

[1 sitting, unp., Gr. 4–6] Gallantly gleaming, meticulously detailed illustrations and a crisply rhyming text highlight the accomplishments of England's famous Elizabethan explorer and scourge of the Spanish Armada. When pursuing a social studies unit on explorers, discuss Drake's life and times before reading this aloud. Perhaps this book will motivate students to write and illustrate new rhymes for other august explorers. CREATIVE WRITING. EXPLORERS. NARRATIVE POETRY. SHIPS. STORIES IN RHYME.

2039   **Gish, Lillian, and Selma Lanes.** *An Actor's Life for Me!* **Illus. by Patricia Henderson Lincoln. Viking, 1987. ISBN 0-670-80416-9**

[12 chapters, 73p., Gr. 4–6] In 1902, at just six years of age, the legendary silent screen star and her sister Dorothy began their acting careers as part of a traveling theatrical company. Her intimate narrative, bolstered with photographs and Lincoln's illustrations, takes us up to the start of her career in the "flickers." Show one of her films, along with a reel or two to go along with Gloria Kamen's biography of another early superstar, *Charlie Chaplin*. ACTORS AND ACTRESSES. AUTOBIOGRAPHY. BIOGRAPHY.

2040   **Goldberg, Rube.** *The Best of Rube Goldberg.* **Illus. by the author. Prentice Hall, 1979. ISBN 0-13-074807-2**

[130p., Gr. 3–6] Demonstrated here through step-by-step instructions and illustrations are ingenious and elaborate mechanical inventions of such outlandish necessities as a self-working corkscrew, self-shining shoes, and many more. Because of the detail, use of an opaque projector might be a good idea. Children will clamor to design their own labor-saving devices. Jim Murphy's *Weird & Wacky Inventions* and its sequel *Guess Again: More Weird & Wacky Inventions* (Bradbury, 1986) give examples of some of the off-the-wall devices that have already been patented, while Webb Garrison's *Why Didn't I Think of That? From Alarm Clocks to Zippers* tells the stories behind ordinary inventions. CAUSE AND EFFECT. INVENTIONS. MACHINES.

2041   **Goodall, Jane.** *The Chimpanzee Family Book.* **Photos by Michael Neugebauer. Picture Book Studio, 1989. ISBN 0-88708-090-1**

[2 sittings, unp., Gr. 3–6] From morning to dusk of one day, naturalist Goodall and photographer Neugebauer followed chimp Gremlin and her infant son, recording their behavior and interactions with others from their community of three dozen chimpanzees. Compare these simians in the wild with lab animals Nim and Koko in Anna Michel's *The Story of Nim: The Chimp Who Learned Language* and Francine Patterson's *Koko's Kitten* and *Koko's Story*; original related fiction for upper grades includes Sandy Landsman's *Castaways on Chimp Island* and Ron Roy's *The Chimpanzee Kid*, all of which should spur interest in research on chimp behavior. CHIMPANZEES.

2042   **Griffin, Judith Berry.** *Phoebe and the General.* **Illus. by Margot Tomes. Coward, 1977.**

[1–2 sittings, 48p., Gr. 2–5] Assigned by her father, the owner of New York City's Queen's Head Tavern, to act as a spy and help uncover a plot to assassinate General Washington, 13-year-old Phoebe Fraunces indeed saved him from eating peas that had been poisoned by a member of his own bodyguard. Based on a real historical incident, the story of a free black innkeeper's daughter is made even more alluring by the fact that Fraunces Tavern not only exists, but still operates as both a museum and a restaurant. Additional true Revolutionary War stories include Drollene P. Brown's *Sybil Rides for Independence*, Patricia Lee Gauch's *This Time, Tempe Wick?* and Ann McGovern's *Secret Soldier*. A young girl disguised as a boy spirits a hidden message to Washington in the fictional *Toliver's Secret* by Esther Wood Brady. AFRICAN AMERICANS. BIOGRAPHY. PRESIDENTS—U.S. U.S.—HISTORY—REVOLUTION. WASHINGTON, GEORGE.

2043   **Grillone, Lisa, and Joseph Gennaro.** *Small Worlds Close Up.* **Illus. with photos. Crown, 1987. ISBN 0-517-53289-1**

[3 sittings, unp., Gr. 4–6, younger for pictures] In three sections—mineral, vegetable, and animal—here is a collection of greatly magnified black-and-white photographs of common substances such as salt, sand, aluminum foil, a leaf, and a snake's fang. Cover up the bold print while young science buffs attempt to identify each electron microscope enlargement, after which you can read aloud the astonishing text. Also see Seymour Simon's *Hidden Worlds: Pictures of the Invisible*. MICROSCOPES AND MICROSCOPY. SCIENCE.

2044 **Gryski, Camilla.** *Cat's Cradle, Owl's Eyes: A Book of String Games.* **Illus. by Tom Sankey. Morrow, 1984. ISBN 0-688-03940-5**

[78p., Gr. 2–6] A step-by-step introduction to dozens of string figures collected worldwide, each clearly illustrated and marked so even *you* can follow the often complex sequence. When you get stuck, your students will be the ones to set you straight, as string games seem to come naturally to them. Give everyone a nice long piece of string for trying out some figures, as these are marvelous for developing sequence and fine motor skills and they are great fun to swap. The follow-up, *Many Stars & More String Games* (1985), is a bit more complex. Anne Pellowski's *The Story Vine* (Macmillan, 1984), an indispensable resource book for storytellers, provides several stories to go along with string games, and instructions on how to make them. GAMES.

2045 **Hazen, Barbara Shook.** *Last, First, Middle and Nick: All about Names.* **Illus. by Sam Q. Weissman. Prentice Hall, 1979. ISBN 0-13-523944-3**

[14 chapters, 130p., Gr. 4–6] Dip into this vast collection of name facts to see how famous people acquired their monikers, how some common names originated, and other gossip-filled trivia. Children can research their own and other family names and write down any unusual anecdotes they pick up from interviewing older family members. Fool around with students' names with the help of Rick and Ann Walton's *What's Your Name, Again? More Jokes about Names.* NAMES.

2046 **Herriot, James.** *Blossom Comes Home.* **Illus. by Ruth Brown. St. Martin's, 1988. ISBN 0-312-02169-0**

[1 sitting, unp., Gr. 2–5] As related by Herriot, the famous Yorkshire veterinarian and author, Mr. Dakin reluctantly sent his favorite old cow to market, only to welcome her back for good when she found her own way back to the farm. See also Pat A. Wakefield and Larry Carrara's true recounting of the year the moose came to Carrara's Vermont farm for an extended visit in *A Moose for Jessica.* COWS. ENGLAND. FARM LIFE.

2047 **Herriot, James.** *Bonny's Big Day.* **Illus. by Ruth Brown. St. Martin's, 1987. ISBN 0-312-01000-1**

[1 sitting, unp., Gr. 2–5] Old John Skipton, a Yorkshire farmer, was persuaded by veterinarian Herriot to enter his old cart-horse, over 20 years old and out to pasture for the past 12 years, in the Family Pets Class of the Darrowby Show, where they won first prize. Both this and *Blossom Comes Home* display the special bond between people and animals. ENGLAND. FARM LIFE. PETS. HORSES.

2048 **Herriot, James.** *The Christmas Day Kitten.* **Illus. by Ruth Brown. St. Martin's, 1986. ISBN 0-312-13407-X**

[1 sitting, unp., Gr. 2–4] Debbie, the stray tabby cat that stops off at Mrs. Pickering's house for meals and a rest in front of the fireplace several days a week, shows up on Christmas morning ill and near death to leave her new kitten with the one person she trusts. As always, Herriot retells this touching anecdote from his practice as an English country veterinarian. CATS. CHRISTMAS. ENGLAND.

2049   Herzig, Alison Cragin, and Jane Lawrence Mali. *Oh, Boy! Babies!* **Photos by Katrina Thomas. Little, Brown, 1980.**

[7 chapters, 106p., Gr. 4–6] The ten boys who sign up for an elective infant-care class at school to learn how to hold, feed, change, bathe, and comfort real babies, earn certificates that qualify them as baby-sitters and, for the future, better fathers. The natural running dialogue of the boys reads like a transcribed recording and makes the listener eager to go find a baby to cuddle. You might arrange for a parent with a new baby to stop in for a class visit. BABIES. BABY-SITTERS.

2050   Hiscock, Bruce. *The Big Rock.* **Illus. by the author. Atheneum, 1988. ISBN 0-689-31402-7**

[1 sitting, unp., Gr. 1–4] Sitting as it does down the hill from Hiscock's studio, at the edge of the Southern Adirondacks in New York State, Hiscock researched the rock's odyssey over the past billion years until now. His resulting explanation, paired with Lisa Westberg Peters's *The Sun, the Wind, and the Rain,* makes a difficult concept comprehensible to young children. Equally absorbing are Joanna Cole's *The Magic School Bus Inside the Earth,* Tomie dePaola's *The Quicksand Book,* and Faith McNulty's *How to Dig a Hole to the Other Side of the World.* GEOLOGY. ROCKS.

2051   Hofer, Angelika. *The Lion Family Book.* **Trans. by Patricia Crampton. Photos by Günter Ziesler. Picture Book Studio, 1988. ISBN 0-88708-070-7**

[1 sitting, unp., Gr. 1–6] Hofer, a zoologist, and her companion, a world-known wildlife photographer, spent a year in the African "Masai Mara" Nature Reserve studying a pride of lions, including one-month old cubs, playing, hunting, and resting together. The astonishing close-up color photographs of lions in action will spoil you for most other big cat books, though Toshi Yoshida's *Young Lions* has gorgeous illustrations. Find out how the animal was created in William Pène du Bois's fanciful *Lion.* LIONS.

2052   Hunt, Bernice. *The Whatchamacallit Book.* **Illus. by Tomie dePaola. Putnam, 1976.**

[unp., Gr. 3–6] This illustrated description of all those common objects you can't readily name, such as uvula, antimacassar, eyelet, and ampersand, is a natural vocabulary enhancer when presented as a fun oral quiz, though you'll be amazed at how many answers you won't know. Make a class list of other vocabulary items whose names you can't supply and see if your researchers can find out what they are called. VOCABULARY.

2053   Hunter, Edith Fisher. *Child of the Silent Night: The Story of Laura Bridgman.* **Illus. by Bea Holmes. Houghton Mifflin, 1963. ISBN 0-395-06835-5**

[10 chapters, 124p., Gr. 3–5] The first blind, deaf, and mute person to be successfully taught to communicate, Laura, born in 1829, helped pave the way for many other multiply handicapped children, among them Helen Keller. BIOGRAPHY. BLIND. HANDICAPS.

2054 Isaacman, Clara, and Joan Adess Grossman. *Clara's Story.* Jewish Publication Society, 1984. ISBN 0-8276-0243-X

[15 chapters, 121p., Gr. 5–6] Unlike Anne Frank, young Clara Isaacman's family was active in the Resistance as they moved from one hiding place to another during their two-and-a-half-year ordeal in Antwerp, Belgium, as this harrowing, gut-wrenching World War II autobiography reveals. Fifty years later, children need to know what happened, and how children suffered, which books like Chana Byers Abels's *The Children We Remember,* Eleanor Coerr's *Sadako & the Thousand Paper Cranes,* Lois Lowry's *Number the Stars,* Johanna Reiss's *The Upstairs Room,* Noel Streatfeild's *When the Sirens Wailed,* Yoshiko Uchida's *Journey Home,* and Eva-Lis Wuorio's *Code: Polonaise* reveal. AUTOBIOGRAPHY. BIOGRAPHY. JEWS. WORLD WAR, 1939–1945.

2055 Jaspersohn, William. *The Ballpark: One Day behind the Scenes at a Major League Game.* Photos by author. Little, Brown, 1980.

[3–4 sittings, 116p., Gr. 4–6] Black-and-white photographs and a wide-ranging text detail everything that goes on at Fenway Park on the day of a Red Sox game—from when the ground crew "dumps the tarp" at 7:00 A.M. until the 35,000 fans go home and the place is cleaned up at 7:00 P.M. Show this in the fall, as World Series fever hits, along with Ernest Lawrence Thayer's *Casey at the Bat.* BASEBALL.

2056 Johnston, Ginny, and Judy Cutchins. *Andy Bear: A Polar Cub Grows Up at the Zoo.* Photos by Constance Noble. Morrow, 1985. ISBN 0-688-05628-8

[2–3 sittings, 62p., Gr. 2–6] Atlanta, Georgia, zookeeper Constance Noble first rescued and then raised the bear cub for five months in her own apartment, to which her own clear photographs attest. Alice Leighner's *Reynard: The Story of a Fox Returned to the Wild* and Betty Leslie-Melville's *Daisy Rothschild: The Giraffe That Lives with Me* are also fascinating animal accounts. BEARS. ZOOS.

2057 Kamen, Gloria. *Charlie Chaplin.* Illus. by the author. Atheneum, 1982. ISBN 0-689-30925-2

[13 chapters, 78p., Gr. 3–6] Do your students a favor and introduce them to some of the silent films of the Little Tramp as you read this poignant biography of Chaplin's impoverished childhood and subsequent fame. From the same era see Lillian Gish's autobiography *An Actor's Life for Me!* ACTORS AND ACTRESSES. BIOGRAPHY.

2058 Kellogg, Steven. *Johnny Appleseed.* Illus. by the author. Morrow, 1988. ISBN 0-688-06418-3

[1 sitting, unp., Gr. 1–4] How the legendary John Chapman cleared his way through Pennsylvania, Ohio, and Indiana, planting and selling his apple trees to pioneer families, inspiring tall tales about his backwoods exploits. Bring in a variety of apples to taste. BIOGRAPHY. FRONTIER AND PIONEER LIFE. FRUIT—FOLKLORE. TALL TALES. TREES.

2059 Kraske, Robert. *Magicians Do Amazing Things.* Illus. by Richard Bennett. Random House, 1979. ISBN 0-394-84106-9

[7 chapters, 69p., Gr. 3–6] Since magicians never reveal the secrets behind their tricks, magic buffs will be fascinated to find out how each of six famous conjurers, including Harry Houdini and Robert Houdin, performed one mystifying illusion, including walking through a brick wall and making a woman float in mid-air.

Before revealing each solution have your class puzzle out how they think each deed was done. Naturally, you will want to read Florence White's *Escape! The Life of Harry Houdini*, along with magic books *Now You See It* by Ray Broekel and Laurence B. White, Jr., and *Mr. Mysterious's Secrets of Magic* by Sid Fleischman. MAGIC. MAGICIANS.

2060   Krupp, E. C. *The Comet and You*. Illus. by Robin Rector Krupp. Macmillan, 1985. ISBN 0-02-751250-9

[1–2 sittings, 48p., Gr. 1–4] This down-to-earth explanation of comet orbits, composition, and other sensible facts, illustrated in glorious black and white, make a complex subject approachable for children with little background in astronomy. It is never too early to begin preparing for the next appearance of Halley's Comet in 2062. ASTRONOMY.

2061   Lauber, Patricia. *Lost Star: The Story of Amelia Earhart*. Illus. with photos. Scholastic, 1988. ISBN 0-590-41615-4

[13 chapters, 106p., Gr. 5–6] Examining the dangers of early plane flights and the heroics of the flyers, Lauber charts the life of an uncommon woman who broke world aviation records and disappeared while pursuing an around-the-globe record flight under circumstances that remain a mystery to this day. Note how she paved the way for others such as Sally Ride, who describes her experiences in *To Space and Back*. AIRPLANES. BIOGRAPHY. FLIGHT. WOMEN–BIOGRAPHY.

2062   Lauber, Patricia. *The News about Dinosaurs*. Illus. by John Gurche. Bradbury, 1989. ISBN 0-02-754520-2

[2 sittings, 48p., Gr. 2–6] What scientists used to believe about dinosaurs versus what they now feel is true, proving that even the experts don't have all the facts. With its magnificent giant color paintings done by a series of specialists in the field, this title sets new standards of quality for nonfiction. Fossil fans will also be absorbed by Caroline Arnold's *Trapped in Tar* about the Rancho La Brea tar pits in California. DINOSAURS.

2063   Lauber, Patricia. *Volcano: The Eruption and Healing of Mount St. Helens*. Illus. with photos. Bradbury, 1986. ISBN 0-02-754500-8

[5 chapters, 60p., Gr. 4–6] Large dramatic color photographs take us through the 1980 eruption and subsequent rebirth of wildlife after the devastation. Seymour Simon's overview, *Volcanoes*, is also breathtaking. Move into fiction with Roger W. Drury's *The Finches' Fabulous Furnace*, where the volcano is in the basement, or William Pène Du Bois's fantastic account of Krakatoa's big bang in *The Twenty-One Balloons*. Ann Grifalconi's *The Village of Round and Square Houses* is an unusual folktale about an African village's response to an eruption. VOLCANOES.

2064   Lavies, Bianca. *It's an Armadillo*. Photos by author. Dutton, 1989. ISBN 0-525-44523-4

[unp., Gr. K–3] Once you've read Rudyard Kipling's *The Beginning of the Armadillos*, your listeners will want to know more about the real McCoy. Former National Geographic Society photographer Lavies went to Florida to trail these shy and homely nocturnal mammals, and her entertaining text and color photos allow us in on some of their secrets. ANIMALS. ARMADILLOS.

2065 **Lehane, M. S.** *Science Tricks.* **Illus. by Terrence M. Fehr. Franklin Watts, 1980.**

[32p., Gr. K–3] Seventeen extremely simple experiments with household items such as eggs, salt, sugar, raisins, and ice. For slightly more complex offerings try Bob Brown's *How to Fool Your Friends* and Vicki Cobb and Kathy Darling's *Bet You Can!* and *Bet You Can't!* SCIENCE–EXPERIMENTS.

2066 **Leighner, Alice Mills.** *Reynard: The Story of a Fox Returned to the Wild.* **Photos by author. Atheneum, 1986. ISBN 0-689-31189-3**

[1–2 sittings, 48p., Gr. 1–5] The six-week-old red fox, found near a New York State Thruway toll booth one rainy April night, was taken in by volunteers of Wildcare, an organization that cares for injured or abandoned wild animals and then releases them back to their natural habitats. After hearing all those antifox tales such as Steven Kellogg's *Chicken Little*, James Marshall's *Wings*, Pat McKissack's *Flossie and the Fox*, and William Steig's *Dr. DeSoto*, it is refreshing to see charming black-and-white photographs that bring out our sympathies for the red-furred rascals. Combine this with pro-fox fiction like Betsy Byars's *The Midnight Fox*, Roald Dahl's *The Fantastic Mr. Fox*, Irina Korschunow's *The Foundling Fox*, and Tejima's *Fox's Dream*. FOXES.

2067 **Leslie-Melville, Betty.** *Daisy Rothschild: The Giraffe That Lives with Me.* **Photos by author. Doubleday, 1987. ISBN 0-385-23896-7**

[5 chapters, 42p., Gr. 2–6] Alarmed at the prospect of the endangered Rothschild giraffe becoming extinct, the author and her husband adopted first Daisy and then Marlon and raised them at their Nairobi, Kenya, estate. Large color photographs of these charming human-thumb-sucking giraffes and a conservationist conversational text ensure children's interest in saving threatened wildlife. Other first-person account close-ups of wild animals include Angelika Hofer's *The Lion Family Book*, Ginny Johnston and Judy Cutchins's *Andy Bear*, Alice Mills Leighner's *Reynard*, Francine Patterson's *Koko's Kitten* and *Koko's Story*, and Bill Peet's *Capyboppy*. GIRAFFES.

2068 **Lyon, George Ella.** *A B Cedar: An Alphabet of Trees.* **Illus. by Tom Parker. Orchard, 1989. ISBN 0-531-08395-0**

[1 sitting, unp., Gr. Pre–6] Elegantly arranged with handholding leaf-and-fruit samples for each tree, one per alphabet letter, and a silhouette drawing of each tree below, this unusual alphabet book is a starting point for botanical research. AL-PHABET BOOKS. TREES.

2069 **McGovern, Ann.** *If You Lived in Colonial Times.* **Illus. by Brinton Turkle. Scholastic, 1969. ISBN 0-590-41948-X**

[16 chapters, 79p., Gr. 2–5] Included are more than 50 questions children might ask about colonial times and interesting, easy-to-fathom answers. This book is one in a series of you-are-there books now issued in paperback by Scholastic and makes history real and fun to boot. More terrific books in the series include: Ruth Belov Gross's *If You Grew Up with George Washington* (1982); Ellen Levine's *If You Traveled on the Underground Railroad* (1988) and *If You Traveled West in a Covered Wagon* (1986); Elizabeth Levy's *If You Were There When They Signed the Constitution* (1987); and McGovern's *If You Grew Up with Abraham Lincoln* (1966), *If You Lived with the Sioux Indians* (1972), and *If You Sailed on the Mayflower* (1969). Other valuable read-alouds about colonial days include Jean Fritz's *Who's That Stepping on*

Plymouth Rock?, Marcia Sewall's *The Pilgrims of Plimoth*, and Kate Waters's *Sarah Morton's Day: A Day in the Life of a Pilgrim Girl*. Laugh it up a bit with David A. Adler's *Remember Betsy Floss and Other Colonial American Riddles*. U.S.–HISTORY–COLONIAL PERIOD.

2070   **McGovern, Ann.** *Runaway Slave: The Story of Harriet Tubman*. **Illus. by R. M. Powers. Scholastic, 1965.**

[11 chapters, 62p., Gr. 2–5] Between 1850 and the start of the Civil War, the ex-slave called "Moses" led over 300 slaves north to freedom on the Underground Railroad. For another detailed account of slavery also read Ellen Levine's *If You Traveled on the Underground Railroad* (Scholastic, 1988). Also pertinent and sobering are Stacy Chbosky's *Who Owns the Sun*, Monjo's *The Drinking Gourd*, and Jeanette Winter's *Follow the Drinking Gourd*. AFRICAN AMERICANS–BIOGRAPHY. BIOGRAPHY. SLAVERY. U.S.–HISTORY–1783–1865.

2071   **McGovern, Ann.** *The Secret Soldier: The Story of Deborah Sampson*. **Illus. by Ann Grifalconi. Four Winds, 1987. ISBN 0-02-765780-9**

[11 chapters, 107p., Gr. 3–6] In 1782, at the age of 21, Deborah disguised herself as a man and enlisted in the army as a Continental soldier, where she remained for a year-and-a-half until her secret became known. Three other courageous females during that time can be found in Drollene P. Brown's *Sybil Rides for Independence*, Patricia Lee Gauch's *This Time, Tempe Wick?* and Judith Berry Griffin's *Phoebe and the General*. BIOGRAPHY. SOLDIERS. U.S.–HISTORY–REVOLUTION. WOMEN–BIOGRAPHY.

2072   **McNulty, Faith.** *How to Dig a Hole to the Other Side of the World*. **Illus. by Marc Simont. Harper & Row, 1990. ISBN 0-06-443218-1**

[1 sitting, 32p., Gr. 1–4] If you could dig way down and had access to a diving suit and a jet-propelled fireproof submarine, McNulty shows how you could tunnel through topsoil, granite, steam, basalt, and magma to get to the mantle and keep going until you came up at the bottom of the Indian Ocean. Joanna Cole takes us on a similar journey, with more emphasis on identifying rocks, in *The Magic School Bus Inside the Earth*. EARTH. GEOLOGY.

2073   **Maestro, Betsy.** *A More Perfect Union: The Story of Our Constitution*. **Illus. by Giulio Maestro. Lothrop, 1987. ISBN 0-688-06840-5**

[1 sitting, 43p., Gr. 2–5] As basic an explanation as you will find in elegant picture book format. For more details go to Jean Fritz's *Shh! We're Writing the Constitution* and Elizabeth Levy's *If You Were There When They Signed the Constitution* (Scholastic, 1987). U.S.–CONSTITUTIONAL HISTORY.

2074   **Maestro, Betsy.** *The Story of the Statue of Liberty*. **Illus. by Giulio Maestro. Lothrop, 1986. ISBN 0-688-05774-8**

[1 sitting, 45p., Gr. 2–5] Along with a simple but intelligent text, dramatic, often spectacular watercolors chronicle the creation of New York harbor's most famous lady with the lamp. Tie this in with Russell Freedman's *Immigrant Kids*, so many of whom glimpsed the statue as they first sailed to Ellis Island on their way to a new life. MONUMENTS.

2075   Matthews, Downs. *Polar Bear Cubs.* Photos by Dan Guravich. Simon & Schuster, 1989. ISBN 0-671-66757-2

[1 sitting, unp., Gr. 1–4] In the frozen north, a male and female polar bear cub become self-sufficient over the course of two years of close supervision and instruction by their mother. Contrast this color photo essay with Ginny Johnston and Judy Cutchins's *Andy Bear: A Polar Bear Grows Up at the Zoo,* Joanne Ryder's dramatic *White Bear, Ice Bear,* and the lighthearted story *Don't Ever Wish for a 7-Foot Bear* by Robert Benton. BEARS.

2076   Michel, Anna. *The Story of Nim, the Chimp Who Learned Language.* Photos by Susan Kuklin and Herbert S. Terrace. Knopf, 1980. ISBN 0-394-84444-0

[2 sittings, 59p., Gr. 3–6] Columbia University behavioral psychologist Herbert S. Terrace directed Project Nim, where he and his staff raised a chimpanzee whom they named Nim Chimpsky and taught him American sign language, much as Francine Patterson did with gorilla Koko as described in *Koko's Kitten* and *Koko's Story.* The dramatic black-and-white photo essay will impel your students to learn some sign language. For older students Sandy Landsman's *Castaways on Chimp Island* and Ron Roy's *The Chimpanzee Kid* are both interesting fiction tie-ins. CHIMPANZEES. COMMUNICATION. SIGN LANGUAGE.

2077   Mowat, Farley. *Owls in the Family.* Illus. by Robert Frankenberg. Little, Brown, 1962. ISBN 0-316-58641-2

[11 chapters, 107p., Gr. 3–5] In a series of very funny episodes, the famous Canadian author describes the two wild horned owls, Wols and Weeps, that he found and tamed when he was a boy. More pets from the wild include Sterling North's *Rascal* and Bill Peet's *Capyboppy.* AUTOBIOGRAPHY. CANADA. DOGS. OWLS. PETS.

2078   Murphy, Jim. *Weird and Wacky Inventions.* Illus. Crown, 1978.

[9 chapters, Gr. 3–6] Original drawings of 90 of the oddest inventions patented by the U.S. Patent Trademark Office are each captioned with four choices so the reader will deduce the correct one. Answers with explanations, printed on the back of each page, are often amazing and always amusing. Look for more in *Guess Again: More Weird and Wacky Inventions* (Bradbury, 1986). Rube Goldberg's *The Best of Rube Goldberg,* full of outlandish contraptions, and Webb Garrison's *Why Didn't I Think of That? From Alarm Clocks to Zippers* will put everyone in the mood for inventing something. INVENTIONS.

2079   North, Sterling. *Rascal: A Memoir of a Better Era.* Illus. by John Schoenherr. Penguin, 1990. ISBN 0-14-034445-4

[8 chapters, 189p., Gr. 4–6] North's autobiographical account of when he caught and raised a wild baby raccoon in Wisconsin. Pair with Farley Mowat's *Owls in the Family. Little Rascal* (Dutton, 1965) is an easier-to-read version of the same story for grades two to four. ANIMALS. PETS. RACCOONS.

2080   Patterson, Francine. *Koko's Kitten.* Photos by Ronald H. Cohn. Scholastic, 1985. ISBN 0-590-33811-0

[1 sitting, unp., Gr. 2–6] Taught by Patterson to communicate through American sign language, the famous gorilla continues to live in California with her gorilla friend Michael and their pet cat Smoky. *Koko's Kitten* makes a touching Christmas story, about her first cat, the tailless All Ball, while *Koko's Story* (1987) is an overview of the gorilla's life and training. Also, don't miss *The Story of Nim, the Chimp Who Learned Language* by Anna Michel, as it was Nim's accomplishments that interested Patterson in beginning her gorilla project. Venture to learn and then pass along some basic sign language to your students. COMMUNICATION. GORILLAS. SIGN LANGUAGE.

2081   **Peet, Bill.** *Capyboppy.* **Illus. by the author. Houghton Mifflin, 1967. ISBN 0-395-24378-5**

[1–2 sittings, 62p., Gr. 2–5] Brought home as a pet, the guinea pig-resembling South American capybara, world's largest rodent, adapted well to life with the Peet family until he grew bigger and more headstrong. Children who have been exposed to Peet as an animal-loving picture book writer will be charmed to cast an eye on his family life. Also difficult as pets were Farley Mowat's *Owls in the Family* and Sterling North's *Rascal.* ANIMALS. PETS.

2082   **Peters, Lisa Westberg.** *The Sun, the Wind and the Rain.* **Illus. by Ted Rand. Henry Holt, 1988. ISBN 0-8050-0699-0**

[1 sitting, unp., Gr. Pre–2] Two stories in one, side by side, the first showing how a mountain is created and then worn down and changed by the forces of nature; the second, on facing pages, parallels the first, as Elizabeth constructs a sand "mountain" at the beach, only to have it erode from wind and rain. Bring in sand and reproduce a small-scale version of Elizabeth's mountain and show how it was flattened. Gorgeous dark watercolors make this an exciting partner to other easy-to-understand geology books such as Joanna Cole's *The Magic School Bus Inside the Earth,* Tomie dePaola's *The Quicksand Book,* Bruce Hiscock's *The Big Rock,* and Faith McNulty's *How To Dig a Hole to the Other Side of the World.* GEOLOGY. MOUNTAINS. NATURE. SEASHORE.

2083   **Phillips, Louis.** *263 Brain Busters: Just How Smart Are You, Anyway?* **Illus. by James Stevenson. Viking, 1985. ISBN 0-670-80412-6**

[87p., Gr. 3–6] A perfect after lunch warm-up of puzzlers to test math, language, logic, and listening skills in an amusing and clever way. Answers at the back of the book will have you slapping your forehead with dismay, as even you will be tricked by some of these stumpers. If you crave more see E. Richard Churchill's *Devilish Bets to Trick Your Friends* and Laurence B. White, Jr., and Ray Broekel's *The Surprise Book* and *The Trick Book* (Doubleday, 1979). MATHEMATICS. WORD GAMES.

2084   **Provensen, Alice, and Martin Provensen.** *The Glorious Flight: Across the Channel with Louis Blériot.* **Illus. by the authors. Viking, 1983. ISBN 0-670-34259-9**

[1 sitting, 39p., Gr. K–6] In 1909, Frenchman Blériot became the first person to successfully fly the English Channel in a mere 36 minutes, as chronicled picture book style in a stunning portrayal of the man's obsession with airplanes. Update advances in the field with some research and astronaut Sally Ride's *To Space and Back.* Just for fun see also Peter Spier's *Bored, Nothing to Do,* where two boys build and fly their own plane one afternoon. AIRPLANES. BIOGRAPHY. CALDECOTT MEDAL. FLIGHT. PICTURE BOOKS FOR ALL AGES.

2085   **Reit, Seymour.** *Behind Rebel Lines: The Incredible Story of Emma Edmonds, Civil War Spy.* **Harcourt, 1988. ISBN 0-15-200416-5**

[16 chapters, 102p., Gr. 5–6] Like Deborah Sampson, described in Ann McGovern's Revolutionary War biography *The Secret Soldier,* Edmonds disguised herself as a man and spent two years as a battlefront nurse and a spy for the Union Army. In a study of the Civil War, Edmonds's remarkable story, coupled with Russell Freedman's *Lincoln: A Photobiography*, Zachary Kent's *The Story of Ford's Theater and the Death of Lincoln* (Childrens, 1986), and Ann McGovern's *Runaway Slave: The Story of Harriet Tubman*, draws a compelling and tragic portrait of a nation wrenched apart. BIOGRAPHY. SPIES. U.S.—HISTORY—CIVIL WAR. WOMEN—BIOGRAPHY.

2086   **Ride, Sally, and Susan Okie.** *To Space and Back.* **Illus. with photos. Lothrop, 1986. ISBN 0-688-06159-1**

[96p., Gr. 3–6] The first American woman astronaut, Sally Ride, is an inspiring role model for girls and her personal explanation of what it is like in space is as close to a space shuttle flight as most of us are likely to get. Huge color photographs and detailed descriptions of fellow astronauts working, eating, and sleeping give us a vicarious taste of flight conditions. Ride even fills us in on how the bathroom works! Link this with Patricia Lauber's *Lost Star: The Story of Amelia Earhart* to meet another courageous aeronautical pioneer who opened doors for women. ASTRONOMY. SPACE FLIGHT.

2087   **Ryden, Hope.** *Wild Animals of America ABC.* **Illus. by the author. Dutton, 1988. ISBN 0-525-67245-1**

[unp., Gr. Pre–2] Children can identify those U.S. animals they recognize in this combination of known and obscure animals, with a full-page color photograph for each letter. Final pages include "About These Animals" information. Pair fact and fiction as you read aloud additional books about the 26 creatures included. ALPHABET BOOKS. ANIMALS.

2088   **Ryder, Joanne.** *Catching the Wind.* **Illus. by Michael Rothman. Morrow, 1989. ISBN 0-688-07171-6**

[1 sitting, unp., Gr. Pre–3] When the autumn wind comes calling, it carries you into the sky, where you soar on feathered wings over your town and join the rest of the geese flying in V formation. This lyrical and compelling "Just for a Day" book would add depth and vicarious experience to those stories where humans become birds or vice versa, such as Hans Christian Andersen's *The Wild Swans*, Molly Bang's *Dawn*, Mordicai Gerstein's *Arnold of the Ducks*, and Beatrice Gormley's *Mail-Order Wings*. BIRDS. GEESE. TRANSFORMATIONS.

2089   **Ryder, Joanne.** *Chipmunk Song.* **Illus. by Lynne Cherry. Dutton, 1987. ISBN 0-525-67191-9**

[unp., Gr. Pre–2] Stunning detailed illustrations and a poetic "you-are-there" text detail a chipmunk's lot as it prepares for winter hibernation. Any nature/winter/animals units will be made more meaningful after reading and acting this out in narrative pantomime. Other stories about hibernation include Don Freeman's *Bearymore*, Michele Lemieux's *What's That Noise?* and Millicent Selsam and Joyce Hunt's *Keep Looking!* CHIPMUNKS. HIBERNATION. SEASONS. WINTER.

2090   **Ryder, Joanne.** *Lizard in the Sun.* **Illus. by Michael Rothman. Morrow, 1990. ISBN 0-688-07173-2**

[1 sitting, unp., Gr. Pre–3] One bright morning, the sun slips into your room, changing you into an anole, a lizard small and thin, light as a handful of popcorn. As in *Catching the Wind* and *White Bear, Ice Bear*, each listener can become a new animal for a day, pantomiming the lizard's sunning, eating, drinking, and changing color from green to brown. CREATIVE DRAMA. LIZARDS. REPTILES. TRANSFORMATIONS.

2091 Ryder, Joanne. *White Bear, Ice Bear*. Illus. by Michael Rothman. Morrow, 1989. ISBN 0-688-07175-9

[1 sitting, unp., Gr. Pre–3] From child to polar bear, your metamorphosis takes you across a white frozen sea, hunting for seals through a hole in the Arctic ice. From the realism and color photographs of Downs Matthews's *Polar Bear Cubs* and Ginny Johnston and Judy Cutchins's *Andy Bear: A Polar Bear Grows Up at the Zoo*, use Ryder's "Just for a Day" book as a slide into the fiction of Robert Benton's *Don't Ever Wish for a 7-Foot Bear*. BEARS. TRANSFORMATIONS.

2092 Schwartz, Alvin. *Gold and Silver, Silver and Gold: Tales of Hidden Treasure*. Illus. by David Christiana. Farrar, 1988. ISBN 0-374-32690-8

[10 chapters, 128p., Gr. 4–6] After reading a fiction story of a hunt for buried or missing treasure such as John Bellairs's *The Treasure of Alpheus Winterborn* or Sid Fleischman's *The Ghost in the Noonday Sun*, regale your gold-fevered listeners with these mostly true descriptions of searches for sunken ships and other booty. Hide a prize of your choosing somewhere on school grounds and either devise a map and code for seekers to decipher or have your class create them for another class to figure out. For a recent heart-stopping search see also Robert Ballard's firsthand *Exploring the Titanic* (Scholastic, 1988). BURIED TREASURE. MONEY.

2093 Schwartz, David M. *How Much Is a Million?* Illus. by Steven Kellogg. Lothrop, 1985. ISBN 0-688-04050-0

[1 sitting, unp., Gr. 1–4] As ever, Kellogg's zillions of details are not so easy for a group to see, but if you want your math-minded crew to find out just how big a million, billion, and trillion really are, do not miss this trip through Earth and stars with Marvelosissimo the Mathematical Magician and friends. A note from Schwartz at the back of the book explains how he made his amazing computations. Keep counting with his *If You Made a Million*. MATHEMATICS.

2094 Schwartz, David M. *If You Made a Million*. Illus. by Steven Kellogg. Lothrop, 1989. ISBN 0-688-07017-5

[1 sitting, unp., Gr. 2–4] Marvelosissimo the Mathematical Magician returns to explain how money, banks, and interest work for children who are planning to start investing in their future fortunes. Kellogg's illustrations teem with hard-to-see details, so have everyone sit close. Math teachers will find this a gold mine for lesson starters. MATHEMATICS. MONEY.

2095 Selsam, Millicent, and Joyce Hunt. *Keep Looking!* Illus. by Normand Chartier. Macmillan, 1989. ISBN 0-02-781840-3

[1 sitting, 32p., Gr. Pre–2] Though the snow-covered house and yard look empty, closer inspection reveals creatures such as chickadee, chipmunk, skunk, and woodchuck going through their routines. Pair this with Joanne Ryder's *Chipmunk Song*, Tejima's *Fox's Dream*, and Jane Yolen's *Owl Moon* for an up-front look at animals in winter. ANIMALS. NATURE. WINTER.

2096 Seuling, Barbara. *The Last Cow on the White House Lawn & Other Little-Known Facts about the Presidency*. Illus. by the author. Doubleday, 1978.

[95p., Gr. 3–5] Arranged chronologically from George Washington through Jimmy Carter, the array of often humorous facts will help you put a human face on each president. When researching individual presidents, students can compile other unusual tidbits and, after presenting oral reports, students can play a Presidents' Trivia Game, where they attempt to identify each president from the facts. FACTS. PRESIDENTS—U.S.

2097   Seuling, Barbara. *You Can't Eat Peanuts in Church: And Other Little-Known Laws.* Illus. by the author. Doubleday, 1975.

[64p., Gr. 3–5] Seuling has compiled a list of past and current laws that are outstanding for their outrageousness. Reading aloud assorted snippets of outlawed behavior, from putting tomatoes in clam chowder to spitting against the wind, will bring mirth to your class, as will the companion book *It Is Illegal to Quack Like a Duck & Other Freaky Laws* (Lodestar, 1988), and Seuling's accompanying fact compendiums including *The Last Cow on the White House Lawn & Other Little-Known Facts about the Presidency* and *You Can't Sneeze with Your Eyes Open & Other Freaky Facts about the Human Body* (Lodestar, 1986). FACTS.

2098   Sewall, Marcia. *The Pilgrims of Plimoth.* Illus. by the author. Atheneum, 1986. ISBN 0-689-31250-4

[2 sittings, 48p., Gr. 2–6] A narrative account of life then, told by the Pilgrims' Menfolk, Womenfolk, and Youngfolk in the vernacular of the settlement. Pair this with Jean Fritz's *Who's That Stepping on Plymouth Rock?* and Kate Waters's photo essay of Plimoth Plantation, *Sarah Morton's Day: A Day in the Life of a Pilgrim Girl.* PILGRIMS. U.S.—HISTORY—COLONIAL PERIOD.

2099   Simon, Seymour. *Animal Fact / Animal Fable.* Illus. by Diane de Groat. Crown, 1979.

[1 sitting, unp., Gr. 1–4] Each page makes a statement with which children must agree or disagree and then identifies and explains the scientific facts behind it. This is a good way to demonstrate the difference between fact and fable and the large amusing animal paintings give children a chuckle as they puzzle out if bats are blind or if porcupines shoot their quills. Continue the questions with Simon's *The Dinosaur Is the Biggest Animal That Ever Lived, and Other Wrong Ideas You Thought Were True.* More of the same, plus black-and-white photographs, can be found in Edward R. Ricciuti's *Do Toads Give You Warts? Strange Animal Myths Explained* (Walker, 1975) and Susan Sussman and Robert James's much more detailed *Lies (People Believe) about Animals* (Albert Whitman, 1987). ANIMALS.

2100   Simon, Seymour. *The Dinosaur Is the Biggest Animal That Ever Lived and Other Wrong Ideas You Thought Were True.* Illus. by Giulio Maestro. Lippincott, 1984. ISBN 0-397-32076-0

[2 sittings, 63p., Gr. 2–5] Like the preceding, simpler *Animal Fact/Animal Fable,* Simon details the facts behind more than 24 science-related misconceptions. Older children can research other science fallacies and stump the class with their findings. SCIENCE.

2101   Simon, Seymour. *Galaxies.* Illus. with photos. Morrow, 1988. ISBN 0-688-08004-9

[1 sitting, unp., Gr. 3–6] Seymour Simon makes the inconceivable accessible and facts about the 200 billion stars that comprise the Milky Way, one of over one million known galaxies, are a revelation to children who think Cleveland is very far away. Read with *Stars* as a first step into the amazing universe. ASTRONOMY.

2102   **Simon, Seymour.** *Hidden Worlds: Pictures of the Invisible.* **Illus. with photos. Morrow, 1983. ISBN 0-688-02465-3**

[1–2 sittings, 47p., Gr. 4–6] From the microscopic to the telescopic, detailed photographs show astonishing sights such as blood cells, a speeding bullet, and Hurricane Allen. A complement to Lisa Grillone and Joseph Gennaro's *Small Worlds Close Up.* MICROSCOPES AND MICROSCOPY.

2103   **Simon, Seymour.** *Icebergs and Glaciers.* **Illus. with photos. Morrow, 1987. ISBN 0-688-06187-7**

[1 sitting, unp., Gr. 3–5] Enormous magnificent color photographs and an unusually clear text make another fascinating subject understandable. OCEAN. SNOW.

2104   **Simon, Seymour.** *Stars.* **Illus. with photos. Morrow, 1986. ISBN 0-688-05856-6**

[1–2 sittings, unp., Gr. 3–6] With its gigantic color photographs and mind-shaking facts and figures this book will make you feel very small and insignificant in the scheme of things—what with all the talk of billions of stars in the Milky Way or Andromeda being a cool 12 quintillion miles away. This is another staggeringly successful presentation of complex information made comprehensible for the beginner. Math possibilities abound; for example, if stars move ten miles a second, how many miles do they move in an hour? How many inches is the circumference of Earth? Read Paul Goble's *Her Seven Brothers* to see how the Cheyenne Indians explain the birth of one major constellation. Pair with *Galaxies*, above, for the even larger picture. ASTRONOMY. STARS.

2105   **Simon, Seymour.** *Storms.* **Illus. with photos. Morrow, 1989. ISBN 0-688-07414-6**

[1 sitting, unp., Gr. 4–6] For a weather unit or just a rainy day, the huge color photos and well-chosen facts will inspire awe and ah's; information on what to do in a thunderstorm and imposing shots of tornadoes in action are enough to spark multiple research projects. Ivy Ruckman's *Night of the Twisters*, a fiction book based on a true account, will also appeal to readers. STORMS. WEATHER.

2106   **Simon, Seymour.** *Volcanoes.* **Illus. with photos. Morrow, 1988. ISBN 0-688-07412-X**

[1 sitting, unp., Gr. 2–6] Simon's easy-to-understand introduction to volcanoes is made riveting by full-page fiery color photographs focusing on Mount St. Helens and Mauna Loa, but includes information on all four groups: shield, cinder cone, stratovolcanoes, and cone. Focus further with Patricia Lauber's *Volcano: The Eruption and Healing of Mount St. Helens* and try a little folklore with Ann Grifalconi's *The Village of Round and Square Houses* or some fiction with Roger W. Drury's *The Finches' Fabulous Furnace* or William Pène Du Bois's *The Twenty-One Balloons.* GEOLOGY. VOLCANOES.

2107   **Stein, Sara Bonnett.** *Cat.* **Illus. by Manuel Garcia. Harcourt, 1985.**

[1 sitting, unp., Gr. Pre–1] Along with its companion book *Mouse* (1985), here is an easily understood explanation of how cats hunt and how mice are hunted. Both books sport larger-than-life-size paintings of the black-and-white cat and the mouse family it stalks through house and yard. Sumiko's *Kittymouse* and Paul O.

Zelinsky's *The Maid and the Mouse and the Odd-Shaped House* provide some fictional comic relief. CATS.

2108   **Swan, Robert.** *Destination: Antarctica.* **Illus. with photos. Scholastic, 1988. ISBN 0-590-41285-X**

[1–2 sittings, unp., Gr. 4–6] In 1986, Swan and two companions made the 900-mile trek through Antarctica to the South Pole to duplicate Robert Scott's historic journey in 1912. This color photo essay documents their modern-day undertaking for readers studying that continent and its explorers or those who relish true adventure. EXPLORERS. WINTER.

2109   **Swinburne, Irene, and Laurence Swinburne.** *Behind the Sealed Door: The Discovery of the Tomb and Treasures of Tutankhamen.* **Illus. with photos. Sniffen Court, 1977.**

[6 chapters, 96p., Gr. 4–6] How archaeologist Howard Carter located and excavated the fabulous tomb of the ancient Egyptian boy-king in 1922, with dazzling photographs of the legendary shrine he found there. Once your students become delirious over Egypt also read the ancient folktales *The Egyptian Cinderella* by Shirley Climo and *The Voyage of Osiris* by Gerald McDermott, as well as Mary Stolz's fictional *Zekmet the Stone Carver* about how the Sphinx may have been carved. ARCHAEOLOGY. BURIED TREASURE. EGYPT, ANCIENT.

2110   **Tayntor, Elizabeth, Paul Erickson, and Les Kaufman.** *Dive to the Coral Reefs: A New England Aquarium Book.* **Illus. with photos. Crown, 1986. ISBN 0-517-56311-8**

[1 sitting, unp., Gr. 3–6] These large knockout color photographs of animals and plants were taken by scientist-divers on a Jamaican coral reef. A brief text explains the ecology and introduces us to a glorious underwater world. For more detailed information about ocean dwellers see Gilda Berger's *Whales.* Also go back to Leo Lionni's impressionistic fish survival story *Swimmy* for an artist's view. FISHES. ISLANDS. OCEAN.

2111   **Wakefield, Pat A., and Larry Carrara.** *A Moose for Jessica.* **Photos by Larry Carrara. Dutton, 1987. ISBN 0-525-44342-8**

[2–3 sittings, unp., Gr. 3–6] When the 6-foot moose came to the Carrara family's Vermont pasture and spent 72 days mooning over their Hereford cow it made national headlines. While Larry Carrara never touched the moose, feeling that to do so would take some of its wildness from it, Betty Leslie-Melville tamed an African giraffe in *Daisy Rothschild: The Giraffe That Lives with Me.* For another true cow tale see James Herriot's *Blossom Comes Home.* COUNTRY LIFE. COWS. MOOSE.

2112   **Waters, Kate.** *Sarah Morton's Day: A Day in the Life of a Pilgrim Girl.* **Photos by Russ Kendall. Scholastic, 1989. ISBN 0-590-42634-6**

[1 sitting, 32p., Gr. 1–5] A firsthand narration, in period dialect with matching color photographs, of a typical day, by a nine-year-old Plimoth Plantation girl. Correlate her situation to the modern-day saga of a Russian émigré schoolgirl in *Molly's Pilgrim* by Barbara Cohen. Also see Jean Fritz's pragmatic *Who's That Stepping on Plymouth Rock?* and Marcia Sewall's intimate *The Pilgrims of Plimoth.* PILGRIMS. U.S.–HISTORY–COLONIAL PERIOD.

2113   **White, Florence.** *Escape! The Life of Harry Houdini.* **Illus. with photos. Messner, 1979.**

[11 chapters, 108p., Gr. 3–6] From a poor Hungarian Jewish necktie cutter to the world's most famous magician and escape artist, the astonishing career of Erich

Weiss is documented with period photographs. Uncover the secret behind one of his greatest tricks as revealed in Robert Kraske's *Magicians Do Amazing Things* and demonstrate sleight of hand with the aid of Roy Broekel and Laurence B. White, Jr.'s *Now You See It* and Sid Fleischman's *Mr. Mysterious's Secrets of Magic*. BIOGRAPHY. MAGICIANS.

2114   **White, Laurence B., Jr., and Ray Broekel.** *The Surprise Book.* **Illus. by Will Winslow. Doubleday, 1981.**

[87p., Gr. 2–6] Word games, magic, and other tricks to play on your students before they try them on you. Find more word-oriented examples in Gyles Brandreth's *Brain Teasers and Mind-Benders*, E. Richard Churchill's *Devilish Bets to Trick Your Friends*, Louis Phillips's *263 Brain Busters*, and Alvin Schwartz's *Tomfoolery* and *Witcracks*. GAMES. TRICKS. WORD GAMES.

2115   **Williams, Gurney.** *True Escape and Survival Stories.* **Illus. by Michael Deas. Franklin Watts, 1977.**

[8 chapters, 84p., Gr. 4–6] In spite of great odds, these seven victims made it out of Auschwitz, Indian captivity, a mountain blizzard, the *Apollo 13* spaceship, a Pacific Island, the Springhill, Nova Scotia coal mine disaster, and an Andes plane crash. Listeners will also thrill to Walter R. Brown and Normal D. Anderson's *Rescue!* ADVENTURE AND ADVENTURERS. BIOGRAPHY. COURAGE. HEROES. SURVIVAL.

2116   **Yoshida, Toshi.** *Young Lions.* **Illus. by the author. Philomel, 1989. ISBN 0-399-21546-8**

[1 sitting, unp., Gr. 1–4] On their first hunt, in the shadow of Mt. Kilimanjaro, three young lions observe or chase a wide array of game, including rhinoceros, water buffalo, zebras, impalas, and cheetahs. An uncomplicated, direct text and shimmering, heat-blurred color-pencil illustrations make this an exciting entry to life on the African plain. Also don't miss Angelika Hofer's splendid photographs in *The Lion Family Book*. AFRICA. ANIMALS. LIONS.

2117   **Young, Ruth.** *Starring Francine & Dave: Three One-Act Plays.* **Illus. by the author. Orchard, 1988. ISBN 0-531-08381-0**

[1 sitting, unp., Gr. Pre–2] "Foodies," be prepared to hand out refreshments after reading aloud the dialogue and stage directions for these three skits about two friends who make a peanut butter sandwich, fine-tune a pitcher of lemonade, and divvy up a chocolate cake. (Nadine Bernard Westcott's *Peanut Butter and Jelly* is a must here.) Children can act these out in pairs, make up new playlets, and read other books about plays like Remy Charlip's *Mother, Mother, I Feel Sick, Send for the Doctor Quick, Quick, Quick*, Miriam Cohen's *Starring First Grade*, Joan Lowery Nixon's *Gloria Chipmunk, Star*, and Joanne Oppenheim's *Mrs. Peloki's Class Play*. CREATIVE DRAMA. FOOD. PLAYS.

Illustration by Tomie dePaola reprinted by permission of G. P. Putnam's Sons from TOMIE DEPAOLA'S BOOK OF POEMS, copyright © 1988 by Tomie dePaola.

Bibliography
and Indexes

From JENNY ARCHER, AUTHOR by Ellen Conford, with illustrations by Diane Palmisciano. Illustrations copyright © 1989 by Diane Palmisciano. By permission of Little, Brown and Company.

PROFESSIONAL BIBLIOGRAPHY

OVERVIEW OF CHILDREN'S LITERATURE: TEXTS

2118   Cullinan, Bernice E. *Literature and the Child*. Harcourt, 1989. ISBN 0-15-551111-4

Interspersed with the highly competent text exploring each genre are practical "Teaching Idea" pages that show ways to use books being discussed and "Profile" pages of well-known authors and illustrators.

2119   Huck, Charlotte. *Children's Literature in the Elementary School.* 4th ed. Holt, Rinehart & Winston, 1987. ISBN 0-03-041770-8

A thorough study of the field encompassing every aspect of developing a successful literature program. No professional collection is complete without this invaluable text.

2120   Lacy, Lyn Ellen. *Art and Design in Children's Picture Books: An Analysis of Caldecott Award-Winning Books.* American Library Association, 1986. ISBN 0-8389-0446-7

An in-depth look at 13 winners.

2121   Lukens, Rebecca J. *A Critical Handbook of Children's Literature.* 4th ed. Scott, Foresman, 1990. ISBN 0-673-38773-9

How to evaluate children's books in terms of genre, characters, plot, setting, theme, point of view, style, and tone.

2122   Norton, Donna E. *Through the Eyes of a Child: An Introduction to Children's Literature.* 2nd ed. Merrill, 1987. ISBN 0-675-20725-8

A competent, attractive, and detailed overview designed for children's literature classes.

2123   Sutherland, Zena, et al. *Children and Books.* 7th ed. Scott, Foresman, 1986. ISBN 0-673-18069-7

Under each genre major authors and their works are discussed in detail.

READING, WRITING, AND BOOKTALKING: IDEAS AND ANNOTATIONS

2124   **Baring-Gould, William, and Cecil Baring-Gould, eds.** *The Annotated Mother Goose.* **Clarkson N. Potter, 1982. ISBN 0-517-54629-9**

Explanations of the history behind the rhymes.

2125   **Barstow, Barbara, and Judith Riggle.** *Beyond Picture Books: A Guide to First Readers.* **R. R. Bowker, 1989. ISBN 0-8352-2515-1**

An annotated bibliography of more than 1,600 books at a first-to-second grade beginning-to-read level that children can handle independently.

2126   **Bauer, Caroline Feller.** *Celebrations: Read-Aloud Holiday & Theme Book Programs.* **Illus. by Lynn Gates. H. W. Wilson, 1985. ISBN 0-8242-0708-4**

Innovative children's book-related holiday activities.

2127   **Bauer, Caroline Feller.** *This Way to Books.* **Illus. by Lynn Gates. H. W. Wilson, 1983. ISBN 0-8242-0678-9**

A grand and attractive collection of children's book-related projects.

2128   **Bodart, Joni.** *Booktalk! Booktalking and School Visiting for Young Adult Audiences.* **H. W. Wilson, 1980. ISBN 0-8242-0650-9**

The hows and whys of booktalking. This book is geared to older children though the principles of booktalking remain the same for all ages.

2129   **Bodart, Joni.** *Booktalk! 2: Booktalking for All Ages and Audiences.* **2nd ed. H. W. Wilson, 1985. ISBN 0-8242-0716-5**

This book describes how to give a booktalk.

2130   **Bodart, Joni, ed.** *Booktalk! 3: More Booktalks for All Ages and Audiences.* **H. W. Wilson, 1988. ISBN 0-8242-0764-5**

More booktalks for elementary school audiences.

2131   **Carlson, Ruth Kearney.** *Enrichment Ideas: Sparking Fireflies.* **2nd ed. William C. Brown, 1976. ISBN 0-697-06209-0**

Hundreds of suggestions for extending the classroom reading program with children's books.

2132   **Carlson, Ruth Kearney.** *Writing Aids Through the Grades.* **Teachers College Press, 1970. ISBN 0-8077-1141-1**

Developmental activities for writing poetry and prose.

2133   **Cullinan, Bernice E., and Carolyn Carmichael, eds.** *Literature and Young Children.* **National Council of Teachers of English, 1977. ISBN 0-8141-2972-2**

Sensible strategies for presenting books to children. Includes bibliographies after each chapter, plus a list of 100 best books and authors for young children.

2134   **Dreyer, Sharon Spredemann.** *The Bookfinder: A Guide to Children's Literature about the Needs and Problems of Youth Ages 2 to 15.* **Volume 1. American Guidance Service, 1977. ISBN 0-913476-45-5**

Indexed by subject, this book is a well-annotated bibliography of children's books useful in bibliotherapy. Volumes 2, 3, and 4, published in 1981, 1985, and 1989, respectively, are necessary updates.

2135   Edwards, Margaret A. *The Fair Garden and the Swarm of Beasts: The Library and the Young Adult.* Hawthorne, 1969.

Geared for those who work with older children this book includes excellent practical advice on booktalking.

2136   Gillespie, John T. *More Juniorplots: A Guide for Teachers and Librarians.* R. R. Bowker, 1977. ISBN 0-8352-1002-2

This book includes a marvelous introduction on booktalking by Mary K. Chelton, plus booktalk material on 72 novels for grades five and up.

2137   Gillespie, John T., and Diana Lembo. *Introducing Books: A Guide for the Middle Grades.* R. R. Bowker, 1970. ISBN 0-8352-0215-1

A thematically arranged, generously annotated guide for booktalkers. Eighty-eight well-chosen book reviews include a plot analysis along with thematic booktalk and other suggestions for using with children.

2138   Gillespie, John T., and Diana Lembo. *Juniorplots: A Book Talk Manual for Teachers and Librarians.* R. R. Bowker, 1967. ISBN 0-8352-0063-9

A continuation of *Introducing Books.*

2139   Gillespie, John T., and Corinne J. Naden, eds. *Best Books for Children: Preschool through Grade 6.* 4th ed. R. R. Bowker, 1990. ISBN 0-8352-2668-9

Over 11,000 annotated titles arranged under general subject categories.

2140   Hopkins, Lee Bennett. *Pass the Poetry, Please!* 2nd ed. Harper & Row, 1987. ISBN 0-06-446062-2

Poetry-shy teachers can unwind with biographical sketches and a poem for each of 20 well-loved children's poets. Also includes descriptions of types of poetry and a plethora of activities to try out with students.

2141   Kennedy, DayAnn M., Stella S. Spangler, and Mary Ann Vanderwerf. *Science & Technology in Fact and Fiction: A Guide to Children's Books.* R. R. Bowker, 1990. ISBN 0-8352-2708-1

An attractive bibliography of more than 300 science-related fiction and nonfiction books. Each entry includes a detailed summary and an evaluation of illustrations and text.

2142   Kimmel, Mary Margaret, and Elizabeth Segel. *For Reading Out Loud! A Guide to Sharing Books with Children.* Rev. ed. Delacorte, 1988. ISBN 0-385-29660-6

Full-page detailed write-ups of 300 good books to read aloud, with advice on how to do it.

2143   Kobrin, Beverly. *Eyeopeners! How to Choose and Use Children's Books about Real People, Places, and Things.* Penguin, 1988. ISBN 0-14-046830-7

An annotated subject guide to activities and tips for using nonfiction books with children.

2144   Larrick, Nancy. *A Parent's Guide to Children's Reading*. 5th rev. ed. Westminster, 1983. ISBN 0-664-32705-2

Hundreds of suggested titles and activities to try at home.

2145   Laughlin, Mildred, and Letty S. Watt. *Developing Learning Skills Through Children's Literature: An Idea Book for K-5 Classrooms and Libraries.* Oryx, 1986. ISBN 0-89774-258-3

An interesting and appealing subject approach to introducing books to children with a lifetime supply of suggestions for literature-based activities.

2146   Leonard, Charlotte. *Tied Together: Topics and Thoughts for Introducing Children's Books*. Scarecrow, 1980. ISBN 0-8108-1293-2

Hundreds of titles, with ways to present them.

2147   Lima, Carolyn W., and John A. Lima. *A to Zoo: Subject Access to Children's Picture Books*. 3rd ed. R. R. Bowker, 1989. ISBN 0-8352-2599-2

An enormous bibliography of nearly 12,000 titles cataloged under 700 subjects. The only comprehensive guide of its kind.

2148   Lipson, Eden Ross. *The New York Times Parent's Guide to the Best Books for Children*. Times Books, 1988. ISBN 0-8129-1649-2

A competent, well-chosen, annotated booklist of more than 900 titles broken into wordless, picture, story, early reading, middle reading, and young adult books.

2149   Paulin, Mary Ann. *Creative Uses of Children's Literature*. Shoe String Press, 1986. ISBN 0-208-01861-1

A vast compendium of ideas.

2150   Polette, Nancy. *Nancy Polette's E Is for Everybody: A Manual for Bringing Fine Picture Books into the Minds and Hearts of Children*. 2nd ed. Scarecrow, 1982. ISBN 0-8108-1579-6

Annotations and activities for 126 picture books, plus a section on interpreting literature through art and media.

2151   Polette, Nancy. *Picture Books for Gifted Programs*. Scarecrow, 1981. ISBN 0-8108-1461-7

Your students do not need to be geniuses to appreciate the wealth of activities here, which incorporate cognitive development, visual literacy, language development, and productive and critical thinking skills.

2152   Polette, Nancy, and Marjorie Hamlin. *Celebrating with Books.* Illus. Scarecrow, 1977. ISBN 0-8108-1032-8

Holiday tie-ins using children's books.

2153   Reasoner, Charles F. *Releasing Children to Literature*. Dell, 1976.

Annotated titles with pre- and postreading discussion questions.

2154   Reasoner, Charles F. *Where the Readers Are*. Dell, 1972. ISBN 0-685-29120-0

Teaching units for independent reading with Dell paperbacks. Pre- and postreading discussion questions and suggested activities accompany each title.

2155   Sloan, Glenna Davis. *The Child as Critic: Teaching Literature in Elementary and Middle School*. Teachers College Press, 1984. ISBN 0-8077-2705-9

Includes a fascinating explanation of literary imagery and the four types of literature: comedy, romance, tragedy, and irony-satire.

2156   Thomas, Rebecca L. *Primaryplots: A Book Talk Guide for Use with Readers Ages 4–8.* R. R. Bowker, 1989. ISBN 0-8352-2514-3

A quality reading-guidance directory of 150 easy-to-read and picture book titles, with each entry supplying bibliographic information, a plot summary, thematic material, booktalk ideas and activities, and a list of related titles.

2157   Trelease, Jim. *The New Read-Aloud Handbook.* Rev. ed. Penguin, 1989. ISBN 0-14-046881-1

Why and what to read aloud; a treasury of nearly 300 annotated titles.

2158   Winkel, Lois. *The Elementary School Library Collection: A Guide to Books and Other Media.* 16th ed. Bro-Dart, 1988. ISBN 0-87272-092-6

An enormous, annotated catalog, issued yearly, of suggested new and favorite titles for children. Arranged like a library shelflist, and including copious indexes, reference and audiovisual material, and subject headings for each entry, this is a tool no librarian should be without.

2159   Zavatsky, Bill, and Ron Padgett, eds. *The Whole Word Catalogue 2.* McGraw-Hill, 1977. ISBN 0-915924-67-6

Myriad creative ideas for writing poetry and prose.

STORYTELLING AND CREATIVE DRAMATICS

2160   Baker, Augusta, and Ellin Greene. *Storytelling: Art and Technique.* 2nd ed. R. R. Bowker, 1987. ISBN 0-8352-2336-1

A sensible manual for beginning and experienced storytellers alike.

2161   Bauer, Caroline Feller. *Handbook for Storytellers.* American Library Association, 1977. ISBN 0-8389-0293-6

From planning to delivery, a gold mine of ideas.

2162   Bauer, Caroline Feller. *Presenting Reader's Theater: Plays and Poems to Read Aloud.* Illus. by Lynn Gates Bredeson. H. W. Wilson, 1987. ISBN 0-8242-0748-3

More than 50 read-aloud scripts based on children's literature.

2163   Bettelheim, Bruno. *The Uses of Enchantment: The Meaning and Importance of Fairy Tales.* Random House, 1989. ISBN 0-679-72393-5

Fascinating interpretations by the famous child psychologist.

2164   Bosma, Bette. *Fairy Tales, Fables, Legends, and Myths: Using Folk Literature in Your Classroom.* Teachers College Press, 1987. ISBN 0-8077-2827-6

Comprehension, critical reading, writing, and other creative activities for incorporating the study of folklore into a classroom program.

2165   Breneman, Lucille, and Bren Breneman. *Once Upon a Time: A Storytelling Handbook.* Nelson-Hall, 1983. ISBN 0-8304-1007-4

The basics.

2166   Briggs, Nancy E., and Joseph A. Wagner. *Children's Literature Through Storytelling &*
Drama. 2nd ed. William C. Brown, 1979. ISBN 0-697-06212-0

A thoroughly professional, pragmatic, and accessible guide, with scads of useful
exercises and examples involving children as tellers and actors.

2167   Chambers, Dewey W. *The Oral Tradition: Storytelling and Creative Drama.* 2nd ed.
William C. Brown, 1977. ISBN 0-697-06210-4

Another useful guide, laced with practical suggestions.

2168   Champlin, Connie, and Nancy Renfro. *Storytelling with Puppets.*   American Library
Association, 1985. ISBN 0-8389-0421-1

A competent overview, including puppet patterns, techniques for storytelling and
puppet manipulation, participatory activities, story bibliographies, and sensible
advice.

2169   Clarkson, Atelia, and Gilbert B. Cross. *World Folktales: A Scribner Resource Collection.*
Scribner, 1980. ISBN 0-684-16290-3

Over 60 known and not-so-known stories for telling, including notes, principal
motifs, and parallel stories for each selection.

2170   Colwell, Eileen. *Storytelling.* Bodley Head, 1983. ISBN 0-370-30228-1

From an old hand.

2171   De Wit, Dorothy. *Children's Faces Looking Up: Program Building for the Storyteller.*
American Library Association, 1979. ISBN 0-8389-0272-3

Develops storytelling programs on a multitude of themes, with suggestions for
tales that tie in.

2172   Heinig, Ruth Beall, and Lydia Stillwell. *Creative Drama for the Classroom Teacher.* 3rd
ed. Prentice Hall, 1988. ISBN 0-13-189424-2

An exhaustive guide that relates children's literature to drama activities.

2173   Livo, Norma J., and Sandra A. Rietz. *Storytelling: Process and Practice.* Libraries Unlimited, 1986. ISBN 0-87287-443-5

Practical and comprehensive guidance through every aspect of the art of storytelling.

2174   MacDonald, Margaret Read. *Storyteller's Sourcebook.* Gale, 1982. ISBN 0-8103-0471-6

A comprehensive index of more than 700 editions of folktales, by story subject,
motif, and title. A necessity for all folklore-minded library collections.

2175   MacDonald, Margaret Read. *Twenty Tellable Tales: Audience Participation for the*
Beginning Storyteller. Illus. by Roxane Murphy. H. W. Wilson, 1986. ISBN 0-8242-0719-X

Step-by-step, for people who are afraid to tell stories.

2176   MacDonald, Margaret Read. *When the Lights Go Out: Twenty Scary Tales to Tell.* Illus.
by Roxane Murphy. H. W. Wilson, 1988. ISBN 0-8242-0770-X

Includes extensive notes on how to tell scary stories, with sources and variants for
each tale.

2177   **Pellowski, Anne.** *The Family Storytelling Handbook: How to Use Stories, Anecdotes, Rhymes, Handkerchiefs, Paper and Other Objects to Enrich Your Family Traditions.* **Illus. by Lynn Sweat. Macmillan, 1987. ISBN 0-02-770610-9**

A gem that parents and all storytellers will treasure.

2178   **Pellowski, Anne.** *The Story Vine: A Source Book of Unusual and Easy-to-Tell Stories from Around the World.* **Illus. by Lynn Sweat. Macmillan, 1984. ISBN 0-02-770590-0**

Indispensable "gimmicks," with instructions for string, picture-drawing, sand, doll, fingerplay, and musical instrument stories.

2179   **Sawyer, Ruth.** *The Way of the Storyteller.* **Rev. ed. Penguin, 1977. ISBN 0-14-004436-1**

Engrossing commentary on the art by a famous American storyteller, with a sampling of her favorite tales.

2180   **Schimmel, Nancy.** *Just Enough to Make a Story: A Sourcebook for Telling.* **Rev. ed. Sisters' Choice Press, 1987. ISBN 0-932164-02-1**

Practical, down-to-earth advice and an assortment of good stories to tell.

2181   **Shedlock, Marie L.** *The Art of the Story-Teller.* **3rd ed. Dover, 1952. ISBN 0-486-20635-1**

Instructions and tales from a renowned American storyteller; originally published in 1915.

2182   **Yolen, Jane.** *Favorite Folktales from Around the World.* **Pantheon, 1988. ISBN 0-394-72960-9**

An intelligent assortment of tellable stories grouped by types of tales and characters.

2183   **Yolen, Jane.** *Touch Magic: Fantasy, Faerie and Folklore in the Literature of Childhood.* **Putnam, 1981. ISBN 0-399-20830-5**

Lyrical essays on the art and artistry of storytelling.

2184   **Ziskind, Sylvia.** *Telling Stories to Children.* **H. W. Wilson, 1976. ISBN 0-8242-0588-X**

The chapter on "Mastering Technique" should be required for beginning storytellers.

AUTHOR INDEX

Authors are arranged alphabetically by last name. Authors' and joint authors' names are followed by book titles—also arranged alphabetically—and the text entry number.

Boyd, Pauline (jt. author). *I Met a Polar Bear*, 340

Boyd, Selma, and Pauline Boyd. *I Met a Polar Bear*, 340

Boynton, Sandra. *A Is for Angry*, 341

Bozzo, Maxine. *Toby in the Country, Toby in the City*, 25

Brady, Esther Wood. *Toliver's Secret*, 1148

Brady, Irene. *Doodlebug*, 620

Brandenberg, Franz. *I Wish I Was Sick, Too*, 26
No School Today, 342

Brandreth, Gyles. *Brain-Teasers and Mind-Benders*, 1997
The Super Joke Book, 1754

Brandreth, Gyles (comp.). *The Biggest Tongue Twister Book in the World*, 1753

Branley, Franklyn M. *Tornado Alert*, 1998

Breneman, Bren (jt. author). *Once Upon a Time*, 2165

Breneman, Lucille, and Bren Breneman. *Once Upon a Time*, 2165

Brenner, Barbara. *A Dog I Know*, 621
Little One Inch, 1407
Mr. Tall and Mr. Small, 343
A Year in the Life of Rosie Bernard, 1149

Brett, Jan. *The First Dog*, 622
Goldilocks and the Three Bears, 1408
The Mitten, 1409
The Twelve Days of Christmas, 1755

Brewton, John E. (jt. comp.). *My Tang's Tungled and Other Ridiculous Situations*, 1759
Shrieks at Midnight, 1758

Brewton, John E., and Lorraine A. Blackburn, comps. *They've Discovered a Head in the Box for the Bread*, 1756

Brewton, John E., Lorraine A. Blackburn, and George M. Blackburn, III, comps. *In the Witch's Kitchen*, 1757

Brewton, Sara, and John E. Brewton, comps. *Shrieks at Midnight*, 1758

Brewton, Sara, John E. Brewton, and G. Meredith Blackburn, III, comps. *My Tang's Tungled and Other Ridiculous Situations*, 1759

Briggs, Nancy E., and Joseph A. Wagner. *Children's Literature Through Storytelling & Drama*, 2166

Briggs, Raymond. *Jim and the Beanstalk*, 623

Briggs, Raymond (comp.). *The Mother Goose Treasury*, 1885

Brimner, Larry Dane. *Country Bear's Good Neighbor*, 27

Brink, Carol Ryrie. *The Bad Times of Irma Baumline*, 1150
Caddie Woodlawn, 1151

Brittain, Bill. *All the Money in the World*, 1152
Devil's Donkey, 1276
Dr. Dredd's Wagon of Wonders, 1277
The Wish Giver, 1278

Broekel, Ray (jt. author). *The Surprise Book*, 2114

Broekel, Ray, and Laurence B. White, Jr. *Now You See It*, 1999

Brooke, L. Leslie. *The Golden Goose Book*, 1658

Brooks, Walter Rollin. *Jimmy Takes Vanishing Lessons*, 876

Brown, Bob. *How to Fool Your Friends*, 2000

Brown, Drollene P. *Sybil Rides for Independence*, 2001

Brown, Jeff. *Flat Stanley*, 624

Brown, Marc. *Arthur's April Fool*, 625
Arthur's Baby, 344
Arthur's Birthday, 626
Arthur's Eyes, 345
Arthur's Halloween, 627
Arthur's Teacher Trouble, 628
Arthur's Tooth, 629
Hand Rhymes, 1760
Spooky Riddles, 1761

Brown, Marc, and Stephen Krensky. *Dinosaurs, Beware!*, 2002
Perfect Pigs, 2003

Brown, Marcia. *Cinderella*, 1410
Dick Whittington and His Cat, 1411
How, Hippo!, 28
Peter Piper's Alphabet, 1762
Stone Soup, 1412

Brown, Margaret Wise. *The Important Book*, 630
The Runaway Bunny, 29
The Steamroller, 346
Wheel on the Chimney, 631

Brown, Ruth. *A Dark, Dark Tale*, 347
If at First You Do Not See, 348
Our Cat Flossie, 632

Brown, Walter R., and Norman D. Anderson. *Rescue!*, 2004

Browne, Anthony. *Bear Hunt*, 30
Gorilla, 349
Willy the Wimp, 350

Bruchac, Joseph. *Iroquois Stories*, 1659

Bucknall, Caroline. *One Bear in the Picture*, 31

Bulla, Clyde Robert. *The Sword in the Tree*, 877

Bunting, Eve. *Ghost's Hour, Spook's Hour*, 351
The Mother's Day Mice, 32
Scary, Scary Halloween, 352
The Valentine Bears, 353
The Wall, 354
The Wednesday Surprise, 633

Burch, Robert. *Ida Early Comes Over the Mountain*, 1153

478

Wallace, Daisy (comp.). *Ghost Poems*, 1970

Wallace, Ian. *Chin Chiang and the Dragon Dance*, 843

Walsh, Jill Paton. *See* Paton Walsh, Jill

Walton, Ann (jt. author). *What's Your Name, Again?*, 1971

Walton, Rich, and Ann Walton. *What's Your Name, Again?*, 1971

Ward, Lynd. *The Biggest Bear*, 844
The Silver Pony, 1024

Warner, Gertrude Chandler. *The Boxcar Children*, 1025

Waters, Kate. *Sarah Morton's Day*, 2112

Waterton, Betty. *Petranella*, 845
A Salmon for Simon, 846

Watson, Clyde. *Father Fox's Pennyrhymes*, 1972
How Brown Mouse Kept Christmas, 847

Watson, Pauline. *Wriggles the Little Wishing Pig*, 582

Watt, Letty S. (jt. author). *Developing Learning Skills Through Children's Literature*, 2145

Watts, Bernadette (reteller). *Mother Holly*, 1502

Weil, Lisl. *Owl and Other Scrambles*, 1026

Weinberg, Larry. *The Forgetful Bears Meet Mr. Memory*, 583

Weiss, Nicki. *Hank and Oogie*, 584
If You're Happy and You Know It, 1973

Weller, Frances Ward. *Riptide*, 848

Wells, Rosemary. *Good Night, Fred*, 285
Hazel's Amazing Mother, 585
Max's Chocolate Chicken, 286
Max's Christmas, 287
Peabody, 288
Shy Charles, 586
Timothy Goes to School, 587

Weng, Virginia (jt. author). *The Magic Boat*, 1699

West, Colin. *The King of Kennelwick Castle*, 289

Westcott, Nadine Bernard. *I Know an Old Lady Who Swallowed a Fly*, 588
The Lady with the Alligator Purse, 290
Peanut Butter and Jelly, 291
Skip to My Lou, 292

Westwood, Jennifer. *Going to Squintum's*, 1624

Wetterer, Margaret. *The Giant's Apprentice*, 1130

Whelan, Gloria. *A Week of Raccoons*, 589

Whipple, Laura (comp.). *Eric Carle's Animals, Animals*, 1974

White, E. B. *Charlotte's Web*, 1027
Stuart Little, 1131
The Trumpet of the Swan, 1253

White, Florence. *Escape!*, 2113

White, Laurence B., Jr. (jt. author). *Now You See It*, 1999

White, Laurence B., Jr., and Ray Broekel. *The Surprise Book*, 2114

Whitney, Alma Marshak. *Just Awful*, 293
Leave Herbert Alone, 294

Wiesner, William. *Happy-Go-Lucky*, 1625
Turnabout, 1626

Wilder, Laura Ingalls. *Farmer Boy*, 1132
Little House in the Big Woods, 1028

Wildsmith, Brian. *The Hare and the Tortoise*, 1627
The Lion and the Rat, 1628

Wilhelm, Hans. *Tyrone the Horrible*, 590

Willard, Nancy. *Papa's Panda*, 295
Simple Pictures Are Best, 849

Williams, Barbara. *Albert's Toothache*, 296
Donna Jean's Disaster, 850

Williams, Gurney. *True Escape and Survival Stories*, 2115

Williams, Jay. *Everyone Knows What a Dragon Looks Like*, 1029
The Magic Grandfather, 1254
One Big Wish, 1030

Williams, Jay, and Raymond Abrashkin. *Danny Dunn and the Homework Machine*, 1255
Danny Dunn, Time Traveler, 1256

Williams, Linda. *The Little Old Lady Who Was Not Afraid of Anything*, 591

Williams, Vera B. *A Chair for My Mother*, 851
Cherries and Cherry Pits, 852

Willis, Jeanne. *The Monster Bed*, 592

Willis, Val. *The Secret in the Matchbook*, 593

Willoughby, Elaine. *Boris and the Monsters*, 297

Wilner, Isabel (comp.). *The Poetry Troupe*, 1975

Wilson, Gahan. *Harry the Fat Bear Spy*, 1133

Winkel, Lois. *The Elementary School Library Collection*, 2158

Winn, Marie (comp.). *The Fireside Book of Fun and Game Songs*, 1976

Winter, Jeanette. *Follow the Drinking Gourd*, 1134

Winthrop, Elizabeth. *Bear and Mrs. Duck*, 298
The Castle in the Attic, 1374
Lizzie & Harold, 594
Maggie & the Monster, 299
Shoes, 300
Sloppy Kisses, 595

Wiseman, David. *Jeremy Visick*, 1375

Wisniewski, David. *The Warrior and the Wise Man*, 1031

Withers, Carl. *I Saw a Rocket Walk a Mile*, 1735
Tale of a Black Cat, 853

Withers, Carl (comp.). *A Rocket in My Pocket*, 1977

TITLE INDEX

Note: References are to entry numbers, not page numbers.

ILLUSTRATOR INDEX

Illustrators and joint illustrators are listed here, as well as names of photographers. Authors' names are shown in parentheses following the book title. If no author name is given parenthetically, then the illustrator is also the author of the book. References are to entry numbers, not page numbers.

SUBJECT INDEX

All references are to entry numbers, not page numbers. Recommended reading
levels appear in brackets, following the title.

Feelings, Muriel. *Jambo Means Hello: Swahili Alphabet Book* [2-5], 1798

Folsom, Michael, and Marcia Folsom. *Easy as Pie: A Guessing Game of Sayings* [1-2], 670

Gardner, Beau. *Have You Ever Seen . . .?: An ABC Book* [K-1], 403

Hoguet, Susan. *I Unpacked My Grandmother's Trunk* [1-2], 689

Ipcar, Dahlov. *I Love My Anteater with an A* [3-4], 1078

Lobel, Arnold. *On Market Street* [K-1], 483

Lyon, George Ella. *A B Cedar: An Alphabet of Trees* [Pre-6], 2068

MacDonald, Suse. *Alphabatics* [K-1], 490

Martin, Bill, Jr., and John Archambault. *Chicka Chicka Boom Boom* [Pre-K], 205

Merriam, Eve. *Where Is Everybody?: An Animal Alphabet* [K-1], 508

Neumeier, Marty, and Byron Glaser. *Action Alphabet* [1-2], 758

Ryden, Hope. *Wild Animals of America ABC* [Pre-2], 2087

Sendak, Maurice. *Alligators All Around* [K-1], 550

Seuss, Dr. *Dr. Seuss' ABC* [K-1], 553
On Beyond Zebra [1-2], 805

Steig, William. *CDB* [2-6], 1959

Talon, Robert. *Zoophabets* [2-3], 1014

Weil, Lisl. *Owl and Other Scrambles* [2-3], 1026

AMERICAN REVOLUTION
SEE U.S.–History–Revolution

ANGER
SEE Emotions

ANIMALS
SEE ALSO Domestic Animals; Pets; also under individual animals, e.g., Bears

Bacon, Peggy. *The Magic Touch* [3-4], 1043

Barrett, Judi. *Animals Should Definitely Not Wear Clothing* [2-3], 870

Brady, Irene. *Doodlebug* [1-2], 620

Burningham, John. *Mr. Gumpy's Outing* [Pre-K], 33

Burton, Marilee Robin. *Tails, Toes, Eyes, Ears, Nose* [Pre-K], 34

Carle, Eric. *The Grouchy Ladybug* [Pre-K], 37

Carlson, Natalie Savage. *Marie Louise's Heyday* [1-2], 638

Cherry, Lynne. *Who's Sick Today?* [Pre-K], 47

Cole, Joanna. *Golly Gump Swallowed a Fly* [K-1], 372

Dahl, Roald. *The Enormous Crocodile* [1-2], 656

De Regniers, Beatrice Schenk. *May I Bring a Friend?* [Pre-K], 69

Ehlert, Lois. *Color Zoo* [Pre-K], 76

Eichenberg, Fritz. *Ape in a Cape: An Alphabet of Odd Animals* [Pre-K], 79
Dancing in the Moon: Counting Rhymes [K-1], 380

Flack, Marjorie. *Ask Mr. Bear* [Pre-K], 87

Forrester, Victoria. *The Magnificent Moo* [Pre-K], 89

Fox, Mem. *Koala Lou* [K-1], 389

Freeman, Don. *Quiet! There's a Canary in the Library* [Pre-K], 96

Gammell, Stephen. *Once upon MacDonald's Farm* [K-1], 401

Gardner, Beau. *Guess What?* [Pre-K], 110

George, William T. *Box Turtle at Long Pond* [Pre-2], 2037

Ginsburg, Mirra. *Mushroom in the Rain* [Pre-K], 115

Goodspeed, Peter. *A Rhinoceros Wakes Me Up in the Morning* [Pre-K], 116

Grahame, Kenneth. *The Wind in the Willows* [5-6], 1305

Guarino, Deborah. *Is Your Mama a Llama?* [Pre-K], 123

Hadithi, Mwenye. *Crafty Chameleon* [Pre-K], 124
Greedy Zebra [Pre-K], 125

Hall, Malcolm. *Headlines* [2-3], 932

Hoban, Tana. *A Children's Zoo* [K-1], 430

Howard, Jane R. *When I'm Sleepy* [Pre-K], 141

Ipcar, Dahlov. *I Love My Anteater with an A* [3-4], 1078

Jacques, Brian. *Redwall* [5-6], 1315

Jorgensen, Gail. *Crocodile Beat* [Pre-K], 159

Kessler, Leonard. *Old Turtle's Baseball Stories* [1-2], 709

Kherdian, David. *The Cat's Midsummer Jamboree* [K-1], 457

Kipling, Rudyard. *How the Camel Got His Hump* [2-3], 947
Just So Stories [2-3], 948

Koide, Tan. *May We Sleep Here Tonight?* [Pre-K], 172

Langstaff, John. *Over in the Meadow* [Pre-K], 180

Lavies, Bianca. *It's an Armadillo* [K-3], 2064

Leydenfrost, Robert. *The Snake That Sneezed* [Pre-K], 188

Lionni, Leo. *Frederick's Fables: A Leo Lionni Treasury of Favorite Stories* [1-2], 728

Lobel, Arnold. *Fables* [4-5], 1207

Lofting, Hugh. *The Story of Doctor Dolittle* [3-4], 1091

Ellis, Anne. *Dabble Duck* [K-1], 382

Gaeddert, Lou Ann. *Noisy Nancy Norris* [Pre-K], 102

Gretz, Susanna. *It's Your Turn, Roger!* [K-1], 412

Hill, Elizabeth Starr. *Evan's Corner* [1-2], 687

Hurwitz, Johanna. *Busybody Nora* [1-2], 694
Superduper Teddy [1-2], 696

Keats, Ezra Jack. *Apt. 3* [2-3], 942

Levy, Elizabeth. *Frankenstein Moved in on the Fourth Floor* [2-3], 951

Williams, Vera B. *A Chair for My Mother* [1-2], 851

APPLES
SEE Fruit

ARCHAEOLOGY
Donnelly, Judy. *True-Life Treasure Hunts* [3-5], 2020

Swinburne, Irene, and Laurence Swinburne. *Behind the Sealed Door: The Discovery of the Tomb and Treasures of Tutankhamen* [4-6], 2109

ARITHMETIC
SEE Counting Books; Mathematics; Measurement

ARMADILLOS
Kipling, Rudyard. *The Beginning of the Armadillos* [2-3], 945

Lavies, Bianca. *It's an Armadillo* [K-3], 2064

ART
Fox, Dan. *Go In and Out the Window: An Illustrated Songbook for Young People* [Pre-6], 1801

Koch, Kenneth, and Kate Farrell, comps. *Talking to the Sun: An Illustrated Anthology of Poems for Young People* [Pre-6], 1849

ARTISTS
Agee, John. *The Incredible Painting of Felix Clousseau* [2-3], 862

Baker, Alan. *Benjamin's Portrait* [K-1], 326

dePaola, Tomie. *The Art Lesson* [2-3], 907

Du Bois, William Pène. *Lion* [2-3], 912

Freeman, Don. *Norman the Doorman* [1-2], 671

McPhail, David. *The Magical Drawings of Mooney B. Finch* [1-2], 737
Something Special [K-1], 497

Peet, Bill. *Encore for Eleanor* [1-2], 768

Rylant, Cynthia. *All I See* [2-3], 988

Stolz, Mary. *Zekmet, the Stone Carver* [4-5], 1244

Zelinsky, Paul O. *The Lion and the Stoat* [1-2], 859

ARTISTS–Folklore
Bang, Molly. *Tye May and the Magic Brush* [K-3], 1398

ASTRONOMY
SEE ALSO Moon; Space flight; Stars; Sun

Krupp, E. C. *The Comet and You* [1-4], 2060

Ride, Sally, and Susan Okie. *To Space and Back* [3-6], 2086

Simon, Seymour. *Galaxies* [3-6], 2101
Stars [3-6], 2104

AUNTS
Brooks, Walter Rollin. *Jimmy Takes Vanishing Lessons* [2-3], 876

Cooney, Barbara. *Miss Rumphius* [1-2], 654

Fleischman, Sid. *The Ghost on Saturday Night* [2-3], 918

Greenwald, Sheila. *The Atrocious Two* [4-5], 1184

Schwartz, Amy. *Her Majesty, Aunt Essie* [1-2], 796

Wallace, Barbara Brooks. *Peppermints in the Parlor* [5-6], 1372

AUSTRALIA
Cox, David. *Bossyboots* [1-2], 655

Fox, Mem. *Koala Lou* [K-1], 389

Vaughn, Marcia K. *Wombat Stew* [1-2], 836

AUTHORS
SEE ALSO Writing

Dahl, Roald. *Boy: Tales of Childhood* [5-6], 2012

Krauss, Ruth. *Is This You?* [1-2], 714

Nixon, Joan Lowery. *If You Were a Writer* [2-3], 972

AUTOBIOGRAPHY
SEE ALSO Biography

Dahl, Roald. *Boy: Tales of Childhood* [5-6], 2012

dePaola, Tomie. *The Art Lesson* [2-3], 907

Fitzgerald, John D. *The Great Brain* [4-5], 1171

Gish, Lillian, and Selma Lanes. *An Actor's Life for Me!* [4-6], 2039

Isaacman, Clara, and Joan Adess Grossman. *Clara's Story* [5-6], 2054

Mowat, Farley. *Owls in the Family* [3-5], 2077

Wilder, Laura Ingalls. *Little House in the Big Woods* [2-3], 1028

AUTOMOBILES
SEE ALSO Bicycles; Buses; Transportation; Trucks

Karlin, Bernie, and Mati Karlin. *Night Ride* [K-1], 446

Pinkwater, Daniel. *Tooth-Gnasher Superflash* [K-1], 523

BEARS–Folklore

Brett, Jan. *Goldilocks and the Three Bears* [Pre-1], 1408

Cauley, Lorinda Bryan. *Goldilocks and the Three Bears* [Pre-2], 1415

Dasent, George Webbe. *The Cat on the Dovrefell: A Christmas Tale* [Pre-2], 1432

Eisen, Armand. *Goldilocks and the Three Bears* [Pre-1], 1450

Galdone, Joanna. *The Little Girl and the Big Bear* [Pre-2], 1455

Galdone, Paul. *The Three Bears* [Pre-1], 1472

Hague, Kathleen, and Michael Hague. *East of the Sun and West of the Moon* [3-5], 1513

Marshall, James. *Goldilocks and the Three Bears* [Pre-1], 1561

Stevens, Janet. *Goldilocks and the Three Bears* [Pre-1], 1611

BEARS–Poetry

Yolen, Jane. *The Three Bears Rhyme Book* [Pre-2], 1981

BEDTIME–Poetry

Merriam, Eve. *You Be Good & I'll Be Night: Jump-on-the-Bed Poems* [Pre-1], 1871

Prelutsky, Jack. *My Parents Think I'm Sleeping* [Pre-3], 1910

BEDTIME STORIES

Aylesworth, Jim. *Two Terrible Frights* [Pre-K], 18

Bond, Felicia. *Poinsettia and the Firefighters* [K-1], 338

Browne, Anthony. *Gorilla* [K-1], 349

Christelow, Eileen. *Five Little Monkeys Jumping on the Bed* [Pre-K], 48

Henry and the Dragon [Pre-K], 49

Cole, William. *Frances Face-Maker: A Going to Bed Book* [Pre-K], 53

Crowe, Robert L. *Clyde Monster* [Pre-K], 60

Gackenbach, Dick. *Hurray for Hattie Rabbit* [Pre-K], 99

Gerstein, Mordicai. *William, Where Are You?* [Pre-K], 113

Goodspeed, Peter. *A Rhinoceros Wakes Me Up in the Morning* [Pre-K], 116

Hoban, Russell. *Bedtime for Frances* [K-1], 428

Holabird, Katharine. *Alexander and the Dragon* [Pre-K], 140

Johnston, Johanna. *Edie Changes Her Mind* [Pre-K], 155

Kalman, Maira. *Hey Willy, See the Pyramids* [2-3], 941

Kandoian, Ellen. *Under the Sun* [K-1], 445

Lobel, Arnold. *Mouse Tales* [K-1], 482

Mayer, Mercer. *There's a Nightmare in My Closet* [Pre-K], 207

There's an Alligator under My Bed [Pre-K], 208

There's Something in My Attic [Pre-K], 209

Nixon, Joan Lowery. *The Alligator under the Bed* [Pre-K], 218

Paxton, Tom. *Jennifer's Rabbit* [Pre-K], 224

Polushkin, Maria. *Mother, Mother, I Want Another* [Pre-K], 230

Pomerantz, Charlotte. *Posy* [Pre-K], 232

Robison, Deborah. *No Elephants Allowed* [Pre-K], 243

Root, Phyllis. *Moon Tiger* [K-1], 535

Ross, Tony. *I'm Coming to Get You!* [K-1], 536

Ryder, Joanne. *The Night Flight* [K-1], 540

Rylant, Cynthia. *Night in the Country* [K-1], 541

Sharmat, Marjorie Weinman. *Go to Sleep, Nicholas Joe* [Pre-K], 263

Stevenson, James. *What's Under My Bed?* [1-2], 826

Tobias, Tobi. *Chasing the Goblins Away* [1-2], 831

Viorst, Judith. *My Mama Says There Aren't Any Zombies, Ghosts, Vampires, Creatures, Demons, Monsters, Fiends, Goblins or Things* [1-2], 840

Waber, Bernard. *Ira Sleeps Over* [1-2], 842

Wells, Rosemary. *Good Night, Fred* [Pre-K], 285

Willis, Jeanne. *The Monster Bed* [K-1], 592

Willoughby, Elaine. *Boris and the Monsters* [Pre-K], 297

Winthrop, Elizabeth. *Maggie & the Monster* [Pre-K], 299

Zemach, Harve. *Mommy, Buy Me a China Doll* [Pre-K], 305

BEHAVIOR

Allard, Harry. *Miss Nelson Is Missing* [1-2], 601

Blundell, Tony. *Joe on Sunday* [K-1], 337

Carlson, Natalie Savage. *Runaway Marie Louise* [Pre-K], 43

Cassedy, Sylvia. *Behind the Attic Wall* [5-6], 1287

Caudill, Rebecca. *Did You Carry the Flag Today, Charlie?* [1-2], 643

Chase, Mary. *Loretta Mason Potts* [4-5], 1157

Clymer, Eleanor. *My Brother Stevie* [3-4], 1054

Cole, Brock. *Nothing but a Pig* [1-2], 651

Collodi, Carlo. *The Adventures of Pinocchio* [4-5], 1160

Corbett, Scott. *The Lemonade Trick* [3-4], 1056

Delton, Judy. *I'm Telling You Now* [Pre-K], 65

Gantos, Jack. *Rotten Ralph* [K-1], 402

Greenwald, Sheila. *The Atrocious Two* [4-5], 1184

Hurwitz, Johanna. *Class Clown* [2-3], 936

Hutchins, Pat. *The Very Worst Monster* [Pre-K], 150

Where's the Baby? [K-1], 435

Jeffers, Susan. *Wild Robin* [1-2], 699

Kline, Suzy. *Don't Touch!* [Pre-K], 170

Lester, Helen. *Cora Copycat* [K-1], 468

Pookins Gets Her Way [K-1], 470

Lindgren, Barbro. *The Wild Baby* [K-1], 473

MacDonald, Betty. *Mrs. Piggle-Wiggle* [3-4], 1092

Manes, Stephen. *Be a Perfect Person in Just Three Days* [3-4], 1095

Marshall, James. *The Cut-Ups* [1-2], 743

Nostlinger, Christine. *Konrad* [4-5], 1219

Potter, Beatrix. *The Tale of Peter Rabbit* [K-1], 528

Rey, H. A. *Curious George* [Pre-K], 238

Riley, James Whitcomb. *The Gobble-Uns'll Git You Ef You Don't Watch Out* [3-4], 1108

Robinson, Barbara. *The Best Christmas Pageant Ever* [4-5], 1230

Ross, Tony. *Super Dooper Jezebel* [1-2], 786

Thayer, Jane. *The Popcorn Dragon* [Pre-K], 273

Viorst, Judith. *Alexander and the Terrible, Horrible, No Good, Very Bad Day* [1-2], 838

Wade, Barrie. *Little Monster* [Pre-K], 284

Zakhoder, Boris. *How a Piglet Crashed the Christmas Party* [1-2], 858

BEHAVIOR – Poetry

Cole, William. *Beastly Boys and Ghastly Girls* [2-6], 1775

Kennedy, X. J. *Brats* [3-6], 1845

Livingston, Myra Cohn. *Higgledy-Piggledy: Verses & Pictures* [2-3], 953

BICYCLES

SEE ALSO Transportation

Douglass, Barbara. *The Great Town and Country Bicycle Balloon Chase* [Pre-K], 73

Drury, Roger W. *The Champion of Merrimack County* [4-5], 1169

Say, Allen. *The Bicycle Man* [1-2], 791

BIOGRAPHY

Brown, Drollene P. *Sybil Rides for Independence* [2-4], 2001

Brown, Walter R., and Norman D. Anderson. *Rescue!: True Stories of Winners of the Young American Medal for Bravery* [3-6], 2004

Coerr, Eleanor. *Sadako & the Thousand Paper Cranes* [3-6], 2007

Cross, Helen Reeder. *The Real Tom Thumb* [3-6], 2011

Dahl, Roald. *Boy: Tales of Childhood* [5-6], 2012

D'Aulaire, Ingri, and Edgar Parin D'Aulaire. *Benjamin Franklin* [2-6], 2013

Epstein, Sam, and Beryl Epstein. *Secret in a Sealed Bottle: Lazzaro Spallanzani's Work with Microbes* [5-6], 2022

Freedman, Russell. *Lincoln: A Photobiography* [5-6], 2028

Fritz, Jean. *And Then What Happened, Paul Revere?* [3-6], 2029

Can't You Make Them Behave, King George? [3-6], 2030

The Double Life of Pocahontas [4-6], 2031

What's the Big Idea, Ben Franklin? [3-6], 2033

Where Do You Think You're Going, Christopher Columbus? [4-6], 2034

Gish, Lillian, and Selma Lanes. *An Actor's Life for Me!* [4-6], 2039

Griffin, Judith Berry. *Phoebe and the General* [2-5], 2042

Hunter, Edith Fisher. *Child of the Silent Night: The Story of Laura Bridgman* [3-5], 2053

Isaacman, Clara, and Joan Adess Grossman. *Clara's Story* [5-6], 2054

Kamen, Gloria. *Charlie Chaplin* [4-6], 2057

Kellogg, Steven. *Johnny Appleseed* [1-4], 2058

Lauber, Patricia. *Lost Star: The Story of Amelia Earhart* [5-6], 2061

McGovern, Ann. *Runaway Slave: The Story of Harriet Tubman* [2-5], 2070

The Secret Soldier: The Story of Deborah Sampson [3-6], 2071

Provensen, Alice, and Martin Provensen. *The Glorious Flight: Across the Channel with Louis Blériot* [K-6], 2084

Reit, Seymour. *Behind Rebel Lines: The Incredible Story of Emma Edmonds, Civil War Spy* [5-6], 2085

Rylant, Cynthia. *Waiting to Waltz: A Childhood* [5-6], 1941

White, Florence. *Escape!: The Life of Harry Houdini* [3-6], 2113

Williams, Gurney. *True Escape and Survival Stories* [4-6], 2115

BIRDS

SEE ALSO Chickens; Ducks; Geese; Owls; Parrots; Roosters

Andersen, Hans Christian. *It's Perfectly True* [1-2], 602

The Nightingale [3-4], 1039

The Ugly Duckling [1-2], 603

The Wild Swans [3-4], 1040

Tomb and Treasures of Tutankhamen [4-6], 2109

BUSES

SEE ALSO Automobiles; Transportation; Trucks

Alexander, Martha. *Move Over, Twerp* [K-1], 315

Kovalski, Maryann. *The Wheels on the Bus* [Pre-K], 173

Raffi. *Wheels on the Bus* [Pre-K], 235

Sheldon, Dyan. *A Witch Got on at Paddington Station* [Pre-K], 265

BUTTERFLIES

SEE ALSO Insects

Brown, Ruth. *If at First You Do Not See* [K-1], 348

Carle, Eric. *The Very Hungry Caterpillar* [Pre-K], 42

CAKE

SEE Cookery; Food

CALDECOTT MEDAL

Aardema, Verna. *Why Mosquitoes Buzz in People's Ears* [Pre-2], 1386

Ackerman, Karen. *Song and Dance Man* [1-2], 599

Bemelmans, Ludwig. *Madeline's Rescue* [K-1], 335

Brown, Marcia. *Cinderella: Or, The Little Glass Slipper* [1-4], 1410

Brown, Margaret Wise. *Wheel on the Chimney* [1-2], 631

Burton, Virginia Lee. *The Little House* [1-2], 634

De Regniers, Beatrice Schenk. *May I Bring a Friend?* [Pre-K], 69

Emberley, Barbara. *Drummer Hoff* [Pre-K], 80

Haley, Gail E. *A Story, a Story* [K-3], 1517

Hall, Donald. *Ox-Cart Man* [2-3], 931

Hodges, Margaret, adapt. *Saint George and the Dragon: A Golden Legend* [3-6], 1526

Hogrogian, Nonny. *One Fine Day* [Pre-2], 1528

Keats, Ezra Jack. *The Snowy Day* [Pre-K], 165

Lobel, Arnold. *Fables* [4-5], 1207

McCloskey, Robert. *Make Way for Ducklings* [1-2], 734
  Time of Wonder [2-3], 957

Mosel, Arlene. *The Funny Little Woman* [Pre-3], 1571

Ness, Evaline. *Sam, Bangs and Moonshine* [1-2], 757

Provensen, Alice, and Martin Provensen. *The Glorious Flight: Across the Channel with Louis Blériot* [K-6], 2084

Ransome, Arthur. *The Fool of the World and His Flying Ship* [2-4], 1583

Sendak, Maurice. *Where the Wild Things Are* [Pre-K], 255

Steig, William. *Sylvester and the Magic Pebble* [1-2], 821

Thurber, James. *Many Moons* [2-3], 1015

Udry, Janice May. *A Tree Is Nice* [Pre-K], 278

Van Allsburg, Chris. *Jumanji* [2-3], 1020
  The Polar Express [1-2], 835

Ward, Lynd. *The Biggest Bear* [1-2], 844

Yolen, Jane. *Owl Moon* [1-2], 857

Young, Ed. *Lon Po Po: A Red-Riding Hood Story from China* [K-2], 1633

Zemach, Harve. *Duffy and the Devil* [2-5], 1635

CALIFORNIA

Fleischman, Sid. *By the Great Horn Spoon* [5-6], 1300

CALL-AND-RESPONSE STORIES

Carlson, Bernice Wells. *Listen! And Help Tell the Story* [Pre-2], 1765

Crews, Donald. *Freight Train* [Pre-K], 58

Duke, Kate. *Seven Froggies Went to School* [K-1], 377

Galdone, Paul. *Over in the Meadow: An Old Nursery Counting Rhyme* [Pre-K], 108

Jones, Maurice. *I'm Going on a Dragon Hunt* [Pre-K], 158

Leedy, Loreen. *A Number of Dragons* [Pre-K], 182

Martin, Bill, Jr. *Brown Bear, Brown Bear, What Do You See?* [Pre-K], 204

Rosen, Michael. *We're Going on a Bear Hunt* [Pre-K], 245

Sivulich, Sandra Stroner. *I'm Going on a Bear Hunt* [Pre-K], 267

CAMELS

Kipling, Rudyard. *How the Camel Got His Hump* [2-3], 947

Tworkov, Jack. *The Camel Who Took a Walk* [K-1], 571

CAMPING

Henkes, Kevin. *Bailey Goes Camping* [Pre-K], 131

Howe, James. *Nighty-Nightmare* [4-5], 1194

Roy, Ron. *Nightmare Island* [4-5], 1234

CANADA

SEE ALSO Folklore–Canada

Andrews, Jan. *Very Last First Time* [2-3], 867

Burnford, Sheila. *The Incredible Journey* [5-6], 1279

Mowat, Farley. *Owls in the Family* [3-5], 2077

Waterton, Betty. *A Salmon for Simon* [1-2], 846

CANADA–Poetry

Service, Robert W. *The Cremation of Sam McGee* [5-6], 1355

CANDY

Balian, Lorna. *The Sweet Touch* [K-1], 329

Catling, Patrick Skene. *The Chocolate Touch* [2-3], 884

Dahl, Roald. *Charlie and the Chocolate Factory* [3-4], 1058

Kroll, Steven. *The Candy Witch* [K-1], 462

Smith, Robert Kimmell. *Chocolate Fever* [2-3], 1003

Wells, Rosemary. *Max's Chocolate Chicken* [Pre-K], 286

CAREERS

SEE Occupations

CATERPILLARS

SEE ALSO Insects

Brown, Ruth. *If at First You Do Not See* [K-1], 348

Carle, Eric. *The Very Hungry Caterpillar* [Pre-K], 42

CATS

Alexander, Lloyd. *The Cat Who Wished to Be a Man* [5-6], 1259

The Town Cats and Other Tales [5-6], 1261

Alexander, Martha. *The Story Grandmother Told* [Pre-K], 2

Balian, Lorna. *Amelia's Nine Lives* [Pre-K], 19

Brandenberg, Franz. *I Wish I Was Sick, Too* [Pre-K], 26

No School Today [K-1], 342

Brown, Ruth. *A Dark, Dark Tale* [K-1], 347

Our Cat Flossie [1-2], 632

Bunting, Eve. *Scary, Scary Halloween* [K-1], 352

Burchardt, Nellie. *Project Cat* [2-3], 878

Burnford, Sheila. *The Incredible Journey* [5-6], 1279

Calhoun, Mary. *Cross-Country Cat* [1-2], 635

Carlson, Natalie Savage. *Spooky Night* [K-1], 357

Cauley, Lorinda Bryan. *The Three Little Kittens* [Pre-K], 45

Clifford, Sandy. *The Roquefort Gang* [3-4], 1053

Coombs, Patricia. *Dorrie and the Weather Box* [1-2], 653

The Magician and McTree [2-3], 900

Everitt, Betsy. *Frida the Wondercat* [K-1], 384

Fenton, Edward. *The Big Yellow Balloon* [1-2], 667

Ferguson, Alane. *That New Pet!* [K-1], 386

Flack, Marjorie. *Angus and the Cat* [Pre-K], 84

Foreman, Michael. *Cat and Canary* [K-1], 388

Frascino, Edward. *My Cousin the King* [K-1], 390

Gag, Wanda. *Millions of Cats* [Pre-K], 104

Gantos, Jack. *Rotten Ralph* [K-1], 402

Graeber, Charlotte. *Mustard* [2-3], 927

Herriot, James. *The Christmas Day Kitten* [2-4], 2048

Hildick, E. W. *The Case of the Condemned Cat* [3-4], 1073

Hiller, Catherine. *Abracatabby* [K-1], 424

Howe, Deborah, and James Howe. *Bunnicula: A Rabbit-Tale of Mystery* [4-5], 1193

Howe, James. *The Fright before Christmas* [2-3], 935

Nighty-Nightmare [4-5], 1194

Keats, Ezra Jack. *Pet Show!* [Pre-K], 163

Kherdian, David. *The Cat's Midsummer Jamboree* [K-1], 457

King-Smith, Dick. *Martin's Mice* [3-4], 1085

Lear, Edward. *The Owl and the Pussycat* [Pre-K], 181

Le Guin, Ursula K. *Catwings* [2-3], 950

A Visit from Dr. Katz [Pre-K], 183

Lisle, Janet Taylor. *The Dancing Cats of Applesap* [4-5], 1205

Low, Joseph. *Mice Twice* [K-1], 488

McMillan, Bruce. *Kitten Can* [Pre-K], 198

McPhail, David. *Great Cat* [K-1], 495

Minarik, Else Holmelund. *It's Spring!* [Pre-K], 213

Morey, Walt. *Sandy and the Rock Star* [5-6], 1333

Ness, Evaline. *Sam, Bangs and Moonshine* [1-2], 757

Nolan, Dennis. *Witch Bazooza* [1-2], 762

Panek, Dennis. *Catastrophe Cat* [Pre-K], 222

Park, Barbara. *Skinnybones* [4-5], 1222

Peppé, Rodney. *The Mice Who Lived in a Shoe* [1-2], 772

Pinkwater, Daniel. *The Wuggie Norple Story* [K-1], 524

Ravilious, Robin. *The Runaway Chick* [Pre-K], 236

Reeves, Mona Rabun. *I Had a Cat* [Pre-K], 237

Robinson, Nancy K. *Just Plain Cat* [2-3], 986

Samuels, Barbara. *Duncan & Dolores* [Pre-K], 251

Selden, George. *The Cricket in Times Square* [4-5], 1237

Seuss, Dr. *The Cat in the Hat* [Pre-K], 258

Stadler, John. *Animal Cafe* [1-2], 819

Steig, William. *Solomon the Rusty Nail* [2-3], 1008

Stein, Sara Bonnett. *Cat* [Pre-1], 2107

Stolz, Mary. *Cat Walk* [3-4], 1121

Turkle, Brinton. *Do Not Open* [2-3], 1016

Viorst, Judith. *The Tenth Good Thing about Barney* [K-1], 575

Waber, Bernard. *Rich Cat, Poor Cat* [K-1], 579

Wagner, Jane. *J. T.* [3-4], 1129

Wagner, Jenny. *John Brown, Rose and the Midnight Cat* [K-1], 581

Whitney, Alma Marshak. *Leave Herbert Alone* [Pre-K], 294

Withers, Carl. *Tale of a Black Cat* [1-2], 853

Zelinsky, Paul O. *The Maid and the Mouse and the Odd-Shaped House* [1-2], 860

CATS–Folklore

Brown, Marcia. *Dick Whittington and His Cat* [1-4], 1411

Cauley, Lorinda Bryan. *Puss in Boots* [K-4], 1419

Galdone, Paul. *King of the Cats* [2-4], 1463
Puss in Boots [K-4], 1470

Hurlimann, Ruth. *The Proud White Cat* [Pre-2], 1532

Kent, Jack. *The Fat Cat* [Pre-2], 1539

Pevear, Richard. *Mr. Cat-and-a-Half* [1-3], 1578

Uchida, Yoshiko. *The Two Foolish Cats* [Pre-2], 1620

Zaum, Marjorie. *Catlore: Tales from Around the World* [2-6], 1738

CATS–Poetry

Chapman, Jean. *Cat Will Rhyme with Hat: A Book of Poems* [3-6], 1767

De Regniers, Beatrice Schenk. *This Big Cat and Other Cats I've Known* [Pre-2], 1793

Eliot, T. S. *Old Possum's Book of Practical Cats* [4-6], 1795

Hopkins, Lee Bennett. *I Am the Cat* [K-6], 1823

Larrick, Nancy. *Cats Are Cats* [3-6], 1851

Livingston, Myra Cohn. *Cat Poems* [2-5], 1858

CATS–Riddles

Keller, Charles. *It's Raining Cats and Dogs: Cat and Dog Jokes* [2-5], 1837

CAUSE AND EFFECT

Aylesworth, Jim. *Hush Up!* [K-1], 323

Barton, Byron. *Buzz Buzz Buzz* [Pre-K], 21

Charlip, Remy. *Fortunately* [1-2], 645

Goldberg, Rube. *The Best of Rube Goldberg* [3-6], 2040

Goodsell, Jane. *Toby's Toe* [K-1], 407

Lester, Helen. *It Wasn't My Fault* [K-1], 469

Lexau, Joan. *That's Good, That's Bad* [Pre-K], 187

Noble, Trinka Hakes. *The Day Jimmy's Boa Ate the Wash* [1-2], 761

Numeroff, Laura. *If You Give a Mouse a Cookie* [K-1], 514

Zolotow, Charlotte. *The Quarreling Book* [1-2], 861

CAVES

Taylor, Mark. *Henry the Explorer* [K-1], 564

CHAIRS

Graham, Thomas. *Mr. Bear's Chair* [Pre-K], 119

Williams, Vera B. *A Chair for My Mother* [1-2], 851

CHAMELEONS

SEE ALSO Reptiles

Carle, Eric. *The Mixed-Up Chameleon* [Pre-K], 38

Hadithi, Mwenye. *Crafty Chameleon* [Pre-K], 124

Massie, Diane Redfield. *Chameleon Was a Spy* [2-3], 960

CHANTABLE REFRAIN

Aardema, Verna. *The Riddle of the Drum* [1-4], 1383

Anderson, Leone Castell. *The Wonderful Shrinking Shirt* [1-2], 604

Arnold, Tedd. *Ollie Forgot* [1-2], 607

Asch, Frank. *Just Like Daddy* [Pre-K], 13

Blia, Xiong. *Nine-in-One, Grr! Grr!: A Folktale from the Hmong People of Laos* [K-3], 1404

Bowden, Joan Chase. *The Bean Boy* [Pre-1], 1405

Brown, Ruth. *A Dark, Dark Tale* [K-1], 347

Carle, Eric. *The Grouchy Ladybug* [Pre-K], 37

Carlson, Bernice Wells. *Listen! And Help Tell the Story* [Pre-2], 1765

Cauley, Lorinda Bryan. *The Pancake Boy: An Old Norwegian Folk Tale* [1-3], 1418

Christelow, Eileen. *Five Little Monkeys Jumping on the Bed* [Pre-K], 48

Cook, Scott. *The Gingerbread Boy* [Pre-1], 1429

Dobbs, Dayle-Ann. *Wheel Away!* [Pre-K], 71

Domanska, Janina. *Little Red Hen* [Pre-1], 1447

Duff, Maggie. *Rum Pum Pum* [Pre-2], 1449

Gag, Wanda. *Millions of Cats* [Pre-K], 104

Galdone, Joanna, and Paul Galdone. *Gertrude the Goose Who Forgot* [Pre-K], 107

Galdone, Paul. *The Gingerbread Boy* [Pre-1], 1459
The Greedy Old Fat Man: An American Folktale [Pre-2], 1460
Henny Penny [Pre-1], 1461
The Little Red Hen [Pre-1], 1464
Old Mother Hubbard and Her Dog [Pre-1], 1468
The Old Woman and Her Pig [Pre-1], 1469

Harper, Wilhelmina. *The Gunniwolf* [Pre-1], 1519

Hutchins, Pat. *Don't Forget the Bacon!* [K-1], 434

Ishii, Momoko. *The Tongue-Cut Sparrow* [Pre-3], 1535

Johnston, Tony. *The Vanishing Pumpkin* [K-1], 443

Yonder [2-3], 939

Kalan, Robert. *Jump, Frog, Jump* [Pre-K], 160

Koide, Tan. *May We Sleep Here Tonight?* [Pre-K], 172

Lamont, Priscilla. *The Troublesome Pig: A Nursery Tale* [Pre-2], 1543

Levitin, Sonia. *Nobody Stole the Pie* [1-2], 722

Little, Jean, and Maggie De Vries. *Once Upon a Golden Apple* [K-1], 478

Lobel, Arnold. *The Rose in My Garden* [K-1], 485

Martin, Bill, Jr. *Brown Bear, Brown Bear, What Do You See?* [Pre-K], 204

Mosel, Arlene. *Tikki Tikki Tembo* [Pre-3], 1572

Oppenheim, Joanne. *You Can't Catch Me!* [K-1], 516

Patz, Nancy. *Pumpernickel Tickle and Mean Green Cheese* [K-1], 520

Perkins, Al. *Hand, Hand, Fingers, Thumb* [Pre-K], 228

Polushkin, Maria. *Mother, Mother, I Want Another* [Pre-K], 230

Prelutsky, Jack. *The Mean Old Mean Hyena* [2-3], 983

The Terrible Tiger [1-2], 778

Preston, Edna Mitchell. *Pop Corn & Ma Goodness* [K-1], 529

Sawyer, Ruth. *Journey Cake, Ho!* [Pre-2], 1591

Stern, Simon. *The Hobyas: An Old Story* [Pre-1], 1609

Stevens, Janet. *The House That Jack Built: A Mother Goose Nursery Rhyme* [Pre-K], 271

Thomas, Patricia. *"Stand Back," Said the Elephant, "I'm Going to Sneeze!"* [K-1], 568

West, Colin. *The King of Kennelwick Castle* [Pre-K], 289

Westcott, Nadine Bernard. *The Lady with the Alligator Purse* [Pre-K], 290

Peanut Butter and Jelly: A Play Rhyme [Pre-K], 291

Willard, Nancy. *Simple Pictures Are Best* [1-2], 849

Wood, Audrey. *King Bidgood's in the Bathtub* [1-2], 855

CHEMISTRY

SEE Science—Experiments

CHICKENS

SEE ALSO Birds; Ducks; Geese; Owls; Parrots; Roosters

Allard, Harry. *I Will Not Go to Market Today* [K-1], 316

Andersen, Hans Christian. *It's Perfectly True* [1-2], 602

Anderson, Margaret. *The Brain on Quartz Mountain* [3-4], 1041

Cazet, Denys. *Lucky Me* [K-1], 360

Flora, James. *Little Hatchy Hen* [2-3], 923

Fox, Mem. *Huttie and the Fox* [Pre-K], 91

Ginsburg, Mirra. *The Chick and the Duckling* [Pre-K], 114

Heine, Helme. *The Most Wonderful Egg in the World* [Pre-K], 129

Hutchins, Pat. *Rosie's Walk* [Pre-K], 149

Kasza, Keiko. *The Wolf's Chicken Stew* [Pre-K], 162

Kellogg, Steven. *Chicken Little* [1-2], 704

Kent, Jack. *Little Peep* [K-1], 455

Lester, Helen. *The Wizard, the Fairy and the Magic Chicken* [Pre-K], 185

McCleery, William. *Wolf Story* [K-1], 489

Manes, Stephen. *Chicken Trek: The Third Strange Thing That Happened to Oscar J. Noodleman* [4-5], 1211

Marshall, James. *Wings: A Tale of Two Chickens* [1-2], 745

Pinkwater, Daniel. *The Hoboken Chicken Emergency* [3-4], 1104

Ravilious, Robin. *The Runaway Chick* [Pre-K], 236

CHICKENS—Folklore

Cauley, Lorinda Bryan. *The Cock, the Mouse and the Little Red Hen* [Pre-2], 1414

Domanska, Janina. *Little Red Hen* [Pre-1], 1447

Galdone, Paul. *Henny Penny* [Pre-1], 1461

The Little Red Hen [Pre-1], 1464

CHIMPANZEES

SEE ALSO Gorillas; Monkeys

Browne, Anthony. *Willy the Wimp* [K-1], 350

Goodall, Jane. *The Chimpanzee Family Book* [3-6], 2041

Hoban, Lillian. *Arthur's Christmas Cookies* [K-1], 425

Arthur's Great Big Valentine [K-1], 426

Arthur's Honey Bear [Pre-K], 136

Arthur's Loose Tooth [K-1], 427

Landsman, Sandy. *Castaways on Chimp Island* [5-6], 1323

Michel, Anna. *The Story of Nim, the Chimp Who Learned Language* [3-6], 2076

Roy, Ron. *The Chimpanzee Kid* [5-6], 1348

CHINA

SEE ALSO Folklore—China

Sundgaard, Arnold. *Meet Jack Appleknocker* [Pre-K], 272

Wakefield, Pat A., and Larry Carrara. *A Moose for Jessica* [3-6], 2111

Whelan, Gloria. *A Week of Raccoons* [K-1], 589

COURAGE

Avi. *Shadrach's Crossing* [5-6], 1269

Brady, Esther Wood. *Toliver's Secret* [4-5], 1148

Brown, Walter R., and Norman D. Anderson. *Rescue!: True Stories of Winners of the Young American Medal for Bravery* [3-6], 2004

Calhoun, Mary. *The Night the Monster Came* [2-3], 880

Coombs, Patricia. *Molly Mullett* [2-3], 901

Gackenbach, Dick. *Harry and the Terrible Whatzit* [Pre-K], 98

Green, Norma B. *The Hole in the Dike* [K-1], 409

Henkes, Kevin. *Sheila Rae, the Brave* [Pre-K], 132

Hoban, Lillian. *Arthur's Loose Tooth* [K-1], 427

Kraus, Robert. *Noel the Coward* [Pre-K], 175

McSwigan, Marie. *Snow Treasure* [5-6], 1330

Monjo, F. N. *The Drinking Gourd* [2-3], 966

Peet, Bill. *Cowardly Clyde* [2-3], 976

Sperry, Armstrong. *Call It Courage* [4-5], 1242

Steig, William. *Brave Irene* [1-2], 820

Ullman, James Ramsay. *Banner in the Sky* [5-6], 1371

Williams, Gurney. *True Escape and Survival Stories* [4-6], 2115

Wuorio, Eva-Lis. *Code: Polonaise* [5-6], 1377

COURAGE–Folklore

Grant, Joan. *The Monster That Grew Small: An Egyptian Folktale* [1-4], 1484

COUSINS

Clifford, Eth. *Harvey's Horrible Snake Disaster* [3-4], 1052

Giff, Patricia Reilly. *The Winter Worm Business* [4-5], 1177

COWS

Ernst, Lisa Campbell. *When Bluebell Sang* [K-1], 383

Forrester, Victoria. *The Magnificent Moo* [Pre-K], 89

Herriot, James. *Blossom Comes Home* [2-5], 2046

Wakefield, Pat A., and Larry Carrara. *A Moose for Jessica* [3-6], 2111

COWS–Folklore

Cooper, Susan. *The Silver Cow: A Welsh Tale* [2-5], 1430

CREATIVE DRAMA

SEE ALSO Acting

578

Adams, Adrienne. *A Woggle of Witches* [Pre-K], 1

Agee, John. *The Incredible Painting of Felix Clousseau* [2-3], 862

Aliki. *At Mary Bloom's* [Pre-K], 4

Allard, Harry. *I Will Not Go to Market Today* [K-1], 316

Allen, Pamela. *Bertie and the Bear* [Pre-K], 7

Arnold, Tedd. *Ollie Forgot* [1-2], 607

Artis, Vicki K. *Gray Duck Catches a Friend* [Pre-K], 9

Asch, Frank. *Happy Birthday, Moon* [Pre-K], 12
Just Like Daddy [Pre-K], 13

Bond, Michael. *A Bear Called Paddington* [4-5], 1146

Boynton, Sandra. *A Is for Angry: An Animal and Adjective Alphabet* [K-1], 341

Brown, Margaret Wise. *The Steamroller* [K-1], 346

Burningham, John. *Mr. Gumpy's Outing* [Pre-K], 33

Charlip, Remy, and Burton Supree. *Mother, Mother, I Feel Sick, Send for the Doctor Quick, Quick, Quick* [1-2], 646

Cole, Brock. *No More Baths* [Pre-K], 52

Cole, William. *Frances Face-Maker: A Going to Bed Book* [Pre-K], 53

Cooney, Nancy Evans. *The Umbrella Day* [Pre-K], 57

dePaola, Tomie. *Charlie Needs a Cloak* [K-1], 376

Duke, Kate. *Guinea Pigs Far and Near* [Pre-K], 75

Eichenberg, Fritz. *Dancing in the Moon: Counting Rhymes* [K-1], 380

Emberley, Barbara. *Drummer Hoff* [Pre-K], 80

Fenton, Edward. *The Big Yellow Balloon* [1-2], 667

Flack, Marjorie. *Ask Mr. Bear* [Pre-K], 87

Freeman, Don. *Quiet! There's a Canary in the Library* [Pre-K], 96
A Rainbow of My Own [Pre-K], 97

Gage, Wilson. *Cully Cully and the Bear* [K-1], 399

Gannett, Ruth Stiles. *My Father's Dragon* [1-2], 674

Gantos, Jack. *Greedy Greeny* [Pre-K], 109

Gerstein, Mordicai. *Arnold of the Ducks* [1-2], 677
Follow Me! [Pre-K], 112

Ginsburg, Mirra. *The Chick and the Duckling* [Pre-K], 114
Mushroom in the Rain [Pre-K], 115

Glazer, Tom. *Eye Winker, Tom Tinker, Chin Chopper: Fifty Musical Fingerplays* [Pre-2], 1804

Goodsell, Jane. *Toby's Toe* [K-1], 407

Hellsing, Lennart. *Old Mother Hubbard and Her Dog* [Pre-K], 130

CREATIVE DRAMA – Folklore

CREATIVE WRITING

Keller, Beverly. *The Genuine, Ingenious Thrift Shop Genie, Clarissa Mae Bean and Me* [4-5], 1198

Lobel, Arnold. *Ming Lo Moves the Mountain* [K-1], 481

McKissack, Patricia C. *Mirandy and Brother Wind* [2-3], 958

Martin, Bill, Jr., and John Archambault. *Barn Dance!* [K-1], 505

Quinn-Harkin, Janet. *Peter Penny's Dance* [1-2], 779

Schertle, Alice. *Bill and the Google-Eyed Goblins* [1-2], 792

Shannon, George. *Dance Away* [Pre-K], 260

Wallace, Ian. *Chin Chiang and the Dragon Dance* [1-2], 843

DANCING–Folklore

Grimm, Jacob. *The Twelve Dancing Princesses* [1-4], 1509

DAYS OF THE WEEK

Balian, Lorna. *Amelia's Nine Lives* [Pre-K], 19

Blundell, Tony. *Joe on Sunday* [K-1], 337

Sundgaard, Arnold. *Meet Jack Appleknocker* [Pre-K], 272

Wood, Audrey. *Heckedy Peg* [1-2], 854

DAYS OF THE WEEK–Folklore

Maitland, Antony. *Idle Jack* [K-3], 1559

DEATH

Bauer, Marion Dane. *On My Honor* [5-6], 1273

Cohen, Miriam. *Jim's Dog Muffins* [K-1], 368

Cohn, Janice. *I Had a Friend Named Peter: Talking to Children about the Death of a Friend* [Pre-K], 51

Graeber, Charlotte. *Mustard* [2-3], 927

Keller, Holly. *Goodbye, Max* [K-1], 452

Kennedy, Richard. *Come Again in the Spring* [3-4], 1080

Little, Jean. *Home from Far* [4-5], 1206

Miles, Miska. *Annie and the Old One* [4-5], 1213

Paterson, Katherine. *Bridge to Terabithia* [5-6], 1340

Viorst, Judith. *The Tenth Good Thing about Barney* [K-1], 575

DEER

Carrick, Donald. *Harald and the Great Stag* [2-3], 883

DEMONS

SEE Monsters

DESERTS

Bash, Barbara. *Desert Giant: The World of the Saguaro Cactus* [2-5], 1994

DESERTS–Poetry

Baylor, Byrd. *Amigo* [1-2], 613

Siebert, Diane. *Mojave* [2-3], 1000

DEVIL

Babbitt, Natalie. *The Devil's Storybook* [5-6], 1270

Brittain, Bill. *Devil's Donkey* [5-6], 1276

Carey, Valerie Scho. *The Devil & Mother Crump* [3-4], 1049

Hooks, William H. *Mean Jake and the Devils* [3-4], 1074

Small, David. *Paper John* [1-2], 814

DEVIL–Folklore

Barth, Edna. *Jack-O'-Lantern* [3-6], 1400

Basile, Giambattista. *Petrosinella: A Neopolitan Rapunzel* [4-6], 1401

Belpré, Pura. *Oté* [1-4], 1402

Conger, Leslie. *Tops and Bottoms* [Pre-3], 1427

Grimm, Jacob. *The Bearskinner* [2-4], 1486

The Devil with the Three Golden Hairs [2-4], 1489

McCurdy, Michael. *The Devils Who Learned to Be Good* [K-3], 1549

Scribner, Charles. *The Devil's Bridge* [2-4], 1596

Turska, Krystyna. *The Magician of Cracow* [2-5], 1619

Zemach, Harve. *Duffy and the Devil* [2-5], 1635

DICTIONARIES

Babbitt, Natalie. *The Search for Delicious* [4-5], 1139

Rosenbloom, Joseph. *Daffy Definitions* [4-6], 1927

DINOSAURS

SEE ALSO Animals, prehistoric

Brown, Marc, and Stephen Krensky. *Dinosaurs, Beware!: A Safety Guide* [Pre-3], 2002

Butterworth, Oliver. *The Enormous Egg* [4-5], 1154

Carrick, Carol. *Patrick's Dinosaurs* [K-1], 358

What Happened to Patrick's Dinosaurs? [1-2], 642

Kellogg, Steven. *Prehistoric Pinkerton* [1-2], 707

Kroll, Steven. *The Tyrannosaurus Game* [1-2], 719

Lauber, Patricia. *The News about Dinosaurs* [2-6], 2062

Schwartz, Henry. *How I Captured a Dinosaur* [Pre-K], 546

Talbott, Hudson. *We're Back!* [2-3], 1013

Thayer, Jane. *Quiet on Account of Dinosaur* [K-1], 567

Wilhelm, Hans. *Tyrone the Horrible* [K-1], 590

DINOSAURS-Poetry

Cole, William. *Dinosaurs and Beasts of Yore* [1-4], 1776

Hopkins, Lee Bennett. *Dinosaurs* [K-6], 1821

Prelutsky, Jack. *Tyrannosaurus Was a Beast* [1-6], 1922

DINOSAURS-Riddles

Rosenbloom, Joseph. *The Funniest Dinosaur Book Ever* [Pre-3], 1928

DIVORCE

Park, Barbara. *Don't Make Me Smile* [4-5], 1220

Roy, Ron. *The Chimpanzee Kid* [5-6], 1348

DOGS

Adler, David A. *My Dog and the Birthday Mystery* [K-1], 313

Armstrong, William. *Sounder* [5-6], 1264

Bare, Colleen Stanley. *To Love a Dog* [Pre-2], 1992

Bemelmans, Ludwig. *Madeline's Rescue* [K-1], 335

Berger, Terry. *The Turtle's Picnic: And Other Nonsense Stories* [1-2], 615

Brenner, Barbara. *A Dog I Know* [1-2], 621

Brett, Jan. *The First Dog* [1-2], 622

Bunting, Eve. *Ghost's Hour, Spook's Hour* [K-1], 351

Burnford, Sheila. *The Incredible Journey* [5-6], 1279

Byars, Betsy. *The Not-Just-Anybody Family* [4-5], 1156

Carrick, Carol. *Ben and the Porcupine* [1-2], 640
The Foundling [1-2], 641

Chapman, Carol. *Barney Bipple's Magic Dandelions* [1-2], 644

Cleary, Beverly. *Henry Huggins* [2-3], 888
Ribsy [2-3], 891

Cohen, Miriam. *Jim's Dog Muffins* [K-1], 368

Cuyler, Margery. *Shadow's Baby* [Pre-K], 61

Davidson, Margaret. *Seven True Dog Stories* [2-4], 2015

DeJong, Meindert. *Hurry Home, Candy* [3-4], 1060

Dillon, Barbara. *What's Happened to Harry?* [2-3], 910

Ellis, Anne. *Dabble Duck* [K-1], 382

Flack, Marjorie. *Angus and the Cat* [Pre-K], 84
Angus and the Ducks [Pre-K], 85
Angus Lost [Pre-K], 86

Gackenbach, Dick. *Beauty, Brave and Beautiful* [K-1], 395
Dog for a Day [K-1], 396
What's Claude Doing? [Pre-K], 101

Gardiner, John Reynolds. *Stone Fox* [3-4], 1067

Garfield, James B. *Follow My Leader* [4-5], 1174

Gipson, Fred. *Old Yeller* [4-5], 1180

Graham, Margaret Bloy. *Benjy and the Barking Bird* [Pre-K], 118

Griffith, Helen V. *Plunk's Dreams* [Pre-K], 122

Hayes, Sarah. *This Is the Bear* [Pre-K], 128

Hazen, Barbara Shook. *Fang* [K-1], 417

Heath, W. L. *Max the Great* [5-6], 1309

Hoff, Syd. *Lengthy* [Pre-K], 139

Howe, Deborah, and James Howe. *Bunnicula: A Rabbit-Tale of Mystery* [4-5], 1193

Howe, James. *The Fright before Christmas* [2-3], 935
Nighty-Nightmare [4-5], 1194

Juster, Norton. *The Phantom Tollbooth* [5-6], 1316

Keats, Ezra Jack. *Goggles!* [K-1], 449
Whistle for Willie [Pre-K], 166

Keller, Holly. *Goodbye, Max* [K-1], 452

Kellogg, Steven. *Pinkerton, Behave* [1-2], 706
Prehistoric Pinkerton [1-2], 707

Lauber, Patricia. *Clarence and the Burglar* [1-2], 720

Lexau, Joan. *I'll Tell on You* [1-2], 724

Low, Joseph. *Mice Twice* [K-1], 488

Modell, Frank. *Tooley! Tooley!* [1-2], 752

Molarsky, Osmond. *Take It or Leave It* [2-3], 965

Mowat, Farley. *Owls in the Family* [3-5], 2077

Myller, Rolf. *A Very Noisy Day* [1-2], 755

Peet, Bill. *The Whingdingdilly* [2-3], 979

Pinkwater, Daniel. *The Magic Moscow* [3-4], 1105

Porte, Barbara Ann. *Harry's Dog* [1-2], 777

Rinkoff, Barbara. *The Remarkable Ramsey* [2-3], 985

Robart, Rose. *The Cake That Mack Ate* [Pre-K], 241

Schwartz, Amy. *Her Majesty, Aunt Essie* [1-2], 796
Oma and Bobo [K-1], 545

Selden, George. *The Cricket in Times Square* [4-5], 1237

Seligson, Susan, and Howie Schneider. *Amos: The Story of an Old Dog and His Couch* [K-1], 549

Sharmat, Marjorie Weinman. *Chasing after Annie* [2-3], 998
Nate the Great [1-2], 810

FAMILY LIFE – Poetry

FAMILY PROBLEMS

FAMILY STORIES

FANTASY

FARM LIFE

There's an Alligator under My Bed [Pre-K], 208
There's Something in My Attic [Pre-K], 209
Nixon, Joan Lowery. *The Alligator under the Bed* [Pre-K], 218
Pfeffer, Susan Beth. *What Do You Do When Your Mouth Won't Open?* [5-6], 1344
Pittman, Helena Clare. *Once When I Was Scared* [1-2], 775
Polacco, Patricia. *Thunder Cake* [K-1], 525
Robison, Deborah. *No Elephants Allowed* [Pre-K], 243
Ross, Tony. *I'm Coming to Get You!* [K-1], 536
Stevenson, James. *That Terrible Halloween Night* [1-2], 824
What's Under My Bed? [1-2], 826
Stolz, Mary. *Storm in the Night* [1-2], 828
Tobias, Tobi. *Chasing the Goblins Away* [1-2], 831
Udry, Janice May. *Alfred* [K-1], 572
Viorst, Judith. *My Mama Says There Aren't Any Zombies, Ghosts, Vampires, Creatures, Demons, Monsters, Fiends, Goblins or Things* [1-2], 840
Whitney, Alma Marshak. *Just Awful* [Pre-K], 293
Williams, Barbara. *Donna Jean's Disaster* [1-2], 850
Williams, Linda. *The Little Old Lady Who Was Not Afraid of Anything* [K-1], 591
Willis, Jeanne. *The Monster Bed* [K-1], 592
Willoughby, Elaine. *Boris and the Monsters* [Pre-K], 297
Winthrop, Elizabeth. *Maggie & the Monster* [Pre-K], 299

FEAR – Folklore

Bennett, Jill. *Teeny Tiny* [Pre-2], 1403
Dasent, George Webbe. *East o' the Sun & West o' the Moon: An Old Norse Tale* [2-6], 1433
Galdone, Paul. *The Teeny-Tiny Woman: A Ghost Story* [Pre-2], 1471
Grant, Joan. *The Monster That Grew Small: An Egyptian Folktale* [1-4], 1484

FEET

SEE Foot

FIGHTING

Kraus, Robert. *Noel the Coward* [Pre-K], 175
Udry, Janice May. *Thump and Plunk* [Pre-K], 277

FIGURES OF SPEECH

SEE English language – Idioms

FINGERPLAYS

Brown, Marc. *Hand Rhymes* [Pre-2], 1760
Carlson, Bernice Wells. *Listen! And Help Tell the Story* [Pre-2], 1765

Delamar, Gloria T. *Children's Counting-Out Rhymes, Fingerplays, Jump-Rope and Bounce-Ball Chants and Other Rhythms: A Comprehensive English-Language Reference* [Pre-3], 1788
Glazer, Tom. *Eye Winker, Tom Tinker, Chin Chopper: Fifty Musical Fingerplays* [Pre-2], 1804
Langstaff, Nancy, and John Langstaff, comps. *Jim Along Josie: A Collection of Folk Songs* [Pre-2], 1850
Pooley, Sarah. *A Day of Rhymes* [Pre-1], 1903
Tashjian, Virginia. *Juba This and Juba That: Story Hour Stretches for Large or Small Groups* [Pre-4], 1961
Westcott, Nadine Bernard. *Peanut Butter and Jelly: A Play Rhyme* [Pre-K], 291

FIRE

Bond, Felicia. *Poinsettia and the Firefighters* [K-1], 338
Brenner, Barbara. *Mr. Tall and Mr. Small* [K-1], 343
Gramatky, Hardie. *Hercules* [Pre-K], 120
Roy, Ron. *Nightmare Island* [4-5], 1234
Williams, Vera B. *A Chair for My Mother* [1-2], 851

FISHES

Cohen, Barbara. *The Carp in the Bathtub* [2-3], 892
Griffith, Helen V. *Grandaddy's Place* [1-2], 682
Lionni, Leo. *Fish Is Fish* [K-1], 474
Swimmy [K-1], 476
McCloskey, Robert. *Burt Dow, Deep-Water Man* [2-3], 955
O'Dell, Scott. *The Black Pearl* [5-6], 1338
Palmer, Helen. *A Fish Out of Water* [Pre-K], 221
Seuss, Dr. *McElligot's Pool* [1-2], 804
Tayntor, Elizabeth, Paul Erickson, and Les Kaufman. *Dive to the Coral Reefs: A New England Aquarium Book* [3-6], 2110
Waber, Bernard. *I Was All Thumbs* [2-3], 1023
Waterton, Betty. *A Salmon for Simon* [1-2], 846

FISHES – Folklore

Grimm, Jacob. *The Fisherman and His Wife* [2-4], 1492
Louie, Ai-Ling. *Yeh-Shen: A Cinderella Story from China* [3-5], 1548

FLIES

SEE Insects

FLIGHT

Adams, Adrienne. *A Woggle of Witches* [Pre-K], 1

HUMOROUS FICTION

HUSBANDS AND WIVES–Folklore

Grimm, Jacob. *The Fisherman and His Wife* [2-4], 1492

Hague, Kathleen, and Michael Hague. *The Man Who Kept House* [K-4], 1514

Wiesner, William. *Happy-Go-Lucky* [1-4], 1625
Turnabout [K-4], 1626

HYGIENE

Bottner, Barbara. *Messy* [K-1], 339

Schwartz, Mary Ada. *Spiffen: A Tale of a Tidy Pig* [K-1], 547

IDIOMS

SEE English language–Idioms

ILLNESS

SEE Sick

ILLUSTRATION OF BOOKS

Brown, Ruth. *If at First You Do Not See* [K-1], 348

Drescher, Henrik. *Simon's Book* [1-2], 664

Jonas, Ann. *Reflections* [1-2], 700
Round Trip [1-2], 701

Krauss, Ruth. *Is This You?* [1-2], 714

Withers, Carl. *Tale of a Black Cat* [1-2], 853

IMAGINATION

Balian, Lorna. *The Aminal* [K-1], 327

Boyd, Selma, and Pauline Boyd. *I Met a Polar Bear* [K-1], 340

Burningham, John. *Would You Rather . . .* [K-1], 355

Byars, Betsy. *The Two-Thousand Pound Goldfish* [5-6], 1283

Carrick, Carol. *Patrick's Dinosaurs* [K-1], 358
What Happened to Patrick's Dinosaurs? [1-2], 642

Conford, Ellen. *Jenny Archer, Author* [2-3], 898

Cooney, Nancy Evans. *The Umbrella Day* [Pre-K], 57

Craig, M. Jean. *The Dragon in the Clock Box* [K-1], 375

Faulkner, Matt. *The Amazing Voyage of Jackie Grace* [1-2], 666

Fife, Dale. *Who's in Charge of Lincoln?* [2-3], 917

Freeman, Don. *A Rainbow of My Own* [Pre-K], 97

Gardner, Beau. *The Look Again . . . and Again, and Again, and Again Book* [1-2], 675

Greenfield, Eloise. *Me and Neesie* [K-1], 411

Griffith, Helen V. *Plunk's Dreams* [Pre-K], 122

Haas, Dorothy F. *Tink in a Tangle* [2-3], 929

Heller, Nicholas. *An Adventure at Sea* [1-2], 685

Henkes, Kevin. *Jessica* [K-1], 418

Keats, Ezra Jack. *Regards to the Man in the Moon* [1-2], 703

Lionni, Leo. *Fish Is Fish* [K-1], 474

Long, Claudia. *Albert's Story* [K-1], 487

Lystad, Mary. *Jennifer Takes Over P.S. 94* [1-2], 733

Pittman, Helena Clare. *Once When I Was Scared* [1-2], 775

Rylant, Cynthia. *All I See* [2-3], 988

Shaw, Charles G. *It Looked Like Spilt Milk* [Pre-K], 264

Small, David. *Imogene's Antlers* [K-1], 558

Stevenson, Robert Louis. *Block City* [K-1], 563

Townson, Hazel. *Terrible Tuesday* [K-1], 569

Van Allsburg, Chris. *The Mysteries of Harris Burdick* [4-5], 1250

Vreeken, Elizabeth. *The Boy Who Would Not Say His Name* [K-1], 576

Ward, Lynd. *The Silver Pony* [2-3], 1024

Zhitkov, Boris. *How I Hunted the Little Fellows* [3-4], 1136

IMMIGRATION AND EMIGRATION

Cohen, Barbara. *Molly's Pilgrim* [2-3], 893

Freedman, Russell. *Immigrant Kids* [4-6], 2027

Waterton, Betty. *Petranella* [1-2], 845

INDIANS OF NORTH AMERICA

SEE ALSO Folklore–Indians of North America

Banks, Lynne Reid. *The Indian in the Cupboard* [5-6], 1272

Brink, Carol Ryrie. *Caddie Woodlawn* [4-5], 1151

Freedman, Russell. *Buffalo Hunt* [5-6], 2025

Gardiner, John Reynolds. *Stone Fox* [3-4], 1067

Miles, Miska. *Annie and the Old One* [4-5], 1213

O'Dell, Scott. *Island of the Blue Dolphins* [5-6], 1339

Speare, Elizabeth George. *The Sign of the Beaver* [5-6], 1363

INDIANS OF NORTH AMERICA–Biography

Fritz, Jean. *The Double Life of Pocahontas* [4-6], 2031

INDIVIDUALITY

Conford, Ellen. *And This Is Laura* [5-6], 1289

dePaola, Tomie. *The Art Lesson* [2-3], 907

Seuling, Barbara. *The Triplets* [1-2], 800

Swope, Sam. *The Araboolies of Liberty Street* [1-2], 829

Willard, Nancy. *Simple Pictures Are Best* [1-2], 849

Yashima, Taro. *Crow Boy* [2-3], 1032

INSECTS

Aylesworth, Jim. *Hush Up!* [K-1], 323

Cameron, Polly. *"I Can't," Said the Ant* [1-2], 636

Seeger, Pete. *Abiyoyo* [K-1], 548

Seuss, Dr. *Bartholomew and the Oobleck* [2-3], 994

Smith, L. J. *The Night of the Solstice* [5-6], 1362

Stanley, Diane. *The Good-Luck Pencil* [2-3], 1005

Steig, William. *Solomon the Rusty Nail* [2-3], 1008

Sterman, Betsy, and Samuel Sterman. *Too Much Magic* [3-4], 1119

Turkle, Brinton. *Do Not Open* [2-3], 1016

Vande Velde, Vivian. *A Hidden Magic* [4-5], 1251

Williams, Jay. *The Magic Grandfather* [4-5], 1254

Wright, Jill. *The Old Woman and the Jar of Uums* [1-2], 856

MAGIC–Folklore

dePaola, Tomie. *Strega Nona* [K-4], 1444

Galdone, Paul. *The Magic Porridge Pot* [Pre-2], 1465

Johnston, Tony. *The Badger and the Magic Fan: A Japanese Folktale* [Pre-2], 1536

MAGICIANS

Cole, Joanna. *Doctor Change* [2-3], 896

Coombs, Patricia. *The Magician and McTree* [2-3], 900

Kraske, Robert. *Magicians Do Amazing Things* [3-6], 2059

Lewis, C. S. *The Magician's Nephew* [4-5], 1204

McGowen, Tom. *The Magician's Apprentice* [5-6], 1329

Mayer, Mercer. *A Special Trick* [2-3], 961

Seuss, Dr. *Bartholomew and the Oobleck* [2-3], 994

Van Allsburg, Chris. *The Garden of Abdul Gasazi* [2-3], 1019

White, Florence. *Escape!: The Life of Harry Houdini* [3-6], 2113

MAGICIANS–Folklore

Turska, Krystyna. *The Magician of Cracow* [2-5], 1619

MAINE

McCloskey, Robert. *Burt Dow, Deep-Water Man* [2-3], 955

Time of Wonder [2-3], 957

Van de Wetering, Janwillem. *Hugh Pine* [3-4], 1127

MANNERS

SEE Etiquette

MATHEMATICS

SEE ALSO Counting books; Measurement

Birch, David. *The King's Chessboard* [3-4], 1045

Brandreth, Gyles. *Brain-Teasers and Mind-Benders* [3-6], 1997

Churchill, E. Richard. *Devilish Bets to Trick Your Friends* [3-6], 2005

Matthews, Louise. *Gator Pie* [K-1], 506

Phillips, Louis. *263 Brain Busters: Just How Smart Are You, Anyway?* [3-6], 2083

Schwartz, David M. *How Much Is a Million?* [1-4], 2093

If You Made a Million [2-4], 2094

MATHEMATICS–Folklore

Dee, Ruby. *Two Ways to Count to Ten: A Liberian Folktale* [K-3], 1436

MATURITY

Kraus, Robert. *Leo the Late Bloomer* [K-1], 460

McPhail, David. *Pig Pig Grows Up* [Pre-K], 202

MEASUREMENT

SEE ALSO Counting books; Mathematics

Lionni, Leo. *Inch by Inch* [K-1], 475

Myller, Rolf. *How Big Is a Foot?* [2-3], 970

Russo, Marisabina. *The Line Up Book* [Pre-K], 247

MEMORY

Arnold, Tedd. *Ollie Forgot* [1-2], 607

Galdone, Joanna, and Paul Galdone. *Gertrude the Goose Who Forgot* [Pre-K], 107

Hoguet, Susan. *I Unpacked My Grandmother's Trunk* [1-2], 689

Hutchins, Pat. *Don't Forget the Bacon!* [K-1], 434

King-Smith, Dick. *Farmer Bungle Forgets* [K-1], 458

MacGregor, Ellen. *Theodore Turtle* [K-1], 491

Patz, Nancy. *Pumpernickel Tickle and Mean Green Cheese* [K-1], 520

Weinberg, Larry. *The Forgetful Bears Meet Mr. Memory* [K-1], 583

MENTALLY HANDICAPPED

SEE Handicaps

MEXICO

Garrett, Helen. *Angelo the Naughty One* [1-2], 676

Lewis, Thomas P. *Hill of Fire* [1-2], 723

MICE

Alexander, Sue. *Dear Phoebe* [1-2], 600

Aylesworth, Jim. *Two Terrible Frights* [Pre-K], 18

Brenner, Barbara. *Mr. Tall and Mr. Small* [K-1], 343

Bunting, Eve. *The Mother's Day Mice* [Pre-K], 32

Cleary, Beverly. *The Mouse and the Motorcycle* [3-4], 1050

Watson, Pauline. *Wriggles the Little Wishing Pig* [K-1], 582
White, E. B. *Charlotte's Web* [2-3], 1027
Winthrop, Elizabeth. *Sloppy Kisses* [K-1], 595
Zakhoder, Boris. *How a Piglet Crashed the Christmas Party* [1-2], 858

PIGS–Folklore
Cauley, Lorinda Bryan. *The Three Little Pigs* [Pre-2], 1420
Galdone, Paul. *The Amazing Pig* [2-4], 1457
  The Three Little Pigs [Pre-1], 1474
Hooks, William H. *The Three Little Pigs and the Fox* [Pre-2], 1530
Lamont, Priscilla. *The Troublesome Pig: A Nursery Tale* [Pre-2], 1543
Marshall, James. *The Three Little Pigs* [Pre-1], 1563
Zemach, Margot. *The Three Little Pigs: An Old Story* [Pre-2], 1639

PIGS–Poetry
Lobel, Arnold. *The Book of Pigericks* [2-6], 1861

PILGRIMS
Cohen, Barbara. *Molly's Pilgrim* [2-3], 893
Fritz, Jean. *Who's That Stepping on Plymouth Rock?* [3-6], 2035
Kroll, Steven. *Oh, What a Thanksgiving!* [1-2], 718
Sewall, Marcia. *The Pilgrims of Plimoth* [2-6], 2098
Waters, Kate. *Sarah Morton's Day: A Day in the Life of a Pilgrim Girl* [1-5], 2112

PIONEERS
SEE Frontier and pioneer life

PIRATES
Cohen, Caron Lee. *Renata, Whizbrain and the Ghost* [2-3], 894
Faulkner, Matt. *The Amazing Voyage of Jackie Grace* [1-2], 666
Fleischman, Sid. *The Ghost in the Noonday Sun* [5-6], 1301
Haynes, Betsy. *The Ghost of the Gravestone Hearth* [4-5], 1185
McNaughton, Colin. *Anton B. Stanton and the Pirats* [1-2], 736
Peet, Bill. *Cyrus the Unsinkable Sea Serpent* [1-2], 767

PLANETS
SEE Astronomy; Space flight

PLANTS
SEE ALSO Flowers; Gardens; Vegetables; Trees

Back, Christine. *Bean and Plant* [Pre-3], 1989
Bash, Barbara. *Desert Giant: The World of the Saguaro Cactus* [2-5], 1994
Flora, James. *The Great Green Turkey Creek Monster* [2-3], 921
Gardiner, John Reynolds. *Top Secret* [5-6], 1303
Krauss, Ruth. *The Carrot Seed* [Pre-K], 178
Zion, Gene. *The Plant Sitter* [K-1], 598

PLAY
SEE ALSO Games
Heller, Nicholas. *An Adventure at Sea* [1-2], 685
Henkes, Kevin. *A Weekend with Wendell* [K-1], 420
Kent, Jack. *Jim Jimmy James* [K-1], 454
Phelan, Terry Wolfe. *The Week Mom Unplugged the TVs* [3-4], 1102

PLAYS
Aardema, Verna. *Who's in Rabbit's House?* [2-4], 1385
Charlip, Remy, and Burton Supree. *Mother, Mother, I Feel Sick, Send for the Doctor Quick, Quick, Quick* [1-2], 646
Cohen, Miriam. *Starring First Grade* [K-1], 371
Freeman, Don. *Hattie the Backstage Bat* [K-1], 393
Gormley, Beatrice. *Fifth-Grade Magic* [4-5], 1181
Johnston, Johanna. *Speak Up, Edie* [K-1], 440
Nixon, Joan Lowery. *Gloria Chipmunk, Star!* [1-2], 760
Oppenheim, Joanne. *Mrs. Peloki's Class Play* [1-2], 763
Robinson, Barbara. *The Best Christmas Pageant Ever* [4-5], 1230
Young, Ruth. *Starring Francine & Dave: Three One-Act Plays* [Pre-2], 2117

POETRY–Anthologies
Arbuthnot, May Hill. *Time for Poetry* [Pre-6], 1744
Cole, Joanna. *A New Treasury of Children's Poetry: Old Favorites and New Discoveries* [Pre-6], 1773
Corrin, Sara, and Stephen Corrin, comps. *Once Upon a Rhyme: 101 Poems for Young Children* [K-3], 1783
dePaola, Tomie. *Tomie dePaola's Book of Poems* [Pre-4], 1790
De Regniers, Beatrice Schenk. *Sing a Song of Popcorn: Every Child's Book of Poems* [Pre-4], 1792
Foster, John. *A First Poetry Book* [K-2], 1800
Hopkins, Lee Bennett. *More Surprises* [Pre-3], 1825

Side by Side: Poems to Read Together [K-2], 1827

Hopkins, Lee Bennett, and Misha Arenstein, comps. *Thread One to a Star: A Book of Poems* [4-6], 1829

Kennedy, X. J. *Knock at a Star: A Child's Introduction to Poetry* [4-6], 1847

Koch, Kenneth, and Kate Farrell, comps. *Talking to the Sun: An Illustrated Anthology of Poems for Young People* [Pre-6], 1849

Larrick, Nancy. *Piping Down the Valleys Wild* [2-6], 1852

Lewis, Richard. *Miracles: Poems by Children of the English-Speaking World* [1-6], 1856

Moore, Lilian. *Go with the Poem* [3-6], 1874

Prelutsky, Jack. *The Random House Book of Poetry for Children* [1-5], 1916

Read-Aloud Rhymes for the Very Young [Pre-3], 1917

Saunders, Dennis. *Magic Lights and Streets of Shining Jet* [1-4], 1943

Untermeyer, Louis. *The Golden Treasury of Poetry* [2-6], 1968

Whipple, Laura. *Eric Carle's Animals, Animals* [K-4], 1974

Wilner, Isabel. *The Poetry Troupe: An Anthology of Poems to Read Aloud* [K-4], 1975

POETRY – Single Author

SEE ALSO Narrative poetry; Stories in rhyme

Adoff, Arnold. *Eats* [2-6], 1742

Bodecker, N. M. *Let's Marry Said the Cherry and Other Nonsense Poems* [K-5], 1751

A Person from Britain Whose Head Was the Shape of a Mitten and Other Limericks [3-6], 1752

Ciardi, John. *Doodle Soup* [1-4], 1769

Fast and Slow: Poems for Advanced Children and Beginning Parents [2-5], 1770

The Hopeful Trout and Other Limericks [3-6], 1771

You Read to Me, I'll Read to You [1-3], 1772

De Regniers, Beatrice Schenk. *This Big Cat and Other Cats I've Known* [Pre-2], 1793

Eliot, T. S. *Old Possum's Book of Practical Cats* [4-6], 1795

Esbensen, Barbara Juster. *Cold Stars and Fireflies: Poems of the Four Seasons* [3-6], 1797

Greenfield, Eloise. *Honey, I Love* [2-5], 1807

Under the Sunday Tree [2-5], 1808

Hoban, Russell. *Egg Thoughts and Other Frances Songs* [K-2], 1813

Hughes, Langston. *Don't You Turn Back* [3-6], 1830

Kennedy, X. J. *Ghastlies, Goops & Pincushions: Nonsense Verse* [3-6], 1846

Klein, Robin. *Snakes and Ladders: Poems about the Ups and Downs of Life* [3-6], 1848

Lear, Edward. *How Pleasant to Know Mr. Lear!* [4-6], 1853

Lee, Dennis. *Alligator Pie* [Pre-4], 1854

Jelly Belly: Original Nursery Rhymes [Pre-3], 1855

Livingston, Myra Cohn. *A Song I Sang to You: A Selection of Poems* [K-3], 1860

Lobel, Arnold. *The Book of Pigericks* [2-6], 1861

Whiskers & Rhymes [Pre-3], 1862

McCord, David. *One at a Time* [K-4], 1864

Margolis, Richard J. *Secrets of a Small Brother* [1-4], 1867

Merriam, Eve. *Blackberry Ink* [Pre-2], 1868

Chortles: New and Selected Wordplay Poems [3-6], 1869

A Poem for a Pickle: Funnybone Verses [K-4], 1870

You Be Good & I'll Be Night: Jump-on-the-Bed Poems [Pre-1], 1871

Milne, A. A. *Now We Are Six* [Pre-3], 1872

Mizamura, Kazue. *Flower Moon Snow: A Book of Haiku* [2-6], 1873

Nash, Ogden. *Custard and Company* [3-6], 1893

O'Neill, Mary L. *What Is That Sound!* [2-5], 1898

Peck, Robert Newton. *Bee Tree and Other Stuff* [4-6], 1899

Pomerantz, Charlotte. *If I Had a Paka* [K-4], 1902

Prelutsky, Jack. *The Baby Uggs Are Hatching* [K-4], 1904

The New Kid on the Block [K-5], 1911

Nightmares: Poems to Trouble Your Sleep [3-6], 1912

The Queen of Eene [2-4], 1914

Ride a Purple Pelican [Pre-2], 1918

The Sheriff of Rottenshot [2-4], 1920

The Snopp on the Sidewalk and Other Poems [K-3], 1921

Zoo Doings [K-4], 1924

Rylant, Cynthia. *Waiting to Waltz: A Childhood* [5-6], 1941

Sandburg, Carl. *Rainbows Are Made* [5-6], 1942

Silverstein, Shel. *Where the Sidewalk Ends* [Pre-6], 1952

Simmie, Lois. *Auntie's Knitting a Baby* [2-5], 1953

Smith, William Jay. *Laughing Time: Nonsense Poems* [K-3], 1955

Starbird, Kaye. *The Covered Bridge House and Other Poems* [3-6], 1957

631

Viorst, Judith. *If I Were in Charge of the World and Other Worries: Poems for Children and Their Parents* [2-5], 1969

Watson, Clyde. *Father Fox's Pennyrhymes* [Pre-1], 1972

Worth, Valerie. *Small Poems* [2-6], 1979

Yolen, Jane. *The Three Bears Rhyme Book* [Pre-2], 1981

Zolotow, Charlotte. *Everything Glistens and Everything Sings* [K-4], 1984

POETS

Byars, Betsy. *Beans on the Roof* [2-3], 879

Clifford, Sandy. *The Roquefort Gang* [3-4], 1053

Corbett, Scott. *The Limerick Trick* [3-4], 1057

Lionni, Leo. *Frederick* [1-2], 727

Moore, Lilian. *I'll Meet You at the Cucumbers* [2-3], 967

Nikly, Michelle. *The Emperor's Plum Tree* [1-2], 759

POLICE

McCloskey, Robert. *Make Way for Ducklings* [1-2], 734

Sauer, Julia L. *Mike's House* [Pre-K], 252

POLLUTION

Madden, Don. *The Wartville Wizard* [1-2], 738

Peet, Bill. *The Wump World* [2-3], 980

Seuss, Dr. *The Lorax* [2-3], 997

POND LIFE

George, William T. *Box Turtle at Long Pond* [Pre-2], 2037

POPCORN

Asch, Frank. *Popcorn* [Pre-K], 15

dePaola, Tomie. *The Popcorn Book* [1-4], 2018

Thayer, Jane. *The Popcorn Dragon* [Pre-K], 273

PORCUPINES

Carrick, Carol. *Ben and the Porcupine* [1-2], 640

Lester, Helen. *A Porcupine Named Fluffy* [K-1], 471

Van de Wetering, Janwillem. *Hugh Pine* [3-4], 1127

POURQUOI TALES

Aardema, Verna. *Why Mosquitoes Buzz in People's Ears* [Pre-2], 1386

Bowden, Joan Chase. *Why the Tides Ebb and Flow* [1-6], 1406

Climo, Shirley. *King of the Birds* [K-3], 1425

Goble, Paul. *Iktomi and the Boulder: A Plains Indian Story* [K-3], 1483

Hadithi, Mwenye. *Greedy Zebra* [Pre-K], 125

Kipling, Rudyard. *The Elephant's Child* [2-3], 946

How the Camel Got His Hump [2-3], 947

How the Whale Got His Throat [1-2], 712

Just So Stories [2-3], 948

Lester, Julius. *The Knee-High Man and Other Tales* [K-4], 1706

Roth, Susan L. *Kanahena: A Cherokee Story* [Pre-2], 1587

Steptoe, John. *The Story of Jumping Mouse: A Native American Legend* [Pre-4], 1608

Troughton, Joanna. *How the Birds Changed Their Feathers: A South American Indian Folk Tale* [Pre-3], 1616

PREHISTORIC ANIMALS

SEE Animals, prehistoric; Dinosaurs

PREJUDICE

Estes, Eleanor. *The Hundred Dresses* [2-3], 914

Taylor, Mildred D. *The Gold Cadillac* [4-5], 1248

Uchida, Yoshiko. *Journey Home* [5-6], 1370

PRESENTS

SEE Gifts

PRESIDENTS–U.S.

Freedman, Russell. *Lincoln: A Photobiography* [5-6], 2028

Griffin, Judith Berry. *Phoebe and the General* [2-5], 2042

Seuling, Barbara. *The Last Cow on the White House Lawn & Other Little-Known Facts about the Presidency* [3-5], 2096

PRINCES AND PRINCESSES

Andersen, Hans Christian. *The Princess and the Pea* [K-1], 322

Elkin, Benjamin. *The Loudest Noise in the World* [K-1], 381

Fleischman, Sid. *The Whipping Boy* [4-5], 1172

Houseman, Laurence. *Rocking-Horse Land* [1-2], 690

Laroche, Michel. *The Snow Rose* [3-4], 1086

Nesbit, E. *Melisande* [4-5], 1218

Stanley, Diane. *Fortune* [3-4], 1117

Thurber, James. *Many Moons* [2-3], 1015

Vande Velde, Vivian. *A Hidden Magic* [4-5], 1251

Vesey, A. *The Princess and the Frog* [1-2], 837

Yolen, Jane. *Sleeping Ugly* [2-3], 1033

PRINCES AND PRINCESSES–Folklore

Brown, Marcia. *Cinderella: Or, The Little Glass Slipper* [1-4], 1410

Carrick, Carol. *Aladdin and the Wonderful Lamp* [2-4], 1413

Galdone, Paul. *Cinderella* [1-4], 1458

Willis, Val. *The Secret in the Matchbook* [K-1], 593

Wittman, Sally. *The Wonderful Mrs. Trumbly* [K-1], 596

Yashima, Taro. *Crow Boy* [2-3], 1032

SCHOOLS–Riddles

Keller, Charles. *School Daze* [2-5], 1842

SCIENCE

Grillone, Lisa, and Joseph Gennaro. *Small Worlds Close Up* [4-6], 2043

Simon, Seymour. *The Dinosaur Is the Biggest Animal That Ever Lived and Other Wrong Ideas You Thought Were True* [2-5], 2100

SCIENCE–Experiments

Adler, David A. *Eaton Stanley & the Mind Control Experiment* [4-5], 1137

Brown, Bob. *How to Fool Your Friends* [3-5], 2000

Cobb, Vicki, and Kathy Darling. *Bet You Can!: Science Possibilities to Fool You* [3-6], 2006

Cole, Joanna. *The Magic School Bus at the Waterworks* [2-4], 2008

The Magic School Bus Inside the Earth [2-4], 2009

Corbett, Scott. *The Lemonade Trick* [3-4], 1056

The Limerick Trick [3-4], 1057

Gardiner, John Reynolds. *Top Secret* [5-6], 1303

Hayes, William. *Project: Genius* [5-6], 1308

Hughes, Dean. *Nutty Knows All* [5-6], 1312

Lehane, M. S. *Science Tricks* [K-3], 2065

Simon, Seymour. *Einstein Anderson, Science Sleuth* [4-5], 1239

Williams, Jay, and Raymond Abrashkin. *Danny Dunn and the Homework Machine* [4-5], 1255

SCIENCE FICTION

Alcock, Vivien. *The Monster Garden* [5-6], 1257

Ames, Mildred. *Is There Life on a Plastic Planet?* [5-6], 1263

Beatty, Jerome. *Matthew Looney's Invasion of the Earth* [4-5], 1142

Corbett, Scott. *The Donkey Planet* [4-5], 1163

Etra, Jonathan, and Stephanie Spinner. *Aliens for Breakfast* [2-3], 915

Fisk, Nicholas. *Grinny: A Novel of Science Fiction* [5-6], 1297

Harding, Lee. *The Fallen Spaceman* [3-4], 1070

L'Engle, Madeleine. *A Wrinkle in Time* [5-6], 1325

Marshall, Edward. *Space Case* [1-2], 742

Marshall, James. *Merry Christmas, Space Case* [1-2], 744

Paton Walsh, Jill. *The Green Book* [5-6], 1341

Pinkwater, Daniel. *Fat Men from Space* [3-4], 1103

Lizard Music [4-5], 1225

The Slaves of Spiegel: A Magic Moscow Story [4-5], 1226

Roberts, Willo Davis. *The Girl with the Silver Eyes* [5-6], 1345

Ross, Tony. *I'm Coming to Get You!* [K-1], 536

Sadler, Marilyn. *Alistair in Outer Space* [1-2], 787

Alistair's Time Machine [1-2], 789

Service, Pamela F. *Stinker from Space* [5-6], 1354

Sleator, William. *Into the Dream* [5-6], 1359

Slobodkin, Louis. *The Spaceship under the Apple Tree* [3-4], 1113

Slote, Alfred. *My Robot Buddy* [2-3], 1002

My Trip to Alpha I [3-4], 1114

Sterman, Betsy, and Samuel Sterman. *Too Much Magic* [3-4], 1119

Williams, Jay, and Raymond Abrashkin. *Danny Dunn, Time Traveler* [4-5], 1256

Yorinks, Arthur. *Company's Coming* [2-3], 1034

SCIENTISTS

Anderson, Margaret. *The Brain on Quartz Mountain* [3-4], 1041

Butterworth, Oliver. *The Enormous Egg* [4-5], 1154

Epstein, Sam, and Beryl Epstein. *Secret in a Sealed Bottle: Lazzaro Spallanzani's Work with Microbes* [5-6], 2022

Ormondroyd, Edward. *David and the Phoenix* [3-4], 1100

Ungerer, Tomi. *The Beast of Monsieur Racine* [2-3], 1018

SCOTLAND

Hunter, Mollie. *Wicked One: A Story of Suspense* [5-6], 1313

Selden, George. *Sparrow Socks* [1-2], 799

SCULPTORS

Freeman, Don. *Norman the Doorman* [1-2], 671

Schotter, Roni. *Captain Snap and the Children of Vinegar Lane* [1-2], 793

Stolz, Mary. *Zekmet, the Stone Carver* [4-5], 1244

SEA

SEE Ocean; Seashore

SEASHORE

SEE ALSO Ocean

Haynes, Betsy. *The Ghost of the Gravestone Hearth* [4-5], 1185

Jonas, Ann. *Reflections* [1-2], 700

Ness, Evaline. *Sam, Bangs and Moonshine* [1-2], 757

Peters, Lisa Westberg. *The Sun, the Wind and the Rain* [Pre-2], 2082

Robbins, Ken. *Beach Days* [Pre-K], 242

Samton, Sheila White. *Beside the Bay* [Pre-K], 250

Stevenson, James. *Clams Can't Sing* [K-1], 560

Tresselt, Alvin. *Hide and Seek Fog* [1-2], 833

Turkle, Brinton. *Do Not Open* [2-3], 1016

Weller, Frances Ward. *Riptide* [1-2], 848

Zion, Gene. *Harry by the Sea* [Pre-K], 307

SEASHORE-Folklore

Hodges, Margaret. *The Wave* [K-4], 1527

SEASHORE-Poetry

McMillan, Bruce. *One Sun: A Book of Terse Verse* [Pre-2], 1865

SEASONS

SEE ALSO Autumn; Months; Spring; Summer; Winter

Alexander, Sue. *There's More . . . Much More* [Pre-K], 3

Andrews, Jan. *Very Last First Time* [2-3], 867

Aylesworth, Jim. *One Crow: A Counting Rhyme* [Pre-K], 17

Borden, Louise. *Caps, Hats, Socks, and Mittens: A Book about the Four Seasons* [Pre-K], 24

Burton, Virginia Lee. *Katy and the Big Snow* [Pre-K], 35

The Little House [1-2], 634

Clifton, Lucille. *The Boy Who Didn't Believe in Spring* [1-2], 650

Coleridge, Sara. *January Brings the Snow: A Book of Months* [Pre-K], 54

Fowler, Susi Gregg. *When Summer Ends* [Pre-K], 90

Hall, Donald. *Ox-Cart Man* [2-3], 931

Johnson, Crockett. *Will Spring Be Early? or Will Spring Be Late?* [K-1], 439

Johnston, Tony. *Yonder* [2-3], 939

Laroche, Michel. *The Snow Rose* [3-4], 1086

Lemieux, Michele. *What's That Noise?* [Pre-K], 184

Major, Beverly. *Playing Sardines* [1-2], 741

Minarik, Else Holmelund. *It's Spring!* [Pre-K], 213

Ryder, Joanne. *Chipmunk Song* [Pre-2], 2089

Sendak, Maurice. *Chicken Soup with Rice* [K-1], 551

Tejima, Keizaburo. *Fox's Dream* [K-1], 565

Udry, Janice May. *A Tree Is Nice* [Pre-K], 278

Van Allsburg, Chris. *The Stranger* [3-4], 1124

SEASONS-Folklore

Proddow, Penelope. *Demeter and Persephone* [5-6], 1581

SEASONS-Poetry

Esbensen, Barbara Juster. *Cold Stars and Fireflies: Poems of the Four Seasons* [3-6], 1797

Hopkins, Lee Bennett. *Moments: Poems about the Seasons* [1-5], 1824

The Sky Is Full of Song [K-3], 1828

Hughes, Shirley. *Out and About* [Pre-1], 1831

Mizamura, Kazue. *Flower Moon Snow: A Book of Haiku* [2-6], 1873

Prelutsky, Jack. *It's Snowing! It's Snowing!* [Pre-3], 1907

What I Did Last Summer [K-3], 1923

Singer, Marilyn. *Turtle in July* [1-4], 1954

SELF-CONCEPT

Ames, Mildred. *Is There Life on a Plastic Planet?* [5-6], 1263

Andersen, Hans Christian. *The Ugly Duckling* [1-2], 603

Blume, Judy. *Freckle Juice* [1-2], 618

Byars, Betsy. *The Summer of the Swans* [5-6], 1282

Caple, Kathy. *The Biggest Nose* [K-1], 356

Carle, Eric. *The Mixed-Up Chameleon* [Pre-K], 38

Chapman, Carol. *The Tale of Meshka the Kvetch* [2-3], 885

Cohen, Miriam. *No Good in Art* [K-1], 370

Conford, Ellen. *Impossible Possum* [1-2], 652

Revenge of the Incredible Dr. Rancid and His Youthful Assistant, Jeffrey [4-5], 1162

dePaola, Tomie. *Big Anthony and the Magic Ring* [2-3], 908

Holman, Felice. *The Blackmail Machine* [4-5], 1191

Howe, James. *I Wish I Were a Butterfly* [1-2], 692

Kasza, Keiko. *The Pigs' Picnic* [Pre-K], 161

LeSieg, Theo. *I Wish That I Had Duck Feet* [K-1], 467

Lexau, Joan. *Benjie* [K-1], 472

Lionni, Leo. *Fish Is Fish* [K-1], 474

Lisle, Janet Taylor. *The Dancing Cats of Applesap* [4-5], 1205

Marshall, James. *Portly McSwine* [K-1], 503

Peet, Bill. *The Spooky Tail of Prewitt Peacock* [1-2], 771

The Whingdingdilly [2-3], 979

Pfeffer, Susan Beth. *What Do You Do When Your Mouth Won't Open?* [5-6], 1344

Schertle, Alice. *The April Fool* [2-3], 991

Ungerer, Tomi. *One, Two, Where's My Shoe?* [Pre-K], 281

Winthrop, Elizabeth. *Shoes* [Pre-K], 300

SHOES–Folklore

Grimm, Jacob. *The Elves and the Shoemaker* [Pre-2], 1491

SHOPPING

Allard, Harry. *I Will Not Go to Market Today* [K-1], 316

Daly, Niki. *Not So Fast, Songololo* [Pre-K], 62

Grossman, Bill. *Tommy at the Grocery Store* [K-1], 414

SHORT STORIES

Ainsworth, Ruth. *The Phantom Carousel and Other Ghostly Tales* [4-5], 1138

Alexander, Lloyd. *The Town Cats and Other Tales* [5-6], 1261

Babbitt, Natalie. *The Devil's Storybook* [5-6], 1270

Bauer, Caroline Feller. *Windy Day: Stories and Poems* [1-4], 1746

Dahl, Roald. *The Wonderful Story of Henry Sugar and Six More* [5-6], 1293

Hunter, Mollie. *A Furl of Fairy Wind* [3-4], 1076

Kipling, Rudyard. *Just So Stories* [2-3], 948

Levitt, Paul M., Douglas A. Burger, and Elissa S. Guralnick. *The Weighty Word Book* [5-6], 1326

Lionni, Leo. *Frederick's Fables: A Leo Lionni Treasury of Favorite Stories* [1-2], 728

Mendoza, George. *Gwot!: Horribly Funny Hairticklers* [2-3], 962

Pollack, Pamela. *The Random House Book of Humor for Children* [4-5], 1228

Rylant, Cynthia. *Children of Christmas: Stories for the Seasons* [5-6], 1349

Salway, Lance. *A Nasty Piece of Work and Other Ghost Stories* [5-6], 1351

Slote, Alfred. *The Devil Rides with Me and Other Fantastic Stories* [5-6], 1360

SIBLING RIVALRY

Blume, Judy. *The Pain and the Great One* [1-2], 619

Caseley, Judith. *Silly Baby* [Pre-K], 44

Dragonwagon, Crescent. *I Hate My Brother Harry* [1-2], 663

Kellogg, Steven. *Much Bigger than Martin* [K-1], 453

Park, Barbara. *Operation: Dump the Chump* [3-4], 1101

Roche, P. K. *Good-Bye, Arnold* [K-1], 533

Root, Phyllis. *Moon Tiger* [K-1], 535

Russo, Marisabina. *Only Six More Days* [Pre-K], 248

Stevenson, James. *Worse Than Willy!* [1-2], 827

Viorst, Judith. *I'll Fix Anthony* [K-1], 574

Yorinks, Arthur. *Oh, Brother* [2-3], 1036

SIBLING RIVALRY–Poetry

Margolis, Richard J. *Secrets of a Small Brother* [1-4], 1867

SICK

Brandenberg, Franz. *I Wish I Was Sick, Too* [Pre-K], 26

Charlip, Remy, and Burton Supree. *Mother, Mother, I Feel Sick, Send for the Doctor Quick, Quick, Quick* [1-2], 646

Cherry, Lynne. *Who's Sick Today?* [Pre-K], 47

Coerr, Eleanor. *Sadako & the Thousand Paper Cranes* [3-6], 2007

Gackenbach, Dick. *What's Claude Doing?* [Pre-K], 101

Gretz, Susanna. *Teddy Bears Cure a Cold* [K-1], 413

Le Guin, Ursula K. *A Visit from Dr. Katz* [Pre-K], 183

Schotter, Roni. *Captain Snap and the Children of Vinegar Lane* [1-2], 793

Slote, Alfred. *Hang Tough, Paul Mather* [4-5], 1241

Smith, Robert Kimmell. *Chocolate Fever* [2-3], 1003

Thurber, James. *Many Moons* [2-3], 1015

Williams, Barbara. *Albert's Toothache* [Pre-K], 296

SIGN LANGUAGE

Michel, Anna. *The Story of Nim, the Chimp Who Learned Language* [3-6], 2076

Patterson, Francine. *Koko's Kitten* [2-6], 2080

SINGING GAMES

Glazer, Tom. *Eye Winker, Tom Tinker, Chin Chopper: Fifty Musical Fingerplays* [Pre-2], 1804

Langstaff, Nancy, and John Langstaff, comps. *Jim Along Josie: A Collection of Folk Songs* [Pre-2], 1850

SISTERS

SEE ALSO Brothers; Brothers and sisters

Cleary, Beverly. *Beezus and Ramona* [2-3], 887

Galbraith, Kathryn O. *Waiting for Jennifer* [K-1], 400

Henkes, Kevin. *Sheila Rae, the Brave* [Pre-K], 132

Howard, Ellen. *A Circle of Giving* [4-5], 1192

Naylor, Phyllis Reynolds. *Witch's Sister* [4-5], 1217

Samuels, Barbara. *Duncan & Dolores* [Pre-K], 251

Schwartz, Amy. *Annabelle Swift, Kindergartner* [1-2], 794

Seuling, Barbara. *The Triplets* [1-2], 800

SISTERS-Folklore

Grimm, Jacob. *Mother Holly* [Pre-2], 1502

San Souci, Robert. *The Talking Eggs* [1-4], 1590

Steptoe, John. *Mufaro's Beautiful Daughters: An African Tale* [1-4], 1607

Young, Ed. *Lon Po Po: A Red-Riding Hood Story from China* [K-2], 1633

SIZE

Andersen, Hans Christian. *Thumbelina* [2-3], 864

Banks, Lynne Reid. *The Indian in the Cupboard* [5-6], 1272

Brenner, Barbara. *Mr. Tall and Mr. Small* [K-1], 343

Chase, Mary. *Loretta Mason Potts* [4-5], 1157

Du Bois, William Pène. *The Giant* [5-6], 1294

Hadithi, Mwenye. *Crafty Chameleon* [Pre-K], 124
  Tricky Tortoise [Pre-K], 126

Heide, Florence Parry. *The Shrinking of Treehorn* [3-4], 1071

Joyce, William. *George Shrinks* [K-1], 444

McNaughton, Colin. *Anton B. Stanton and the Pirats* [1-2], 736

McPhail, David. *Great Cat* [K-1], 495

Nesbit, E. *Melisande* [4-5], 1218

Norton, Mary. *The Borrowers* [5-6], 1336

Parish, Peggy. *No More Monsters for Me* [K-1], 517

Peet, Bill. *Big Bad Bruce* [1-2], 766

Pinkwater, Daniel. *The Wuggie Norple Story* [K-1], 524

Sleator, William. *Among the Dolls* [4-5], 1240

Tapp, Kathy Kennedy. *Moth-Kin Magic* [4-5], 1247

White, E. B. *Stuart Little* [3-4], 1131

Winthrop, Elizabeth. *The Castle in the Attic* [5-6], 1374

SIZE-Folklore

Brenner, Barbara. *Little One Inch* [K-4], 1407

SKELETONS

SEE Bones

SKIING

Calhoun, Mary. *Cross-Country Cat* [1-2], 635

Fife, Dale. *North of Danger* [5-6], 1296

SKUNKS

Service, Pamela F. *Stinker from Space* [5-6], 1354

SKY

Cummings, Pat. *C.L.O.U.D.S.* [2-3], 903

Shaw, Charles G. *It Looked Like Spilt Milk* [Pre-K], 264

SLAPSTICK

Allard, Harry. *The Stupids Die* [K-1], 318

Noble, Trinka Hakes. *The Day Jimmy's Boa Ate the Wash* [1-2], 761
  Meanwhile Back at the Ranch [2-3], 974

Rose, Anne. *The Triumphs of Fuzzy Fogtop* [1-2], 784

Silverstein, Shel. *A Giraffe and a Half* [1-2], 811

SLAVERY

Chbosky, Stacey. *Who Owns the Sun?* [4-5], 1158

Hurmence, Belinda. *A Girl Called Boy* [5-6], 1314

McGovern, Ann. *Runaway Slave: The Story of Harriet Tubman* [2-5], 2070

Monjo, F. N. *The Drinking Gourd* [2-3], 966

Winter, Jeanette. *Follow the Drinking Gourd* [3-4], 1134

SLEEP

Howard, Jane R. *When I'm Sleepy* [Pre-K], 141

Johnston, Johanna. *Edie Changes Her Mind* [Pre-K], 155

Kandoian, Ellen. *Under the Sun* [K-1], 445

Keats, Ezra Jack. *Dreams* [K-1], 448

Koide, Tan. *May We Sleep Here Tonight?* [Pre-K], 172

Kraus, Robert. *Milton the Early Riser* [Pre-K], 174

Lemieux, Michele. *What's That Noise?* [Pre-K], 184

Murphy, Jill. *Peace at Last* [Pre-K], 214

Sharmat, Marjorie Weinman. *Go to Sleep, Nicholas Joe* [Pre-K], 263

Stevenson, James. *What's Under My Bed?* [1-2], 826

Wood, Audrey. *The Napping House* [Pre-K], 301

SLEEP-Folklore

Grimm, Jacob. *The Sleeping Beauty* [2-5], 1505
  Thorn Rose: or, The Sleeping Beauty [1-4], 1508

SLEEP-Poetry

Prelutsky, Jack. *My Parents Think I'm Sleeping* [Pre-3], 1910

SNAILS

King-Smith, Dick. *Sophie's Snail* [1-2], 711

Marshall, James. *The Guest* [Pre-K], 203

Ryder, Joanne. *The Snail's Spell* [Pre-K], 249

SNAILS–Folklore

Wolkstein, Diane. *White Wave: A Chinese Tale* [2-6], 1631

SNAKES

Clifford, Eth. *Harvey's Horrible Snake Disaster* [3-4], 1052

Kipling, Rudyard. *The Elephant's Child* [2-3], 946

Kudrna, C. Imbior. *To Bathe a Boa* [K-1], 463

Leydenfrost, Robert. *The Snake That Sneezed* [Pre-K], 188

Moore, Lilian. *The Snake That Went to School* [2-3], 968

Noble, Trinka Hakes. *The Day Jimmy's Boa Ate the Wash* [1-2], 761

Rounds, Glen. *Mr. Yowder and the Train Robbers* [4-5], 1232

Ungerer, Tomi. *Crictor* [K-1], 573

SNAKES–Folklore

Aardema, Verna. *What's So Funny, Ketu?* [1-4], 1384

Steptoe, John. *Mufaro's Beautiful Daughters: An African Tale* [1-4], 1607

SNAKES–Riddles

Burns, Diane L. *Snakes Alive!: Jokes about Snakes* [1-4], 1763

SNOW

SEE ALSO Rain and rainfall; Storms; Weather; Winter

Burton, Virginia Lee. *Katy and the Big Snow* [Pre-K], 35

Calhoun, Mary. *Cross-Country Cat* [1-2], 635
The Night the Monster Came [2-3], 880

Fleming, Susan. *Trapped on the Golden Flyer* [4-5], 1173

Keats, Ezra Jack. *The Snowy Day* [Pre-K], 165

Lindgren, Astrid. *The Tomten* [1-2], 725

Moskin, Marietta. *The Day of the Blizzard* [3-4], 1098

Nietzel, Shirley. *The Jacket I Wear in the Snow* [Pre-K], 217

Noble, Trinka Hakes. *Apple Tree Christmas* [2-3], 973

Sauer, Julia L. *Mike's House* [Pre-K], 252

Simon, Seymour. *Icebergs and Glaciers* [3-5], 2103

Slobodkin, Florence. *Too Many Mittens* [Pre-K], 268

Steig, William. *Brave Irene* [1-2], 820

Taylor, Mark. *Henry the Explorer* [K-1], 564

Ziefert, Harriet. *Snow Magic* [Pre-K], 306

Zolotow, Charlotte. *Something Is Going to Happen* [Pre-K], 311

SNOW–Poetry

Prelutsky, Jack. *It's Snowing! It's Snowing!* [Pre-3], 1907

Service, Robert W. *The Cremation of Sam McGee* [5-6], 1355

SOLDIERS

McGovern, Ann. *The Secret Soldier: The Story of Deborah Sampson* [3-6], 2071

SOLDIERS–Folklore

Brown, Marcia. *Stone Soup* [1-4], 1412

Grimm, Jacob. *The Bearskinner* [2-4], 1486

Hutton, Warwick. *The Nose Tree* [2-5], 1533

McCurdy, Michael. *The Devils Who Learned to Be Good* [K-3], 1549

Reuter, Bjarne. *The Princess and the Sun, Moon and Stars* [1-4], 1585

SONGBOOKS

SEE ALSO Music; Songs; Stories with songs

Fox, Dan. *Go In and Out the Window: An Illustrated Songbook for Young People* [Pre-6], 1801

Garson, Eugenia. *The Laura Ingalls Wilder Songbook* [2-5], 1802

Glazer, Tom. *Eye Winker, Tom Tinker, Chin Chopper: Fifty Musical Fingerplays* [Pre-2], 1804
Tom Glazer's Treasury of Songs for Children [Pre-6], 1805

Hart, Jane. *Singing Bee!: A Collection of Favorite Children's Songs* [K-2], 1810

Hoban, Russell. *Egg Thoughts and Other Frances Songs* [K-2], 1813

John, Timothy. *The Great Song Book* [Pre-5], 1832

Langstaff, Nancy, and John Langstaff, comps. *Jim Along Josie: A Collection of Folk Songs* [Pre-2], 1850

Mother Goose. *Songs from Mother Goose: With the Traditional Melody for Each* [Pre-2], 1890

Nelson, Esther L. *The Funny Song Book* [Pre-6], 1894

Quackenbush, Robert. *The Holiday Songbook* [Pre-5], 1925

Raffi. *The Raffi Singable Songbook: A Collection of 51 Songs from Raffi's First Three Records for Young Children* [Pre-2], 1926

Seeger, Ruth Crawford. *American Folk Songs for Children* [Pre-4], 1951

Weiss, Nicki. *If You're Happy and You Know It: Eighteen Story Songs Set to Pictures* [Pre-2], 1973

SQUIRRELS

Drummond, V. H. *Phewtus the Squirrel* [Pre-K], 74

Shannon, George. *The Surprise* [Pre-K], 262

STARS

SEE ALSO Astronomy; Moon; Space flight; Sun

Moeri, Louise. *Star Mother's Youngest Child* [3-4], 1097

Sachs, Marilyn. *Matt's Mitt and Fleet-Footed Florence* [2-3], 990

Simon, Seymour. *Stars* [3-6], 2104

STARS–Folklore

Esbensen, Barbara Juster. *The Star Maiden: An Ojibway Tale* [2-5], 1451

Goble, Paul. *Her Seven Brothers* [3-6], 1482

STEALING

SEE ALSO Honesty

Devlin, Harry, and Wende Devlin. *Cranberry Thanksgiving* [1-2], 660

Kroll, Steven. *Amanda and Giggling Ghost* [1-2], 715

Shyer, Marlene Fanta. *My Brother, the Thief* [5-6], 1356

STORIES IN RHYME

SEE ALSO Narrative poetry; Poetry–Single author

Aardema, Verna. *Bringing the Rain to Kapiti Plain* [Pre-2], 1380

Aesop. *Aesop's Fables* [3-6], 1646

Aylesworth, Jim. *One Crow: A Counting Rhyme* [Pre-K], 17

Baer, Edith. *Words Are Like Faces* [K-1], 324

Barrett, Judi. *Pickles Have Pimples: And Other Silly Statements* [1-2], 611

Baylor, Byrd. *Amigo* [1-2], 613

Bemelmans, Ludwig. *Madeline's Rescue* [K-1], 335

Brenner, Barbara. *Mr. Tall and Mr. Small* [K-1], 343

Bunting, Eve. *Scary, Scary Halloween* [K-1], 352

Cameron, Polly. *"I Can't," Said the Ant* [1-2], 636

Cauley, Lorinda Bryan. *The Three Little Kittens* [Pre-K], 45

Causley, Charles. *"Quack!" Said the Billy-Goat* [Pre-K], 46

Cherry, Lynne. *Who's Sick Today?* [Pre-K], 47

Cole, William. *Frances Face-Maker: A Going to Bed Book* [Pre-K], 53

Coleridge, Sara. *January Brings the Snow: A Book of Months* [Pre-K], 54

Coletta, Irene, and Hallie Coletta. *From A to Z: The Collected Letters of Irene and Hallie Coletta* [2-3], 897

Crews, Donald. *Ten Black Dots* [Pre-K], 59

Degen, Bruce. *Jamberry* [Pre-K], 64

dePaola, Tomie. *The Comic Adventures of Old Mother Hubbard and Her Dog* [Pre-1], 1438

De Regniers, Beatrice Schenk. *May I Bring a Friend?* [Pre-K], 69

Dobbs, Dayle-Ann. *Wheel Away!* [Pre-K], 71

Eichenberg, Fritz. *Ape in a Cape: An Alphabet of Odd Animals* [Pre-K], 79

Dancing in the Moon: Counting Rhymes [K-1], 380

Emberley, Barbara. *Drummer Hoff* [Pre-K], 80

Emberley, Ed. *The Wing on a Flea* [Pre-K], 81

Gag, Wanda. *Millions of Cats* [Pre-K], 104

Galdone, Joanna, and Paul Galdone. *Gertrude the Goose Who Forgot* [Pre-K], 107

Galdone, Paul. *The History of Mother Twaddle and the Marvelous Achievements of Her Son, Jack* [K-3], 1462

Old Mother Hubbard and Her Dog. [Pre-1], 1468

Over in the Meadow: An Old Nursery Counting Rhyme [Pre-K], 108

Gerrard, Roy. *Sir Francis Drake: His Daring Deeds* [4-6], 2038

Goodspeed, Peter. *A Rhinoceros Wakes Me Up in the Morning* [Pre-K], 116

Grossman, Bill. *Tommy at the Grocery Store* [K-1], 414

Guarino, Deborah. *Is Your Mama a Llama?* [Pre-K], 123

Hale, Sarah Josepha Buell. *Mary Had a Little Lamb* [Pre-K], 127

Hayes, Sarah. *This Is the Bear* [Pre-K], 128

Heller, Ruth. *Kites Sail High: A Book about Verbs* [3-5], 1812

Hellsing, Lennart. *Old Mother Hubbard and Her Dog* [Pre-K], 130

Hennessy, B. G. *The Missing Tarts* [Pre-K], 133

Hoberman, Mary Ann. *A House Is a House for Me* [K-1], 431

Hutchins, Pat. *Don't Forget the Bacon!* [K-1], 434

The Tale of Thomas Mead [1-2], 697

Where's the Baby? [K-1], 435

Ivimey, John W. *The Complete Story of the Three Blind Mice* [Pre-K], 151

Complete Version of Ye Three Blind Mice [Pre-K], 152

Kudrna, C. Imbior. *To Bathe a Boa* [K-1], 463

Langstaff, John. *Frog Went a-Courtin'* [Pre-K], 179

Over in the Meadow [Pre-K], 180

STORIES TO TELL

STORIES WITH SONGS

STORIES WITH SONGS–Folklore

STORIES WITHOUT WORDS

STORMS

STORMS–Folklore

STORYTELLING

TRANSPORTATION

SEE ALSO Airplanes; Automobiles; Bicycles; Buses; Trucks

Douglass, Barbara. *The Great Town and Country Bicycle Balloon Chase* [Pre-K], 73

Kimmel, Eric A. *Charlie Drives the Stage* [2-3], 943

Kovalski, Maryann. *The Wheels on the Bus* [Pre-K], 173

Merrill, Jean. *The Pushcart War* [5-6], 1331

Peterson, Esther Allen. *Penelope Gets Wheels* [1-2], 774

Pinkwater, Daniel. *Tooth-Gnasher Superflash* [K-1], 523

Seuss, Dr. *Marvin K. Mooney, Will You Please Go Now* [K-1], 554

Shaw, Nancy. *Sheep in a Jeep* [K-1], 556

Siebert, Diane. *Truck Song* [Pre-K], 266

TREASURE

SEE Buried treasure

TREES

SEE ALSO Flowers; Gardens; Plants; Vegetables

Cherry, Lynne. *The Great Kapok Tree: A Tale of the Amazon Rain Forest* [1-2], 647

Kellogg, Steven. *Johnny Appleseed* [1-4], 2058

Lyon, George Ella. *A B Cedar: An Alphabet of Trees* [Pre-6], 2068

Nikly, Michelle. *The Emperor's Plum Tree* [1-2], 759

Noble, Trinka Hakes. *Apple Tree Christmas* [2-3], 973

Seuss, Dr. *The Lorax* [2-3], 997

Silverstein, Shel. *The Giving Tree* [2-3], 1001

Udry, Janice May. *A Tree Is Nice* [Pre-K], 278

TREES-Folklore

Say, Allen. *Once Under the Cherry Blossom Tree: An Old Japanese Tale* [1-4], 1592

Troughton, Joanna. *Tortoise's Dream* [Pre-2], 1618

TRICKS

SEE ALSO Magic

Baum, Arline, and Joseph Baum. *Opt: An Illusionary Tale* [3-4], 1044

Brandreth, Gyles. *Brain-Teasers and Mind-Benders* [3-6], 1997

Brown, Marc. *Arthur's April Fool* [1-2], 625

Churchill, E. Richard. *Devilish Bets to Trick Your Friends* [3-6], 2005

Flora, James. *The Joking Man* [2-3], 922

White, Laurence B., Jr., and Ray Broekel. *The Surprise Book* [2-6], 2114

TRICKSTER TALES

Aardema, Verna. *Rabbit Makes a Monkey Out of Lion* [Pre-3], 1382

Appiah, Peggy. *Tales of an Ashanti Father* [3-6], 1653

Arkhurst, Joyce Cooper. *The Adventures of Spider: West African Folktales* [1-4], 1654

Coatsworth, Emerson, and David Coatsworth, comps. *The Adventures of Nanabush: Ojibway Indian Stories* [2-5], 1665

Courlander, Harold. *The Hat-Shaking Dance: And Other Tales from the Gold Coast* [2-6], 1668

The Piece of Fire and Other Haitian Tales [3-6], 1669

Courlander, Harold, and George Herzog. *The Cow-Tail Switch and Other West African Stories* [2-6], 1670

Goble, Paul. *Iktomi and the Boulder: A Plains Indian Story* [K-3], 1483

Kimmel, Eric A. *Anansi and the Moss-Covered Rock* [Pre-2], 1541

Lester, Julius. *The Tales of Uncle Remus: The Adventures of Brer Rabbit* [2-5], 1707

Parks, Van Dyke, and Malcolm Jones. *Jump!: The Adventures of Brer Rabbit* [2-5], 1714

Robinson, Gail. *Raven the Trickster: Legends of the North American Indians* [4-6], 1719

Roth, Susan L. *Kanahena: A Cherokee Story* [Pre-2], 1587

TROLLS

SEE ALSO Fairies; Giants; Leprechauns; Monsters; Ogres

Marshall, Edward. *Troll Country* [K-1], 501

Torgersen, Don Arthur. *The Girl Who Tricked the Troll* [1-2], 832

TROLLS-Folklore

Asbjørnsen, P. C. *The Three Billy Goats Gruff* [Pre-2], 1396

Dasent, George Webbe. *The Cat on the Dovrefell: A Christmas Tale* [Pre-2], 1432

East o' the Sun & West o' the Moon: An Old Norse Tale [2-6], 1433

D'Aulaire, Ingri, and Edgar Parin D'Aulaire. *D'Aulaire's Trolls* [K-3], 1434

Galdone, Paul. *The Three Billy Goats Gruff* [Pre-1], 1473

TRUCKS

SEE ALSO Automobiles; Buses; Transportation

Lyon, David. *The Biggest Truck* [Pre-K], 193

Merrill, Jean. *The Pushcart War* [5-6], 1331

Siebert, Diane. *Truck Song* [Pre-K], 266

TURKEYS

Schatell, Brian. *Farmer Goff and His Turkey Sam* [K-1], 543

TURTLES

SEE ALSO Reptiles

Asch, Frank. *Turtle Tale* [Pre-K], 16

Balian, Lorna. *The Aminal* [K-1], 327

Berger, Terry. *The Turtle's Picnic: And Other Nonsense Stories* [1-2], 615

George, William T. *Box Turtle at Long Pond* [Pre-2], 2037

Hadithi, Mwenye. *Tricky Tortoise* [Pre-K], 126

MacGregor, Ellen. *Theodore Turtle* [K-1], 491

Williams, Barbara. *Albert's Toothache* [Pre-K], 296

TURTLES–Folklore

Aesop. *The Tortoise and the Hare: An Aesop Fable* [Pre-2], 1388

Roth, Susan L. *Kanahena: A Cherokee Story* [Pre-2], 1587

Wildsmith, Brian. *The Hare and the Tortoise* [Pre-3], 1627

TWINS

Cleary, Beverly. *The Growing-Up Feet* [Pre-K], 50

Conford, Ellen. *Me and the Terrible Two* [4-5], 1161

Seuling, Barbara. *The Triplets* [1-2], 800

Slobodkin, Florence. *Too Many Mittens* [Pre-K], 268

Wisniewski, David. *The Warrior and the Wise Man* [2-3], 1031

UNCLES

Bellairs, John. *The House with a Clock in Its Walls* [4-5], 1143

Byars, Betsy. *The Winged Colt of Casa Mia* [3-4], 1048

Lobel, Arnold. *Uncle Elephant* [K-1], 486

Martin, Jacqueline Briggs. *Bizzy Bones and the Lost Quilt* [Pre-K], 206

Pinkwater, Daniel. *Yobgorgle: Mystery Monster of Lake Ontario* [4-5], 1227

Tripp, Wallace. *My Uncle Podger* [3-4], 1123

Wetterer, Margaret. *The Giant's Apprentice* [3-4], 1130

U.S.–Constitutional History

Fritz, Jean. *Shh! We're Writing the Constitution* [4-6], 2032

Maestro, Betsy. *A More Perfect Union: The Story of Our Constitution* [2-5], 2073

U.S.–History

Freedman, Russell. *Immigrant Kids* [4-6], 2027

U.S.–History–Civil War

Reit, Seymour. *Behind Rebel Lines: The Incredible Story of Emma Edmonds, Civil War Spy* [5-6], 2085

U.S.–History–Colonial Period

Fritz, Jean. *The Double Life of Pocahontas* [4-6], 2031

Who's That Stepping on Plymouth Rock? [3-6], 2035

McGovern, Ann. *If You Lived in Colonial Times* [2-5], 2069

Sewall, Marcia. *The Pilgrims of Plimoth* [2-6], 2098

Waters, Kate. *Sarah Morton's Day: A Day in the Life of a Pilgrim Girl* [1-5], 2112

U.S.–History–Colonial Period–Fiction

Avi. *Night Journeys* [5-6], 1268

Sauer, Julia L. *Fog Magic* [5-6], 1353

Speare, Elizabeth George. *The Sign of the Beaver* [5-6], 1363

U.S.–History–Revolution

Brown, Drollene P. *Sybil Rides for Independence* [2-4], 2001

D'Aulaire, Ingri, and Edgar Parin D'Aulaire. *Benjamin Franklin* [2-6], 2013

Fritz, Jean. *And Then What Happened, Paul Revere?* [3-6], 2029

Can't You Make Them Behave, King George? [3-6], 2030

What's the Big Idea, Ben Franklin? [3-6], 2033

Griffin, Judith Berry. *Phoebe and the General* [2-5], 2042

Longfellow, Henry Wadsworth. *Paul Revere's Ride* [4-6], 1863

McGovern, Ann. *The Secret Soldier: The Story of Deborah Sampson* [3-6], 2071

U.S.–History–Revolution–Fiction

Avi. *The Fighting Ground* [5-6], 1267

Brady, Esther Wood. *Toliver's Secret* [4-5], 1148

Collier, James Lincoln, and Christopher Collier. *My Brother Sam Is Dead* [5-6], 1288

Gauch, Patricia Lee. *This Time, Tempe Wick?* [2-3], 926

Lawson, Robert. *Ben and Me* [5-6], 1324

U.S.–History–Riddles

Adler, David A. *Remember Betsy Floss: And Other Colonial American Riddles* [2-6], 1740

Wild Bill Hickok and Other Old West Riddles [2-5], 1741

Keller, Charles, and Richard Baker, comps. *The Star-Spangled Banana and Other Revolutionary Riddles* [2-6], 1844

U.S.–History–1783–1865

Blumberg, Rhoda. *The Incredible Journey of Lewis & Clark* [5-6], 1996

Freedman, Russell. *Lincoln: A Photobiography* [5-6], 2028

McGovern, Ann. *Runaway Slave: The Story of Harriet Tubman* [2-5], 2070

Winter, Jeanette. *Follow the Drinking Gourd* [3-4], 1134

U.S.–History–1783–1865–Fiction

Brink, Carol Ryrie. *Caddie Woodlawn* [4-5], 1151

Fleischman, Sid. *By the Great Horn Spoon* [5-6], 1300

Hurmence, Belinda. *A Girl Called Boy* [5-6], 1314

Kirby, Susan. *Ike and Porker* [4-5], 1200

Monjo, F. N. *The Drinking Gourd* [2-3], 966

Mooser, Stephen. *Orphan Jeb at the Massacree* [4-5], 1215

U.S.–History–1865–1898

Freedman, Russell. *Buffalo Hunt* [5-6], 2025

Children of the Wild West [3-6], 2026

U.S.–History–1865–1898–Fiction

Beatty, Patricia. *That's One Ornery Orphan* [5-6], 1274

Wilder, Laura Ingalls. *Farmer Boy* [3-4], 1132

Little House in the Big Woods [2-3], 1028

U.S.–History–20th Century–Fiction

Brenner, Barbara. *A Year in the Life of Rosie Bernard* [4-5], 1149

Burch, Robert. *Ida Early Comes Over the Mountain* [4-5], 1153

Fitzgerald, John D. *The Great Brain* [4-5], 1171

VALENTINE'S DAY

Bunting, Eve. *The Valentine Bears* [K-1], 353

Carlson, Nancy L. *Louanne Pig in the Mysterious Valentine* [1-2], 637

Hoban, Lillian. *Arthur's Great Big Valentine* [K-1], 426

Modell, Frank. *One Zillion Valentines* [1-2], 751

Sharmat, Marjorie Weinman. *The Best Valentine in the World* [1-2], 807

Stevenson, James. *Happy Valentine's Day, Emma!* [1-2], 823

VALENTINE'S DAY–Poetry

Prelutsky, Jack. *It's Valentine's Day* [Pre-3], 1909

VEGETABLES

SEE ALSO Cookery; Flowers; Food; Fruit; Gardens; Plants; Soup

Ehlert, Lois. *Eating the Alphabet: Fruits and Vegetables from A to Z* [Pre-K], 77

Growing Vegetable Soup [Pre-K], 78

Krauss, Ruth. *The Carrot Seed* [Pre-K], 178

McMillan, Bruce. *Growing Colors* [Pre-K], 197

Nolan, Dennis. *Witch Bazooza* [1-2], 762

VEGETABLES–Folklore

Domanska, Janina. *The Turnip* [Pre-1], 1448

Morgan, Pierr. *The Turnip: An Old Russian Folktale* [Pre-1], 1569

Tolstoi, Alexei. *The Great Big Enormous Turnip* [Pre-1], 1614

VEGETABLES–Riddles

Keller, Charles. *Alexander the Grape: Fruit and Vegetable Jokes* [2-6], 1834

VERBS

SEE English language–Grammar

VISUAL PERCEPTION

Brown, Ruth. *If at First You Do Not See* [K-1], 348

Gardner, Beau. *Guess What?* [Pre-K], 110

The Look Again . . . and Again, and Again, and Again Book [1-2], 675

Hoban, Tana. *Look Again!* [1-2], 688

Jonas, Ann. *Reflections* [1-2], 700

Round Trip [1-2], 701

MacDonald, Suse. *Alphabatics* [K-1], 490

Shaw, Charles G. *It Looked Like Spilt Milk* [Pre-K], 264

Ungerer, Tomi. *One, Two, Where's My Shoe?* [Pre-K], 281

Yektai, Niki. *What's Missing?* [Pre-K], 303

What's Silly? [Pre-K], 304

VOCABULARY

SEE ALSO English language; Language; Word games

Babbitt, Natalie. *The Search for Delicious* [4-5], 1139

Baer, Edith. *Words Are Like Faces* [K-1], 324

Day, Alexandra. *Frank and Ernest* [2-3], 906

Duke, Kate. *Guinea Pigs Far and Near* [Pre-K], 75

Hoban, Tana. *A Children's Zoo* [K-1], 430

Hunt, Bernice. *The Whatchamacallit Book* [3-6], 2052

Ipcar, Dahlov. *I Love My Anteater with an A* [3-4], 1078

Juster, Norton. *The Phantom Tollbooth* [5-6], 1316